LEGAL SYSTEMS

Blair J. Kolasa

Ph.D., University of Pittsburgh
J.D., Duquesne University
Dean and Professor of Behavioral Science
School of Business and Administration
Duquesne University

Bernadine Meyer

Ed.D., Columbia University
J.D., Duquesne University
Associate Professor of Law Administration
School of Business and Administration
Duquesne University

Prentice-Hall, Inc., Englewood Cliffs, New Jersey 07632

Library of Congress Cataloging in Publication Data

KOLASA, BLAIR JOHN
    Legal Systems.

    Bibliography: p.
    Includes index.
    1. Justice, Administration of—United States.
    2. Procedure (Law)—United States.   I. Meyer,
Bernadine,   joint author   II. Title.
KF8700.K64   347'.73   77-20657
ISBN 0-13-529404-5

This book is dedicated to our families, colleagues, and students.
—The Authors

© 1978 by Prentice-Hall, Inc., Englewood Cliffs, N.J. 07632

Printed in the United States of America.

10 9 8 7 6 5 4 3 2

PRENTICE-HALL INTERNATIONAL, INC., *London*
PRENTICE-HALL OF AUSTRALIA PTY. LIMITED, *Sidney*
PRENTICE-HALL OF CANADA, LTD., *Toronto*
PRENTICE-HALL OF INDIA PRIVATE LIMITED, *New Delhi*
PRENTICE-HALL OF JAPAN, INC., *Tokyo*
PRENTICE-HALL OF SOUTHEAST ASIA PTE. LTD., *Singapore*
WHITEHALL BOOKS LIMITED, *Wellington, New Zealand*

CONTENTS

**PART III
DECISION ANALYSIS
OF THE
CRIMINAL PROCESS   223**

PREFACE

The impact of law upon the daily lives of individuals today is of such significance that men and women not only accept its pervasiveness but look to the law when seeking means to improve the quality of their lives. So influential is the law that persons who seek to understand their society, its institutions, and governance must have a basic understanding of the nature and functions of law, as well as of the legal system and the legal process. For this reason, study of law is essential in everyone's general education, not just for those intending to enter the legal profession. To meet this need, legal studies programs have become an increasingly important element in the offerings of universities and colleges.

This text has been prepared for use in undergraduate or graduate courses in law, primarily those offered outside the law school. Its objective is to help the student understand the legal process as well as such substantive areas of the law as contracts, torts, crimes, organizations, and commercial transactions. It is equally suitable for use in legal studies in liberal arts programs and in law courses offered in the professional schools, notably the business school. For programs in law enforcement or the administration of legal systems, it is supportive of the objectives of the course work.

The approach is analytical. Law is viewed as much more than a set of rules. It is seen as a dynamic system and process, one in which human beings interact and influence not only one another but also the law and the legal system. Thus, law is considered not as an isolated discipline, but as one influenced by and influencing such other spheres of life as the economy, politics, ethics, social life, and business.

Rather than merely explain to the student what law, the legal system, and the legal process are, the text draws the student into examination of them through analysis of the decision making that takes place within the civil, criminal, and administrative agency processes. Decisions and procedures are flow charted so the student can visualize not only the steps in the process but also the outcomes of decision making. It is this decision analysis which is the unique contribution of the text.

The book consists of five major divisions. Part I is introductory; it provides a framework of reference for the parts that follow and deals with law, the legal process, the systems approach, and the methodology of decision analysis. Part II is concerned with a decision analysis of the civil process; Part III, the criminal; and Part IV, the administrative agency. In each of these three parts, the student is presented with a situation occurring in the life of hypothetical persons, eventually involving them in the legal system. The student follows these fictional persons, step by step, as they go all the way through the legal process. As he does so, the student finds that knowledge of substantive law is as important to resolution of the matter as is knowledge of procedural law. Thus, the student realizes the significance of Part V, which treats substantive areas.

As in any complex area of disciplinary activity, one small volume will not contain all or even most of the material to be gained. Neither this book nor any one of similar length will satisfy those with a desire to delve more deeply into the discipline. Further professional pursuit of the law will take the student so inclined to many texts and several courses in a law program beyond the scope of this work.

In summary, the text can be used for such courses as introduction to law, legal process, legal systems, law and society, legal environment, business law, survey of law. In introducing the student to the law, it provides a base for learning through the use of a systems format to delineate steps in the legal process and analysis of the myriad factors at work in the decisions that are made by various actors in that social process. That it might serve to increase public understanding and appreciation of the law has been the aim of the authors.

NOTE TO READERS

The hypothetical cases in Parts II, III, and IV of this book refer to fictional persons, organizations, and places. If the names of persons or companies bear any similarity to those of actual persons or companies, the similarity is purely fortuitous.

Legal requirements vary among the different jurisdictions. The legal procedures, forms, and documents in Parts II, III, and IV of this text are illustrative of those generally in use. They have been incorporated in the text solely for educational purposes in acquainting the student with the nature of the legal process. They may not meet specific legal requirements of particular states. *Under no circumstances* should procedures, forms, or documents be used or adapted for self-help purposes by persons not admitted to the bar. Readers with specific legal problems should consult an attorney.

ACKNOWLEDGEMENTS

The authors wish to express their appreciation to all those who have contributed to the preparation of this text. We are especially grateful to Professor Edwin W. Tucker of the University of Connecticut and the late Hendrik Zwarensteyn of Michigan State University whose manuscript reviews were of great help and a source not only of encouragement but also of valuable suggestions and comments. Substantial portions of the manuscript were read by Dr. Barry Baroni of the University of New Orleans, Prof. A. Richard Grant of Boise State University, and Prof. Dwight D. Murphy of Wichita State University, to all of whom we are indebted for their critiques and helpful recommendations. It is with much gratitude that we acknowledge similar assistance from our colleague at Duquesne University, Kathy Gamble, and David Johnson, a recent graduate of Duquesne University School of Law.

Very special thanks is extended to Mrs. Mary Beth Johnson, whose contribution was a major one. Not only did she research and edit, but she also typed much of the manuscript. Additional typing was done by Mrs. Donna Mills, Mrs. Donna Repic, and Ms. Mary Ann Vranesevich, whom we also thank. We are indebted to Ms. Susan Anderson, David C. Hildebrand, and Robert Smith for editorial assistance.

Acknowledgement is also gratefully made to the American Law Institute and the National Conference of Commissioners on Uniform State Laws for permission to quote from the official text of the 1972 Uniform Commercial Code, and to the West Publishing Company and the Institute for Defense Analysis for permission to reproduce figures.

Blair J. Kolasa
Bernadine Meyer

PART I
INTRODUCTION

Part I begins the study of law in a basic and fundamental manner, in order to provide a brief overview of the area and a foundation for later, more in-depth study. Discussion in this first part of the book of legal concept and systems and implementing them will serve only as an introduction to the field and *not* as a complete and comprehensive survey of the law. Greater exposure and awareness is meant to come through repetition and elaboration in subsequent stages of discussion of legal concepts and their use in realistically portrayed incidents.

The sound educational basis for this method is further enhanced by the use of what is called the Analysis of Decision Systems approach whereby the flow of the legal process is pictured and each step in that process is subjected to an analysis that is intended to aid learning.

CHAPTER 1
LAW AND LEGAL QUESTIONS

Law is a form of order
                              —Aristotle
The welfare of the people is the highest law
                                        —Cicero
The Law, which is perfection of reason
                                        —Sir Edward Coke
Law is what the judge says it is
                                  —Anonymous

What then is law? The learned discussions in the past on this topic would probably fill more space than is available in many college libraries and still not provide answers to satisfy everyone. The various opinions and the problems connected with them have undoubtedly been responsible for the omission of definitions of law in many texts that have been written to outline "The Law." With the feeling that such scant attention is improper, the authors venture to provide a starting point for the systematic analysis of the law.

DEFINITION

When faced with the need for understanding the meaning of a word, people often open a dictionary and get the definition. While this approach may raise more questions than answers, that may be a good place to start. Webster's *New Collegiate Dictionary*, for instance, defines law as

the binding custom or practice of a community; rules of conduct enforced by a controlling authority; also, any single rule of conduct so enforced . . . a rule of conduct or action prescribed by the supreme governing authority and enforced by a sanction, as any whole body of such rules; also the control or regulation, or state of society, brought about by the existence and enforcement of such rules.

Several aspects can be seen in this definition; it includes the concepts of

1. Rules,
2. Conduct,
3. Sanctions,
4. Control,

but there is no direct statement of the ultimate reason for the existence of law; the answers to the question *why* may be the most important of all.

The notion that law is a set of rules that governs the actions of people in a community is probably the most common. This view sees law as a set of fixed principles known to lawyers and judges (ignorance of which excuses no one, not even the less knowledgeable or less affluent members of society). The approach seeks out the specific precepts that must be followed by citizens and that, if not followed, give rise to a cause of action in the courts. It is also the view of law that may be reinforced by a course in law or business law in which the student may feel that he must memorize all the rules and regurgitate them during a later examination. Not that all memorization is unnecessary; memorization is detrimental if it excludes analyzing the basic factors involved in the development of law and the reasons, if any, for the continuation of legal rules.

This approach to law as a logical set of rules by which behavior is to be governed has been responsible for most of the traditional classifications or distinctions as well as implementations made today in the legal order. When a famous early English jurist, Sir Edward Coke, stated, "law . . . is perfection of reason" he was only one in a long series of law men who focus on the basis for law in reason and point to its logical arrangement (but who are sometimes unaware when its "logic" breaks down). A look into the development of broad systems has been the basis for the differentiation between the Anglo-American system of law (common law) and the continental system or Civil law. If one looks to the seat of authority or jurisdiction then one refers to *federal law*, *state law*, or *international law*. A further differentiation may be made on the basis of whether society has an overriding interest in the matter because the interests of the state are deeply involved. If the activity is such that officials of the state must play a greater role because of society's concern, the matter may be placed in the category of *criminal law*. If, however, the limited personal and economic rights of individuals or organizations are affected then the legal process becomes a suit in the *civil* area (civil law in this usage differs from the use of the term *Civil* when we refer to the continental law system).

If we focus upon some systematic breakdown of the total area into categories according to legal content, the differentiation may result in labels such as *contracts*, *torts*, and *decedents' estates*. The elements of these content areas are known as *substantive* law, and a concentration on the process in which these rules are applied is referred to as *procedural* law. Finally, this same recourse to law as a set of rules has been outlined on philosophical grounds where a distinction has been made between *positive* law and *natural* law. Positive law is established by persons and organizations in authority, whereas natural law most generally refers to a more basic or "higher law" in human behavior. This last distinction has caused much controversy in history, as it has been subject to differing interpretations.

A further view of law inherent in the dictionary definition is that it is a method of social control, a means of establishing order through the expression of an authority deriving from the social group. Earlier treatises often looked upon this in terms of a command of a ruler and defined law in that simple way. That view may persist in some approaches today. The broader and more socially valid view of social group control is, however, an analysis that reaches back to remote times. Aristotle believed law to be "a form of order, and good law must necessarily mean good order." To maintain good order, however, a complex society must have some social unit assigned to perform that job. More recently, Max Weber, a perceptive observer of law and society, has pointed out that law comes about only when, "there exists a coercive apparatus, i.e., that there are one or more persons whose special task it is to hold themselves ready to apply specially provided means of coercion (legal coercion) for the purpose of norm enforcement."[1] A primitive social group may have norms or guidelines, but law begins only when a special group is set up to enforce the social norms. In this case there may be some truth to the facetious comment that law is the second oldest profession. Weber adds that the coercive apparatus need not be limited to agents of the political community but can exist in the influence of a labor, business, or church group on its members and the coercion can be psychological as well as physical. Most observers still recognize, however, that law exists only in a formal framework of a judicial and enforcement system of a political body. "What these officials do about disputes is . . . the law itself."[2] This attitude is the basis for the formal definitions focusing more on social control rather than rules—"law is defined as the formal means of social control that involves the use of rules that are interpreted, and are enforceable, by the courts of a political community."[3] This view includes rules but the stress is upon the means of formal social control.

A variation of this is the belief that the key concept underlying law is that of authority, the obligation to act in line with norms authoritatively determined.[4] Even more important, however, is the insistence of Selznick that an adequate theory of law not only emphasizes the authoritative atmosphere but also identifies other aspects such as

1. The distinctive work done by law and society,
2. The resources of law,
3. The characteristic mechanisms brought into play.

This approach can be much more meaningful than a simple view of law as a means of either rules or social control and forms a good basis for the systems approach to the study of legal process.

A further sociological definition of law can be seen in an approach like the interactional social systems of Parsons[5] where the legal system can be viewed as "a structure of relations between actors"—a web of interaction.[6] In this approach roles and role relationships are significant; relationships between employer and employee, husband and wife, seller and buyer, or landlord and tenant, are significant parts of the interactional process that must be focused upon to understand the nature of law. This view does not eliminate the control aspects, however, as sanctions are viewed as being important in the process of regulations of the social order. The focus is still upon interactions between actors in the social system.

After all of the above perhaps we can finally focus upon a comprehensive definition that seems to cover all the aspects discussed.

> Law is . . . a body of binding obligations regarded as a right by one party
> and acknowledged as a duty by the other which has been reinstitutionalized
> within the legal institution so that society can continue to function in an
> orderly manner on the basis of rules so maintained.[7]

Note that not only are elements present but processes as well; the interpersonal bases in the existence of law are included with an analysis of how the framework is developed (institutionalization) and the purpose for which it functions.

TRADITIONAL CLASSIFICATIONS

Law can be understood further by considering ways in which the entire field has been subdivided for one purpose or another. It must be pointed out first, however, that the categories to be given are not mutually exclusive; that means there are many ways in which to subdivide the entire area. Differing subdivisions can be made depending upon the primary focus of interest or purpose under consideration at one time.

Basic Development of Systems

Law in Western societies has developed along two lines. In the countries of continental Europe and those areas influenced by them, the governing law dates back to Roman law and is known as the *Civil law system*. The law with which U.S. citizens are more familiar is known as the *common law*, the system that developed in English-speaking countries. For many purposes, however, some differences between the two systems are more historical than real at the present time.

The major difference between the two systems lies in the operation of judicial processes. Adjudication under the Civil law is made by the judge following principles established by the earliest developments of Roman law as embodied at present under an extensive code of law in effect in that particular country. The judge must apply the appropriate section of the code to the case in court. The common law develops more through the decisions of judges applying prior decisions of courts to the new facts at hand. When Mr. Justice Holmes stated "the life of the law has not been logic; it has been experience"[8] he was writing the first sentence of his treatise on the common law. This emphasis upon case-by-case decisions has been kept in order to maintain the flexibility that comes with continuing challenges to the validity of certain legal positions that can be made through the participation of a greater number of individuals. Again it must be stated that there may not be much difference between the two great systems of law, especially these days when legislation in the common law countries is proceeding more rapidly than before.

A few more words might be said here about the common law since it is the system under which we in America function. It has been noted that the prior decisions of judges in similar cases have been noted in deciding a present case. This adherence to precedent is known by the Latin term *stare decisis.* It would seem at first glance that this obedience to precedent makes common law more rigid than it is flexible. Actually the judge can distinguish between the facts of the different cases or find some other reasons for going his own way. The outstanding characteristic of the system still remains the great opportunity for judicial decision making without discarding the experience built up from prior court decisions.

There are a few more aspects of the general legal process in common law countries that might be mentioned briefly to help in understanding some possibly puzzling distinctions that occur later in the text. At present little reason exists to differentiate concepts of equity or principles of business law from the rest of the large body of common law. These concepts are based, however, upon early developments outside the common law and their use of form at this time may bear some vague relationship to that historical fact. In early feudal times common law courts were very rigid and limiting in the kinds of cases that would be entertained. Very frequently many persons could obtain no relief in the courts and had to petition the king for redress. The king's chancellor concerned himself with meting out justice in a court system that became known as the *courts of equity*. Present-day courts (because equity courts were absorbed into the common law courts) enforce equitable remedies which include

1. Injunction—a direction to persons to refrain from committing a particular act,

2. Specific performance—compelling the party to perform, usually under a contract,

3. Reformation—the alteration of a contract or other instrument where errors were made,

4. Enforcement of a trust—directing performance of duties owed benefiting someone else.

Equity cases do not have as strict rules of evidence and the judge ordinarily sits as the court without a jury.

Most of the elements of commercial or business law have their origin in the Middle Ages in the body of laws known as the law merchant. As with equity matters the courts of common law either could not or were not interested in settling problems arising between merchants and the merchants themselves had to do so. By the time of the settlement of America, however, most of these merchants courts had been absorbed into the general legal system so that all cases in controversy were being handled by the same set of judges.

Degree of Societal Interest

The magnitude of concern of a society in the relationships of its members will determine the extent to which the officials of that society play a role. Various kinds of controversies can be handled by the courts but selected officials of the legal system will step in to actively prosecute a case in which the seriousness of the cause is deemed sufficient for the political unit to take over. This is the distinction between *civil* law and *criminal* law. In civil law problems the authorities are concerned primarily with providing a forum for the resolution of controversies between individuals or groups. In criminal law there is a concern for public safety and order or "morals." A criminal is one who violates those portions of the statutes which were set up to ensure the public welfare and stability of the society. Where the public interest becomes this strong, the public officials must move to protect the interests of society.

It must be noted that the use of the term civil law in this context is quite different from the use of that term to refer to the continental European legal systems stemming from Roman law. To differentiate between the two the word civil when used in the present context will not be capitalized.

Content Versus Process

A focus upon the specific kinds of rights and duties created among individuals is a concentration upon the substance of the law or, as the domain is most often called, *substantive* law. The ways in which these rights and duties are maintained or enforced is the area of *procedural* law. In a specific case or controversy the lawyer will be interested in both aspects. He may want to know, for instance, whether the elements for a valid case of law are present; on the other hand, he will be concerned with how to proceed to secure a remedy. Both areas can be quite complex, but as the areas of substantive law are more easily distinguishable it would be well to concentrate on those.

Substance

Substantive law itself can be divided into *public* law and *private* law. The public law category concerns broader questions covering activity under the governmental system such as *constitutional* law. In addition to this, *administrative* law covers those areas dealing with the activities of governmental agencies acting in implementation of broader social and political policy.

The area of private law has a greater number of differentiations as follows

1. *Contracts*—including various relationships under agreements, such as agreements to buy or sell, *negotiable instruments, secured transactions,* and *bailments.*

2. *Property*—laws relating to the ownership or use of whatever may be claimed or controlledby someone. *Real property* is land and anything permanently attached to it, while *personal property* covers all other objects or interests owned.

3. *Persons*—legal precepts covering the interrelationships among individuals. These can be of a more personal nature, such as *family law* or *domestic relations,* or they can have a more business or commercial flavor such as those relationships encompassed under *agency, partnerships,* and *corporations.*

4. *Torts*—this substantive area of law refers to wrongs or injuries of a noncriminal nature. These can be physical as in *assault* and *battery* or they can be verbal as in *libel* or *slander.* By far the greatest number of tort cases arise when individuals are physically injured through the action of another, as in an automobile accident or in an injury caused by a defective product.

Each of the substantive areas can be subdivided further for analysis.

Process

Legal procedure is a more cohesive topic than substantive law from the standpoint of logical distinctions. The application of substantive law focuses more upon steps in a sequence. Process will be a prime orienting concept in the development of this book.

LAW IN ACTION

Verbal definitions, no matter how complete, or logical structures, even if they are valid in their internal consistency, are not enough to provide adequate coverage of any area, especially the law. What really happens in a complex environment becomes more important than the academic outlines of a discipline if a fuller understanding of the problems is to be achieved. Many of the questions or approaches to problems can be introduced at this point with fuller discussion later.

While there might be considerable interest in the functioning of law in simpler societies of the past or in present primitive groups, the main thrust of approaches labelled law-in-action usually focuses on modern, complex environments for study. Actual behavior in a social setting—rather than abstract legal concepts or distinctions—is emphasized here.

The broad impact of social changes on law may be summarized by referring to the overall view of a prominent commentator[9] who sees the capacity of the present legal order challenged by three main thrusts.

1. a "drift toward mass society marked by high rates of mobility, fragmented social experience, rising demands for short run gratification, and more active participation."
2. "the emergence of the large scale organization as the representative institution of modern society."
3. "the ascendance of social interest over parochial interests."

All three are viewed as emerging from the weakening of social controls based upon close kinship and community ties.

Functions of Law

Definitions of law are apt to be more deficient in providing some inkling of the purposes served by the functioning of law. While there may be some variation over time or as a result of geographic location, prevailing patterns of thought and analysis provide a basis for further study.

One current business law text[10] traces the function of law from simple peace keeping in primitive societies to the promotion of social justice in modern complex environments. More specifically the authors outline the historically changing functions as

1. *Peace keeping*—primary in primitive societies but still a concern today.
2. *Maintenance of the Status Quo*—trying to keep each person in his appointed role, as in ancient Greece or Rome and medieval society.

3. *Maximum individual self-assertion*—protection from arbitrary power and development of individual rights as in the "Age of Enlightenment."

4. *Promotion of social justice*—providing all citizens access to economic and political benefits, as in recent civil rights enactments.

In addition the authors list other functions of law.

1. Influencing and enforcing standards of law,
2. Facilitating orderly change,
3. Facilitating planning,
4. Promoting realization of reasonable expectations,
5. Providing compromise solutions.

It can be seen that some of these latter functions could be included with the first group.

A complementary socio-psychological analysis of the functioning of law would develop an outline that shows law

1. Fulfilling social needs,
2. Meeting social aspirations,
3. Developing individual rights,
4. Preserving group consensus,
5. Building legitimacy,
6. Providing a basis for social control,
7. Stimulating social change,
8. Acting as an instrument of public policy,
9. Embodying certain values,
10. Expressing authority,
11. Strengthening social solidarity,
12. Serving common interests.

While these descriptions represent somewhat of a departure from the usual categories in the law as outlined earlier, they do not represent rejection of the familiar concepts met in traditional legal studies. This outline does, however, point out that the purely legalistic concepts represent a view which encompasses a smaller part of the total functioning of law in the entire spectrum of social activity. Concern with the pure-law aspects of torts, contracts, and property seldom provides a clear enough focus of activity, or the basis for broad and fundamental policy, or decision making in business and society. The twelve categories should be kept in mind in analyzing all legal problems and questions to follow.

The Empirical Basis of Law

Perhaps the most fundamental of newer conceptual approaches is the attempt to determine the real variables that underlie behavior in a legal and social order. When researchers are interested in uncovering bases of decision making and policy making, they concern themselves with aspects that are of prime importance yet which may be taken for granted and glossed over. When real-life decisions are made, as when laws are enacted, people assume certain relationships between the rule and the behavior that the rule is intended to influence. Intuitively one may say that a particular regulation will prevent a specific type of behavior which is considered as undesirable by a social body. It takes no great amount of insight, however, to find that in many cases the regulation enacted proves to be ineffective. In a more fundamental way we might ask the question, "Does punishment actually deter?" On the basis of limited personal experience it may be evident that punishment does influence in some way. The question really is not a good one; what we really should ask is "What sort of punishment deters, how often, who is deterred and who is not, and why not?" Detailed and well-controlled studies into the variables affecting legal behavior in specific circumstances can be encouraged.

Control may be the question in the regulation of activity in the social area, an issue that might be stated in terms of a philosophy of control. Very often clearly antithetical positions may be recognized early. In a particular case there may be either a demand for punishment or simply a hope for the re-education of individuals who have violated the prescriptions of the legal order. These orientations are evident in emphases on enforcement on the one hand or for correction on the other. This might be referred to as the difference between a *laissez-faire* approach and a more paternal view of the forces of authority. In the former instance people are considered more on their own and are responsible for their actions in the world. In the paternal approach governmental agents may take the position that they are acting as concerned parents in prescribing particular procedures which will make better students, better workers, and, therefore, better citizens of the community. Instead of taking a punitive approach, the more humanitarian approach of society would seek to help the offender, young or old, intelligent or not.

The notion of education may be widely accepted but there is a danger in the educational approach. Often a particular type of "correction" may involve a punitive process rather than an educational one. In practice what is called correction or re-education of the individual means far less than that and this "treatment" may even contribute to further criminality upon release from correctional institutions. It is little wonder that mass processing of individuals and the aftereffects of improper treatment can arouse anxieties in a large segment of the population, which feels threatened by the return of released prisoners.

There is the paramount question of individual rights in this and other settings. At the present time if one is adjudged responsible and guilty, one is faced with a specified penalty of certain maximum duration. Critics of the less formal approaches with an educational or paternal flavor are concerned that the treatment is very often worse in terms of separation from society than the ordinary punishment for the crime. Also, this determination might be reached without procedures which are intended to protect the rights of individuals, as in juvenile or commitment cases. This concern has been stated well by a long time professional researcher in the field of correction, the late Paul Tappan.

> There is one telling argument against wholesale abandonment of legal rule and procedural form to accomplish social objectives: wholly to free the law from the "dead hand of the past" one must entrust unlimited discretion to judge, reformer, or clinician and his personal views of expedience. Unless he be circumscribed in some degree by established instrumental or traditional rule and form, the fate of the defendant, the interest of society, the social objectives themselves must hang by the tenuous thread of the wisdom and personality of the particular administrator.[11]

This is another repetition of the oft-quoted maxim that we live under a rule of laws and not of man.

Law and Morals

Another area containing issues for contemporary society lies in the province that may be described as the overlap between law and morality. The relationship between law and morals has been hotly debated for centuries with little consensus on major points. At the present time controversy still exists in the current concern about pornography, whether it be in books, in the movies, or some other form. Constitutional lawyers consider the issue in terms of the provisions of the First Amendment relating to free speech and free expression. It has been suggested, however, that a better understanding of the problems involved might come about if these are treated in the light of more fundamental aspects, namely, those involving the relationships between the enactments of a legislature and the prevailing moral sentiments of the community. Other issues that may be placed in the same category are those arising from the laws regulating all types of sexual activities and those concerned with drug addiction or abortion. All these problems not only have their medical bases but their behavioral ones as well; sometimes neither of these aspects is looked at sufficiently in the development of laws regulating this broad area. At times only the moral sentiments of single individuals or those of small groups in limited areas of the country are brought into the determination.

Mass Society

The great task facing the modern law system that Selznick[12] mentioned first (above) is an area of the legal order that is the object of general concern—the area of administration of justice in a complex and changing society or the "Mass Society." With a larger population and greater mobility the opportunities for social friction and discontent increase. Even simple matters in the administration of justice become overpowering through sheer numbers alone. The protection of individual rights becomes difficult when agents of the law must operate with procedures tailored for a much smaller and cohesive society of the eighteenth century. The situation becomes a fertile ground for what has been called "bargain-basement justice." Justice is apt to be more casual and bargaining takes place when, in return for a guilty plea on a lesser charge, the prosecutor is instrumental in obtaining a shorter sentence or probation. More hinges on the effectiveness of defense counsel in "getting a deal made" than on the application of proper techniques or placement in therapeutic surroundings.

An important point to remember in all of this is that a legal system is an adversary system. Each side is represented by counsel charged with the responsibility of working diligently toward a result favorable to the client, although various notions of what constitutes a favorable outcome may exist in the minds of the litigants or representatives of society. Since representation is crucial, a point of social concern has been the lack of proper representation of defendants unable to obtain legal assistance. Various recent Supreme Court decisions have generated action by states and municipalities toward the development of aid in representation for all defendants, particularly in serious criminal matters, and for plaintiffs in civil suits.

Recent developments have taken place also to provide more legal representation of groups—tenants, consumers, or citizens of a community. As a result of the problems raised in "Mass Society," the traditional close personal relationship between lawyer and client is undergoing change. It may well be that the entire complexion of legal practice (and, therefore, the legal profession itself) will change. The deluge of accident and personal injury cases before the courts accounts for most of the backlog of cases; in some jurisdictions this backlog runs to three years and more. Whether this and other factors will lead to different procedures such as no-fault insurance in automobile claims is one of the prime topics of discussion. A radically different approach worries some practitioners, yet there have been some departures from the traditional advocacy-in-court system in the area of injury at work. Workmen's compensation superimposed an almost completely new system upon the traditional pattern, without, apparently, any serious denial of traditional rights.

Just as distressing and perhaps more important are the problems related to differential enforcement of the law that takes place along socio-economic lines. Arrest and incarceration are more likely to happen to those who are at the lower end of the social scale. The basis for this does not lie completely in the fact that more crime occurs as the result of unfavorable economic conditions but in the more subtle variation in law enforcement influenced by the attitudes and values of law officials. Prosecution is more likely to take place for an activity that violates the sensitivities of the prosecutor. What at one level of society can be regarded as inoffensive behavior may be looked upon by persons at other levels, because of their different set of values and attitudes, as an undesirable or even immoral act. Middle-class values of law men will influence official activity in the community.

Organizations and Law

Still another significant contributor to pressures on the law, as Selznick[13] stated above, is the area of "private government." One of the most obvious aspects of mass society is the fairly recent and continuing growth in the size and number of organizations of all types—economic, educational, social, religious, and communications. Each has at least some power to influence the daily activities of many individuals, and some may have even more control over their members than do the agents of the legal and political order. The role of governmental agencies is an active and easily visible one; the moves of private government are less easily seen but nonetheless effective in influencing individuals and groups. This influence, furthermore, may be all out of proportion to the numbers involved. A few economic decision makers may establish a policy with an impact on hundreds within the organization and thousands outside it.

The question is not whether public government or private government is too strong or not strong enough. The concern with this phenomenon lies, instead, in whether the same basic checks on the power of the group over the individual that are preserved in the area of public government should not be transferred as well to private organizations. In this view due process of law, judicial review, and other constitutional rights deserve a place in the procedures that could confront a single individual in a corporation, labor union, or even in an educational institution. Dismissal from a company has long been referred to as "industrial capital punishment." A union member who may not completely agree with a particular union policy may find himself cut off from the opportunity to earn a living (or be barred in the first place). The dismissal of a student from a university can be, in this day, a matter that affects his future more than many sentences or punishments by a civil or criminal court acting as an agent of public government. Safeguards similar to those available to the individual under a public legal system may be desirable in the private organization.

Quality of Life

Much attention at the present centers upon issues that relate to individual and group welfare in existence in a modern environment. Perhaps this final section is the culmination of all concerns expressed above in that the beneficial condition of man, physically and psychologically, should be the ultimate measure of success of legal efforts.

Invasion of a human being's physical life space has been a concern of law for centuries; tort and trespass actions have been a traditional and usually effective legal recourse. Protection against psychological intrusions such as the invasion of privacy, however, have a short history. Not yet a century old, the legal relief of individuals from having personal information bandied about has been hastened by reactions to the greater effectiveness (not necessarily accuracy) of collecting and storing large amounts of data. Technological advancements have gone hand-in-hand with commercial expansion and changes in social views. Huge data banks with mountains of information now serve business and governmental units in the rush to a credit-conscious society and the expansion of public services. How much others need to know in all this is a growing personal concern.

Concern for the environment is an even more recent phenomenon; only in the past decade has there been any serious movement toward the alleviation of physical conditions that are detrimental to human functioning. Previous attitudes fostered economic growth or furthered individual rights at the expense of efforts to preserve environmental balance. Ecology has become a prime topic overnight and the growing awareness of others beyond a small band of "environmentalists" has been responsible for the enactment of a long series of statutes and the revival of long dormant and little used laws to conserve resources and protect health. One of the most significant of the statutes, the National Environmental Policy Act of 1969, states the intent of Congress to assure "for all Americans safe, healthful, productive, and esthetically and culturally pleasing surroundings."[14] The thrust of this Act and others goes beyond dealing with air and water pollution as it also encompasses the preservation of natural resources and valuable elements of the national heritage.

There is little serious disagreement over the general goals in the environmental crusade; controversy comes when implementation of policy takes place. Economic costs must be allocated and various painful trade-offs made. Law has long served to settle controversies, and its extensive role in these matters extends well into the future.

FOOTNOTES

[1]Max Weber, *Law in Economy and Society*, ed. M. Rheinstein (Cambridge, Massachusetts: Harvard University Press, 1954) p. 13.

[2] Karl Llewellyn, *The Bramble Bush* (New York: Oceana Publications, 1960) p. 12.

[3] F. James Davis, "Law as a Type of Social Control," in *Society and the Law*, F. James Davis et al. (New York: Free Press, 1962) p. 41.

[4] Philip Selznick, "The Sociology of Law," in *International Encyclopedia of the Social Sciences*, Vol 9. ed. D. Sills (New York: Macmillan Co. and Free Press, 1968).

[5] Talcott Parsons, *The Social System* (Glencoe, Illinois: Free Press, 1951).

[6] Julius Stone, *Law and the Social Sciences* (Minneapolis: University of Minnesota Press, 1966).

[7] Paul Bohannon, "Law and Legal Institutions," in *International Encyclopedia of the Social Sciences*, Vol. 9, ed. D. Sills (New York: Macmillan Co. and Free Press, 1968) p. 33.

[8] Oliver Wendell Holmes, *The Common Law* (Boston: Little, Brown & Co., 1881) p. 1.

[9] Selznick, "The Sociology of Law", p. 57.

[10] Harold F. Lusk et al., *Business Law; Principles and Cases* (Homewood, Illinois: Richard D. Irwin, 1974).

[11] Paul Tappan, *Delinquent Girls in Court* (New York: Columbia University Press, 1947).

[12] Selznick, "The Sociology of Law", p. 57.

[13] Selznick, "The Sociology of Law", p. 57.

[14] The National Environmental Policy Act, P.L. 91-190, 83 Stat. 852.

CHAPTER 2
SYSTEMS AND LEGAL PROCESS

One of the most common labels used at the present time is the term *system*. In various ways it is used to describe a complex situation or area of activity, but in virtually every case the use is very general or colloquial. Youth might rebel against "the system," a vague and general description of the many factors they might believe must be changed in the social environment. Legal scholars might speak of the legal system and mean the entire conglomerate of concepts and processes with which they work. Neither of these uses adequately describes the orientation that will be used here from now on. What is meant by the systems approach and, therefore, a legal system, refers to a more precise and scientific method of analysis and description of the complex structure and functioning of the parts and whole of the law.

THE SYSTEMS APPROACH

The complexity of modern life is one of the most obvious facts facing us. In any situation an attempt at administration must take into account the many factors that enter into the problems to be solved. In the law, as in every other significant activity, there are just too many things happening at one and the same time for any simple handling of one facet to be effective; as many streams of action must be brought together simultaneously or in an orderly sequence the common description of administration as "getting it all together" is certainly apt. Getting everything together when it is all so complex undoubtedly requires thinking and acting in the systematic fashion that has come to be known as the systems approach.

A more complex knowledge of the systems approach requires the definition of *system*, what distinguishes it from other approaches, its characteristics, and any subclass of systems. A focus on structure leads to a definition like "system is an organized or complex whole; an assemblage or combination of things or parts forming a complex or unitary whole."[1]   A concentration on the reasons for the existence of a system provides something that indicates that: "The basic function of administration appears to be co-alignment, not merely of people (in coalition) but of institutionalized action—of technology and task environment into a viable domain, and of organizational design and structure appropriate to it."[2]

Churchman,[3] in noting the wide diversity in descriptions of what a system is, summarizes a series of steps in thinking that must be taken in order to grasp the full meaning of a system. Five complementary considerations must be kept in mind.

1. The total system objectives,
2. The environment of the system,
3. Its resources,
4. Components of the system,
5. The management of the system.

System objectives include, most specifically, performance measures of the system. The environment includes fixed constraints while resources include human and physical resources. Activities, goals, performance measures, and so on are included among the components of the system.

From these and other definitions, descriptions like the following can be applied to the systems approach.

1. Systematic in working from an information data base,
2. Integrative, in collating all information and operations,
3. Interdisciplinary in bringing together diverse techniques and skills,
4. Decision oriented,
5. Holistic, that is, concerned with the interaction of the human elements with all other parts of an organized system.

Many of these characteristics can be present in other views of organizational activity, but the presence of all is what illustrates the systems approach. A system, then, may be defined as a set of elements becoming interrelated through pursuit of a goal. This common activity occurs along systematic lines on the basis of many inputs being combined to produce some outcome. A system in law would combine human elements with more material ones such as equipment to reach a goal, the stability of society.

Working in a systematic way from facts is a characteristic of an empirical science. In this approach knowledge is based upon data gathered in an organized and unbiased fashion. Fact, not speculation, is important for use—we are concerned with what *is*, not what ought to be. The data can be gathered in many ways—through experiments, surveys, or tests—as long as it is collected in a systematic fashion.

There is, however, a word of caution that must be included. It is the position that Churchman[4] describes as the "arrogance" of the management scientist who feels that he is the one who sees the whole system. The old story about the seven blind men describing the elephant when they have touched only part of it (saying it is like a palm tree after feeling its leg, etc.) is the basis for such arrogance on the part of the story teller because it assumes that he does have the full picture. No one, emphasizes Churchman, really has complete grasp of the system, although we may certainly seek this fuller description.

The systems approach is integrative in collating and combining as many inputs as are possible to include in the system. The end result is that the whole is greater than the sum of its parts (when the parts are put together properly). Another recent popular way to describe this outcome is taken from biological sciences. *Synergy* is the working together of products or medicines to provide a result greater than would be achieved by simple addition.

Because of its attempts to handle all aspects of complex problems, the systems approach is, of necessity, interdisciplinary. This means that it draws upon personnel, concepts, and techniques from many and varied areas of activity. Today's problems do not align themselves neatly into the often artificial categories we use in our schools or professional groupings. It takes more than contributions from a limited professional area such as the one represented by the psychologist, lawyer, or mathematician. All must be involved in the solving of social problems, on a broad scale or within a more restricted organizational setting. As a system implies complexity regardless of the size of the system, no one person these days can really do all that must be done. The coordination of all these activities, however, is the job of the administrator. Needless to say, that is a very challenging assignment calling for one who has more than familiarity with many different disciplines and approaches. Such persons are always in demand.

SYSTEMS ADMINISTRATION

The job of the administrator is popularly regarded as making decisions in an organization. Helping in the choice of alternatives that point to optimum results is an important contribution that the systems approach can make to the administrator. Further, the administration of modern systems in any setting calls for administrators who are flexible and able to deal with changing circumstances. They must be able to adapt the functioning of the coordinated organization to novel conditions—a true test is the ability to tolerate ambiguity and make decisions under uncertainty in complex situations.

The systems approach provides an administrator with a means of solving problems of a total system, not just part by part in piecemeal fashion. In an organization this means

1. Calling upon all skills and abilities of different individuals in the organization,

2. Focusing upon the interactions of the individuals in the total organization without becoming bogged down with the limited problems of a specific department,

3. Recognizing that the organization exists in a complex environment and that an openness to all inputs from the outside is critical,

4. Individual, group, and societal problems are met through a scientific and organized manner.

Systems analysis and the implementation of it cut across all lines and bring all together to aid the decision maker in solving problems.

There may really be nothing new, basically, in the approach to organizations and their functioning in terms of systems. For a long time executives have described their activities as "organizing and controlling" or "coordination of several diverse activities." This is the essence of the systems approach even if the term has not been used. Actually, however, there is more to it than has been apparent. New concepts and tools have brought current decision makers to a point where an analysis of the modern systems methods and techniques shows much more than has been present up to now. It is more than merely pasting a new label on an old idea or approach.

The systems approach can be used and is applied in organizations of all kinds. There is no doubt that administrators in any kind of organization—industrial, governmental, legal, social, educational, or religious—are faced with pretty much the same complex problems with the necessity to resolve them in an effective way. The validity of and the opportunities inherent in the systems approach lie even more, however, in the broader social systems that envelop all organizations. Most, if not all, of society's problems have developed in such a complex way that the systems approach is necessary. In an earlier day (but perhaps not even then!) social situations were simple and the demands upon citizens and servants of the people were not great. Each problem was treated in its own limited context and there was little need to recognize the interrelationships between events. Now the problems of housing, education, control of pollution, traffic, delinquency, as well as the production and marketing of goods or services, are so interdependent that none can be approached without a consideration of the entire galaxy of interacting events. One area alone, for that matter, can be so complex in and of itself that a systems way of thinking and acting may be called for in solving its problems. So it is with the systems of law and its subsystems. Courts, correctional organizations, and the control agencies (law enforcement) are wholes that have many parts that must be synchronized as well as having each of the three systems mesh for the proper and effective administration of justice.

DECISION MAKING

Decisions are the central force in any rational individual, organizational, or societal activity. Making a decision means a choice between alternatives and taking a specific action. Decision making usually occurs in a problem-solving situation and any complex set of circumstances calls for a sequence of decisions to handle the problem. The elements of the process can be identified as

1. Recognition of basic assumptions,
2. Determination of goals,
3. Setting means of proceeding,
4. Limiting parameters of procedures,
5. Acceptance or rejection of inputs of data,
6. Selection from among alternatives,
7. Implementation of choice,
8. Evaluation of action.

This sequence requires coordination of material and human resources in a systematic and logical way in the search for ways to achieve goals set.

The decision-making process depends upon many factors. Information is basic in the activity as rational choices should be based on data obtained. There are quality as well as quantity aspects to the information gathering. In addition to having the best kind of information, the decision maker, ideally, wishes to have as much information as possible before making the decision. That means the executive problem solver wants to *maximize* in terms of information received and used. Since this is not efficient, if not impossible, the decision maker is urged to *satisfice*, that is, to make timely decisions with a requisite amount of input data rather than waiting for the impossible maximum.[5]

Information systems present data for decision making. The material conditions of the information system and the reception factors determine not only the extent of the information but its form as well. The way information is presented shapes the decision, but even more influential is the reception and perception by the human actors in the process. While both aspects cause *filtering* and *distortion*, the human factors come into play more significantly. Broad social and cultural factors are further transformed into individual psychological influences upon the problem solver in the decision-making system. National cultural preferences and social values influence the shaping of decisions, in legal systems, as well as in other situations. Attitudes and values in the United States often differ from those of other cultures and determine much of what is later enacted into statutes or followed by legal procedures. Individual personality patterns, abilities, perceptions, and aspirations further influence decisions.

Finally, decision-making situations may be identified as involving either programmed or nonprogrammed decisions. Programmed decisions are those that are repetitive or routine and are ones that can be handled by either habitual responses or by set policy or decision rules. Nonprogrammed situations and decisions are unstructured or difficult to pin down because they may be novel or infrequent and, therefore, may require much more than routine attention or handling. Because programmed decision making is simple and regular, the attention of decision makers is often directed to the drawing up of decision rules for individual and organizational activity.

MODELS OF A SYSTEM

Models are useful in the systems approach because they enable a decision maker to focus on aspects of a situation that is too complex to handle effectively if one intends to consider all the variables that are present. Models are a representation of reality that enables viewers to get a better idea of that reality by cutting through the complexity and presenting some key features of the situation.

There are many kinds of models under several classifications. While an extensive review of classes of models is beyond the scope of this discussion,[6] there are some aspects that not only sketch the area but also provide a basis for the departure upon which the present text will rely for the treatment of the substance and the procedure of law and legal systems.

Models may be divided into those that are *static*, that is, those not reflecting changes over time, and those that are *dynamic* and reflect changes in state or structure. An example of a static model is an organizational chart that portrays related elements in a system. Figure 2-1 shows the various kinds of courts at different levels in a typical state judicial system. Dynamic models, on the other hand, show steps in an ongoing process. Figure 2-2 is a simple model that illustrates the basic elements of

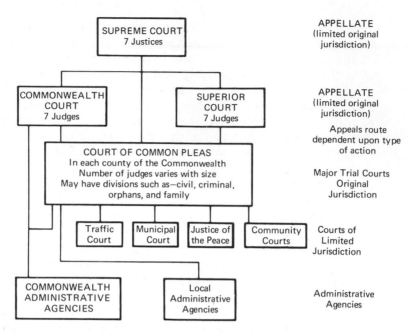

FIGURE 2-1. A State Judicial System. Adapted from Pennsylvania Code, (Harrisburg, Pa.: Legislative Reference Series, 1975) 204 Sec. 201.2

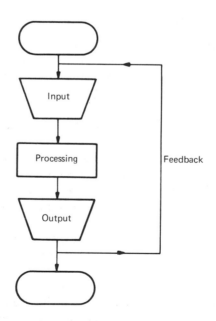

FIGURE 2-2. Simple Dynamic Systems Model

a dynamic system—inputs, process, system logic, outputs, and information requirements. A more specific model of a legal system appears in Figure 2-3 which provides a rough overview of the movement of criminal cases through a total system by showing virtually all steps possible in the process in addition to providing an awareness of the relative frequency of cases being determined at each step. The size of the black lines in Figure 2-3 indicates the relative number of cases at each disposition point.

A similar technique has been used in connection with the development of models used to simulate the processing of felony defendants in a trial court system. The dynamic chart (Figure 2-4) shows processing unit (circles), paths (lines) leading from one unit to another, and the percentage of defendants following those paths (numbers on the lines). The model, as descriptive models are intended to do, was developed to reflect the system accurately as it existed when observed.

These two examples of basically the same technique look a lot like an already established approach in industry. The Critical Path Method, CPM, is a scheduling technique that identifies steps in a total project, usually in manufacturing a product, and allows an educated estimate of the time for the steps and the total time for completing the project rather than numbers of individuals moving through a legal system. The total time it will take to complete the job is the sum of the activity times along the longest path in the network. This longest path is called the critical path.

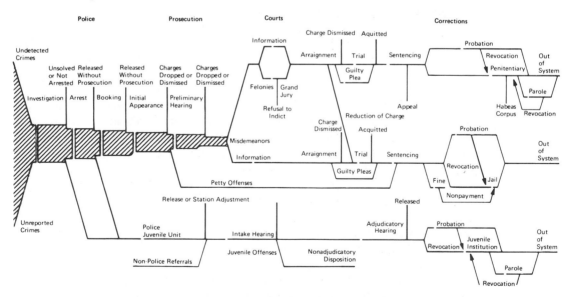

FIGURE 2-3. A Model of a Legal System. *From:* Challenge of Crime in a Free Society (Washington, D.C.: President's Commission on Law Enforcement and Administration of Justice, 1967).

ACQ	Acquittal
ARG	Arraignment
CAL	Calendar
CNV	Conviction
CON	Continuance
DCC	Nonjury trial
DCJ	Jury trial
MFD	Motion filing
MOE	Motions ended
MOF	Motion heard
PLD	Guilty plea
SEN	Sentencing

FIGURE 2-4. A Dynamic Model of Part of the Criminal Justice System. *From:* Jean G. Taylor and others, Data Analysis and Simulation of the District of Columbia Trial Court System for the Processing of Felony Defendants (Arlington, Virginia: Institute for Defense Analysis, 1968).

Focusing on the form of a model provides at least two different types. An *iconic* model is familiar from childhood attempts at building model ships or airplanes. An iconic model has some physical characteristics of the real thing it represents. *Symbolic* models use mathematical or other symbolic representation of the real situation.

Models may be *descriptive*, *predictive*, or *normative* depending upon what they are set up to do. A descriptive model describes the situation as it exists. Prediction is the function of the second type of model where an outcome is predicted if a certain set of circumstances exists. Normative models presumably provide an optimum or "best" result when elements of the model are sketched.

Finally, models may incorporate references to a degree of certainty represented by the model. *Deterministic* models operate under conditions of certainty in which inputs lead to specific outputs. Models under conditions of uncertainty are called *game* models in which conditions and their

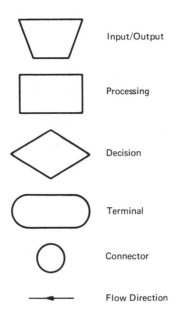

FIGURE 2-5. Flow Chart Conventional Figures.

outcomes are faced without any specific knowledge of the elements of a relationship. *Probabilistic* models operate between the preceding two, they are models in which decisions are made under risk conditions in terms of expectations of outcomes, i.e., probabilities.

There are certain conventional figures that are more useful in drawing models of a dynamic system (Figure 2-5). Just as road signs now are shaped in standard forms to match the message written on them so the shape of a drawing can represent a particular kind of step or operation. The steps are arranged in a more descriptive flow chart to show the progression through different functional phases of a system.

ANALYSIS OF DECISION SYSTEMS

The techniques sketched above are dynamic and descriptive—they report actual or modeled happenings as they occur in a sequence. Since they are merely descriptive of events in a process they do not lead to an analysis of the situation or provide an understanding per se of the factors that might cause a decision maker to choose one option over another. In many actual situations there is greater value in knowing what the choices are and how they might be made than in merely knowing how many individuals pass through the system or how much time elapses for completion of a project, interesting as that information might be in itself.

An approach which can be called the Analysis of Decision Systems (ADS) will attempt to picture steps in a process but also focus inquiry into the basic factors present at each point so that important questions may be asked. In the legal process, the progression through the network should focus upon the inquiry into the questions that are critical for an understanding of the facts and concepts underlying the action; from this understanding can come more intelligent coping with the legal problems that face individuals in a society. Appreciating and grasping the substantive aspects of law and legal systems thus comes from an analysis of process, if the basic reasons for decision making at each decision point are analyzed.

Figure 2-6 is a dynamic and descriptive model of a trial subsystem, a model which, though it provides some valuable information, stops short of being as helpful as it might be. It must be remembered that the factors in each geometric figure in the flow chart must be analyzed.

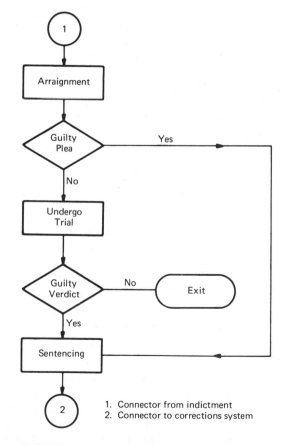

1. Connector from indictment
2. Connector to corrections system

FIGURE 2-6. Flow Chart of Trial Subsystem.

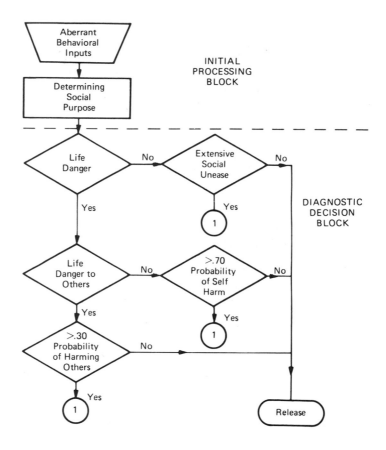

A more balanced model of the analysis of decision systems approach appears in Figure 2-7 in a matter involving the handling and treatment of individuals under certain limited circumstances. While each step is identified in terms of the action needed, the analysis of the basic decisions that accompany those actions still must be made. In addition to the descriptive and dynamic features of the model, however, there is a probabilistic approach added. The determination of whether a person is to be deprived of his liberty because his mental state represents a danger to himself or others is a legal process that proceeds according to the governing statutes. Many nonlegal questions, however, arise in the process and must be addressed. Decisions are required at frequent intervals in the flow chart, and it must be emphasized that these decisions are based not only upon the "fact" but upon judgments. In the model those judgments are quantified (somewhat arbitrarily, to be sure) and the probabilities that represent judgments help focus attention upon the underlying bases for decisions. Where do the probabilities come from? The person analyzing the situation arrives at the probability of a particular outcome. For

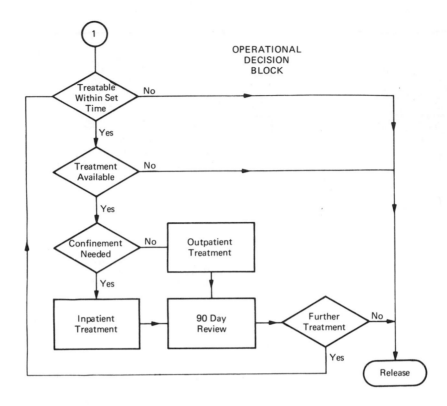

FIGURE 2-7. Flow Chart of Legal Commitment Decision Processes in Analysis of Decision Systems Approach.

instance the decision maker may, on the basis of all he knows about the circumstances, determine that the chances of success are one in two (a probability of .50) and answers the question of whether or not to proceed on that basis. In the model illustrated in Figure 2-7 there is a more subtle addition in that the determinations represent more of a value judgment whereby the decision maker begins to decide what *ought* to be. In Figure 2-7, for instance, there is a determination that society may be able to tolerate a higher level of risk of self-harm, for instance, than the chances of harm to others. Differing positions on this issue and, therefore, other probabilities assigned, are of course possible.

In the remainder of this book there will be a substantial number of simpler or more complex sketches of process as the areas of law will be treated in terms of analyzing steps in the legal procedure.

FOOTNOTES

[1] Fremont Kast and James Rosenzweig, *Organization and Management: A Systems Approach* (New York: McGraw-Hill, 1970) p. 110.

[2] James D. Thompson, *Organizations in Action* (New York: McGraw-Hill, 1967) p. 157.

[3] C. West Churchman, *The Systems Approach* (New York: Delacorte Press, 1968) pp. 29–30.

[4] Churchman, *The Systems Approach*, 1968.

[5] Herbert Simon, *Administrative Behavior*, (New York: Free Press, 1957).

[6] Robert G. Murdick and Joel E. Ross, *Information Systems for Modern Management* (Englewood Cliffs, N.J.: Prentice-Hall, 1971). Chapter 11, for example, provides more detail.

CHAPTER 3
THE LEGAL SYSTEM

The functioning of law can be identified within the systems framework just sketched. In the criminal system one can further subdivide that total complex into three rather well-known subsystems—control, court, and correctional.

Control subsystems comprise the law enforcement area; the judicial and penal subsystems comprise the courts and correctional units of the legal system.

The descriptions that follow will focus upon the three subsystems individually, and each may be referred to as a system in itself. It should be remembered, however, that the three areas are subsystems of the entire system and the use of the term system is for the reader's convenience.

CONTROL SYSTEMS

The usual initial phase of the criminal system is the area more often referred to as law enforcement. While these control units most often come into action in connection with an individual infraction, there are many opportunities for state and federal regulatory agencies to perform similar control operations in organizational activity. Their functioning occurs almost exclusively in a criminal law context, of course.

Federal Control Systems

The wide diversity of federal law enforcement agencies can be determined to a great extent from viewing Tables 3-1 and 3-2. These agencies

TABLE 3-1. Federal agencies with extensive control functions.

Agency	Mission	Personnel
Department of Justice		
Federal Bureau of Investigation	Detection and apprehension of violators of federal laws; protecting security of U.S.	Special agents; technical specialists
Immigration and Naturalization Service	Prevention of entry of illegal persons into the country	Immigration inspectors Border patrolmen
Drug Enforcement Administration	Control under drug laws through inspection and detection	Compliance investigators and undercover agents
Bureau of Prisons	Administration of Federal Penal Institutions	Correctional officers, counselors and treatment specialists
Criminal Division	Supervision of enforcement of Federal criminal laws	Attorneys, investigation, scientific technicians
U.S. Marshals	Support court activities—serving summons, protecting courts	U.S. Marshals in all judicial districts
Law Enforcement Assistance Administration	Improvement of Criminal Justice System (created by the Omnibus Crime Control Safe Streets Act of 1968)	Expert consultants, researchers, government grants personnel
Department of the Treasury		
Internal Revenue Service	Detection of evasion of income, alcohol, tobacco, and other taxes	Internal revenue agents (accountants, examiners, technicians); intelligence agents; alcohol, firearms, and tobacco tax investigators
Bureau of Customs	Prevention of illegal entry of goods into the country	Customs inspectors, security officers, patrolmen
Secret Service	Protection of the President and other officials; prevention of counterfeiting	Special agents, analysts, investigators; scientific personnel in Bureau of Engraving and Printing

all perform the functions of maintaining security of individuals and organizations in the specific duties entrusted to them by the Constitution, statutes, and perhaps agency regulation. Table 3-1 outlines the divisions and activities of the two federal departments most active in the investigative and control area. Other agencies, as illustrated in Table 3-2, have more limited external activities but all have an internal audit function for self-policing. The tables do not include still other organizations that may

TABLE 3-2. Federal agencies with limited control activities.

Agency	Mission	Personnel
Department of Defense		
Department of the Air Force, Army, and Navy	Promoting efficient armed services in support of national security	Investigators, security police, special investigators, military police, correctional officers, and criminal investigators
Department of State		
Office of Security	Providing security in department and installations abroad	Special agents
Agency for International Development	Assistance for law administration in developing countries	Investigators and public safety advisors
Department of the Interior		
National Park Service	Providing effective police services in national parks	U.S. Park Police
Bureau of Sport, Fisheries, and Wildlife	Enforcement of U.S. wildlife conservation statutes	U.S. game management agents
Department of Health, Education and Welfare		
Internal Security Office	Investigations to maintain effectiveness of agency	Investigative officers
Public Health Service, Food and Drug Commission	Enforcement of laws protecting consumers	Consumer safety officers

ALSO,

Department of Transportation	Civil Service Commission
Department of Agriculture	General Services Administration
Department of Commerce	Federal Trade Commission
United States Courts	Federal Maritime Commission
	United States Postal Services

be considered a part of the overall structure of law enforcement. The CIA, the National Security Agency, and various branches of military intelligence, for instance, have certain enforcement activities, but their primary thrust is the protection of our society by gaining information on external threats to the continuing existence of the country.

Federal agencies are able to act only when there is a specific statute or agency regulation that invokes their involvement. A specific federal law enables the federal agencies to exist and perform their duties. Where there is no such statute, the offenses come under the jurisdiction of state agencies. When a federal agency is called in, there is either evidence that state lines have been crossed or it is presumed that because of a lapse of time state lines have been crossed in the commission of the crime. In addition to this establishment of jurisdiction, states can, of course, request the assistance of federal agencies.

State Control Systems

State police forces operate under the statutes of their particular state and their jurisdiction extends, at least theoretically, across the entire state. In reality most state police forces leave much of the work to local units at the municipal or county level. There is a dearth of coverage in thinly populated rural areas by local forces, but even here the state police are seldom very active because they are understaffed. Most of the activity of the state police takes the form of highway patrol and accident investigation. Occasional serious crimes in rural areas will be investigated, however, and special task force programs hitting a specific crime target also take place. Apart from these activities most enforcement activity takes place at the local level.

Local Control Systems

By far the most common control system of which the average citizen is aware is that represented by the police, a sheriff, a constable, or, on rarer occasions, the county police. At this level there are over 30,000 separate police units all over the country ranging in size from the one-man police force in a village or township to the more than 37,000 members of the police force of New York City. It can be expected that large municipal departments are complexly structured, and Figure 3-1 illustrates a model organizational arrangement of a larger city police department.

Variation in duties of officials with the same title may be somewhat confusing. A sheriff in many states, particularly those in the Southwest, may have extensive law enforcement duties while the sheriff in an urban county in the east is often limited to activity such as service of court summons upon defendants in court actions. In Massachusetts, for instance, the sheriff maintains the peace and dignity of the courts and administers the jail and house of correction, in addition to serving writs of the court. There, as well as in most organized urban areas, local police units have taken over most of the criminal work that the movie-stereotyped sheriff may still perform in the more open areas of the country.

County police, as well, may show variation in duties. Some are truly investigative and active detective agencies while others are restricted to patrolling county parks and directing traffic at airports and other facilities.

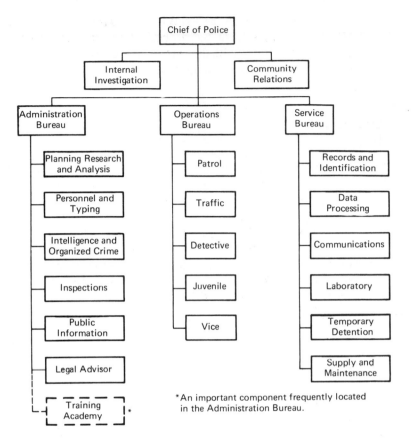

FIGURE 3-1. A Model Organizational Chart of A Municipal Police Department, *From:* George T. Felkenes, The Criminal System, (Englewood Cliffs, N.J.: Prentice Hall, Inc., 1973) P. 22.

COURT SYSTEMS

A court is a political entity organized for the purpose of administering justice. From a basic legal viewpoint the court consists of a judge and a jury, but discussions about court systems must include many other personnel. A court system needs a large number of support personnel in order to administer the activities that surround the basic cases.

Judicial activity in the United States takes place within two separate systems—the federal and the state courts. Each system has many tiers or levels, from the inferior magistrate's court to the ultimate court of appeals. In the federal system that final appellate body is, of course, the Supreme Court of the United States (it has limited original jurisdiction, however.) The cases that reach it upon appeal started out long before at an initial court, either at the federal district court located within one of the judicial districts of the United States or at a trial court in a particular state.

Some confusion may arise because of the apparent overlapping of state and federal courts and the number of special courts in the federal system. Even more confusing, however, is the variation in names of courts at the state level. An observer must be very careful to recognize at which level the court is operating when he hears the terms *superior* or *supreme* court used in different states.

The Federal Court System

The Constitution of the United States established only one court by name, the Supreme Court, but provided also that inferior courts could be established by Congress. There is no limit, therefore, on the number and types of federal courts that Congress may establish. The Constitution also established that the jurisdiction of federal courts would extend to all cases arising under the Constitution, laws of the United States, controversies where citizens of different states or different states themselves were involved—in short, all matters that could not be handled or considered within the boundaries of the single state. There is the added statutory provision that, at this point in time, controversies between citizens of different states must amount to individual claims of more than $10,000.

There are a large number of different courts in the federal judicial system, a fact that might be more readily appreciated by looking at Figure 3-2. It must be remembered, however, that the actual structure and functioning of the federal system is even more complex than it is pictured. It will be sufficient to note here that the usual activity begins with an original case in one of the 94 Federal District Courts in the fifty states and

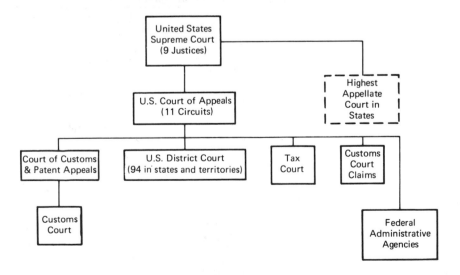

FIGURE 3-2. The Federal Judicial System.

territories (populous states have more than one district). Appeals go to the United States Court of Appeals covering the larger area in which that district fits geographically. Further appeals from those decisions go to the United States Supreme Court.

State Courts

Designations of the courts in different states can be quite misleading at times. Usually the term *Supreme Court* refers to the court of last resort in the state system. As Table 3-3 shows, however, the highest court can be called by some other name. Even more confusing is the situation in New York where the Supreme Court is the basic trial court. In California that basic court is called the Superior Court, whereas in Pennsylvania the court by that name is a statewide intermediate (and sometimes final) court of appeal.

The inferior tribunals also carry a variety of titles. Most familiar are the terms *municipal* and *traffic* courts, or *justices of the peace*. Recently housing courts have been added to the list of other lower-level courts.

TABLE 3-3. Comparison of three state judicial systems. Information taken from: The Book of the States, 1974–75, Vol. 20 (Lexington, Kentucky: The Council of State Governments, 1974) p. 21.

Level of Court	Selected States (Number of Judges in Parentheses)		
	New York	*Pennsylvania*	*Minnesota*
Court of Last Resort	(7) Court of Appeals	(7) Supreme Court	(9) Supreme Court
Intermediate Appeals Court	(28) Appellate Division of Supreme Court	(7) Superior Court ——————— (7) Commonwealth	None
Major Trial Court	(221) Supreme Court	(234) Court of Common Pleas	(72) District Court
How Elected	all elected by partisan ballot, except Governor appoints Judge of Court of Appeals and members of appellate division of Supreme Court. Mayor appoints judges of some local courts.	all elected by partisan ballot to serve for 10 years, nonpartisan retention thereafter.	All elected by ballot.

Other courts, such as probate, surrogate, family, and juvenile courts, are considered to be more important and, therefore, handled in the basic level, the court of original jurisdiction. The basic court may have divisions incorporating those functions. In Pennsylvania, for example, the Court of Common Pleas (the basic trial court) has juvenile and family divisions, as well as the criminal and civil trial divisions. A simplified structuring of a more extensive state judicial system appears in Figure 3-3. Again it should be noted that the actual situation in detail is much more complex than can be presented in one figure.

Judges

The administration of justice in the court system is fundamentally in the hands of the judge. As a matter of fact, the judge has so critical a role in the process that he is often referred to as the court. The title judge may also have a more specific term attached to it such as *district—presiding—* or *juvenile court—* to designate the jurisdiction or assignment; often the judge may be called a justice (as on the U.S. Supreme Court) or chancellor. The justice of the peace or magistrate, however, is the lowest office in the judicial system and the holder of that post is seldom regarded in the same way as those mentioned above.

Judges are chosen in various ways. In the federal judicial system the President of the United States, with the advice and consent of the Senate, appoints judges, who serve for life.

Prior to making the appointment the President consults with the Senators from the state where the vacancy exists; in addition, steps are usually taken to assure that the nominee is competent. Both approaches keep the number of rejections by the Senate at a minimum.

At the state level various ways exist for selection of judges. In over half the states judges are elected by popular vote. In some states nomination at a political primary pits two candidates in a partisan campaign, in other states the voting occurs on a nonpartisan basis. In half a dozen states the legislature selects the judges and in a few others the governors choose from a slate on the basis of merit determined by a panel or nonpartisan group. The candidate must then be approved or rejected by the electorate after a period of judicial service. This procedure is often called the Missouri Plan after its first use in that state.

The Legal Profession

A fact often forgotten is that a legal system is, to a great extent, an adversary one. Without lawyers to protect the rights of individuals in the process it may be ventured that justice would be more difficult to attain.

FIGURE 3-3. A State Judicial System; *From:* Pennsylvania Code, (Harrisburg, Pa: Legislative Reference Bureau, 1975) 204 Sec. 201.2.

While defendants in criminal matters need the protection of knowledgeable counsel, the prosecution must also discharge its responsibilities. In civil cases, as well, both sides need help. Thus there is no doubt that any discussion of legal systems must include a description of the legal profession and the role it plays in the system of justice.

Development of the legal profession proceeded slowly under English Common Law; at first, when trial by ordeal was abolished, judges permitted anyone to appear as counsel for the parties. Gradually it became evident that, for better representation of persons and control by the court, a program of training and selection was necessary. Educational development of lawyers was still somewhat casual, however, as prospective lawyers were tutored in the offices of practitioners; only at the end of the past century did law schools take over a significant role in the preparation of lawyers. Most states these days require graduation from law school as a prerequisite for admission to the bar (and law schools generally require graduation from college). Admission to the bar means that the lawyer may represent litigants in court at the same time that he submits himself to regulation by the court and his peers and accepts the provisions of the code of ethics of the profession.

In addition to their professional activity as advocates in a specific cause, lawyers are seen to play a significant role in shaping statutes and governmental processes. Their influence, as Mayer[1] and other observers have pointed out, may be all out of proportion to their numbers in society (although even here the United States has more lawyers per capita than any other major nation in the world).

Public Lawyers

Attorneys general and other prosecuting officers occupy so important a segment of the legal system that some descriptions of the system set them apart from the courts. Their major role is in the administration of justice through the judicial system and they are known as officers of the court, but they are elected or appointed in actions separate from those initiated by the courts. Nevertheless, they are part of the court system more than any other subdivision, and as such they are treated here.

The position of attorney general developed early in England where the king appointed an attorney to represent him in all legal actions. The post was adopted in America in colonial times and carried over into cabinet status in the federal government as well as in the states, one by one. Over this time span the role of the attorney general in all jurisdictions was remarkably similar to the role known today.

The Attorney General of the United States, in addition to advising the President on points of law, provides legal services to other departments of the government. In addition, he supervises the functioning of the most extensive legally-related federal department (Table 3-1). The Attorney General appoints the U.S. attorney in each judicial district of the United States. At that level the U.S. attorney presents evidence to and advises the grand jury. He is also in charge of all litigation and helps to conduct all those activities in his district for which the Attorney General of the United States is responsible.

The attorney general at the state level performs much the same function, except that he may extend legal opinions to the legislature as well as to the chief executive. In 42 states the attorney general is an elected official while in most of the remaining eight states he is selected by the governor and reports to him. The opinions of the attorney general are quasi judicial in nature as his advisory opinions are often regarded as representing the status of the law.

At the local level, usually for a county unit, the enforcement of criminal law in the judicial system is in the hands of an officer of the court who is usually referred to as the county prosecutor or district attorney. In this discussion the local prosecutor is included in the court subsystem, but may be considered by some as an entity separate from it. He is elected or appointed as provided by statute and acts as any other public servant. At the federal and state level the attorney general operates more in the executive area, but the independence of the district attorney from the judicial and executive branches is almost complete at the local county or district level.

Attorneys For the Defense

Counsel for defendants have traditionally been selected in the course of the direct contacts that exist in the usual attorney-client relationships of both civil and criminal law. This is still a significant aspect of the functioning of the judicial system, but recent greater concern for adequate representation has put the focus on publicly supported counsel. Courts appoint attorneys for indigent defendants, usually on a random basis from the general panel of local lawyers. Legal Aid Societies may also assist individuals in securing the assistance of counsel. Some limitation in this system has led to more formal arrangements through a permanently established office of a public defender. With increased workloads, particularly in large metropolitan areas, an organized system is needed to operate more efficiently than the more casual ad hoc appointment system. A public defender's office is, with luck, as well staffed as the local prosecutor's office, with public revenues supporting investigators and clerks, as well as lawyers. Even by the late 1960s, however, public defenders' offices were handling about one third of the indigent cases while assigned counsel still took care of the majority of cases.[2]

The Jury

The strength of the jury, especially in criminal trials, comes from a strong tradition in Anglo-American Common Law. Probably as the result of arbitrary acts of the king's judges during colonial times, the founding fathers were determined that a panel of their peers would function to check the possible arbitrariness of a single judicial officer. The U.S. Constitution established the right of trial by jury in Article III while two amendments, in the Bill of Rights, confirmed the right to speedy and public trial by jury (Sixth Amendment) and a right to jury trial in suits at common law where the value exceeds twenty dollars (Seventh Amendment). Each state followed with somewhat similar guarantees in state courts and subsequent federal court decisions have extended the federal level of rights in criminal cases to those states with fewer safeguards (invoking the Fourteenth Amendment).

The jury has traditionally consisted of twelve persons selected from a larger list of eligible (competent) candidates. While the number twelve has a long history, the trend today is toward juries of six persons. The U.S. Supreme Court has ruled that this size does not violate one's constitutional rights.[3]

In selecting the jury prosecution and defense can exercise a set number of challenges, for a specific reason involving possible bias (challenge for cause) or for no reason (peremptory challenge). Jurors, once selected, are to determine the facts under the guidance of the judge who instructs them in the law. The verdict reached by the jury stands unless the judge believes that he must set aside the verdict because of valid legal reasons. That verdict may be reached by less than a unanimous decision if the law permits. Moreover, a jury trial may even be waived by a defendant and the judge sits as trier of both fact and law.

The best-known type of jury is the *petit jury*, which hears the criminal or civil case at first resort. There are other juries, also determining factual situations, such as the *coroner's jury* or a *grand jury*. The grand jury (the name comes from the greater number of persons on it) inquires into matters brought before it by district attorney, sheriff, or other officer to determine if a basis exists for bringing the matter to trial. The grand jury also can be called to investigate other general matters such as corruption or related concerns in government or society. Many states are in the process of eliminating the grand jury and relying upon an *information* presented to the court by the prosecutor.

ADMINISTRATIVE AGENCIES

Because of the increasing complexity of society, particularly that of an industrially developed one, there are many matters that cannot be handled by the limited facilities of the existing three branches of government—the legislative, the executive, and the judicial. Matters that arise every day are often so involved that transfer of many of the functions in the legal system is made to a governmental agency established for the purpose of either investigating, monitoring, or regulating the activities of individuals or corporate entities. Administrative agencies have proliferated from nothing almost 100 years ago to present regulation of atomic energy, radio and television, labor relations, the securities market, and countless other areas. The extensiveness of federal agencies (Table 3-4) is to a great extent parallelled by the comparable agencies at the state level. Almost all states will have a Public Utility Commission to regulate rates of utilities operating within the state, a Human Relations Commission, and myriad additional agencies that can even include a Liquor Control Board (Table 3-5).

Administrative agencies are established by specific act of either the executive or legislative branch. There is no provision in the Constitution for them. The act of legislature or executive order, which establishes the

TABLE 3-4. Selected federal agencies.

Action	Inter-American Foundation
Administrative Conference of the United States	Interstate Commerce Commission
American Battle Monuments Commission	National Aeronautics and Space Commission
Appalachian Regional Commission	National Credit Union Administration
Atomic Energy Commission	National Foundation of the Arts and
Canal Zone Government	Humanities
Civil Aeronautics Board	National Labor Relations Board
Commission of Fine Arts	National Mediation Board
Commission on Civil Rights	National Science Foundation
Consumer Product Safety Commission	Occupational Safety and Health Review
Delaware River Basin Commission	Commission
District of Columbia	Overseas Private Investment Corporation
Economic Stabilization Program	Panama Canal Company
Environmental Protection Agency	Postal Rate Commission
Equal Employment Opportunity Commission	Railroad Retirement Board
Export-Import Bank of the United States	Renegotiation Board
Farm Credit Administration	Securities and Exchange Commission
Federal Communications Commission	Selective Service System
Federal Deposit Insurance Corporation	Small Business Administration
Federal Home Loan Bank Board	Smithsonian Institution
Federal Maritime Commission	Susquehanna River Basin Commission
Federal Mediation and Conciliation Service	Tennessee Valley Authority
Federal Power Commission	U.S. Arms Control & Disarmament Agency
Federal Reserve System	U.S. Civil Service Commission
Federal Trade Commission	U.S. Information Agency
Foreign Claims Settlement Commission of	U.S. Postal Service
the United States	U.S. Tariff Commission
General Services Administration	Veterans Administration
Indian Claims Commission	

TABLE 3-5. Selected state agencies (Commonwealth of Pennsylvania).

Commissions and Boards

Pennsylvania Board of Probation and Parole
Civil State Service Commission
Historical and Museum Commission
State Horse Racing Commission
Pennsylvania Liquor Control Board
Milk Marketing Board
State Tax Equalization Board (Independent Administrative Board)
Pennsylvania Turnpike Commission
Pennsylvania Public Television Network Commission
Bicentennial Commission
Fish Commission
Pennsylvania Game Commission
Pennsylvania Public Utility Commission (quasi-judicial agency of the Legislature)
Workmen's Compensation Appeal Board (in Dept. of Labor and Industry)

Authorities
(Separate Public Corporation Created by the Legislature)

The General State Authority
State Highway and Bridge Authority
State Public School Building Authority
Pennsylvania Higher Educational Facilities Authority
Pennsylvania Transportation Assistance Authority

agency, may also prescribe the policies for it and outline the general procedures that are to be followed. An agency may be placed within one of the three branches of government—executive, legislative, judicial—or it may be classified as an "independent" agency. The independent agency has more latitude than those in the branches as its members generally enjoy a specific term of office. Some agencies have received the power to act in a quasi-judicial capacity and, therefore, are often significant adjuncts to the judicial system. Needless to say, their decisions are subject to appeal in the regularly established channels in the court system. Even if the agency has no judicial powers, the ability to establish specific rules and procedures governing its actions is a lawmaking function. In the final instance, however, both functions are under the ultimate control of the legislature—which determines its existence and continuing budget—and of the courts, which review administrative decisions.

THE CORRECTIONS SYSTEM

As much as our present-day correctional institutions are in need of improvement, there is no doubt that we have come a long way from the barbaric means of retribution that passed for correction of a transgression.

Little useful purpose will be served by cataloging the cruel and unusual punishments that have been imposed in the past or perhaps even exist today in some parts of the world. What is important to keep in mind is that current practice in correctional institutions may lean more toward retribution than positive rehabilitation.

Penal Institutions

Jails and prisons have existed for centuries but their expansion to a system that encompassed the totality of a political unit came as recently as the rise of the industrial revolution.[4] Earlier the care and feeding of prisoners might have been a nuisance to the community; when the rapid development of industry called for more labor, the jail population could supply that in quantity and at low cost. The rise in penal legislation and capacity of prisons began to match the industrial needs of the day. No longer was the local jailer dependent upon the meager fees for food and services that he could squeeze from prisoners—the political unit could pay jailers a wage and hire out convicts profitably. While now the practice of chain gangs on farms and road building has almost completely disappeared under the positive actions of concerned citizens, the compensating need for more financial support to maintain the prison population in a semblance of humaneness is not being met. Reluctance to pay the costs of proper incarceration has hampered prison reform.

City and county units are the base of the correctional system. There are over 4000 municipal or county jails in the country, a majority of them very old and inadequate. They get more than two million commitments a year, most of them for such misdemeanors as drunkenness or motor vehicle charges.[5] Some may be held for trial for a longer period than they would serve if convicted and many eventually are found not guilty after the long wait for trial.

Local jails are under the control of municipal police or county officers such as the sheriff. Standards of care and operation either do not exist or are very difficult to meet under the usual limitations of funding of correctional facilities at any level. Local facilities are especially subject to these conditions, and the resulting shortage of trained personnel, poor physical and health conditions, and slack supervision encourage demeaning or even brutal responses on the part of guards and prisoners, as well.

State correctional facilities can demonstrate more professional planning and implementation than most local jails can. Development of facilities has been matched by changes of attitudes to the point where positive correctional re-education has been slowly introduced in that more favorable physical setting. Punitive philosophy on the part of officials may not have been completely eliminated, but general civic concern has stimulated improvements upon past conditions.

The number of prisoners in state and federal prisons has risen in recent years. In 1971 approximately 160,000 persons were incarcerated in institutions of various types,[6] but on January 1, 1976 that figure rose to 250,000 and is projected to increase even further in the near future.[7]

Probation and Parole

The correctional system includes activity that does not involve confinement as a means for returning an individual to society. *Probation* is a program selected by the court to rehabilitate the offender outside of prison under the supervision of a court case worker. The judge's decision leaves the offender at liberty during his period of testing and proving his worthiness. *Parole* is the conditional release from a correctional institution of a person who has served part of his sentence. His release into the custody of a parole officer is based upon the assumption that he is ready to be received in society and has, in a sense, given his word that his behavior will be above reproach (parole comes from the French term or word for promise).

Probation is based upon the power of the court to suspend a sentence or impose conditions other than incarceration. While a sentence may be suspended unconditionally (in which case the defendant is discharged), probation is a period for observation of a person under a suspended sentence in which certain conditions are imposed. The offender is then required to meet the conditions imposed by the court and is monitored by the probation officer to see that he does so. If not, the probationer can be sent to a correctional institution to serve the term appropriate for the offense when the court revokes the suspension.

Parole is determined by a board selected or appointed for that purpose. The members of the board meet to set policy and procedure, fix appropriate periods of trial before eligibility for parole, study individual cases, and decide whether the offender merits release on parole. As with probation, the parolee must report to an officer maintaining contact who also provides counseling and guidance in the period of parole. Violation of the conditions under which parole is granted will put the parolee back in prison.

Probation offices are also attached to the juvenile court where young offenders (who may be one of society's growing problems on the basis of numbers alone) are directed. The realization that an adolescent should receive more attention has caused courts to treat juveniles with greater care than adults receive. Juvenile probation officers, therefore, often may be selected with more deliberation and followed more closely by the court and community.

Probation and parole officers have more to do than counsel and supervise the offenders. At the very outset, the court or parole board needs to know as much as possible about the offender so that it can arrive at a better decision about the treatment most likely to be effective in the individual case. Extensive investigation prior to sentencing may also be the job of the probation officer. Similarly, gathering the life history of the inmate as well as testing and evaluating him is the task of the case workers in the parole office. The parole officer in the field must, in some way, investigate and file reports on the parolees under his supervision.

Continuing concern about recurring deficiencies in the correctional process has generated attempts to approach the old problems in newer ways. Variations of long-standing probation and parole techniques or completely innovative approaches have been suggested to supplement or supplant the one-to-one relationship that has existed between the offender and the agency officer.

Work Release is a program developed in the federal corrections system, as well as in many states, which is intended to release inmates so that they can be productively and gainfully employed under previously set conditions. Either a complete exit or release during working hours prepares the inmate for return to society and reduces the financial strain on the corrections system when the inmate reimburses it and pays taxes.

External treatment centers, usually in the home area, are intended to reintroduce the offender gradually to the community. The centers can be either governmental units or those developed with the participation of private organizations. The Federal Bureau of Prisons has initiated community treatment centers and some states may follow suit. Halfway houses are set up for the same reasons by local governmental units or community agencies. These may have numerous volunteers involved or the services can be carried out in many supporting ways in the community, either in group projects or in the individual type of counseling that the probation or parole officer traditionally has provided.

FOOTNOTES

[1] Martin Mayer, *The Lawyers* (New York: Harper and Row, 1971).

[2] The President's Commission on Law Enforcement and Administration of Justice, *The Challenge of Crime in a Free Society* (Washington, D.C.: Government Printing Office, 1967).

[3] *Williams v. Florida*, 399 U.S. 78 (1970).

[4] George T. Felkenes, *The Criminal Justice System: Its Function and Personnel* (Englewood Cliffs, N.J.: Prentice-Hall, 1973).

[5] President's Commission, *The Challenge of Crime*, p. 72.

[6] *Statistical Abstract of the United States* (Washington, D.C., U.S. Bureau of the Census, 1973).

[7] *Wall Street Journal*, July 20, 1976, p. 1.

CHAPTER 4
LEGAL SUBSTANCE
AND PROCEDURE

Substantive law represents the foundation upon which the actors in the legal system base their approach to the solution of the problems in society that are susceptible to such treatment. These elements are brought into play as the system swings into action in the legal process as described. The factors of substance and process are intertwined in this phase of societal activity just as they are in other human events.

CRIMES

One of the basic distinctions made in Chapter 1 was between criminal and civil law. This differentiation applies to the matter of how a particular act affects society. When society considers an act to be a wrong committed against society, the commission of that act is a crime. An injury done as a private wrong to a person is considered a tort, a civil injury, and one to be redressed in a civil action.

The same set of circumstances can be the basis for both a criminal and civil action. If, for instance, Smith strikes Jones, Jones may sign a complaint and have Smith prosecuted for assault and battery in a criminal court. Jones also may file a separate tort action in civil court for monetary damages. In the criminal case the state proceeds against Smith:

Commonwealth v. Smith
State v. Smith
People v. Smith

(The exact caption varies from state to state.) In a civil case the matter carries the caption "Jones v. Smith," identifying the plaintiff and the defendant, in that order.

Crimes themselves can be distinguished on the basis of severity—some are more shocking to society than others. A basic twofold distinction in common law has been made between a *felony* and a *misdemeanor*. Under old English law a felony was an act punishable by forfeiture of life and property; all other, lesser offenses were misdemeanors (in addition there was treason, an even more serious offense against the Crown).

At this time the criminal statutes differentiate between the two on the basis of the penalty imposed:

1. Length of term, and
2. Place of incarceration.

The level of crime is specified in the statute or is recognized as *existing at common law*. Place of imprisonment and term vary accordingly. Some states have now extended the two classes and refer to felonies and misdemeanors of the first, second, and third degree, in that order of severity.

There are some general factors that must be considered. For a crime to have been committed, two elements must be present:

1. *Act* and
2. *Intent.*

Both must be considered; there is no crime if either is absent.

An actual act must be shown to have taken place; this is not as difficult as showing intent. That requisite criminal mental state goes under the Latin term *mens rea* or "thing of the mind." This state of the mind can be

1. Specific intent,
2. General intent,
3. Transferred intent,
4. Criminal negligence.

Specific intent must be shown as part of the act. Theft, for example, is unlawful control over the property of another with the intent to deprive him thereof. Here the intent is specifically mentioned and must be shown for the act to be considered a crime. General intent refers to a situation where no special frame of mind is present; if an overall intention to do the act can be shown, the crime exists. General intent also covers cases in which the act is criminal, even though the person does not intend it. A motorist traveling an interstate highway at 75 miles per hour gets a speeding ticket because (unknown to him) the limit is now 55 mph in order to conserve gasoline nationally. Transferred intent occurs when an individual intends to commit a wrongful act but makes a mistake and injures someone else. While he did not intend those specific results he did have a criminal frame of mind that is transferred to the action. In certain cases there may be such gross lack of care that this negligent action is criminal negligence. This is the *mens rea* that provides the requisite intent to make the act a crime. If Mr. Z accidentally wildly discharges a gun in a crowd and someone is killed, the negligence is criminal and enough to make out a malevolent frame of mind.

The various acts that constitute crimes are cataloged in a criminal code enacted by the legislature of that particular state and in federal statutes. Such codes are usually very specific in describing the prohibited acts and the penalties associated with them. The codes are also quite comprehensive, and the student with specific questions is directed to the code for his jurisdiction or to the more general substantive supplement available as Part V of this text.

THE CRIMINAL PROCESS

Those serious acts against society that are called crimes involve the individual charged with the act and various agents of government assigned the task of maintaining law and order. The major steps taken in this activity are sketched in Figure 4-1.

The legal process in criminal matters begins with the police and community reaction to the initial incident. A crime may be observed by a police officer or instituted by a complainant—a witness to or victim of the criminal act. Investigation and the apprehension of the purported criminal can employ a series of witnesses, leads, or "tips" from informants or continuous surveillance.

Arrest and Booking

Arrest occurs when a person is taken into custody by law officers in order to charge him with a crime—a search may take place, a reasonable search without a warrant, or search with a warrant or with the consent of the suspect. Most encounters of police with those questioned do not end in arrest; interrogation on the street or in the home may be the only contact a person has with the criminal process.

Booking takes place immediately after the arrest. This is merely a clerical process where the basic information is placed on the police record or *blotter*. In serious offenses the suspect will be fingerprinted and photographed. In minor matters the officer at the desk may decide that the best approach lies in taking care of the problem in an informal process in the station and releasing the person detained. Even more, the officer

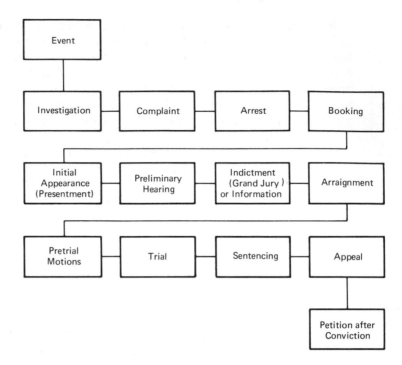

FIGURE 4-1. General Overview of the Criminal Law Process.

in charge may determine, after hearing the evidence, that no basis exists for further detention.

The booking is reported to the prosecutor's office, where the decision is made as to whether the defendant should be charged with the crime and continued in the system. Deciding not to prosecute may happen as often as half the time. Charging the defendant means that the prosecutor prepares the complaint identifying him and specifying the charge against him.

Arrested persons in most jurisdictions are to be taken before a magistrate without unreasonable delay. For many reasons (e.g., numbers or time of day) the time span may be longer than would ordinarily be thought reasonable. In some states this appearance before a magistrate is known as a *presentment* but may be called a *preliminary arraignment*. In federal court it would be called an *appearance*. The defendant is advised of the charges, of his right to a preliminary hearing, and the right to assigned or retained counsel. The magistrate sets bail at a figure that matches the severity of the crime charged or, more rarely, makes use of new plans to provide release without regular bail, that is, release on recognizance, or nominal bail. If money bail is required, a nearby bondsman is usually ready to provide it at a cost that ordinarily runs to ten percent of the bail set. About half the defendants cannot afford this and are sent to jail for further processing.

The Preliminary Hearing

Further action on the case does not proceed until the magistrate is convinced by the prosecutor that there is probable cause that a felony was committed by .the defendant. Cross-examination is available to the defendant but very few go to this length; a vast majority of accused persons waive their right to a preliminary hearing. If the magistrate finds probable cause (and he does almost all the time) he will *bind over* or hold the defendant for trial.

Indictment by Grand Jury or by Information

In many jurisdictions the grand jury serves as an additional screening device through which the case passes before it comes to a full trial. This body is chosen from a larger panel of citizens to make a group of at least twelve but seldom more than twenty-four to decide whether the prosecutor has established probable cause. If more than half vote to indict, the defendant will stand trial. Those states that have eliminated the grand jury have substituted the process of *information*, a procedure whereby the court receives a statement prepared by the prosecutor showing wrongdoing by a party.

The Arraignment

This is the step in the process in which the defendant is brought to the trial court and receives information on the charges against him. The defendant is also informed of the pleas that he can choose—guilty, not guilty, or *nolo contendere* (noncontesting). At this point as many as three-fourths of the defendants plead guilty. This comes about as the result of several factors. First of all, many individuals have been diverted out of the criminal justice system at one point or another, and most of the cases remaining are those that the prosecution feels with some degree of certainty should go to trial. In addition there is often *plea bargaining* in which the defendant's attorney may be able to obtain a reduction of the charge to a lesser offense in return for a plea of guilty by the defendant.

Pretrial Motions

Objections of various kinds, if they have not been raised before, are made at this time before trial. A motion to supress illegally obtained evidence is perhaps the most common. This motion is frequently seen in narcotics cases and, when the motion is successful, the case is often dismissed for lack of evidence. When the defendant feels that too much publicity in the area has been prejudicial to his case, he may move to have a change in venue. Various other motions, such as sufficiency of indictment, prior jeopardy, or improper procedures of the grand jury are more likely to have been raised earlier.

The Trial

Defendants in felony cases have a right to a trial by jury but they often waive the right and have the judge sit as judge and jury. There does not seem to be much difference in the percentage of acquittals; in either case the percentage of acquittals seldom goes above one-third of the cases. A criminal trial has more rigorous standards than a civil trial in some respects. The defendant is presumed innocent, he has a right not to take the stand, and such action is not to redound to his detriment, evidence obtained illegally is not admitted, and proof beyond a reasonable doubt is required for conviction.

Sentencing

In most situations the judge has widespread discretion as to the sentence to be imposed. He may consign the defendant to prison or place him on probation. The sentence to imprisonment may be for a specific span of time or for an indeterminate period. Both are usually bound by a minimum and a maximum period of imprisonment, terms that vary by statute from state to state. In some jurisdictions the judge will delay sentencing until he receives advice from a behavior clinic or a similar group of professional evaluators if there is some doubt in the judge's mind as to the kind of sentence that will best achieve the goals of the criminal justice system. It is not unusual for about one-half of the convicted defendants to be sent to prison while the other half receive a probation or suspended sentence.

Appeal

Defendants who are found guilty may appeal to a higher court, and these days about a fourth of them do. If an appeal is successful (and less than one-fourth of them are) the appellate court reverses the conviction (but in many cases the defendant may be retried and quite possibly convicted).

Petitions After Conviction

Incarceration does not end the possibilities for the convicted prisoner's matter to come to the attention of the courts. Petitions for collateral relief from prison can be framed simply and presented to the courts, although they are rarely successful. Apparently prisoners are becoming more sophisticated in this area, or there is a greater recognition of availability of the right to petition, since the number of such petitions has increased considerably over the past few years.

CIVIL LAW

A wrong that is not considered by society to be an offense against that entity to a degree that would seriously damage it is placed in the category of civil law rather than criminal law. In the civil area, government agents play a lesser role in the process. Even on the civil side, however, there must be a source in law for the remedy or right residing in the plaintiff before the wrong can be taken to the judicial agents of the society for settlement.

The source in law for civil remedies in the United States is seen, as has been introduced earlier, in remote beginnings in early English history. The two main streams of Anglo-American jurisprudence date from the twelfth century when equity concepts developed under the chancellor in a reaction against the rigidity of common law mechanisms. Major common law remedies were recovery of possession (*replevin* for objects or *ejectment* for land) or *damages* (compensation for injury). Because pleas to common law courts had to be specifically addressed in proper language in a limited number of forms, there were many petitions for special relief that were not covered by common law. With a great increase in petitions the lord chancellor was given the task of dispensing justice in these cases in the name of the king. Equity, too, has its specific remedies, however. The major ones are rescission (cancelling the contract), injunction (order to cease an act), and specific performance (order to do something).

These two thrusts can still be identified in civil law even though they have merged in the court system. There is still an emphasis on form of action and the reliance on past decisions (*stare decisis*) in common law, whereas equity actions are more flexible, as in the beginning, in order to obtain justice that cannot be fitted easily into common law concepts. It may be due to this feature of flexibility that equity actions are expanding in our legal system.

To these two basic sources of contemporary law must be added the third significant area of civil law, the law merchant. The customary rules of dealing in the marketplace have entered the law and enriched it, primarily in the extensive codifications of the Uniform Commercial Code.

A party seeking a remedy for a wrong, once it is determined that the requirements for entry are present, can then use the court system for the attempt to settle the dispute. The question at this point is which specific court can be used. A case in controversy can be brought to a court if that court has

1. Jurisdiction
    (a) over subject matter
    (b) over parties
2. Venue.

Jurisdiction refers to authority of power of a court to act; venue is a matter of physical location.

One division of a state court of original jurisdiction will generally hear a case arising within the borders of that state. A federal court has more requirements to be met before entry into the system. There must be:

1. A federal question—one arising under the Constitution or the laws of the United States, and amount over $10,000, or

2. Diversity of citizenship—citizens of different states or foreign states, and amount in controversy exceeding $10,000, or

3. Matter restricted by statute to federal courts.

If an action is brought in a state court it may be removed to a federal court by the defendant if the action is based on a federal question or if there is diversity of citizenship and the over $10,000 requisite is satisfied.

Jurisdiction over the parties extends to the persons (*in personam*) or their property (*in rem*). For a state court to have jurisdiction over the person it must be able to provide a copy of the summons and a complaint to the defendant who is present or domiciled in the state. This is known as personal service of process. Jurisdiction *in rem* (of the object or thing) exists for a state court if the object is within the boundaries of the state. Land, physical objects, or even such status as marriage can be the subject of court action not only when there is personal service on the defendant but also when there is substitute service such as publication in a newspaper if personal service cannot be obtained.

Venue refers to the location where the court can act. Usually the plaintiff can bring an action in the county where the cause of action arose or where the defendant resides. A court might have jurisdiction but not have venue, in which case the action may be challenged.

The two major classes of cases in controversy in civil disputes are those relating to contracts and torts. A contract is a promise to do something in the future; it gives rise to rights in the parties to the promise and grants remedies if the promises are breached. A tort is a breach of a duty imposed by society upon individuals to refrain from doing a specific sort of harm to others intentionally or unintentionally through lack of due care.

If a contract meets all the requirements that are set forth in the law of contracts or a statute, the courts will consider it a valid contract and will proceed to enforce it if asked to do so. The elements of a contract are

1. Capacity of the parties,
2. Offer,
3. Acceptance,
4. Consideration,
5. Legal purpose.

In addition, some contracts may be required by statutes to be in writing. If all the elements are present a valid contract comes into existence. Other agreements or purported contracts will not fare as well. A void agreement is not a contract and has no legal effect as, for instance, a gambling debt in most states will not be enforced by a court. A voidable contract is one in which a party may withdraw if he wishes but the other party is bound by it. An unenforceable contract is one that may meet the general requirements for a contract but a statute provides that such a contract cannot be enforced.

The contract may be either express or implied. An express contract is worded such that specific promises and conditions are set forth. An implied contract does not have those essential elements but must be determined from the surrounding circumstances and the conduct of the persons. It must be evident, however, that there is a mutual understanding between the parties as to what each will give and receive in order for a contract to exist.

Parties usually arrive at a contract through a stage of negotiations. One side will come forth with an offer which, if accepted by the other, will result in a contract. The offer that is communicated, if not withdrawn by the offeror, can be accepted by the offeree. A rejection of the offer terminates it as does a lapse of reasonable time (unless otherwise specified) or an incapacity of the parties in the interim. An acceptance of the offer communicated establishes the contract. Silence on the part of the offeree does not ordinarily mean consent. Consent, as a matter of law, must be shown on both sides. If parties were induced to enter into an otherwise valid contract by duress, fraud, or misrepresentation, a valid contract does not exist. Nor can a valid contract exist if parties do not have the capacity to enter into a binding contract. In this instance capacity is the ability to perform in a manner that the law regards as valid. Insane and underage persons often are under this type of protection. Finally, there must be a bargaining between the parties and the emergence of consideration. The promisee must take on a legal burden or give up a legal right in order for consideration to exist.

The above fundamental principles of contract law form the basis for court action when disputes arise. Some variations have been introduced under the *Uniform Commercial Code*, which has been adopted relatively recently by all states except Louisiana, which has adopted only a part.[1] One provision, for instance, requires that contracts for the sale of goods in excess of $500 must ordinarily be in writing. Without this the contract is unenforceable.

In a well-regulated society each individual has a duty not to damage the person or property of others in that society and a breach of that duty is a tort. Torts may be classified in the following way:

1. Intentional:
   (a) Interference with the person,
   (b) Interference with property,
2. Nonintentional.

Intentional torts on the person may consist of such physical acts as assault, battery, and false imprisonment or they may consist of words or acts that defame a person, invade his privacy, or place him in mental distress. Interference with property rights include the interference of possession of both real and personal property (trespass) as well as any action where economic advantage is gained over another through wrongful means. The injured party may recover actual, nominal, or punitive damages in some or all of the above situations.

Nonintentional torts are based primarily upon the concept of negligence, the failure to use due care in an injury to another that might have been avoided had due care been exercised. There are four elements that must be demonstrated before a tort action alleging negligence can be the subject of recovery:

1. Duty of care,
2. Breach of duty,
3. Proximate cause,
4. Injury or damage.

The actions of a reasonable and prudent person represent the standards by which courts will judge whether the duty of due care was breached. In addition the injury in the incident must be judged to have been the probable result of the plaintiff's actions. Defenses in actions of negligence include *contributory negligence* and *assumption of the risk*. Contributory negligence defenses allege that the plaintiff failed to exercise due care himself while assumption of the risk alleges that the injured party was aware of the risks faced and deliberately proceeded in spite of the foreseeable danger. In some special cases courts have gone further than failure to exercise due care and have imposed a standard of *strict liability* for actions. This makes a person liable even if he exercised all possible due care. This doctrine is applied when hazardous situations exist and the courts have decided that there is some social utility in protecting others through this rigorous interpretation. Mounting a spring gun in one's home to foil intruders or keeping vicious wild animals on the premises fall into this category. In the commercial area this concept is being applied more and more with respect to products when the item is placed upon the market in a defective condition which would make it more dangerous than the consumer would reasonably expect.

It is important to determine whether the elements for an action in tort or on a contract exist. It may be more beneficial, however, to determine the relative strengths of means of proof and the defenses available in the development of a case. This is because in many cases a cause of action may be brought in tort or on the contract. An injury received from using an allegedly defective product may be recoverable in a tort action showing negligence or strict liability, as well as in a contract action showing a breach of contract exemplified by the warranty which expressly or by law accompanies the product.

THE CIVIL PROCESS

A civil proceeding arises when a dispute occurs in an area of law that is not criminal in nature. One party feels wronged by another, whether this arises under a contract or through a tort or other actions, and recourse to the court of law appears to be the only remedy available to the plaintiff. A flow chart of the general process appears as Figure 4-2.

The plaintiff must now select the proper court to hear his case and initiate a civil action by filing a complaint in that court. As with all steps to be subsequently described in this process, the exact form and timing of the complaint will vary according to the procedural law of that jurisdiction. Complaints can be quite simple, alleging the nature of the dispute with the defendant or the format can be somewhat complex. Whatever the form, a copy of the complaint must not only be presented to the court, but also to the defendant, along with the *summons*, a statement of the court calling the defendant to appear in the proceeding. This presentation of the summons of the court is known as *service* upon the defendant.

It is now the turn of the defendant to take action. In answering the complaint the defendant has several options open to him (sketeched in Figure 4-3). If the defendant files preliminary objections he can state that the complaint is defective in some way, the court has no jurisdiction or does not have venue, or that the statute of limitations has been tolled (the time set for bringing the action has passed). The defendant may deny the allegations of the complaint in general or may do so with regard to any specific allegations. The defendant may also counterclaim in that he may allege a cause of action on his own behalf and ask for relief on his complaint. The defendant may admit the facts in the complaint but bring out additional facts which serve as a defense to the allegations of the plaintiff. In a similar response a defendant may file a *demurrer*, which claims that

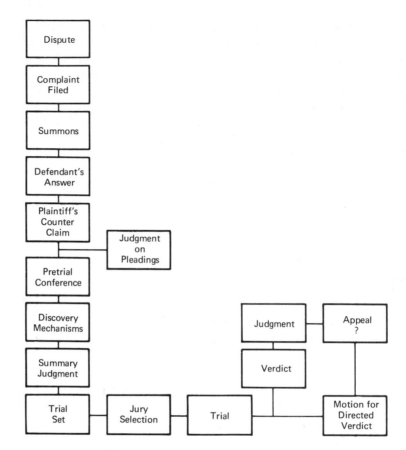

FIGURE 4-2. General Overview of the Civil Law Process.

the complaint does not sufficiently state the cause of action, that no legal wrong has been alleged.

Finally, the defendant can choose not to respond. In this case the court may consider that this lack of response means that the defendant acquiesces and a default judgment by the court may be made.

The plaintiff may file a response to the answers by the defendant that may be in the nature of objections to a counterclaim or to add to his pleas.

Once the responses have been made, it may be argued by either party that there are no questions of fact to be decided by either judge or jury and that the only question is a matter of law. In this case either party may ask the judge for a judgment on the pleadings, a motion that claims a trial is not needed.

If the judgment on the pleadings is not requested or is denied by the judge, the next step is for the two sides to enter into pretrial procedures in which all elements of both parties' cases are extensively aired. The intent here is to improve the litigation process by providing as much information as possible to prevent any surprises at the later trial.

Discovery mechanisms of various kinds provide further pretrial information to improve adjudication. *Depositions*, oral or written statements under oath by witnesses in the case, may be taken if such witnesses are likely to be unavailable for the trial. These are sometimes confused with written interrogatories, which are questions framed to the opposing party that must be answered before the trial. Similar requests may be made for admissions when the opposing party is asked to state whether a particular matter or document is true. Documents or other tangible materials that may be pertinent in the controversy may be produced under a motion for the production of real evidence. The physical or mental condition of a party may also be determined through a motion to require a physical or mental examination if those factors may be part of the matter.

The case is now ready to go on trial and is placed on the court calendar to be tried on a set date. If the case is to be tried before a jury the first order of business is the selection of the jurors (a process known as *voir-dire*). Each attorney would, without doubt, like to have jurors sympathetic to his case. How to achieve this has been the subject of

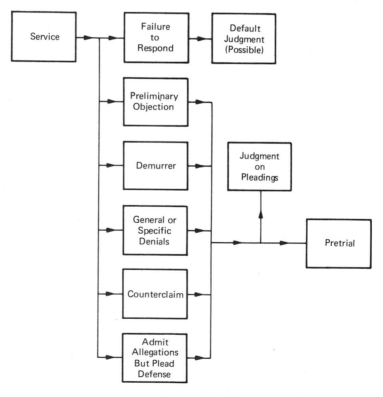

FIGURE 4-3. Alternatives in Responding to a Complaint.

fascinating folklore and more recent attempts to apply behavioral science to help in the selection process. Jurors may be challenged for cause when there is clear reason for believing that bias may exist or the challenge may be peremptory, and no reason need be given. Peremptory challenges are limited in number while challenges for cause are unlimited.

The trial itself begins when attorneys for both sides make their opening statements during which time they may outline their case and what they intend to prove in the trial. The first witness for the plaintiff is then called by the plaintiff's attorney who questions him in what is called direct examination. The defendant's attorney then is allowed to cross-examine the witness on the earlier direct examination, as well as to test the witness's credibility. Questioning by the plaintiff's attorney of the same witness (redirect examination) and recross-examination by the defendant's attorney usually suffice. The plaintiff's attorney will do this with each of his witnesses and then will rest his case. The attorney for the defendant will follow the same procedure in questioning witnesses for the defendant and, when all the witnesses have testified, will rest the case for the defendant. At this point each attorney will make a summation of his case.

After the summation by both attorneys, either one of them may make a motion for a directed verdict, in which the judge is asked to direct the jury to render a verdict for either party. Under such motion the plaintiff or defendant states that even if the facts are as his opponent has stated them, there is no legal basis for the complaint or defense.

If a motion for a directed verdict is denied, the judge will then charge the jury, which means summarizing the evidence and explaining the law. The jury then leaves the courtroom to deliberate and decide on the facts and to apply the law. Upon return to the courtroom the jury informs the judge of its verdict.

After the verdict is rendered the judge will ordinarily pronounce judgment. If the verdict is for the plaintiff and the wrong is to be righted, the end result is an award for damages and/or suffering, both usually expressed in monetary terms. If the defendant prevails he is exonerated, and an action for the same act can never be brought (*res judicata*).

ADMINISTRATIVE LAW

The wide range of activity of governmental agencies has been discussed in Chapter 3. No matter what the charge to the agency may be, however, the fundamental principles of the legal system apply to its functioning.

The fact that administrative agencies can seemingly exercise the powers of the traditional three branches of government would indicate a violation of the traditions of separation of powers, a basic conceptual approach that is looked to as the strength of the democratic form of government exemplified by the United States. The concerns of many observers in this area are met by responses that point out that the legislature really is not delegating its powers to make laws, it is merely allowing administrative officials to fill in any gaps in the laws, although some courts have permitted limited delegation under a grant of authority that contains sufficient standards for the action of the administrative agency. Further review by the legislature is possible through providing legislation that would alter the rules of the administrative agency or, as a final resort, abolish the agency entirely. Executive control over the administrative agencies comes through the appointment by the President or a governor of the members of the agency. The judiciary exercises a control over administrative agency functioning through a review of the activities of the agencies itself. This covers the judicial review of the rules and regulations under which the agency operates but can extend to the actual results of the operations of the agency. In the latter kind of review, however, courts will not disturb the findings of fact by the agency unless it is clear that no reasonable person would find as the agency personnel did.

The extensive number of agencies at both the federal and the state levels may raise further problems, in that areas of activity of the various agencies may begin to overlap. Various agencies in the past may have been called upon—or taken upon themselves—to address various problems and frequently several act concurrently. In addition, there are so many agencies and, therefore, so many rules and regulations that no single individual could ever hope to keep up with all of them. While the publication, *The Federal Register* prints all the rules and regulations of administrative agencies, the output over a very short period of time makes a very extensive volume indeed. These rules are subsequently placed in the *Code of Federal Regulation.*

ADMINISTRATIVE PROCESS

The functioning of administrative agencies is sketched in Figure 4-4; it can be seen that judicial activity occupies much of the diagram. The nature of the administrative process has been described and contrasted with pure judicial process as

> a means by which a Governmental agency clothed with delegated legislative authority or performing a quasi judicial function, regulates activities of groups of persons within specified channels. In its operation the judicial process contemplates a proceeding in which each party is represented in

INTERACTION OF THE ACTORS IN THE ADMINISTRATIVE PROCESS

FIGURE 4-4. Fundamentals of the Federal Administrative Process. *From:* Edwin W. Tucker, Text-Cases-Problems on Administrative Law, Regulation of Enterprise and Individual Liberties (St. Paul, Minn.; West Publishing Co., 1975) p. 5.

person or by counsel, with the tribunal acting as an arbiter. The Administrative process envisages a proceeding in which the regulatory body may be represented before itself by its own counsel, who presents evidence in support of an action which he suggests that the agency should take, while parties who may be affected by the proposed action may be heard in person or by counsel. In one case, there is a determination of controversy by an impartial tribunal, while in the other instance, the regulatory agency or officer is in part an interested party and in part a trier of the respective contentions advanced by its counsel and the counsel for other parties represented at the hearing.[2]

In an appeal the difference between the two—administrative and judicial processes—is more pronounced as the administrative agent is a defendant or respondent in the review process and seeks to sustain the original action. A trial court has no more interest or role in the appeal.

Attempts by the bar to provide some guidance for the development and activity of administrative agencies particularly at the state level have led to the drafting of a Model State Act. The Act attempts to provide some uniformity so that all state administrative procedures would show

1. Uniformity in procedure for defining agencies in inclusive terms.
2. Adoption of well defined rules of procedure.
3. Proceedings to be publicly known.
4. That interested parties have a hand in establishing agency rules.
5. Prompt publication of agency rules.
6. Speedy determination of questions though declaratory judgment.
7. Cases decided speedily and fairly with an accurate record of proceedings.
8. Limits on deprivation of licenses.
9. Speedy and simple judicial review of decisions.

These reasonable guides to effective and fair administrative action should relieve most people's concern over the validity of the procedures and outcomes.

THE LAW OF ECONOMIC REGULATION

Agencies of government, acting in the interests of society, are vitally concerned with the activities of individuals or groups. There is particularly great concern in industrialized societies in the influence and impact of business groupings upon the economy. Government regulation of business and other organizations occurs in all three avenues of the legal process mentioned above—the criminal, the civil, and the administrative law systems. Because of its importance, however, this area of regulation of industrial activity deserves a separate brief mention here.

Establishment of an Entity

A corporation, from the moment of its creation, must meet certain requirements, of the state in which it exists, as a legal person to do business (a corporation is considered a person in the law). Other forms of business entities must also fulfill certain requirements. The issuance of shares of stock by the corporation comes under the scrutiny of the proper agencies at the state level and probably also under review of the Securities and Exchange Commission, the federal body that regulates such business activity. Depending on the type of organization and what it intends to do, other regulatory agencies may be involved. No broadcasting station, for example, can function legally without a license from the Federal Communications Commission. Trucking and other transportation companies are regulated by the State Public Utilities Commission, and their interstate activity is monitored by the Interstate Commerce Commission.

Antitrust

A major area of concern in the early years of the unfolding industrial revolution in the United States has been on the avoidance of concentrated economic power, to insure that industrial entities be restrained from exercising influence in the society all out of proportion to their place in the system. Some balance has been thought to be desirable and the control on size and influence of business enterprises has been a feature of the social scene since the rise of huge combinations after the Civil War. Congress passed the first antitrust law in 1890 in the form of the Sherman Act which provided that any combination in restraint of trade was illegal. Some serious attempts by the government were made to prosecute under the Act but "trust-busting" was difficult. In 1914 both the Clayton Act and the Federal Trade Commission Act were passed. The latter act created the Federal Trade Commission, which was established to enforce the more specific provisions of the Clayton Act and provide for other activities in enforcement of antitrust action. Several other refinements in the struggle to maintain economic competitiveness were deemed necessary, as in 1936 when the Robinson–Patman Act focused on price discrimination and added criminal penalties to the Clayton Act. The Celler–Kefauver Act of 1950 took note of the growing trend of industrial mergers and proscribed those that made monopoly probable in "any line of commerce in any section of the country."

Economic Maintenance

On the other side of the coin, when economic conditions seemed to call for them, statutes were enacted to protect enterprises from what might be damaging effects of competition. The Capper-Volstead Act of 1922 permitted farmers to associate in getting their agricultural products to market. The National Recovery Act of 1933, in an attempt to promote economic recovery during the big depression of that period, provided many exemptions from the existing antitrust legislation. During those troubled economic times of the 1930s virtually every state enacted the so-called Fair Trade Act whereby retailers were permitted to agree to a maintenance of the sale prices set in a contract with the manufacturers. Patents and copyrights may also be considered in the same light for in these cases, the government permits the inventor of a product or the author of a literary and artistic creation to use it in an exclusionary way. There is a limitation on their use, however, in that they may not be employed as a means to effect a distinct restraint of trade.

Consumer Protection

Government activity in the regulation of the impact of business practices in the marketplace also has some history. The Food and Drug Act of 1906 was the first in a series of statutes intended to protect the consumer. It was concerned with the misbranding of foods and drugs, but the protection under this pioneer act was very limited. Further legislation was called for, of course, but few statutes were passed in the half-century after the pioneer act of 1906. Except for the establishment of the Federal Trade Commission by the Clayton Act and the setting up of the Federal Power Commission, consumer-minded legislative efforts were limited. Starting, for the most part, in 1964 and continuing in rapid succession, a series of significant statutes on the federal level highlighted the concern for consumer protection and maintenance of a high quality of life through environmental controls: the Federal Cigarette Labelling and Advertising Act of 1964, the Motor Vehicle Safety Standards Act (1966), the Fair Packaging and Labelling Act (1966), the Air Quality Act (1967), the Securities Markets Review Act (1968), the Consumer Product Safety Act of 1972, the Consumer Product Warranty Act of 1975, and a host of other acts covering meat and poultry inspection, electrical equipment, insecticides, consumer counseling, and many other concerns. In addition to all these, the President of the United States created a new Office of Consumer Affairs to help support governmental action under these various enactments. Clearly the tide has turned from a situation of buyer beware (*caveat emptor*) to *caveat venditor*, the reverse.

Labor Law

Attitudes toward collective action in labor matters were generally negative in the United States until relatively recent times. While viable unions existed from 1878 (the founding of the Knights of Labor), it was only during the years of the Great Depression that union activity received significant governmental support. The National Labor Relations Act of 1935 (Wagner Act) introduced collective bargaining on the industrial scene. That legislation marked the real emergence of a union presence although the earlier Norris-LaGuardia Act of 1932 limiting the use of injunctions in labor disputes paved the way. During World War II unions grew to a position thought by many to be too powerful, so the pendulum swung the other way in the enactment of the Taft—Hartley Act, the Labor

Management Relations Act of 1947. This legislation imposed controls on unions that made the give-and-take somewhat more even. More overall monitoring by government agencies on the industrial front was achieved through legislation in 1959, the Labor Management Reporting and Disclosure Act (Landrum—Griffin Act).

Conditions in the working environment also received closer scrutiny from Congress, even though it took some time to take positive action. Long after the evils of child labor were exposed by crusading journalists and others, the Fair Labor Standards Act of 1938, which covers business in interstate commerce was enacted. In addition to prohibiting child labor the Act established a basic living wage and a limit to forty hours of the work week at regular pay with additional compensation thereafter. The minimum wage has been raised several times in the years after (from forty cents an hour in 1938 to well over two dollars at present).

While safe working conditions have been the concern of government regulators down through the years, the extensive general legislation in this area is very recent in the form of the Occupational Safety and Health Act of 1970. Specific and stringent criteria for conditions of the work place are outlined with concomitant measures for enforcement.

Prohibition against discrimination in employment practices on the basis of sex, race, age, or national origin was firmed up in the Civil Rights Act of 1964. This federal legislation has been followed by similar enactments at the state level throughout the country.

Perhaps the most significant departure from basic legal concepts in the area of employment came quite a bit earlier than most of the legislation heretofore mentioned. Soon after the turn of this century most states enacted Workmen's Compensation statutes to simplify the problem arising from industrial injuries. Traditional concepts of tort law limited liability of employers and made recovery by injured employees a long and usually expensive process. Workmen's Compensation statutes establish, instead, a set schedule of payments to the injured party or his beneficiary upon the showing of injury in the course of employment. Little else in the way of proof is necessary. The entire schedule of payments is supported by an insurance program paid for by employers.

FOOTNOTES

[1] *Uniform Laws Annotated; Uniform Commercial Code* (St. Paul, Minn.: West Publishing Co., 1975, Cumulative Annual Pocket Part).

[2] Edwin W. Tucker, *Text-Cases-Problems on Administrative Law, Regulation Enterprise and Individual Liberties* (St. Paul, Minn.: West Publishing Co., 1975).

PART II
DECISION ANALYSIS OF THE CIVIL PROCESS

Part II focuses upon the civil process. Through analysis of the decisions involved in a hypothetical case, insight is provided into the working of the legal system. While the persons and organizations are fictional, the events in which they participate are those of the legal process. The case continues through the four chapters in Part II as the actors move through various stages of the civil process. Excerpts from actual cases appear at the end of each chapter, *a propos* legal principles discussed within the chapter.

CHAPTER 5
ENTRY INTO THE SYSTEM:
A CASE ARISES

August 26 is a date Mary (Mrs. John Q.) Worker will always remember. It was that day when unexpected tragedy struck, with such rippling effects that the John Q. Worker incident became legal history and eventually came to be as well known to lawyers and law students as the name of Shakespeare is to students of English literature.

The newspapers in Big City on August 26 reported merely that John Q. Worker, at age 42, was dead as a result of an accident that occurred while he operated a cypres machine at The Firm, Inc., where he had been employed for 23 years.

Peter Superior, John's foreman, as well as his close friend and neighbor for many years, had difficulty reading the newspaper that evening. His thoughts kept returning to events of that afternoon when a new zagger on a cypres machine John Q. Worker had been operating had shattered while spinning at 2600 revolutions per minute. One of the pieces struck John Q. in the stomach with such force that it pierced his abdomen, causing instantaneous death. Within minutes every machine operator in the cypres department walked off the job, leaving Peter to describe what had happened to Tom Newboy, the firm's personnel manager, and to Fred Famous himself, president and son of the founder of The Firm.

Newspaper accounts of the accident were read avidly that same evening in the United Cypres Operators of America Building, where John Q.'s co-workers congregated after leaving their jobs. Robert Leader, president of Local 135 and operator of the machine next to John Q.'s, held several pieces of the shattered zagger in his hand as he recounted what happened.

Because of his experience and recognized skill, John Q. had been the first man assigned to work on the initial production of a new type of chattel, which the firm had announced it would be placing on the market soon. Regular zaggers could not be used for this job, and a specially designed zagger had been manufactured by the company's usual zagger supplier. John Q. had just returned from the supplies department with a box of the new zaggers, opened it, put one on his machine, and started it up when the accident occurred. Neither Robert nor any of the other men had ever seen a zagger shatter with such explosive force and violence.

There was a general consensus that the new zaggers must not be safe. Members of the union safety committee were asked to check whether the new zaggers met the Safety Code for Zaggers promulgated by the Occupational Safety and Health Administration. Some of the cypres operators suspected that short cuts that disregarded safety standards may have been taken with the new zaggers, in order to get the new chattels into early production.

As the group disbanded, a number of the men left with Robert Leader to visit Mary Worker.

At home that evening, Mary Worker read the newspaper account of the accident and reflected on the drastic change that had occurred in her life in just one day. Married to John Q. Worker for twenty-one years, she was the mother of five children: a son, age 19, who was a college student; a 16-year old daughter, a high school student; another daughter, age 10, a fourth grader; and four-year-old twins.

What would she do now? The death of John Q. was not only a great personal loss to her and the children, but it would create even more serious financial problems for the family. John Q.'s income as a cypres operator had sustained them in a modest way of life, but they had no substantial savings. She had not been employed outside the home since she resigned her secretarial job almost twenty years ago. She didn't know if she could find a job today, and—even if she did—who would care for the children? The twins were still preschoolers. She hoped her son would not have to leave the university. Long ago she and John Q. had determined to give their children a college education, something which neither of them had had. Her thoughts were interrupted by the arrival of members of Local 135, who spent some time talking with her about the accident. As they left, Robert Leader, holding several fragments of the zagger in his outstretched palm, said: "Remember, Mary, if there's anything we can do for you, be sure to call."

The next day engineers who had worked on development of the new zaggers were brought in from Zagger Supply, Inc. to consult with Sam Scott, chief plant safety engineer at The Firm. They attributed the accident to human error: improper placement or clamping of the zagger on the cypres machine or a momentary lapse of care by John Q. when he first brought the chattel form into contact with the zagger. The union safety committee was not satisfied with this explanation, and said so.

"It's a whitewash," they claimed, "nobody tested the new zaggers while they were revolving on the cypres machines."

When Peter Superior asked Timothy O'Goode to take over work on the new chattels, Timothy balked. He relented, however, after both Peter Superior and Sam Scott operated cypres machines using the new zaggers to demonstrate their safety and after Jim Boss, the plant manager, told him he would either work on the new chattels or lose his job.

At last, production of the new chattels began. Jim Boss breathed a sigh of relief. He knew the company had a deadline to meet in getting the new chattels on the market. Fred Famous had made a large loan to the firm from his personal funds to develop the new product. He had done so in the hope that this would give the firm a much needed boost and help it to recover a sizable share of the market, which had been lost to competitors in recent years. Jim knew Fred would have been furious with any delay, even one resulting from something so tragic as John Q.'s death.

THE FIRM'S LIABILITY

Little did Jim know that at that very moment Fred was involved in a long, serious conference dealing with the company's legal liability arising from the death of John Q. Worker. Tom Newboy and Leo Lex, the firm's legal counsel, were the other participants.

Leo Lex was explaining that under the Workmen's Compensation Law of Great State an employer was responsible for injury or death that occurred to an employee during the course of his employment, regardless of fault. There were two exceptions, neither of which was applicable in this case. They were in cases of employee intoxication or self-inflicted injury. He went on to say that the statute limited the liability of employers, even in cases where the company was negligent, to the benefits specified in the act. These consisted of weekly payments to the widow for 700 weeks plus an additional sum for minor children. (In Great State a person reached legal majority at age 18.) Payments were determined by reference to a schedule in the act and were based upon the deceased employee's average weekly earnings.

After a series of calculations, all three agreed that the payments required for the Worker family were minimal and did not begin to approach John Q.'s take-home pay. Leo Lex noted that many persons had criticized workmen's compensation laws because they believed the payments required were inadequate, and in 1970 the Congress had established a National Commission on States Workmen's Compensation Laws to study state statutes and recommend improvements.[1]

That, however, did not change the fact that present Great State law applied to the matter at hand. Therefore, the one and exclusive remedy the John Q. Worker family had against The Firm was workmen's compensation benefits. The reason for such a provision in the statute, Leo said, was to place a uniform and definite limit on an employer's liability in cases of injury and death. It would be entirely discretionary with The Firm, he added, to make any additional payments.

Tom Newboy pointed out that the widow would receive the proceeds from a life insurance policy, which the firm carried on each of its employees as a fringe benefit. This would provide an immediate, large, lump sum payment to her. He added that he would also assist her in applying for social security benefits. These would supplement her benefits under workmen's compensation, and he believed his assistance would serve as a goodwill gesture to the family.

It was Fred Famous who made the decision regarding discretionary payments. Although he was sympathetic to the Worker family needs, he decided that company policy should limit payments to those required by law. His reasons were: (1) the strained financial position of the company; (2) the precedent that would be established for the future; (3) his conviction that the company had in no way contributed toward the employee's death by negligence or willful lack of care. The flow chart in Figure 5-1 of Fred's decision indicates that he believed The Firm, after payment to the Worker family of workmen's compensation benefits, would have discharged its legal, social, and moral obligations to them. That flow chart also indicates that, in Fred's judgment, discharge of a legal obligation would not necessarily automatically discharge one's social and moral obligations.

MARY'S REACTION

Mary Worker was dismayed when she learned of the financial arrangements. Even when the social security and workmen's compensation benefits were added together, her family's standard of living would be lowered considerably. It might even mean that her oldest son would have to leave the university. She felt the company was responsible for her husband's death and should make arrangements to put her and her children in at least the same financial condition as they had enjoyed prior to John Q.'s death. She asked the company to reconsider. It was to no avail.

Mary went to see Robert Leader. It was he who first suggested that John Q.'s death might have been caused by an unsafe zagger. Since the accident, several of the new zaggers had shattered. No one had been seriously injured. However, the frequency with which this was occurring caused him to suspect that the zaggers were not sufficiently strong for the use to which they were being put. Robert told her that the union safety committee had lodged a complaint with the local office of the Occupational Safety and Health Administration, alleging violation of the safety standards for zaggers at The Firm.

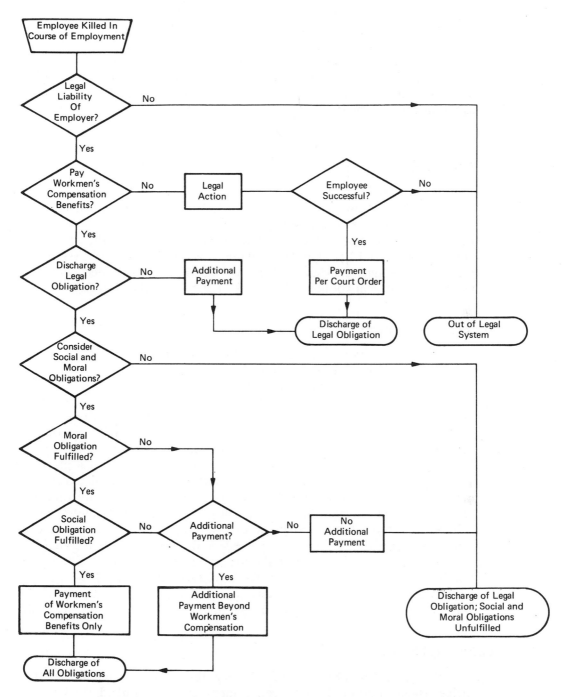

FIGURE 5-1. Fred Famous' Decision to Pay Only Workmen's Compensation Benefits to Worker Family.

"Remember, Mary, I still have zagger fragments from the accident, if you or your attorney ever need them," he said in parting.

The germ of an idea had been planted.

"Why not?" she thought. "I really should talk with a lawyer. John Q. didn't have a will, and I have questions about what to do about such things as the house and the car."

FINDING A LAWYER

Having made up her mind, Mary discovered her first problem was that she did not know a lawyer. Nor did she know how to choose one from the hundreds listed in the yellow pages of the Big City telephone directory. Because she was also concerned about cost, she followed the advice of a neighbor who told her that the Neighborhood Legal Services Association provided free legal assistance. Mary visited the nearest office, where she learned a great deal about legal services programs available in Big City.

Legal Services Programs

Originally established under the Equal Opportunity Act of 1964[2] to provide legal assistance for persons living in poverty, the NLSA office she visited now operated under the Legal Services Corporation Act.[3] The latter was enacted in 1974 to provide for a private, nonmembership, nonprofit corporation, which would be funded through Congressional appropriation as well as private grants. Its purpose was to continue to provide legal services to the poor but through a nongovernmental agency. It was hoped that this would remove the program from political pressures. The act authorized legal aid in civil matters (and only in exceptional instances, in criminal matters) to persons who were financially unable to afford it. The Corporation was authorized to develop guidelines for different parts of the country for determining eligibility for assistance, using such criteria as income, total assets, and other available resources.

Mary discovered that she could not qualify for assistance. She learned that she would be ineligible, too, for legal services provided by the Legal Aid Society. This was a public service organization funded by the United Way in Big City. It, also, rendered legal help in civil matters to the needy.

Prepaid Legal Services

Searching for some way to aid Mary, the young woman in the NLSA office asked if John Q. had been a member of a prepaid legal services plan. She explained that many employers and unions in the Big City area sponsored such plans, which were similar to medical and health care plans. Members and their families were eligible for legal advice and services covered by the plan. The cost was covered through payments which were either absorbed entirely by the employer, or shared with employees as a fringe benefit. Some of these plans provided for selection of an attorney of one's choice, others for selection from a specific list of attorneys. Often these plans were developed in association with the local bar, sometimes by insurance companies. Mary was skeptical about John Q.'s membership in any such plan. Before leaving the NLSA office, she was given the address and telephone number of the lawyer referral service of the local bar association. She continued her search for legal aid there.

Lawyer Referral Service

At bar association headquarters, Mary learned that lawyers who were members of the referral panel agreed to provide one-half hour of consultation at a very minimal fee. During that time, she could explain her situation to an attorney, learn what legal action—if any—would be possible, be given an explanation of the costs and fees for any such undertaking, and then decide for herself whether she wished to retain the particular lawyer and proceed with any action. Mary decided to pay the minimum fee for a thirty-minute consultation.

CONSULTATION

She was referred to attorney Henry Law who, after asking question upon question about her husband's accident, finally said:

"Do I understand correctly that your husband's death occurred during the course of his employment and as a result of an accident which you allege was due to a zagger which shattered while he operated a cypres machine?"

"That's right," Mary replied.

"And the Firm has made you an offer for financial settlement which you do not believe is adequate."

"Yes," said Mary.

"Do you know—or do you have any indication—that the zagger your husband was using at the time of his death was defective?," he asked.

Mary told him about the fragments in Robert Leader's possession and the complaint filed by the union with OSHA.

"Because of the limited liability of employers under the state's workmen's compensation act, the only hope I can hold out for you, Mrs. Worker, is to seek damages from the supplier or manufacturer of the zagger—provided, that is, it can be proved the zagger was defective and that this was the cause of your husband's death."

"But I don't even know who they are." Mary was skeptical.

"That would be my job—to learn that as well as a great many more facts." Henry Law explained that one could not charge another party with liability upon mere supposition; a factual basis was needed. Therefore, before he could render an intelligent opinion about any legal claim she might have against the zagger manufacturer or supplier, he would have to gather more information. For instance, he would want to talk with Robert Leader and possibly other witnesses to the accident; he would have the zagger fragments tested for defects; he would inquire into what action, if any, OSHA had taken with regard to the union's complaint.

Henry explained that he was not seeking enough evidence to prove a case in a court of law, but rather sufficient factual data to enable him to make an informed judgment about whether she had grounds or the basis for instituting legal proceedings—and what the expectations for success might be. Sometimes, he said, it becomes necessary for lawyers to inform their clients that they have no cause which can be pursued at law. Sometimes, he added, they must tell their clients that while there is a basis for legal action, it would not be worth pursuing for any number of reasons, such as lack of means of proof or costs that would far outstrip any possible recovery.

Therefore, he said, it would be necessary for him to undertake some fundamental investigative work about the cause of her husband's death. Once he possessed sufficient factual information, he would research the relevant law. Because this involved a civil matter, the requirements in litigation would be proof by a preponderance of the evidence. *Preponderance of the evidence,* he explained, does not mean the greater number of witnesses. It does mean evidence that is more credible and convincing than that offered by the opposing party; in other words, the evidence that meshes best with reason and probability. Therefore, Henry continued, he would assess the facts along with the appropriate law, in order to arrive at a judgment as to whether the preponderance of the evidence and the law were in her favor.

If he believed she had no legal claim, he would tell her so and remove himself from the case. However, he would have to bill her for the costs incurred in connection with his investigative work. On the other hand, if he believed that there was a basis for legal action, he would so inform her, explain the courses of action open to her together with possible outcomes, and then ask her to indicate her wishes as to future action.

ENGAGING LEGAL COUNSEL

If she wished to retain him to do this, he added, he would require a small down payment—a retainer—now. He would also ask that she sign a contract providing for legal fees to be paid on a contingent fee basis. He read through the contract form with her:

FORM 5-1. Agreement with Lawyer.

Henry Law

Attorney-at-Law

Big City, Great State

    I, the undersigned client, hereby retain and employ Henry Law as my attorney to represent me in my claim for damages against the supplier and/or manufacturer of zaggers to The Firm, Inc. and/or any other persons, firms or corporations liable therefor, resulting from an accident that occurred on August 26, 19XX, in which John Q. Worker, my late husband, was killed as he was engaged in the course of his employment at The Firm, Inc.

    As compensation for said services, I agree to pay for the costs of investigation and court costs, if necessary, and to pay my attorney from the proceeds of recovery, the following fees:

33-1/3% if settled without suit

40%   if suit is filed

50%   if an appeal is taken by either side.

    It is agreed that this employment is on a contingent fee basis, so that if no recovery is made, I will not owe my attorney any amount for attorney's fees.

        Dated this _____ day of _____ 19 _____ .

_____(SEAL)
                Client

I hereby accept the above employment.

_____(SEAL)
        Henry Law, Attorney

When Mary said she was not sure she understood the contingent fee system, he asked her to assume the following: jury verdict for $100; court costs of $20; contingent fee according to the contract. The amount Mary would receive would be determined as follows:

Jury verdict $100
LESS 40% contingent fee payable to attorney . . . . − 40
                                                                          $ 60
LESS court costs payable by client . . . . − 20
Actual amount client would take home . . . . $ 40

While that didn't leave much for the client to take home, Mary felt she would have everything to gain and nothing to lose by such an arrangement. Henry Law also explained that if she recovered nothing, he would receive no fee and she would pay only the $20 court costs.

In answer to Mary's question, Henry Law explained that the courts of Great State had always held that a client has an implied right to discharge an attorney if he so wishes, even when there is a written agreement. However, the client must pay for all costs and fees earned by the attorney up to that point. On the other hand, an attorney could only withdraw for a good reason (for example, discovering his client had an unjust or immoral cause), and then only in such a way as to be sure that the client was fully protected at all times.

Positive that it was what she wanted to do, Mary signed the contract. Before leaving the office, she was asked by Henry Law to be sure not to get in touch with, talk with, or in any other way communicate with any persons who might be or might represent the other party. In order to be positive she would not jeopardize her case in any way, she should refer all such persons to him. Mary replied that she would be happy to do this. She felt good that at last someone would be taking action in her behalf.

INVESTIGATION

Henry Law proceeded to do just that. The turning point for him came in the report of the tests made on the zagger fragments by Professor Ira Learned at Great Scientific University. One of the outstanding zagger experts in the nation, Professor Learned examined the fragments under a microscope. He discovered a flaw "consisting of a pocket—or collection of crystals which are not bonded—within the composition of the zagger." Such imperfections, his report stated, would cause a zagger to shatter even when it was revolved at a relatively low speed, and definitely at 2600 rpm. Neither visual inspection nor tapping for sound would reveal these flaws. Had the zaggers been subjected to a test approximating actual use of zaggers in motion at 2600 rpm, they would have disintegrated or shattered, thus indicating the presence of a defect. Professor Learned's report concluded that such "in-motion" testing was required by the safety code for zaggers promulgated by the Occupational Safety and Health Administration.

From the local OSHA office, Henry secured a copy of the zagger safety requirements. He learned, too, that action had not yet been taken on the union's complaint. Robert Leader also supplied Henry with information.

LEGAL RESEARCH

With this information at hand, Henry Law began his research of the law to determine if there was a legal cause of action arising out of the facts he now had. He knew that in cases of defective products, the law of torts regarding negligence and strict liability was applicable. It was the common law to which he would have to refer. Therefore, he checked the *Restatement of the Law of Torts 2d,* with annotations for Great State. Henry knew that in a recent decision the Supreme Court of Great State had adopted as the law of the state §402A of that Restatement.

Because the common law is "unwritten," that is, not codified, it is found in judicial decisions. In order to facilitate research, these decisions have been compiled into what is referred to as the *Restatement of the Law.* This is a reiteration of judicial holdings arranged according to subject matter and categories, with appropriate references to the cases in which the decisions were handed down. There is a separate Restatement for each of the major substantive areas of the law, including torts, contracts, and agency. *Annotations* are relevant comments from specific decisions, provided as an aid in understanding the delimitations of the decisions.

The court opinions themselves are collected as handed down. Those from state trial courts are not always printed and bound in volumes. Instead, they may be found in the appropriate clerk of courts office. Federal district court opinions are printed in the *Federal Supplement,* those of the federal circuit courts of appeals in the *Federal Reporter,* and those of the United States Supreme Court in the *United States Reports*, as well as in the *Supreme Court Reporter* and the *United States Supreme Court Reports, Lawyer's Edition.* State appellate decisions can be found in state reporters or in regional reporters.

To facilitate research the citation for each case includes the location, with volume number preceding and page number following identification of the reporter in which a case is to be found. For example, the citation for the appellate decision excerpted at the end of this chapter is as follows: *Webb v. Zern*, 422 Pa. 424, 220 A2d 853 (1966). This indicates that the case, decided in 1966, can be found in two places: volume 422, page 424 of the *Pennsylvania State Reports* (the reporter for the supreme court of that state) and in volume 220, page 853 of the *Atlantic Reporter, Second Series* (the regional reporter).

Precedent

Henry Law also checked the most recent decisions of Great State's supreme court in defective products cases. He did so because of the doctrine of *stare decisis*, or the determining role of precedent in the common law. Precedent refers to the common law as it has been judicially declared in previously adjudicated cases involving the same or substantially the same issues and facts. Henry checked the supreme court's decisions because, as the highest court in Great State, its decisions were controlling and binding upon the lower courts of the state. He found no cases involving defective zaggers. In that respect, this would be a case of "first impression" in the state. For this reason he checked other states for defective zagger cases. He knew those decisions would not be controlling in Great State since they were "foreign" law. However, courts often refer to decisions of other states as a guide when they are faced with a case of first impression. Again, he found none.

He did, however, find in Great State a number of other cases involving defective products. From them he selected those similar in basic characteristics and concepts to the Worker case—employee injury, product used on the job, recovery from the manufacturer, for example. Once he found such comparability, Henry checked for the legal principle emerging from the case. He looked for the court's *holding*, that is, the rule of law that the court decided applied in the case at hand and determined its outcome. He did not want *dictum*, that is, an extraneous remark or additional pronouncement made by the court not essential to the determination of the case. In other words, he was looking for rules of law he could abstract from prior cases. Having found appropriate holdings of law, he could then quote them to the judge as precedent for the Mary Worker case. Given sufficient similarity in the fact situation, the judge would undoubtedly follow that precedent.

Thus it is that the common law evolves. A rule of law is set in one case, is followed in similar cases, and becomes fixed as the law. Predictability of outcome is possible. However, that does not mean the common law is stagnant. It may in later decisions be overruled or slowly eroded as social conditions, technological knowledge, and times, in general, change. Thus, there is also a flexibility, adaptability, and a dynamic quality to the common law. It is important to note that decisions are made on an *ad hoc* basis; that is, they are applied to a particular set of facts at a given period of time. If one can distinguish, differentiate, or find important differences in fact, then the court can be expected to decide differently.

"Once you change the facts, you change the law," is a very old but true saying.

This kind of reasoning by analogy, from particular to general and back to particular again, is sometimes referred to as legal reasoning. It consists of finding from the specifics of prior cases generalizations that will fit the specifics of the present case. That was what Henry Law was engaged in doing.

Tort Actions

Henry found that in recent years more cases involving defective products had been brought as strict liability cases than as negligence cases. After considering the elements of the two torts, one readily understands why. Elements are those ingredients of which the tort consists. They are the matters that have to be proved to a court to establish a *prima facie* case, that is, one sufficiently strong for the opposing party to be required to answer the charges or defend against it.

Since Mary Worker was the plaintiff, she would have the *burden of proof*. That meant she would have to go forward with the evidence to prove that a *prima facie* case existed. If that was not done, the judge would grant a defendant's motion for either a dismissal or for a directed verdict. This would mean the defendant would not even be required to "put in his case," that is, to call any witnesses or enter any testimony on his behalf. It would be similar to saying that Mary Worker did not have a sufficiently good case to be able to go forward with or continue the trial. Therefore, Henry Law understood the importance of the plaintiff's being able to establish each of the elements of the cause of action under which he was proceeding. He contemplated the proof that would be necessary in a negligence action.[4]

Negligence is the failure to exercise the degree of care that a reasonably prudent person would use under the circumstances, such conduct being the proximate cause of harm or injury to a person or property. One test of whether action is negligent involves *foreseeability*. This means the individual could reasonably have anticipated and foreseen the likelihood of harm resulting from his conduct. The elements which the plaintiff must establish to prove negligence are

1. Duty of care,
2. Breach of that duty,
3. Proximate cause,
4. Injury or damage.

As for the duty of reasonable care owed to the plaintiff, Henry thought there would be little problem proving there was such a duty. The OSHA standards, having the force of law, would establish that zaggers must be manufactured according to certain stated requirements. Reasonable care, that of the ordinary, prudent person under similar circumstances, did not mean perfection. Henry Law would have to show there was a lack of reasonable care in the manufacture of the zagger involved. To do this, he would have to seek the manufacturer's records regarding quality control, inspection, production, and even records regarding complaints from other customers and return of unsatisfactory goods.

On the other hand, strict liability created legal liability regardless of the care exercised. That eliminated the need for all the proof necessary in establishing negligence. It would be easier, less expensive, require less fact finding. The evidence would have to establish that the product was unreasonably and dangerously defective at the time of sale and that this condition was still true at the time of use.

Both torts required proof of causation, of proximate cause. In other words, Henry would have to prove that the defective zagger was the cause of the accident. Both torts also required a showing of injury or damage. With John Q.'s death following the injury, that would be no problem.

Different defenses were available under each tort action. In negligence, a showing that the plaintiff by his own negligence had contributed to the injury—contributory negligence—would be a complete defense in Great State. Other states, following a doctrine of comparative negligence, make it a partial or proportionate defense. However, in strict liability, the defendant would have to show that John Q. had voluntarily assumed a known risk. This means that of his own will and with knowledge of the risk involved, he undertook to do what he did. Henry Law believed that with a latent defect John Q. could not be said to have assumed a known risk.

Since both negligence and strict liability were tort actions, both had the same time requirements for bringing suit. Henry decided there was a legal cause of action in tort under either negligence or strict liability, but the advantages of strict liability far outweighed those of negligence.

Contract Actions

However, before he would make a final decision Henry checked contract law to investigate the possibilities of a contract cause of action. There is a common law of contracts, but Henry Law knew that all states following the common (as distinguished from the civil) law have adopted the Uniform Commercial Code (UCC). As statutory law, it takes precedence over the common law. Its provisions cover contracts involving the sale of goods. *Goods* are personal or movable property as distinguished from real or fixed property. Since the sale of zaggers would be a contract for the sale of goods, he consulted both the UCC as enacted in Great State and annotations of Great State decisions involving the breach of warranty provisions of the UCC.

While statutory law is enacted by legislators, interpretation of that law is a function of the courts. It is true that the judiciary looks for legislative intent when the meaning of a statute is not clear. They also check the law's stated purpose, and study statements made at hearings and in committee before the law is passed. However, in the end, it is they who decide what the words mean. In this sense, they can be said to "make law."

Henry found examples of just this very thing in Great State. Contract cases had been brought involving defective products on grounds of breach of warranty. Breach of warranty occurs when there is failure or falsehood of a promise or statement that is part of the basis of the bargain in the sale of goods, unless there is a disclaimer. One such warranty is that goods shall be merchantable.[5] That includes being fit for the ordinary purposes for which such goods are used. Another implied warranty is that of fitness for a particular purpose when goods are purchased in reliance on the seller's knowledge of that purpose and expertise regarding the product.[6] These warranties are breached when the goods do not meet the standards of the warranties; in other words, when the goods are defective with respect to the qualities covered by the warranty.

Henry knew that in a contract action he would have to prove there was a contract of sale between the manufacturer and John Q.'s employer, that there were no disclaimers to eliminate warranties, and that the zagger was defective. To prove the contract would mean getting records of both The Firm and Zagger Supply.

In some states there would have been an added problem since John Q. was not the purchaser of the goods. That meant there existed no privity between him and the seller. In other words, there was lacking the close relationship that exists between contracting parties. When he checked the Great State decisions, Henry found that the state's supreme court had permitted recovery by a buyer's employees even when privity did not exist. The court stated that this was done to make it possible to achieve the same result when the case is brought in contract as when it is brought in tort. This was a good example of judicial interpretation of statutory meaning, Henry Law thought to himself. The reason for his so thinking was that the UCC is not explicit about recovery by persons lacking privity in industrial situations.[7]

One advantage of the contract action was that it allowed for twice the time for bringing suit—four years—as did tort. However, additional time was not one of Henry's concerns.

Causes of Action Compared

Comparison of the elements of each of these causes of action—negligence, strict liability, and contract—appears in Table 5-1, along with the time requirements for bringing action and the disadvantages associated

TABLE 5-1. Comparison of negligence, strict liability, and contract actions.

	Tort	Contract
Elements of Tort Negligence	*Elements of Tort Under §402A—Strict Liability*	*Elements of Action Under UCC—Breach of Warranty*
1. Duty of care	1. Defective product	1. Valid contract for sale of goods
2. Breach of duty	a. Unreasonably dangerous	2. Warranty—express or implied
3. Proximate cause	b. Defective at time of sale	3. Breach of warranty
4. Injury or damage	c. Substantially unchanged from condition at sale	4. Injury or damage
	d. Sold by seller engaged in business of selling	5. Privity—in some states
	2. Proximate cause	
	3. Injury or damage	
Defense	*Defense*	*Defense*
Contributory negligence	Voluntary assumption of a known risk	Lack of valid contract
		Lack of warranty
		Lack of privity—in some states
Time Limitations	*Time Limitations*	*Time Limitations*
2 years from date of injury*	2 years from date of injury*	4 years from date of delivery of goods
Disadvantage	*Disadvantage*	*Disadvantage*
Need to prove lack of due care in manufacturing specific product, resulting in defective product—records with defendant	Need to prove defect existed at time of sale and continued to exist	Need to prove contract and existence of warranties between third party and defendant—records with third party and defendant

*may vary from state to state

with each. As Henry reflected upon these matters, he realized that three different possible causes of action existed in the Mary Worker case. He felt he was fortunate, for it is not often that lawyers find three different possible actions. The more usual situation is to find just one.

Having weighed the advantages and disadvantages of each of the three actions, Henry decided that his first preference was strict liability. Having decided that, he made a list of the items he would have to prove and his sources of proof. His list looked like this:

Facts to be Proved	Sources of Proof
1. Death of John Q.	1. Death certificate.
2. Death caused by defective zagger manufactured by Zagger Supply (he had learned their identity through Leader and Learned).	2. Testimony of Leader and other union members who witnessed the accident, or purchasing and production personnel at The Firm.

3. Death occurred because the zagger was defective—unreasonably and dangerously so.

3. Testimony of OSHA personnel and Professor Learned; offering of zagger fragment test results and OSHA standards into evidence.

4. Defect present when zagger was sold by Zagger Supply, and zagger substantially unchanged at time of accident.

4. Testimony of Leader, Superior, supplies room personnel who witnessed John Q. remove zagger from shipping box and place on machine to use.

5. Zagger Supply engaged in the business of selling zaggers.

5. Testimony of corporate personnel, if necessary. (Would probably be admitted by Zagger Supply.)

It would be up to the defense to rebut the plaintiff's case. Aware that a good lawyer not only attempts to predict his adversary's position but also plans how to refute it, Henry made another list. In one column, he noted possible defenses. In the second, he listed his means of refutation.

Defenses

1. Zagger was not defective.

Refutation

1. Testimony of Professor Learned; offering of zagger fragment test results and OSHA standards into evidence.

2. Death was due to improper use of the zagger or actions of John Q., and not to a defective zagger.

2. Testimony of Leader, other cypres operators, Superior as to John's skill, his safety record; perhaps testimony of Professor Learned as to effect of improper use on machine.

He wondered. Would the defendant attempt to disclaim responsibility for any defects by charging that The Firm had the duty to inspect the zaggers before using them and had failed in this duty? If so, he believed he could answer that by referring to the fact that OSHA standards have the force and effect of law.[8] Therefore, zaggers which do not meet those standards cannot legally be used. Would Zagger Supply want to admit they sold zaggers that were not legally usable? He would ask the Zagger Supply witnesses if it were not the normal expectation of anyone purchasing zaggers to expect to receive and pay for zaggers which could be used. That should place the onus of inspection for OSHA standards on the manufacturer—and that would be all he would need. However, he would also refer to normal practice in the cypres industry: boxes of zaggers were opened and put on machines for use, not tested first. And since John Q.

was starting a production run—not a trial run—normal expectations would be that testing processes were finished and usual operating procedures were in order.

After all of this, Henry was finally satisfied that Mary had a worthy cause of action. He had completed the decision making summarized in Figure 5-2, except for the financial considerations. Therefore, he set about determining the amount of money damages that Mary could seek. John Q.'s potential work years until retirement at age 65 numbered 23. When his annual salary during that time was considered, along with normally expected increases of even a minimal amount, the sum was enormous: $250,000. Even when reduced to present value, the amount was great: approximately $150,000 when compounded annually at 6%. He would have to be sure Mary Worker understood that this was the asking sum, that judges and juries often do not award the amount asked, and that adverse parties often will settle only for much less. (Mary already understood that she would not be able to recover twice for the same cause, and that the form she signed accepting workmen's compensation benefits from The Firm provided that the corporation had a right of subrogation. That is the right of one person to substitute for or take the place of another with respect to a legal claim.)

REQUEST TO SETTLE

Henry called Mary to inform her that he believed she had a reasonably good case, although he would not and could not guarantee results. Henry suggested the first step should be an attempt to arrive at an amicable settlement without litigation. Mary agreed. Therefore, Henry wrote to Zagger Supply, requesting compensation for John Q.'s death caused by a defective zagger which the company had manufactured and sold to The Firm, Inc.

His letter caused much activity at Zagger Supply. President Will Very took it to the corporation's legal department where he consulted W. E. Just, the attorney in charge. Both then called upon Charles Sell, engineering sales manager, seeking background information. They learned that the new zaggers had been developed after Charles had gone to The Firm's plant to discuss with Sam Scott and Jim Boss zaggers for use on the new chattels. Sell's staff worked on an adaptation of the zagger The Firm usually bought, since the latter wanted the new zaggers to be interchangeable with the old ones on the cypres machines. Sixty dozen had been manufactured for the first order from specifications prepared by the Zagger Supply development engineers. Of these, only half a dozen had been tested prior to shipment. When the static test results coincided with those of the other zaggers manufactured at Zagger Supply, dynamic testing was not considered necessary and was omitted so that the promised delivery

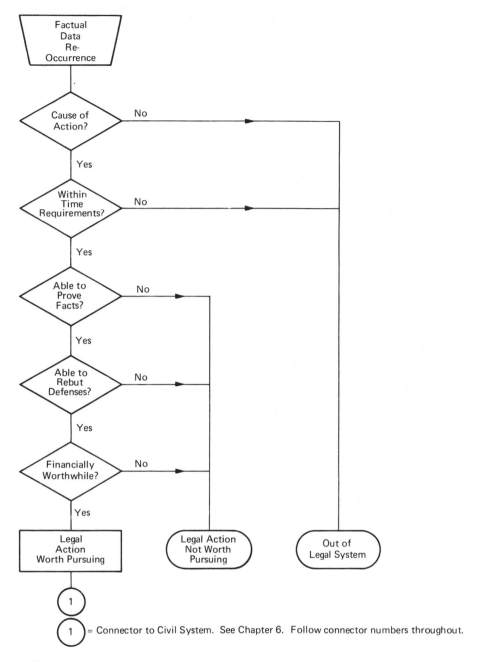

FIGURE 5-2. Henry Law's Decision That Mary's Cause Warrants Pursuing in the Legal System.

dates could be met. Charles also recounted the staff's trip to The Firm the day after John Q. Worker's death.

Will Very walked away from the discussion, saying to Attorney Just: "Fight it. We won't pay—not a nickel."

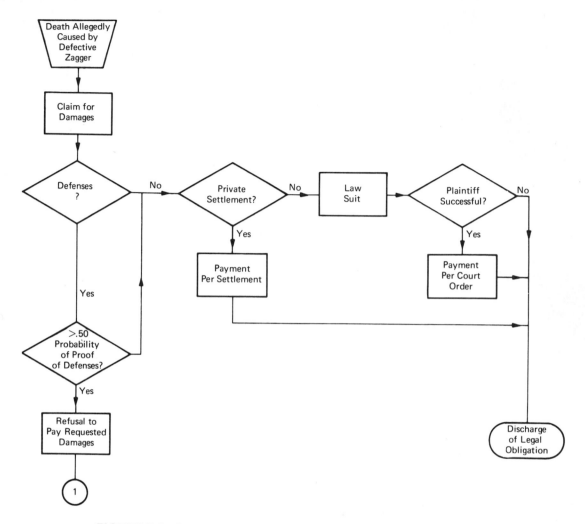

FIGURE 5-3. Decision of Manufacturer to Refuse Request for Payment to Mary Worker.

W. E. decided it would take a minor miracle to be able to do that, knowing only what he did at the present time. Therefore, he started upon his own investigation. His first step was to request that available fragments of the shattered zagger be sought and sent to Acme Industrial Laboratories for testing. He scheduled interviews with the engineers and production personnel who had worked on The Firm's order; gathered production and quality control reports related to the order; and then scheduled several sessions with cypres engineers to learn all he could about the use of zaggers on those machines.

The report from Acme Laboratories was a blow. It said essentially what Professor Learned's report did.

"If they have this kind of information—and at this time I have no way of knowing that they do—then they have a basis for claiming the zagger was defective. If that's true, our best line of defense would be to deny that death occurred because of a defective zagger," W. E. said as he met with Will Very and Charles Sell several days later. "The zagger might have shattered for a number of reasons. The cypres engineers tell me it's entirely plausible that a zagger could shatter if improperly mounted or if an operator becomes distracted and is careless for a few minutes."

"Can you prove that?"

"Oh, yes. Based on prior defective zagger experience, I'd estimate there's a better than two to one chance of proving that."

"Anything over 50 per cent would be good enough for me," said Will Very. "In fact, that should be enough to cool any desire they may have to sue."

"Perhaps," replied W. E. "We don't know yet how seriously they intend to pursue this, but in view of the lab report I believe we should be prepared in case of follow-up."

"Keep fighting," was Very's reply. "Under no circumstances are we going to pay." That decision of his has been flow charted in Figure 5-3.

Will Very was a determined man, willing to assume the accompanying risks or to do the unusual if he believed it would help him accomplish his purposes. That, W. E. Just believed, was one of the reasons the company had changed over to self-insurance for its product liability when rates increased. Many had advised against it, including W. E. Just, even when Will Very had agreed to additional legal staff if increased work resulted. Therefore, W. E. Just realized he would, indeed, have little choice in this matter but "to fight it."

After that conversation Henry Law received a letter from W. E. Just stating that Zagger Supply denied that John Q. Worker's death was caused by a defective zagger manufactured by them. Therefore, they also denied any liability and would make no payment. Attorney Law followed up with a telephone call to W. E. Just, indicating that his client was serious and would maintain suit if necessary. W. E. could only reply that Zagger Supply's position was clear; it continued to deny liability and would defend any legal action brought against it.

DECISION TO BRING CIVIL SUIT

When Henry Law discussed the Zagger Supply response with Mary, the two reviewed the entire situation. Mary then asked Henry to pursue the matter further, and it was agreed that Henry should take the action necessary to institute civil suit against Zagger Supply. The decision to do

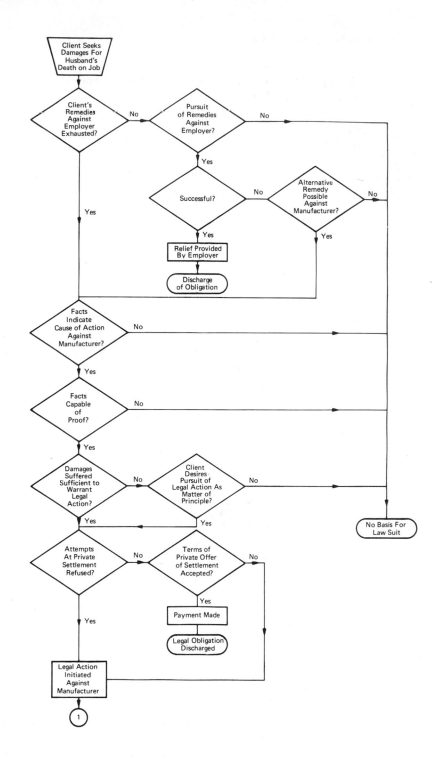

FIGURE 5-4. Decision to Institute Legal Action.

this, as it evolved from the very beginning, has been flow charted in Figure 5-4.

It was in this way that Mary Worker became the plaintiff in a civil action. When she found herself thinking about how it all came about, she discovered that she could diagram mentally the steps which led her to this point. Those steps have been flow charted in Figure 5-5. Mary would learn soon that there were many to follow. What happened to her in succeeding stages is discussed in the next chapters, which report the events that took place once she was in the civil system.

QUESTIONS

Mary's entry into the legal system as the plaintiff in a law suit has been the result of the decisions made by the various persons who have been involved in all of the steps through which she has passed. There is

FIGURE 5-5. Steps in Mary Worker's Pursuit of Legal Action to Recover Damages for John Q. Worker's Death.

Fred Famous' decision that The Firm would pay her only the amount required by the Great State Workmen's Compensation Act. It is a decision made in full compliance with the law—Fred acted in consultation with the firm's legal counsel—yet it is also an example of the interaction of business and law. Fred himself indicated that the firm's financial condition influenced him in his thinking.

Would his decision have been different if the company had been in a more affluent state? Had he offered additional payments, would Mary have pursued legal action? Has he really, while acting in full compliance with the law, shifted some of the economic burden and responsibility arising from an employee's death to others in the marketplace? If that is the effect of the statute, should it be amended? Or, is it a proper allocation of economic risks? Is it a result desired by the legislators who enacted the statute?

Certainly Henry Law had a great influence upon Mary's entry into the legal system. Not only did legal issues concern him, but his decision was influenced greatly by factual considerations. In his conversations with Mary, he stated that he must have facts and not just suppositions. He also considered mentally the problems involved in meeting the burden of proof.

What does this suggest regarding the legal system's capabilities for achieving justice for persons who have been wronged but do not have the means of proof? Is there anything that can be done to change that?

Henry Law's first approach, once he believed there was a basis for legal action, was to try to effectuate a private, out-of-court settlement. Does this not suggest a "private judicial system"? What are the consequences? Should the legal system tolerate this? Should the law provide for procedures to be followed in private settlements? Why are most disputes settled out of court? Why does the law encourage this kind of settlement?

The decision of Zagger Supply to refuse payment for John Q.'s death is apparent from Will Very's first response to Henry Law's letter, "We won't pay." Could he have sustained that position if W. E. Just had been unable to come up with some reasonable defenses? Attorney Just is in the position of having to deal with and defend the company against a *fait accompli*. What does this say about the need for, or advisability of, consultation with the corporate legal staff regarding everyday business transactions? Is this a realistic suggestion?

The influence of other persons whose decisions have not been flow charted upon Mary Worker's entry into the legal system must be recognized. For instance, there is Robert Leader's decision to pick up several fragments of the shattered zagger at the time of the accident. There is also his twice-made statement to Mary that he had the fragments if she needed help. Had he not acted in this manner, would Mary be starting legal action against Zagger Supply?

There is also the role played by the young woman at the NLSA office who did her best to be of assistance to Mary.

Can you flow chart her actions and decisions in eventually leading Mary to the lawyer referral service? Would you have as much difficulty as Mary Worker had in finding a lawyer? How would you locate one if you needed legal counsel today? If you moved to another area of the country and needed a family doctor, how would you find one? A family lawyer? Should professional codes regulate lawyer and doctor advertising? What is the maximum allowable income and net worth of eligibility for NLSA or the Legal Aid Society in your community? Should these criteria be changed? Do you know of any prepaid legal services plans? What suggestions do you have for improving the delivery of legal services? Do Mary's experiences indicate that the hurdles for entry into the legal system (1) are too many and too great? (2) Of reasonable difficulty for the purpose of testing one's seriousness of purpose? (3) Should be increased or made more difficult in order to eliminate frivolous lawsuits and reduce the caseloads of the courts? What changes would you suggest? Prepare a flow chart for entry into the civil system as you believe it should be. Will it be optimal, yet realistic, in achieving justice for everyone? Can it be? What compromises, if any, must you make to achieve your goal?

CASES

Webb v. Zern
422 Pa. 424, 220 A.2d 853 (1966)

MR. JUSTICE COHEN: This appeal is from the dismissal of a suit in trespass seeking damages for injuries resulting from the explosion of a beer keg purchased by the plaintiff's father.

Charles Webb purchased a quarter-keg of beer from a distributor, John Zern. That same day, plaintiff's brother tapped the keg and about a gallon of beer was drawn from it. Later that evening, when plaintiff entered the room in which the keg had been placed, the keg exploded, severely injuring plaintiff. . . .

[The issue determinative of this appeal] is the nature and scope of the liability in trespass of the one who produces or markets a defective product for use or consumption. . . .[M]odern case law and commentaries. . .extend and recommend the extension of the law of strict liability in tort for defective products. The new Restatement of Torts reflects this modern attitude. Section 402A thereof states:

"(1) One who sells any product in a defective condition unreasonably dangerous to the user or consumer or to his property is subject to liability for physical harm thereby caused to the ultimate user or consumer, or to his property, if (a) the seller is engaged in the business of selling such a product, and (b) it is expected to and does reach the user or consumer without substantial change in the condition in which it is sold."

"(2) The rule stated in Subsection (1) applies although (a) the seller has exercised all possible care in the preparation and sale of his product, and (b) the user or consumer has not bought the product from or entered into any contractual relation with the seller." Restatement 2d, Torts, §402A (1965).

We hereby adopt the foregoing language as the law of Pennsylvania.

The plaintiff in this litigation, therefore, must be given an opportunity to plead and prove his case. Since the plaintiff has broadly pleaded those facts necessary to a cause of action for defective products liability, plaintiff will be permitted to amend his complaint to explicitly state a cause of action in trespass for defective products liability. . . .

DISSENTING OPINION BY MR. CHIEF JUSTICE BELL:

I very emphatically dissent.

If such a drastic change in the field of tort *liability without fault* is to be made in our law—even the majority admit that "we are today adopting a new basis of liability"—it is difficult to imagine a more unlawyerlike judicial Opinion than the majority Opinion. . . .

The new role adopted by the majority so completely changes, not by legislative action but by judicial ukase, the law with respect to trespass actions for injuries resulting from noninherently dangerous products that are either manufactured or bottled or sold by any vendor—even a retail druggist—that in my opinion it is not only very unfair but absolutely *unjustifiable* in Justice or in Law. . . .

Today, no one knows from month to month or whenever the Supreme Court of Pennsylvania or the Supreme Court of the United States meets, what the law will be tomorrow—or, by retrospectivity, what the Court will now say it always should have been—or what anyone's rights, privileges, liabilities and duties are. The net result is uncertainty, confusion, dismay, and constantly diminishing respect for Law and for our Courts—and, of course, is one of the major causes of the constantly and rapidly increasing litigation which is literally swamping our Courts.

In a Constitutional form of government such as ours, which is based upon Law and Order, *certainty and stability are essential.* Unless the Courts establish and maintain *certainty and stability* in the Law, (1) public officials will not know from week to week or from month to month the powers and limitations of the Government, (2) Government cannot adequately protect law-abiding citizens or peaceful communities against criminals, (3) private citizens will not know their rights and obligations, (4) the meaning of wills, bonds, contracts, deeds, leases and other written agreements will fluctuate and change with each change in the personnel of a Court or their individual ideas of what the writing should and would have said if the present situation had been visualized in the light of today's conditions, (5) property interests will be jeopardized and frequently changed or lost, (6) businessmen cannot safely and wisely make agreements with each other or with their employees.

The basic need for certainty and stability in the law has been recognized for centuries by English-speaking peoples. LORD COKE, Chief Justice of England, thus wisely expressed (circa 1600) these truths: "The knowne certaintie of the law is the safetie of all." Until very recently, this has been a beacon light for Anglo-American Courts, for text authorities, and for law-abiding Americans ever since the foundation of our Country. In the realm of the Law it is usually expressed in the principle known as Stare Decisis. Stare Decisis is one of the bedrocks upon which the House of Law has been built and maintained.

If such a radical change in the Law is to be made—as is now made in the majority Opinion—it should be made and must be made only by the Legislature. It appears to be completely forgotten that we are not a super or Supreme Legislature or indeed a Legislature at all, desirable as that sometimes would be; or, as Mr. Justice FRANKFURTER pointedly reminded the Supreme Court of the United States in his concurring Opinion in *Green v. United States*, 356 U.S. 165, "Decision-making is not a mechanical process, but neither is this Court an originating lawmaker. The admonition of Mr. Justice BRANDEIS that we are not a third branch of the Legislature should never be disregarded." (page 193).

Too many appellate Judges envision themselves, not as interpreters of the Constitution and the laws, which is the role and province assigned and limited to them by the Constitution, but as possessing the right, the power and the duty to change and, if necessary, rewrite the Constitution and any and every Law, in order to bring it in accord with what they believe is or will be best for the social, political or economic interests of our State or Country.

I can never approve or condone such a Judge-made revolutionary and unfair rule as the majority promulgate.

I very vigorously dissent.

FOOTNOTES

[1] 29 U.S.C. §676. This refers to Title 29, section 676 of the *United States Code.*
[2] 42 U.S.C. §2809.
[3] 42 U.S.C. §2996 *et seq.*
[4] *Swayne v. Connecticut Co.,* 86 Conn. 439, 84 A. 634, 635 (*1913*).
[5] U.C.C. 2-314.
[6] U.C.C. 2-315.
[7] U.C.C. 2-318.
[8] 29 U.S.C. §655 (a).

CHAPTER 6
PRETRIAL: DEVELOPMENT OF A CASE FOR TRIAL

PREPARATION FOR PLEADING

Henry Law was now ready to take the steps necessary to institute a law suit on behalf of Mary Worker. This involved much more than merely walking down to the nearest courthouse and filling out an application or request to begin litigation against Zagger Supply.

Justiciable Action

Henry's mental process at this time consisted of thoughtful review of a number of decisions he made in his earlier determination that Mary Worker had a legal basis for bringing suit. A chain of decisions had led to his conclusion that the John Q. Worker case was *justiciable*, that is, proper for action by the courts. In addition to the existence of a cause of action, he had also decided:

1. There existed a case or controversy.
2. The plaintiff had standing to sue.
3. The defendant was a proper party to the action.
4. The suit would be brought within the time period of the applicable Statute of Limitations.

How did Henry arrive at these determinations? Further inquiry is in order.

Consider first the decision as to case or controversy.[1] Recourse to the courts is possible when there is an actual dispute between adverse parties. The courts do not exist to settle theoretical issues, to determine answers to problems that might arise in the future, to provide a forum for friendly—as contrasted with adversarial—parties, or to pursue an intellectually stimulating question for its own sake. Nor will the courts decide moot questions, those of a kind where a judicial decision would have no legal effect upon an existing controversy.

That there existed a real dispute between Zagger Supply and Mary Worker concerning payment to her for John Q.'s death, there could be no doubt. Determining the existence of a live controversy was one of the easier decisions Henry had had to make.

Henry Law's next decision regarding proper parties was more involved. He knew that Mary as the *plaintiff*—the party bringing the action—must have standing to sue. In other words, she must have been personally wronged in some manner. One of her legally protected interests must have been invaded by the defendant. This requirement prevents an interested but unharmed spectator or bystander from bringing legal action. It also precludes bringing suit for no reason other than mere desire to take legal action against another or to harass him.

Obviously the standing to sue requirement meant that Robert Leader would not have the right to bring suit against Zagger Supply for John Q.'s death. What may not be quite so obvious is Mary's position.

The person suffering legal injury from the alleged wrong was John Q., now dead and unable to bring suit. Had this occurred in the very early days of the common law, the legal claim for personal injury would have died with John Q. However, modern law has remedied that by passage of death statutes. These take two forms: *survival* acts and *wrongful death* acts. Today each state has enacted either one or both of these death statutes. They commonly provide for two types of action which may be brought following one's death.

A *survival action* is a legal action that the deceased could have brought had he lived and which, as its name indicates, survives his death. It is brought by the deceased's personal representative on behalf of and for the benefit of the decedent's estate. Recoverable damages include compensation for hospital and medical expenses, lost earnings, and pain and suffering sustained by the deceased as a result of injury to him.

A *wrongful death action*, on the other hand, is a legal action brought on behalf of persons dependent upon the deceased to recover for losses they have suffered as a result of his death. Damages are recoverable by them rather than by the estate. Examples include not only funeral expenses but also compensation to a decedent's surviving spouse and children for loss of both financial and nonpecuniary benefits, such as the deceased's services as a spouse and parent as well as the financial support provided by the decedent to the family.

Great State had enacted the two death statutes. They provided that both actions might be brought in the event of death but must be joined for trial so that double recovery would not result. Therefore, Henry Law realized that the Great State statutes conferred upon Mary standing to sue in her capacity as administratrix[2] of John Q.'s estate.

Satisfied that Mary was a proper plaintiff, Henry Law next determined that Zagger Supply was a proper defendant—the party against whom legal action is brought. In referring to §402A of the *Restatement of Torts 2d,* he found that in cases of dangerously defective products which result in physical harm to the user, the seller of the product—provided he is engaged in the business of selling such products—can be held strictly liable. There is no requirement that the user also be the purchaser. While he had previously decided he would prefer to proceed in tort; i.e., *ex delicto,* Henry mentally noted that the supplier of the product would also be a proper defendant if one were to proceed in contract, or *ex contractu.* This was in accordance with the interpretation by the Great State courts of the Uniform Commercial Code. Henry Law had received verification from two sources, Robert Leader and Professor Learned, that Zagger Supply was the manufacturer and supplier of the zagger that had shattered at the time of John Q.'s death. Therefore, he knew that he had no problem with respect to the proper defendant.

The next item for Henry Law's concern was the time period that had elapsed since John Q.'s death. He checked this because of the Statute of Limitations, which sets specific time limits for bringing various kinds of legal actions. The purpose of the statute is to encourage timely suit. Unreasonable delay in instituting legal action makes the rendering of justice difficult. Witnesses may die or move away, those who are still available find it difficult to remember events occurring in the distant past, evidence is lost or destroyed. Therefore, it is a defense to a legal action if it is brought after expiration of the time period provided in the Statute of Limitations.

The Statute of Limitations can be tolled; that is, there is a holding action on the time. One event that precipitates this is the official beginning of a law suit. It is not necessary that the legal action be concluded prior to the expiration of the time period set in the statute. There are variations from state to state regarding other situations that will toll the statute and regarding the time limitations. The Great State Statute of Limitations provided that wrongful death actions must be brought within one year and survival actions within two years of the death of the decedent. Since only three months had elapsed since John Q.'s death, Henry Law knew that the law suit would be filed in ample time to meet Statute of Limitations requirements.

Discussion of Henry Law's determination that there had been a wrong committed for which the law provides a remedy—that there was a cause of action—appears in Chapter 5.

Pleadings

Thus it was that Henry Law concluded that the Mary Worker case was justiciable. He realized his next step would be to initiate the *pleadings.* These are formal, written documents filed with the court prior to trial. They contain statements of the two parties concerning the controversy. The plaintiff actually commences a civil action by filing the first statement, generally referred to as the *complaint*, with the court. This document identifies the parties, states the nature of the dispute, contains the plaintiff's charges against the defendant, and states the relief sought. The defendant responds to those charges. His reply is commonly referred to as an *answer*. Other statements may follow. Each court system has its own rules of procedure for the preparation of these documents, known as *Rules of Civil Procedure*. These vary from state to state and between the federal and state systems.

Choice of Court

Obviously, Henry would have to know in which court he would file suit before he could know which court's rules of procedure he must follow in his pleadings. That meant making another decision, one that involved answers to these questions:

1. In which level of the court system is it proper to bring this case?
2. Is this case properly brought in the federal or state court system, and, if the state system, which state?
3. Which court has subject matter jurisdiction?
4. Which court has personal jurisdiction, and, can that jurisdiction be perfected?
5. Which is the court with proper venue?

Answers to these questions include concepts that are basic to *due process of law.* That term is used here to refer to fair and orderly legal proceedings which protect the rights and liberty of the persons involved.

Henry's first decision, that of proper level of a court system, was easily made. He knew that the amount of damages to be sought was far in excess of the maximum which the minor judiciary can properly handle. Since this was not an appeal from a decision already rendered by a lower court, he also realized it would not be within the province of an appellate court. Therefore, the proper level would be a trial court.

His next determination would be of a specific trial court, but should it be one in a state or in the federal court system? Henry knew that, as a general rule, courts in both systems have the power to hear and decide cases involving either state or federal law. There is an exception regarding a few special subject matter areas which have been specifically restricted to one system either constitutionally or by statute. In many situations both a state and a federal court can properly hear a case, and in some instances the courts of several states can do so.

As the party initiating legal action, the plaintiff makes the choice of court, or *choice of forum* as it is called. However, he must choose from among those courts which can properly hear the case. It should be noted that in some instances a defendant, after petitioning the court and showing sufficient cause, can have the case removed from a state to a federal court. He can also request a change of venue.

The proper court to hear and decide a case is one that has jurisdiction over the subject matter, jurisdiction over the defendant or property involved, and proper venue. *Jurisdiction* is the power or authority of the court to hear a case. *Venue* refers to geographical location. Hence, change of venue refers to change of location of the trial site.

Jurisdiction

Jurisdiction of the courts can be determined by referring to the sources of judicial power: the constitution (state or federal, depending upon which court system is involved) and legislation enacted pursuant to constitutional provisions. Could litigation in the Mary Worker case properly be brought in a federal trial court? Referring to the United States Constitution[3] and the United States Code,[4] Henry found that the United States District Court has jurisdiction in civil matters as follows:

1. Where the sum in controversy exceeds $10,000 and arises under the Constitution, laws or treaties of the United States;

2. Where the matter involved is one which by federal statute is restricted to the federal courts regardless of the sum involved. Some examples of this are civil rights, bankruptcy, patent and copyright, antitrust, and admiralty cases;

3. Where the sum in controversy exceeds $10,000 and there is diversity of citizenship.

Diversity of citizenship means that the parties are citizens of different states or that one is a citizen of the United States and the other, a citizen of a foreign country. Complete diversity is required. Should there be more than one plaintiff or defendant, it is necessary that all persons on one side be citizens of different states from the states of which the persons on the other side are citizens. For purposes of diversity, a corporation is considered to be a citizen of both the state in which it is incorporated and the state in which it has its principal place of business. That meant Zagger Supply was a citizen of only Nearby State.

Therefore, federal jurisdiction existed in the Mary Worker case on the basis of the amount involved and diversity of citizenship. Knowing this,

Henry asked himself if the courts of Great State and Nearby State also had jurisdiction.

The Great State Constitution provided for the following special purpose courts:

1. A probate court to handle primarily matters related to the wills and estates of deceased persons;
2. A family court which was concerned with the area of domestic relations;
3. A juvenile court to deal with cases involving youthful offenders;
4. A criminal court to hear criminal cases.

It also provided for a court of common pleas with more general jurisdiction, covering all matters not coming under the aegis of the specialized courts or the minor judiciary. The latter's jurisdiction included civil cases involving not more than $1000.

Consequently, Henry Law realized that the Court of Common Pleas of Great State would have subject matter jurisdiction in the Mary Worker case. He also found that in Nearby State the trial court of general jurisdiction, known as the Circuit Court, had subject matter jurisdiction in civil cases in excess of $500. Thus far, Henry had his choice of the federal, Great State, and Nearby State court systems; all would be proper in the Mary Worker case.

He knew, however, that jurisdiction over subject matter alone is not sufficient. A court must also have jurisdiction over the person of the defendant or the property of the case, depending upon whether the action is *in personam* or *in rem.*

In personam jurisdiction is required when the controversy is of such a nature that the plaintiff seeks to have the court render a judgment against a specific person or persons who are the defendants.[5] In an in personam action, the defendant's obligation to do something or to give something is to be decided. The Mary Worker case is an example. In contrast, in rem jurisdiction applies when the plaintiff requests the court to render a judgment affecting an interest in property. An example would be a case in which ownership of a piece of land is the issue to be decided.

A court can acquire in personam or personal jurisdiction over a person if he is physically present or domiciled within the state in which the court sits.[6] That physical presence in the state may be temporary. It can consist of simply passing through. (Persons entering a state to give testimony in a judicial proceeding or who are brought in by force or trickery do not have jurisdictional presence.) Would it be possible for the state and federal courts to perfect jurisdiction over Zagger Supply, Henry asked himself?

Service of Process

To perfect jurisdiction requires that the defendant receive proper notice that a legal action is being brought against him. This is known as *service of process*. Service is accomplished by delivering to the defendant a copy of the plaintiff's complaint, along with a summons ordering him to appear in court. The summons and complaint may be handed to the defendant personally, may be left at his usual place of abode with a person of suitable age and discretion residing there, or may be delivered to an agent authorized to receive service of process. Service upon an officer or agent is made in the case of a corporation, partnership, or association defendant.

A person may voluntarily consent to a court's jurisdiction. Foreign corporations are considered to have done so when they register to do business within a state other than the one in which they were incorporated. Many states have *long arm statutes* which provide for jurisdiction over nonresidents who come into the state and cause injury or loss while there. Most of these statutes include provisions for jurisdiction over nonresident motorists, nonresidents entering into a contract or transacting business within the state, and nonresidents who commit a tort within the state. Many of these statutes state that nonresidents, by coming into the state and engaging in activity there, impliedly give their consent to appointment of a state official, usually the secretary of state, to receive service of process should legal action be filed against them as a result of their activities within the state. Service upon the state's secretary is generally followed by notice to the nonresident by mail. This is referred to as *substitute service.*

In rem jurisdiction exists when the rights in property (a "thing") are to be determined by the court, and the property is located within the geographical boundaries of the court's jurisdiction. If personal service is not possible because the defendant is neither a resident of, nor physically present in, the state, *constructive service* is possible. This may consist of notice of suit by newspaper publication or posting notice on the property itself. In rem jurisdiction will not exist, however, in the absence of requisite "minimum contacts" within the state.

In the Mary Worker case, it was evident to Henry that there would be no problem insofar as in personam jurisdiction was concerned. Zagger Supply was a resident of Nearby State, and personal service was possible there. The firm had registered as a foreign corporation doing business in Great State, and the Great State statute provided for substitute service in that event. Since the Federal Rules of Civil Procedure provide for both personal service and substitute service upon foreign corporations in accordance with state statute, personal jurisdiction over Zagger Supply could also be perfected in a federal action. At this point, Henry found that he had not yet eliminated the federal courts or the courts of either

Great State or Nearby State as proper places for entering the Mary Worker suit.

Venue

He thereupon set about determining the question of proper venue. Venue is regulated by statute. With regard to the federal courts, the United States Code[7] provides

1. In civil actions based only on diversity, action may be brought in the judicial district where all plaintiffs or all defendants reside or in which the claim arose;

2. A corporation may be sued in any judicial district in which it is incorporated or licensed to do business or is doing business.

Since the Mary Worker claim arose in the Great State District and since Zagger Supply was doing business in that same district, a proper location for the trial in the federal court system would be in the United States District Court for the Great State District. At the same time, Zagger Supply was a resident of Nearby State, had been incorporated there, and carried on business there. Consequently, a second proper location for the trial would be in the United States District Court for the Nearby State District.

State venue statutes typically provide that legal action may be brought in the county where the defendant resides or is doing business or in the county where the cause of action arose. These were the Great State and Nearby State provisions. Since Zagger Supply was doing business in Local County of Great State and since the cause of action also arose there, proper venue in the Great State system for the Mary Worker case would be the Common Pleas Court of Local County. In Nearby State, Zagger Supply was a resident of This County. Therefore, proper venue in that system would be in the Circuit Court of This County.

Henry Law concluded that, all other factors being equal, his choice of location would be the Great State District because most of the witnesses—Robert Leader, other employees of The Firm and Local 135 members, as well as Mary Worker herself—resided there. To transport them to Nearby State District would be expensive.

Forum Non Conveniens

Before concluding with venue, Henry Law considered one other matter. That was the doctrine of *forum non conveniens*. This permits a court to dismiss an action when it appears to the satisfaction of the court that the suit might more appropriately be tried elsewhere. Henry also remembered that the United States Code[8] provides that a district court may, in the interest of justice and for the convenience of parties and witnesses, transfer a civil action to another district where it might have been brought. Great State and Nearby State change of venue statutes were typical of those in many states. They provided for relocation under conditions similar to those in the federal law.

Because Henry's reason for preferring Great State over Nearby State was the appropriateness of the place, he concluded that there would be little likelihood of a request for change of venue—and still less for grant of a request for such—if he proceeded in either the Great State District Court or in Local County Common Pleas Court. However, he would wait to make a firm choice until after he reviewed the conflict of laws situation.

Choice of Law

Would a difference in the law that a specific court followed work as an advantage to his client? In a state court, he could expect state procedural and substantive law to be applied. In diversity cases, a federal court must follow the substantive law of the state in which it is sitting but federal procedure will apply. This is known as the "Erie doctrine", since it evolved from the United States Supreme Court decision in *Erie R. Co. v. Tompkins*, 304 U.S. 64 (1938). The reason for this rule is to prevent a federal and state court sitting in the same state from reaching different results regarding the same legal question.

Entering into Henry Law's choice of forum was consideration of yet another factor. In the Mary Worker case, most of the events—including John Q.'s death—occurred in Great State. However, the zaggers were manufactured in Nearby State by a Nearby State corporation. Would the laws of Nearby State or Great State apply? Suppose the provisions of Great State law differed from those of Nearby State law. This situation is referred to as *conflict of laws.*

The answer, Henry knew, could be found in that portion of the law referred to as *choice of law.* Each state, either by judicial decision or statute, has provisions specifying which state's laws should be used by its courts in deciding cases that involve events occurring in more than one state. For instance, Great State law provided that in tort cases the law of the place of injury, referred to as *lex loci delicti,* would apply. This meant that since John Q. was injured in Great State, the laws of Great State would be applicable. Henry Law found that Nearby State also followed the lex loci delicti rule. This would mean that even if the case were tried in the Nearby State courts, the court would follow the law of Great State in reaching its decision. That gave Henry more flexibility in his choice of forum than he would have had if the Nearby State choice of law rules had called for application of Nearby State law regarding John Q.'s accident.

Because of differences in state law, the lawyer is sometimes faced with a situation in which there is a conflict in the laws regarding choice of law. For instance, not all states follow the rule of lex loci delicti. There is a trend toward interest analysis and test of significant relationship; that is, which state has the greater interest or concern with the events and the parties involved. There are other variations. In contract cases, for example, the law to be applied may be that of a number of different states. It may be, among others, the law of the state where the action is brought, the state where the contract was made, the state where the contract was to be performed, the state that the parties have specified in the contract itself, or the state where there is the greatest interest and relationship.

When there is a conflict in the laws regarding choice of law, then the law of the forum state with respect to choice of law controls. As can be seen, the rules regarding conflict of laws can be quite complicated. They are an important factor in the attorney's selection of the court in which to bring an action. Given a choice of forum, the attorney will ordinarily decide upon the one that will apply laws most favorable to his client's cause.

Henry Law was fortunate in that the rules regarding choice of laws would not limit his choice of forum. His choice of Great State over Nearby State was now firm. He had only one more decision to make regarding the court: would it be federal or state?

Selection of Court Decision

As Henry Law continued this decision-making process, he checked the calendar of both the Common Pleas Court of Local County and the United States District Court for Great State District. He discovered that he could expect almost half the waiting time for trial in that particular federal court since it did not have as great a backlog of cases as did the Local County court. That was the decisive factor as far as he was concerned.

Therefore, and after all those considerations, Henry Law decided to file suit in the United States District Court for the Great State District. Whereupon he brought out his copy of the *Federal Rules of Civil Procedure* (F.R. Civ. P.) for handy reference and proceeded to prepare a complaint in the civil case of Mary Worker, Administratrix of the Estate of John Q. Worker, v. Zagger Supply, Inc., a corporation.

PLEADINGS

Complaint

As Henry Law sat at his desk preparing to draft the complaint,[9] he mentally considered its function. The complaint serves to acquaint the court with the matters in dispute and to give the defendant notice of the claim being asserted by the plaintiff.

Form and content of the complaint would be governed by the Federal Rules. Noting that they were simpler and allowed for greater flexibility than did the Great State rules, Henry found the complaint must have

1. A short and plain statement of the grounds upon which the court's jurisdiction depends;

2. A short and plain statement of the claim showing that the pleader is entitled to relief;

3. A demand for judgment for the relief. Relief in the alternative, or of several different types, may be demanded.

Henry also considered that the action was being brought as both a wrongful death and survival action and on the basis of strict liability in tort for a defective product. As a guide to the content of the complaint, he prepared the worksheet, which appears as Table 6-1. Using it, he was able to complete the complaint, Form 6-1.

TABLE 6-1. Henry Law's guide to contents of complaint.

Nature of Suit	Reference	Contents of Complaint
Federal court action	F.R.Civ.P. 8(a)	Statement of Jurisdiction:
Diversity action	29 U.S.C. § 1331, 1332	citizenship of plaintiff
		citizenship of defendant (corporate defendant: place of incorporation and principal place of business)
		over $10,000 in controversy
Strict liability in-tort for defective product	F.R.Civ.P. 8(a)	Statement of claim:
	§ 402A, Restatement of Torts 2d	defendant sold the product involved
		defendant is a seller in the business of selling the product involved
		product was defective at the time of sale
		product reached user without substantial change
		plaintiff's decedent was a user
		product was being used for the purpose and in the manner intended by the seller
		product was unreasonably dangerous
		user suffered harm
		proximate cause
Wrongful death and survival action	F.R.Civ.P. 8(a)	Prayer for relief:
	Great State Statutes	damages—wrongful death
		damages—survival action
		capacity of plaintiff re these two actions

FORM 6-1. Complaint.

DISTRICT COURT OF THE UNITED STATES
FOR THE DISTRICT OF GREAT STATE

MARY WORKER,
    Administratrix of the
    ESTATE OF JOHN Q.
    WORKER, deceased,
        Plaintiff

        v.   Civil Action
                    No. _____

ZAGGER SUPPLY, INC.,
    a corporation,
        Defendant

COMPLAINT

Plaintiff alleges as follows:

COUNT ONE

1. Plaintiff Mary Worker is a citizen of Great State and is administratrix of the estate of John Q. Worker, deceased, who was killed on August 26, 19XX in the accident referred to herein.

2. Defendant Zagger Supply, Inc., is a corporation incorporated under the laws of Nearby State and having its principal place of business in Nearby State. Defendant is engaged in the business of manufacturing and selling zaggers.

3. The matters in controversy exceed, exclusive of interest and costs, the sum of $10,000.

4. On or about August 15, 19XX defendant manufactured and sold to The Firm, Inc., the zagger involved in the incident referred to herein. The zagger was especially manufactured and sold by the defendant for the specific use being made of it at the time of the accident.

5. On August 26, 19XX at approximately 2:00 P.M., plaintiff's decedent, John Q. Worker, was killed when the zagger manufactured and sold by the defendant shattered with great violence and a fragment pierced his abdomen while he was engaged in operating a cypres machine on

which the zagger was being used in the course of his employment and the performance of his duties as a cypres operator at The Firm, Inc. in Big City, Local County, Great State.

6. At the time of the accident, plaintiff's decedent was a user of the zagger and was using it in the manner and for the purpose expected and intended by the defendant.

7. At the time of the accident the zagger existed without substantial change from the condition in which it was manufactured and sold. It was in a defective condition in that it was defectively manufactured and unreasonably dangerous to users. Defendant knew or should have expected that the zagger would reach users without substantial change in the condition in which it was manufactured and sold.

8. Death of plaintiff's decedent and resulting damages were caused by the conduct of the defendant in defectively manufacturing such zagger and selling it in a defective condition unreasonably dangerous to intended users as well as to persons reasonably expected to be within the orbit of such use. Defendant corporation is strictly liable for the death and damages herein set forth.

9. By reason of the aforesaid wrongful acts of the defendant which directly and proximately caused the death of John Q. Worker, plaintiff administratrix claims damages of defendant on behalf of the wife and children of the deceased as follows: (a) for loss to the wife of the society, services, comfort and companionship of her husband; (b) for loss to the children of the care, companionship, nurture, and parental guidance of their father; (c) for funeral, burial, cemetery, and grave monument expenses.

Wherefore, plaintiff Mary Worker, administratrix of the estate of John Q. Worker, deceased, demands judgment of the defendant Zagger Supply, Inc., a corporation, on behalf of the family of the deceased under the Wrongful Death Act in an amount in excess of the sum of $10,000.

COUNT TWO

10. Plaintiff incorporates herein the allegations made in paragraphs 1 through 8 of this complaint.

11. By reason of the aforesaid wrongful acts of the defendant which directly and proximately caused the death of John Q. Worker, plaintiff administratrix claims damages

of the defendant Zagger Supply, Inc., a corporation, on behalf of the estate as follows: (a) for loss of established earnings and earning power of the deceased for a period of time beginning August 26, 19XX and continuing to the termination of his natural life, which earnings and earning power would have continued but for his death on August 26, 19XX; (b) for expenses incident to the administration of the estate of the deceased; (c) for other expenses caused by the accident.

Wherefore, plaintiff demands judgment of the defendant Zagger Supply, Inc., a corporation, on behalf of the estate of the decedent under the Survival Act in an amount in excess of the sum of $10,000.

A JURY TRIAL IS DEMANDED.

_____
Attorney for Plaintiff
789 Main Street
Big City, Great State

Request for Jury Trial

Notice that the last item in the complaint is a request for a jury trial. Henry knew that the Federal Rules provided that a request for a jury trial could be included in the pleadings. Before he took action on this, he telephoned Mary Worker and asked if she would come to his office. There he reviewed with her the contents of the complaint and the steps in the litigation now underway and also asked her wishes about a trial by jury.

"I didn't know there was a choice," she said. "I thought all trials had a jury."

"No," replied Henry Law. "The right to trial by jury in the federal courts in civil matters is guaranteed by the Seventh Amendment to the United States Constitution."

Seventh Amendment

When Mary looked puzzled at this response, he explained that the Constitution is the supreme law of the land. No law that is in conflict with it is valid, nor would any legal procedure which resulted in depriving an individual of a constitutional right be valid. As Mary nodded, indicating understanding, Henry continued. The federal constitution, he said, reflects the thoughts of its authors who came to this country steeped in the traditions of the English common law. That included the jury system. It had developed over the centuries following man's early attempts to determine guilt or innocence through trial by ordeal, which was usually by fire or water. Early juries in England consisted of twelve local men (no women, in those days) who served as witnesses and testified as to the events that occurred. The role of the jury as an objective, disinterested group came only later, but did exist at the time the original thirteen colonies were being formed into one nation. The framers of the Constitution considered the jury—a group of one's peers acting as decision makers and interposed between the defendant and the authorities—as one means of preventing possible harassment of citizens by those in power. Because the possibility of abuse was greater in criminal matters than in civil cases, the constitutional provisions for the two kinds of action differ.

The Seventh Amendment provides that the right to trial by jury exists in civil matters over $20, that being a sizable sum of money at the time the Constitution was being written, Henry continued. It also restricts the right to a jury trial in civil cases to those matters where it existed under the common law. That excludes all cases in equity as well as actions at law for which the right to trial by jury had never been provided, such as those for divorce or change of name.

Henry went on to say that Mary could waive the right to trial by jury if she so chose. In the federal court system, the assumption is that a person has waived that right when no request for a jury trial is made. On the other hand, said Henry, the reverse assumption is true in the Great State court system. However, the right to trial by jury would be the same, since provisions of the Great State constitution coincided with those in the federal constitution. Because provisions of the Seventh Amendment have not been made applicable to the states, the right to a jury trial in civil cases in state courts is governed by the provisions of the state constitutions.

At this point Mary asked who made decisions in cases in which there was no jury.

Trier of Fact

Henry replied by describing the jury as the *trier of fact*. The jury is the decision maker regarding factual matters. An example of facts to be decided by a jury would be whether the zagger John Q. had been using at the time of the accident was defective. On the other hand, questions of law are the province of the judge. He explains to the jury any matters of law of which jurors must be aware in their decision making. This is exceedingly important when the jury must apply the law to the facts in a particular case. One example of that would be in a negligence case where the jury, after hearing all of the facts surrounding the event as well as having had negligence defined for them by the judge, would be required to decide if the defendant had been negligent or not. When there is no jury, Henry explained, the judge alone is the decision maker and decides both questions of law and fact.

Mary said it was her opinion that she would benefit more from having a jury—a number of persons who could identify with her and her situation—make the decision in her case. They would be more inclined, she believed, to consider the problems of a working-class family who had lost its husband and father in an industrial accident. A judge she felt, would probably be more interested in points of law.

"I have more faith in a jury," she concluded, "and I really wouldn't feel I had a fair trial without one."

Henry smiled. "Your belief in the jury system is shared by many," he replied. "Observers of Americans have commented that as a nation we regard the jury in much the same esteem as we do the right to vote—as a symbol of the democratic process. People in other countries do not view it in the same manner. In many cases, of course, this is because they have different legal systems. However, the jury system does have its critics. There have been suggestions for change, ranging all the way from dispensing with juries to use of only persons professionally trained as jurors. It is interesting that in one study of jury verdicts in civil matters[10] judges agreed with the jury's decision in 80 per cent of the cases."

"And I'm not interested in being part of the other 20 per cent," was Mary's response.

Preparation of Document

After Mary left his office, Henry gave his secretary a draft of the complaint for typing. While it was being prepared, he glanced at the morning newspaper. There was Will Very's picture on page one. He would be in Big City all week at the meeting of the Zagger Manufacturers Association where he was scheduled to be the principal speaker.

"What incredible luck," thought Henry. "I can have him served personally and will instruct the Clerk of Courts accordingly when I file the complaint."

As he signed the complaint, Henry Law realized that according to the Federal Rules his signature constituted certification by him that he had read the complaint and to the best of his knowledge, information, and belief there was good ground to support it. Thus, the attorney bears responsibility if a false or sham legal action is instituted. In contrast, the Great State rules of procedure required that a complaint be accompanied by an affidavit of the plaintiff swearing to the truth of the statements contained therein. Many other states follow that same practice.

Filing Complaint

Henry Law took two copies of the complaint to the office of the Clerk of Courts for the United States District Court for the Great State District. These he filed with the clerk and paid the filing fee. The clerk gave the case a number and entered the case on the court's *docket*. The docket is the formal record of the court's activities. It contains a record of all action taken on every case to come before it from inception to conclusion.

The clerk also assigned the case to Judge Fairness, since his name appeared on the first assignment card in the torts file. A block of these cards for each category of cases had been prepared in advance by the Clerk of Courts. The cards were numbered consecutively, and each bore the name of a judge. The order in which the judges' names appeared was a well-guarded secret, in keeping with the objective of random assignment of judges to cases. In following this assignment procedure, the Clerk of Courts was complying with the District Court's local procedure. Assignment of a case to a judge to follow from the very beginning to its final conclusion is known as the individual calendar system. This contrasts with the master calendar system where different aspects of the same case—motions, pretrial conferences, and the trial itself—are handled by the judge assigned to that specific function. This means that several judges may handle portions of one legal action. More efficient disposition of the court's business is claimed by proponents of each system.

One copy of the complaint was retained by the clerk to be placed in a file that would be opened for the Mary Worker case. That file would contain all the important documents related to the case and would be kept in the office of the Clerk of Courts, the court officer responsible for the record-keeping function. The case number and judge's name were stamped on the file jacket, and notice of the assignment was sent to Judge Fairness.

The clerk also issued a summons. Henry delivered it together with the second copy of the complaint to the United States marshal for service on Zagger Supply, the defendant. That summons has been reproduced in Form 6-2.

Service of Process

The marshal, a federal officer whose duties are similar to those of a sheriff and who executes process for the federal courts, found Will Very at the convention.

"Mr. Will Very, president of Zagger Supply, Inc.?" he asked.

"Yes," was the reply. As the marshal handed him the complaint and summons, Will Very added, "What's this?"

"A summons issued by the United States District Court for the Great State District together with a complaint filed in that court in a law suit

FORM 6-2. Summons.

UNITED STATES DISTRICT COURT
FOR THE DISTRICT OF GREAT STATE
Civil Action, File No. <u>XX-123</u>

Mary Worker,
    Administratrix of the
    ESTATE OF JOHN Q.
    WORKER, deceased,
        Plaintiff
	:
	 :
	 :
	 :
	 :
	 :	

v.	:	SUMMONS

Zagger Supply, Inc.,
    a corporation,
        Defendant
	:
	 :
	 :	

To the above named Defendant:

You are hereby summoned and required to serve upon <u>Henry Law</u>, plaintiff's attorney, whose address is <u>789 Main Street, Big City, Great State,</u> an answer to the complaint which is herewith served upon you, within <u>20</u> days after service of this summons upon you, exclusive of the day of service. If you fail to do so, judgment by default will be taken against you for the relief demanded in the complaint.

SEAL OF THE COURT

<u>*Clark Clark*</u>
Clerk of Court

Dated: <u>November 21, 19XX</u>

Note: This summons is issued pursuant to Rule 4 of the Federal Rules of Civil Procedure.

instituted there against Zagger Supply, Inc. (Showing Identification). As a United States marshal, I am serving you with these papers."

"All right," was Will Very's only reply at that moment.

Service completed, the marshal filled out a "return" form, indicating that he had made service. He returned the form to the Clerk of Courts office where it was placed in the file for the case. Note in Figure 6-1 the activity generated by the complaint prepared by Henry.

Defendant's Reaction

Will Very's immediate reaction was to call W. E. Just and turn the entire matter over to him, repeating his earlier directive to "fight it."

W. E. read through the complaint Will Very forwarded to him. He then asked for the file of information regarding the zagger in the John Q. Worker incident that his paralegal assistant had compiled. A paralegal assistant is a lawyer's aide, much as a nurse is to a medical doctor. The paralegal, although not a lawyer nor a member of the bar, requires special

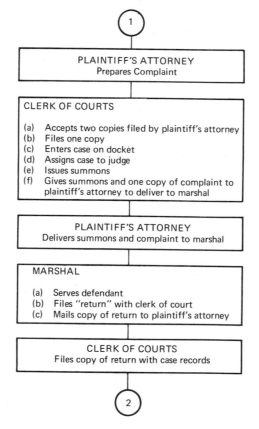

FIGURE 6-1. Processing of the Complaint.

training in legal matters and works directly with, but under the guidance and direction of, the attorney.

In that file was the factual information Attorney Just started to gather at the time he was asked to respond to Henry Law's letter requesting settlement: data regarding the order and sale of the special zaggers to The Firm, Inc., the testing done at Zagger Supply prior to shipment of the order, findings by Acme Labs relative to the zagger fragments, statements of cypres engineers that shattering could result from improper mounting or momentary lapse of care, and Charles Sell's report of the accident investigation he conducted.

Third-Party Defendant

W. E. Just also engaged in researching the law, in the course of which he examined Great State law regarding employer liability in cases of industrial death. He found that there were specific statutory provisions which precluded any employer liability to third parties. He could not,

TABLE 6-2. Attorney Just's list of possible responses to plaintiff's complaint.

Possible Action	Effect of Action
Do Nothing.	Failure to respond will result in judgment (the official decision of a court) against Zagger Supply by default. It indicates the defendant does not wish to contest. The effect is similar to an admission that the allegations made by the plaintiff in the complaint are true. The court will award the relief sought by the plaintiff in the complaint.
File written motions with the court prior to filing an answer:	Motions will precipitate a pretrial hearing before a judge who will determine whether to grant them after hearing arguments from both sides.
Motion requesting court to dismiss the action.	Motion will be granted and action will be dismissed if court finds there is lack of jurisdiction over subject matter, lack of jurisdiction over the defendant, improper venue, insufficiency of process, insufficiency of service of process, failure to state a claim upon which relief can be granted, failure to join an indispensable party.
Motion requesting court to order amendment of complaint.	If the motion is for a more definite statement and is granted, the court will order the plaintiff to amend the complaint to provide information sufficient to enable the defendant to respond.
Motion to strike.	If the motion is to strike and is granted, the court will order that scandalous, impertinent material be striken from the complaint.
File an answer to the complaint in accordance with time requirements in the summons.	This will move the action closer to trial, although there still exists the possibility of disposition by pretrial motions. The answer may admit, deny, or assert defenses to allegations in the complaint, indicate lack of knowledge sufficient to form a belief as to the truth of the allegations, or enter a counterclaim against the plaintiff.

therefore, even consider bringing in The Firm, Inc., as a third-party defendant in the case.

Had W. E. been able to do that, Zagger Supply, in addition to being the defendant in the case, would also have been a third-party plaintiff. As such, it would have asserted against The Firm a claim for damages arising out of the accident. This would mean that should the jury find that Mary Worker and her family were entitled to recover damages, the possibility existed that The Firm would have to pay some or all of the award. This would have involved questions of whether the two firms were joint tortfeasors (a tortfeasor being one who commits a tort); of whether there should be contribution (a pro-rata distribution of the loss among tortfeasors) or indemnification (repayment by the primary tortfeasor to the secondary tortfeasor for the entire loss). The procedure for bringing in a third-party defendant is for the defendant, as third-party plaintiff, to have a summons and third-party complaint served on the third-party defendant.

Attorney Just's Decision

Unable to proceed in this fashion, Attorney Just made a list of the alternative courses of action open to him. That list appears in Table 6-2. W. E. really had little choice except to file an answer to the complaint. Failure to respond would be in direct contradiction to Will Very's order to "fight it," and he lacked the necessary grounds on which to base any of the listed motions.

Answer

W. E. therefore proceeded with preparation of the answer. In that answer he would respond to each allegation in the complaint, the possible responses, and their effect being as follows:

1. Admit the allegations in the complaint. Admitted allegations would be considered as proved, and there would be no need to take them up at trial.
2. Deny the allegations in the complaint. This would create "issues" for trial; i.e., matters to be proved at trial.
3. Indicate the defendant presently lacked sufficient information to form a belief as to the truth of the allegations in the complaint. The effect would be the same as that of a denial.
4. Assert affirmative defenses. If these defenses were proved at trial, judgment could be for the defendant even if the plaintiff proved all of his allegations.
5. Assert the plaintiff failed to state a claim for which relief can be granted. If the court agrees with this assertion that there is no basis

for any legal action, judgment will be for the defendant. This is similar to a "demurrer" used in some state courts.

After noting those allegations in the complaint to be admitted, those to be denied, and those for which he lacked sufficient information, W. E. was pleased that he could assert an affirmative defense.

Affirmative Defense

The Great State Supreme Court in prior defective product cases had stated that "voluntarily and unreasonably proceeding to encounter a known danger, commonly known as assumption of the risk, is a defense as it is in other cases of strict liability." W. E. believed he had sufficient facts to be able to establish this defense. He would cite John Q.'s long experience as a cypres operator which should have made him aware of the hazards involved in working with zaggers. Furthermore, Charles Sell's report of the accident investigation contained pictures taken at the scene. These showed that the guard on John Q.'s machine had not been in its proper position. W. E. knew his case would be much stronger if he could go forward with positive assertions for the defense rather than just make denials of the allegations in the complaint.

He also anticipated he would have a strong argument that the plaintiff lacked proof of proximate cause. If so, the plaintiff would be unable to prove a prima facie case. Therefore, W. E. would assert in his answer that the plaintiff failed to state a claim upon which relief can be granted.

Preparation and Filing of Documents

Having completed the foregoing thought process, W. E. Just prepared two documents. The first was a form stating that he was entering his appearance as legal counsel for the defendant. This served as notification of his association with the case. Since he was a member of the Great State bar, he did not have to secure a local associate counsel as required in the case of out-of-state lawyers. He served one copy on Henry Law by mail and he filed the second with the Clerk of Courts.

Next he prepared the answer. The completed document appears in Form 6-3.

In accordance with the Federal Rules, Attorney Just served one copy of the answer on Henry Law by mail and filed the second copy with the Clerk of Courts. This copy was added to the file of the Mary Worker case.

Henry Law read through the answer when it arrived. He found nothing there that he had not anticipated.

Except in cases in which the court orders a reply to an answer or there is a counterclaim or cross-claim, the complaint and answer constitute the pleadings. That was true in this case. Amendments to the pleadings are permitted. However, at this time neither of the parties in the case had cause to consider amendments.

FORM 6-3. Answer.

DISTRICT COURT OF THE UNITED STATES
FOR THE DISTRICT OF GREAT STATE

MARY WORKER,   :
 Administratrix of the :
 ESTATE OF JOHN Q. :
 WORKER, deceased, :
    Plaintiff   :
          :
    v.   :   Civil Action
          :   No. XX-123
ZAGGER SUPPLY, INC., :
 a corporation,   :
    Defendant :
          :

ANSWER

Defendant, a corporation, by its attorneys files the following answer to the plaintiff's complaint:

FIRST DEFENSE

1. Defendant admits the averments in paragraphs 1 and 2 of plaintiff's complaints.
2. Defendant is presently without sufficient information to form a belief as to the truth of the averments in paragraphs 3, 4, 5, and 6 of plaintiff's complaint.
3. Defendant denies the averments in paragraphs 7, 8, and 9 of plaintiff's complaint.
4. In response to averments in paragraph 10 of plaintiff's complaint, defendant incorporates herein and re-iterates paragraphs 1 through 3 of this answer.
5. Defendant denies the averments in paragraph 11 of plaintiff's complaint.

SECOND DEFENSE

6. Plaintiff's complaint fails to state a cause of action upon which recovery can be had by the plaintiff and against the defendant.

THIRD DEFENSE

7. If John Q. Worker's death was caused by defendant's acts as alleged in plaintiff's complaint, John Q. Worker voluntarily assumed the risk.

—————————————————————
Attorney for the Defendant

Zagger Building
That City, Nearby State

CERTIFICATE OF SERVICE

The undersigned hereby certifies that service of the foregoing Defendant's Answer to Plaintiff's Complaint was made on counsel for the plaintiff, Henry Law, 789 Main Street, Big City, Great State, by registered mail return receipt requested.

—————————————————————
W. E. Just

December 3, 19XX

Judgment on the Pleadings

Another possible step at this stage of the proceedings would be for either of the parties to make a motion for a judgment on the pleadings. This can be done when the pleadings show that both parties agree as to the facts in the matter and the only questions remaining are questions of law. A judge can then make a determination and render a judgment without trial. The reason for this is that, as Henry Law had explained to Mary Worker, questions of law are for the judge while the jury is the trier of fact. A judgment on the pleadings, therefore, will not be granted in cases in which there are genuine issues as to material facts. If the matter in the pleadings is supplemented by other matters, such as information in an affidavit, the motion is treated as one for summary judgment.

However, both parties in this case realized there were definite issues of fact involved. One look at the answer reveals many denials, so that the factual issues are apparent from the face of the document. Therefore, each of the parties now began to concentrate on the next stage in the legal process, discovery. The decisions involved from receipt of complaint to this point have been flow charted in Figures 6-2 and 6-3.

Historical Perspective

As Henry Law reflected on the present status of the case, he considered the changes that had occurred over the years in the pleading

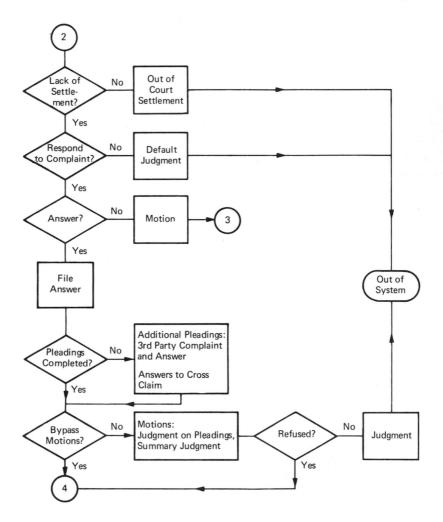

FIGURE 6-2. W. E. Just's Decision to File an Answer.

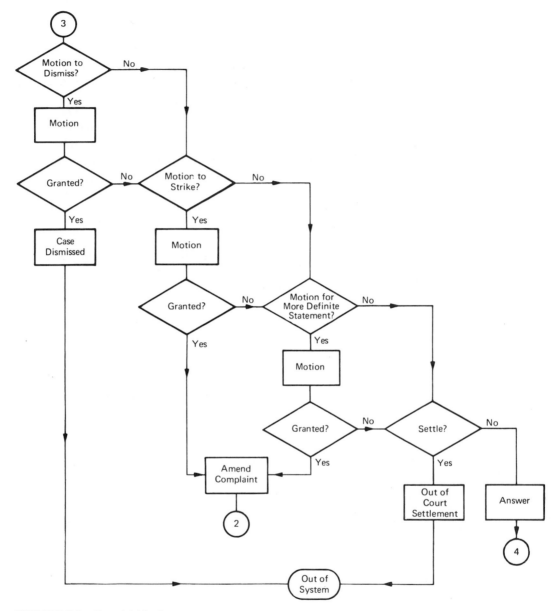

FIGURE 6-3. Pretrial Motions in Response to Complaint.

process and in its objectives. He recalled a conversation he had with his secretary, Albert, at the time the complaint for the Mary Worker case was being prepared. With the rough draft in hand prior to typing, Albert had come into his office to ask if Henry did not wish the complaint to state the action was being brought in trespass.

"No," was the response, "notice pleading is sufficient in the federal courts as contrasted with the common law pleading we do in the Great State courts." It was apparent at once that Albert had not understood this reply. Since Albert was also a law student, Henry asked if he would not like to take five minutes for a short discussion of the different kinds of pleadings.

"I believe it will be easier to understand if I can show you how the pleadings evolved historically," Henry began. "As you know, the heritage of the American legal system is the old English common law as distinguished from the civil or code system which exists in most western European nations. The common law emerged following the Norman Conquest during a feudal period when large landholders presided as lords over their manors, and the king reigned supreme over all. The allegiance owed by the lords to the king created a unified organization with central control in the monarch. Many believe that without this social structure an unwritten law based on precedent created by decisions in ad hoc disputes could not have developed."

"Another example of how law and the social order are intertwined?," Albert asked.

"Yes, and the court system and legal procedures that emerged very clearly reflect this. For instance, each lord dispensed justice and presided over the court of his manor. The king, however, was acknowledged as the source of all justice. Disputes between lords or appeals from the decisions of the lords on extraordinary matters were referred to him. As the volume of work increased, he delegated more and more to his subordinates. There eventually emerged a king's court presided over by appointed officials. However, access to that court was only by writ, a written order granting one the privilege of having the court hear his case. Each different type of law suit had its own specific writ. Thus, there evolved a classification system for legal actions. From that emerged the requirement that pleadings had to be prepared according to the form of action or the pigeon hole into which the case was classified. There were a great many of these, some of which are still retained today in states that follow the common law system of pleading. For instance, in Great State we still use:

1. Assumpsit—the form of action for breach of contract
2. Replevin—the form of action to recover personal property wrongfully taken
3. Case—the form of action to recover damages for an indirect injury to property
4. Trespass—the form of action to recover damages caused by injury to the plaintiff. This was originally known as trespass *vi et armis* to distinguish it from other actions of trespass. Many laymen recognize the word only in connection with the tort of trespass."

"You mean, when people talk about trespassing on their neighbor's property—?"

"Yes, there's both a tort of trespass and a common law form of action known as trespass. As I was saying the early common law had categories of trespass. As you can see, it was a very elaborate classification system. However, that system not only resulted in making pleading a very technical exercise. It was deficient in that it did not provide a classification for every possible matter for which the citizenry looked to the courts for resolution. For instance, if a person wished a court to order another person to refrain from engaging in certain activity—to secure an injunction—there was no writ for this. Therefore, one had no way of availing himself of the court's help in that situation. In other words, there was no remedy at law.

"The only recourse in that case would be to appeal directly to the king for justice or equity. In the course of time, the king delegated this function to his Chancellor. As the number of such appeals increased, there developed a Court of Chancery. Resort to it was possible only when there was no remedy in a court of law or when the remedy at law was inadequate. In the case of a breach of contract, for instance, the injured party could recover money damages in a court of law but only in a court of chancery could he secure an order for specific performance, that is, to secure performance according to the contract terms."

"That sounds very much like the actions in equity we have today," said Albert. "Equitable remedies, such as the injunction and specific performance, aren't granted if there's a remedy at law which is adequate to meet the situation. And I've read some decisions in equity where the judge is referred to as the chancellor."

"That's right," Henry replied. "The courts of chancery eventually became known as courts of equity. There are other practices we still retain in equity. For instance, the Court of Chancery operated much more informally then did a court of law. Writs were not required, and there was no jury. Concern was with 'what ought to be done in order to render justice'."

"All of which is still true."

"Yes, and there also evolved a number of rules, known as equitable maxims. They are still used today as the basis for decisions rendered in actions in equity."

"Some of them come to mind immediately:

He who comes into equity must do so with clean hands.
He who seeks equity must do equity.
Equity will not suffer a right to exist without a remedy.
Equity aids the vigilant.
Equity regards as done that which ought to be done."

"Right," was Henry's response.   "The outgrowth of this was the development, side by side, of two court systems: courts of law and courts of chancery.   Both the common law system of pleading forms of action as well as the system of separate courts for law and equity were brought to this country by the early English settlers. The one exception occurred in Louisiana, where the French influence resulted in a system of law based upon the civil or code system.

"One of the steps toward change to what we have today occurred around 1848 when code pleading was introduced in New York state. The many different common law forms of action were eliminated and replaced by just one form of civil action at law. This makes it possible for the plaintiff to recover on any legal theory applicable to the facts pleaded and proved. In addition, law and equity were merged so that the same court can hear a case whether it is brought at law or equity."

"In other words, the legal process was simplified by combining the actions at law and then by bringing law and equity together in one court."

"Yes. Additional simplification followed. An important development occurred in 1938 when the Federal Rules were adopted. They streamlined the pleading process by providing for notice pleading. That means it is necessary to plead only those circumstances or events necessary to inform the other party of the incident for which he is being sued. The gathering of detailed facts is left for other pretrial activity. The object of pleading is simply to put the other party on notice. In this it differs from both common law and code pleading, where the goal is to formulate the legal issues in the pleadings. As a result, those systems of pleading require that facts be pleaded in support of each of the elements constituting the cause of action.

"Today many of the states have revised their rules of procedure to conform with the federal rules. A few, such as Great State, still follow a revised form of common law pleading. Others, such as Nearby State, use code or fact pleading."

"Hasn't anyone proposed a uniform system? It seems to me that would make things a lot easier," was Albert's response.

"I agree," said Henry. "We have made progress with other uniform laws, the most notable success being the Uniform Commercial Code. That has been adopted by the legislatures of all the states (partly in Louisiana). Many believe this result was achieved since the UCC is concerned with sales, secured transactions, commercial paper, investment securities, and other business matters.   Businessmen, concerned about the effect of differences in state laws on interstate commercial transactions, were convinced that uniformity was a necessity. Of course, we also have other uniform laws, such as the Uniform Partnership Act, which the majority of the states have adopted. There is also some uniformity which is an indirect result of the 'model acts,' which have been developed by the American

Law Institute as guides or patterns which the various state legislatures can follow in enacting legislation. Some similarity is assured when a number of states use the Model Penal Act or the Model Business Corporation Act, for instance, in writing legislation. Additional uniform state laws would truly be a boon and reduce problems arising because of conflict of laws."

"The mention of all those acts makes me realize that we have a great deal of statutory law in our common law system."

"Yes," replied Henry, "but the general policy is still that 'statutes in derogation of the common law' are to be strictly construed. Therefore, while the provisions of a statute may supersede conflicting provisions found in the common law, the latter still prevails when the written law's provisions are not specific."

"So that the common law really fills in any gaps in the statutory law."

At this point their conversation about the historical development of pleadings, common law, equity, and uniform written laws came to an end. Albert commented that the historical perspective increased one's understanding of why certain procedures, such as discovery, are presently in effect.

DISCOVERY

Both Henry Law and W. E. Just now began preparation for the next stage in the Mary Worker case. The pleadings had identified the fact that a controversy between the parties existed regarding strict liability in tort for death allegedly caused by a defective product. The specific matters in controversy were those that had been alleged by the plaintiff in the complaint and denied by the defendant in the answer. In addition, there were the affirmative defenses asserted by the defendant. These were the points "at issue"—each side contending the truth of his position with regard to these items. Since the parties could not agree, each would have to set about proving his case. Each would have to seek out facts that would support his contentions. Fact finding thus became a necessary next step. It is also the objective of the next stage in the civil process, which is known as *discovery*.

Discovery refers to the process of securing relevant information regarding an impending suit, a process engaged in after completion of the pleadings and prior to trial. Each party to an action may use the mechanisms of discovery to secure all the relevant information possessed by any persons, including the opposing party. Failure to provide requested information can lead to being held in contempt of court. Some matter remains privileged, however, and a protective order may be secured from the court limiting or barring discovery of such material. Examples include matter coming within the attorney-client privilege, the work product of the attorney, and that which would be self-incriminatory in a criminal matter. Protection from discovery of unrelated matter or for harassment purposes is also available.

The concept of discovery represents a distinct departure from the old common law and from the impression sometimes created by television courtroom drama, which features the last-minute surprise witness who saves the hero or heroine from certain defeat. It is the purpose of discovery to avoid surprise at trial and to give each party an opportunity to evaluate both his own and the other side's case prior to trial. This enables each to be better prepared and results in improving the quality of the trial process itself. It makes possible collection of information by less formal, less expensive, and less time-consuming methods than characterize the securing of information at the trial itself. Possession of more and better information prior to trial also enables the parties to refine the issues at that point in time. It often leads to pretrial settlement because the parties are each aware of the other's case. Information obtained through discovery may be used at trial in accordance with the provisions of the rules of procedure and the rules of evidence.

Rules 26 through 37 of the Federal Rules of Civil Procedure deal with discovery. Similar rules have been adopted by almost all the states. It was the Federal Rules that both W. E. Just and Henry Law consulted. They also checked the *local rules* of the Great State District Court. Local rules are those prepared by and for use at a particular court. They supplement applicable federal or state rules.

Each attorney now sought information about witnesses, records, or reports that would provide data related to the law suit and that would help him meet his burden of proof. As the plaintiff's advocate, Henry Law was concerned with being able to establish a prima facie case and with being able to rebut any defenses raised by his opponent. W. E. Just, representing the defendant, contemplated how he could not only refute the plaintiff's case but also prove affirmative defenses. Hence each attorney was concerned not just with presentation of his own case but also with being prepared for what his adversary would do.

The two attorneys mentally asked themselves the same questions;

What information do I need?
Who has it?
Where can it be found?
How can I get it?

A large data collection process seemed imminent. Where and how would each attorney begin?

Each had his own list of desiderata, one which would be reviewed and revised as he learned more about what information was available and what his opponent knew. Each prepared his list with the realization he must acquire factual information sufficient to meet his burden of proof. Therefore, it was no haphazard compilation that took place, but rather one accompanied by careful consideration of the pleadings, jurisdictional requirements, the elements of an action brought under §402A as well as a wrongful death and survival action.

Each attorney planned to secure the information he needed by making use of the same means of discovery: interrogatories, depositions, and production of documents. Each also chose to begin his discovery with interrogatories.

Interrogatories

The Federal Rules provide that one party may serve upon any other party written questions (interrogatories) to be answered under oath by the party served. It is an inexpensive method of eliciting information from one's opponent. Interrogatories are often used, as was true in the Mary Worker case, as the initial means of discovery for learning names of witnesses and experts, the existence of records and reports, as well as additional sources of information which the other party has. It is then possible to follow up the answers with either additional interrogatories or with other means of discovery.

One advantage of the interrogatory to the person answering is that he has time to reflect upon his answers. Help in framing those answers is not precluded. An obvious disadvantage to the questioning party is the inability to follow up an incomplete or evasive answer with another question, as is possible when interrogation is oral. Another limitation is that it is not available for use with witnesses who are not parties to the action.

Interrogatories are prepared by the attorney and are served either by mailing or delivering them to the attorney for the other party. (Should there be more than two parties to an action, all other parties must receive a copy not only of the questions when submitted but also of the answers.) The Great State District local rules provided that the Clerk of Courts receive written notification when and upon whom interrogatories are served, that interrogatories be prepared with space for answers to be inserted following each question, that at least three copies be served upon the answering party. They further required that when answers have been inserted, one copy of the completed document must be filed with the Clerk of Courts, one copy returned to the discovering party (and to any other parties), and the final copy retained by the party providing the answers. In this way, every party to the action, as well as the court, is aware at all times of the status of the action being taken.

When interrogatories are received by an attorney, the party involved is informed and generally receives assistance from his attorney in preparation of the answers. Both the signature and affidavit of the party to whom the interrogatories have been directed are required on the answers. Objections to questions may be made by the attorney of the party being questioned. In that case, reasons for the objection are stated in lieu of an answer to the question and the attorney's signature to the objections is required.

Both W. E. Just and Henry Law prepared interrogatories. Because each party's interrogatories were rather extensive, only portions of the one prepared by W. E. Just have been reproduced in Form 6-4 as an illustration.

It was from the answers to interrogatories that W. E. Just learned about plaintiff's witnesses, Leader and O'Goode, and of the testing done by Professor Learned. Thus, the use of the interrogatories had been very worthwhile for him.   He had no idea of what Leader, O'Goode, or

---

FORM 6-4. Interrogatory.

DISTRICT COURT OF THE UNITED STATES
FOR THE DISTRICT OF GREAT STATE

MARY WORKER,   :
   Administratrix of the   :
   ESTATE OF JOHN Q.   :
   WORKER, deceased,   :
      Plaintiff   :
                 :
       v.   :   Civil Action
                 :   No. XX-123
ZAGGER SUPPLY, INC.,   :
   a corporation,   :
      Defendant   :

INTERROGATORY TO PLAINTIFF

Defendant above named pursuant to Rule 33 of the Federal Rules of Civil Procedure demands that the plaintiff, Mary Worker, Administratrix of the Estate of John Q. Worker, deceased, make full and complete answers under oath to the following interrogatories within the time required by the Rules.

1. State names and present addresses of all witnesses to the events immediately preceding alleged accident which are known to plaintiff, plaintiff's attorneys, agents, investigators, or other representatives.

2.   State names and present addresses of all witnesses to the alleged accident which are known to plaintiff, plaintiff's attorneys, agents, investigators, or other representatives.

3.   State names and present addresses of all witnesses to the events immediately subsequent to the alleged accident which are known to plaintiff, plaintiff's attorneys, agents, investigators, or other representatives.

. . . .

7.   Was plaintiff's decedent employed at the time of the alleged accident? If so, state the name and present address of said employer, nature of duties performed for said employer, length of such employment, and amount of hourly, daily, weekly, or monthly wages or salary received from said employer.

8.   State the total amount of income earned by plaintiff's decedent for each of the four calendar years immediately preceding the alleged accident and the year of said accident.

. . . .

12.   State specifically each and every manufacturing defect referred to in Paragraphs seven and eight of plaintiff's complaint.

13.   State the name and address of each and every expert whom you have had examine fragments of the zagger in question and/or similar zaggers and/or who may have given you an opinion without an examination of the zagger, setting forth the area of expertise of said expert.

. . . .

Learned knew or would testify to at the trial. Their testimony might aid his case. On the other hand, it might be devastatingly damaging. Therefore, he realized he could not afford to take the chances attendant with not knowing and decided to take the depositions of all three.

While he made preparations to do this, Henry Law was completing the questions for the interrogatories to be directed to Zagger Supply. In the case of corporations (or other forms of organization), interrogatories may be served upon any officer or agent. The firm must then designate an officer or agent to answer for it. There is a duty to provide all information known to corporate personnel or determinable without undue burden. Henry Law prepared questions concerned with:

1. Manufacture by the defendant of the zagger involved in the lawsuit—when, for whom, existence of production records, persons having possession of such records, persons involved in the manufacturing process.

2. Sale of the zagger—date and place, terms, specific agreements as to design and engineering, persons in charge of design and engineering, existence of blueprints or drawings of the zagger, persons having possession of such representations, shipping terms and arrangements, records regarding such and persons having possession of these, instructions furnished purchaser regarding use of zagger, copies available and persons having possession of such.

3. Testing of zaggers—usual tests made in manufacture of zaggers and descriptions of such, standards to be met, industry standards and persons having copies of such, tests made in connection with this zagger, description of such, persons conducting such tests, existence of test reports and persons having possession of such, any testing of fragments of the shattered zagger, persons conducting such tests, existence of test reports and persons having possession of such.

4. Expert witnesses expected to be called at trial—identity, substance of facts and opinions to which they are expected to testify, summary of grounds for each opinion.

5. Defendant's awareness of defect in the zagger, when and by whom defendant was made aware, description of defect, statement of facts concerning accident of which defendant is aware.

6. In connection with assumption of the risk as a defense—statement of manner in which plaintiff assumed the risk and identity of witnesses to be called to prove this; in connection with defense of failure to state a claim for which relief can be granted—statement of basis for this and identity of witnesses.

7. Persons answering interrogatories for the corporation and their capacity with the firm, persons whose help was secured in answering and their capacity.

Depositions

As might be expected, consultation in connection with answering this set of interrogatories required a great deal of W. E. Just's time. He was happy he had planned for the first taking of depositions to occur several

---

FORM 6-5. Notice of Deposition.

DISTRICT COURT OF THE UNITED STATES
FOR THE DISTRICT OF GREAT STATE

MARY WORKER,   :
   Administratrix of the   :
   ESTATE OF JOHN Q.   :
   WORKER, deceased,   :
          Plaintiff   :
                     :
         v.   :   Civil Action
                     :   No. XX-123
ZAGGER SUPPLY, INC.,   :
   a corporation,   :
          Defendant :

NOTICE OF DEPOSITION

To: Henry Law, Attorney for the Plaintiff

Take notice that the deposition of Robert Leader will be taken for the purpose of discovery and for use at trial pursuant to Rule 26 of the Federal Rules of Civil Procedure, as amended, before a notary public duly authorized by law to administer oaths, on Thursday, the 29th day of December, 19XX at 4:00 PM at the offices of Clyde Partner, Attorney at Law, Lawyers Building, Big City, Great State, at which time and place you are invited to appear and take such part as shall be fitting and proper.

The scope and purpose of this deposition is to inquire into the facts and circumstances surrounding the accident in suit, including the identity and whereabouts of other witnesses.

By   *W.E. Just*
          Attorney for the Defendant

weeks in the future, since his notices of intent to depose had crossed Henry Law's interrogatories in the mail. A copy of the notice regarding the Robert Leader deposition appears in Form 6-5. Notice to all parties is required prior to deposition taking and is served upon the party's attorney.

Had Robert Leader been a party to the action, the notice would have been sufficient to require his attendance. Since he was not, W. E. Just requested that a subpoena be served upon Leader. He did this at the time he filed a copy of the notice with the Clerk of Courts. Similar procedure was followed with both O'Goode and Learned, except that a *subpoena duces tecum* was served on the professor. While a subpoena commands the person to whom it is directed to attend and give testimony at the time and place specified, a *subpoena duces tecum* commands that, in addition, the person bring with him documents or materials in his possession. It was the test report prepared by Professor Learned that W. E. Just wished to obtain.

The depositions were scheduled to be held in the Big City law offices of Clyde Partner, who often did legal work for Zagger Supply. Everyone involved except W. E. Just was located in Big City. In addition to convenience, the location enabled compliance with the Federal Rules that require that depositions be taken either in the county in which the deponent can be served (or within 40 miles of the place of service). Local County was where all three deponents lived and worked.

When Timothy O'Goode asked Robert Leader about the subpoena and the deposition, the men discovered their depositions were scheduled two days apart. Both decided they should consult Henry Law. He explained that deposition taking meant they would be questioned by the defendant's attorney after an oath had been administered to them. Henry Law would be present. He would not only have the right to cross-examine but also to raise objections to improper questions. The entire session would be recorded by a court reporter, who would probably also administer the oath. A transcript would be prepared later. Both deponents would be given the opportunity to read it through before signing. The answers given would be important. They could be introduced at the trial itself and used for such purposes as contradicting testimony the men gave at trial. On the other hand, if they could not be present at the trial because of death or serious illness, the deposition—or parts of it—could be read into the trial record.

Timothy asked if Henry Law knew what questions would be asked. Henry's reply was that he did not know the specific questions. His best estimate was that each man could expect to be asked about the following:

1. Details of the accident—including what occurred just before and after.

2. Explanation of the operation of the cypres machine and especially the use of zaggers on the machine.

3. Safety precautions necessary with use of zaggers.
4. Any prior or subsequent shattering experience with zaggers.
5. John Q.'s reputation as a cypres operator.
6. Experience in the use of the new zaggers.

"In general," he said, "I would say that you can expect questions very similar to the ones I have been asking you in our conversations."

"It sounds just like being on the witness stand," was Robert's comment.

"Yes," Henry agreed. "that's why the oral deposition is so popular as a discovery mechanism. An attorney can learn a lot more through it than he can by using written depositions."

"I thought the written ones are called interrogatories," Robert commented.

"There are differences," was the reply. Henry Law went on to explain that depositions are not restricted to parties but may be taken of any person. In the case of written depositions, the questions are answered before an examining officer who also administers the oath. Cross, redirect, and recross questions may be served later, thus providing some resemblance to the examination possible at the oral deposition taking.

The taking of the depositions of Timothy O'Goode and Robert Leader went very much as Henry Law had predicted. Each lasted approximately an hour. Both men were questioned in detail concerning their recollection of John Q.'s actions: what he did with the zagger, the manner in which he placed it on the machine, how he had checked his machine prior to starting it up, whether the guard was in place, etc. Neither could state definitely that he positively remembered seeing John Q. go through each of the motions involved. However, each said he was confident that John Q., known as a skilled worker who had never had a prior accident, had followed his usual careful pattern of operation. W. E. Just did elicit the fact that there was more than the usual amount of conversation and some air of excitement because of the start of production of the new chattel.

Asked about the new zaggers he had used, Timothy O'Goode testified that he was extremely careful with them. None that he had used had shattered; however, several other cypres operators assigned to production of the new chattel had experienced shattering. The shatterings were not of the violent, explosive type, and no one had been seriously injured. Timothy also stated the new zaggers were not tight fitting and that "you have to be careful to get it on the machine right or the zagger will wobble once you start up the machine."

"And what happens if the zagger wobbles?" W. E. Just wanted to know.

"At high-speed operations, the zaggers shatter," Timothy responded.

Robert testified that he had never been assigned to work on the new chattels.

Following the two depositions, the attorneys began to see their arguments emerging more clearly. Henry Law knew he would have to concentrate on failure of the zagger to meet OSHA standards as proof of a dangerously defective product. W. E. Just was interested in the hubbub surrounding the start of production of the new chattel and John Q.'s knowing use of the zagger without the guard in place on his machine. Each attorney now waited to see what other discovery would reveal.

Just as the depositions of Mary Worker's witnesses proved helpful to W. E. Just, the interrogatories and depositions taken by Henry Law were rewarding to him. Answers to his interrogatories revealed the existence of a number of documents which he believed he should have, such as the report of the testing done at Zagger Supply prior to shipment of the special purpose zaggers, the purchase order and accompanying correspondence for special purpose zaggers for The Firm. Henry also wished to have Professor Learned analyze the fragments in Zagger Supply's possession, and test other zaggers manufactured for The Firm under the special order.

Production of Documents

Consequently, Henry decided to make use of still another form of discovery: request to another party for production of documents and other items in his possession and control. It can also be used to request entry upon the premises of the other party for the purpose of inspection, photographing, sampling, copying, and the like. This mechanism is available only when the item is in the possession of a person who is a party to the action.

A request to the other party is all that is necessary. Therefore, Henry Law prepared the request to produce, portions of which appear in Form 6-6. One copy he mailed to Zagger Supply, the second he filed with the Clerk of Courts.

The Zagger Supply response was prompt and provided Henry with the requested material. Armed with the knowledge acquired in this way, Henry Law embarked upon his own deposition taking.

Additional Depositions

The deposing of Charles Sell revealed that he was thoroughly acquainted with The Firm's operations. He visited frequently with Sam Scott and Jim Boss since Zagger Supply was The Firm's major supplier of zaggers. He acknowledged the special order and admitted there had been dynamic testing of only half a dozen of the special purpose zaggers. This,

FORM 6-6. Request to Produce.

DISTRICT COURT OF THE UNITED STATES
FOR THE DISTRICT OF GREAT STATE

MARY WORKER,
   Administratrix of the
   ESTATE OF JOHN Q.
   WORKER, deceased,
      Plaintiff

         v.

ZAGGER SUPPLY, INC.
   a corporation,
      Defendant

Civil Action
No. XX-123

REQUEST TO PRODUCE

Plaintiff above named hereby requests pursuant to Rule 34 of the Federal Rules of Civil Procedure that defendant, Zagger Supply, Inc., a corporation,

(1) produce and permit plaintiff to inspect and to copy each of the following documents:

    a. reports of tests conducted by defendant on the special zaggers manufactured for The Firm, Inc., and shipped to them in August, 19XX under special order #98765;

    . . . .

(2) produce and permit plaintiff to inspect and to photograph each of the following objects:

    a. fragments of zagger #XXX secured from The Firm, Inc., the day following the accident in which John Q. Worker was killed;

    . . . .

It is requested that the aforesaid production be made on the day of December 15, 19XX, at two o'clock in the P.M. at the offices of Henry Law, Esq., 789 Main Street, Big City, Great State.

By   *Henry Law*
        Attorney for the Plaintiff

789 Main Street
Big City, Great State

he said, was unusual. It occurred because they were behind schedule and the static testing which had been done on all the special-purpose zaggers showed no abnormalities. Henry was interested in pursuing claims made by Zagger Supply in its sales literature regarding bonding defects. Charles Sell testified that Zagger Supply used a patented process in manufacturing zaggers, which resulted in fewer than the industry average number of bonding defects. Their experience record was for such a defect to show up approximately five times in every 10,000 zaggers. The industry statistics, he said, were five in every 1000.

He acknowledged that it would be most unusual for zagger users to test them after purchase. It was the custom in the industry and at The Firm to rely upon manufacturer testing. He also testified that Zagger Supply packed the special-purpose zaggers and delivered them to The Firm's supply department. His investigation following the accident revealed they had been stored under ideal conditions. He admitted to Henry Law that those in the supply department were in substantially the same condition as when shipped.

"Would the zagger John Q. used also have been in substantially the same condition as when shipped?" he was asked.

"Yes," he replied, "unless at the last minute John Q. did something unusual to it or with it."

"Did your investigation reveal any evidence of that?"

His answer was in the negative.

No separate instructions had been prepared regarding use of the special purpose zaggers, he said, since they would not have differed from those for other zaggers. In response to Henry Law's question, he indicated that Zagger Supply normally printed warnings and instructions on its zagger labels. It also cooperated with the Zagger Institute in producing a safety film regarding proper use of zaggers. A copy of the film had been furnished to The Firm and was used by their safety department. Charles said that on several occasions he had been the speaker at safety meetings for cypres operators at The Firm where the film had been shown.

Henry Law mentally debated whether to depose next the Zagger Supply cypres engineer or Sam Scott. It developed that Sam's time commitments resulted in his being scheduled first.

It was a revealing deposition, particularly with regard to the pictures taken after the accident. They showed that there was no guard on John Q.'s machine. Sam stated that guards are bolted to the framework of cypres machines so they cannot be removed easily. However, they must be taken off when a new zagger is installed. He stressed that company safety instructions were explicit in their directive to operators regarding replacement of the guard as soon as a zagger was installed. Asked if the guard could not have been removed after the accident, Sam indicated there had not been sufficient time for anyone to do so before the pictures were taken. He also stated it was his firm conviction that the guard would have been strong enough to stop the flying zagger fragments.

"Even in the case of a shattering of such tremendous force as has been described in this situation?" he was asked. His answer was "yes."

Henry Law asked if fragments could not have come out of the opening in the guard in front where the chattel came in contact with the zagger.

"No one can answer that for sure. It's a 45-degree opening—a small one—some fragments could come out, they'd have to be small."

"But, the more violent the shattering the greater the likelihood that some would come out?"

"Yes."

"And they would come out in the direction in which the machine operator was standing?"

"Yes, provided he was standing in the normal position—directly in front of the machine." In response to Henry's next question, Sam stated that no one had been able to determine just where John Q. had been standing at the time the accident occurred.

"No," Sam replied when asked if he knew of any reason why John Q. would have been in an other-than-normal position.

"And this opening in the guard—its distance from the floor—would you say it would be about waist high for a man of John Q.'s height?"

"Just about—yes."

He testified that the machine setting indicated John Q. had set the speed for that normally expected and anticipated for work on the new chattels.

With regard to the condition of the cypres machine, Sam replied that it had undergone a complete overhaul three days before the accident since it was to be used for the new chattels.

In chronological sequence, the deposition of Professor Learned was next. W. E. Just received no comfort from learning through interrogatories that Professor Learned was the plaintiff's expert and was expected to testify at trial. Professor Learned was recognized in the industry as the foremost zagger expert in the country, and W. E. Just would rather have had so formidable an authority in his corner than in his opponent's. He realized the vital importance of learning what the Professor knew about this situation by deposing him.

Professor Learned testified that he had examined the zagger fragments, was positively able to identify them as parts of the shattered zagger, had definite proof of defectiveness in the zagger bonding which was directly attributable to the manufacturing process. He further stated that the defect was latent but could and should have been discovered through required dynamic testing before the zaggers left the manufacturer, that the reason for the dynamic testing requirement was to prevent just such shattering as had occurred, that he was not only familiar with the standards of OSHA and the Zagger Institute but had been chairperson of the committee of experts who wrote them. W. E. Just asked Professor Learned about the possibility of shattering from improper placement of a zagger on the cypres machine. Professor Learned replied that a zagger not properly clamped on the machine would begin to wobble.

"And the effect of the wobbling?" W. E. began to ask.

"Sometimes—especially if the machine is just being started up and if it is being operated at a relatively low speed—the zagger will right itself, and—"

"Does wobbling ever lead to shattering?" W. E. wanted to know.

"Yes," said Professor Learned, "if the machine is being operated in excess of the maximum safe speeds for that particular zagger or if the zagger is not of the correct size and cannot be made to fit properly on the machine."

W. E. asked if the shattering of the zagger in this case could have been caused by wobbling. Professor Learned was emphatic in his reply:

"The shattering in this case was caused by a defective zagger."

"You are positive that the bonding defect was the one and only possible cause of the shattering?"

"It is the most probable cause. No one can say with absolute certainty that other defects were not present and did not also contribute to the accident. What one can say with certainty is that some combination of defects, which included the bonding, caused the shattering."

When queried about the guard, the professor's testimony was much more positive than that of Sam Scott. The former was of the opinion that there was no question but that the violence of the shattering had been such that fragments would have been propelled with great force through the guard opening, resulting in the fatal injury to John Q. At this point he became quite didactic and ignored Henry's earlier request that he not volunteer information.

"It is common knowledge in the industry," he said, "that machine operators are at times in a hurry or impatient or even careless. Sometimes they leave guards off their machines; sometimes they do not clamp their zaggers into position firmly. That is why the present zagger standards were put into effect as requirements. We have the technical ability today—through proper testing—to eliminate from use those zaggers that do not have the necessary qualities to withstand use without shattering under such adverse conditions. Testing will reveal defects—bonding, size, others—that lead to violent shattering. Zaggers that do not meet such standards are dangerous to human life. There is no need—no excuse—for a death such as the one in this case."

W. E. blanched, but quickly recovered. "Can you say positively, Professor, that a zagger that has been subjected to the required testing will never shatter?"

"Since the standards went into effect just about a year ago, there has not been a single shattering incident reported with zaggers that have been subjected to the required testing."

When the deposition taking was concluded, W. E. mentally noted that his prior assessment of this witness as formidable had indeed been correct.

Professor Learned's testimony was in part confirmed by the Zagger Supply cypres engineer and the Acme Lab zagger research engineer, whose depositions Henry Law took several weeks later. Differences did exist, however, with regard to their opinions as to the cause of the shattering. The cypres engineer testified that improper placement of the zagger on the machine and failure of the operator to concentrate completely on the job at hand were the most probable causes of the shattering. He also believed that serious injury could and would have been prevented had the guard been in position on John Q.'s machine. The Acme Lab test engineer did not believe that the bonding defect could have resulted in the violent shattering which had characterized this incident. He stated that improper clamping was one of the most common causes of the very explosive type of shattering.

Henry Law also deposed Peter Superior who seemed reluctant to discuss the accident. His major contribution was his testimony that there had been five additional shatterings involving the new zaggers in the department he had supervised. While none of these had been serious, the number was a distinct increase over a five-year record of only one or two shatterings a year with the regular zaggers. He also admitted to W. E. Just, on cross-examination, that there had been a general atmosphere of exhilaration in the department that day as John Q. started on the new chattels.

Both attorneys carefully studied transcripts of the depositions. A copy had been prepared for each of the parties and one had been filed with the Clerk of Courts.

Request for Admissions

Use of two other possible discovery mechanisms was ruled out by both attorneys. One of those methods is the written request for admission of any matters within the scope of discovery. It may be served by one party upon any other party. Answers are required. However, if the request relates to a matter that is a genuine issue for trial, the matter may either be denied or the reasons for not answering set forth. Both Henry Law and W. E. Just decided they would forego requests for admissions at this stage. Since this was not a law suit where the mental or physical condition of one of the parties was in controversy, the use of either a mental or physical examination as a discovery mechanism was not appropriate.

Narrowing Issues

Studying the information they now possessed, both attorneys gave thoughtful consideration to whether they had all the relevant and necessary facts. Checking their lists of information to be secured, they found that discovery had not only served its purpose of providing necessary information but also of narrowing the issues. Table 6-3 indicates the status of the major facts and questions following discovery. It is clear from the table that, at this point in time, many facts were no longer in dispute. These would be admitted (or stipulated) prior to trial. In fact, that would be one of the items on the agenda for the forthcoming pretrial conference. Use of discovery in the civil process has been flow charted in Figure 6-4.

Both attorneys looked carefully at those matters on which there still was no agreement. Would further discovery lead to information not yet available that would cause the two parties to agree on these items? A glance at the unresolved matters listed in Table 6-3 reveals that they are facts that had been examined and investigated, for which there was information available, but which could be construed as leading to several results. They represent differing conclusions about factual situations, the differences being of a kind at which reasonable persons could arrive. Given the same set of facts and reasonable disagreement concerning the conclusions that can be derived from them, it becomes evident the two parties now need an arbiter—a third party—to settle their differences. And that is precisely the role of the courts.

With both attorneys satisfied that additional fact finding would not yield results of much value, they were ready for the next stage in the civil process: the pretrial conference.

TABLE 6-3. Status of issues after discovery.

Matters Settled and Not at Issue	Matters Still at Issue
Questions of jurisdiction	Zagger was dangerously defective
Defendant engaged in business of selling zaggers	Zagger shattered because of defects
Defendant sold zagger involved in accident	Shattering was caused by John Q.'s lack of concentration
Zagger reached user substantially unchanged	Shattering was caused by improper placement on machine
Zagger had bonding defect	Use of a guard would have prevented the injury
Zagger was not subjected to dynamic testing	Dynamic testing would have prevented accident
John Q. was killed when struck by zagger fragments	
John Q. did not have guard in place on machine	
John Q. was a careful and experienced machine operator	
Cypres machine John Q. was using was functioning properly	

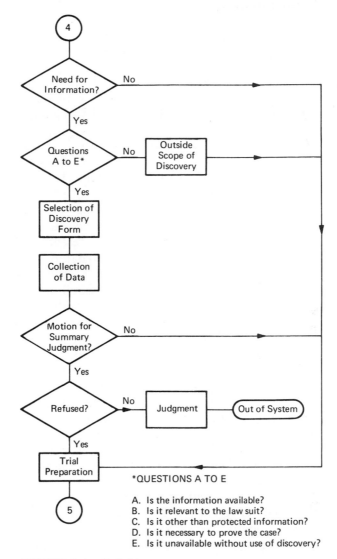

FIGURE 6-4. Civil Discovery.

*QUESTIONS A TO E

A. Is the information available?
B. Is it relevant to the law suit?
C. Is it other than protected information?
D. Is it necessary to prove the case?
E. Is it unavailable without use of discovery?

PRETRIAL CONFERENCE

Henry Law called W. E. Just to ask if he were ready for the pretrial conference. When Attorney Just said he was, the two agreed to meet in Henry's office. This was in keeping with the District Court's local rules which required not only that the two attorneys meet but also that each submit a pretrial memorandum to the court in preparation for a pretrial conference with the judge.

Meeting of Attorneys

As the agenda for their meeting, the attorneys followed the format for the pretrial memorandum in the local rules. Therefore, their discussion concerned the court's jurisdiction, contentions as to liability, discussion of damages, witnesses to be called by each side and identification of those who would serve as experts, review of the pleadings to determine if amendments were in order, matters to be stipulated, estimated length of trial.

They agreed to stipulate; i.e., admit the truth of those matters which are listed in Table 6-3 as no longer being in issue. Each man named the witnesses he expected to call at trial. Henry indicated that his would be Mary Worker, Robert Leader, Timothy O'Goode, Professor Learned, Peter Superior, and Sam Scott, although not necessarily in that order.

W. E. Just indicated that he would call as witnesses Charles Sell, the cypres engineers, and the zagger researcher at Acme Labs. The latter two and Professor Learned were designated as expert witnesses. W. E. Just said he would stipulate Professor Learned's knowledge of OSHA and Zagger Institute standards so that it would not be necessary for Henry Law to call other experts regarding those standards.

The attorneys next began to list their exhibits for trial. Henry's list included photographs at the accident scene, parts of the zagger, pictures of zagger fragments, the invoice for the sale of the special purpose zaggers, instructions for the use of zaggers, zagger labels, hospital record and bill, doctor bill, ambulance bill, death certificate, letters of administration, funeral home bill, bill for grave marker, and John Q.'s W2 forms for the past five years, among others. When the total amount of the bills was added to the $150,000 mentioned previously as the present value of John Q.'s anticipated earnings as well as to a sum for loss of the services of a husband and father, the grand total once again came close to $250,000. As they reviewed the latter, Henry said:

"W. E., I called my client last evening to tell her we would be having this conference today. In the course of that conversation, I asked if she wished me to discuss a settlement with you and what terms might be agreeable with her. I am authorized to ask if you are willing to consider settlement at this point."

Henry's offer to settle was based on his thought that W. E. Just might believe he faced some difficulty in defending Zagger Supply's position, and could save that company the added expense of trial.

However, W. E. Just replied: "Since I anticipated you would bring up the matter of settlement, I discussed it with the president of Zagger Supply. After careful consideration, our position is that we will see you in court."

"That being so, let's see if we can estimate the number of trial days that will be needed for this case. Then we can both get busy drawing up the pretrial memoranda." They decided that three to four days would be necessary for the trial.

The next day Henry Law called Mary Worker to report that no settlement had been effected and that it looked very much as if none ever would be. He explained that the next step would be for each of the attorneys to prepare and file with the Clerk of Courts (as well as with each other) a pretrial memorandum. After that, they would be notified by the Clerk when to appear before Judge Fairness for a pretrial conference. When Mary asked what that involved, Henry explained.

Conference with Judge

The pretrial conference, he said, is a meeting of the attorneys for the parties with the judge prior to trial. Its object is to discuss the case and its impending litigation informally. Some refer to it as a time for "clearing the decks" for trial, because it is a time for simplifying the issues, obtaining admissions in order to avoid unnecessary proof at trial, limiting the number of expert witnesses to be called at trial, and perhaps amending the pleadings. It is available in the federal and in most of the state court systems.

The Federal Rules make the pretrial conference discretionary with the court. Some state and local rules, however, make it mandatory. Procedure varies. Generally, the conference is not held until after the discovery has been completed and shortly before trial. There is no requirement, however, regarding the time nor is there a limit in the Federal Rules on the number of pretrial conferences. Some complex law suits necessitate several.

Henry Law went on to say that some districts hold pretrial conferences in open court; others, in the judge's chambers. Some are very formal in approach; others, informal. Some have a court reporter present; others do not. In some cases, local rules require that the attorneys meet with each other first, prepare pretrial memoranda for the court, and only then confer with the judge. Henry explained that this was true in Great State. In other jurisdictions just one conference of the attorneys with the judge is held.

However, in all cases stipulations and statements made by counsel at the pretrial conference are binding. Following the conference, the judge enters an order relating the action taken. This controls subsequent events.

Henry added that such requirements mean the attorneys for both parties are well prepared for trial. A study[11] of the use of the pretrial conference showed that it resulted in improving the quality of the trial process because of better lawyer preparation. That same study refuted claims that the pretrial conference would effect a reduction in court congestion and delay by increasing the number of pretrial settlements and by saving the judges' time. In fact, the study revealed that use of the conference requires additional judge time to be devoted to a case. In other words, Henry concluded, the study showed that the pretrial conference improves quality rather than quantity.

Mary's only comment was that she hoped that better quality would redound to her benefit.

The pretrial conference went much as expected. Judge Fairness welcomed the attorneys into his chambers. A court reporter, the judge's law clerk, and W. E. Just's paralegal aide were the only others present.

"Let's see what we have here—a product liability case, isn't it?" said the judge. It was apparent throughout the entire discussion that he had done his "homework"—read the entire file of the Mary Worker case and was familiar with its contents.

His agenda included the following: a review of the pretrial memorandum prepared by each attorney, a request to Henry Law for a short statement of the substance of the plaintiff's case, a similar request to W. E. Just regarding the defendant's case, a determination from the attorneys that the pleadings were in order and required no amendment, discussion with the attorneys regarding the exhibits each would place in evidence at trial, determination from each attorney of the witnesses—with identification of those who would serve as experts—he would call at trial, an estimate of the number of days required for trial. The topics for discussion were similar to those covered by the two attorneys in their prior conference. The only new developments consisted of an agreement by W. E. Just to limit the number of cypres engineers he would call as experts to one, and an attempt by the judge to effect a settlement. The latter was to no avail.

Motion for Summary Judgment

Neither attorney presented a motion for summary judgment, although it may be made at this point in the civil process. This motion requests the court to render judgment based on the facts in the pleadings plus those added by discovery and those contained in any affidavits filed with the court. In the sense that it encompasses information beyond that contained in the pleadings, the motion differs from one for judgment on the pleadings.

A motion for summary judgment is properly granted only when the facts are not in dispute and questions of law alone remain to be decided. In the Mary Worker case, not only did facts still remain in dispute but they were the extremely vital ones. One such question concerned the cause of the shattering of the zagger. Both attorneys, realizing such factual determination was a jury matter and an issue for trial, decided against a motion for summary judgment at this time.

Courts office. Record of the status of all cases was kept by a calendar control clerk. With each judge controlling his own calendar, there were times when conflicts could arise if, for instance, two cases involving the same lawyer were scheduled for the same date. This system was in contrast with that in effect in Great State courts, where a master calendar control system was in effect. There, a case was put on the trial list after it had been certified as ready for trial following the pretrial conference. Notification of readiness was then sent to the master calendar control office, presided over by the calendar control judge. There the case was placed in a pool of all cases ready for trial and awaited its turn to be scheduled. Great State had been researching the use of electronic data processing and application of queueing theory to this scheduling process.

Policy decisions regarding calendaring, since they bear a direct relation to adjudication, are made by the court's judges. Execution of such policy, however, is often the function of a court executive or court administrator. Similar to the executive in a business firm, a court administrator is responsible for such "behind the scenes" managerial functions as accounting and budgeting, personnel practices, purchasing, space allocation and acquisition, public relations, data processing functions, as well as calendaring. Therefore, it was not unusual that the calendar control clerk in the District Court reported to the court executive who, in turn, reported directly to the chief judge of the court.

Thus it was that the Mary Worker trial was scheduled to begin on February 28, and notification was sent to all concerned. The attorneys met with their witnesses to review the facts and prepare for trial, and Judge Fairness' law clerk researched the law regarding defective products. The first day of trial would soon be at hand.

QUESTIONS

Consider the number of times attempts have been made to settle this case without going to trial. Why have they not been successful? Have reasons for not settling become more or less substantial as the case has progressed through various stages? With court dockets already crowded, is this the kind of matter that should go to trial or be settled through some alternative method? What method would you suggest?

Concentration has been on the legal aspects of this case. Have you found any social, moral, ethical issues involved? What are they? Any questions of public policy?

Discovery is often referred to as a fact-finding process. Has the case taken on any new aspects as a result of discovery? Has discovery changed the view of the case you held previously? If so, in what ways?

Is the pretrial conference a valuable step in the legal process? Why? What was accomplished through the conference in the Mary Worker case?

Is there any danger that by the time a case comes to trial the attorneys will have worked with the facts so often that a sense of carelessness can develop from overfamiliarity?

What do the statistics regarding civil litigation in your state reveal about the number of civil jury v. nonjury trials? The waiting period between readiness for trial and date a trial is called? Who is responsible for the lapse of time between the readiness date and the day the trial actually commences?

Consider the functions performed by the office of the Clerk of Courts. Is it merely a record-keeping function? What influence, if any, can it have upon litigation? What differences, if any, exist among the roles played by Attorney Just's paralegal aide and Henry Law's secretary? What part in the legal process is played by these "behind the scenes" personnel, such as paralegals, secretaries, clerks in the Clerk of Courts office? What understanding of the legal system should they possess to perform their jobs well?

Do you agree with Henry's secretary in his observation that the present can be better understood if one has some knowledge of history? Are his observations about the intertwining of law and the social order accurate? Could the common law have evolved if its beginnings were in a society such as ours in the United States today? Do the changes that Henry and Albert discuss and which have occurred over a period of time show any adaptation of the law to the times?

Do you agree with Henry that additional uniform state laws would be a boon? Why should laws relating to business have a greater tendency to become standardized than laws relating to other matters? Doesn't the freedom of travel and communication prevalent today mean that most individuals in their daily lives have contact with interstate matters? Are "long arm" statutes another reflection of the need for adjustment or change because of increased interstate activity?

Should the issues for trial be arrived at in the pleadings? Is leaving that process for discovery simply a matter of putting the matter off for a later date? Can you see any reasons for postponing it to the later stage?

Consider the content of the complaint and the answer. Do you find them understandable? written in "legalese?"

The "Erie doctrine" is often advanced as a means of arriving at a similar outcome, whether one is in the state or federal courts. Thus, it is said to be a deterrent to "forum shopping" for the purpose of selecting a court that will apply law more favorable to the plaintiff. Does not the variation in law and the rules regarding choice of law among the states make this very same kind of forum shopping possible? Should it be eliminated? How?

What do the number and kind of decisions made by Henry Law prior to filing the complaint say about the role of the lawyer in the legal process?

CASES

Singleton v. Wulff
428 U.S. 106, 96 S. Ct. 2868, 49 L. Ed. 2d 826 (1976)

MR. JUSTICE BLACKMUN . . . suit was filed in the United States District Court . . . by two Missouri-licensed physicians. Each plaintiff avers . . . that he "has provided, and anticipates providing abortions to welfare patients who are eligible for Medicaid payments." The plaintiffs further allege . . . that all Medicaid applications filed in connection with abortions performed by them have been refused by the defendant, who is the responsible state official. . . .

The defendant's sole pleading in District Court was a pre-answer motion to dismiss. Dismissal was sought upon several alternative grounds: that there was no case or controversy; that the plaintiffs "lacked standing to litigate the constitutional issues raised"; that injunctive relief "cannot be granted" because of absence of "irreparable harm" to the plaintiffs; that the plaintiffs "personally could suffer no harm", and that in any case they "cannot litigate the alleged deprivation or infringement of the civil rights of their welfare patients.". . .

. . . the three-judge panel that had been convened to hear the case dismissed the count now before us "for lack of standing." The court saw no "logical nexus between the status asserted by the plaintiffs and the claim they seek to have adjudicated."

The United States Court of Appeals for the Eighth Circuit reversed.

. . . two distinct standing questions are presented . . . and they are these: first, whether the plaintiff-appellees allege "injury in fact," that is, a sufficiently concrete interest in the outcome of their suit to make it a case or controversy subject to a federal court's Art. III jurisdiction, and, second, whether, as a prudential matter, the plaintiff-appellees are proper proponents of the particular legal rights on which they base their suit.

[1] A. The first of these questions needs little comment, for there is no doubt now that the appellee-physicians suffer concrete injury . . . Their complaint and affidavits . . . allege that they have performed and will continue to perform operations for which they would be reimbursed under the Medicaid program, were it not for the limitation of reimbursable abortions to those that are "medically indicated." If the physicians prevail in their suit to remove this limitation, they will benefit, for they will then receive payment for the abortions. The State (and Federal Government) will be out of pocket by the amount of the payments. The relationship between the parties is classically adverse, and there clearly exists between them a case or controversy in the constitutional sense. . . .

B. The question of what rights the doctors may assert in seeking to resolve the controversy is more difficult. The Court of Appeals adverted to what is perceived to be the doctors' own "constitutional rights to practice medicine." . . . We have no occasion to decide whether such rights exist. Assuming that they do, the doctors, of course, can assert them. It appears, however, that the Court of Appeals also accorded the doctors standing to assert, and indeed granted them relief based partly upon, the rights of their patients. We must decide whether this assertion . . . was a proper one.

Federal courts must hesitate before resolving a controversy, even one within their constitutional power to resolve, on the basis of the rights of third persons not parties to the litigation. The reasons are two. First, the courts should not adjudicate such rights unnecessarily, and it may be that in fact the holders of those rights either do not wish to assert them, or will be able to enjoy them regardless of whether the in-court litigant is successful or not. . . . Second, third parties themselves usually will be the best proponents of their own rights. The courts depend on effective advocacy, and therefore would prefer to construe legal rights only when the most effective advocates of those rights are before them. The holders of the rights may have a like preference, to the extent they will be bound by the courts' decisions under the doctrine of *stare decisis.* . . . These two considerations underlie the Court's general rule: "Ordinarily, one may not claim standing in this Court to vindicate the constitutional rights of some third party.". . .

Like any general rule, however, this one should not be applied where the underlying justifications are absent. With this in mind, the Court has looked primarily to two factual elements to determine whether the rule should apply in a particular case. The first is the relationship of the litigant to the person whose right he seeks to assert. If the enjoyment of the right is inextricably bound up with the activity the litigant wishes to pursue, the court at least can be sure that its construction of the right is not unnecessary in the sense that the rights' enjoyment will be unaffected by the outcome of the suit. Furthermore, the relationship between the litigant and the third party may be such that the former is fully, or very nearly, as effective a proponent of the right as the latter. . . .

The other factual element to which the Court has looked is the ability of the third party to assert his own right. Even where the relationship is close, the reasons for requiring persons to assert their own rights will generally still apply. If there is some genuine obstacle to such assertion, however, the third party's absence from court loses its tendency to suggest that his right is not truly at stake, or truly important to him, and the party who is in court becomes by default the right's best available proponent. . . .

Application of these principles to the present case quickly yields its proper result. . . .

We conclude that it is generally appropriate to allow a physician to assert the rights of women patients as against government interference with the abortion decision. . . . In this respect, the judgment of the Court of Appeals is affirmed. . . .

On this record, we do not agree, however, with the action of the Court of Appeals in proceeding beyond the issue of standing to a resolution of the merits of the case. . . .

. . . petitioner has never been heard in any way on the merits of the case. . . .

Assuming, therefore, that the Court of Appeals had jurisdiction to proceed to the merits in this case, we hold that it should not have done so. To that extent, its judgment is reversed and the case is remanded with directions that it be returned to the District Court so that petitioner may file an answer to the complaint and the litigation proceed accordingly.

International Shoe Co. v. Washington
326 U.S. 310, 66 S.Ct. 154, 90 L.Ed. 95 (1945)

Suit was filed against International Shoe Co. by the state of Washington to collect unemployment compensation taxes which the state alleged were due on commissions paid to salesmen employed by the corporation within the state. Notice was personally served upon a sales solicitor employed by the corporation in Washington. A copy was sent by registered mail to the home office in St. Louis. The corporation contended that service upon its salesmen was not proper service and, further, that subjecting it either to suit or taxation within the state of Washington was a denial of due process of law. The supreme court of the state of Washington having found otherwise, the company appealed to the United States Supreme Court.

MR. CHIEF JUSTICE STONE . . . . The facts . . . are not in dispute. Appellant is a Delaware corporation, having its principal place of business in St. Louis, Missouri, and is engaged in the manufacture and sale of shoes and other footwear. It maintains places of business in several states, other than Washington, at which its manufacturing is carried on and from which its merchandise is distributed interstate through several sales units or branches located outside the State of Washington.

Appellant has no office in Washington and makes no contracts either for sale or purchase of merchandise there. It maintains no stock of merchandise in that state and makes there no deliveries of goods in intrastate commerce. During the years from 1937 to 1940, now in question, appellant employed eleven to thirteen salesmen under direct supervision and control of sales managers located in St. Louis. These salesmen resided in Washington; their principal activities were confined to that state; and they were compensated by commissions based upon the amount of their sales. The commissions for each year totaled more than $31,000. Appellant supplies its salesmen with a line of samples, each consisting of one shoe of a pair, which they display to prospective purchasers. On occasion they rent permanent sample rooms, for exhibiting samples, in business buildings, or rent rooms in hotels or business buildings temporarily for that purpose. The cost of such rentals is reimbursed by appellant.

The authority of the salesmen is limited to exhibiting their samples and soliciting orders from prospective buyers, at prices and on terms fixed by appellant. The salesmen transmit the orders to appellant's office in St. Louis for acceptance or rejection, and when accepted the merchandise for filling the orders is shipped f.o.b. from points outside Washington to the purchasers within the state. All the merchandise shipped into Washington is invoiced at the place of shipment from which collections are made. No salesman has authority to enter into contracts or to make collections. . . .

Appellant also insists that its activities within the state were not sufficient to manifest its "presence" there and that in its absence the state courts were without jurisdiction, that consequently it was a denial of due process for the state to subject appellant to suit. It refers to those cases in which it was said that the mere solicitation of orders for the purchase of goods within a state, to be accepted without the state and filled by shipment of the purchased goods interstate, does not render the corporation seller amenable to suit within the state. . . . And appellant further argues that since it was not present within the state, it is a denial of due process to subject it to taxation or other money exaction. It thus denies the power of the state to lay the tax or to subject appellant to a suit for its collection.

Historically the jurisdiction of courts to render judgment in personam is grounded on their de facto power over the defendant's person. Hence his presence within the territorial jurisdiction of a court was prerequisite to its rendition of a judgment personally binding him. . . . But now that the capias ad respondendum has given way to personal service of summons or other form of notice, due process requires only that in order to subject a defendant to a judgment in personam, if he be not present within the territory of the forum, he have certain minimum contacts with it such that the maintenance of the suit does not offend "traditional notions of fair play and substantial justice.". . .

Since the corporate personality is a fiction, although a fiction intended to be acted upon as though it were a fact, . . . it is clear that unlike an individual its "presence" without, as well as within, the state of its origin can be manifested only by activities carried on in its behalf by those who are authorized to act for it. . . . For the terms "present" or "presence" are used merely to symbolize those activities of the corporation's agent within the state which courts will deem to be sufficient to satisfy the demands of due process. . . . Those demands may be met by such contacts of the corporation with the state of the forum as make it reasonable, in the context of our federal system of government, to require the corporation to defend the particular suit which is brought there. An "estimate of the inconveniences" which would result to the corporation from a trial away from its "home" or principal place of business is relevant in this connection.

"Presence" in the state in this sense has never been doubted when the activities of the corporation there have been not only continuous and systematic, but also give rise to the liabilities sued on, even though no consent to be sued or authorization to an agent to accept service of process has been given. . . . Conversely it has been generally recognized that the casual presence of the corporate agent or even his conduct of single or isolated items of activities in a state in the corporation's behalf are not enough to subject it to suit on causes of action unconnected with the activities there. . . . To require the corporation in such circumstances to defend the suit away from its home or other jurisdiction where it carries on more substantial activities has been thought to lay too great and unreasonable a burden on the corporation to comport with due process. . . .

It is evident that the criteria by which we mark the boundary line between those activities which justify the subjection of a corporation to suit, and those which do not, cannot be simply mechanical or quantitative. The test is not merely, as has sometimes been suggested, whether the activity, which the corporation has seen fit to procure through its agents in another state, is a little more or a little less. . . . Whether due process is satisfied must depend rather upon the quality and nature of the activity in relation to the fair and orderly administration of the laws which it was the purpose of the due process clause to insure. That clause does not contemplate that a state may make binding a judgment in personam against an individual or corporate defendant with which the state has no contacts, ties, or relations. . . .

But to the extent that a corporation exercises the privilege of conducting activities within a state, it enjoys the benefits and protections of the laws of that state. The exercise of that privilege may give rise to obligations; and, so far as those obligations arise out of or are connected with the activities within the state, a procedure which requires the corporation to respond to a suit brought to enforce them can, in most instances, hardly be said to be undue. . . .

Applying these standards, the activities carried on in behalf of appellant in the State of Washington were neither irregular nor casual. They were systematic and continuous throughout the years in question. They resulted in a large volume of interstate business, in the course of which appellant received the benefits and protection of the laws of the state, including the right to resort to the courts for the enforcement of its rights. The obligation which is here sued upon arose out of those very activities. It is evident that these operations establish sufficient contacts or ties with the state of the forum to make it reasonable and just according to our traditional conception of fair play and substantial justice to permit the state to enforce the obligations which appellant has incurred there. Hence we cannot say that the maintenance of the present suit in the State of Washington involves an unreasonable or undue procedure. . . .

Appellant having rendered itself amenable to suit upon obligations arising out of the activities of its salesmen in Washington, the state may maintain the present suit in personam to collect the tax laid upon the exercise of the privilege of employing appellant's salesmen within the state. . . . The activities which establish its "presence" subject it alike to taxation by the state and to suit to recover the tax. . . .

Affirmed.

Hickman v. Taylor
329 U.S. 495, 67 S.Ct. 385, 91 L.Ed. 451 (1947)

MR. JUSTICE MURPHY . . . On February 7, 1943, the tug "J.M. Taylor" sank while engaged in helping to tow a car float of the Baltimore & Ohio Railroad. . . . Five of the nine crew members were drowned. Three days later the tug owners and the underwriters employed a law firm, of which respondent Fortenbaugh is a member, to defend them against potential suits by representatives of the deceased crew members and to sue the railroad for damages to the tug.

A public hearing was held . . . at which the four survivors were examined. Their testimony was recorded and made available to all interested parties. Shortly thereafter, Fortenbaugh privately interviewed the survivors and took statements from them with an eye toward the anticipated litigation; . . . Fortenbaugh also interviewed other persons believed to have some information relating to the accident and in some cases he made memoranda of what they told him. . . . Ultimately claims were presented by the representatives of all five of the deceased; four of the claims, however, were settled without litigation. The fifth claimant, petitioner herein, brought suit in a federal court . . . naming as defendants the two tug owners, individually and as partners, and the railroad.

One year later, petitioner filed 39 interrogatories directed to the tug owners. The 38th interrogatory read: "State whether any statements of the members of the crews of the Tugs 'J.M. Taylor' and 'Philadelphia' or of any other vessel were taken in connection with the towing of the car float and the sinking of the Tug 'John M. Taylor.' Attach hereto exact copies of all such statements if in writing, and if oral, set forth in detail the exact provisions of any such oral statements or reports."

Supplemental interrogatories asked whether any oral or written statements, records, reports or other memoranda had been made concerning any matter relative to the towing operation, the sinking of the tug, the salvaging and repair of the tug, and the death of the deceased. If the answer was in the affirmative, the tug owners were then requested to set forth the nature of all such records, reports, statements or other memoranda.

The tug owners, through Fortenbaugh, answered all of the interrogatories except No. 38 and the supplemental ones just described. While admitting that statements of the survivors had been taken, they declined to summarize or set forth the contents. They did so on the ground that such requests called "for privileged matter contained in preparation for litigation" and constitute "an attempt to obtain indirectly counsel's private files." It was claimed that answering these requests "would involve practically turning over not only the complete files, but also the telephone records and, almost, the thoughts of counsel."

In connection with the hearing on these objections, Fortenbaugh made a written statement and gave an informal oral deposition explaining the circumstances under which he had taken the statements. . . . The District Court . . . held that the requested matters were not privileged. . . .

The Third Circuit Court of Appeals . . . reversed the judgment of the District Court. . . . The importance of the problem, which has engendered a great divergence of views among district courts, led us to grant certiorari. . . .

The pre-trial deposition-discovery mechanism . . . is one of the most significant innovations of the Federal Rules of Civil Procedure. Under the prior federal practice, the pre-trial functions of notice-giving issue-formulation and fact-revelation were performed primarily and inadequately by the pleadings. Inquiry into the issues and the facts before trial was narrowly confined and was often cumbersome in methods. The new rules, however, restrict the pleadings to the task of general notice-giving and invest the deposition-discovery process with a vital role in the preparation for trial. The various instruments of discovery now serve (1) as a device, along with the pre-trial hearing . . . to narrow and clarify the basic issues between the parties, and (2) as a device for ascertaining the facts, or information as to the existence or whereabouts of facts, relative to those issues. Thus civil trials in the federal courts no longer need be carried on in the dark. The way is now clear, consistent with recognized privileges, for the parties to obtain the fullest possible knowledge of the issues and facts before trial. . . . Mutual knowledge of all the relevant facts gathered by both parties is essential to proper litigation. To that end, either party may compel the other to disgorge whatever facts he has in his possession. The deposition-discovery procedure simply advances the stage at which the disclosure can be compelled from the time of trial to the period preceding it, thus reducing the possibility of surprise. But discovery like all matters of procedure, has ultimate and necessary boundaries . . . limitations inevitably arise when it can be shown that the examination is being conducted in bad faith or in such a manner as to annoy, embarrass or oppress the person subject to the inquiry . . . further limitations come into existence when the inquiry touches upon the irrelevant or encroaches upon the recognized domains of privilege.

We also agree that the memoranda, statements and mental impressions in issue in this case fall outside the scope of the attorney-client privilege and hence are not protected from discovery on that basis . . . it suffices to note that the protective cloak of this privilege does not extend to information which an attorney secures from a witness while acting for his client in anticipation of litigation. . . . Petitioner has made more than an ordinary request for relevant, non-privileged facts in the possession of his adversaries or their counsel. He has sought discovery as of right of oral and written statements of witnesses whose identity is well known and whose availability to petitioner appears unimpaired . . . petitioner was free to examine the public testimony of the witnesses. . . . Here is simply an attempt, without purported necessity or justification, to secure written statements, private memoranda and personal recollections prepared or formed by an adverse party's counsel in the course of his legal duties. As such, it falls outside the area of discovery and contravenes the public policy underlying the orderly prosecution and defense of legal claims. Not even the most liberal of discovery theories can justify unwarranted inquiries into the files and the mental impressions of an attorney. . . .

We do not mean to say that all written materials obtained or prepared by an adversary's counsel with an eye toward litigation are necessarily free from discovery in all cases. Where relevant and non-privileged facts remain hidden in an attorney's file and where production of those facts is essential to the preparation of one's case, discovery may properly be had. Such written statements and documents might, under certain circumstances, be admissible in evidence or give clues as to the existence or location of relevant facts. Or they might be useful for purposes of impeachment or corroboration. And production might be justified where the witnesses are no longer available or can be reached only with difficulty. . . . But the general policy against invading the privacy of an attorney's course of preparation is so well recognized and so essential to an orderly working of our system of legal procedure that a burden rests on the one who would invade that privacy to establish adequate reasons to justify production through a subpoena or court order. . . .

. . . forcing an attorney to repeat or write out all that witnesses have told him and deliver the account to his adversary gives rise to grave dangers or inaccuracy and untrustworthiness . . . No legitimate purpose is served by such production. The practice forces the attorney to testify as to what he remembers or what he saw fit to write down regarding witnesses' remarks. Such testimony could not qualify as evidence; and to use it for impeachment or corroborative purposes would make the attorney much less an officer of the court and much more an ordinary witness. . . .

. . . we are not justified in permitting discovery in a situation of this nature as a matter of unqualified right. When . . . the . . . discovery rules were adopted, this Court and the members of the bar in general certainly did not believe or contemplate that all the files and mental processes of lawyers were thereby opened to the free scrutiny of their adversaries. And we refuse to interpret the rules at this time so as to reach so harsh and unwarranted a result.

We therefore affirm the judgment of the Circuit Court of Appeals.

FOOTNOTES

[1] Article III, Section 2 of the United States Constitution extends the federal judicial power to "cases" and "controversies."

[2] The personal representative of the deceased when there is no will is referred to as the *administrator* or *administratrix*; if there is a will, that personal representative is known as the *executor* or *executrix*.

[3] Article III, Section 2.

[4] 28 USC §1331 and 1332.

[5] "Person" includes a corporation, which the law looks upon as an artificial person. The term also includes entities such as partnerships or associations.

[6] Exceptions to this exist by federal statute.

[7] 28 USC §1391.

[8] 28 USC §1404.

[9] In some jurisdictions the complaint is known as the declaration, the petition, or the bill.

[10] Kalven, Harry, Jr. and Hans Zeisel, *The American Jury*, (Boston: Little, Brown & Company), 1966.

[11] Rosenberg, Maurice, *The Pre-Trial Conference and Effective Justice*, (New York: Columbia University Press), 1964.

CHAPTER 7
TRIAL: ARGUMENT AND ADJUDICATION

On the morning of the first day of trial, Mary Worker met Henry Law at his office and together the two went to the federal courthouse in Big City. As they entered the courtroom of Judge Fairness, Mary looked around. This was the first time she had ever been in that court. Since they were the first persons there, Henry explained the physical arrangements to her.

THE COURTROOM

The immediate focus of attention of anyone entering the room was the judge's bench, loftily centered at the very front. The witness stand was to the left of it at a slightly lower level. At the extreme left was the jury box. Directly in front of the judge's bench was a long table. This, Henry explained, would be shared by the court reporter, the court clerk, and the judge's law clerk. To the right of the judge's bench was the chair for the bailiff or tipstaff, as he is sometimes known. His duties, Henry said, included announcing the opening and closing of court sessions, escorting the jury, and serving as a general aide to court.

Mary and Henry took places at a long double table in the center of the room, below the judge's bench and in front of the railing which separated the seating area for members of the general public from the rest of the courtroom. Henry informed Mary that W. E. Just and representatives of Zagger Supply would be seated on the other side of the table, directly across from them. He also said that most courtrooms are arranged in a somewhat similar manner, although a few of the more recently built courthouses have courtrooms "in the round." Proponents of the latter

159

arrangement, he explained, claim that it brings judge, jury, witnesses, and attorneys much closer to each other physically, thus facilitating communication.

LAWYER TO LAWYER

It was not long until W. E. Just and his paralegal assistant arrived. Mary was surprised, almost disheartened, to find that Henry was both friendly and cordial in greeting them. Noticing her concern, Henry thought that a comparison with professional baseball or football players might be helpful in explaining lawyers' relationships with each other. While playing, he told her, professional athletes put all of their energy, effort, and talent into winning for their team or their side. However, it is not uncommon to find they are sometimes close friends off the field with these same athletes who are their opponents on the playing field. So it can be with lawyers, too, he said. Advocates for opposing sides do not necessarily carry that adversarial relationship over into their private and personal lives.

JURY SELECTION

In the meantime, elsewhere in the courthouse, a number of other persons who would play an important role in the trial had already gathered in the jury assembly room. They had been selected randomly from voter lists for the district served by the court, in accordance with the provisions of the Federal Jury Selection and Service Act of 1968.[1] Voter lists are used to secure a fair cross-section of the community.

The United States Supreme Court has held that a "jury of one's peers" does not require that a jury consist of persons whose characteristics are identical with those of the parties to the law suit. Instead, the requirement is that there be equal opportunity and possibility for representation of all segments of the community on the *jury panel*.[2] The jury panel is the larger group from which members of the trial jury are chosen. Systematic exclusion from juries of such groups of people as women or blacks results in jury panels that are not representative of the community, and, therefore, it is not permitted.[3]

Determinants of qualification for jury duty, as set forth in the Federal Jury Selection and Service Act, are: age, citizenship, residence in the district, literacy, mental and physical health, and absence of a criminal record. These criteria were selected in order to prevent disqualification of persons for purely subjective reasons and to eliminate insofar as possible opportunities for the creation of the *blue ribbon juries* sometimes alleged in the past to be characteristic of the juries in the federal courts. A blue ribbon jury is one on which the proportion of managerial and professional persons to all others is much greater than it is in the general population.

Under the act, persons excluded from jury service because of occupation include the police, firefighters, soldiers, and public officers. Others who may be excused upon request include mothers with young children, clergy, physicians, lawyers, nurses, teachers, sole proprietors of business, and those able to show "undue hardship or extreme inconvenience." A statute similar to the federal act has been proposed for uniform adoption by the states.

Jury Array

Responsibility for jury selection in this court rested with the court executive and was implemented by the clerk of courts office. In some jurisdictions a jury commissioner assists the clerk. This court had under way study of the feasibility of using the computer for random generation of names on the voter lists. Present procedure was to place the names of all persons on the voter lists in a master jury wheel and to draw names from it manually. This list of names drawn was referred to as the *jury array*. It was subject to challenge by a showing that selection had not been made in accordance with the law.

Once the array had been determined, a qualification form was mailed to every person on the list. Each reply was checked to see if the individual met the requirements for jury duty. If so, that person's name was placed in the "qualified" jury wheel. As the need for jurors was anticipated, names were pulled from that wheel. Notices to report to the jury assembly room on a specified date were mailed to the persons whose names had been drawn. They would constitute the *general jury panel*. Requests for excuse from jury duty were referred to a judge who decided if they were valid.

These steps in selection of the general jury panel have been flow charted in Figure 7-1. Notice that the chart shows that discharge from jury duty may result from either excuse or disqualification.

Trial Panel

When prospective jurors reported to the assembly room, they were welcomed, informed about courthouse facilities and the role of jurors, and given a juror's handbook to study and a juror's identification button to wear. They were instructed to wait in the juror assembly area until a call came for a trial panel. When it did, the names of twenty of the assembled persons were drawn from a jury wheel. This group was then escorted to a courtroom where selection of the jury for a specific trial would be made. If the need arose, additional groups would be sent in order for sufficient persons to be secured to serve on the trial, or *petit, jury*. The procedures followed by this court in the selection of persons for jury duty do not differ markedly from those followed elsewhere.

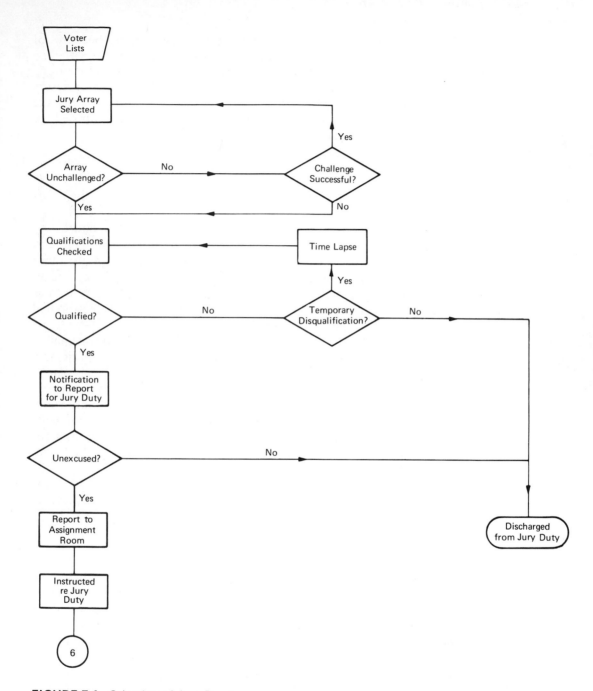

FIGURE 7-1. Selection of Jury Panel.

Jury Size

The traditional petit jury consisted of twelve persons. Today many courts use as few as six persons for reasons of economy and efficiency. When the constitutionality of juries consisting of fewer than twelve persons was challenged, the United States Supreme Court ruled that the guarantee of trial by jury in the federal constitution does not have a number requirement.[4] Therefore, one's right to trial by jury is not infringed if there are fewer than twelve *veniremen* or jurors. The local rules of the district court for the Great State district provided for juries of six with two alternates.

Thus it was that a group of prospective jurors was sent to Judge Fairness' courtroom where the parties, the witnesses scheduled for the first day of trial, the judge's law clerk, the court reporter, and the court clerk were assembled. In some courts, the jury for civil trials is selected near or in the juror assembly room and a judge's presence is not required. That was not true in this court, however. Once all necessary persons were present in the courtroom, Judge Fairness entered. Having identified the case about to be tried, he called for selection of the jury to begin.

Challenges

Henry Law had explained to Mary Worker beforehand that both he and W. E. Just would have a list of the general jury panel showing names, addresses, and occupations. Each attorney checked this list as the clerk now called the names of the twenty members of the trial panel. Mary anticipated that the attorneys would make two kinds of challenges to having specific persons from this panel serve on the jury for her lawsuit. Each successful challenge would mean that the individual would be dismissed from participation on the jury in this trial.

Challenges for cause in an unlimited number are possible by each attorney. These challenges must be based upon a good and sufficient reason, such as a prospective juror's being related to or employed by one of the parties or attorneys. Discovery of such matters is by *voir dire* or questioning of the jury panel. Judge Fairness handled the voir dire himself. Both attorneys were permitted to submit to the judge beforehand questions to be used in the voir dire. ·In some courts, the questioning is done by both the attorneys and the judge. In this case the voir dire resulted in the dismissal for cause of the following members of the jury panel: Clyde Partner's secretary; a shipping clerk employed by The Firm; Will Very's cousin, the publicity director for the Zagger Institute; a local television newscaster, who covered and reported the John Q. Worker accident for his station; a Big City industrial equipment broker, who at times dealt in Zagger Supply products; Professor Learned's laboratory assistant; and the wife of the ambulance driver who had been called to the accident scene.

163

Both attorneys also made use of the *peremptory* challenge. This is, in effect, a rather arbitrary challenge since no reason need be given to exclude a particular person from the jury. Peremptory challenges are limited in number by the rules of civil procedure. Much has been said and written about the importance of selecting jurors with whom rapport can be established. In fact, it is sometimes said that juries "try the attorneys." Henry Law included in his peremptory challenges the owner of a small business and a salesperson for a railway equipment firm. As he told Mary later, he believed that because of their occupations these individuals might tend to be sympathetic with the defendant's cause. W. E. Just's challenges included a widowed housewife and a union steward.

Final Choice

Those finally selected for the jury were:

1. Geraldine Horne, age 26, a saxophone player and member of a quintet which played regularly in a local lounge;
2. Adam Frank, age 52, bookkeeper;
3. Kathleen Logan, age 62, a part-time computer programmer;
4. Martin Lee, age 31, a salesperson at a Big City haberdashery;
5. Nancy Perkins, age 44, a telephone operator;
6. Sam Wells, age 52, a truck driver.

Rosemarie Friday, 21, a waitress, and Joseph Patrick, 33, a janitor, were selected as alternate jurors. They would sit in the jury box during the trial. Should any of the six regular jurors become ill or incapacitated and unable to take part in the deliberations for a verdict, the alternates would replace them. If not, the two would be dismissed and sent home when the jury retired to begin its deliberations.

The panel members who had not been selected for the jury were thanked by Judge Fairness and escorted back to the jury assembly room to await consideration for membership on other juries. Those not selected for any jury would be paid the $20-per-day federal jury fee and sent home. All of this is shown in Figure 7-2 which flow charts selection of the trial jury.

Opening Statements

The jury having been selected and sworn, it was now time for opening statements by the two attorneys. This stage of the trial provides counsel for each party with the opportunity to talk briefly with the jury about the case as well as about the evidence to be offered and the witnesses to be called. Thus the jury is given a preview and has some idea of what to

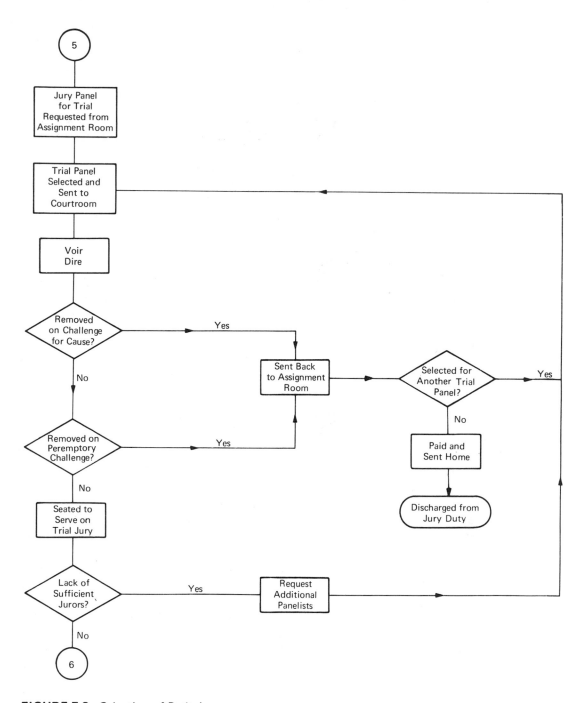

FIGURE 7-2. Selection of Petit Jury.

expect next.   Opening statements are not evidence.   The reason is that they are made by attorneys who are advocates and not witnesses.   As the party bringing the case, the plaintiff is first.   Therefore, Henry began his statement to the jury.

He did so by identifying the parties and their attorneys.   He also told the jury about the various steps in a trial.   Following that, he became specific about the Mary Worker case.   The lawsuit, Henry said, arose from an accident in which John Q. Worker, a cypres machine operator, was killed when a fragment from a shattering zagger pierced his abdomen. Henry explained that the zagger had shattered while being used by John Q. in the course of his employment.   The suit, Henry went on, was being brought by John Q.'s widow to recover from the manufacturer of the zagger for the loss to herself and her family of a husband and father. Henry told the jury he would present witnesses who would testify that the zagger was dangerously defective and was the cause of John Q.'s death. There would also be testimony, he added, that the zagger was being used for its intended purpose at the time of the accident by a careful and skilled machinist, and that testing by the manufacturer prior to shipment could have prevented the accident.   The evidence would show, he concluded, that the zagger manufacturer's actions were the cause of the accident and John Q.'s death.   Finally, he asked that they listen carefully to the testimony that would follow the opening statements.

W. E. Just followed with his opening statement to the jury.   He identified himself as the counsel for Zagger Supply, told the jury he would have the opportunity to cross-examine each of Henry's witnesses after that person had testified and said he would present the case for the defense when Henry had completed the plaintiff's case.   He also said he would present witnesses who would testify that the zagger shattered as it did for reasons other than any defect, that John Q. had used the zagger without a guard on his machine—in such a manner that he knowingly and voluntarily assumed the risk of the accident that resulted.   He ended by saying that the evidence would show that his client was not responsible for the accident.

As they spoke, Mary noticed the court reporter was busily recording everything that was said, the judge's law clerk making notations, the judge listening to each attorney's statements and from time to time referring to documents related to the case, the clerk busy with papers connected with the trial, and the jury listening with apparent interest.   She noticed, too, that so far everything had proceeded much as Henry Law had said it would.

PLAINTIFF'S CASE IN CHIEF

Preparation

The opening statements to the jury completed, Judge Fairness asked Henry if the plaintiff was ready with his first witness.

The examination of each witness called to testify at a trial is conducted in accordance with the following steps:

1. *Direct Examination.* This consists of questioning by the attorney for the party who calls the witness. The objective is to establish the facts or claim of that party.

2. *Cross-examination.* This involves questioning by the opposing counsel and is optional with him. It offers the opportunity for attacking the credibility of the opponent's witness and his testimony. Cross-examination is generally limited to matters covered on direct examination.

3. *Redirect Examination.* Optional requestioning is possible by the attorney who conducted the direct examination. This is generally used to "rehabilitate" the witness following cross-examination; that is, to recapture his lost credibility. The subject matter is usually limited to answering that which was brought out on cross-examination.

4. *Recross-examination.* The opposing counsel has the option of requestioning following the redirect examination. The limits generally imposed are to new matter brought out on redirect.

This process of witness examination is flow charted in Figure 7-3.

Henry Law had devoted his attention prior to trial to the matter of whom would be called as witnesses and the order in which they would be called. Details of the accident and related events would have to be told to a jury, unacquainted with any of the facts, in a manner that they could follow and that would at the same time be as beneficial as possible to Mary's case. Henry reasoned, therefore, that the most understandable sequence for a jury would be to discuss first the accident, then the defect, and finally the damages.

As to the persons who would serve as witnesses, he could select only from those persons with first-hand knowledge of the facts about which he needed testimony. This was because of the *rules of evidence,* which require that witnesses have personal knowledge regarding that to which they testify. Rules of evidence are those that regulate the admission of proof at the trial of a lawsuit. Uniform Rules of Evidence have been proposed but not adopted; however, the rules tend to be very similar as one goes from state to state. For the federal courts, new Rules of Evidence were promulgated in 1975.[5]

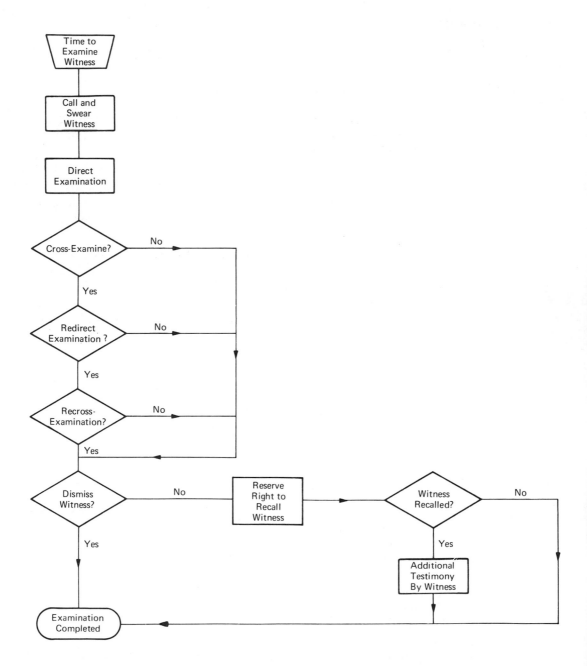

FIGURE 7-3. Examination of Witnesses.

The rules of evidence have been developed from experience in the conduct of trials over the centuries. They are a good example of procedural law, knowledge of which is important to the attorney.

As Henry considered possible witnesses, he naturally looked for persons who would provide testimony favorable to his client. When there was more than one person with the requisite first-hand knowledge, he would choose that person or persons whose manner and appearance would be most convincing to the jury and who would be least likely to damage his client's case on cross-examination.

Henry knew of three witnesses to the accident: Robert Leader, Timothy O'Goode, and Peter Superior. Robert had observed more of the occurrences immediately prior to, during, and immediately following the accident than the other two had. Therefore, he alone would be able to testify regarding certain details. Timothy, as the only one of the three who had worked on production of the new chattels, could testify regarding his experience with the special zaggers. Peter also could make a unique contribution with testimony regarding the five shattering incidents involving the special zaggers, which had taken place in the department he supervised. Therefore, Henry decided he needed all three as witnesses.

Henry realized that for the jury to comprehend the defective qualities of the new zaggers, they would first have to learn about the operation of a cypres machine and how zaggers are used on them. In addition, they must be informed about the order, design, and manufacture of the special zaggers. As the most articulate of these three witnesses and also the most experienced cypres operator, Robert Leader was Henry's choice to provide the jury with a nontechnical explanation of the machine's operation.

For first-hand knowledge of the special zagger order, however, Sam Scott would have to be called. He also qualified to explain differences between the two types of zaggers and could testify regarding the function of the guard on the machine.

Henry planned to rely upon Professor Learned for most of the testimony regarding defectiveness of the zagger and lack of proper testing. In fact, Henry believed the outcome of the trial would be influenced greatly by this man's testimony, not only because of his impressive qualifications and reputation but also because he was an experienced expert witness. As an expert, he could be asked *hypothetical questions;* i.e., those in which the witness is asked to assume a given set of facts and to render an opinion about the result or outcome. The rules of evidence require that witnesses testify as to facts, not conclusions or opinions. An exception is made in the case of *expert witnesses;* that is, witnesses who by reason of experience, training, or education have special knowledge about matters before the court. They are permitted to give opinions in their area of expertise.

Henry realized it was vital to his client's case to have testimony concerning the results that would follow or could be expected to follow if there were bonding or size defects in a zagger. The same necessity prevailed, in his estimation, regarding the effects or absence of the guard. For that reason, Henry planned to present evidence to qualify not only Professor Learned, but also Sam Scott, as expert witnesses.

Finally, testimony regarding damages was necessary. For this, Henry would call Mary to explain what the loss of John Q. had meant to her and her children.

It should be mentioned that Henry had explored what might be added to the plaintiff's case as a result of the OSHA inspection made at The Firm. He found nothing relevant to his purposes that he had not already considered and included in his preparation. He therefore concluded that delving further into that matter would provide no enhancement for his case. He also decided that W. E. Just would conclude similarly with regard to the defendant's case. In this he was correct.

This, then, had been Henry Law's thought process in arriving at decisions regarding witnesses, most of which had been made prior to the pretrial conference. Except for Peter Superior and Sam Scott, Henry telephoned prospective witnesses and arranged to meet with each in preparation for trial. He explained the procedures in testifying, reviewed with them prior statements they had made, told them what he believed they could expect on cross-examination, and answered questions of concern to them about the trial process. Such witness preparation is entirely proper. It is a necessary part of the trial lawyer's job. Contrary to the opinion held by some persons, it is a legitimate task for the trial attorney to permit witnesses to "refresh their recollection" by permitting them to reread memoranda or statements they have previously prepared. The rules of evidence give recognition to the fact that memories dim with time. Witnesses are permitted to refer to their own writings even while testifying, provided all the evidentiary requirements for doing so are met. In no instance, however, is the attorney permitted to suggest to witnesses that they tell anything other than the truth—the whole truth. To do so would be to commit the crime of subornation of perjury.

In the case of Peter and Sam, subpoenas were issued. Previously, when these two men had been subpoenaed for the taking of depositions, they had consulted Leo Lex about the legal ramifications. Following that, Sam Scott called Henry to inform him that both could be present at the time set for the deposition taking. He also indicated The Firm's position was that it would cooperate in the legal process. It would not obstruct justice. However, it did not desire to become the legal antagonist of Zagger Supply with whom it wished to maintain friendly business relations. The two companies, he said, had always been able to settle any problems or differences they might have had between themselves out of court. It was their hope to continue to do so.

When this second subpoena arrived, Sam again called Henry. He asked if he could expect to testify regarding the same matters about which he had been questioned in connection with the deposition. He was informed that this was so. The conversation then turned to the possible use of visual aids for the purpose of making Sam's technical explanations more comprehensible to nonengineers who, in all probability, would constitute the majority of the jury. The two agreed that both a regular and special zagger as well as models of the cypres machine and the new chattel would be appropriate. Such objects are often referred to as *demonstrative evidence,* and may be passed from hand to hand by jurors who have the right to examine them. Henry planned to introduce these objects into evidence at appropriate times during Sam's testimony.

All this preparation having taken place, Robert Leader now took his place in the witness box after having been sworn to tell the truth by the clerk.

The Case in Chief

Anxious at first, Robert soon settled back and responded well to Henry's questions. His testimony contained no surprises. It duplicated information he had provided previously in his deposition and in conversation with Henry Law. However, one incident that occurred during his direct examination is noteworthy.

After the usual preliminary questions dealing with identification, Henry questioned Robert about his twenty years of experience as a cypres machine operator at The Firm, Inc., where he worked at the machine immediately to the right of the one which John Q. had operated. Following that, Robert testified that he had been chairperson of the safety committee of Local 135 for ten years prior to becoming local president. This evidence came in after Judge Fairness overruled W. E. Just's objection that Robert's union activities were not relevant.

A fundamental requirement for the admission of evidence is that it relate to the matters at issue in the trial, that it have a bearing on the truth of the facts in dispute. The purpose of this rule of evidence is to restrict testimony to trial matters. This is to prevent prolonging the trial and confusing jurors by introducing into evidence extraneous matters.

Henry's response to W. E.'s objection was to ask if counsel could approach the bench. Such a request is, in effect, one for a private conversation between judge and attorneys. Henry's purpose in doing so was to make an *offer of proof,* that is, state to the judge what he expected to show by the answer of the witness. Such an offer is made out of the hearing of the jurors. The reason is to prevent their being influenced by having heard it, should the evidence be ruled inadmissible.

Juries and court watchers are often bewildered and some jury members are even resentful when conversations between counsel and judge, such as this one, take place out of their hearing. It is not that the case is being tried in private between judge and attorneys. Instead, the discussion generally involves resolution of such questions as admissibility of evidence or proper trial procedure. In this case, when Judge Fairness heard that Henry wished to establish Robert's experience with a safety committee to lay a foundation for his further testimony regarding zagger safety, he permitted pursuit of the line of questioning.

Both attorneys noted that Robert's description of the accident provoked response from the jury. Geraldine Horne for the first time sat upright in her chair; Mrs. Logan winced; Mr. Frank leaned forward; Jurors Perkins and Wells moved to the edge of their chairs; and Mr. Lee stared intently at the witness. Obviously, an impact had been made.

W. E. Just, on cross-examination, was able to reduce that impact somewhat. In answer to defense counsel's questions, Robert admitted he could not state positively that he had seen John Q. go through each of the motions necessary in properly checking and placing the zagger on the cypres machine. Nor could he state positively that he had seen John Q. replace the guard. Robert also admitted that he had never used any of the new zaggers and that he had never personally examined them.

That brought to a close the first day of the trial. Before court began the next morning, Henry checked to see that the visual aids for Sam Scott's testimony were on hand.

In order to qualify Sam as an expert in cypres and zagger safety, Henry questioned him about his engineering school background and his twelve years of experience in the cypres industry. Sam's testimony included an explanation to the jury that production of the new chattel required zaggers of a different size, shape, and hardness from those regularly used by The Firm.

When the special order for zaggers became the topic, the actual order was introduced into evidence. The fact that the original, rather than just a copy, was placed in evidence was because of the *best evidence* rule. This requires that proof of the contents of a writing be made through production of the writing itself. Where the terms of that writing are material, the original document must be produced except for good cause. The reason for this rule is apparent. Production of a writing results in much greater accuracy regarding its contents than can be expected from oral testimony based on memory. The requirement of an original eliminates the possibility for error or change connected with the copying process. Authentication of written documents is a usual prerequisite to their admission into evidence.

A related rule of evidence is the *parol evidence rule*. This does not permit oral (parol) testimony regarding variation or alteration of the terms of a written contract if the parties regard their writing as the final expression of their intentions. There are exceptions, such as in the case of fraud or typographical error.

"Your purchase order to Zagger Supply for the special zaggers specified they must comply with OSHA standards, did it not? " Henry asked Sam.

W. E. Just objected that Henry was leading the witness. Leading questions are those that suggest or contain the answer. They are not permitted on direct examination because they make it possible for the attorney, rather than the witness, to do the actual testifying by the way the lawyer frames his questions. However, such questions generally are permitted on cross-examination.

W. E. Just's objection was made at the time Henry asked the question. Objections must be made immediately when grounds for inadmissibility are apparent. Failure to object at the time an offer of evidence is made is a waiver of any complaint against its admission. If the attorney could wait until the trial had ended, the evidence would have been heard and taken into consideration by the jury and could constitute such error as to necessitate a new trial. In many jurisdictions, objections must be accompanied by a statement of reasons. These are noted on the trial record. The record stands and other reasons cannot be added at a later time, for example, when an appeal might be contemplated.

In this case, Judge Fairness sustained W. E. Just's objection. Henry then reworded the question to ask Sam to describe the zaggers covered by the purchase order. Sam referred to specifications on the order itself. Henry then requested Sam to read directly from the purchase order. The words were clear: the order was for zaggers that would "meet the standards promulgated by OSHA and the Zagger Institute."

Additional testimony by Sam regarding guards on the cypres machines, inspection of zaggers after purchase, and safety requirements at The Firm was much the same as that given at the taking of his deposition.

On cross-examination, Sam admitted that The Firm purchased primarily from Zagger Supply because of the quality and safety of its zaggers as compared with competitive brands. He also admitted that the zagger shattering record at The Firm was far below industry-wide figures for similar operations. He attributed this to the patented manufacturing process used by Zagger Supply. W. E. elicited from him the information that safety training programs at The Firm, which John Q. had attended several times, stressed the legal requirement in Great State for operation of a cypres machine only with the guard in place.

Timothy O'Goode was Henry's next witness. He testified that he had operated the cypres machine to the left of John Q.'s for the past ten years and that he had been selected to replace John Q. in the first production run of the new chattels. He duplicated testimony given at his deposition, stating that he complied with the directive to use special zaggers only when threatened with the loss of his job and that he had filed a complaint with the union because of fear for his safety in working with new zaggers.

When he said his fellow workers reported that technicians employed at Zagger Supply had told them the new zaggers were not safe, W. E. Just objected to this as hearsay. Judge Fairness sustained the objection and instructed the jury to disregard the statement. One of the more complex rules of evidence, the *hearsay rule,* excludes evidence that consists of what another person has said or written outside of the court when it is offered for the purpose of establishing the truth of what was said or written. The reason is that the person responsible for the out-of-court statement cannot be cross-examined regarding it to check its reliability. There are many exceptions to the hearsay rule, including spontaneous exclamations made at the time an event occurs (sometimes referred to as *res gestae*), admissions made by the other party, and entries made in the regular course of business in books of account.

On cross-examination, Timothy admitted he experienced no shattering incidents with new zaggers, that he had been able to cope with any clamping problems by using extra care in adjusting and placing the new zaggers on the machine. He did this, he testified, to prevent wobbling which could cause shattering at high speeds.

The direct examination of Peter Superior yielded no new information. On cross-examination, W. E. Just asked if he had used the special zagger during the preproduction trial period when Zagger Supply was working with personnel of The Firm in the design of the new zagger. His answer was in the affirmative. Asked if he had used them following the accident, he again answered "yes." He testified that he had demonstrated their use to Timothy O'Goode. W. E. Just then asked if he had experienced difficulties with shattering, fit, or anything else in their use. This time his answer was negative.

On redirect examination, Peter admitted to Henry that the only special zaggers he had used were those that had been prepared on prototypes. He had never used any from the manufacturing lot represented by the special order, not even in his demonstration for Timothy O'Goode.

A person acquainted with Professor Learned's deposition testimony would find his trial testimony repetitious. He told again of the bonding defects in the zagger fragments, how the defects could have been discovered by dynamic testing, and how they would cause shattering when the zagger was revolved at more than 2000 rpm. He maintained the position he had taken at the deposition that a guard could not have prevented the fatal injuries when there was such a violent and explosive shattering. He also reiterated his earlier contention that the accident would not have occurred had proper testing been done.

When W. E. asked him on cross-examination if improper mounting or clamping of a zagger could lead to wobbling and then shattering, his answer was the same as that in his deposition. The defense attorney did not allow that to go unchallenged. He referred to articles and pronouncements by others who the professor acknowledged to be experts and then asked if it was not true that Professor Learned's point of view was neither the prevailing nor the accepted one in the industry.

"It is the correct one," was the response; "popularity is not pertinent."

Repressing a smile, Henry on redirect asked about shattering caused by wobbling when zaggers were used at speeds in excess of those for which they had been tested. This meant, said Professor Learned, that the shattering was the result of improper speed and had nothing to do with improper mounting or clamping. When Henry asked if the zagger could have shattered following wobbling because of an incorrect size, the professor said it had been impossible to reconstruct the zagger from the fragments. Thus, taking measurements had been impossible. However, he added, if there had been a size defect, this would only bear out his conclusion that it was a defective zagger that was responsible for John Q.'s death.

On recross, W. E. asked if the professor meant to infer that a differential in size between regular and special zaggers constituted a defect.

"No," was the response. "There is a defect only when a discrepancy in size prevents a proper fit on the machine, and testing will reveal this."

With that, W. E. said: "Thank you, Professor Learned, that is all."

Henry called Mary Worker next. She testified regarding John Q.'s job, his salary, their children, his activities with and contributions to his family, estate expenses, personal and financial loss to the family resulting from his death. W. E. Just followed his pretrial plan to forego cross-examination of Mary.

With that, Henry rested.

W. E. Just then moved for a *directed verdict* for the defendant. Such a motion, in effect, asks the judge to take the case away from the jury. The judge has the power to do so. The power is properly exercised if the evidence is such that reasonable persons could not find for a party other than the one in whose favor the verdict has been directed. If Judge Fairness were to grant this motion, further evidence would not be put forth. Instead, the judge would instruct the jury to retire and return a verdict for the defendant in accordance with his directions. Judge Fairness, however, denied the motion. In his mind there was no question but that the plaintiff had met its burden of proof, clinching it, in his opinion, with Professor Learned's testimony.

In some state court systems and in federal nonjury trials, the proper motion at this time would have been for dismissal for failure to prove a prima facie case. It is sometimes referred to as a motion for a nonsuit. Such a motion is granted if the judge determines as a matter of law that the plaintiff has not presented sufficient evidence to prove his cause of action. While it is more usual to find the defense making the motion for a directed verdict or for a nonsuit after the plaintiff has rested, it is possible for the plaintiff to make these motions. If the plaintiff's motion were for a directed verdict, the motion would be granted only if reasonable persons could not find for the defendant. That would mean the plaintiff's case in chief had been so strong it was clear—even prior to the presentation of evidence by the defense—that it could not be rebutted. In those states where the plaintiff can move for a voluntary nonsuit, he does so when he finds his case has been so weak that it is to his advantage to seek dismissal without prejudice so that he can proceed at another time more effectively. This motion will not be granted if there has been lack of due diligence by counsel, since the effect of granting such a motion is that the matter is not *res judicata*. *Res judicata* means that the case has been adjudicated and may not be brought again.

DEFENDANT'S CASE IN DEFENSE

Since W. E. Just's motion for a directed verdict was not granted, it was now time for the defendant to present his case in defense. Trial procedure in this country gives the defendant the opportunity to present evidence to rebut the plaintiff's claim and in support of any affirmative defenses put forward. This follows the plaintiff's case in chief. Both the plaintiff and defendant follow the same process of examination with witnesses.

Preparation

W. E. Just's preparation for the case in defense required consideration of how best to controvert what he anticipated the plaintiff would present in the case in chief. One of W. E.'s first decisions was whether he should call any witnesses. In many cases the defense relies entirely on the weaknesses and limitations of the plaintiff's case in chief and on the doubts that can be cast upon credibility through cross-examination. Knowing that the plaintiff had evidence of a man's death and of a shattered zagger, W. E. decided that he could not rely upon inadequacy of the plaintiff's case. His decision, therefore, was to present a case in defense and, in accord with Will Very's wishes, to make the defense as strong as possible. Having made that decision, W. E. Just now had to consider how to present his case. He decided to call three witnesses: Charles Sell, the cypres engineer, and the zagger research engineer from Acme Labs. Charles Sell was an important witness since he could refute implications of a size defect and had first-hand knowledge of John Q.'s difficulty in working with the special zagger. He also had statistical data that W. E. Just hoped might have the effect of downplaying the lack of dynamic testing. The cypres engineer's contribution concerned John Q.'s failure to use a guard.

However, it was the Acme Labs researcher who held what W. E. considered to be the key item for the defense: evidence that the Zagger Supply process precluded violent shattering when there were bonding defects. These were the major defenses planned by W. E. He hoped they would be strong enough to overcome two major but undeniable factors unfavorable to the defendant: the bonding defect and lack of dynamic testing.

W. E. Just's next decision concerned the order in which he would call his witnesses. He realized that by the time they took the stand the jury would already have heard the plaintiff's case. That meant they would not only have some familiarity with the occurrences but also would have begun to form impressions about those events. Therefore, he believed the greatest impact would be made by building up to and ending with the witness who offered the strongest defense testimony. That would be the Acme Laboratories research engineer. W. E. also considered the fact that Charles Sell's testimony would lay the foundation for what the cypres engineer had to say. Therefore, he decided to call Charles Sell, the cypres engineer, and the Acme Labs engineer, in that order.

In preparing his witnesses for trial, W. E. was asked by the Acme Labs researcher about the possibility of videotaping his testimony beforehand. Attorney Just explained that the videotaping of testimony of witnesses (especially those called as experts), and presenting it on the screen in court, is practiced in some but not all jurisdictions. Some courts restrict its use to situations in which the witness will be unable to appear personally or is in such poor health as to be in danger of death before the trial. He added that some advocate a change to totally prerecorded videotaped testimony, filmed beforehand, at times and places that suit the convenience of witnesses and counsel. Others, he said, believe that taping denies the jury the opportunity to observe witnesses first-hand, can create distortions through such photographic effects as closeups, and destroys the psychological effect upon a witness of having to appear in person before judge and jury. The conversation turned to televising of the actual trial for public broadcast and information. W. E. explained that this generally is not permitted, because the presence of the camera and camera crew in the courtroom are distracting to those involved in the case. He commented on the need for dignity and restraint in a court of law so that a trial does not become a "three-ring circus."

However, the time for planning was now at an end. It was, instead, time for W. E. to call his first witness, the trial having already reached the last stage depicted in Figure 7-4 after having progressed through all of the preceding stages as shown in that flow chart.

Case in Defense

Charles Sell, as the first witness for the defense, testified that he and other company design engineers working on the development of the special

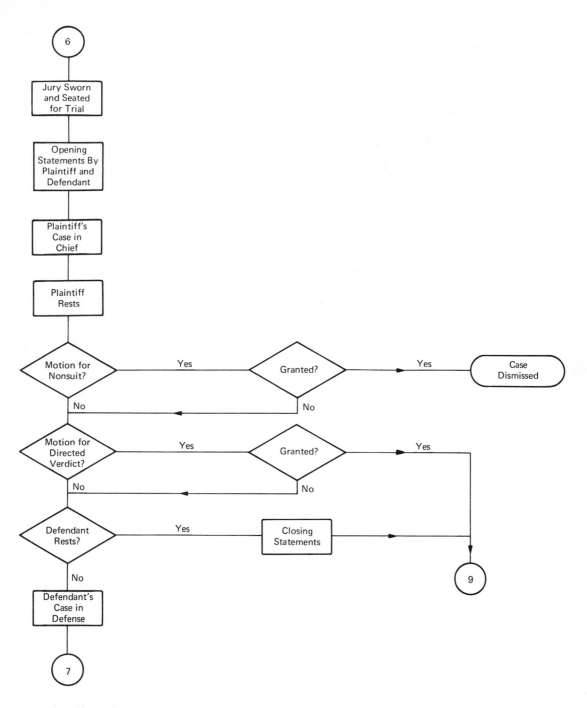

FIGURE 7-4. Trial: From Opening to Defendant's Case in Defense.

zagger had visited The Firm at least a dozen times testing prototypes. The latter had been used in trial runs of the new chattels on The Firm's cypres machines. Not only he and his engineers, but also Sam Scott, Jim Boss, and Peter Superior, had used the prototypes—all without incident. He further testified that John Q. had worked with this group during their last four sessions. John Q. had experienced difficulty in placing the special zagger prototype on the cypres machine and getting it clamped in place securely. In answer to Attorney Just's questions, Charles said that John Q. had been the only one in that group to have such trouble. Extra time had been spent working with John Q. until he appeared to have mastered the technique. Charles also testified that Timothy O'Goode, whom he was asked to train on the day after the accident, was able to adjust to the special zaggers immediately and without any of the difficulties John Q. had experienced.

Sell explained that a different clamping technique was necessary with the special zaggers. This resulted from the fact that a variation in zagger size was required for work on the new chattels. In response to W. E.'s question, Charles characterized the size differential as a necessary adjustment in design, not an imperfection.

On cross-examination, Charles admitted to Henry Law that the order for special zaggers specified conformity with OSHA standards, that dynamic testing was required to meet those standards, and that only six of the special zaggers shipped had been subjected to dynamic testing. Henry then elicited from him confirmation of the fact that size as well as bonding defects could be detected by such testing and that the reason for the testing requirement was prevention of shattering accidents. After that, Henry led an uncomfortable Charles through questioning that clearly conveyed the idea that Charles could not state with absolute certainty that the special zaggers, except for six, would not cause shattering due to dynamic-test detectable defects.

W.E. set out on redirect to "rehabilitate" his witness. Responding to questioning, Charles testified that each of the special zaggers shipped had been subjected to static testing, that this reveals ninety-five percent of the defective zaggers manufactured by the special patented Zagger Supply process, that the patented process resulted in bonding defects in approximately five out of every ten thousand zaggers manufactured, as contrasted with industry figures of five out of each thousand, that this meant dynamic testing was useful in finding defects in Zagger Supply products for only $\frac{1}{400}$ of one percent of the zaggers that they produced. He also testified that The Firm's order for special zaggers had gone through exactly the same production process as the prototypes, and that the latter had been tested and retested to an extent far beyond legal requirements and industry standards.

On recross, Henry Law asked if $\frac{1}{400}$ of one percent did not mean that there was an expectation of twenty-five defective zaggers in every one million produced. Charles Sell answered in the affirmative. Henry asked if it did not then follow that failure to use dynamic testing by a firm, such as Zagger Supply, which manufactured over one million zaggers in a year could cause twenty-five deaths annually due to shattering. W. E. Just was on his feet immediately, objecting strenuously to this question, pointing out that it was argumentative, conclusory, and based on an unproved assumption (that shattering inevitably caused and resulted in death). Judge Fairness sustained the objection. He instructed the jury to disregard it and Henry to withdraw it. Even with that, W. E. Just was concerned that the jury had heard the damaging remarks. Could the jurors really mentally disregard it, he asked himself. If Henry had intentionally asked an improper question for the express purpose of having the jury hear it, he would have acted unethically. Henry's apology for the question, however, seemed to be sincere and to indicate it had not been an intentional attempt to illicitly influence the jury.

W. E. Just's second witness, the cypres engineer, qualified as an expert through undergraduate and graduate study in cypres engineering and twenty years of experience as a cypres engineer. The last ten of these were with Zagger Supply, where his primary duties were design of zaggers for use on the cypres machines of that firm's customers. He confirmed Charles Sell's testimony about development of the special zagger, the prototype, and the training of John Q. He also testified regarding his part in the investigation of the accident. In viewing the accident scene and enlargements of the pictures taken immediately after the accident, he noted at all times the absence of the guard on John Q.'s machine. This, he said, was significant since improper placement of a zagger on a cypres machine makes it difficult to fit the guard in place. One of the reasons, he stated, for construction of cypres machine guards in such a manner is to encourage proper mounting of the zagger on the machine. He confirmed that wobbling results when there is improper placement of the zagger on the machine. Asked for his opinion of the cause of the accident, he said that based on absence of the guard and John Q.'s past difficulty in placement of the zagger on the machine, he believed the accident was caused by wobbling resulting from insecure clamping and improper mounting of the zagger on the machine.

On cross-examination, he did admit to Henry that "I cannot say it would never be impossible" for small zagger fragments to pass through the opening in the guard. When Henry asked if he knew, either directly or indirectly, of any cases of shattering where there was wobbling following improper clamping of a zagger which had been subjected to dynamic testing, his response was:

"No, there have been no reported shatterings with dynamically tested zaggers."

He would not agree with Henry, however, that this proved Professor Learned's contention that improper mounting could not, of itself, be the cause of shattering. He stated that, in his opinion, insufficient time had elapsed since the testing requirement went into effect to have the necessary experience to make such a statement or to prove that the testing would eliminate all shatterings.

Henry then asked if a bonding defect alone could not cause shattering. The engineer replied that a bonding defect could not, in his opinion, have caused the accident which occurred to John Q. Henry responded that that was not what he had asked. He then restated his query as to whether a bonding defect could result in shattering. When the reply was "Yes," Henry Law prevented the engineer's obvious desire to elaborate and explain further.

He simply said:

"Thank you. That is all."

W. E. Just followed up on redirect by asking if, in the engineer's opinion, the violent shattering which had occurred in this case could have resulted from a bonding defect. The answer was: "No. The Zagger Supply process prevents explosive shattering."

The research engineer from Acme Labs qualified as an expert with graduate study in both the cypres and zagger areas and sixteen years of experience in researching the causes of zagger shattering. W. E. Just was careful to point out for the jury the credentials of his witnesses as one means of counteracting the impact of Professor Learned's appearance for the plaintiff.

The Acme Labs researcher testified that he had performed tests on the zagger fragments involved in the John Q. Worker accident at the request of Zagger Supply. He had found bonding defects in the zagger, but he believed that these could not have caused the accident. He testified that the violent shattering that had occurred could have been caused only by wobbling of the zagger while it was being operated at high speeds—in excess of 2000 rpm. This conclusion, he said, was based upon his research studies regarding zagger shatterings that included testing of over one thousand shattered zaggers over a five-year period. These tests included every shattered zagger manufactured by the patented Zagger Supply process, as well as hundreds of shattered zaggers of other manufacturers. His research revealed that the Zagger Supply process resulted in fewer bonding defects. Furthermore, those Zagger Supply products which did have bonding defects did not shatter with an explosive force or in the violent manner connected with the John Q. Worker incident.

Henry followed up, on cross-examination, by asking if the wobbling to which the witness had referred could not have been caused by a size defect in the zagger.

"I have no basis for stating that the zagger was defective with regard to size," was the reply.

He did admit that a size defect could cause wobbling and also acknowledged that size defects commonly accompany bonding defects.

Henry continued, asking if dynamic testing could not have been a factor in the infrequent explosive shatterings of Zagger Supply products. The witness acknowledged that it might have been, since Zagger Supply had voluntarily been doing such testing on random production runs even before the testing was made a requirement.

Continuing with the cross-examination, Henry wanted to know if the research work and testing of zagger fragments at Acme Labs had not been paid for by Zagger Supply and other zagger manufacturers. The answer was that each firm paid for the research it wished to have done.

W. E. Just did not like that last question or its implications. Therefore, on redirect examination he re-established through questioning that Acme Labs, as an independent entity, provided its clientele with an impartial, disinterested means of research regarding their products.

"Has the independence and objectivity of the work done at Acme Labs ever received public recognition? " he asked.

"Yes," answered the engineer, who testified further that the latest such recognition was in an article in the July 19XX issue of the *Zagger Journal.*

"And," asked W. E. Just, "who was the author of that article?"

"Professor Ira Learned," was the reply.

"That is all."

W. E. Just turned to Henry, who, realizing what had happened to his attempt to discredit the testimony of the last witness, had no wish to engage in recross-examination.

With that, W. E. Just rested.

It was now Henry Law who made a motion for a directed verdict. It was denied. Judge Fairness could find no reason to grant such a motion. In his mind, the evidence was sufficiently contradictory to require submission of the case to the jury.

PLAINTIFF'S EVIDENCE IN REBUTTAL

At this point, Henry had to decide if he wished to present plaintiff's evidence in rebuttal. After the defendant rests, the plaintiff has the option of calling new witnesses or recalling those who had testified previously. He is, however, limited to refuting evidence introduced by the defendant. The same process is followed with witnesses as for the case in chief. At the conclusion, the plaintiff's attorney announces that he closes.

Henry decided to forego this stage. He believed that the defense had introduced no evidence that he had not anticipated and already refuted through his earlier witnesses. Any plaintiff's evidence, in his opinion, would now be mere repetition of matters presented in the case in chief.

DEFENDANT'S EVIDENCE IN REJOINDER

Henry's decision eliminated another trial stage: the defendant's evidence in rejoinder. If the plaintiff on rebuttal brings up new points, the defendant has the option of calling witnesses in rejoinder to those matters. He follows the same procedure as with prior witnesses. The defense counsel indicates that he closes at the conclusion of this stage. These proceedings that would have been possible in the trial following the defendant's case in defense have been flow charted in Figure 7-5. Notice the consequences of any of these occurrences.

CLOSING ARGUMENTS

After each attorney has closed his case, final or closing arguments follow. Each attorney is given the opportunity to review for the jury (or the judge in nonjury trials) important evidence and to state again the arguments and contentions in favor of his client. As with the opening statements, these do not constitute evidence. Generally the plaintiff, who is given the first word in the opening statements, is given the last word in the closing arguments. These are sometimes referred to as *closing statements,* the term used in Figure 7-6, which brings the charting of trial stages up to that point.

Defendant's Close

W. E. Just believed he had an advantage in being able to follow the testimony of defense witnesses with his closing argument to the jury. He felt this would serve as a reinforcement for what the jury had just heard. He told the jurors that the real question in this trial was not whether there was a bonding defect in the zagger, but whether the defectiveness of the product had been the cause of John Q.'s death. He reminded them that they had heard from an expert in zagger shatter research, one with vast experience regarding shattering accidents. The same expert, he said, had stated under oath that in his opinion the bonding defect could not have caused the kind of explosive shattering that resulted in John Q.'s death. According to that expert, the bonding defect alone could have caused no more than a mild shattering. He also recalled the testimony about insufficient time having elapsed since inception of the testing requirement to prove that it could completely eliminate shatterings.

Attorney Just reminded the jurors that they had heard testimony not only from the cypres engineers, but also from plaintiff's witnesses who were cypres operators, about the importance of proper placement and clamping of the zagger on the machine, the wobbling resulting from an improper clamping, the fact that this wobbling when combined with high speeds caused violent shattering. He reminded them of accident pictures they had been shown, pictures which revealed that John Q. did not have the guard in position. He recalled that there was testimony by the cypres engineer that an improper placement of the zagger on the machine makes it difficult to position the guard in place. In addition, there was testimony that John Q. had experienced difficulty during training sessions with properly mounting the zagger on his machine. He reminded them that size differences were necessary adjustments in design, not defects. W. E. suggested to the jury there had been sufficient evidence presented to show it was not any defect in the zagger, but rather improper placement of the zagger on the machine—operator failure—which had caused the accident resulting in John Q.'s death.

He reminded them that John Q. was an experienced operator, one who knew he was working with a potentially hazardous instrumentality. Yet, John Q. worked without a guard. Further, there was testimony of a general air of exuberance in the plant that day, a factor that could have precluded John Q.'s full concentration on the job at hand. Finally, he suggested that after careful consideration of all this evidence they, the jurors, would find it indicated very clearly that the defendant should prevail for two reasons: first, John Q.'s accident and resulting death had not been caused by any defect in the zagger; second, John Q. had knowingly and voluntarily assumed any and all risks attached to use of the zagger on the cypres machine.

Plaintiff's Close

It was now Henry Law's turn. He began by stating that this was, indeed, a case of a defective product that had caused a working man's death. He told the jury that John Q. was not the bumbling, incompetent, careless operator his opponent attempted to portray. Instead, John Q. was known to his fellow workers as an extremely careful and skilled worker. In fact, his superiors testified that they had selected him to be the first cypres operator to work on the new chattels for that very reason. He reminded the jurors that this man had not had a prior accident in his twenty-three years with The Firm. If John Q. had some difficulty in working with the new zagger, wouldn't any reasonable person consider this natural on a first attempt? Perhaps it was due to size differences, he suggested, and noted that Professor Learned had testified regarding them.

Henry reminded the jury there had been five other accidents with the special zaggers. "Why?" he asked. Answering his own question, Henry said it was because those zaggers did not meet federal safety standards—legal requirements that had been adopted for the very purpose of preventing accidents such as this one which had resulted in the death of an experienced employee. He reminded the jurors that the foremost zagger authority in

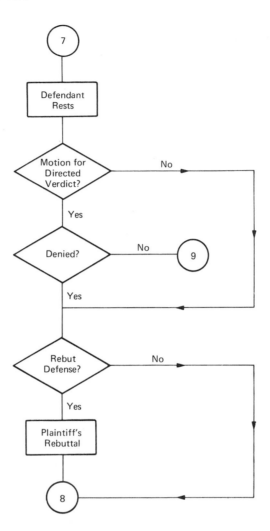

FIGURE 7-5. Trial: From Defendant's Rest to Plaintiff's Rebuttal.

the country, one of the authors of those standards, had testified as to the reasons for promulgating them. That same authority had tested fragments from the shattered zagger and formed the opinion that test-detectable defects had caused the accident.

Finally, he urged the jury to consider all the testimony carefully. He asked that the jury members use their experience in living and their common sense in determining the truth and arriving at a verdict. As a final word he added:

"I am sure you will find that the correct resolution of this issue must be in the plaintiff's favor."

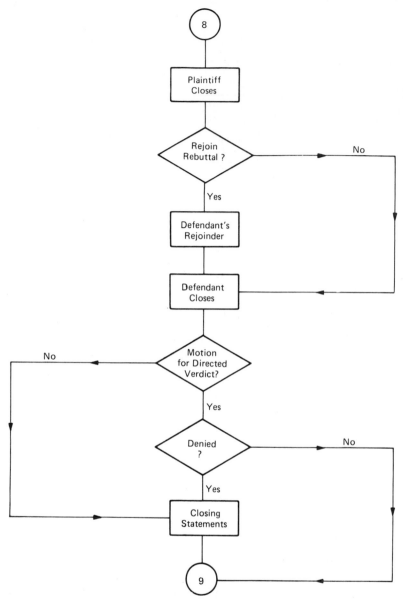

FIGURE 7-6. Trial: From Plaintiff's Close to Closing Statements.

JUDGE'S CHARGE TO THE JURY

At this point in a jury trial, it is the judge's turn to talk with the jury. This stage is referred to as the *charge to the jury* or *jury instructions* since the judge explains the applicable law.   He may review some of the testimony and in some courts, including the federal system, he has the right to comment on it.

Requested and Pattern Instructions

Each attorney may present to the judge matters to be included in the jury instructions. The requested instructions are often submitted in writing to the judge. Some courts have *pattern instructions;* that is, model jury charges prepared by committees of judges and lawyers. Some jurisdictions require use of the pattern instructions exactly as prepared, while others consider them to be guidelines only. Proponents of pattern instructions assert that not only is there a saving of judicial time, but also greater accuracy, impartiality, and uniformity in jury instructions when patterns are used. Critics allege that pattern instructions, when available, tend to be given verbatim and decrease the probability of instructions' being adapted to fit the case at hand.

Both Henry and W. E. submitted to Judge Fairness requested points for inclusion in the instructions to the jury. After studying them, the judge decided not to use any of them. He believed that Henry's points for charge would lead the jurors to feel they must find for the plaintiff automatically if the defendant had violated OSHA standards. On the other hand, he thought that W. E.'s points would burden the plaintiff with an almost impossible standard of proof of causation. Judge Fairness desired the instructions he used to be not only a correct statement of the applicable law but also to be as objective as possible. He conferred with the two attorneys regarding their requests for instruction. He did this prior to the closing arguments and in his chambers, off the record, and out of the jury's hearing.

Effectiveness of Instruction

The instructions he finally prepared and delivered consisted of twenty-four pages of double-spaced material. There has been much discussion of jury instructions. Some allege the instructions are confusing to the jury, worded in legal terminology not easily comprehended by the lay person, so lengthy and detailed that a jury cannot be expected to remember even the major points. Still others point out that the law is explained to the jury only after the jurors have heard all the evidence, the implication being that the jury could listen more effectively to testimony if instructed at the outset of the trial. The contrary view is that earlier instructions would influence or prejudice the jury and could cause jurors to mentally discard important matters. Still others lament the fact that some judges have been known to read jury instructions in a rapid monotone, so that even the most conscientious of jurors finds it hopeless to follow. Judge Fairness, however, did not do this.

Jury Charge

The judge began by telling the jury members that they would be the sole judges of the facts. He explained they must pass on the credibility of witnesses, should not be influenced by any sympathy or prejudice they might feel regarding the parties, must base their verdict entirely on the evidence, i.e., testimony of witnesses, documents and exhibits admitted into evidence.

He then reviewed some of the facts of the case. Judge Fairness said that there was no dispute about the fact that the shattering accident had occurred, that John Q. had been killed, that the special zagger had been manufactured and sold by the defendant, that a bonding defect existed, that the required dynamic testing had not been done, and that the guard had not been in place on John Q.'s machine. Both the testing and the guard matters, he said, represented failure by the respective parties to comply with legal requirements. He explained that the plaintiff contended that defects in the zagger caused the shattering that resulted in John Q.'s death. On the other hand, he said, the defendant contended that death was caused not by any defect in the product but by the deceased's actions in connection with placing the zagger on the machine and then using it without a guard.

He explained to the jury the five questions the jurors would be required to answer. Those questions are listed in Table 7-1.

TABLE 7-1. Questions submitted to jury in Mary Worker case.

1. Was the accident that occurred on August 28, 19XX and which resulted in the fatal injuries to John Q. Worker caused by a defective zagger which he was using at the time?

   Answer YES or NO _____

2. Was that defective condition in existence when the zagger was sold by Zagger Supply, Inc.?

   Answer YES or NO _____

3. Did John Q. Worker use the special zagger knowing the risks involved and voluntarily assuming those risks?

   Answer YES or NO _____

4. What were the damages sustained by the estate of John Q. Worker as a result of his death?

   $ _____

5. What were the damages sustained by the family of John Q. Worker as a result of his death?

   $ _____

Judge Fairness then went on to explain strict liability in tort for a defective product, quoting to the jury from §402A. He described proximate cause as "that cause which, in a natural and continuous sequence, unbroken by any intervening cause, produces the result complained of and without which the result would not have occurred—in other words, a substantial contributing factor in bringing about the result complained of."

He told the jury that the mere happening of an accident did not in and of itself raise a presumption that anyone was liable as a matter of law, that the plaintiff had the burden of establishing by a preponderance of the evidence that there had been a defective product and that it was a proximate cause of John Q.'s death. He said if the jurors did not find this to be so, they need proceed no further. Their verdict would be for the defendant. On the other hand, if they found in the affirmative, they must determine whether John Q. had voluntarily undertaken the task at hand knowing the risks involved and proceeding regardless of those risks. He explained that this constituted a complete defense. Therefore, if they found this to be so, they need go no further. If not, they must proceed to the final two questions. He reviewed for them the bills for estate expenses that had been entered into evidence and also discussed John Q.'s age, salary, and expected work life. Turning to counsel, he asked if they had any points they believed the court should have covered and did not. If so, he asked them to state those now.

Henry Law requested a side bar conference to be recorded by the court reporter. He and W. E. Just both objected to the court's denial of their requests for items to be included in the charge. Judge Fairness again refused, stating his reasons. The attorneys wanted this on the record, since errors in jury instructions can constitute the basis for an appeal.

The judge then turned to the jury. He told the jurors he had concluded the charge and that it was now time for them to retire and deliberate.

He reminded them again that a unanimous verdict was necessary. He excused jurors seven and eight and thanked them for their services. He also asked if counsel objected to having the exhibits which had been admitted into evidence go out with the jury. There was no objection. The jury retired.

Verdicts

Judge Fairness had given the jury five questions to answer. This is referred to as a special verdict. In the federal courts, the judge has discretion to request either a general or special verdict. A *general verdict* is one that requires the jury to decide in favor of one of the parties and, if damages have been sought, to indicate the sum of money to be awarded. A *special verdict* is one that requires answers to specific interrogatories, such as those given to the jury in this case. Advocates of the special verdict maintain that it has the advantage of providing rationale in support of the jury's decision. This is, of course, lacking in a general verdict. The federal rules also give the judge discretion to request a combined special and general verdict; that is, answers to specific questions as well as indication of the party in whose favor the jury finds.

Problems have arisen in cases in which juries returned answers to special interrogatories that were inconsistent with each other or with the general verdict on the combined ballot. In such cases, the judge may enter judgment based upon consistencies he finds within the special interrogatories, he may send the matter back to the jury, or he may order a new trial.

Note that Judge Fairness also instructed the jury to return a unanimous verdict. The federal rules provide that the parties may stipulate that the finding of a stated majority shall be taken as the verdict. That was not done in this case, because W. E. Just would not agree to it. Some states provide for less than a unanimous verdict in their rules of procedure.

JURY DELIBERATIONS AND VERDICT

Following Judge Fairness' charge, the jury was escorted from the courtroom to a conference room where the jury members would deliberate in private. No other persons, including court officials, are permitted in the jury room during this process. All contact with the outside is through the *tipstaff,* who is summoned to notify the judge once the jury reaches a verdict. If the jurors find the need for additional instruction, they may send a message to the judge, who can provide such information to them in open court. Transcripts of depositions or of the testimony during the trial itself are not available to them. In many states they are not permitted to take notes during the trial. Therefore, their deliberations are based upon their recollection of the testimony given during the trial. They normally have available in the jury room materials that have been entered into evidence. Exceptions are possible where undue influence might result.

Inside the jury room, the chairperson, Nancy Perkins, suggested that they might begin by voting on the five questions they had to answer. Adam Frank said he would prefer to vote later, after they had an opportunity to discuss some of the testimony.

"Especially," he added, "what the professor and the engineers had to say about what caused the accident. If I believe the professor, it's the company's fault this man was killed and his widow should win this case. But, if I believe the engineers, then it's his own fault he was killed. I don't know what to believe. It's confusing."

"There's no problem," said Sam Wells. "Here's a working man who was killed on the job, and his widow is suing the big corporation that manufactured the zagger he was using which exploded. Any zagger that explodes isn't safe to use. That corporation knows it. They even skipped the tests they're supposed to do."

"That's right," Kathleen Logan interrupted. "They broke the law."

"But why did he use it—and without a guard? He broke the law, too," said Nancy Perkins.

"What chance did he have?" was Geraldine Horne's response. "You heard what that younger man said about being forced to use it or lose his job."

"Right," said Sam. "It's just the same with the truck I drive. I tell the foreman the tires are bald and he says, 'Use it; use it; they're not that bad.' They wait for a major breakdown before they take it out of service. It costs less. These big companies are all the same. You want a job, you do what they say."

"But surely not something that would kill a man," said Nancy.

"What do they care?" asked Sam. "All they're interested in is how much money they'll make. And if a man gets killed, they go out and hire some engineer who says it's the man's own fault."

"But I thought that last engineer made a lot of sense," said Adam.

"Of course," said Sam. "Why do you think they hired him? They're not going to put someone on the stand who'll say it's all their fault."

"I feel so sorry for that Mrs. Worker," said Kathleen Logan. "With five children to raise. It's such a pity."

"What's worse is that this never should have happened. When a man has to use a zagger in his work, he should be given one that won't explode." Martin Lee spoke for the first time.

"Well, a man should have safe equipment with which to work, I agree," said Adam.

"You're right," replied Sam. "And when he gets killed because he doesn't have it, the company ought to pay. They can afford it."

"Of course," said Geraldine. "Besides, they're insured. Everyone knows that. The insurance company will pay."

"That's the wrong attitude," said Adam. "That's why insurance costs so much these days."

Because it appeared that the two were going to debate the insurance issue, Nancy interrupted to ask if they were ready to vote. Adam still hesitated, but the others said they had made their decision. Finally, Kathleen suggested that they take a first vote to see how close they were to agreement. They could always continue their discussion if the vote indicated it was necessary. That sounded reasonable, and Adam acquiesced.

Nancy read from the verdict ballot the first question, which asked if the accident had been caused by a dangerously defective zagger. They were surprised to find that all had voted in the affirmative. The second question, which asked if the defect existed at the time the zagger was sold, also received a unanimous vote of "yes." It was the third question, which was concerned with whether John Q. had assumed the risk, on which they did not agree. Adam and Nancy voted yes.

"We have to be unanimous," said Nancy.

"Yes," said Martin. "The last jury I was on was a hung jury." In answer to Sam's query he added, "That means the jury's deadlocked. When we reported that to the judge, he declared a mistrial and the same case was tried all over again with another jury."

Kathleen interrupted, addressing Nancy and Adam: "I don't see how you can think a man would intentionally do something that would kill him. That's just like committing suicide."

"But he wasn't using the guard," said Nancy.

"That was probably accidental. We all do things like that at one time or another."

"Even so, that means he caused the accident himself," Nancy replied.

"Read the question again," said Geraldine. "It says he knew the risks and voluntarily assumed them. That's different from being careless."

Nancy reread the question aloud:

"Did John Q. Worker use the special zagger knowing the risks involved and voluntarily assuming those risks?"

"You're right," she said. "I'll change my vote."

"And so will I," said Adam.

It was in this way that they arrived at unanimity with regard to the third question. The two remaining questions dealt with damages. To arrive at the sum to be awarded, they added the bills that had been introduced into evidence and arrived at $4,891.23. It was no quite so easy for them to determine the damages to be awarded for the family. They computed John Q.'s expected salary for the next twenty-three years, but Kathleen was vehement in wanting to add an additional amount as compensation for his unexpected death. This provoked a heated discussion, and they finally agreed on the sum of $300,000.

It had taken them approximately two and a half hours. Nancy completed the verdict ballot, they all signed it, and then summoned the tipstaff to announce they had reached a verdict.

When they returned to the courtroom, the members of the jury were asked if they had reached a verdict. Nancy answered for them that they had. The verdict was read from the ballot by the clerk. W. E. Just asked that the jury be polled. The judge honored that request, and each juror affirmed the verdict.

POST-VERDICT MOTIONS AND JUDGMENT

While the work of the jury was completed and the members could be dismissed, the Mary Worker case was far from being over. Henry Law, as might be expected, was eager for the court to enter judgment in accordance with the verdict. *Judgment* is the decree and order of the court, indicating the successful party and stating the relief to which he is entitled. The judgment is the official decision of the court. It may or may not coincide with the verdict.

The federal rules provide that, in addition to the damages recovered, costs may be allowed to the prevailing party. Costs refer to fees paid to the court and do not include attorney's fees. (Other countries provide that the losing party must pay for the counsel fees of the successful party.)

W. E. Just, on the other hand, would forego no opportunity to win the case. He indicated to the judge that he would file a written motion with the court to have the verdict set aside. This motion is for a *judgment n.o.v.*;[6] that is, judgment notwithstanding the verdict. The motion is properly granted if reasonable persons could not differ on the fact that the jury returned a verdict against the weight of the evidence. This motion is often joined with one for a new trial. Granting a new trial requires a showing of cause, such as error committed during the course of the trial, or some new evidence. It is not intended to provide a losing party with the opportunity to bring a second lawsuit against the same party for the same claim. That would be a violation of the principle of *res judicata,* which, translated, literally means "the matter has been decided." This doctrine is based upon the premise that an individual should be given a fair opportunity to have his controversy decided by a court. Once that occurs, there must be an end to litigation. If not, the same parties would be able to retry the same case *ad infinitum.* The exception occurs when there has been error, in which case there is the right to appeal.

Since the federal rules provide that the motion for judgment n.o.v. must be made no later than ten days after entry of judgment, W. E. Just wasted no time. He set to work immediately after deciding he would ask in the alternative for a new trial. The possible outcomes of such motions are shown in Figure 7-7, which flow charts steps in the trial beginning with the jury instructions. Note the difference in motions possible when there is a jury trial as compared with a nonjury trial. The latter are shown in Figure 7-8.

In support of his motions, W. E. Just gave the following rationale:

1. The plaintiff failed to meet his burden of proving (a) that a defect in the product was the proximate cause of the accident; (b) that the product at the time of the accident was being used as intended, i.e., properly mounted and clamped on a machine with a guard. Therefore, the court erred in permitting the case to go to the jury or, in the alternative, in not properly instructing the jury regarding these matters.

2. The verdict was clearly against the weight of the evidence. The evidence was uncontradicted that the plaintiff's deceased operated the cypres machine without a guard; thus he knowingly and

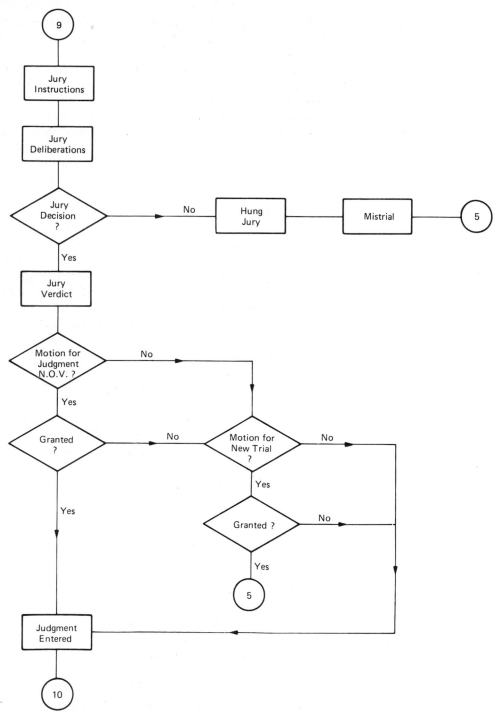

FIGURE 7-7. Trial: From Jury Instructions to Entry of Judgment.

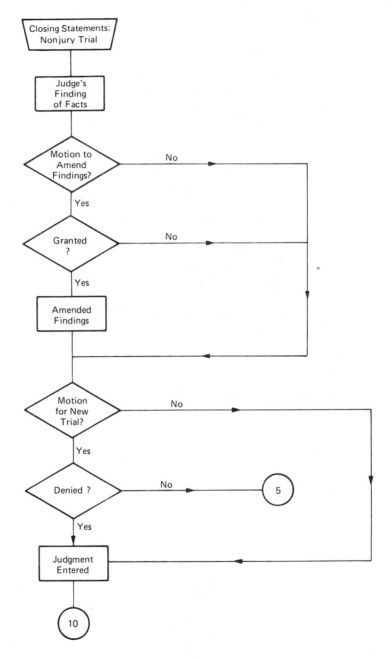

FIGURE 7-8. Nonjury Trial: Closing Statement to Entry of Judgment.

voluntarily exposed himself to a clear danger and assumed the risk of his acting.

3. The damages awarded were excessive.

W. E. filed these motions with the clerk of court. When such motions are made and granted following entry of judgment, that judgment may be reopened and either a new judgment entered or a new trial ordered. Henry Law, who had to tell Mary Worker she would not receive immediate payment of the sum voted by the jury and that there was the prospect of a reversal of that verdict as a result of a post-trial motion, also received a copy of the motions Attorney Just had filed. He prepared replies asking that the motions not be granted.

Judge Fairness, the trial still vivid in his memory, decided the jury's verdict would stand, entered judgment in accordance with it, and denied the defendant's motion. The reasons he gave were as follows:

1. There was sufficient evidence from Professor Learned from which a jury could reasonably conclude that the defective zagger was the cause of the accident.

2. The evidence was uncontradicted that the zagger was being used at the time of the accident for the purpose for which it was intended, i.e., on The Firm's cypres machine in the production of new chattels. Testimony of defendant's experts indicated that lack of a guard and improper mounting were conditions not only reasonably foreseeable but actually known to the defendant to exist at times in general

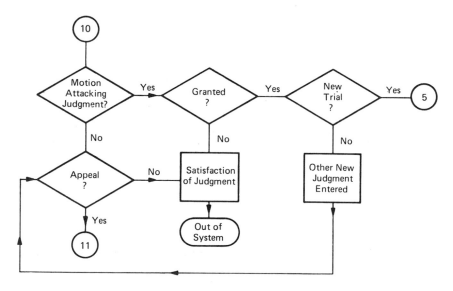

FIGURE 7-9. Post-Judgment Action.

usage. Therefore, the defendant could not claim that these conditions were outside the sphere of intended use.

3. Whether the plaintiff's deceased had voluntarily exposed himself to a clear and known danger was a conclusion of fact, to be determined by the jury from all the testimony and not just those portions cited in the defendant's brief. There having been contradictory evidence by plaintiff's and defendant's experts, different conclusions could reasonably be reached as to whether the danger was clear and known to the plaintiff's deceased.

4. The sums awarded as damages were consistent with the testimony of Mary Worker, both as to estate expenses and her late husband's expected life earnings.

Only to his wife did Judge Fairness reveal that he believed reasonable persons could have arrived at different conclusions in this case.

With entry of the judgment in favor of Mary Worker, the case would be concluded, as shown in Figure 7-9, when the defendant made payment in accordance with that judgment. This is referred to as *satisfaction of the judgment*. However, Zagger Supply had no inclination to make payment at this point. Instead, Will Very was adamant about pursuing the matter further. Since W. E. Just believed there was sufficient cause to allege error, the defense would pursue the alternate course shown in Figure 7-9 by appeal to a higher court. What occurred in the appellate court is discussed in the next chapter.

QUESTIONS

An interesting aspect of the Mary Worker case involves the fact that Judge Fairness, although privately believing differing conclusions are possible, upholds the jury verdict for the plaintiff. Why did he do so? Should he have granted a new trial? W. E.'s request for a directed verdict? Is W. E. correct in his contention that causation has not been proved? Why?

Have the parties in this case each received a fair trial? Has each received justice? Does a losing party ever feel that justice was done?

Considering all the evidence, was either party either all right or all wrong? Do you believe this is typical? If so, how can a jury arrive at a decision?

What is your reaction to the events that took place in the jury deliberation room? Did this jury adequately tackle the task before it? Did the members discuss the real issues in the case? Give reasons for your answer. Has its verdict been unduly influenced by matters extraneous to the trial? If so, what are they? Have you ever served on a jury? How does your experience compare with that reported here? Does this jury's action have any implications for education for jury service? for professional juries? If so, what are they?

A judge's power to enter a judgment n.o.v. gives him yet another opportunity to take a verdict away from a jury. What other opportunities does he have for doing so? Does this give him too much discretionary power? Is it necessary power? Is there any control over its possible abuse? If so, what is that?

Considering the total effort that has gone into this case so far and anticipating that which is yet to come, do you believe this is a matter which should be resolvable in some other way? How? Should there be a "no-fault" products liability law? Why?

Does Zagger Supply really have a good cause to appeal this case? What hope do you believe they might have for success? Would you have appealed? Why? Having the benefit of hindsight, what do you believe W. E. Just could have done differently that would have won the case for the defendant?

The rules of evidence were a factor during the trial several times. In each instance, did the rules help in securing a fair trial for both parties? In what way? Does your exposure to just a few of the rules of evidence give any clue as to the amount of procedural law that must be almost second nature to the trial lawyer? Does it imply anything for those who sometimes wish to serve as their own lawyer? Can you see any difference in the work of a trial lawyer and the attorney who does not engage in trial work?

What has been the role of Judge Fairness in this trial? Has he given any direction to it? If so, in what way?

CASE

Newman v. Los Angeles Transit Lines
262 P.2d 95 (District Court of Appeals, California, 1953)

Action by street car passenger against transit corporation for injuries allegedly sustained in fall caused by jerking of streetcar while passenger was alighting therefrom. The Superior Court of Los Angeles County entered judgment based upon a unanimous verdict rejecting plaintiff's suit for damages for personal injuries, and passenger appealed.

MOORE, Presiding Justice. . . . since the sufficiency of the evidence to support the verdict is not in question, the assignments of error will be discussed in the order presented.

The first assignment is the court's overruling appellant's general objection to the following question propounded to her on cross-examination: "Mrs. Newman, have you ever had a feeling of having a persecution complex?" To which she answered: "I don't." It is not improper to develop any feeling of antagonism or animosity of a witness toward a party. But if such ruling had been error, it could have caused no prejudice since the answer was favorable to appellant. . . .

She complains of the court's adverse ruling on her general objection to the question: "Have you ever accused anybody of spying on you continuously?" She answered that "all kinds of attempts at frameups. . . ." The answer revealed the workings of her mind as intended by the inquisitor. With her own statement about frame-ups against her before the jury, they were more nearly able to weigh her testimony. By means of developing the situation of appellant with respect to her adversary, her interest, her motives, her inclination and prejudices, her powers of discernment and description, the cross-examiner placed the witness in her true light before the jury. Her answer showed that by reason of her suspicions she had created a steel barrier of hate against her adversary. It is a rule of universal application that a witness may be required to answer any question which tends to test his accuracy, veracity or credibility and especially in the case of a party to the action where he appears as a witness. . . . Great latitude should be allowed in developing the existence of bias. . . . Liberal cross-examination is the rule. . . . But appellant made no specific objection to the question asked her. An adverse ruling upon a general objection is never the basis for a reversal except in those instances where the testimony elicited is not admissible upon any ground whatsoever. . . .

Appellant complains that an extraneous, immaterial issue was injected by respondent's asking her: "Is Communism behind this?". . . . Not only was no objection made to such question, nor motion made to forbid their repetition, but appellant appears to have relished the inquiry as another opportunity for denouncing the motorman and all who were opposing her lawsuit. . . .

Appellant contends that it was error for the court over her objection to permit "a demonstration of the mechanical operation of the steps on the streetcar No. 1536; that it was three years after the alleged accident and with a different and skilled operator. . . .

Whether the court should grant the application for a view of a mechanical device whose operation was allegedly the cause of an accident is peculiarly within the discretion of the court. . . . No proof was made that the car used for the demonstration or that the manner of opening the doors was at all different from the condition of the device three years before. No other objection can on appeal be considered. . . .

Appellant assigns as error the conduct of the trial judge in "permitting two jurors to sleep during most of the trial." There is no record to support such assignment. Not an objection was made; not a request by appellant for the court to reprove somnolescent jurors. . . . But if two jurors had slept throughout the trial, no prejudice was suffered. The jury returned a unanimous verdict, whereas the law required only three-fourths of the jury to return a valid verdict. . . . Finally, not only is there no proof of the presence of the sleeping jurors, but at no time did the trial judge observe such phenomenon.

Appellant asserts that she was excluded from the view of the demonstration of the streetcar doors and steps and also that at the demonstration respondent's witnesses were allowed to make statements in the hearing of the jury. In support thereof she claims further that the reporter's transcript is incorrect in its report of the events that transpired.

The transcript, once settled and approved, cannot be impeached by charges contained in a brief. . . . Inasmuch as error is not to be presumed, but must affirmatively appear in the record, it must be held that the criticized acts did not occur. No objection is found in the record to any ruling of the court and there is no evidence that appellant was excluded from the demonstration or that it was suggested. The presumption is that the incidents of the trial occurred as reported.

Error is assigned in that appellant witness, Mrs. Suchman, was not permitted to testify after having been sworn. After respondent had rested, appellant called in rebuttal Mrs. Provin. The latter testified concerning the behavior of appellant after December 19, 1948. Thereupon, it was stipulated that the testimony of Mrs. Suchman would be substantially the same as that of Mrs. Provin. Since the need for the lady's testimony had disappeared, counsel for appellant did not call her. By reason of the fact that an attorney is agent of his client and is empowered to conduct the cause during its pendency, . . . his agreements with reference to calling or excusing a witness are binding upon his client. . . .

Assignment is made that the court admitted the "hearsay" testimony of witnesses Lacy and Spencer. . . . The complaint is too late. No objection was made during the entire examination of these gentlemen. Therefore, error cannot be effectively asserted in the absence of objection to the introduction of the evidence. . . . Having failed to object at the trial, objection to evidence cannot for the first time be interposed in the appellate court.

Because the deposition of witness Prutsman gave two different times of day for the arrival of car No. 1536, appellant charges error in the court's receiving same. Such deposition was read into evidence by appellant's counsel, not by respondent. An appellant cannot base his appeal on the admission of testimony which was read to the jury by his own counsel. . . . Moreover, inconsistencies do not render testimony inadmissible. Such matters are to be resolved by the trial court. . . .

The court gave the following instruction:

"If, prior to the trial, the deposition of a party to the action was taken, and if all or part of it was read into evidence, and if, in said deposition she made contradictory statement or statements in conflict with her testimony here in court, you may consider such conflicts, and any explanation given therefore, in testing her credibility, in like manner as if all such testimony were given originally at the trial. The deposition, too, was given under oath. Also, if any statement in a party's deposition constituted an admission against interest, it may be considered in determining the truth or falsity thereof as well as in judging her credibility."

Notwithstanding that correctness of the foregoing is not questioned, appellant claims it is prejudicial error because it "singles out the plaintiff for the giving of the instruction and does not make it a general instruction applicable to all persons* * *" The fact is that it concerns and is limited to "the deposition of a party to the action." Appellant is the only party who gave a deposition. The instructions which preceded . . . were general and applied to witnesses as well as to depositions of witnesses, setting forth the rules that in judging credibility, a witness is presumed to speak the truth; that such presumption may be overcome by contradictory evidence, by the manner of testifying, by the character of his testimony or by evidence that pertains to his motives; that a witness false in one part of his testimony is to be disregarded in others; the jury may reject the whole testimony of a witness who has wilfully testified falsely on a material point, unless, from all the evidence, the jury believes that the probability or truth favors his testimony in other particulars; that the jury are not to discount testimony received by way of deposition for the sole reason that it was in the form of deposition; that it is entitled to the same rebuttable presumption of verity and the same judgment of the jury with reference to its weight as that of any witness appearing on the stand. By reason of such instructions having preceded . . . it cannot be reasonably asserted that appellant was singled out as the only one whose credibility was to be tested and determined by the jury. Appellant would reverse the rule and weight and consider any one instruction separately from all others instead of reading it in its context. . . .

As to the use of Mrs. Newman's deposition, only two short questions were read from it to contradict the testimony she had just given on the stand. Such was proper practice as an aid to the jury's better understanding of the lady's testimony.

In her reply brief, appellant presents for the first time the question of error of the trial court's failure to instruct the jury on the doctrine of last clear chance. Questions presented in this manner will not ordinarily be considered by the appellant court in the absence of meritorious reason for the delay. But the court may nevertheless examine such matters, and may allow an appellant to discuss new points in a final brief upon application showing a reason such as sickness, inadvertence, or excusable neglect. . . . Appellant has made no such application and in fact failed to mention that this question was raised for the first time in her reply brief.

Appellant does admit that no such instruction was requested. Assuming that such an instruction would have been proper, the rule is that the failure of a trial court to give an instruction may not be reviewed on appeal unless the record specifies the instruction and shows that it was requested and refused. . . . It was not error for the trial court to fail to give the instruction in question on its own motion.

Judgment affirmed.

FOOTNOTES

[1] 28 U.S.C. §1861 *et seq.*

[2] *Fay v. New York,* 332 U.S. 261 (1947); *Apodaca v. Oregon,* 406 U.S. 404 (1970).

[3] *Taylor v. Louisiana,* 419 U.S. 522 (1975); *Peters v. Kiff,* 407 U.S. 493 (1972).

[4] *Colgrove v. Battin,* 413 U.S. 149 (1973).

[5] P. L. 93-595 (1975).

[6] Judgment *non obstante verdicto.*

CHAPTER 8
APPEAL

"Over a quarter of a million dollars! When a man didn't use enough care to place the guard in position on his cypres machine! If every cypres operator who gets hurt while using our zaggers is going to be able to recover from us, no matter how little care he himself exercises, we'll be out of business by the end of this year. Appeal? There's absolutely no question about it. We can't afford not to appeal."

That was how Will Very reacted to the jury verdict as he and W. E. Just discussed Judge Fairness' denial of the motions for judgment n.o.v. and a new trial.

DECISION TO APPEAL

Very's decision was a business judgment, one that W. E. Just privately predicted even before he approached the firm's president about proceeding on appeal. In fact, W. E. did not request a meeting with the president until he had mentally considered these matters with regard to appeal:

1. Is there a legal basis for appeal?
2. What are the possibilities for success?
3. What costs will be involved?
4. What is in my client's best interests?

An appellant (the party bringing an appeal) cannot seek reversal of a lower court's decision upon a ground not raised in the trial court. W. E. had already laid the foundation for appeal in his motions for a directed verdict, for judgment n.o.v., and for a new trial. In each instance, he had raised legal issues and alleged error by the trial court. Thus, he was satisfied that the legal basis for appeal existed. Furthermore, he believed he had sufficient, relevant, Great State precedent in support of his contentions to convince the appellate court of the legal soundness of the appellant's position.

As a lawyer, W. E. did not share the widely held, erroneous belief of many lay persons that there is an automatic right of appeal granted by the federal constitution. Nor do many persons understand that an appellate court's review of facts is much more limited than is its review of the legal issues. Details regarding the limits and possible results of an appeal are shown in Table 8-1. All these matters were considered by Attorney Just in weighing the wisdom of proceeding with an appeal.

TABLE 8-1. The right of appeal in civil matters.

Source Of The Right	Actions From Which Appeal May Be Taken	Considerations Upon Appeal

1. Right exists in the state courts as provided in state constitutions and state statutes.
 	
2. Right is provided in the federal courts although NOT required by the federal constitution (nor considered to be a requirement of due process).
	1. From final judgment of a lower court
	
	2. From certain interlocutory* (not final) orders; e.g.,
	  a. where an injuction is involved.
	  b. when the trial judge certifies a question of law to the appellate court.
		1. Evidence is viewed in a light most favorable to the party prevailing in the lower court.
		
		2. Generally no review of error induced or invited by actions of appealing party.
		
		3. Generally no review of error to which objection was not raised in lower court.

Limits Of The Right	**Restrictions On Matters Reviewed On Appeal**	**Possible Results of Appeal**
1. Usually limited to one appeal to an intermediate appellate court. 2. Additional appeal generally discretionary with the highest court of appeals.	1. Normally limited to review of errors of law. 2. Generally limited to prejudicial (as opposed to harmless) error; i.e., error resulting in miscarriage of justice. 3. Usually no review of facts unless there is NO substantial evidence to support findings of fact made by judge or jury.	1. Action of lower court affirmed. 2. Decision of lower court reversed. 3. Case remanded (sent back) to the lower court with directions as to action to be taken by lower court, such as new trial. 4. In cases of discretionary appeal, denial of petition for review.

*An interlocutory order is not a final decision of the whole controversy; it settles only some point or matter intervening between the commencement and the end of a lawsuit.

NOTE: Appeal in civil cases is distinguished from appeal in criminal matters. The latter are affected by the constitutional provision regarding double jeopardy which normally precludes appeal by the prosecution.

Costs, W. E. believed, would not be as significant a factor in Zagger Supply's decision to appeal as they would be if Mary Worker were making the decision. Although not all trial lawyers also handle appeals, W. E. was one who did. Since he was salaried, no additional counsel fees would be incurred. Court costs are recoverable by a successful appellant from the appellee (his opponent). However, when he compared court costs with the economic benefits that would result if the appeal were a success, W. E. believed the best interests of his client indicated appeal should be undertaken.

W. E. discussed all this with Will Very, since it is the client and not the attorney who makes the decision regarding appeal. Not only was Will positive about his wishes, but he also added:

"Call Charles Sell and tell him I want him to take all the time necessary to prepare and appear in court with you on this."

It was then that W. E. found it necessary to explain that there is neither a jury nor are there witnesses in an appellate court. Instead, the attorneys for both sides present their arguments orally before a panel of judges. The oral arguments supplement written materials. These include a record of what transpired in the lower court as well as each counsel's *brief* or written rationale, which must be submitted to the court prior to the date of argument. This is to give the judges an opportunity to review the materials prior to that day. W. E. characterized appeal as a review, rather than a retrial.

"It's a battle for the lawyers, is that it?," Will Very asked. W. E. realized then that the president understood.

INITIATING APPEAL

Following this conference, W. E. took the first step necessary to initiate an appeal. He filed notice of appeal in the office of the clerk of the same United States District Court in which the trial had been held. A copy of that notice appears as Form 8-1. At the same time he filed a bond as security. This had the effect of staying execution or enforcement of the trial court's judgment against Zagger Supply, pending outcome of the appeal.

A copy of the notice of appeal was sent to Henry Law by the clerk of courts as official notification. The clerk also recorded all of these transactions on the court's docket. W. E. was happy that he had been able to meet the deadline for filing notice of appeal, which was thirty days following entry of judgment. Note that this appeal was in accord with what is sometimes referred to as the "final judgment" rule. This requires that final judgment be entered before appeal can be made. However, there are exceptions for situations in which delay of appeal would be harmful or

---

FORM 8-1. Notice of Appeal

DISTRICT COURT OF THE UNITED STATES
FOR THE DISTRICT OF GREAT STATE

MARY WORKER,
    Administratrix of the
ESTATE OF JOHN Q.
WORKER, deceased,
        Plaintiff
	:
	:
	:
	:
	:
	:
	:
		Civil Action
		XX-121

v.	: :	Notice of Appeal

ZAGGER SUPPLY, INC.,
    a corporation,
            Defendant
	:
	:
	:	

Notice is hereby given that Zagger Supply, Inc., corporate defendant above named, hereby appeals to the United States Court of Appeals for the Y Circuit from the final judgment entered in this action on the sixteenth day of March, 19XY.

W. E. Just
_____
W. E. Just, Attorney for
Zagger Supply, Inc.
Zagger Building
That City, Nearby State

---

wasteful. Appeal prior to final judgment is referred to as an *interlocutory* appeal.

While he was at the district court, W. E. ordered from the court reporter a transcript of the entire trial in order to complete the record of the case on file in the clerk of courts office. (He also ordered a copy for his own use in preparing for the appeal.) That record, consisting of the original papers and exhibits filed in the district court, the transcript of the proceedings, and a certified copy of the docket entries prepared by the clerk of the district court, would have to be transmitted to the clerk of the Court of Appeals of the Y Circuit. Responsibility for actual forwarding of the record rested with the clerk of the district court, but it was W. E.'s responsibility to request that it be sent. This he did.

Selection of the Y Circuit Court of Appeals represented the only possible course of action. The sole question that had to be resolved was which was the proper appellate court for review of a case tried in the federal district court for the Great State District. Direct appeal from a federal district court to the United States Supreme Court is possible in only a few situations. As shown in Table 8-2, one example is a final judgment which holds an act of congress unconstitutional in a civil action to which the United States is a party. The Mary Worker case, however, did not qualify for direct review by the United States Supreme Court. Therefore, review of her case would be by an intermediate federal court of appeals, and by the one for that circuit covering the Great State district. That was the Y Circuit. Oral arguments would be held in the federal court house located in Center City, Great State.

TABLE 8-2. Appeal to the United States Supreme Court.

From The Federal Court System	From The State Court Systems
Review of decisions of the lower federal courts:	Review of final judgment of the highest court in a state:
1. Review from federal courts of appeal	
a. by certification by the court of appeals of a question of law,	1. By appeal
b. by appeal by a party relying on a state statute held unconstitutional by the court of appeals,	a. if a United States statute or treaty is involved and the state court has held it invalid,
c. by writ of *certiorari* granted by the Court upon petition of a party to the case.	b. if a state court has upheld a state statute which is alleged to be in violation of the constitution, treaties, or statutes of the United States.
2. Direct appeal from federal district courts only in limited cases specified by Congress.	2. By writ of *certiorari*
	a. in any of the situations listed above,
	b. if any right, privilege, or immunity is claimed under the constitution, treaties, or statutes of the United States.

Mary Worker's first official word regarding the appeal came from Henry Law who telephoned her when he received the copy of the notice of appeal. She had experienced a sense of victory when the jury's verdict was read in open court and again when Henry informed her that Judge Fairness had entered judgment in accordance with that verdict. It was a distinct letdown to hear now that her legal battle was far from being over, that the possibility existed that she could lose on appeal everything she had gained as an outcome of the trial. She felt she had no choice but to continue to fight. Although Henry explained to her that he had limited appellate experience, she asked him to stay with the case.

In the meantime, W. E. had forwarded the docket fee to the clerk of the court of appeals so that the appeal could be entered on that court's docket. It would be listed under the title given to the action in the district court. (Not all appellate courts follow this practice, some listing the appeal as the appellant v. appellee.) Soon after that, the record was transmitted from the lower court. The clerk sent notice to both W. E. and Henry of the date on which that record was filed. W. E. now had forty days in which to prepare and file his brief.

APPELLATE BRIEFS

The brief is an exceedingly important document in the appeal process. It contains the legal arguments upon which a party bases his contention that the lower court's decision should either be reversed or upheld. Some appeals are decided on the basis of the contents of the brief, since oral arguments may be dispensed with either at the request of the parties or by the court on its own motion. The panel assigned to decide a case on appeal may consist of three, five, seven, or nine judges, depending upon the court and the case. In the federal court of appeals, panels of three are common. In unusual situations, a court may sit *en banc* which means that a panel consisting of all the judges of that court will hear the case.

Multiple copies of the brief are required to be filed with the clerk of courts, so that each judge will receive his own copy. The brief contains each attorney's statement of the questions to be decided by the court on review, the action he wishes the court to take, and—most importantly—the reasons to support his position. That rationale generally includes reference to authoritative sources, such as the precedent of prior court decisions, statutes, and legal treatises. Therefore, finding relevant authoritative support for his position is vital in the attorney's legal research.

Copies of the appellant's brief must be served on the appellee who is given thirty days in which to prepare and file copies of his own brief with the clerk of the court of appeals. An appellant has the option of filing another brief in reply to that of the appellee.

Failure of either party to file a brief can be disastrous to his cause. If the appellant fails to file within the time provided, the appellee may move for dismissal of the appeal. If the appellee fails to file his brief, he cannot take part in the oral argument before the court except by special permission. This is shown in Figure 8-1, which flow charts procedure prior to the appellate decision.

With all this in mind, W. E. began work on the appellant's brief. The required contents included:

1. A statement of the legal issues to be presented to the court for review.

2. A brief history of the case: the facts, the proceedings and disposition by the trial court.

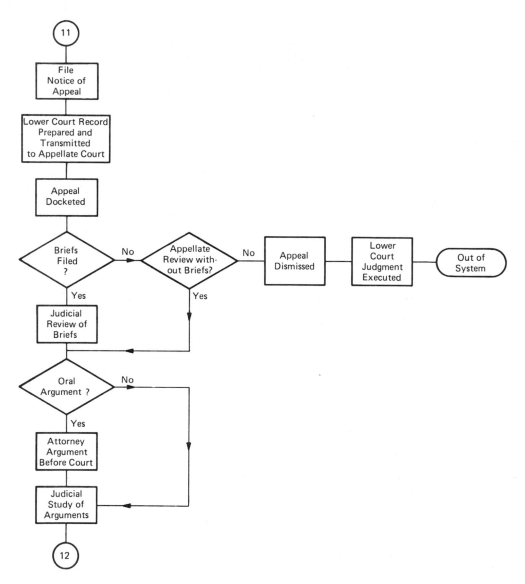

FIGURE 8-1. Procedure on Appeal Prior to Appellate Decision.

3. Appellant's argument: contentions as well as supporting rationale.
4. A statement of the relief sought on appeal.

W. E.'s brief necessarily contained many matters already known to the reader. Therefore, discussion is limited to the legal issues and points of argument he presented for review.

In asking the court to reverse the judgment of the lower court, W. E. raised the following issues, which he charged constituted reversible error:

1. In a case brought in strict liability in tort for an allegedly defective product, the court erred in refusing to grant appellant's motion for a directed verdict:

    (a) when the appellee failed to prove that a defective and unreasonably dangerous condition of the product manufactured by the appellant was the proximate cause of the accident and injury and death to appellee's decedent;

    (b) when there was uncontradicted testimony clearly showing appellee's decedent voluntarily proceeded, with full knowledge of the risks involved, to expose himself to a clear and known danger.

2. The court erred in failing to give sufficient and proper instructions to the jury:

    (a) in not explaining that in order for the appellee to meet his burden of proof as to causation, he must not only prove which defect caused the accident but must also eliminate such other causes of the accident as fairly arose from the evidence;

    (b) in not explaining that the appellee decedent's voluntary actions in exposing himself to a clear and known danger constituted assumption of the risk and thus denied to the appellee any right of recovery.

3. In light of both of the above and a jury verdict that was clearly against the weight of the evidence, the court erred in refusing to order a judgment n.o.v. for the appellant or, in the alternative, a new trial.

In support of his contention that the appellee had not met his burden of proof regarding causation, W. E. referred to *Carlin v. Goodbar,* 248 G.S. 334, 19XW[*], which involved a service station operator who sought to recover from the manufacturer after a snow tire exploded while the operator was working with it. The court said in this 402A case that the operator "had the burden of proving that there was a defect in the tire, that the defect existed when the tire left the manufacturer's hands, that the defect was unreasonably dangerous to the user, and that there was a causal connection between the defect and the explosion." W. E. charged that Mary Worker had failed with respect to the latter two required proofs. Referring to specific pages of the trial transcript, W. E. noted that Professor Learned had admitted under cross-examination that he could not state positively that the bonding defect in the zagger was the only possible cause of the shattering. W. E. also pointed to explanation by appellant's

[*]Years are indicated as −XV or −XW, etc., to show their occurrence prior to the year 19XX; as −XY, etc., to show occurrence thereafter.

witnesses as to why the bonding defect could not have caused the accident and their testimony advancing other possible reasons for the shattering. He urged that the trial judge had erred in failing to instruct the jury properly with regard to causation or, in the alternative, in failing to grant a directed verdict for the defendant.

In connection with the issue of assumption of the risk, W. E. referred to the Great State statute requiring that cypres machines be operated only with the guard properly positioned. He called attention to the picture exhibits as well as to specific pages of the transcript to show that the testimony had been uncontradicted regarding John Q.'s failure to have the guard in place. As support for his contention that failure to use the guard constituted assumption of the risk, W. E. referred to the case of *Farmer v. Glass Crushers, Inc.,* 256 G.S. 156, 19XX, involving an experienced operator of a glass-crushing machine. That operator was injured when, instead of using the long-handled device provided for such purposes, he reached with his hand into the machine to dislodge glass that had jammed. The lower court entered judgment for the plaintiff in accordance with the jury's verdict. The Great State Supreme Court reversed, ruling as a matter of law that the plaintiff's actions constituted voluntary assumption of a known risk. W. E. noted the similarities between that glass worker's actions and John Q.'s failure to use a guard. He alleged that Judge Fairness had erred in instructing the jury, by failing to charge that if the jurors found that John Q. had been an experienced worker, trained in safety procedures, who had operated his machine without the guard in place, then they must find that there was no right to recover.

Henry's brief, submitted in reply, asked that the appellate court affirm the lower court's judgment. He noted Professor Learned's testimony that the injury could have been prevented by the required testing. Thus, he urged, there had been proof that the accident was caused by a test-detectable defective zagger. He contended that the appellant's attempt to explain the accident as operator failure was not only rebutted by the appellee's expert witness but further denigrated by the very proponents of that explanation under cross-examination. He noted, too, that the appellant had not only stipulated as to the expertness of the appellee's witness but also to his recognition as the foremost zagger authority in the country. Therefore, he concluded, there was ample evidence of causation upon which to send the matter to the jury.

Henry contended that not only proximate cause but also assumption of the risk were jury questions and that both had been properly submitted to them. He called attention to the Great State Supreme Court decision in *Franke v. James Machinery,* 234 G.S. 922, 19XV, a case involving industrial machinery shown to be defective in certain respects. In that case testimony regarding a defective condition was admitted as circumstantial evidence as to the cause of injury. The question of proximate cause was submitted to the jury. The Great State Supreme Court upheld this action of the lower court. Henry contended that the decision as to whether a defense had been refuted was for the jury.

With regard to the assumption of the risk issue, Henry charged that the *Glass Crushers* case had important factual differences from the instant case. He agreed the *Glass Crushers* decision stood for the proposition that an experienced worker who reached into moving machinery with his hand had voluntarily assumed the risk, but he noted that there had been no allegations of defective functioning or manufacture of the equipment in that case. The allegations of defectiveness were of design in not providing a shield to prevent insertion of an employee's hand into the moving mechanism. That, he said, was quite different from the instant case in which John Q. had been working with zaggers, which, even the appellant had admitted, contained bonding defects. Therefore, he concluded, the *Glass Crushers* case must be considered inappropriate as precedent for this appeal.

He urged that W. E.'s concept of what constituted voluntary assumption of the risk in cases of strict liability for defective products did not coincide with that of §402A of the *Restatement of Torts* 2d as adopted by the courts of Great State. Henry argued that voluntary assumption of the risk referred to the situation in which an individual had knowledge of a product's defect, realized that using it in its defective state would be unreasonably dangerous, and then proceeded to do so regardless of the hazards involved. He noted that John Q. could not have knowingly assumed the risk of the bonding defect, since it was latent.

JUDICIAL ACTION

Only the two briefs were filed. The case was assigned to Judges Quest, Looke, and Search, who first read the list of legal issues involved as well as the summary of the arguments of both the appellant and the appellee. All three recognized that issues of substance were raised. Therefore, the appeal was neither frivolous nor subject to dismissal. They read further, then checked the decisions cited as precedent by both parties. Assistance in this research was provided by the judges' law clerks. Two judges sent for the trial record to reread Judge Fairness' charge to the jury and the testimony of the expert witnesses.

Judge Quest believed he could reach a decision from the written materials, but the others had questions they wished to pursue with counsel at oral argument. A hearing date was set by the clerk of courts who also informed all the parties of the time and place.

ORAL ARGUMENT

When Henry called Mary to tell her the date for oral argument had been set, she asked for additional information about what would transpire at that time. In his explanation, Henry told her that each side would have thirty minutes for argument. The appellant was entitled to both open and close the argument; he would begin with a brief review of the case and would then launch into the legal arguments. Henry also explained that the lawyers could expect to be interrupted at any point by judges who had questions. He also said that sometimes the arguments seem rather technical to the lay person.

What was most important to Mary was that no decision would be announced that day. Instead, the judges would restudy the matter after hearing the oral arguments. Their opinion would not be forthcoming for several weeks. This caused Mary to decide that, although this was an event of great importance to her, she would not make the trip to Center City to observe the arguments.

And that was how it came to be that on June 4, 19XY five individuals—three judges and two lawyers—participating in one hour of legal arguments in an appellate courtroom were the determining forces of Mary Worker's case.

The oral arguments took an interesting turn, with each judge seeming to focus on one particular issue. W. E. had not gone far in his presentation to the court and was contending that the appellee had failed to prove proximate cause when he was interrupted by Judge Quest.

"Tell me, counselor, just what is the standard of proof you allege the appellee should have met? Is the interpretation of Great State law that you are urging upon this court one that would require a standard of proof beyond a reasonable doubt?"

"No," replied W. E., but went on to urge that, "when the appellant's expert witnesses have shown that the reasons alleged by the appellee for the accident could not have caused it, then I submit causation has not been proved and, further, that the weight of the evidence—the preponderance—is contrary to a jury verdict in favor of the appellee."

Judge Quest followed up on this when it was Henry's turn. He asked Henry to answer W. E.'s contention that the weight of the evidence regarding causation was clearly in favor of the appellant. Henry replied that the jury, making its own decisions as to credibility of experts, as well as other witnesses, apparently did not agree with appellant's counsel that the latter's expert witnesses had refuted the appellee's proof of causation but believed, instead, that the weight of the evidence was in favor of the appellee. He reiterated that there had been ample evidence submitted by the appellee to enable the jury to reasonably arrive at that conclusion.

When W. E. began his discussion of assumption of the risk, Judge Looke asked him about the interpretation of the *Glass Crusher* decision in Henry's brief and why that did not make it an inappropriate precedent for this case. W. E. replied that John Q. was an experienced employee whose accident had been caused by his own action in failing to use a guard and not by any defect in the product he was using. That, he said, made the two cases similar. Later during the argument, Henry insisted that since the zagger had a defect—one admitted to exist by the appellant—the cases differed.

Judge Looke pursued with W. E. the matter of John Q.'s actions. Where in the record, he wanted to know, was there testimony that John Q. had intentionally used the machine without a guard; where had there been testimony to prove that John Q.'s actions were anything more than mere inadvertence at the most. W. E. replied that removing the guard was certainly deliberate and required conscious action. Pressed by the judge, however, he had to admit there had been no testimony that failure to replace the guard had been deliberate. When Henry's turn came, he contended any failure by John Q. to use required safety measures must be construed to be, at the most, momentary lapse of attention. He quoted *Cross v. Book Binders,* 248 G.S. 15, 19XW, where momentary lapse of attention by a machine operator was not accepted as a defense in a 402A case, the court noting that it did not constitute voluntary assumption of the risk.

Judge Search asked W. E. to defend his contention that the zagger had not been used for the purpose for which it was intended. Didn't the record indicate, he wanted to know, that the appellant realized that operators at times used zaggers improperly mounted and without a guard on cypres machines? Therefore, weren't such uses foreseeable?

W. E. responded that failure to use a guard was a violation of Great State law. He urged that illegal usage was certainly not one intended by the manufacturer. Henry, on the other hand, contended that foreseeability of such uses was evident from the very requirement of dynamic testing.

The hearing ended when time expired. Both attorneys went home to await the court's decision, as eager to know the outcome as their clients were.

JUDGES' CONFERENCE

At a conference held a week later the three judges discussed the Mary Worker case along with others that had been argued that week. In the meantime, they reread selected portions of the record and briefs, rechecked the cases cited as precedent, and engaged in other necessary research.

"I have reread Judge Fairness' charge at least three times," said Judge Quest, "and I can find no error in it."

"I agree," said Judge Looke. "Nor can I find any legal basis for disturbing the jury's verdict. Resolution of the conflicting evidence regarding cause of the accident was clearly a jury function, and it was properly submitted to them. Furthermore, there was sufficient evidence from Professor Learned from which the jurors could reasonably arrive at the conclusion they did. I hasten to add that I agree with their decision that the cypres operator's actions did not constitute voluntary assumption of the risk. There was no evidence that he acted other than inadvertently."

"Gentlemen," said Judge Search, "we are in agreement in one respect. We all find that we should affirm the lower court's decision. However, I find this is just one more of a long line of product liability cases in which we are left with a gnawing impression that a panel of professionals, knowledgeable about zaggers and cypres machines, would be the logical persons to resolve these technical disputes. Furthermore, this is another case involving state law that comes into the federal courts as a diversity action, proceeding to clog our calendars, and requiring that we interpret the law of a specific state. It is time to speak out, to urge not only that different procedures be adopted for product liability cases involving technical testimony but also that diversity actions be removed from the jurisdiction of the federal courts. Therefore, I intend to write a concurring opinion stating these views even if the two of you elect to issue no more than a 'judgement affirmed' announcement."

Judge Search was referring to the fact that when appellate courts reach a decision in what they consider to be a clear-cut affirmation of a lower court's decision, involving no new law, they seldom write an explanatory opinion. Instead, they merely issue an announcement affirming the lower court's decision. To do otherwise would result in filling the appropriate *Reporter* with duplication.

Both Judges Quest and Looke said they would prefer the short statement of affirmation. However, they would read the Search concurring opinion before deciding if they wished to join in it. As it turned out, neither wished to be associated with it. Thus it was Judge Search who made the Mary Worker appeal famous. While the decision itself was unspectacular, the concurring opinion was quoted by the Chief Justice of the United States, denounced and exalted in numerous law review articles, read and studied by lawyers, judges, and law students so that the Mary Worker case was known to almost all of them.

The appellate decision was a unanimous one. While unanimity is not required, a majority of the judges hearing an appeal must agree upon the disposition to be made of it. At times an appellate judge may agree with the final result reached by his colleagues but not with the reasons they have set forth. He may then decide to write a concurring opinion, so that his views will be publicly known. On the other hand, when an appellate judge disagrees with the majority, he may write a dissenting opinion. In the regular reading of dissenting opinions of a particular court, trends are often discernible. Certainly added insight into the thinking of the court is provided.

In the Mary Worker appeal, the actions of the lower court were affirmed. Had the appellate court found that the trial judge had committed prejudicial error (either during the trial or, later, in denying the defense

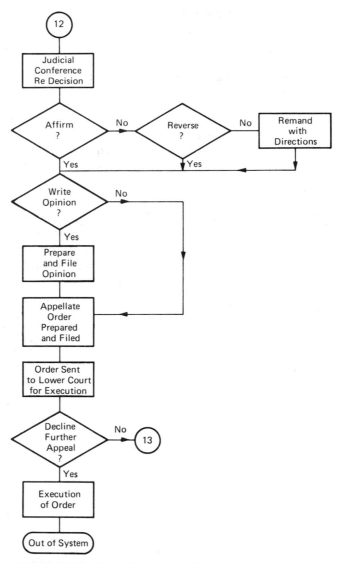

FIGURE 8-2. Procedure re Appellate Decision.

motions for judgment n.o.v. and a new trial) or that there had been no evidence from which the jury could reasonably have reached the verdict it did, then the decision would have been to reverse. Prejudicial error is that which results in a miscarriage of justice. Harmless error does not occasion reversal. There can be partial as well as complete reversal or affirmation. Appellate courts frequently remand—that is, send back—a case to the lower court with specific directions, such as ordering a new trial. In any case, appellate decisions are transmitted to the lower court so that appropriate implementation or execution may be taken.

The procedures involved in the appellate decision have been flow charted in Figure 8-2.

REACTION TO APPELLATE OPINION

When the opinion was finally prepared, it was filed with the clerk of the court of appeals who sent copies immediately to Judge Fairness and to both Henry and W. E. The latter discussed the outcome with Will Very. His first reaction was to appeal further—to the United States Supreme Court. However, W. E. explained that they had already had one review in an appellate court. Their recourse to the United States Supreme Court would have to be by writ of *certiorai,* best described as a request that the high court review a case that is within its discretionary province. He explained that review by the highest court in the land is a matter of right if an appellate court holds a state statute to be unconstitutional or contrary to federal law, or if a state supreme court holds a federal law to be unconstitutional. None of these had occurred in this case. One other means of access to the high court, he said, takes place when a court of appeals certifies a question of law to that court. After discussion, Will reluctantly agreed to consider the litigation to be at an end. The procedures that would have been involved have been flow charted in Figure 8-3. Payment of the judgment to Mary Worker was another matter. Will Very reluctantly ordered payment, thus satisfying the judgment, and then reconsidered the matter of self-insurance.

For Mary Worker, the news was a joy which diminished only when the financial realities became evident. The total jury award was for $304,891.23. Her contract with Henry Law called for counsel fees of 50 percent if the case were appealed. Therefore, calculation of the monetary return by her was as follows:

Jury verdict	$304,891.23
Less counsel fee	152,445.61
	$152,445.62
Less fees and expenses	3,402.35
Net return to Mary Worker	$149,043.27

Then Henry Law explained that there was still the matter of complying with the provisions of the subrogation agreement with the workmen's compensation carrier for The Firm. (Great State law provided that such carriers must assume a pro-rata share of the expenses and counsel fees, based on benefit to them from the litigation.)

Like all lower court judges, Judge Fairness was interested in learning what the higher court said regarding his decision in the Mary Worker case. Appellate review, in reality, is an evaluation of a trial judge's work by a

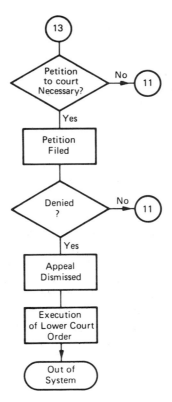

FIGURE 8-3. Procedure for Further Appeal.

group of judges. There is a modicum of truth in the old saying that the lower courts try the case but the appellate courts try the trial judges.

After the opinion had been printed and all the documents and records were gathered together in the case file in the office of the clerk of the court of appeals, the latter completed the docket entry showing that the case had been affirmed on appeal and arranged for permanent storage of the entire file. In the district court, the clerk not only noted the affirmation on appeal on the docket for the case, but also satisfaction of the judgment after payment into court was made by Zagger Supply. Had Zagger Supply not paid, then Mary could have requested the court's assistance in enforcement of the judgment. In that case, the clerk of courts would have directed an order to the sheriff instructing the latter to seize such Zagger Supply property as approximately equaled in value the amount of the judgment, sell it, and turn proceeds equivalent to the judgment over to Mary. Any remainder would be returned to the owner of the sold property. As should be obvious from this, it is possible to secure judgment against another party and then find that the latter is without sufficient assets to make payment. While there is an extended time period during which one has the right to collect, some judgment creditors never become able to make satisfaction in full.

This, then, marked the official end of the Mary Worker case. It was now *res judicata*. As a civil case, pursued through both trial and appellate stages, it provides a background for comparison with the criminal case, which follows in Part III.

QUESTIONS

How do you reconcile the concept of appellate review of a lower court's judgment with the statement made by the appellate judge in this case about a "gnawing impression" that a panel of professionals would be the logical decision makers? Shouldn't the appellate court have reversed on those grounds?

What actually happens on appeal? Has the appellate court fulfilled its function in this case? Is the appellate decision here one that might be included among the "hard cases that make bad law"? Consider the arguments put forth by both sides. Were they sound? Was the court's decision reasonable and logical? Why? Was the position of the appellant influenced by the desire of the corporate president for appeal?

Consider the appellate procedure. Is it consistent with the concept of review? Does it make review possible? How could it be improved?

Do you believe that the decision to appeal this case was a wise one? Why? Did W. E. make the best use of the opportunity? Should he have sought certiorari in the United States Supreme Court? What would have been his chances for success?

Should the right of appeal be extended so that it is an automatic right? What protections does a client have if his counsel fails to raise objections leading to the right to have error corrected (assuming that there was error in the lower court) on appeal? Why do parties and witnesses play so insignificant a role in the appellate process? Should it be changed to provide more participation by them?

Now that you have had the opportunity to follow a civil case from its inception through appeal, a relevant question is whether there can truly be said to be a civil "system"? Are the characteristics of a system, as explained in Chapter 2, present? Explain. If so, are any subsystems present within it? What are they? If it is a nonsystem, what is lacking?

Are there overall goals for the civil process? Who sets them? Who determines the priorities? Are these consistent with those society or the general public expects of the process? What does society expect of it? How is this determined? Are there any conflicting objectives pursued independently by various elements within the process? Give examples. In what ways, if any, does this interefere with attainment of expected objectives? Is there any method for measuring the effectiveness of the "system"? What is it? Is it pursued formally or informally? What feedback is there? Is any action taken with regard to it?

Is the civil process composed of such steps and procedures as best effectuate desired goals and objectives? Explain. What improvements do you suggest? How is input of information made into the civil process? Is this done effectively? Can it be improved? Is information available to those who need it for decision-making purposes? Give examples. Who defines the problems to be resolved within the civil process? How is this done? Can it be improved? How? Who are the decision makers within the process? Are they primarily persons within or persons from outside the "system"? Is their approach to problem solving an interdisciplinary one? Does it consider the total environment? Does it focus narrowly on one approach? Explain these answers.

Who manages the "system"? Can you suggest alternative models for the present civil process that would more effectively attain desired goals? Does attainment of those goals involve changes without the process as well as within it? rather than within it? In what areas?

Do you see the civil process as a part or "subsystem" or some larger system? What is it? Where is the place of the civil process within it?

CASES

Sturm v. Chicago & N.W. RY. Co.
157 F.2d 407 (8th Cir., 1946)
[Appeal from the District Court of the United States for the District of Minnesota.]

PER CURIAM. Gustav C. Sturm (who will be referred to as plaintiff), while employed by the defendant Railway Company (appellee) as a brakeman in Chicago, Illinois, fell from the top of a box car and was injured. He brought this action under the Federal Employers' Liability Act, 45 U.S.C.A. §51–60, to recover damages for his injuries. In his complaint the plaintiff charged that the Railway Company was negligent in failing to equip the car from which he fell with an efficient hand brake as required by the Federal Safety Appliance Act of 1910, §2, 45 U.S.C.A. §11, and that his injuries were the proximate result of such negligence. The Railway Company denied that the brake was inefficient and that its alleged failure to operate properly caused the plaintiff's injuries. The issues were tried to a jury. The evidence of the plaintiff tended to prove that the brake was inefficient and inoperative and that his injuries were due to its failure to operate. The evidence of the defendant tended to show that the brake was efficient and that the plaintiff's injuries could not have resulted from a defect in the brake. Neither party moved for a directed verdict at the close of the evidence. The issues were submitted to the jury. There were no requests for instructions. No exceptions were taken to the trial court's charge. The jury returned a verdict for the defendant, upon which a judgment was entered. The plaintiff has appealed from the judgment.

It is obvious that this appeal presents no question which is reviewable by this court. No ruling of the trial court is challenged. The question of the sufficiency of the evidence to support the verdict is not subject to review, since that question was not presented to the trial court by a motion for a directed verdict or any other equivalent action. . . . This court is without power to retry this case. It cannot concern itself with the credibility of witnesses or the weight of evidence. . . . The verdict of the jury, whether right or wrong, was completely determinative of the issues of fact tried and submitted.

The judgment is affirmed.

Ferraro v. Ford Motor Company
423 Pa. 324, 223 A.2d 746 (1966)

EAGEN, JUSTICE. William G. Ferraro instituted this action in trespass to recover damages for loss resulting from a unique automobile accident. The named defendants were the Ford Motor Company (Ford) and the Toohey Motor Company (Toohey). Since Toohey, a corporation, had been dissolved, service was never effected on this defendant. Ford was properly served, and the action proceeded against it alone.

After trial, the jury awarded the plaintiff the sum of $107,851. Ford filed motions for a new trial and judgment notwithstanding the verdict. The lower court granted the latter motion and directed the entry of judgment for the defendant. After judgment was so entered, the plaintiff, Ferraro, appealed.

The record discloses the following: Ferraro, a contractor, purchased a new Ford dump truck, for use in the operation of his business, from Toohey, an authorized Ford dealer, . . . He used and operated the truck . . . for a period in excess of two months (and a total of approximately 500 miles . . .), when the accident involved occurred. . . . as Ferraro was engaged in operating the truck on a public highway and executing an extreme left-hand turn at an intersection, the left front wheel locked in the turned position. Ferraro attempted to apply the brake when his foot accidentally bumped the gas accelerator pedal, dislodging it from the ball socket underneath and causing the motor to race. The truck shot forward, left the highway, hit a house, and as a result, Ferraro was seriously injured.

In his testimony Ferraro admitted that on two occasions prior to the day of the accident, he experienced similar instances of the front wheel locking as he executed a turn with the truck; . . . He also admitted experiencing trouble with the accelerator pedal dislodging before the day of the accident. This could be corrected temporarily by manually readjusting the ball under the pedal.

As a result of these known malfunctions, Ferraro brought the truck to the Toohey garage on at least three separate occasions before the day of the accident and complained about its condition. . . . On each occasion he was reassured by employees of Toohey and told that the malfunctions were not serious, dangerous or sufficient to worry about; that the worst he could do would be to rub a little rubber off the tire and once it rubs off, "You're all right"; that Toohey didn't want him bringing the truck to the garage every week and to wait until he had more mileage on the truck and then bring it back for a thorough check and repairs. On these occasions Toohey did nothing to correct the locking problem, but an employee did show Ferraro how to install the displacement-prone ball underneath the gas pedal.

The lower court concluded that Ferraro was grossly negligent in continuing to operate the truck for a period of about six weeks after knowing the existence of the malfunctions and the fact that they were not permanently remedied.

In Webb v. Zern, . . . this Court recently adopted Restatement (Second), Torts §402A (1965), as the law of this Commonwealth in tort actions involving the liability of those who sell products in a defective condition. The question was not reached or ruled upon therein, as to whether or not contributory negligence or assumption of risk by the buyer would constitute a defense in such actions. After studied consideration, it appears to us that if the buyer knows of the defect and *voluntarily* and *unreasonably* proceeds to use the product or encounter a known danger, this should preclude recovery and constitute a complete defense to the action even in cases of strict liability. . . .

Therefore, the crucial issue in this case in determining if Ferraro's own actions preclude recovery is, whether or not, in view of his knowledge, he continued to use the truck and unreasonably encounter a known danger. Our conclusion is that this cannot be said as a matter of law, under the circumstances established by the record. . . .

In the present case the essential facts are not disputed; however, crucial inferences proceeding from these facts are rationally susceptible to opposing interpretations. . . .

Rather we do believe, that, under the circumstances, reasonable men could honestly differ as to what impact, if any, the dealer's assurance would or should have had on the mind of a reasonably prudent automobile driver. Hence a jury question was presented. We will, therefore, reverse the entry of judgment n.o.v.

While the lower court did not dispose of the new trial motion, since it granted judgment n.o.v., it did strongly manifest its thinking in this regard. It said in part: "The verdict for Ferraro against the Ford Motor Company in the amount of $107,851.00 was startlingly excessive. It shocked the conscience of the court. It would be an injustice to allow the verdict to stand. The court would have felt impelled to grant the motion for a new trial because of the excessiveness of the verdict and other grounds. It cannot be rectified by a remittitur." We do not regard this view of the lower court as either arbitrary or a clear abuse of discretion.

Judgment reversed and new trial ordered.

PART III
DECISION ANALYSIS OF THE CRIMINAL PROCESS

Part III is the tale of Harvey Worker. Son of the fictional John Q. and Mary Worker, Harvey Worker is a mythical character who, like Harvey in Mary C. Chase's drama of the same name, exists only in the human imagination. As the principal character in the hypothetical case that runs through Part III, Harvey becomes involved in the steps and procedures of the criminal system as they exist in actuality. His decisions, as well as those of other participants, are examined for further insight and understanding of the criminal process. The hypothetical case is supplemented with excerpts from real cases, which are provided at the end of each chapter.

To provide uniformity of terminology in Part III, the term *magistrate* is used to refer to any member of the minor judiciary. For the same reason, the term *initial appearance* is used to refer to that stage of the criminal process following arrest in which the accused is informed of the charges against him and the bail decision is made. In some areas this may be known as the preliminary appearance, preliminary arraignment, or presentment. In Part III, 19XX indicates the year of arrest.

CHAPTER 9
ENTRY INTO THE SYSTEM: CONTROL SUBSYSTEM AND ENTRY INTO THE COURT SUBSYSTEM

Harvey Worker would have been surprised had he known that executives at The Firm were aware that cypres parts were missing. He would have been even more surprised had he known that he was under surveillance in connection with their disappearance.

It had all started about a year ago when Harvey, shortly after his father's death, dropped out of college and went to work at The Firm. A cypres buff, he soon discovered that the supply room at The Firm stocked in great quantity the very kind of pieces he used in his basement workshop. One day he unobtrusively slipped into his pocket a small but expensive piece he needed at home. Apparently its disappearance went unnoticed. Questions were asked of employees in the department when the third and fourth pieces he took were found to be missing. After that, Harvey worked out a method of changing inventory and production requisition records so that he was able to take additional pieces apparently without his being detected or their being missed. When he found that some of his former college classmates were willing to pay for parts that he offered them at bargain prices, Harvey increased the number and frequency of his takings.

INVESTIGATION

In fact, discrepancies between parts actually on hand and the number which should have been on hand were noted when Chester, Porter, and

Adams, CPAs, conducted the annual audit at The Firm. When they suggested the possibility of employee theft to Fred Famous, he was at first incredulous. Shown the figures which revealed that over $8,000 in parts were unaccounted for, he assigned to Al Chase, manager of security at The Firm, responsibility for investigative work in uncovering the source of the loss. It was Al who persuaded a reluctant Fred that Big City police should be notified about the missing parts and provided with their serial numbers. Al knew that once Big City detectives were alerted, he would have their assistance and cooperation in his investigation. He also hired a young private detective named Ed Under to work in the plant. Ed made it a point to become friendly with everyone, including Harvey. When he learned that Harvey's hobby was working with cypres, he watched intently for signs that Harvey might be involved in some way in the disappearance of the parts. He was, however, exceedingly careful to avoid any form of conduct which might later involve him in some form of criminal activity.

Criminal Involvement

Ed realized he must not induce, counsel, plan with, nor aid and abet Harvey in theft of cypres parts. His instructions were that he could not participate in any activity that would ordinarily lead to criminal charges. These charges might be either solicitation or conspiracy, or acting as an accessory. Further, if he induced Harvey to steal and, in so doing, could be said to have acted on behalf of an officer of the law, then he would have created a defense for Harvey through entrapment. These forms of involvement in criminal activity, other than as the principal perpetrator of the crime, are defined and further distinguished in Table 9-1. Their legal effect is also shown.

Surveillance

Realizing all of this, Ed continued to observe, listen, and report his findings. In the meantime, Al Chase's early decision to involve Big City police bore fruit. Detective Sergeant Dick Find called Al to report that an employee of The Firm named Harvey Worker had been identified as the source of the stolen cypres parts, which had been found in the apartment of a fence when the latter was arrested for receiving stolen goods. While it was now known that Harvey was involved, there was still no evidence as to whether he was working alone or with others. Therefore, Ed Under was assigned to center his surveillance on Harvey. That paid off.

One afternoon Ed saw Harvey unlatch a side entrance door soon after it had been secured by one of the plant guards on his regular rounds just prior to closing time. Ed notified Al. Plans were made. Al would watch the side entrance that evening. Ed would be inside the building in a

TABLE 9-1. Forms of involvement in criminal activity other than as principal perpetrator.

Involvement	Characteristics and Definition	Legal Effect
Entrapment	Entrapment occurs when a law enforcement officer, for the purpose of instituting criminal prosecution, induces a person to commit a crime that the person did not contemplate committing. It is distinguished from the situation in which the criminal intent is already present in the accused's mind, and he is simply furnished with an opportunity to do what he already intended to do. A private citizen acting for, on behalf of, or by direction of an officer of the law may be treated as a law enforcement officer in a situation that might involve entrapment.	Entrapment can be raised as defense by the person charged with committing the crime.
Solicitation	Solicitation consists of hiring, procuring, or counseling another person to commit a crime, even if that crime is not committed. In some states it is necessary that the crime involved be a felony.	Solicitation is a crime in and of itself.
Conspiracy	Conspiracy occurs when two or more persons combine or agree to do an unlawful act or to do a lawful act by unlawful means. The wrong associated with conspiracy exists in the agreement or the forming of a scheme between the parties. Conspiracy exists even if the crime planned is not committed.	Conspiracy is a crime in and of itself.
Accessory	An accessory is one who aids and abets another in criminal activity. He need not actually be present at the scene of the crime. It is sufficient if he advises, counsels, or otherwise acts to forward the crime or assists the criminal in preventing or hindering his being apprehended. This may occur before or after the fact. A crime must have been committed for there to be an accessory.	Acting as an accessory is a criminal offense if the actual crime is committed.

spot where he could see the supply room without being observed himself. Uncertain of what to expect, they agreed that Ed would signal Al to come to the supply room or to call the police if either seemed advisable.

The Incident

When Harvey appeared alone that evening, Al was surprised. Surprise, however, did not deter him from calling the Big City police when signaled by Ed. Responding to a call reporting burglary in progress at The Firm, the police were met at the entrance by Al. He led them to the supply room, where they found Harvey in the act of taking cypres parts from the shelves. He had a large plastic bag with him into which he was placing those parts.

While many of the events of that evening were a confused blur in his mind, Harvey found that some stood out prominently. He remembered how, while busily engaging in selecting the parts he wanted, he had turned around and was unexpectedly greeted by two uniformed policemen, Al Chase, and Ed Under. How well he remembered these words:

"Harvey Worker, you're under arrest."

He recalled being read "his rights" and being patted down. In his opinion, this had included some unnecessary roughing up. He was then taken from the building to Big City police headquarters. Except for sounds emitted by the police car radio, the ride there had been an unpleasantly silent one. His mind reeled with the thought that he had been arrested.

Arrest was something he had not anticipated. Harvey was apprehensive. He did not know why various procedures were being followed and assumed the worst. At this point, some discussion of arrest law should contribute to a better understanding of Harvey's experiences that evening.

ARREST

Arrest occurs when a person is taken into custody to answer for the commission of an offense. Most arrests, as in Harvey's case, are made by law enforcement officers. They may enlist the aid of private persons in effecting arrest. State laws vary, regarding the conditions under which a private citizen has the right to make an arrest. Great State law provided that a private citizen is privileged to arrest, without a warrant, when a felony has actually been committed or is being committed, and he has reasonable grounds to suspect that the person to be arrested has committed it. A private citizen must turn the person he arrests over to authorities without unnecessary delay. Both the private citizen and the police can incur civil liability for false arrest or for the use of excess force in making an arrest.

Great State law provided that a police officer is justified in using as much physical force as necessary to effect arrest or to defend himself or others from bodily harm while making the arrest. It further provided that the individual being arrested does not have the right to use force in resisting the officer, even if the arrest is unlawful. In these respects, Great State law was similar to that of most states.

So, too, were the Great State statutory provisions that permitted a law enforcement officer to arrest without a warrant for a crime committed in his presence or for a felony committed out of his presence when he had reasonable grounds to believe that the individual had committed the felony. An arrest warrant was necessary in other cases.

Arrest Warrant

An arrest warrant is a court order which commands that the individual named by it be taken into custody and brought before the court. It is issued by a judicial authority, usually a magistrate. The warrant is directed to a law enforcement officer or another person authorized by law to execute it.

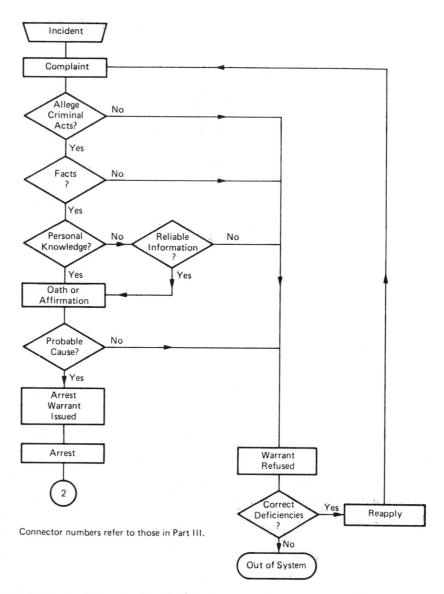

FIGURE 9-1. Decisions Involved in Securing and Issuing an Arrest Warrant.

Application for an arrest warrant is in the form of a complaint, which accuses an individual of actions in violation of the law. The person filing the complaint is generally a police officer but may be a private citizen. The complainant must provide facts. Conjecture or suspicion will not suffice. The facts must be given either under oath or by affirmation. When the accuser lacks personal knowledge, the facts stated may be on the basis of information and belief. In that case, the accuser must show that the information has been received from a trustworthy and reliable source.

If, on the basis of the information provided him, the magistrate finds probable cause to believe that the offense has been committed and that the accused has committed it, the warrant will be issued. Probable cause is more than mere suspicion. However, it does not require the degree of certainty that would be necessary to justify a conviction.

When issuance of a warrant is denied, further investigation may lead to the ability to correct the deficiencies that existed in the original application. A warrant may then be issued on the basis of a second application. These decisions involved in securing and issuing an arrest warrant have been flow charted in Figure 9-1.

An improperly issued warrant can result in an illegal arrest. In such cases, the accused can still be brought to trial. However, any evidence obtained as a result of the unlawful arrest must be excluded.

In some states and according to the Federal Rules of Criminal Procedure,[1] when a person arrested without a warrant is brought before a magistrate a complaint must be filed. As we will see later, this was done in Harvey's case.

Constitutional Considerations

When arrested, a person is no longer free to go his own way. He has been deprived of his liberty. This gives rise to constitutional considerations. As a result the procedure surrounding arrest is complicated.

The predominant constitutional considerations at this stage of the criminal process are provisions of the Fourth, Fifth, and Sixth Amendments of the United States Constitution: the right provided by the Fourth Amendment against unreasonable search and seizure, the privilege provided by the Fifth Amendment against compulsory self-incrimination, and the right provided by the Sixth Amendment to the assistance of legal counsel. These provisions of the federal constitution have been held by the United States Supreme Court to be applicable to the states.[2] This means that the relevant provision of the federal constitution is binding upon the states in their actions. The result is that neither in a federal nor in a state action can a person be deprived of these particular rights. The basis for making these rights applicable to the states is the Fourteenth Amendment, which states that "no state shall. . .deprive any person of life, liberty, or property without due process of law." The rights made applicable to the states may be said to have been incorporated in the Fourteenth Amendment and to be part of the due process required by it. In addition, almost every state constitution has counterparts of these provisions of the Fourth, Fifth, and Sixth Amendments. Those three amendments read as follows:

FOURTH AMENDMENT

The right of the people to be secure in their persons, houses, papers, and effects, against unreasonable searches and seizures, shall not be violated, and no Warrants shall issue, but upon probable cause, supported by Oath or affirmation, and particularly describing the place to be searched, and the persons or things to be seized.

FIFTH AMENDMENT

No person shall be held to answer for a capital, or otherwise infamous crime, unless on a presentment or indictment of the Grand Jury, except in cases arising in the land or naval forces, or in the Militia, when in actual service in time of War or public danger; nor shall any person be subject for the same offence to be twice put in jeopardy of life or limb; nor shall be compelled in any criminal case to be a witness against himself, nor be deprived of life, liberty, or property, without due process of law; nor shall private property be taken for public use, without just compensation.

SIXTH AMENDMENT

In all criminal prosecutions, the accused shall enjoy the right to a speedy and public trial, by an impartial jury of the State and district wherein the crime shall have been committed, which district shall have been previously ascertained by law, and to be informed of the nature and cause of the accusation; to be confronted with the witnesses against him; to have compulsory process for obtaining witnesses in his favor, and to have the assistance of counsel for his defense.

The procedures and practices followed in the criminal process must be such that they do not deny an accused these constitutional rights. Evidence obtained in a manner that violates these rights of an accused can be subject to the *exclusionary rule.* That means it must be suppressed or excluded; it is not admissible against the accused as evidence of his guilt. However, it has been held admissible for impeachment purposes and before the grand jury.[3] The exclusionary rule leads to motions by defense counsel for suppression of evidence. When suppression motions are granted, the prosecution is often left without sufficient admissible evidence to prove its case. In this way, the exclusionary rule can serve as a deterrent to unconstitutional practices. It should be of interest to note the care exercised by all concerned to protect Harvey's constitutional rights.

At the same time, it is important to remember that a whole body of law has developed in connection with constitutional criminal procedure, only the more significant aspects of which are highlighted in this account of Harvey's experiences. Much of this law is embodied in the case law made by the courts in their interpretation of constitutional provisions. As such, it reflects the dynamic and changing characteristics of case law as well as development in connection with ad-hoc factual situations. Constitutional interpretation by the United States Supreme Court, in the opinion of many, is dramatically revealing of the impact of social forces upon the law. Had Harvey Worker's arrest taken place fifty years earlier, there would have been no "Miranda requirements," as described in the pages to follow.

Search and Seizure

The pat down search made by police at the time of Harvey's arrest brings into focus provisions of the Fourth Amendment. The general rule is that searches and seizures made without a warrant (or with one improperly issued) are illegal.[4] There are exceptions to the warrant requirement, the most important of which is search incident to lawful arrest.[5] Among the reasons why a law enforcement officer has the right to search the person being arrested are to find concealed weapons, to prevent destruction of evidence which that individual may have in his possession, and to deprive him of the means of escape. The officer may also search the area within the arrestee's immediate control;[6] i.e., the area from which he might gain possession of a weapon or destructible evidence. This explains the pat down at the time of Harvey's arrest. A warrantless search also meets constitutional standards when it occurs after the appropriate individual voluntarily consents to the search.[7] The United States Supreme Court has also recognized as constitutional warrantless searches that were reasonable under exceptionally compelling circumstances, such as those involved in the "hot pursuit" of a suspect or when contraband is being transported in a moving vehicle.[8]

Distinction is made between the *search and seizure* referred to in the Constitution and the practice often referred to as *stop and frisk*. A *stop* does not involve taking the individual into custody. Therefore, it is less than an arrest or a seizure. A *frisk* is a superficial pat down, generally for weapons, and is less than a search.

With respect to the right of the police to stop and frisk, the United States Supreme Court has said that when a police officer observes unusual conduct which leads him to reasonably conclude, in the light of his experience, that criminal activity may be afoot and that the person with whom he is dealing may be armed and presently dangerous; when, in the course of investigating this behavior, he identifies himself as a policeman and makes reasonable inquiries; and when nothing in the initial stages of the encounter serves to dispel his reasonable fear for his own or other's safety, he is entitled, for the protection of himself and others in the area, to conduct a carefully limited search of the outer clothing of such a person in an attempt to discover weapons that might be used to assault him.[9]

Miranda Requirements

The reading of "his rights" to Harvey at the time of his arrest was only the first of a number of times that he was informed of his constitutional rights. This practice flows from the United States Supreme Court decision in *Miranda v. Arizona,* 384 U.S. 436 (1966). That decision sets forth specific instructions regarding treatment of an accused to assure protection of constitutional rights, especially those arising from provisions of the Fifth and Sixth Amendments. The five protective measures outlined by the Court are as follows:

1. If a person in custody is to be subjected to interrogation, he must first be informed in clear and unequivocal terms that he has the right to remain silent.

2. The warning of the right to remain silent must be accompanied by an explanation that anything said can and will be used against the individual in court.

3. An individual held for interrogation must be clearly informed that he has the right to consult with a lawyer and to have the lawyer with him during interrogation.

4. It is necessary to warn the individual not only that he has the right to consult with an attorney, but also that if he is indigent a lawyer will be appointed to represent him.

5. If the individual indicates in any manner at any time prior to or during questioning that he wishes to remain silent, the interrogation must cease.

These protective measures are required when an individual is interrogated "while in custody at the station or otherwise deprived of his freedom of action in any way."[10] They apply with respect to an accused or a suspect, to one who will be in jeopardy of criminal prosecution. Questioning of a person who is merely an innocent onlooker or witness does not impose the same obligation.

The Miranda requirements apply to custodial interrogations by law enforcement officers or persons acting on their behalf. Thus, one must distinguish situations in which private citizens act in a purely private capacity. Incriminating statements made by an accused to persons such as friends, family, or employers who are not acting for or on behalf of the police are not excludable because Miranda requirements were not met. And this is so whether those incriminating statements were volunteered or in answer to questioning.

Furthermore, the Miranda decision does not prohibit waiver of his rights by an accused. It does, however, require that any such waiver be knowing, intelligent, and voluntary.[11]   The Court stressed that the prosecution would have to bear the "heavy burden" of proving that the waiver was so. As a result, the police and judiciary normally follow the practice of asking a person who waives his rights if he is acting on his own volition and with full understanding. This is then made a part of the record.

Citation and Summons

Arrest was the means by which Harvey entered the criminal system. As shown in Figure 9-2, it is not the only mode of entry. The initiating action may be the issuance of a citation or a summons. These are orders

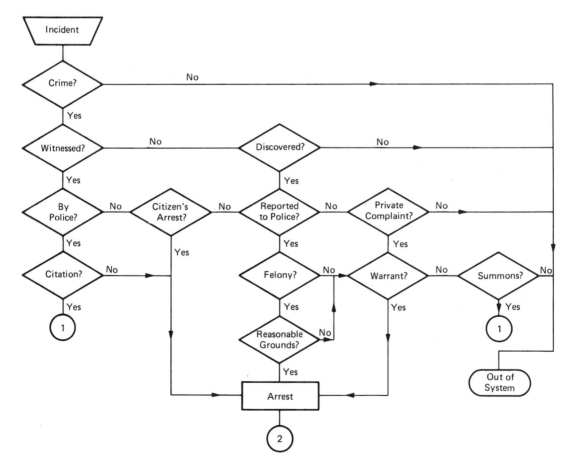

FIGURE 9-2. Entry Into Criminal System.

directing the accused to appear before the proper authority at a specified time and date to answer the charges against him. As noted on the summons in Form 9-1, failure to appear as ordered can result in the issuance of an arrest warrant. Some jurisdictions use the citation procedure, rather than arrest, for the less serious offenses. A citation is issued by the police. A summons, on the other hand, is generally issued by a magistrate after a complaint alleging criminal activity has been filed. Although the complaint is usually filed by the police, a private citizen may also do so. Some jurisdictions require a magistrate to send all private complaints to the district attorney for a determination as to whether probable cause exists to have either a summons or an arrest warrant issued. Which of the two is

---

FORM 9-1. Summons

SUMMONS

STATE OF GREAT STATE   :
                               :   SS

COUNTY OF _____   :

TO_____
           Defendant

    You are notified that _____
                                              Affiant

of _____ has filed a
                          Address

complaint, a copy of which is hereto attached, charging

that on _____ 19____ , you committed the

offense of _____ .

    You are commanded therefore to appear before the

undersigned at ___M, on _____
                                    Date

at _____ in _____
                    Place

for a preliminary hearing upon said charges according to

law and if you fail to appear at the time and place men-

tioned, a warrant will be issued for your arrest. You have

the right to be represented by a lawyer.

_____ (SEAL)
Issuing Authority

_____
Magisterial District

Date _____ 19____

issued generally depends upon the offense involved. Private complaints may also be lodged directly with the district attorney. The citation and summons procedures are flow charted in Figure 9-3.

Having looked at some aspects of the initial stages of the criminal process, it is time to return to the activities in which Harvey Worker was involved.

Booking and Custodial Interrogation

Following Harvey's ride to police headquarters, an administrative process referred to as *booking* occurred. This consists of preparation of the official arrest records. Harvey's name, address, and age were recorded along with the offenses with which he was charged and the time and place of their occurrence. He was being held on two counts, burglary and theft. The Great State Criminal Code defined the two crimes as follows:

> Section 3502. A person is guilty of **burglary** if he enters a building or occupied structure with intent to commit a crime therein, unless the premises are at the time open to the public or the actor is licensed or privileged to enter.
> Section 3921. A person is guilty of **theft** if he unlawfully takes, or exercises unlawful control over, movable property of another with intent to deprive him thereof.

Burglary was classified as a felony, as was theft when it involved property worth more than $2000.

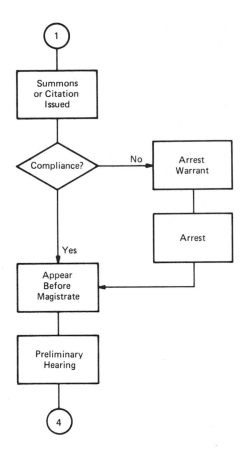

FIGURE 9-3. Entry Into Criminal System by Summons or Citation.

The arresting officers prepared a detailed report of the circumstances surrounding the arrest. Record was also made of the plastic bag full of parts which had been taken up at the scene by the police. The parts were appropriately tagged and labeled.

Harvey was thoroughly searched and given a receipt for his car keys, wallet, and the other personal belongings taken from him. For identification purposes, he was fingerprinted and photographed. Informed that he could notify one person, he called Mary Worker, his mother. She, in turn, called Henry Law. Both started for police headquarters.

In the meanwhile, police began a check to determine if Harvey had a prior record of arrests or if there were warrants outstanding against him. They also verified The Firm's previous report of theft of cypres parts.

At the same time, Detective Find and his partner, Hubert Seek, took Harvey to an interrogation room. After reading him his rights and the charges against him, they asked if he understood these. He replied that he did. He also said that he did not want a lawyer. Under questioning, he informed the detectives that he had been stealing cypres parts for almost a year, that he was working alone, that he sold most of the parts he stole, and that he had an unsold supply at home in his basement workshop. When Detective Find asked Harvey if he would be willing to tape record a statement to that effect, Harvey replied that he would. As the taping began, Detective Find asked Harvey for his name, if he understood the charges against him, and if he understood his rights. Both the charges and his rights were read again to Harvey in connection with the question. When he had completed his statement, Harvey was asked if it had been voluntarily given without either coercion or threat by the police, if it had been given without promise of clemency, and if he had been treated well. His answer to all of these questions was in the affirmative. That completed, Harvey was told he would shortly be taken to a magistrate for what was referred to as an *initial appearance*. In response to Harvey's question, Detective Find told him this was essentially a hearing to determine if he could be released on bail. As Harvey waited for police to make the necessary arrangements, both his mother and Henry Law arrived.

Mary and Henry were distressed when they learned of the serious charges on which Harvey was being held. The Great State Criminal Code provided for a maximum of twenty years imprisonment and fine of not more than $25,000 for a conviction of burglary; and a maximum of seven years imprisonment and fine of not more than $15,000 for a conviction of theft when the value of the property stolen was more than $2000.

Henry asked why Harvey had confessed.

"They caught me in the act," was all Harvey could say.

Soon all left for the magistrate's office. Henry inquired about the time at which each event occurred that evening. He determined that Harvey's arrest at The Firm took place somewhere between 7:15 and 7:30, Harvey arrived at police headquarters at approximately 8:20, and it was around 10:00 when the initial appearance began. Henry's concern with time was because the Great State Rules of Criminal Procedure provided that "when a defendant has been arrested without a warrant, he shall be taken without unnecessary delay before the proper authority where a complaint shall be filed agianst him and the initial appearance shall begin immediately." Had there been unnecessary delay? That would become an issue later. This Great State procedural rule made possible compliance with the requirements of the Fourth Amendment, as interpreted by the United States Supreme Court, that a judicial determination of probable cause is a prerequisite to extended restraint on liberty following arrest.[12]

Events following Harvey's arrest are shown in Figure 9-4. Note the possibilities for exercise of police discretion at the time of booking. It exists at many other stages of the criminal process and is a controversial issue. The police have an obligation to enforce the law, but can or should it be an automatic process, devoid of discretion?

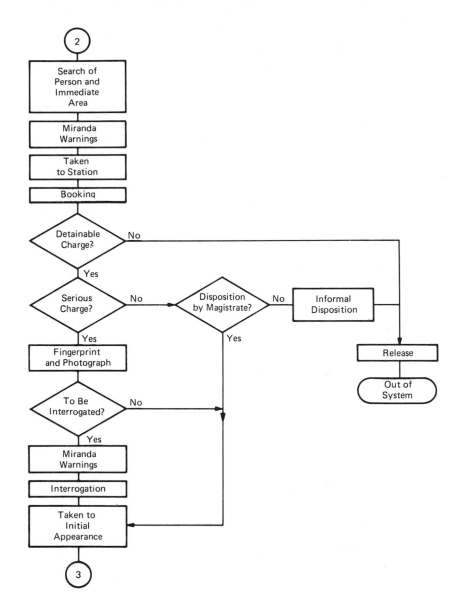

FIGURE 9-4. From arrest to Initial Appearance.

INITIAL APPEARANCE

Magistrate Joseph Mann's office and courtroom were in another wing of the same building in which police headquarters were located. Detective Find filed the complaint shown in Form 9-2 with the magistrate, and took

FORM 9-2. Criminal Complaint

STATE OF GREAT STATE v <u>Harvey Worker</u>
Defendant

Big City, Great State   Address:
Magisterial District __1__   200 Ninth St. , Big City _____

I, the undersigned, do hereby state under oath (affirmation):

(1) My name is __Detective Sgt. Richard Find__ and
I live at __Police Station #1, Big City, Great State;__

(2) I accuse __Harvey Worker__ who lives at
__600 Fifth Street, Big City__ with violating the penal laws of
the State of Great State;

(3) The date when the accused committed the
offense was on __Tuesday__ , __May 20__ , 19<u>XX;</u> and __on or__
__about June 14, 19XW; October 11, 19XW; January 20, 19XX;__
__April 3, 19XX.__

(4) The place where the offense was committed was
in the County of __Local__ ;

(5) The acts committed by the accused were:
__Burglary and Theft   On May 20, 19XX, defendant unlaw-__
__fully and feloniously did willfully and maliciously enter a__
__building located at the Terminal St. Extension, belonging__
__to The Firm, with intent to commit a felony therein and,__
__being therein, did feloniously and burglarously steal, ex-__
__ercise unlawful control over, take and carry away per-__
__sonal property of The Firm consisting of cypres parts__
__numbering two dozen and valued at $2400 with intent of__
__depriving the owner thereof and converting it to a use__
__other than that of the owner and without his consent. All__
__of the above in violation of Sections 3502 and 3921 of the__

Great State Criminal Code. And defendant did further, on prior dates listed above, at all such times, unlawfully and feloniously take and carry away personal property of The Firm consisting of cypres parts valued in all in excess of $10,000 with intent of depriving the owner thereof and converting it to a use other than that of the owner and without his consent in violation of Section 3921 of the Great State Criminal Code.

(6) I ask that the accused be required to answer the charges I have made; and

(7) I swear to (or affirm) the within complaint upon my knowledge, information and belief, and sign it on ____May 20____, 19XX before ____*Joseph Mann*____ whose office is that of __Magistrate__.

Richard Find
Signature of Affiant

STATE OF GREAT STATE   :
                        : SS
COUNTY OF LOCAL   :

Personally appeared before me on ____May 20____, 19XX, the affiant above named who, being duly sworn (affirmed) according to law, signed the complaint in my presence and deposed and said the facts set forth therein are true and correct to the best of his knowledge, information and belief.

Joseph Mann(SEAL)
Issuing Authority

an oath as to the truth of its contents. In it, Harvey was accused of burglary and theft. Magistrate Mann was satisfied that there had in fact been probable cause for Harvey's arrest. When the complaint had been executed, the magistrate noted Henry's appearance as counsel for the accused and continued the proceedings. Magistrate Mann realized that he would be making a determination regarding bail and also that the initial appearance served to provide the accused with notice of the charges against him. The Great State Rules of Criminal Procedure stated specifically that the judicial authority at the initial appearance "shall not question the defendant respecting the offense charged." Turning to Harvey, therefore, he

1. Informed him of the charges against him and gave him a copy of the complaint. Harvey indicated he understood the charges;

2. Informed him of "his rights." Harvey indicated he understood them;

3. Informed him of his right to have a preliminary hearing on the charges against him and that, unless he waived that right, the hearing would be held on May 26 at one o'clock in the afternoon in the Big City Magistrate's Court. After consultation with Henry, Harvey indicated he understood this and would not at this time waive the right to the preliminary hearing;

4. Informed him that until the hearing he could be released on bail; otherwise, he would be committed to the county jail until the time of the preliminary hearing.

Bail

The purpose of bail is to assure that an accused, if he is not detained in jail, will appear for court at the proper time. To guarantee this, money or other property is posted as security with the understanding that it will be returned when the accused appears as required. It is, of course, forfeited if he does not. The word *bail*, when used as a verb, refers to the act of procuring the accused's release by posting security. Used as a noun, it refers to the guarantee of the accused's appearance or to the sum of money required as security.

Many accused persons do not have the personal resources to provide the necessary security. They, therefore, seek others who can post that security for them. Those who do so are referred to as the *surety* since they serve to assure appearance of the accused in court. The United States Supreme Court has held that a surety is authorized to retrieve a defendant when he fails to appear.[13]

Those individuals who are in the business of acting as sureties are known as professional *bail bondsmen.* Their fee is usually from ten to fifteen percent of the amount required for release of the accused on bail.

The term *bondsman* derives from the fact that the document signed by the accused and his surety guaranteeing the accused's appearance is referred to as a bail *bond.*

The bail system has often been a hardship on an indigent accused. Unable either to post security himself or to find a surety who will do so, he is detained in jail until time for his appearance in court. Because of that, such alternatives as ROR, nominal bail, and court-administered bail systems have been given attention recently.

ROR, or *release on one's own recognizance,* means that the accused is released on his promise that he will appear in court. No security is required. ROR is limited to cases involving the less serious crimes and to persons with indicia that they will appear as required. These include residence in the area, family and other ties to the community, history of employment, and the absence of prior conviction for serious crime. The appearance record for persons on ROR has been good but not perfect.

Nominal bail may be used as an alternative to ROR in cases in which it is desirable to have a surety. A deposit of $1 is required and a bond is executed. The surety incurs no financial liability but acts to assure the accused's appearance.

Court-administered bail systems enable an accused to procure a bond at low cost through the court. Security, usually around ten percent of the total amount of bail, is deposited with the clerk of courts. As with the nominal bond, a responsible party must be named as surety. When the accused appears as scheduled, his deposit is refunded except for a small fee to cover the cost of administering the system. This may be as low as $10 or may be a percentage of the deposit. The usual amount is ten percent of the deposit.

The setting of bail is usually the function of a judicial officer. In some cases, it may be set by the police following arrest. In cases in which the accused represents a potential hazard to society if released, sound judgment dictates that bail be denied. Some state laws prohibit a magistrate from releasing on bail persons accused of murder or voluntary manslaughter. When persons released from custody fail to appear as required, necessary warrants may be issued to bring the defendant before the court.

A decision regarding release of the accused on bail is made several times during the criminal process. That decision has been flow charted in Figure 9-5, which also shows the course of events flowing from that decision.

In Harvey's case, Henry urged the magistrate to give consideration to ROR since Harvey had no prior criminal record, lived in Big City with his mother, and had been regularly employed. The magistrate declined to do so because of the seriousness of the charges against him. He did agree that Harvey was a sufficiently good bail risk so as not to require the setting of bail in a large amount. Therefore, he decided upon nominal bail since there would be a surety. Mary agreed to serve as such. After the bond was

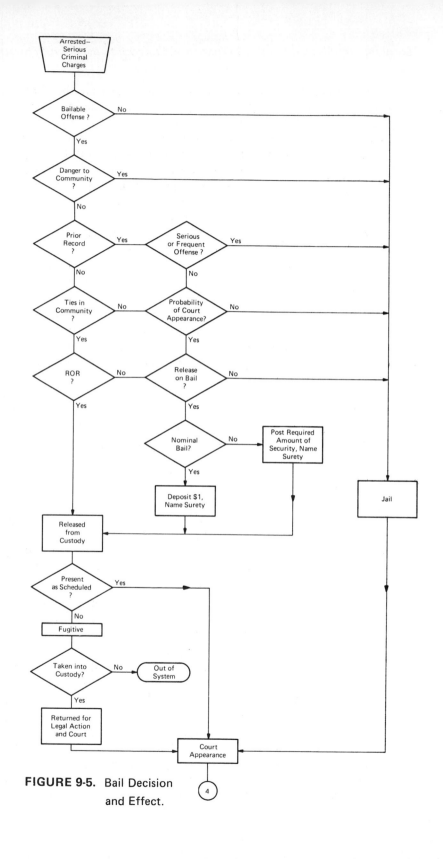

FIGURE 9-5. Bail Decision and Effect.

executed, the initial appearance came to an end. Harvey was free until the preliminary hearing.

The proceedings at the initial appearance have been flow charted in Figure 9-6. The initial appearance need not occur in cases when entry into the system has been by other means than arrest. This is for two reasons: (1) the accused is informed in writing of the charges against him

FIGURE 9-6. Initial Appearance.

since they appear on the citation or summons that he receives; (2) because he has not been taken into custody, there is no need to consider bail nor is there need for judicial determination of probable cause for restraint of liberty. Both of these may be considerations at the hearing at which the accused has been directed to appear.

IN THE MEANTIME

While Harvey's initial appearance was in progress, other events related to the case were taking place. In his confession, Harvey had admitted that stolen parts were stored in his basement workshop at home. As the fruit of prior thefts, they were of concern to the police not only as evidence but also that they might be returned to their rightful owner. If Harvey were released on bail after his initial appearance that evening, as they fully expected, the possibility existed that he would hide, destroy, or otherwise dispose of the parts. Therefore, they felt a sense of urgency about getting those parts into police custody before Harvey returned home. To do this, a search warrant would be needed.

Search Warrant

In Great State, searches conducted after 11:00 PM were considered to be night time searches. A magistrate could authorize them only under certain conditions. Therefore, the first action following Harvey's confession was to prepare an application for a search warrant which Detective Seek would take to Magistrate Dixon, whose office was located on the way to the Worker home. Arrangements were also made for Detective Seek to meet, after the warrant was issued, four officers who would assist in the search. Provided no complications occurred, police expected to be at the Worker home before 10:00 PM. Since they knew where the parts were stored, an hour seemed to be ample time for their search.

The application that Detective Seek presented to Magistrate Dixon is shown in Form 9-3. In applying for a search warrant, the police officer must file with the appropriate judicial authority a deposition or affidavit showing probable cause to believe that illegal goods are located in a certain place. *Illegal goods* may consist of contraband or the fruits of a crime; items criminally possessed, such as drugs; property that is, has been, or will be used in the commission of a crime; goods that are evidence that a crime has been committed. The same requirements that apply to an arrest warrant exist with regard to facts, personal knowledge, and probable cause.

In this situation, Magistrate Dixon was satisfied that probable cause did exist and issued the warrant shown in Form 9-4.

FORM 9-3. Application for Search Warrant

STATE OF GREAT STATE   :
                               : SS

COUNTY OF   Local   :

APPLICATION FOR SEARCH WARRANT

    Hubert J. Seek   of   Big City Police Department
           Name   Police Department

being duly sworn (or affirmed) according to law, deposes and says that he has probable cause to believe that certain property is evidence of or the fruit of a crime or is contraband or is unlawfully possessed or is otherwise subject to seizure, and is located at particular premises, as described below:

IDENTIFY ITEMS TO BE SEARCHED FOR AND SEIZED (be as specific as possible)

        Cypres parts

DESCRIPTION OF PREMISES TO BE SEARCHED (e.g., street or other address, including apartment number, or specific description of vehicle, safe deposit box, etc.):

Dwelling house at 600 Fifth Street, Big City, Great State, including workshop and basement at said premises.

NAME OF OWNER, OCCUPANT OR POSSESSOR OF SAID PREMISES (give alias or description if name is unknown):

Owner of premises is Mary Worker, who occupies said premises with Harvey Worker, her son, and her other children, names unknown.

CRIME WHICH HAS BEEN OR IS BEING COMMITTED (describe conduct or specify statute):

Theft of cypres parts from The Firm, in violation of
Section 3921 of Great State Criminal Code

PROBABLE CAUSE BELIEF IS BASED ON THE
FOLLOWING FACTS AND CIRCUMSTANCES (Special
instructions: 1 - If information was obtained from another
person, e.g., an informant, a private citizen, or fellow
officer, state specifically what information was received,
and how and when such information was obtained. State also
the factual basis for believing such other person to be
reliable.

2 - If surveillance was made, state what
information was obtained by such surveillance, by whom it
was obtained, and state date, time and place of such
surveillance.

3 - State other pertinent facts within personal
knowledge of affiant.

4 - If "nighttime" search is requested (i.e.,
11:00 p.m. to 6:00 a.m.) state additional reasonable cause
for seeking permission to search in night time.

5 - State reasons for believing that the items
are located at the premises specified above.

6 - State reasons for believing that the items
are subject to seizure.

7 - State any additional information considered
pertinent to justify this application.):

On May 20, 19XX Big City Police Officers Teresa Copp and
Vincent Polise arrested Harvey Worker whose address is
600 Fifth Street, Big City, charging burglary and theft,
upon finding him at approximately 7:30 P.M. in the closed
factory building of The Firm, Terminal Street Extension,

Big City, taking cypres parts from the shelves in the factory supply room and placing them in a plastic bag belonging to said Harvey Worker. Following arrest, Harvey Worker gave a statement (copy attached) to Big City Detectives Hurbert Seek and Richard Find at approximately 9:40 P.M. at Big City Central Police Headquarters, in which he confessed to burglary and theft of cypres parts from The Firm and stated that these stolen parts are presently stored in the basement workshop in his home at 600 Fifth Street, Big City. Cypres parts have been reported stolen by The Firm in reports filed with Big City Police on June 14, 19XW, October 11, 19XW, January 20, 19XX, and April 3, 19XX; copies attached.

Hurbert Seek
Signature of Affiant

SEAL:

Magisterial District 14

Office Address:

204 Fifth Street

Big City, Great State

Date Commission Expires:

December 31, 19XX

89   10
Badge Number   District/Unit
Sworn to and subscribed before
me this 20 day of May, 19XX.

Anthony Dixon
Signature of Issuing Authority

A search warrant is a written order issued by a judicial officer in the name of the state. It is directed to an officer of the law. It commands him to search specified persons or premises, or both, for specific property alleged to be illegal goods and to bring the goods, when found, before the issuing authority. It may also include a provision to bring along the persons occupying the searched premises in order that they may be dealt with according to law.

FORM 9-4. Search Warrant

STATE OF GREAT STATE   :
                        : SS
COUNTY OF ___Local___

SEARCH WARRANT

TO LAW ENFORCEMENT OFFICER:

　　　　WHEREAS, facts have been sworn to or affirmed before me by written affidavit(s) attached hereto from which I have found probable cause, I do authorize you to search the following described premises or person:

Dwelling house at 600 Fifth Street, Big City, Great State, including workshop and basement at said premises

And to seize, secure, inventory, and make return according to the Great State Rules of Criminal Procedure the following items:

　Cypres parts as described on reverse side.

As soon as practicable but in no event later than

___May 21___, 19XX and only during the daytime hours 6:00 a.m. to 11:00 p.m.

SEAL:

Issued under my hand this 20th day of __May__, 19XX, at __9:45__ P.M. o'clock. (Time of issuance must be specified.)

Anthony Dixon
Signature of Issuing Authority

Magisterial District 14

Office Address:

204 Fifth Street

Big City, Great State

Date Commission Expires:

　December 31, 19XX

Entry to Search

While the warrant provides the police officer with the right to search specific premises, he cannot execute that search until he first secures entry. Federal and many state statutes provide that in the absence of exigent circumstances, a law enforcement officer does not have the right of forcible entry. Prior to entry, he must give notice of his identity and purpose. He must then wait a reasonable time for a response from the occupants. If not admitted after a reasonable period, he may use as much physical force to effect entry as necessary. Evidence secured as a result of an illegal entry is subject to the exclusionary rule.[14]

Detective Seek and the accompanying police officers arrived at the Worker home shortly before ten o'clock, while Mary was at police headquarters with Harvey. Betsy Worker, at home with her younger brothers and sisters, heard a loud knock followed by the words: "Police. Search Warrant. Open Up." Looking out the window, she saw that indeed there were uniformed police standing at the door. She opened it. Detective Seek showed her identification as well as the search warrant. Although she was a high school senior, she did not understand what a search warrant was and said so. After Detective Seek explained, she took the police to the basement where they soon discovered cypres parts neatly stored in an unlocked cabinet. They gathered these up, prepared a receipt for the parts which they gave to Betsy, and left.

Reports

One copy of the receipt and a copy of the police report of the search were delivered to the magistrate. This was in compliance with the warrant, which required that the police officer executing it make a return and deliver to the magistrate an inventory of all property seized. After reports had also been filed at police headquarters, the seized parts would be checked against the list of stolen items reported by The Firm. Al Chase would later be called to identify them.

DENIAL OF JUSTICE?

Mary and Harvey learned of the search when they arrived home.

"Henry didn't tell us about this," Mary said. She was referring to the conversation she and Harvey had had with Henry following the initial appearance.

They had been confused by what had occurred. Both had previously appeared before a magistrate for traffic violations. In each instance, they had been found guilty by the magistrate and a fine had been imposed.

They had expected much the same procedure to be followed this evening and were greatly surprised that Harvey had not been given an opportunity to speak in his own behalf. In fact, both were greatly concerned about this. They asked if there had been a denial of justice.

"No," said Henry.

Petty Offenses

He explained that the criminal process is shortened in cases involving offenses of a less serious nature than a misdemeanor. These are sometimes referred to as petty or summary offenses and include minor traffic violations. A magistrate has jurisdiction to make final disposition, from which there is the right of appeal, at the preliminary hearing in cases involving those offenses and some misdemeanors. At that time, he may accept a guilty plea, hold a trial to determine guilt or innocence, and impose a fine or jail sentence if the accused is found to be guilty.

With the serious crimes, Henry said, such disposition is reserved for the trial court, a court of record. In Local County, this would be the Criminal Court. Harvey's case would be heard in the state rather than the federal court system. Both crimes, burglary and theft, were state offenses.

The process followed in the magisterial court when there is final disposition of a case at the preliminary hearing has been flow charted in Figure 9-7. Note that appeal from the judgment of the magistrate is to the criminal court. There the case is heard *de novo;* that is, afresh or anew.

An initial appearance is often not necessary in these cases, because they involve the type of offense for which a citation or summons may be used. When an appearance is necessary, it may be scheduled to immediately precede the preliminary hearing. This is seldom done with cases involving serious offenses, which Henry termed the *court cases.*

Court Cases

The Great State Rules of Criminal Procedure required that the preliminary hearing in court cases be held within three to ten days following the initial appearance. The purpose of the preliminary hearing, Henry continued, is to determine if probable cause exists to believe that a crime has been committed and the accused committed it. That is not the same, he hastened to add, as determining the accused's guilt beyond a reasonable doubt, which is the standard required for a guilty verdict at trial. The object of the hearing, he said, is to determine if reasonable grounds exist for holding the accused for the next step in the criminal process. If there are not, the charges against him are dismissed. If there are, he is "bound over for the grand jury."

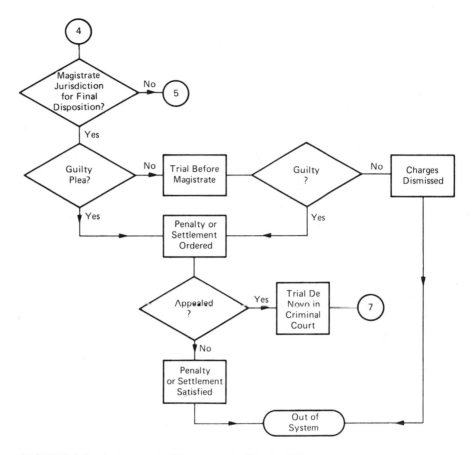

FIGURE 9-7. Judgment by Magistrate in Criminal Case.

Thus, Henry continued, for *court cases* the preliminary hearing is a screening device to determine if the accused should be held for the next step in the criminal process. For the less serious cases, the preliminary hearing is the stage at which final disposition is made.

In answer to Harvey's question about different procedures followed in Nearby State, Henry explained that not only is there variation among the states but federal criminal procedure can differ from state procedure. The same variation exists with regard to terminology, he said. However, as he told Harvey, Great State criminal procedure was in most respects not unlike that of many states.

That, in essence, had been the extent of their conversation. No mention had been made of any search. One reason was that Henry was not yet aware of all the facts. Actually, it was only after they arrived home that evening that Mary Worker learned all of the details.

THE NEXT DAY

The next day, as might be expected, Harvey's employment at The Firm was terminated effective immediately. Fred Famous was adamant that preventive measures be taken so that a similar occurrence would be less likely in the future. Jim Boss was assigned responsibility for implementing new methods of internal control as suggested by Chester, Porter, and Adams. Improvement of security was deemed necessary, and Al Chase was so informed. Fred Famous, although originally reluctant to involve the police, now believed there would be some deterrent effect flowing from the criminal prosecution. Others would realize that there would be no private resolution of such matters at The Firm, he told himself. He became so adamant that subsequent efforts by Harvey, at the urging of both Mary and Henry, to effect rapprochement and attempt to work out some method of restitution were to no avail.

Defense Counsel

Harvey spent the next afternoon conferring with Henry Law. Although Mary Worker had enlisted Henry's aid the previous evening, Henry had not been retained for Harvey's defense. That, however, was merely because of the pressures of time. As Harvey told his mother, Henry was definitely his choice of advocate.

The Worker family did not qualify as indigents and therefore could not avail themselves of court-appointed counsel. In Local County that would have involved a lawyer from the Public Defender's office, a tax-supported office. The application for securing such assistance appears in Form 9-5.

Right to Counsel

Harvey felt some sense of relief in knowing that now he had legal counsel. The United States Supreme Court has held that the right to representation by legal counsel exists at "every stage of a criminal proceeding where substantial rights of a criminal accused may be affected."[15] Examples of such stages, referred to as *critical stages,* include custodial interrogation, the preliminary hearing, the entry of a guilty plea, as well as the trial itself.[16] The right to counsel applies with regard to all criminal cases, even those for petty offenses where a sentence involving loss of liberty may be imposed,[17] and it does not preclude self-representation.[18]

FORM 9-5. Application for Appointment of Legal Counsel

STATE OF GREAT STATE   Charge _____

          V.   No. _____ Term _____

_____

APPLICATION FORM FOR THE ASSIGNMENT OF COUNSEL

The applicant _____ residing at

_____ shows that:

1. I am a defendant in the above entitled criminal cause of action alleging that I did commit the crime of _____ at the _____ of _____ in the County of _____ and State of Great State, on the _____ day of _____, 19___.

2. I am unable to obtain funds from anyone, including my family and associates, by way of compensation for counsel and represent that the answers to the following questions are true to the best of my information and belief:

    a. Do you have any money? _____ If so, how much?

        (1) On the person $_____

        (2) In the bank $_____

        (3) At home $_____

        (4) In custody of the Warden $_____

        (5) Elsewhere $_____

    b. Do you own an automobile? _____

        (1) Year and Make   _____

        (2) Cost $_____

        (3) I owe $_____ to _____

        (4) It is now at _____

c. Do you own any real estate? _____ If so, give location: _____

d. Do you own any other property or do you have any other assets? _____ If yes, furnish description thereof and specify its present location: _____

_____

e. Does anyone owe you money? _____ If yes, give the person's name and address and the amount he owes you:

_____

_____

f. If married, what is the name, age, and address of your spouse? _____

_____

_____

   (1) When did you last live with your spouse?

    _____

   (2) Does your spouse work? _____

   (3) What is the name and address of your spouse's employer?

    _____

    _____

    _____

g. Do you have any children? _____ If yes, give names, ages, and addresses: _____

_____

_____

h. What is your home address? _____

_____

_____

i. Where did you last work? _____

j. What is your social security number?

_____

k. What salary or wages were you receiving?

$_____ per _____

l. What was the total amount of your income during
the past 12 months? $_____

m. Is there a job waiting for you? _____ If yes,
specify what and where: _____

4. Line out a or b, whichever does NOT apply:

a. I am presently in jail and unable to obtain bail.

b. I am presently released from jail on bail in the
amount of $_____. The cost of such
bail was defrayed and paid by _____

_____, in the sum of

$_____.

5. I have not previously been represented by an
attorney in any case in court except: (give name of attorney,
name of case in which you were represented and state
whether or not your attorney was paid in this case and by
whom.) _____

_____

_____

_____

WHEREFORE, petitioner prays:

That this Honorable Court assign counsel to represent (him) (her) in the above entitled criminal cause of action without fee or cost to the defendant.

_____

STATE OF GREAT STATE :
                       :   SS
County of _____ :

_____ , being duly sworn according to law, upon (his) (her) oath, deposes and says:

1. I am the petitioner in the above entitled action.

2. I have read the foregoing petition and know the contents thereof and the same are true to my own knowledge, except as to matters therein stated to be alleged as to persons other than myself, and, as to those matters I believe it to be true.

3. This affidavit is made to inform the Court as to my status of indigency and to induce the Court to assign counsel to me as an indigent defendant for my defense against the criminal charges that have been made against me.

4. In making this affidavit I am aware that perjury is a felony and that the punishment is a fine of not more than $3,000 or imprisonment for not more than seven years or both.

_____
Signature of Defendant

Attorney-Client Privilege

After agreeing to defend him, Henry explained to Harvey how necessary it was that he confide in his attorney and provide him with the entire truth.

"What you tell me confidentially in the course of my professional relationship with you is privileged information. It is a privilege which you, as the client, have the right to assert so that the information cannot be used against you. You can, of course, waive the privilege. However, the reason for its existence is to encourage and enable individuals to confide in their attorneys so that the latter can do the best possible job for their clients."

Advice and Plans

Henry was frank in telling Harvey that his chances were not good in view of his being caught in the act and his confession. Henry asked a great many questions about Harvey's treatment by the police and the circumstances surrounding his confession. In addition, the two discussed the preliminary hearing. Henry indicated that Harvey would not be required to plead. His best advice at this point, he said, would be for Harvey to exercise his right to remain silent. In response to Henry's question, Harvey said that he did not wish to waive the preliminary hearing. This would be the first event in the criminal process for which he was prepared and knew beforehand what to expect. Henry decided to make use of the opportunity he would have of hearing first-hand from the state the evidence against Harvey. He planned to tape the preliminary hearing.

PRELIMINARY HEARING

At the preliminary hearing, the magistrate began by once again informing Harvey of his rights and the charges against him. Henry's presence as his legal counsel was noted. The witnesses against him, Detectives Find and Seek and the arresting officers, were placed under oath and then questioned by the magistrate. No representative from the Local County District Attorney's office was present. Henry introduced no evidence on behalf of the defense, although he did cross-examine about Miranda warnings at the time of arrest and interrogation. The magistrate decided that since Harvey had been arrested in the very act of burglarizing and stealing parts, there was indeed probable cause to hold him for the grand jury. He continued bail as it had been set at the initial appearance. That meant Harvey was once again free, awaiting further action.

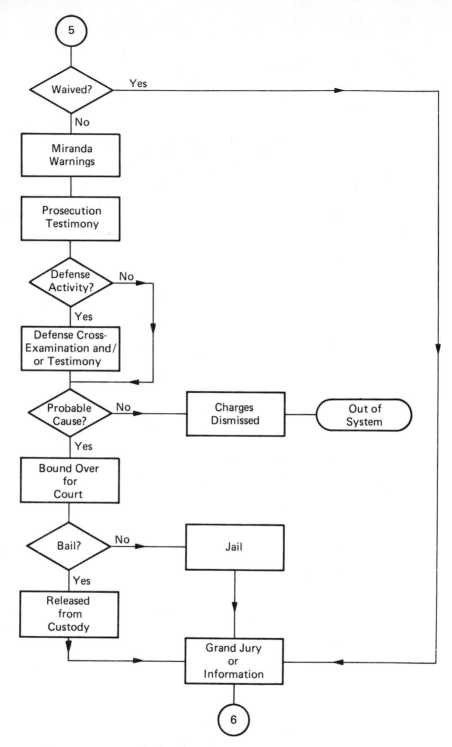

FIGURE 9-8. Preliminary Hearing.

The flow chart of the preliminary hearing appears in Figure 9-8. Following the hearing, the magistrate sent to the clerk of the criminal court a transcript of the hearing, the complaint filed against Harvey along with Detective Find's affidavit, the copy of the bail bond on which Harvey had been released, and a copy of the search warrant and return. In the clerk's office the case was assigned a number, 1246 of 19XX, and two additional copies of the file materials were made. The district attorney's office and the public defender's office picked up, on a daily basis, files of cases bound over for court at preliminary hearings. In Local County the majority of criminal defendants received the legal assistance of the public defender's office. Since Henry had entered his appearance as Harvey's counsel, the file for the Harvey Worker case had been marked to show private defense by Henry Law.

Decision making crucial to Harvey's future would now take place in the district attorney's office and will be discussed in the next chapter.

QUESTIONS

Three groups of persons have made decisions which have had a major effect upon Harvey's life: executives at The Firm, members of the Big City police, and members of the minor judiciary in Big City. It was Fred Famous' decision which triggered events leading ultimately to Harvey's arrest. Why was Fred reluctant at first to file a report with the police about stolen parts? Should businesses handle employee theft privately by simply firing the individuals involved? Is that consistent with the concept of crime? Should "white collar crime" be treated differently from other crime? Should restitution be required in cases of theft? If so, should there also be prosecution? Do you agree with Fred Famous' later thoughts that this incident will have a deterrent effect upon others?

How much discretion were the police really able to exercise in Harvey's case? Cite specific instances. Consider the decision making required of a police officer called to the scene of a crime, remembering that he must give thought to at least the following matters and often must do so within seconds:

1. Safety—what dangers exist in this situation? What measures can I take in my own defense? in defense of others? How much force may I use? May I call upon bystanders for assistance if I need it?

2. Crime—does the incident involve criminal activity? If so, what crime or crimes? Are these felonies, misdemeanors, or summary offenses? May I arrest in this situation? If so, under what conditions? Do I need a warrant? What facts must I have in order to get a warrant? Do I have time to get a warrant? Is this a crime for which a citation is issued? What must

I include on the form so that it does not lack legal effectiveness? Is this a crime for which I must apply to the magistrate for a summons? If so, what information must I have to present to him? What are my chances for success in getting one? If I arrest, may I search this person? how thoroughly? his surroundings? to what extent? May I enter the premises? under what conditions? What procedures must I follow before entering? Do I need a search warrant? If so, do I have sufficient facts to show probable cause? Will the evidence be destroyed and the individual gone before I can get one?

3. Constitutional rights—is this a situation where Miranda warnings must be given? If I question the suspect, search him or the premises, or effect entry to the premises, will the evidence I secure be subject to exclusion?

Can you add to this list? What other jobs of which you know require such crucial decisions with split second timing under tense and often dangerous conditions?

Did you find any instances where Harvey's constitutional rights were denied him? Cite the specific instances.

Do you agree with the decisions of the magistrate regarding bail for Harvey? why? regarding probable cause for the issuance of the search warrant? for holding Harvey for court at the preliminary hearing? why?

Should the state go to the trouble and expense of taking Harvey through all the steps in the criminal process when he is "obviously guilty" and has already confessed? Why not just sentence him now? Why would Henry Law defend an "obviously guilty" man? Should an accused have to pay for private defense counsel when the public defender's office is operated with tax monies? Is Harvey "obviously guilty"? Why?

The criminal process has been described as a screening device. What kind of screening took place in this case? At what points?

The police and other law enforcement agencies are often referred to as the control subsystem within the total criminal system. In the Harvey Worker case, what aspects of control did you find in the police participation? Prevention of crime is considered by many to be an important—if not the most important—function of control. Could the police have prevented Harvey's criminal activity? Was there a natural transition from the control subsystem to the court subsystem? How much "control" has the court subsystem over the control subsystem and the manner in which the latter operates? What relation, if any, exists between this and the court's function in interpreting the Constitution? What examples, if any, have you seen that illustrate the primacy of the federal constitution?

What differences have you seen so far between the criminal process and the civil process? Can you think of reasons which explain why these differences exist?

CASES

Malloy v. Hogan
378 U.S. 1, 84 S.Ct. 1489, 12 L.Ed. 2d 653 (1964)

Petitioner was adjudged in contempt of court and committed to prison after refusing to answer "on the grounds it may tend to incriminate me" questions put to him in an investigation by a state court into alleged gambling activities. His application for habeas corpus relief was denied by the court and also by the state supreme court on appeal.

MR. JUSTICE BRENNAN ... We reverse. We hold that the Fourteenth Amendment guaranteed the petitioner the protection of the Fifth Amendment's privilege against self-incrimination. ... In other words the person must not have been compelled to incriminate himself. We have held inadmissible even a confession secured by so mild a whip as the refusal, under certain circumstances, to allow a suspect to call his wife until he confessed. *Haynes v. Washington,* 373 U.S. 503 (1963). ... the American system of criminal prosecution is accusatorial, not inquisitorial, ... the Fifth Amendment privilege is its essential mainstay. ... The Fourteenth Amendment secures against state invasion the same privilege that the Fifth Amendment guarantees against federal infringement—the right of a person to remain silent unless he chooses to speak in the unfettered exercise of his own will, and to suffer no penalty ... for such silence. This conclusion is fortified by our recent decision in *Mapp v. Ohio* [367 U.S. 643 (1961)]. ...*Mapp* held that the Fifth Amendment privilege against self-incrimination implemented the Fourth Amendment in such cases, and that the two guarantees of personal security conjoined in the Fourteenth Amendment to make the exclusionary rule obligatory upon the states. ... We have held that the guarantees of the First Amendment ... the prohibition of unreasonable searches and seizures of the Fourth Amendment, ... and the right to counsel guaranteed by the Sixth Amendment, ... are all to be enforced against the States under the Fourteenth Amendment according to the same standards that protect those personal rights against federal encroachment. In the coerced confession cases, involving the policies of the privilege itself, there has been no suggestion that a confession might be considered coerced if used in a federal but not a state tribunal. The Court thus has rejected the notion that the Fourteenth Amendment applies to the states only a "watered-down, subjective version of the individual guarantees of the Bill of Rights,".... What is accorded is a privilege of refusing to incriminate one's self, and the feared prosecution may be by either federal or state authorities. ... the same standards must determine whether an accused's silence in either a federal or state proceeding is justified.

United States v. Robinson
414 U.S. 218, 94 S.Ct. 467, 38 L.Ed. 2d 427 (1973)

Respondent Robinson was arrested by Police Officer Jenks who had reason to believe that respondent was operating a motor vehicle after the revocation of his operator's permit. During a pat down, Jenks felt an object in the left breast pocket of the heavy coat respondent was wearing and pulled out a crumpled up cigarette package. It contained capsules of white powder, which later analysis proved to be heroin. The heroin was admitted into evidence at respondent's trial, which resulted in his conviction for possession and facilitation of concealment of heroin. The court of appeals reversed, holding that the heroin introduced in evidence against respondent had been obtained as a result of a search which violated the Fourth Amendment to the United States Constitution. Respondent concedes that Jenks had probable cause to arrest respondent and that he effected a full custody arrest.

MR. JUSTICE REHNQUIST. ... We conclude that the search conducted by Jenks in this case did not offend the limits imposed by the Fourth Amendment, and we therefore reverse the judgment of the court of appeals.

It is well settled that a search incident to a lawful arrest is a traditional exception to the warrant requirement of the Fourth Amendment. This general exception has historically been formulated in two distinct propositions. The first is that a search may be made of the person of the arrestee by virtue of the lawful arrest. The second is that a search may be made of the área within the control of the arrestee. ... In *Chimel* [*Chimel v. California,* 395 U.S. 752 (1969)] ... full recognition was given to the authority to search the person of the arrestee:

> "When an arrest is made, it is reasonable for the arresting officer to search the person arrested in order to remove any weapons that the latter might seek to use in order to resist arrest or effect his escape. Otherwise, the officer's safety might well be endangered and the arrest itself frustrated. In addition, it is entirely reasonable for the arresting officer to search for and seize any evidence on the arrestee's person in order to prevent its concealment or destruction." 395 U.S. at 762–763.

... The authority to search the person incident to a lawful custodial arrest, while based upon the need to disarm and to discover evidence, does not depend on what a court may later decide was the probability in a particular arrest situation that weapons or evidence would in fact be found upon the person of the suspect. A custodial arrest of a suspect based on probable cause is a reasonable intrusion under the Fourth Amendment; that intrusion being lawful, a search incident to the arrest requires no additional justification. It is the fact of the lawful arrest which establishes the authority to search, and we hold that in the case of a lawful custodial arrest a full search of the person is not only an exception to the warrant requirement of the Fourth Amendment but is also a "reasonable" search under that Amendment. ... Having in the course of a lawful search come upon the crumpled package of cigarettes, he [Jenks] was entitled to inspect it; and when his inspection revealed the heroin capsules, he was entitled to seize them as "fruits, instrumentalities, or contraband"; probative of criminal conduct. ...

FOOTNOTES

[1] Fed. R. Crim. P. 5(a).

[2] *Malloy v. Hogan,* 378 U.S. 1 (1964); *Mapp v. Ohio,* 367 U.S. 643 (1961); *Gideon v. Wainwright,* 372 U.S. 335 (1963).

[3] *Harris v. New York,* 401 U.S. 222 (1971); *United States v. Calandra,* 414 U.S. 338 (1974).

[4] *Katz v. United States,* 389 U.S. 347 (1967); *Coolidge v. New Hampshire,* 403 U.S. 443 (1971); *Chambers v. Maroney,* 399 U.S. 42 (1970).

[5] *United States v. Robinson,* 414 U.S. 218 (1973).

[6] *Chimel v. California,* 395 U.S. 752 (1969).

[7] *Davis v. United States,* 328 U.S. 582 (1946); *Zap v. United States,* 328 U.S. 624 (1946); *United States v. Matlock,* 415 U.S. 164 (1974).

[8] *Warden v. Hayden,* 387 U.S. 294 (1967); *Carroll v. United States,* 267 U.S. 132 (1925).

[9] *Terry v. Ohio,* 392 U.S. 1 (1968).

[10] *Miranda v. Arizona,* 384 U.S. 436 (1966).

[11] *Ibid.,* at 444.

[12] *Gerstein v. Pugh,* 420 U.S. 103 (1975).

[13] *Frisbie v. Collins,* 342 U.S. 519, rehearing denied 343 U.S. 937 (1952).

[14] *Ker v. California,* 374 U.S. 23 (1963).

[15] *Mempa v. Ray,* 389 U.S. 128 (1967),

[16] *Escobedo v. Illinois,* 378 U.S. 478 (1964); *Miranda v. Arizona,* 384 U.S. 436 (1966); *Coleman v. Alabama,* 399 U.S. 1 (1970); *Gideon v. Wainwright,* 372 U.S. 335 (1963).

[17] *Argersinger v. Hamlin,* 407 U.S. 25 (1972).

[18] *Faretta v. California,* 422 U.S. 806 (1975).

CHAPTER 10
INITIAL PROCESSING PHASE: COURT SUBSYSTEM

Jim Solicitor was a young assistant district attorney in Local County. It was his job to review the cases that had been bound over for the grand jury at preliminary hearings. On this June third morning he became intrigued as he read the file on the Harvey Worker case. He remembered having processed a case not too long ago involving a fence charged with receiving stolen cypres parts. Some college students who had been buying parts from the fence had been incensed when the stolen goods were traced to them and they were asked to return them. Could Harvey Worker have been the fence's supplier?

This recent local activity in stolen cypres parts was something new. The parts were expensive and small. This made them desirable as well as easy to steal. Interest in cypressing had increased recently, especially on college campuses. Was Local County now seeing the start of a wave of theft of cypres parts? Did this rash of thefts warrant stern measures designed to discourage any further development? Could it possibly be that this young man was part of some larger operation, as yet unknown?

Jim decided that he would like to know more about this case than appeared on paper. A telephone call to Detective Find revealed that both he and Detective Seek were out on assignment. Jim left a message, requesting that his call be returned.

As an assistant district attorney, Jim Solicitor was one of fifty-two lawyers on the staff of the Local County public prosecutor. As has already been seen, public prosecutors exist at the federal, state, and local levels. Their positions are usually that of attorney general or district attorney. Because crimes are acts done in violation of the duties one owes to the community, the law provides that the offender shall make satisfaction to the public when that duty is breached. Therefore, legal action in criminal cases is brought by the government, and not by private plaintiffs, as in the case of civil actions. Proceeding against a person criminally is referred to as *prosecution.* The attorneys who bring these actions are known as *prosecutors.*

In Local County the district attorney's office served a large metropolitan area. In contrast with more sparsely populated areas where there is often only a part-time district attorney, Local County required a staff of lawyers. Some engaged in trial work; others, in appellate work; and some, such as Jim, in such out-of-court activities as case review and preparation.

PROSECUTOR DISCRETION

Jim studied the materials in the Harvey Worker file. His was a screening function, and the decision of whether or not to send a case to the grand jury was entrusted to him. He also decided upon such alternative disposition of cases as diversion to rehabilitative programs.

Nolle Prosequi

One of the discretionary powers of the public prosecutor is that of *nolle prosequi.* The abbreviated form, *nol pros* or *nolle pros,* is often used. Nolle prosequi is the authority not to proceed any further with the action, even though there is sufficient evidence that the accused has committed a crime. This power of the prosecutor has been upheld by the United States Supreme Court.[1] It has also been the subject of much critical comment. In reality, it permits selective enforcement, as well as prosecution, for less than the full extent possible under the law.

The cases that often prompt a prosecutor to exercise his discretion to nolle pros include those in which an accused has cooperated in the apprehension or conviction of others, those in which victims are reluctant to testify, those in which there is insufficient admissible evidence, those in which the prosecutor believes that diversion of the accused to a program of rehabilitation will accomplish more for that individual and for society than prosecution will. Among rehabilitative programs are those for alcoholism, drug addiction, and mental illness. Great State also had a program for persons with no prior convictions who were accused of nonviolent crime of a less serious nature. It was referred to as *accelerated rehabilitation,* since the accused could be placed on probation without being convicted and sentenced. A closer look at it should provide a better understanding of these diversionary programs.

The district attorney could request that an individual be placed into the accelerated rehabilitation program by filing a motion with the criminal court. A hearing on the motion was required to be held in open court, and the defendant, his attorney, and any victims notified of the time and place. Determination of whether or not the accused would be accepted into the program was made by the criminal court judge who presided at the hearing. Acceptance resulted in placement of the accused under the supervision of a probation officer for a designated period of time. If the accused successfully completed the program of probation, the charges against him were dismissed. If he failed to live up to any of the conditions imposed, he was eliminated from the program. When that occurred, the district attorney sent the case to the grand jury, as he also did in those cases in which the accused was not accepted into the program. The purpose of accelerated rehabilitation was to encourage first offenders to make a fresh, new start under supervision and to free other facilities of the criminal system for use with habitual and violent criminals.

Because Harvey was charged with felonies, he would not be eligible in Great State for accelerated rehabilitation. Nor were other rehabilitation programs appropriate in his case. Jim Solicitor studied the file again. If he agreed with the magistrate's decision that probable cause existed, this case would go to the grand jury.

Decision to Prosecute

The grand jury was created to protect the innocent from the harassment of trial when there are not reasonable grounds to believe that the person has committed a crime. It serves as an impartial buffer between the accused and the public prosecutor. Its function is to determine if probable cause exists to bring the accused to trial for the crime (or crimes) with which he is charged. This is the same decision that the magistrate makes at the preliminary hearing. Note that it is also the same decision that Jim Solicitor was making in his review of cases. In this way, the grand jury and magistrate can act as a check on the prosecutor's decision. In all, Great State procedure resulted in three different and independent determinations of probable cause to prosecute before an accused was brought to trial. In some states this determination occurs only twice because either the preliminary hearing or the grand jury is omitted. In still others, the prosecutor makes the sole determination. This is often restricted to cases involving the less serious crimes.

CHARGING ALTERNATIVES

Table 10-1 shows the screening and charging phases of the criminal process. It gives some indication of the wide variety of procedures followed in the various states. The United States Supreme Court has indicated there is no single preferred pretrial procedure.[2]

TABLE 10-1. Screening and charging phases of the criminal process.

Steps	Variations in Practice in Different Jurisdictions		
	Information	*Indictment*	*Information or Indictment**
1. Screening by prosecutor prior to formal charging.	1. Screening by prosecutor.	1. Screening by prosecutor.	1. Screening by prosecutor.
2. Alternate methods of formal charging.	2. Preliminary hearing.	2. Grand Jury.	2. Preliminary hearing.
EITHER	3. Information filed.	3. Indictment.	3. Information OR Grand Jury and Indictment.
Information prepared and filed by prosecutor after determination of probable cause by magistrate at preliminary hearing.	OR	OR	OR
	1. Screening by prosecutor.	1. Screening by prosecutor.	1. Preliminary hearing.
	2. Information filed.	2. Preliminary hearing.	2. Screening by prosecutor.
OR		3. Grand Jury.	3. Information OR Grand Jury and Indictment.
Indictment issued by grand jury after finding by them of probable cause.		4. Indictment.	
		OR	
		1. Preliminary hearing.	
		2. Screening by prosecutor.	
		3. Grand Jury.	
		4. Indictment.	

In some states an option is available in each county regarding the charging instrument. Rule 7 of the Federal Rules of Criminal Procedure provides as follows with regard to charging instruments:

Offense	Charging Instrument
Punishable by death.	Indictment.
Punishable by imprisonment for more than one year.	Indictment or by information if indictment is waived.
All others.	Indictment or information.

The Court has permitted the states the option of using either a grand jury *indictment* or a prosecutor's *information* as the instrument for formally charging an accused with crime.[3]   The provision of the Fifth Amendment of the United States Constitution that "no person shall be held to answer for a capital, or otherwise infamous crime, unless on a presentment or indictment of a Grand Jury" has not been made applicable to the states. However, it does apply to federal prosecutions. As noted in Table 10-1, the Federal Rules of Criminal Procedure require an indictment in cases involving crimes punishable by death.

An indictment is a written accusation by a grand jury charging that there is probable cause to believe, based on evidence presented to it, that the person or persons named in it have committed the criminal offenses specified.   The document itself is sometimes referred to as the bill of indictment.   Note that it merely charges the person with crime. It does not represent a finding of guilt beyond a reasonable doubt.   An information, on the other hand, is a document drafted by a prosecutor who charges an accused with crime. It may follow testing for probable cause before a magistrate at a preliminary hearing. Use of the information eliminates the need for a charging grand jury.

GRAND JURY

Grand juries can have both an investigative and a charging function. Generally, special grand juries are convened to carry out investigatory work. They may bring charges on their own when they uncover criminal activity.

The grand jury has substantial powers. It may compel the production of evidence or the testimony of witnesses.[4] The exclusionary rule is not applicable.[5] Miranda warnings need not be given.[6] Immunity may be granted to witnesses in order to secure needed testimony that would incriminate the witness.[7]

Grand jurors serve not to hear presentations regarding just one case, but to hear those for many cases over a period of time referred to as a term. This may be as long as eighteen months in some jurisdictions.

The circumstances surrounding Harvey Worker's arrest left no doubt in Jim Solicitor's mind but that there was probable cause to prosecute. Following his conversation with Detective Find, he scheduled Harvey's case for the grand jury, the charges being burglary and theft. This prosecutor's screening decision and its possible consequences have been flow charted in Figure 10-1.

Subpoenas were issued for the appearance of witnesses. A copy of a grand jury subpoena appears as Form 10-1. Notice was sent to Harvey in accordance with Great State requirements that an accused be notified at least ten days prior to presentation of his case to the grand jury. This was to inform him of action being taken against him, not to assure or even request his presence. Neither a defendant nor his attorney is permitted to be present during presentations by witnesses against him to the grand jury.

Harvey did have the right to waive grand jury proceedings. In Great State, waiver of the grand jury was permitted in all cases except those involving murder or voluntary manslaughter. Both the defendant and his attorney were required to sign a waiver statement on the bill of indictment. Harvey, however, did not choose to exercise his right of waiver. He considered the possibility that a grand jury might not find probable cause in his case.

Juror Selection

Grand jurors are selected from voter lists, just as are members of petit juries. The number of persons on a grand jury is not the same in all states. Great State required not less than 16 nor more than 23 persons on

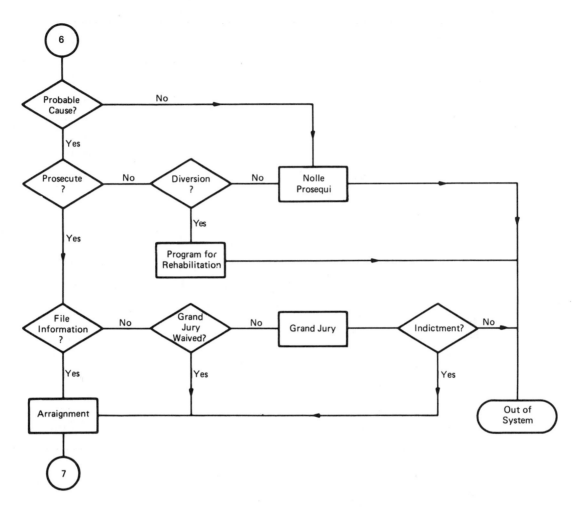

FIGURE 10-1. Prosecutor's Screening Decision.

a grand jury. Great State further required that a list of the persons selected for grand jury service be posted in the offices of the clerk of courts and the district attorney. An accused held for court, his attorney, and the district attorney had the right to challenge the array on the basis that the grand jury had not been selected according to law. If sustained, the challenge resulted in dismissal of that grand jury, and selection of another was begun. Individual members of the grand jury could be challenged for cause. This could result in discharge of a juror or jurors, in which case replacements would be selected. All challenges were required to be in writing. There was, however, no right to voir dire. Henry examined the grand jury list but filed no challenge.

FORM 10-1. Subpoena for Grand Jury Witness.

COURT OF LOCAL COUNTY
CRIMINAL DIVISION

STATE OF GREAT STATE   :

V.   :   **CHARGE:**

<u>   Harvey Worker   </u>   :   <u>Burglary and Theft</u>

GRAND JURY SUBPOENA

You are ordered to appear before the Grand Jury, Third Floor, Local County Court House, 1 Courthouse Square, Big City, Great State, on <u> June </u> <u> 17 </u>, 19<u>XX</u>, at <u> 9:30 </u>, <u> A.M. </u>, to testify in the above case.

Failure to do so may subject you to fine and/or imprisonment.

Date: <u>   June 4, 19XX   </u>

Attest: <u> Connie Scribe </u>   <u>S. Jean Ruhle </u>
           Clerk of Courts   President Judge

Members of the grand jury are sworn to secrecy, and their sessions are held in private. Their work is not done in a typical trial setting presided over by a judge. In addition to jurors, the only persons permitted to be present are the witness who is testifying, the prosecuting attorney, a court reporter in cases in which a transcript is permitted to be made of the proceedings, and an interpreter if one is required. The prosecutor calls witnesses against the defendant. The oath is administered to those witnesses by the grand jury foreperson. In many jurisdictions only prosecution testimony is heard; there is no evidence in defense.

Indictment

When the presentations are finished, the jury retires to deliberate in private. If the members decide to approve the charges against the accused, the foreperson signs the bill of indictment which has been prepared beforehand by the district attorney's office. The signed bill is sometimes

FORM 10-2. Bill of Indictment.

COURT OF LOCAL COUNTY
CRIMINAL DIVISION

STATE OF GREAT STATE   :

         V.   :   Criminal Action No.

      Harvey Worker   :   _1246_ of 19XX

          The Grand Jury of _Local_ County by this indictment charges that, on or about _May 20_, 19XX, in said county, _Harvey Worker_ did _willfully, unlawfully, feloniously, and maliciously enter a building belonging to The Firm, and located at the Terminal Street Extension in Big City with intent to commit a felony therein and, being therein, feloniously and burglarously did steal, take, exercise unlawful control over, and carry away property of The Firm consisting of two dozen cypres parts valued at $2400._

          The Grand Jury does further charge that Harvey Worker on the day and year aforesaid unlawfully and feloniously did then and there steal, take, exercise unlawful control over and carry away those certain goods and property as set forth above, with intent of depriving the owner thereof and of converting it to a use other than that of the owner and without his consent.

          The Grand Jury does further charge that Harvey Worker on or about June 14, 19XW, and on or about October 11, 19XW, and on or about January 20, 19XX; and on or about April 3, 19XX did at all such times unlawfully and feloniously steal, take, exercise unlawful control

over, and carry away personal property of The Firm consisting of cypres parts valued in all in excess of $10,000
with intent of depriving the owner thereof and converting
it to a use other than that of the owner and without his consent.

        All of which is against the peace and
dignity of the State of Great State and in violation of
Sections 3502 and 3921, Great State Criminal Code.

Ray Jacob
Foreperson

James Bethann
by *James Solicitor*
Attorney for the State

WITNESSES:
Teresa Copp
Vincent Polise
Hurbert Seek
Richard Find

Note: Notice of time, date, and place of arraignment on
reverse side.

referred to as a *true bill*. A copy of the one in the Harvey Worker case
appears as Form 10-2. A unanimous decision is not required to indict. In
Great State, the minimum vote necessary for indictment was 12. The
foreperson reports the decisions of the grand jury in open court at least
once a day in the presence of all members of that grand jury. Great State
required that a copy of the indictment be sent to the defendant. A copy
was also sent to the clerk of courts where it served as the triggering
document for scheduling the next step in the criminal process, the
arraignment.

If a grand jury decides to dismiss charges against the accused, the bill of indictment is marked "not found" or "not a true bill" and is said to be ignored. When that occurs, any bail is refunded. If a defendant has been confined to jail, he is released from custody. In Great State, the district attorney could not resubmit a dismissed case to another grand jury unless the criminal court granted permission to do so. Request was made to the court by a motion of the prosecutor.

Grand juries in Local County approved 94 percent of the bills of indictment presented to them during the calendar year 19XX. To those who asserted that this was proof that the grand jury was merely a rubber stamp for the prosecutor, Jim Solicitor replied that it was more a reflection of efficient screening prior to grand jury action. There were those who responded by asking if there really was a need, under these conditions, for a grand jury.

In Harvey's case, the grand jury members, after hearing Detectives Find and Seek and the two arresting officers, agreed unanimously and without hesitation that Harvey should be indicted. Had Harvey's case occurred in a jurisdiction where the charging instrument was an information rather than an indictment, a similar document would have been prepared by the district attorney and filed with the criminal court without any grand jury action.

Information Compared

Arraignment follows the filing of an information just as it does an indictment. At least half of the states do not use the indictment process. There are some that allege that the grand jury is a cumbersome, costly, and outmoded procedure, whose functions are better served through a preliminary hearing. A comparison of characteristics of the two is revealing:

Preliminary Hearing	Grand Jury
1. Determination of probable cause.	1. Determination of probable cause.
2. Decision by magistrate [one person [a professional.	2. Decision by grand jurors [a group [laypersons.
3. Prosecution testimony.	3. Prosecution testimony.
4. Public.	4. Secret.
5. Accused present.	5. Accused not present.
6. Right of accused to assistance of counsel.	6. No right to counsel for accused.
7. Right of accused to cross-examine.	7. No right to cross-examine by accused.

8. Defense testimony permitted.	8. No defense testimony.
9. Accused's counsel may record.	9. No recording by accused.
10. Transcript required.	10. Transcript often not permitted.
11. Waiverable (with exceptions).	11. Waiverable (with exceptions).
12. Miranda warnings required.	12. No Miranda warnings required.
13. Suppression of illegally secured evidence.	13. Exclusionary rule not applicable.
14. Self-incriminating testimony not required.	14. Grant of immunity possible to secure incriminating testimony.

In Great State, the district attorney had yet another opportunity to exercise his discretion. He could file postindictment motions requesting that the defendant be accepted for accelerated rehabilitation or for nolle prosequi. Neither of these was considered in Harvey's case.

RIGHT TO SPEEDY TRIAL

The copy of the indictment sent to Harvey contained a notice of the time and place for which his arraignment had been scheduled. Time was important, since Great State had adopted a statute which required that the trial of criminal cases must begin no later than 180 days after a criminal complaint has been filed. At the federal level, the Speedy Trial Act of 1974[8] generally requires that an accused be brought to trial within 100 days from the date of his arrest, with a maximum time schedule as follows:

Arrest to indictment or information . . . . 30 days
Indictment or information to arraignment . . . . 10 days
Arraignment to trial . . . . 60 days

These laws were enacted for the purpose of furthering the Sixth Amendment right to a speedy trial, a right that has been made applicable to the states by the United States Supreme Court.[9] The legislation is the result of public and legislative concern about the effect of a backlog of criminal cases in the courts. This is of vital significance to those accused who are unable to obtain bail and must await trial while in custody.

PLEA ALTERNATIVES

Harvey asked many questions of Henry Law concerning the forthcoming arraignment. When he learned that he would be called upon to plead to the charges, Harvey asked for advice.

"I can explain the alternatives to you and the consequences of each," said Henry, "but the final decision must be yours."

The two explored the possible pleas: guilty, not guilty, nolo contendere, and silence. A plea of *guilty*, Henry said, would mean that Harvey would forego trial and would be sentenced. It was the equivalent of being found guilty by a jury, he added. A *not guilty* plea, on the other hand, would mean that Harvey would go to trial. He would have the right to a trial by jury but could waive the jury if he so chose. A plea of *nolo contendere* could be entered with consent of the court. It meant that Harvey did not intend to contest the charges. One effect was the same as if he had pleaded guilty: sentencing would result. However, the plea could not be used against Harvey later should a civil suit be brought against him for the same wrong. Finally, there was *silence*, which meant that the accused stood mute before the court. In that case, Henry explained, the judge was required to consider the silence of the accused as the equivalent of a not guilty plea.

"It's really a choice between guilty and not guilty, isn't it?" asked Harvey.

Henry nodded affirmatively.

"With a not guilty plea, I still have a chance. With a guilty plea, I have none," Harvey commented.

Henry suggested that they take a realistic look at Harvey's chances should he go to trial. He reminded Harvey that the district attorney had witnesses who saw Harvey in the plant stealing parts; that the police had in their possession stolen goods that had been recovered from his home workshop; and that they also had a tape recording of his confession. That, Henry added, would establish a very tight case against Harvey. Continuing, Henry noted that there was not much to be offered in defense.

DEFENSE CONSIDERATIONS

Henry had considered the position of the defense for some time. Defense counsel in a criminal action looks for measures that can result in either exculpating the defendant or mitigating the seriousness of the offense. Some measures were obviously not appropriate in this case. For instance, it was out of the question for Harvey to claim either that he did not unlawfully enter the building on the night in question or that, while there, he did not take cypres parts belonging to The Firm. This was not a case in which an alibi could be introduced.

Criminal Act and Intent

But Henry asked, did the fact that the acts took place mean that a crime or crimes had been committed? The Great State Criminal Code retained the common law concept that a crime requires both an act and an evil intention. (Exceptions to that did exist. By statutory provision certain acts were in and of themselves offenses against the Great State Criminal Code, regardless of criminal intent. In common parlance these acts are referred to as crimes, although scholars question if they are "true crimes.") Therefore, Henry mentally considered if there had been present the two elements necessary to the commission of crime:

1. the *actus reus*—criminal acts or deeds.
2. the *mens rea* and criminal intent—the mental intent.

The actus reus, or the guilty act, generally differs from crime to crime. The acts or deeds that constituted the two crimes with which Harvey had been charged were to be found in Sections 3502 and 3921 of the Great State Criminal Code. Referring to the Code, Henry once again quickly went down the list of items that made up each crime:

Burglary: entered a building,
            building not open to the public,
            no license or privilege to enter,
            intent to commit a crime therein.
Theft: unlawfully,
            take and exercise control over,
            movable property of another,
            intent to deprive owner of the property.

Henry asked himself if each existed in Harvey's situation. He found that he had no choice but to say YES with regard to each item, whether it represented an act or an intent.

A wrongful or blameworthy mental state is required for crime in general. Some crimes, such as burglary and theft, require an additional mental element. For them, the specific intent is as much an element of the offense as the act itself, and proof of general malice will not suffice. The terms *criminal intent* and *mens rea* are at times used interchangeably. However, some writers have pointed out that the first term properly refers to a general guilty or evil state of mind, whereas the latter includes many different ones for the many different offenses.

Henry asked himself about his client's mental capacity at the time the acts were committed. Harvey had been neither drugged nor intoxicated. Nor was he mentally impaired. He had acted consciously, understanding what he was doing and knowing that it was wrong. Furthermore, Henry could not find that Harvey had acted under duress, out of fear, or because of threats. Instead, he had acted voluntarily. He had fully intended to do exactly what he did, having been compelled in no way to do so. Henry concluded that both the requisite criminal act and mental intent had been present. In addition, insanity and duress, which can serve as defenses in some criminal matters, were inapplicable. Also inapplicable were such affirmative defenses as entrapment, consent, and self-defense.

Burden of Proof

Henry considered other defense matters. Since this was a criminal action, the prosecution had the burden of proving the defendant's guilt beyond a reasonable doubt. Would the district attorney be able to do so? If he could not, Henry's task would be easy. He would simply move at the close of the prosecution's case for a judgment of acquittal because of the state's failure to establish a prima facie case. What evidence, he asked himself, did the district attorney have? He came up with this list:

> eyewitnesses to the burglary and theft: two police officers, Ed Under, and Al Chase;
> cypres parts in Harvey's plastic bag recovered at the burglary scene;
> other cypres parts which had been recovered from Harvey's basement;
> Harvey's confession to the police;
> witnesses who had purchased cypres parts from Harvey at extremely low prices.

With regard to burglary and theft on the night of May 20, the eyewitnesses and the plastic bag of cypres parts could well serve to prove the *corpus delicti,* that is, the body of the crime (*not* the body of a homicide victim, as is commonly assumed). Furthermore, Henry believed this was competent evidence, not subject to the exclusionary rule.

Proof of the other thefts was another matter. There were witnesses who could testify to purchasing cypres parts from Harvey at extremely low prices, but none knew the source of the parts he sold. Furthermore, Henry believed he could create doubt in the minds of the jurors as to the credibility of the fence, should the latter be called as a witness. Much more damaging evidence existed in Harvey's confession and the cypres parts recovered from his basement workshop with the search warrant.

Suppressible Evidence

However, Henry believed that the confession might be subject to suppression. It had been secured during a delay between Harvey's arrest and the initial appearance. If that had been an unnecessary delay, it violated Rule 118 of the Great State Rules of Criminal Procedure. And in *Great State v. Futch,* 447 G.S. 389 (19XR), the Great State Supreme Court had held that a confession resulting from such violations of Rule 118 was excludable along with all evidence flowing from the confession.

"If I can convince the court that the delay was unnecessary," Henry said to himself, "suppression of the confession and the seized cypres parts should leave the prosecution unable to meet the burden of proving beyond a reasonable doubt the thefts prior to May 20. Then, even if Harvey is convicted on the charges stemming from the May 20 incident, the sentence should be lighter." That made suppression worth striving for, Henry decided. If he wished to have evidence excluded, he would have to file a motion for suppression with the court prior to trial. A hearing would be held before one of the criminal court judges who would then decide whether or not the facts warranted granting the motion.

As Henry thought more about it, he decided there could be additional arguments raised in support of suppression of Harvey's confession. Harvey had been apprehensive and fearful at the time of his confession; he had just been "roughed up" at the scene of his arrest. Could he, under those circumstances, have made a truly voluntary statement?

"I should be able to prepare a persuasive argument," Henry thought.

Other Defenses

However, he did not end his consideration of the defense there. He carefully re-examined the documents related to the case, such as the criminal complaint and the indictment. A defense might emerge from them. For example, there might be error intrinsic to a document, such as an indictment which did not charge a crime. Or, there might have been an indictment for charges on which the defendant had previously been acquitted or convicted. In that case, the defense could file a motion to quash the indictment on the grounds that it was in violation of the Fifth Amendment protection against double jeopardy, that is, being placed in jeopardy twice for the same offense. This provision has been held applicable to the states by the United States Supreme Court.[10] If granted, such a motion would remove the accused from the criminal system. Double jeopardy, it should be noted here, means that one must twice actually be in jeopardy. A prior invalid legal action, such as one in a court lacking jurisdiction, does not constitute a jeopardy. It should also be noted that a defendant, by his actions, may waive the bar of jeopardy. Instances when this may occur include those when he asks for a new trial or appeals his verdict.[11] However, in Harvey's case, these were not applicable.

Henry next determined that the Statute of Limitations could not be raised as a defense. The time limit for the initiation of prosecution for burglary and theft in Great State was four years.

Nor did problems of jurisdiction exist. The case was before the criminal division of the state trial court in Local County. No federal offense had been committed. Therefore, the action properly belonged in the state court system. Great State law, like that of many other states, provided that any person who committed a crime "in whole or in part" within the territorial limits of that state could be convicted there of crime.

So long as the suspect was arrested within the state, no problem arose in bringing him before its courts. However, when the accused fled beyond the state's borders, *extradition* became necessary. Extradition is a formal process by which a person is transferred from one state to another to be tried on criminal charges pending against him in that second state. He has the opportunity for a hearing to show cause why he should not be extradited. However, this was not the situation in Harvey's case.

No venue problem existed. Proper venue in criminal cases generally is the county in which the crime was committed. Nor had the publicity been so great in Harvey's case as to cause Henry to believe that Harvey would not receive a fair trial in Local County. Therefore, no request for change of venue was contemplated.

GUILTY PLEA?

Henry conveyed his assessment of the defense to Harvey explaining that the suppression motion represented just about the only possibility. Furthermore, he could not guarantee that it would be granted. Even if it were, it would help only with respect to the thefts prior to the time of the burglary.

"In this country, one is presumed to be innocent until proven guilty." Henry added, "However, that does not mean that persons who perpetrate criminal acts should expect that they will not be proven guilty. To think otherwise is foolhardy and unrealistic."

"Why bother with a defense, then?" Harvey wanted to know.

Henry explained that defense counsel can act to protect the defendant's rights and to see that he is accorded due process at all times.

Realizing that Henry was not holding out a great deal of hope, Harvey asked:

"Suppose I plead guilty. What kind of sentence do you think I'd get then?"

Bargaining

Henry said he would talk with the prosecutor's office about this. There were mitigating factors: this was a first offense, and about half of the stolen parts had been recovered and would be returned to The Firm. Henry sought out the assistant district attorney to whom Harvey's case had been assigned for trial. That was Bob Barrister. The latter had reviewed the materials in the Harvey Worker file. He remarked to Henry that it seemed rather clear that the defense had little to offer. However, were Henry's client to plead guilty, the prosecutor's office could forego the time, expense, and work involved in having to prove guilt beyond a reasonable doubt. In view of this and of Harvey's lack of prior convictions, he was prepared to recommend probation at the time of sentencing if a guilty plea were entered. Henry indicated that he would discuss this offer with his client.

Henry and Bob had been involved in a practice known as *plea bargaining*. This occurs when the prosecutor and defense counsel (and, at times, the defendant, also) engage in negotiations about the plea, the charges, and the sentence recommendation. The usual outcome is a reduction in charges or a promise by the prosecutor to recommend a more lenient sentence in return for the defendant's plea of guilty.

The vast majority of criminal cases in this country are resolved by a guilty plea. While this has been attributed to good police work and efficient pretrial screening, many believe that plea bargaining is the most important reason for it. At the same time, many critics of plea bargaining allege that it leads to guilty pleas by innocent persons who are frightened and distrustful of the consequences of going to trial. Still others have contended that justice is not something that can be negotiated and have recommended that plea bargaining be completely abolished. On the other hand, there are those who claim that plea bargaining is a necessity if the courts are to be able to cope with the multitude of criminal cases coming before them. The United States Supreme Court has recognized that plea bargaining is a phase of the criminal process and, in one opinion, stated that "properly administered" plea bargaining should be encouraged.[12]

The Great State Rules of Criminal Procedure set forth the following specific requirements regarding plea bargaining:

1. The trial judge is not permitted to participate in the plea negotiations.

2. Counsel for both sides are required to state on the record in open court in the presence of the defendant the terms of the agreement.

3. The judge is required to conduct an inquiry of the defendant to determine if he understands and concurs in the agreement.

4. The judge is permitted to accept the agreement if he is satisfied that the guilty plea is understandingly and voluntarily offered.

5. The judge is not required to be bound by the plea agreement unless he accepts it. If he does not, the accused must be permitted to withdraw the guilty plea.

These rules were developed to eliminate secret deals and to assure, insofar as possible, the voluntariness of confessions of guilt.

Decision

Henry took Bob Barrister's offer back to Harvey. The two discussed it. Henry asked Harvey to consider it very carefully. In answer to Harvey's question, he said that a guilty plea could be entered at the forthcoming arraignment, at a later date prior to trial and after a decision had been rendered by the court regarding the suppression motion, or even during the trial. While Harvey relished the thought of release on probation, he realized there could be no guarantee of this. He also decided that he preferred to try every possible avenue of defense before he would plead guilty. The list of pros and cons he considered in arriving at a decision not to accept the prosecution's offer at least for the present is shown below:

Plead Guilty	**Plead Not Guilty**
1. Quick disposition.	1. Longer time required.
2. No trial.	2. Must stand trial.
3. Less legal fees to be paid.	3. Greater legal fees.
4. Probability of leniency in sentencing.	4. Uncertainty as to leniency.
5. Criminal record.	5. Uncertainty as to criminal record.
6. No chance for acquittal.	6. Chance for acquittal.
	7. Henry's a good lawyer, interested in me, will do his utmost.

The final decision had not been easy. Henry had suggested taking time to reconsider "carefully and realistically" after the first indication of similar intention. He pointed to Harvey's commission of the acts, as well as the paucity of defenses. In a telephone conversation one day Mary explained to Henry that neither she nor Harvey would ever feel satisfied if they did not exhaust every possibility. The death of John Q. had resulted in a severe and detrimental impact upon Harvey's life, including his dropping out of college and "now this," she said. Therefore, she had determined to provide him with every opportunity and all the support she could, not only now but "all the way through an appeal, if that becomes necessary."

ARRAIGNMENT

As scheduled, Harvey appeared with Henry before Judge Joseph Roe in the Local County Criminal Court at ten o'clock on the morning of July 3, 19XX, for arraignment. Bob Barrister was present representing the district attorney's office. In Great State, arraignment was required to be held in open court at least ten days prior to trial. Harvey was read the charges against him which appeared in the indictment. At this point, he would have been given a copy of that document had he not already received one. He was again advised of his rights. Because the arraignment is considered a critical stage in the criminal process, note was made of the

fact that he was present and represented by legal counsel. When the judge asked how he wished to plead, he answered:
"Not guilty."

Record of Plea

The case was set for trial. Harvey indicated he wished to have a jury trial. The judge reviewed his bail and continued it as it had been set at the initial appearance. A transcript of the arraignment was filed with the clerk of court's office. Notice to set a trial date was sent to the deputy court administrator in charge of the criminal trial list.

Voluntariness of Plea

Had Harvey pleaded guilty, the judge would have exerted effort to determine the voluntariness of that plea. Coerced confessions clearly violate the Fifth Amendment privilege against compulsory self-incrimination. Before accepting a plea of guilty, therefore, the judge's concern is that the accused is entering that plea knowingly and of his own accord. One test frequently used to determine this is to elicit answers to questions such as these:

Do you understand the nature of the charges to which you are pleading?

What is the factual basis for your plea? What, in fact, did you do?

Do you understand that you have the right to trial by jury?

Do you understand that you are presumed innocent until found guilty?

Do you know the range of sentences for the offense for which you are charged?

Do you know that the judge is not bound by the terms of any plea bargain unless the judge accepts the agreement?

If the judge were satisfied that the plea had been voluntarily given, he could either impose sentence then or schedule sentencing for a later date. Prior to sentencing, withdrawal of a guilty plea is possible with leave of court.

The arraignment process has been flow charted in Figure 10-2.

DISCOVERY

Henry now engaged in trial preparation. Since this was a criminal case, the extent of discovery in civil actions was not applicable. Great

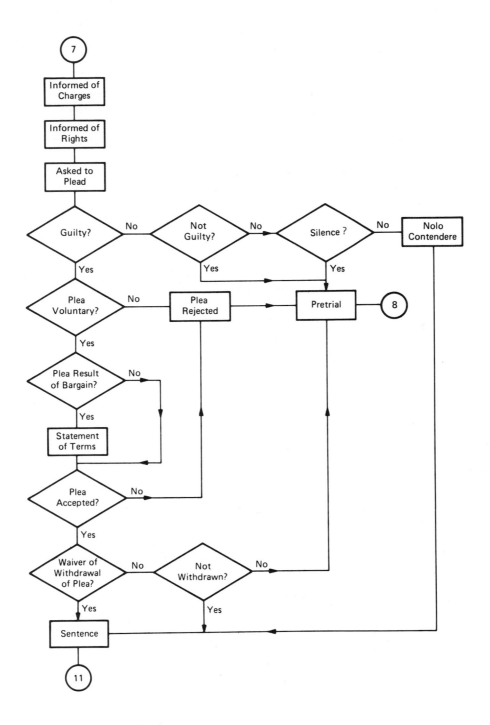

FIGURE 10-2. Arraignment.

State Rules of Criminal Procedure provided, in general, that the prosecution must provide the defense with substantial, material evidence in its possession. However, the prosecutor was not required to turn over the complete file on the case. Deposition taking was limited to that of prospective witnesses whose testimony was considered to be material and who would be unable to attend the trial. The United States Supreme Court has held that a prosecutor has a constitutional duty to provide material exculpatory evidence to the defense, whether or not a request is made.[13]

Many commentators have taken issue with limitations on criminal discovery. Because of the privilege against self-incrimination, some restrictions that would not exist in a civil case appear to be necessary.

MOTION TO SUPPRESS

The court granted Henry's motion to secure a copy of the tape recorded confession which Harvey had given to the police. Henry's next step was to prepare an application for the suppression of evidence, a copy of which appears as Form 10-3. Note that he based his request for suppression upon the delay between arrest and initial appearance and also upon an allegation that Harvey's confession was the product of undue pressure and coercion.

FORM 10-3. Application to Suppress Evidence.

COURT OF LOCAL COUNTY
CRIMINAL DIVISION

STATE OF GREAT STATE   :   No. 1246 of 19XX
          V.   :   Burglary and Theft

HARVEY WORKER   :

APPLICATION TO SUPPRESS EVIDENCE AND
CONFESSIONS AND/OR ADMISSIONS

And now this tenth day of July 19XX comes the above defendant by his attorney pursuant to Great State R. Crim. Pro. 323, 324, and 2001 and respectfully represents as follows:

    1. This matter was set for trial following arraignment before Judge Joseph Roe on July 3.

---

2.   Defendant was arrested on May 20, 19XX for the above mentioned charges.

3.   Defendant believes there will be introduced into evidence at the time of the trial of this case certain written, taped, and/or oral statements and/or admissions which may amount to a confession or which may contain admissions implicating the defendant in the subject case.

4.   That said incriminating statements were made while defendant was being held at Central Police Headquarters in Big City and in fact in police custody.

5.   That said incriminating statements were made by defendant without the presence of legal counsel to advise him.

6.   That the circumstances warranted the defendant being warned of his constitutional rights enunciated in the Fourth, Fifth, Sixth, and Fourteenth Amendments of the United States Constitution and in the case of   Miranda v. Arizona , 384 U.S. 436 (1966).

7.   That even assuming defendant was warned of said constitutional rights before giving a statement, he did not intelligently waive those rights because of the overbearing nature of the circumstances in which he found himself because authorities pressed for answers to questions and overbore his will to resist making a statement.

8.   That the statements above mentioned were not voluntarily and intelligently and knowingly given to the police but were the product of undue pressure, influence, coercion, design, and/or trickery, all of which prompted defendant in making the statements.
All of which above described violates the Fourth, Fifth, Sixth, and Fourteenth Amendments to the Constitution of the United States and the case law made pursuant thereto.

9.   That subsequent to arrest, certain cypres parts were seized from the premises at 600 Fifth Street in Big City pursuant to a search warrant executed and issued on the basis of the information illegally and unconstitutionally secured from the defendant as described above and are therefore "fruit of the poisonous tree."

10.   That defendant's detention at Central Police Headquarters was prolonged following the completion of

booking procedures and the defendant's initial appearance before a magistrate was delayed by the police for the purpose of the above described interrogation of the defendant.

11.   That such delay in the initial appearance is in violation of Great State R. Crim. Pro. 118.

12.   That all evidence obtained as a result of such unnecessary delay in violation of Rule 118 is inadmissible. Great State v. Futch, 447 G.S. 389 (19XR).

Whereupon defendant requests a rule to issue upon the State to show cause why all the evidence seized and the written, taped, and/or oral statements given and the evidence which flows therefrom should not be suppressed.

Respectfully submitted,

Attorney for the Defendant

A copy of the application was filed with the clerk of courts and another with the district attorney. Bob Barrister prepared a request to the court to deny the application. A copy of this appears as Form 10-4. Not only did he contend that any delay following Harvey's arrest was necessary and reasonable, but he also stated that according to Harvey's own admission there had been no undue influence exerted upon him to confess. Notice, too, that Bob concluded by requesting that a hearing on the application be scheduled for as soon as possible in order not to delay the date of trial.

The Great State Criminal Court followed a master calendar plan instead of the individual calendar system. Therefore, different aspects of any one case might be assigned to different judges. For instance, all pretrial applications, petitions, and motions were assigned to the administrative judge. It was in this way that the hearing on Henry's suppression motion came to be scheduled before Judge Homer Grant.

Suppression Hearing

A private hearing was required because the issue of the inadmissibility of a confession would be considered. Were the contents of the confession to be revealed in a public hearing, a grant of the motion to suppress the confession would be of little value! The only persons permitted to be

FORM 10-4. States Request for Denial.

COURT OF LOCAL COUNTY
CRIMINAL DIVISION

STATE OF GREAT STATE   :

         V.   :   No. 1246 of 19XX

HARVEY WORKER   :   Burglary and Theft

STATE'S REQUEST FOR DENIAL OF DEFENDANT'S
APPLICATION TO SUPPRESS EVIDENCE
AND CONFESSIONS AND/OR ADMISSIONS

And now this fourteenth day of July comes James Bethann, District Attorney, by Assistant District Attorney, Robert Barrister, and in answer to Defendant's Application to Suppress Evidence and Confessions and/or Admissions respectfully shows:

    1. Defendant was arrested on May 20, 19XX at 7:30 p.m. at The Firm's factory and transported immediately to Central Police Headquarters in Big City, arriving there at 8:20 p.m. Booking, fingerprinting, and photographing followed. At 9:10 p.m. defendant began a statement to the police which was concluded at 9:40 p.m. Defendant's initial appearance before the magistrate began at 10:00 p.m.

    2. The time between arrest and initial appearance is fully accounted for and was consumed by the above described necessary police procedures. There was no unnecessary delay, in terms of the requirements of Great State R. Crim. Pro. 118, between the time of arrest and initial appearance.

    3. Limited police interrogation of an arrestee is permissible under Great State v. Futch, 447 G.S. 389 (19XR) where at 392 the Court quoted from Adams v. United States, 399 F.2d 574, 579 (D.C. Cir., 1968) as follows:

"Necessary delay can reasonably relate to time to administratively process an accused with booking, fingerprinting and other steps and sometimes even to make same (sic) limited preliminary investigation into his connection with the crime for which he was arrested, especially when it is directed to possible exculpation of the one arrested."

4. Defendant was warned of his constitutional rights at the time of his arrest, at the time he was booked, prior to police interrogation, and again immediately before he provided his taped statement to the police.

5. Defendant is 20 years of age, has attended college for one year, understands and speaks the English language well, and is fully capable of understanding and comprehending the meaning of statements of his constitutional rights.

6. By defendant's own admission, recorded on his taped statement, he was neither coerced, tricked, threatened, subjected to physical harm, made any promises of deals, nor was he in any other way influenced or pressured to give his statement to the police.

7. By defendant's own admission, recorded on his taped statement, he voluntarily and knowingly waived his right to remain silent and to have legal counsel present during the time he gave his statement to the police.

8. Seizure of cypres parts was made at the defendant's home pursuant to a legally issued and executed search warrant and in full accord with defendant's constitutional rights.

For all these reasons, the State requests that defendant's application to suppress evidence and confessions and/or admissions should be denied.

The State further requests that a hearing on the matter of the defendant's application be held at the earliest possible date in order not to delay the date of trial.

James Bethann
James Bethann, District Attorney

Robert Barrister
Assistant District Attorney

present included Harvey, Henry, Bob Barrister, court officers, and the witness testifying. Other witnesses waited in the hall until called. The judge heard from Harvey (who, as Henry explained beforehand, did not in that way waive his right to remain silent at trial), Detectives Find and Seek, Al Chase and Ed Under, and the two arresting officers. He also listened to the tape recorded confession.

At one point during the hearing the judge himself undertook questioning of Harvey regarding the circumstances surrounding his confession. Portions of that examination follow:

Judge: Did you know you had the right to have a lawyer present?

Harvey: Yes.

J: How did you know?

H: The police told me.

J: When did they tell you that?

H: Several times.

J: When would that have been?

H: When I was arrested . . . out at The Firm, when they brought me to the police station, when the detectives took me into the interrogation room where I made the statement, before I made the tape recording.

J: At all of these times?

H: Yes.

J: Did the police tell you anything else at these times?

H: Yes.

J: What was that?

H: That I could remain silent, that anything I said would be held against me.

J: Did they say anything more about a lawyer?

H: Yes.

J: And what was that?

H: If I wanted one and couldn't get one, they'd get one for me.

J: And what did you say about a lawyer?

H: That I didn't want one.

J: That you didn't want one? Why was that?

H: I didn't think then that he could do me any good.

J: Was that because the police advised you of that?

H: No. That was what I thought then. I know better now.

J: Did the police advise you either way: that you needed a lawyer or that you didn't need one?

H: No. They just told me I could have one if I wanted one.

J: And you said?

H: I didn't want one.

J: Did the poliee force you or in any way threaten you to say that?

H: No.

J: Were you tricked into saying that?

H: I didn't know then that a lawyer could help me.

J: Does that mean you know that now?

H: Yes.

J: How did you learn that?

H: I have a lawyer, and he helps me. He explains things. He tells me what's going to happen. I know what to expect.

J: And you didn't then?

H: No I thought they'd probably just lock me in jail.

J: What else did you think would happen to you?

H: I didn't know.

J: Well, did you think, for instance, the police might abuse you? beat you?

H: No.

J: Did they mistreat you at any time?

H: I was roughed up when I was arrested.

J: By the police?

H: Yes.

J: The arresting officers?

H: Yes.

J: What did they do to you?

H: Kicked me in the shins and punched me in the ribs when they were patting me down.

J: Did you require medical attention?

H: No.

J: Did you consult a physician?

H: No.

J: Why not?

H: I didn't need one.

J: Why not?

H: I knew it would get better by itself.

J: How serious was it? Did you, for instance, have bruises, marks, welts, or discolorations on your body from the blows?

H: No.

J: Were you incapacitated in any way?

H: No.

J: What discomfort, if any, did you suffer from the roughing up?

H: It hurt.

J: At the time?

H: Yes.

J: Did the pain continue?

H: Yes.

J: For how long?

H: I don't know.

J: Were you still feeling pain at the time you arrived at the police station?

H: Yes.

J: Did it continue?

H: Yes.

J: For how long?

H: I don't remember.

J: Did you tell the police at the station you were in pain?

H: No.

J: Why not?

H: I guess I was too frightened.

J: Did any other police officer, at any time, either rough you up or in any way beat, hit, or otherwise cause physical harm to you?

H: No.

J: Did any of them threaten to do so?

H: No.

Motion Denied

Several days later, the judge issued an order denying the relief requested. At the same time, he filed a statement of findings of fact and conclusions of law with regard to the defendant's application to suppress evidence. Pertinent portions of that document, later quoted to the appellate court, were as follows:

FINDINGS OF FACT

1. Defendant was arrested without a warrant by police officers who, responding to a call reporting burglary in progress at The Firm, found defendant in The Firm's building after business hours and in the process of removing parts from shelves where they were stored and placing them in a plastic bag.

2. Defendant was given Miranda warnings by the police at the time of his arrest, at the time of booking, and again before his statement to the police regarding his participation in the felonies.

3. Defendant is 20 years of age, has completed one year of college, understands and uses the English language well.

4. Defendant admits he understood he had the right to legal counsel and to remain silent when questioned by the police and further admits that he waived those rights.

5. Defendant admits he was neither threatened nor physically abused by the police at the time he gave them his confession, nor was he made any promises or special deals in return for his confession.

6. While there is some discrepancy in the testimony as to whether defendant was "roughed up" physically at the time of his arrest, defendant neither required medical attention nor suffered any bruises, marks, or discoloration as a result of the alleged treatment.

7. Defendant was arrested at approximately 7:30 PM at The Firm's factory; was transported to central police headquarters where he arrived at 8:20 PM; was booked, fingerprinted, and photographed; gave a statement to the police beginning at 9:10 PM and concluding at 9:40 PM; appeared before a magistrate for his initial appearance beginning at 10:00 PM.

CONCLUSIONS OF LAW

1. Defendant's warrantless arrest was legal, having been made by police who witnessed the defendant in the act of theft and had probable cause to believe he had also committed burglary.

2. The lapse of time between arrest and initial appearance did not constitute unnecessary delay, nor was it unreasonable, in terms of the requirements of Rule 118 of the Great State Rules of Criminal Procedure. The time having been used for necessary police procedures, the initial appearance began within a period that fully complied with the requirements of Rule 118.

3. Defendant's confession was voluntary, having been made after he had been fully informed of his rights and had knowingly and voluntarily waived his right to remain silent and to have counsel present.

4. The search and seizure of cypres parts at defendant's home was valid, since it was conducted pursuant to a search warrant issued and based upon probable cause.

5. The application of defendant to suppress the evidence should be denied.

PRETRIAL PLANNING

Defense Plans

Harvey was disappointed but still determined to go to trial. He and Henry discussed the course of action to be taken should Harvey be found guilty. Henry noted that his first act would be to urge leniency in sentencing. He believed the mitigating factors of a first offense and partial restitution made it likely this would be granted. In addition, Henry planned to quote to the court from the Model Penal Code, which recommends probation unless imprisonment is necessary for "protection of the public." Finally, he and Harvey decided that any other action following that would have to remain indefinite, pending outcome of the trial.

One decision Henry made about this time concerned whether or not Harvey should take the stand in his own defense. Henry concluded that it would be to Harvey's advantage to exercise his privilege against self-incrimination by not testifying. By taking the stand, he would become subject to cross-examination by the prosecution whose skillful questioning could lead Harvey to fatal admissions. Henry also planned to call character witnesses. He and Harvey decided upon the dean of the college Harvey had attended as well as Harvey's former summer employer.

Pretrial Conference

A pretrial conference could be ordered by the court in criminal cases in Great State. This was generally reserved for complicated cases. None was requested in this case. Many persons have advocated an omnibus pretrial hearing for criminal cases, at which time all pretrial motions would be made and means of discovery would be open to both sides. In addition to suppression motions, other possible pretrial motions include those:

> to nolle prosequi,
> to disqualify a judge,
> to request a psychiatric examination of the accused,
> to request a pretrial conference,
> to request a change of venue,
> to quash the indictment,
> to request a bill of particulars (in effect, a means of discovery, since it is a request for information).

Proponents of the omnibus hearing claim it will enable defense counsel to make more intelligent recommendations to their clients regarding guilty pleas, going to trial, and taking the stand in their own defense.

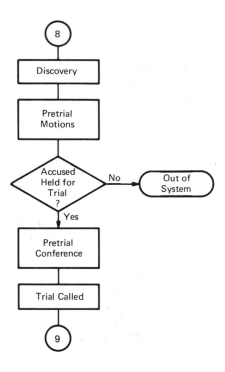

FIGURE 10-3. Pretrial Procedures Following Arraignment.

Prosecutor's Preparation

While the defense was thus at work, Bob Barrister also took steps in connection with the Harvey Worker case. He caused subpoenas to be issued to insure attendance at the trial of these witnesses: the two arresting officers, Detectives Find and Seek, Ed Under, Al Chase, and two of Harvey's former customers. He also made sure that the tape recording of Harvey's confession was in good condition. He planned to play it for the jury.

TRIAL SCHEDULING

At this point the district attorney's office sent to the court administrator's office a list of cases ready for trial. Harvey Worker's case was among them. It was placed on the trial list. Great State rules required that the trial list be called ten days prior to trial. Written notice to both the defendant and his surety was also required. Accordingly, all parties involved were notified that the trial of Harvey Worker on charges of burglary and theft was scheduled for August 28, 19XX before Judge Shirley Wolfe. Cases came to trial more slowly in the summer months in Local County because of court employee vacations.

And so almost 100 days following his arrest, Harvey Worker would come to trial. That trial is described in the next chapter.

QUESTIONS

The chances for Harvey's acquittal appear to be slim. Still he has not yet changed his mind about pleading guilty.

Do you agree with him in this decision? Did Henry make the best use of the negotiations with the prosecutor? Would accepting his offer have been of any advantage to Harvey? any disadvantage? Do you agree with those who advocate elimination of plea bargaining?

Does Henry's suppression motion have merit? Or, is it really a desperate attempt to take some defense action in a case in which there is very little hope?

In comparing the indictment and the information as charging instruments, have you reached an opinion as to which represents the better procedure? Can the grand jury ever be replaced? Is the preliminary hearing a suitable replacement? The preliminary hearing has been compared in function with the summary judgment and the demurrer in the civil process. Do you agree? Are all the screening steps in the criminal process necessary? Do you find any duplication of effort? Where?

In this case there has been considerable pretrial activity, none of which involved The Firm, which was the entity actually suffering a loss because of the crime. What happened to its participation in this process? Should it be excluded? Do you agree that the limited discovery in the criminal process should be changed? Why?

Is the discretionary power of the prosecutor one that should be curbed? How? Why? Has it any value? Is it any greater than the discretion available to the police? Is the discretionary power of the prosecutor one that allows him to ignore the social policy established on behalf of the public by the legislature through enactment of the criminal code? Does the fact that many public prosecutors are elected officials have any bearing on your answer? Are rehabilitation programs into which some criminal cases are diverted an indication that some acts which are classed as criminal should not be so considered? Does it have any other implications? What are they?

What advantages would accrue if the charging procedure in the various states were to be made uniform? Which procedure would you advocate for that? Do you agree with charges that provisions of speedy trial laws tend to overdo speed? Are such laws really an overreaction to publicity about court congestion? Reaction by whom?

Because of specialization in both the Local County prosecutor's office and in the criminal court of Local County, more than one prosecuting attorney and more than one judge will have been involved in this case. What benefits do you see to this? Any disadvantages? To whom?

The criminal process, including those phases which occur between the initial appearance and trial, has been subject to much criticism. What recommendations do you have for improvement? What practices would you change? How can change within the criminal system be effectuated?

CASES

United States v. Mandujano
425 U.S. 564, 96 S.Ct. 1768, 48 L.Ed. 2d 212 (1976)

MR. CHIEF JUSTICE BURGER. This case presents the question whether the warnings called for by *Miranda v. Arizona*, 384 U.S. 436 (1966), must be given to a grand jury witness who is called to testify about criminal activities in which he may have been personally involved; and, whether absent such warnings, false statements made to the grand jury must be suppressed in a prosecution for perjury based on those statements. ...

The grand jury is an integral part of our constitutional heritage which was brought to this country with the common law. The Framers, most of them trained in the English law and traditions, accepted the grand jury as a basic guarantee of individual liberty; notwithstanding periodic criticism, much of which is superficial, overlooking relevant history, the grand jury continues to function as a barrier to reckless or unfounded charges. ... Its historic office has been to provide a shield against arbitrary or oppressive action, by insuring that serious criminal accusations will be brought only upon the considered judgment of a representative body of citizens acting under oath and under judicial instruction and guidance. ...

... the law vests the grand jury with substantial powers, ... Indispensable to the exercise of its power is the authority to compel the attendance and the testimony of witnesses, ... and to require the production of evidence, ...

When called by the grand jury, witnesses are thus legally bound to give testimony. ... The grand jury's authority to compel testimony is not, of course, without limits. The same Amendment that establishes the grand jury also guarantees that "no person ... shall be compelled in any criminal case to be a witness against himself. ..."

Under settled principles, the Fifth Amendment does not confer an absolute right to decline to respond in a grand jury inquiry ... The privilege cannot, for example, be asserted by a witness to protect others from possible criminal prosecution. ... Nor can it be invoked simply to protect the witness' interest in privacy. ...

. . . Moreover, the Court has expressly recognized that "[T]he obligation to appear is no different for a person who may himself be the subject of the grand jury inquiry."

Accordingly, the witness, though possibly engaged in some criminal enterprise, can be required to answer before a grand jury, so long as there is no compulsion to answer questions that are self-incriminating; the witness can, of course, stand on the privilege, . . . The witness must invoke the privilege, however, as the "Constitution does not forbid the asking of criminative questions.". . .

. . . If in fact "there is reasonable ground to apprehend danger to the witness from his being compelled to answer," . . . the prosecutor must then determine whether the answer is of such overriding importance as to justify a grant of immunity to the witness.

If immunity is sought by the prosecutor and granted by the presiding judge, the witness can then be compelled to answer, on pain of contempt, even though the testimony would implicate the witness in criminal activity. . . .

In this constitutional process of securing a witness' testimony, perjury simply has no place whatever. Perjured testimony is an obvious and flagrant affront to the basic concepts of judicial proceedings. . . .

. . . our cases have consistently—indeed without exception—allowed sanctions for false statements or perjury; they have done so even in instances where the perjurer complained that the Government exceeded its constitutional powers in making the inquiry. . . .

. . . [Miranda] warnings were aimed at the evils seen by the Court as endemic to police interrogation of a person in custody. . . . But the Miranda Court simply did not perceive judicial inquiries and custodial interrogation as equivalents; . . .

. . . Indeed, the Court's opinion in Miranda reveals a focus on what was seen by the Court as police "coercion" derived from "factual studies [relating to] police violence and the 'third degree, . . . physical brutality—beating, hanging, whipping—and to sustained and protracted questioning incommunicado in order to extort confessions. . . .'" *Miranda, supra.* at 445–446. To extend these concepts to questioning before a grand jury inquiring into criminal activity under the guidance of a judge is an extravagant expansion never remotely contemplated by this Court in Miranda. . . .

. . . To extend the concepts of Miranda, . . . would require that the witness be told that there was an absolute right to silence, and obviously any such warning would be incorrect, for there is no such right before a grand jury. Under Miranda, a person in police custody has, of course, an absolute right to decline to answer any question, incriminating or innocuous . . . whereas a grand jury witness, on the contrary, has an absolute duty to answer all questions, subject only to a valid Fifth Amendment claim. And even when the grand jury witness asserts the privilege, questioning need not cease, except as to the particular subject to which the privilege has been addressed. . .

. . . A witness "before a grand jury cannot insist, as a matter of constitutional right, on being represented by counsel. . . ." . . . Under settled principles the witness may not insist upon the presence of his attorney in the grand jury room. . . .

Santobello v. New York
404 U.S. 257, 92 S.Ct. 495, 30 L.Ed. 2d 427 (1971).

Santobello entered a guilty plea to a lesser charge as a result of bargaining between defense counsel and the prosecutor. The latter agreed to make no recommendation as to sentence, but at the time of sentencing had been replaced by another prosecutor who recommended imposition of the maximum sentence on the reduced charge. Over defense counsel's objections, the judge imposed the maximum sentence. It was upheld in the state appellate courts.

MR. CHIEF JUSTICE BURGER. We granted *certiorari* in this case to determine whether the State's failure to keep a commitment concerning the sentence recommendation on a guilty plea required a new trial. . . .

. . . The disposition of criminal charges by agreement between the prosecutor and the accused, sometimes loosely called "plea bargaining," is an essential component of the administration of justice. Properly administered, it is to be encouraged. If every criminal charge were subjected to a full-scale trial, the States and the Federal Government would need to multiply by many times the number of judges and court facilities.

Disposition of charges after plea discussions is not only an essential part of the process but a highly desirable part for many reasons. It leads to prompt and largely final disposition of most criminal cases; it avoids much of the corrosive impact of enforced idleness during pretrial confinement for those who are denied release pending trial; it protects the public from those accused persons who are prone to continue criminal conduct even while on pretrial release; and by shortening the time between charge and disposition, it enhances whatever may be the rehabilitative prospects of the guilty when they are ultimately imprisoned. . . .

This phase of the process of criminal justice and the adjudicative element inherent in accepting a plea of guilty, must be attended by safeguards to insure the defendant what is reasonably due in the circumstances. Those circumstances will vary, but a constant factor is that when a plea rests in any significant degree on a promise or agreement of the prosecutor, so that it can be said to be part of the inducement or consideration, such promise must be fulfilled.

On this record, the petitioner "bargained" and negotiated for a particular plea in order to secure dismissal of more serious charges, . . . It is now conceded that the promise to abstain from a recommendation was made, . . . That the breach of agreement was inadvertent does not lessen its impact.

The judgment is vacated and the case is remanded for reconsideration not inconsistent with this opinion.

FOOTNOTES

[1] *Oyler v. Boles,* 368 U.S. 448 (1962).

[2] *Gerstein v. Pugh,* 420 U.S. 103 (1975). Note that the Court also said: "We do not imply that the accused is entitled to judicial oversight or review of the decision to

prosecute. Instead we adhere to the Court's prior holding that a judicial hearing is not prerequisite to prosecution by information."

[3]*Hurtado v. California*, 110 U.S. 516 (1884).

[4]*United States v. Calandra*, 414 U.S. 338 (1974).

[5]*Ibid.*

[6]*United States v. Mandujano*, 425 U.S. 564 (1976).

[7]*Kastigar v. United States*, 406 U.S. 441 (1972).

[8]18 U.S.C. §3161, P.L. 93–619, 88 Stat. 2067.

[9]*Klopfer v. North Carolina*, 386 U.S. 213 (1967).

[10]*Benton v. Maryland*, 395 U.S. 784 (1969).

[11]*United States v. Tateo*, 377 U.S. 463 (1964).

[12]*Santobello v. New York*, 404 U.S. 257 (1971).

[13]*United States v. Agurs*, 427 U.S. 97 (1976).

CHAPTER 11
TRIAL, SENTENCING, AND APPEAL:
COURT SUBSYSTEM AND EXIT TO CORRECTIONS SUBSYSTEM

"All rise."

The words were familiar to Mary Worker, who sat in the first row of the observer's section in the courtroom as Judge Shirley Wolfe entered. The trial of Harvey Worker was about to begin.

TRIAL

At the defendant's table Harvey had been engaged in earnest conversation with Henry Law. Their concern was with selection of the jury, which was about to take place now that the judge had directed that the Harvey Worker trial begin. A group of fifty prospective jurors sat in the courtroom.

According to Great States Rules of Criminal Procedure, Harvey could have agreed to a jury of fewer than twelve, the minimum number being six. Since the prospect of clemency seemed greater to Harvey with larger numbers, he had not done so. Consequently, the clerk drew the names of fourteen persons from the jury wheel. They took seats in the jury box as their names were called.

Jury Selection

In his pretrial conversations with Harvey, Henry had expressed the opinion that careful selection of a jury was vital. Therefore, Harvey listened with interest to the questioning that took place as the voir dire progressed.

"Would you be inclined to give more weight to the testimony of a police officer than you would any other witness?"

When one prospective juror raised her hand in affirmative response to that question, Henry was quick to react.

"Call another," he said.

Thereupon the woman was asked to step down from the jury box. The clerk drew the name of another person from the wheel, and that individual took the seat that had just been vacated in the jury box. Voir dire continued.

"Do you or does anyone in your family know Harvey Worker? know any member of his family?"

"Have you read, seen or heard any news or other items regarding this defendant, who is charged with burglary and theft at The Firm?"

"Do you know anyone seated at counsel table or anyone in the district attorney's office?"

The questioning went on, challenging for cause. Then, both Bob and Henry exhausted the peremptory challenges. At last twelve jurors and two alternates were selected.

Bob Barrister had excluded college students and younger persons, while Henry had eliminated business proprietors, such as the owner of a gasoline station and of a dairy store. The result was that the jury had no members under age 25. Eight of the 12 were women, as were the two alternates. The juror's occupations were diverse. Two were housewives. There was also a taxi driver, a meteorologist, an unemployed photographer, a highway construction worker, a plumber, a chemist, a lumber salesperson, a public relations writer, a barber, and an auto mechanic. Both alternates were housewives.

Harvey studied their faces. His immediate future was in their hands. Mary, too, studied the jury. She and Harvey had discussed the possible outcomes of a jury trial versus a *bench trial;* i.e., trial by a judge without a jury. Henry had told them that most criminal defendants do not elect to go to trial, and of those who do, most do not choose to exercise their right to trial by jury. He had explained that the right to trial by an impartial jury in criminal prosecutions is guaranteed by the Sixth Amendment of the United States Constitution.[1] The United States Supreme Court has made this provision applicable to the states.[2] It pertains to prosecutions for serious crimes, as distinguished from petty offenses. Offenses which carry a potential sentence of more than six months have been termed "serious" by the Court.[3] Harvey had decided at the time of his arraignment that he would not waive this right. Influenced perhaps by his mother's experience in a civil suit, he was inclined to believe that his chances for success were greater with a jury.

Judge's Remarks

After the jury had been impaneled and sworn, the judge asked the clerk to read the indictment. She then addressed the jury, telling them that the defendant had pleaded "not guilty" to the charges they had just heard. She stressed the importance of remembering that a person is presumed to be innocent until proven guilty. That was why, she said, during the trial that followed, the district attorney would have the burden of proving the defendant's guilt beyond a reasonable doubt. The defense, she added, had no obligation to present evidence. However, should the defense desire, it could present its evidence after the prosecution rested.

She outlined trial procedure briefly. The judge told the jurors that the district attorney would talk with them briefly about the case and would then call witnesses to testify. Next, the defense would have the option of presenting evidence. When all testimony had been heard, the jury would hear closing arguments from the attorneys. After that, she would explain the applicable principles of law to the jury. They would then retire to deliberate.

She asked them to listen carefully and not to discuss the case with anyone. Their primary function, she explained, was a finding of the facts in the case since "a trial is a search for the truth of the matter. You, the jury, will be the ones who say in the end what actually happened at times and places that are important to the ultimate decision in this case of the guilt or innocence of the defendant on the charges you are considering."

Trial Procedure

As Henry had explained to Mary earlier, trial proceedings in civil and criminal cases and in the different jurisdictions tend to follow much the same order. He cautioned, however, that some variations do exist. He also told her that generally the rules of evidence were much the same for civil and criminal cases, with statutory and constitutional considerations accounting for most of the differences.

Therefore, following her conversation with Henry, Mary anticipated the following:

1. Opening statement by the district attorney. (In some states opening remarks by defense counsel would follow. In Great State, however, these were deferred until the state rested.)

2. Evidence by the state.

3. Opening statement by defense counsel.

4. Evidence by the defense.

5. Rebuttal testimony, if any, first by the state and then by the defense.

6. Closing statements to the jury, first by the defense and then by the district attorney.

7. Judge's charge to the jury with instructions on those matters of law which are at issue in the case. The judge could also review testimony. (The judge's right to comment on the evidence varies greatly among the different jurisdictions. In some states, the judge may also give the jury instructions on the law before evidence is entered.)

Prosecution's Case in Chief

Bob Barrister began his opening statement to the jury by reminding them this was a case involving burglary and theft. The witnesses he would call, he said, included two police officers who had arrested the defendant on the evening of May 20. They would testify that they had found him in the factory building of The Firm taking cypres parts. Other witnesses, he went on, included two employees of The Firm. One would testify that he had observed the defendant enter the building that evening; the other, that he had seen the defendant take cypres parts from the shelves in the supply room. Finally, Bob continued, there would be testimony by two Big City police detectives who had investigated the case and two persons who had purchased cypres parts from the defendant. His statement was, essentially, a preview of the prosecution's case.

At this time, Bob Barrister called as his first witness police officer Teresa Copp. The witnesses had been sequestered; that is, placed out in the hall to await their turn to testify. Therefore, the tipstaff now escorted Officer Copp into the courtroom.

Most of the testimony during the trial duplicated the recital of events thus far and will not be repeated here. Instead, the description is limited to new matter.

On cross-examination, the arresting police officers told Henry that they remembered that Harvey had been cooperative. Furthermore, they insisted that, if it were true that Harvey had received blows to the ribs and had been kicked in the shins, it would only have been because such force was needed at the time. Detectives Find and Seek described Harvey as no more frightened than many other first-time offenders and insisted that he had been made aware of his rights at all times. When Henry asked Al Chase why he did not attempt to prevent the burglary by locking the side entrance at The Firm following Ed Under's report to him, Al stated it would have hampered his inquiry into the persons involved in the thefts occurring at The Firm as well as their *modus operandi* (manner of operation). All of the prosecution evidence came in, but not without real effort by Henry to keep it out. At one point a sharp exchange developed between Henry and the judge during a side bar conference regarding suppression of evidence. It came after Henry had repeatedly objected to the introduction into evidence of Harvey's confession, photographs of cypres parts seized from the Worker home, and testimony about Harvey's admissions concerning his long period of theft. Finally, the judge asked both attorneys to approach the bench. In rather certain terms she told Henry she had already ruled on his objections, that the objections were being duly noted on the record and thus would be preserved in case of appeal, that she had granted his motion to incorporate by reference into the trial record material from the suppression hearing, that he had introduced no new or additional reasons for the exclusion of evidence other than those already ruled upon at the suppression hearing, that the purpose of suppression hearings was to dispose of such matters prior to trial and to avoid repetition of the very same matters during the trial, that she had studied the record of the suppression hearing and given careful consideration to all the arguments he had made at that time, and that she would find additional objections which were repetitious of those on which there had already been a ruling to be a form of harassment and delay. Henry's annoyance at this point matched hers. He remarked that, if she continued, he would move for a mistrial, adding that "it is obvious Your Honor got out on the wrong side of bed this morning." Her response was that such frivolous remarks were unworthy of counsel. It was Bob Barrister who brought a close to the incident by suggesting a fifteen-minute recess. That recess helped to cool tempers and when the trial continued it did so without further similar incident.

Defense Demurrer

When the prosecution rested, Henry moved to demur to the evidence. This is the counterpart of the defendant's motion for a nonsuit in a civil action. It requires the court to consider the evidence presented by the prosecution. If the motion is granted, the defendant is discharged without any deliberation by the jury. If the motion is denied, the case proceeds as if the demurrer had not been made. It tests, in effect, the sufficiency of the evidence against the defendant. Judge Wolfe did not consider long. In her mind there had been more than sufficient evidence to indicate that Harvey had been engaged in criminal activity. Therefore, she overruled the demurrer and ordered the trial to continue, asking Henry if the defense wished to present any evidence.

Defense

In his opening statement to the jury, Henry said that they had already heard from investigating police detectives that Harvey was a frightened young man, not a hardened criminal. He reminded them that not just guilty persons are brought to trial. He also said the defense would present witnesses who would testify to Harvey's good character and reputation, as well as the effect upon him of his father's untimely death. The testimony of both character witnesses, the dean and Harvey's former employer, confirmed Henry's statement. At the conclusion of his case, Henry moved that the court direct a verdict of acquittal. Judge Wolfe refused to do so. It was her opinion that there had been ample evidence by the prosecution, uncontradicted by the defense, to establish a prima facie case.

Closing Arguments

In his closing statements, Bob Barrister concentrated on the testimony by prosecution witnesses that Harvey had actually committed those acts that constituted burglary and theft. He added that no refutation of this had been made by the defense. He also told the jury that personal grief or hardship did not justify commission of a crime. Henry, on the other hand, concentrated on Harvey's apprehension upon being arrested, his intimidation and treatment by the police, and the pressures exerted upon him to make statements he would not have made of his own free choice.

Judge's Charge to Jury

In her charge to the jury, the judge asked the jurors to remember that statements by counsel were not evidence. She reminded them again of the presumption of innocence until proven guilty and that the standard of proof was beyond a reasonable doubt. Judge Wolfe defined both burglary and theft. She explained that a defendant in a criminal case has a right not to take the stand and not to testify; furthermore, when he does not do so, this cannot be held against him nor should it be considered by the jury as either proof or indication of guilt. She also told them that a unanimous verdict would be necessary and that they must return a separate verdict on each count. (The unanimous verdict was a Great State requirement. The United States Supreme Court has held that unanimous verdicts in criminal cases are not always necessary to meet due process requirements of the Federal Constitution.[4])

Jury Deliberations and Verdict

The jury began deliberations by discussing the case. It soon became obvious that there was agreement that Harvey had committed the acts of

FORM 11-1. Verdict Slip.

COURT OF LOCAL COUNTY
CRIMINAL DIVISION

STATE OF GREAT STATE   :

V.

      Harvey Worker   :

: Criminal Action
No. 1246 of 19XX

VERDICT

This day, _____ *August 29* _____, 19 XX, we the jurors selected to serve in the above described case find the defendant, Harvey Worker, on the

first count: burglary   *Guilty*

second count: theft   *Guilty*

third count: theft   *Guilty*

               Eve Juron
               Foreperson

Instructions: When the jury has reached a unanimous verdict on the counts submitted, the foreperson shall enter in the blank space opposite each count "guilty" or "not guilty" as the jury has unanimously determined. The foreperson shall then sign the verdict slip.

which he was accused. Although they believed this was serious criminality, they did not view him as a hardened criminal. However, they were of the opinion that he might become one if sent to the kind of prisons about which they had read. Since they had received no instructions from the judge about sentencing, they sent a note with the tipstaff to the judge asking for further instructions. Reassembled in the courtroom, they learned that their only decision was to be whether Harvey was guilty or not guilty of burglary and theft. Sentencing, said the judge, was her function. Although she did not say so, in only a few states is there jury sentencing in noncapital cases. Retiring again, the jury took a vote and unanimously found Harvey guilty on all counts. Their foreperson then prepared the verdict slip, shown as Form 11-1, and the jury returned to the courtroom. After the verdict was announced, Henry asked that the jury be polled. They were found to be in agreement. The jurors were then dismissed.

TABLE 11-1. Postconviction remedies of defendant.

In the Trial Court

1. POST-TRIAL MOTIONS

A. In Arrest of Judgment — Counterpart of judgment n.o.v. in civil cases. Grounds include insufficient evidence, court lack of jurisdiction, error intrinsic on the record such as an indictment which charges no crime.

B. New Trial — Grounds include improper admission of evidence, error in charge to jury, verdict contrary to court's instructions.

Trial court's denial of post-trial motions is appealable.

2. POSTCONVICTION HEARING STATUTE REMEDIES

By statute (Postconviction Hearing Statute) in Great State, one basic procedure exists for relief from convictions obtained and sentences imposed without due process of law. This procedure encompasses all prior procedures including Coram nobis and habeas corpus.[+]

Trial court's denial of relief is appealable.

In the Appellate Courts

3. APPEAL

A. Review of Final Judgment (Judgment of Sentence) — Direct appeal from judgment of sentence. A matter of right in Great State by statutory provision.

B. Review of Interlocutory Order — Available in Great State where necessary to safeguard basic rights.

C. Review of Denial of Post-trial Relief — See above.

In the Federal Courts

4. FEDERAL HABEAS CORPUS

In cases of a state conviction, recourse to the federal courts is possible if state remedies are unavailable and if federal constitutional rights have been violated. Arises from Article I, §9, cl. 2 of United States Constitution. Denial of writ is appealable.

By Executive Grace

5. EXECUTIVE ORDERS

A. Pardon — Relieves offender from further punishment; removes all legal disabilities resulting from conviction.

B. Commutation of Sentence — Reduces severity of sentence or penalty.

Both of these are matters of privilege rather than of right. In Great State, they may be granted by the governor upon favorable recommendation of the Great State Board of Pardons. This is by state constitutional provision.

[+]Coram nobis is a civil writ for the purpose of review of a criminal judgment in the trial court; it is similar in many ways to a motion for a new trial. A writ of habeas corpus seeks the release of a person in custody; it is not limited to post conviction stages but may be invoked at any stage of the criminal proceedings.

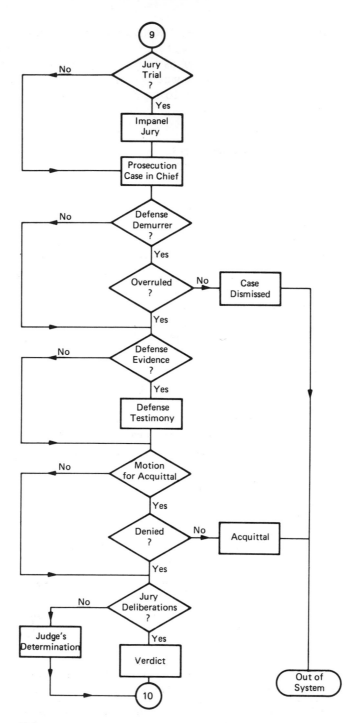

FIGURE 11-1. The Criminal Trial.

Judge Wolfe asked Harvey to come forward. As he stood before her, she informed him that he had been found guilty of the felonies of burglary and theft. She advised him of his right to file postverdict motions for a new trial or in arrest of judgment. This, she said, must be done within seven days and Harvey would have the right to the services of counsel in doing so. Asked if he had any questions, Harvey indicated he did not. Henry requested that sentencing be stayed until he had an opportunity to file post verdict motions. The judge granted that request. She also continued Harvey's nominal bail. As Mary, Harvey, and Henry left the courthouse, Henry noted that although the trial, which is flow charted in Figure 11-1, was over, the case was far from being over. Henry had explained that there were many forms of post conviction relief, as shown in Table 11-1.

Post-Trial Motions

Within the time requirements, Henry filed a motion for a new trial and in arrest of judgment. A copy of this motion appears as Form 11-2. Judge Wolfe asked that a brief be filed by both parties prior to a hearing on the motion to be held before a panel of three judges of the criminal court. Henry's brief alleged that the verdict was based upon evidence unlawfully admitted at the trial. He reiterated arguments made at the time of the suppression motion. In addition, he charged that the trial judge had prejudiced the case against the defendant by her remarks to defense counsel. The contentions in the reply brief prepared by Bob Barrister were similar to those made by the prosecution at the time of the pretrial motion to suppress. He denied the court's remarks were prejudicial. The hearing on the motions was held before Judges Wolfe, Grant, and Roe. It resulted in denial of the motions for the same reasons as had been articulated by Judge Grant in his statement of facts and conclusions of law and, as added reason, that remarks at a side bar could not be prejudicial. The postverdict motions have been flow charted in Figure 11-2.

SENTENCING

Great State required that, absent extenuating circumstances, sentencing be done by the judge who presided at the criminal trial. Therefore, following denial of the post verdict motions, Judge Wolfe requested that a presentence report be prepared by the county probation office. Sentencing would occur after she had received and studied that report. Had this been a case of murder, voluntary manslaughter, or one involving a sex offense, she would have requested a psychiatric examination and report by the county behavior clinic. She could still do so in this case,

FORM 11-2. Motion for New Trial and in Arrest of Judgment.

COURT OF LOCAL COUNTY
CRIMINAL DIVISION

STATE OF GREAT STATE   :

        V.   :   Criminal Action No.

Harvey Worker   :   <u>1246</u> of 19<u>XX</u>

Motion for New Trial and In Arrest of Judgment

      And now this fourth day of September, 19XX comes defendant by his attorney and respectfully requests a new trial and in arrest of judgment for the following reasons:

1. The verdict is against the law.
2. The verdict is against the evidence.
3. The verdict is against the law and the evidence.
4. The court erred in failing to grant the motion to suppress.
5. The defendant was denied a fair and impartial trial because of prejudicial remarks of the Court.

Respectfully submitted,

Henry Law
_____
Counsel for the Defendant

should the probation officer's report indicate a need for it. In the meantime, the judge continued nominal bail.

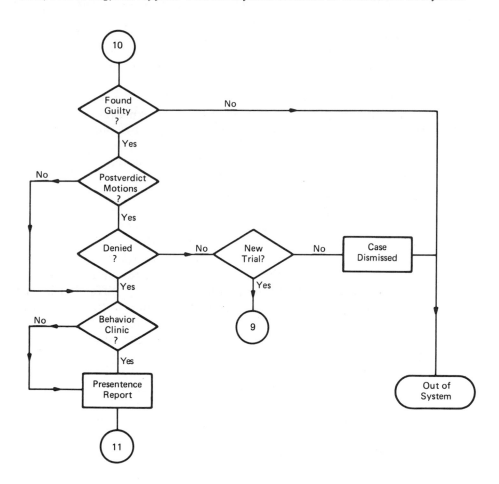

FIGURE 11-2. Postverdict Motions in Criminal Cases.

Presentence Investigation and Report

Probation officer Maria Will did extensive interviewing. She talked with the police; with Jim Solicitor, Bob Barrister, and Henry Law; with Jim Boss and Peter Superior, both of whom had supervised Harvey's work at The Firm; with Harvey and Mary; with Harvey's high school principal and the dean of the college he had attended; with his former summer employer. She learned a great deal about him.

In Great State, the probation officer's presentence report was confidential and could be disclosed only to the sentencing judge. The district attorney and defense counsel had the right of inspection. They also had the right to comment to the judge on the report and to point out any inaccuracies it might contain. By order of the sentencing judge, a copy could be made available to professionals with a legitimate interest in the case, for example, a psychiatrist appointed to assist the court in sentencing, a correctional institution, or the department of probation or parole. The desirability of confidentiality of presentence reports is still an unresolved and controversial issue.

In Harvey's case, the report indicated that he had a very stable and satisfactory home situation and had been known to be reliable and trustworthy, normally industrious, and a reasonably good student and employee. All who knew him at the time detected a change after his father's death, but did not consider it abnormal under the circumstances. His supervisors at The Firm said that he had worked hard and displayed great interest and enthusiasm for his work. In fact, they still found it hard to believe that Harvey had been the person who had been doing the stealing. Most of his young friends were of good character. However, the probation officer expressed concern about his association with a small group of students who had introduced him to the fence. She concluded her report by expressing the opinion that this young man was not disposed to a life of crime and that he had learned a very difficult lesson through this experience. She recommended that, as one means of rehabilitation, he be given an opportunity to make restitution and that discontinued association with the one group be made a condition precedent to his release into the community. Judge Wolfe considered the report, together with a request from Henry for leniency. The latter emphasized that this was a first offense, that partial restitution was already possible, and voiced a conviction that rehabilitation would be enhanced if Harvey could be placed on probation and given an opportunity to work in the community rather than be sentenced to prison. He also cited the Model Penal Code's recommendations.

Judge's Considerations

In arriving at her decision, Judge Wolfe considered the following factors to be significant:

Factors Favoring Leniency	Factors Negating Leniency
1. first-time offender.	1. seriousness of offenses—felonies.
2. healthy home environment.	
3. history of prior acceptable behavior.	2. defendant's continued and increased participation in theft over a long time.
4. temporary emotional crisis following father's death.	3. association with some persons of questionable character.
	4. need to prevent recurrence.

Of those factors, Judge Wolfe's greatest concern was with deterring Harvey from engaging in criminal activity in the future. His continued participation in theft and his undesirable associations caused her to look for some means of providing Harvey with professional assistance to prevent his becoming a *recidivist;* i.e., a habitual criminal.   In determining just what those measures might be, she also considered

1. The options open to her in sentencing according to Great State law,
2. The conditions and programs available in local and state facilities.

The Great State Criminal Code imposed upon a judge maximum but not minimum limitations for sentences. Those for burglary and theft were reported in the previous chapter. No fixed sentences were provided for felonies. In most jurisdictions, judges are given some sentencing discretion.[5] Wide differences do exist, however, with regard to the degree of discretion granted and the situations in which it may be exercised. As with opportunities for exercise of discretion by the police and the prosecutor, the discretionary power of the judge has been subject to much criticism. Some of the options and choices available to Judge Wolfe in Harvey's case included

1. Fine or restitution,
2. Incarceration in jail or prison,
3. Diversion program, such as halfway house or work release,
4. Split sentence,
5. Suspended sentence or probation,
6. Fixed or indeterminate sentence.

Restitution

In deciding upon a sentence, Judge Wolfe's major concern was what would redound to the greatest good for Harvey. She viewed a fine as a means of punishment that, if it created a financial obligation Harvey was unable to meet, could encourage him to further theft in order to pay the fine. At the same time, Judge Wolfe looked with favor upon the idea of restitution. It provided for compensation to the victim of the crime by the perpetrator of that crime. Judge Wolfe considered this to be not only just, but also a deterrent to further crime. If she could determine that Harvey would be able to meet the financial burden of restitution, she would not negate restitution in connection with the thefts. However, there was also the matter of sentencing for the burglary.

Incarceration

Incarceration would have the effect of depriving Harvey of his home and family life. At the same time, it would remove him from the community and from present undesirable associations he had there. If

Harvey were to be sentenced to a detention facility, Judge Wolfe determined it must be to a rehabilitative facility. She shared the jury's concern about the effect of imprisonment upon Harvey as she mentally considered the possibility of incarceration in jail or prison.

Jails and Prisons

A distinction is usually made between those correctional institutions termed jails and those referred to as prisons or penitentiaries. *Jail* refers to a facility, generally operated by city or county authorities, where persons are detained while awaiting trial. It also houses persons who are serving short sentences, usually a term of less than one year. The concept of jail generally refers to a place of confinement rather than a place of punishment. On the other hand, a *prison* is a facility housing persons convicted of the more serious crimes who are serving longer sentences. Prisons are generally state or federally operated. There are also military prisons. Jails are usually found within the community, often at its center, while prisons are most likely to be located in outlying areas. Programs of education, vocational training, counseling, and other forms of rehabilitation are more frequently found in prisons than in jails. Quality of these programs varies greatly.

The Local County Jail in Big City was overcrowded, understaffed, inadequately funded, dirty, and lacking recreational or educational programs. Of all of this Judge Wolfe was keenly aware. In fact, one of the reasons she had continued Harvey's nominal bail was to avoid sending him to that jail. She believed that the jail environment would have had a pernicious influence upon Harvey. On the other hand, a new Great State prison facility located in Little Town had good programs of counseling, therapy, education, recreation, vocational training, as well as a work release program, which she considered would be beneficial in Harvey's case. Residents of the facility who qualified were released during the day to work at regular jobs in the community and returned to the institution at night. Part of their wages could be used in making restitution.

Halfway Houses

While the judge was favorably inclined toward this program for Harvey, she was not inclined to send him to a halfway house located in Big City. More like a home than a prison, it had space for fifteen persons. They were confined there overnight and during weekends but left during the day to go to work, to school, or for treatment. Both a counselor and a case worker were available to the residents. Judge Wolfe believed there was an advantage to this noninstitutional atmosphere. At the same time, she knew that better counseling services existed at the Little Town facility.

She believed the halfway house was better suited to assisting persons who had been confined to prison to return to life in the community, although she knew that some of her fellow judges had been sentencing there directly in certain cases.

Probation and Suspended Sentence

Judge Wolfe weighed the possible effect upon Harvey of institutional life over permitting him to live at home as a result of either a suspended sentence or probation. Were she to sentence Harvey to probation, incarceration would be suspended and he would be placed under the supervision of a probation officer. Certain conditions would also be imposed for his continued freedom from institutionalization. Those conditions generally include restriction on travel outside the state, abstinence from alcohol and other drugs, and continued employment. A suspended sentence, on the other hand, would mean that she would impose sentence, but Harvey, instead of being incarcerated, would be released immediately without supervision. Judge Wolfe believed that Harvey's long period of theft indicated that he needed supervision. Probation would place him right back in the community with those acquaintances whose influences had led him toward crime rather than away from it. Her mind kept coming back to the Little Town facility as the most desirable alternative.

Fixed and Indeterminate Sentence

She discarded the possibility of a split sentence, that is, a jail—rather than prison—term followed by probation. It would have all of the characteristics of jail and probation, neither of which she found suitable for Harvey. The only undecided matter now was whether to impose a sentence for a fixed or an indeterminate time. An indeterminate sentence is one in which the individual is to be incarcerated for a period of time extending somewhere between a minimum and a maximum period, the ultimate being a minimum of one day and a maximum of life. This is sometimes referred to as a *completely indeterminate* sentence, and the term *partially indeterminate* is used to designate a sentence with a spread of a specified period of time, such as three to five years. Judge Wolfe was not so positive about Harvey's future conduct as to feel she could pinpoint a precise and fixed time in which he would positively be rehabilitated. Therefore, she was inclined to set a maximum term with a recommendation that he be considered for parole at the end of a designated minimum term. Generally, when there is no judicial recommendation regarding eligibility for parole, such eligibility, by statutory provision, occurs after one-third of the sentence has been served.

Parole

Parole is distinguished from probation, in that *probation* means serving a term in the community without going to a correctional institution, whereas *parole* means release to the community following a period of confinement in an institution. Just as with probation, parole involves release under supervision. Usually certain conditions are imposed for continued parole. Complete discharge from the criminal system follows at the end of the term to which one has been sentenced. Release on parole is a privilege, not a right, and the decision to parole an individual is influenced not only by the judge's recommendation at the time of sentencing but also by the inmate's behavior and experiences during institutionalization. These sentencing alternatives have been flow charted in Figure 11-3.

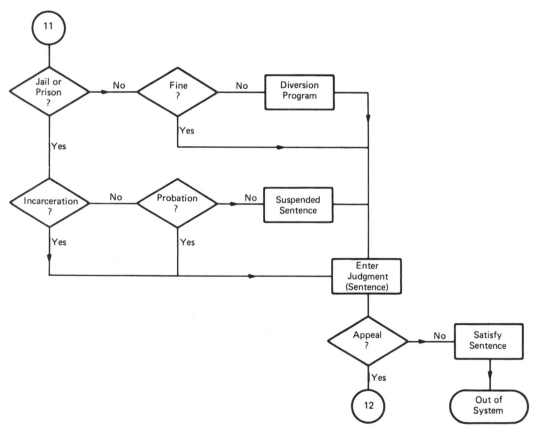

FIGURE 11-3. Sentencing Decision.

Judge's Decision

Judge Wolfe thought that the Little Town personnel would have sufficient opportunity to observe Harvey in one year to make some valid judgment as to his future conduct. Were he placed in a work release program, she believed he could earn enough within that time to make complete financial restitution. She thought he might be ready for parole at the end of one year. However, were he not, continued confinement and treatment would be required. She believed that an additional two years would provide more than ample time for the counseling and therapy that would be necessary. She therefore settled upon a minimum of one and a maximum of three years.

It was in this way that she arrived at the decision to sentence Harvey to the following concurrent sentences:

1. For theft—restitution to be made to The Firm, with credit given for those cypres parts recovered and returned. (The net effect was that Harvey would owe approximately $4700.)
2. For burglary—detention for a minimum of one and a maximum of three years in the Little Town Correction Center, with a recommendation that Harvey be placed in a work release program with portions of his earnings designated for restitution and that he be considered for parole at the end of the first year.

Judge Wolfe would later discover that this decision, to which she had devoted so much careful thought, pleased very few people. Harvey, Mary, and Henry considered it to be unjustly severe and harsh. They had hoped for probation. Although The Firm eventually received complete restitution, Fred Famous publicly stated that one to three years was a real indication that the courts were "soft on criminals." That same feeling was shared by Detective Find and police officer Teresa Copp, who noted that a sentence of twenty years was possible under the Great State Criminal Code for burglary. When Judge Wolfe ran for re-election the following year, Harvey's sentence was listed in a newspaper editorial as one example of sentencing disparities. It was compared with the twenty-year term given by Judge Wolfe to a bank burglar who had stolen $4000. Judge Wolfe found it significant that the editorial did not state that this was the bank burglar's fifth conviction for burglary.

Sentencing

Having determined what sentence she would impose, Judge Wolfe set a time for sentencing two days later. Harvey, Henry, and Bob Barrister were notified. Some delay occurred at the start of the sentencing session, because Harvey, who had gone out for a cup of coffee, was late in returning.   The Sixth Amendment of the United States Constitution provides that "in all criminal prosecutions, the accused shall enjoy the right . . . to be confronted with witnesses against him . . . ," and the United States Supreme Court has held that the right of confrontation is applicable to the states.[6]   The right of confrontation cannot exist unless the accused is present at those proceedings which constitute criminal prosecution.   That includes the preliminary hearing, the arraignment, every stage of the trial when his substantial rights may be affected by the proceedings against him, and the imposition of sentence.   The right may be waived.   In some cases, a defendant may lose the right through continued disruptive behavior in the courtroom.[7]   In Great State, the Rules of Criminal Procedure were specific in stating not only that the defendant must be present during criminal prosecutions, but also that the record of the proceedings must contain a statement to that effect, as well as of representation by counsel.

Note should be made of the fact that the right of confrontation does not apply in the case of investigatory proceedings, such as the grand jury.

When Harvey had returned to the courtroom and the proceedings did get underway, the judge asked Harvey to come forward.   She asked if either he or his counsel wished to make a statement.   Harvey indicated that Henry would speak for him, and there followed a short request for leniency.   The prosecutor had no statement to make.

Judge Wolfe then addressed Harvey.   In imposing sentence, she told him of her concern for his future and his rehabilitation, and explained why she had decided upon the particular sentence.   She also advised him of his right to appeal, informed him that he must file notice of intent to do so within ten days, and stated that he had the right to the assistance of counsel in doing so.

Henry told the judge that notice of appeal would be filed that very day.   He then requested that Harvey be released on bail pending the outcome on appeal.   In cases in which the maximum sentence imposed exceeded two years, Great State provided that bail could be granted at the discretion of the judge.   Since the bail request followed conviction and sentencing, Judge Wolfe set bail at $30,000.   Henry helped Mary to arrange for an eight-percent bond.   That meant that Mary would deposit with the clerk of courts $2400, or eight percent of the amount at which bail was set.   All but ten percent of this deposit would be returned to her when and if Harvey appeared as required until final disposition of the case.   The remaining ten percent would be retained to cover costs of processing the bond.   Mary was named in the bond as surety.   A copy of the form used for the bail bond appears as Form 11-3.   In this way Harvey came to be at liberty once again.   Judge Wolfe entered judgment of sentence, which the clerk of courts entered on the court's records.

FORM 11-3. Bail Bond.

CERTIFICATION OF BAIL
AND DISCHARGE   No.

	Police Case No. J. P. No	C. P. Term & No.

State vs.   (Defendant Name and Address)

Charges	Date of Charges

Police I. D. No.	Indictment No.	District of Arrest

NEXT COURT ACTION FOR FURTHER HEARING

Date and Time	Date and Time

☐ ROR (no surety)
☐ Bail (total amount set, if any):

Nominal Bail
$

Location (Room No.)	Location

Conditions of Release (aside from appearing at court when required:)

_____

_____

DISCHARGE THE ABOVE-NAMED DEFENDANT FROM CUSTODY IF DETAINED FOR NO OTHER CAUSE THAN THE ABOVE STATED.

(attach addendum, if necessary)

Given under my hand and the Official Seal of this Court, this____day of_____,19__.

Security or Surety (if any):

☐ Cash in full   ☐ Surety
   amount of bail   Company

☐ Percentage cash   ☐ Professional
   bail   Bondsman

Money furnished by   ☐ Realty
☐ Defendant   ☐ Other:
☐ 3rd Party

_____
(Clerk of Court or Issuing Authority)

Judge or Issuing Authority

APPEARANCE OR BAIL BOND

TO: ☐ Detention Center

             ☐ Other

I hereby certify that sufficient bail has been entered

☐ by the defendant

☐ on behalf of the defendant by:

THIS BOND IS VALID FOR THE ENTIRE PROCEEDINGS AND UNTIL FULL AND FINAL DISPOSITION OF THE CASE INCLUDING FINAL DISPOSITION OF ANY PETITION FOR WRIT OF CERTIORARI OR APPEAL TIMELY FILED IN THE SUPREME COURT OF THE UNITED STATES.

(Name & Address of Surety)

Refund of cash bail will be made within 20 days after final disposition.
Bring Cash Bail Receipt to Clerk of Court.

STATE OF GREAT STATE

v.

_____

WE, THE UNDERSIGNED, defendant and surety, our successors, heirs and assigns, are jointly and severally bound to pay to the State of Great State the sum of _____ dollars ($_____).

The CONDITIONS of this bond are that the defendant will:

(1) Appear before the issuing authority and in the Courts of the County of _____, Great State, at all times as his presence may be required, ordered or directed, until full and final disposition of the case, to plead, to answer and defend as ordered the aforesaid charge or charges.

(2) Submit himself to all orders and process of the issuing authority or Court.

(3) The DEFENDANT and the SURETY must give written notice to the issuing authority, Clerk of Courts, the district attorney AND Court Bail Agency,_____Street, of any change in his address within forty-eight hours of the date of his change of address.

(4) Comply with any specific requirement of release imposed by the issuing authority or Court, such as satisfactory participation in a designated program.

(5) Obey such other conditions as the Court, or Court Bail Agency with leave of issuing authority or Court, may impose.

If defendant performs the conditions as set forth herein, then this bond is to be void, otherwise the same shall remain in full force and this bond in the full sum thereof shall be forfeited.

And further, in accordance with law, we do hereby empower any attorney of any court of record within the State of Great State or elsewhere to appear for us at any time, and with or without declarations filed, and whether or not the said obligation be in default, to confess judgment against us, and in favor of the State of Great State for use of the County of_____ and its assigns, as of any term or session of a court of record of the County of _____ for the above sum and costs, with release of all errors, without stay of execution, and inquisition on and extension upon any levy or real estate is hereby waived, and condemnation agreed to, and the exemption of personal property from levy and sale on any execution hereon is also hereby expressly

THIS BOND IS SIGNED ON
_____ 19 __,
AT_____,
GREAT STATE.

Signed and acknowledged
before me

this _____ day_____
_____ 19 __
_____
(Clerk of Court or Issuing
Authority)

*In case of corporate
surety bail, Power of
Attorney must be affixed
to bond or otherwise bond
is invalid.

*In case of "Percentage
Cash Bail" or "Nominal
Bail," Power of Attorney
is not required.

APPLICABLE PORTION OF
FOLLOWING PAGES MUST
BE COMPLETED.

waived, and no benefit of
exemption is claimed under
and by virtue of any exemption law now in force or
which may be passed here-
after.
And for so doing this shall
be sufficient warrant. A
copy of this bond and warrant being filed in said
action, it shall not be necessary to file the original
as a warrant of attorney,
any law or rule of the
Court to the contrary, notwithstanding.

I ACKNOWLEDGE THAT I
AM LEGALLY RESPONSI-
BLE FOR THE FULL
AMOUNT OF THE BAIL.

_____ SEAL
Signature of Defendant

_____ SEAL
Signature of Surety (May
be Bondsman, Bail Agency,
or private individual or
organization). Except when
defendant is released on
his own recognizance
(ROR), this must be signed
in all bail situations, including nominal bail.

_____
Address of Surety, Surety
Company or Defendant

_____
Surety Number of Profes-
sional Bondsman

License Number and
Expiration Date

NOTE: DETENTION CENTERS AND POLICE--To release prisoner, you must receive valid bond and immediately forward it to the issuing authority or Court.

CERTIFICATION OF COUNTY INDEMNITY AND PREMIUM (APPLICABLE ONLY WHEN SURETY IS A CORPORATION)

_____ , Principal, and _____
Surety, hereby certify that the amount paid by said Principal to said Surety for bail in the above matter is $_____ and that no further sum or sums is to be paid therefore by the said Principal or anyone on his behalf.

    We further certify that said Principal has given to said Surety counter indemnity consisting of _____ of the value of $_____ and no further counter indemnity is to be given the said Surety except as follows:

_____

_____

    We further certify that there are no judgments against the said corporate surety outstanding and unpaid for a period of more than thirty days from the date of the entry of such judgment except those in which a petition to open or vacate the judgment has been filed and remains undisposed of.

Dated: _____ , 19___

_____ SEAL
(Principal)

_____ SEAL
(Surety)

MUST BE SIGNED IN PERSON BY THE APPROVED AGENT

* * * * * * * * * * * * * * *

JUSTIFICATION OF SURETY

(Questions 3, 4, 5, 7, 8 and 9 are applicable only when real estate is posted as security.)

The undersigned about to become Surety in the case cited herein, being duly sworn, deposes and says:

1. I reside at _____

    and my occupation is _____

2. I have no undisposed of criminal cases against me pending in the Courts of _____ County, except as follows: _____

    _____

3. ☐ (I am/We are) the sole owner(s) of

    ☐ (I am/We are) joint tenant(s) in   } real estate situated

    ☐ (I am/We are) tenant(s) by the entirety in

    in the said County of _____, as follows, viz:

    a lot of ground, in size _____ feet, situated at

    _____ Street in the _____ ward,

    which is improved with the following buildings _____

    _____

    _____

    (All other joint tenants or tenants by the entirety must co-sign this bond and state their addresses at the bottom of this page or on an attachment hereto.)

4. The said property was obtained by me by ☐ Deed

    ☐ Will from _____

    _____

    _____

5. The ☐ Deed ☐ Will is dated _____

    and is recorded in the office of the ☐ Dept. of Records

    ☐ Register of Wills of _____ County,

    in ☐ Will Book Vol. _____ Page _____ , and

    the title is in ☐ my name and ☐ my spouse's name.

    Also a lot of ground, in size _____ feet,

    situated at _____ Street in the _____

    Ward. The said property was obtained by me by

    ☐ Deed ☐ Will from _____. The

    ☐ Deed ☐ Will is dated _____ and is

    recorded in ☐ Deed ☐ Will Book Vol. _____

    Page _____ in said _____ County,

    and is in ☐ my name and ☐ my spouse's name.

6. I am not Surety on any bond of any kind except as follows:
    follows:

DATE	AMOUNT	DEFENDANT

7. There are no mortgages, or other liens or encumbrances
    of any kind or description, upon the said premises, and
    there are no judgments against me except as follows:
    Mortgages as set forth in the Dept. of Records on first
    property _____
    Mortgages as set forth in the Dept. of Records on
    second property _____
    Judgments and Liens _____
    Real estate taxes have been paid except: _____

8. The assessed valuation of said premises is: _____
    _____

9. No judgment has been entered or action instituted again
    against me upon a forfeited recognizance except _____
    _____

10. I have read carefully the foregoing affidavit and know that it is true and correct.

Sworn and subscribed   _____SEAL
before me this day of   (Surety)
                                        _____SEAL
_____   (Co-surety, if any, co-joint
                                        tenant or co-tenant by the
                                        entirety)
_____
                                        _____SEAL
                                        (Address)

APPEAL

In Great State appeal in criminal cases was a matter of right by statutory provision. It is so by constitutional provision in some of the states. Persons convicted and sentenced for felonies in Great State could appeal directly to the state's supreme court. Misdemeanor cases went to an intermediate appellate court. Considering the time table within which the state supreme court had been working recently, Henry calculated it would take about six months at the most to appeal and for an appellate decision to be handed down.

Mary and Harvey had talked with Henry about appeal prior to the time of sentencing. Henry has been authorized to appeal immediately should imprisonment be imposed, and he was now deeply involved in the decision making connected with that appeal.

Issues

As counsel for the appellant, he was the one who would determine the issues to be raised on appeal. As early as the trial, he had been paving the way. He had been very careful to enter objections at appropriate times in order to preserve all rights on appeal. Judge Wolfe might even say that he had been somewhat overeager in this respect.

Preparing his brief for the Great State Supreme Court, Henry asked himself if his client had at any time been denied his legal rights, if he had received a fair and impartial trial, if error that could be the basis for reversal had occurred. He had before him materials which the appellate judges would have available: a transcript of the trial and the suppression hearing, a copy of Judge Grant's findings of fact and conclusions of law and of Judge Wolfe's order denying his request for an arrest of judgment and new trial.

Three bases for appeal emerged from his reflection, and he made a note of these issues to present to the court:

1. The unnecessary delay between arrest and initial appearance was in violation of Rule 118, making inadmissible all evidence directly related to the delay. Therefore, the trial court erred in refusing to grant defendant's motion to suppress this evidence.

2. Defendant's confession was involuntary, as a result of statements made to the police without the presence of legal counsel while defendant was in a state of apprehension after having been physically "roughed up" at the time of arrest and after having waived his rights without fully comprehending the legal effect of doing so. Therefore, the confession and all evidence flowing from it were inadmissible, and the trial court erred in refusing to grant the defendant's motion to suppress this evidence.

3. The trial judge's criticism and rebuke of defense counsel in connection with his efforts to have the foregoing evidence suppressed reflected unfavorably upon the defendant, thus prejudicing his case and denying him a fair and impartial trial.

Appellate Briefs

With this as a beginning, he started to work on the appellant's brief, portions of which appear in Form 11-4. He also made arrangements for

---

FORM 11-4. Appellant's Brief.

IN THE SUPREME COURT OF GREAT STATE

STATE OF GREAT STATE,   :
              Appellee   :
                   v.   :   BRIEF FOR APPELLANT
Harvey Worker,   :
              Appellant   :

Table of Contents

. . . .

Table of Cases

. . . .

Questions Presented for Review

1. Where appellant following warrantless arrest was taken to police headquarters at 8:20 p.m. and where after the administrative chores of booking were completed appellant was interrogated by police until a confession had been obtained resulting in delay of the initial appearance of appellant before a magistrate until 10:00 p.m., is the delay between the time of the appellant's arrest and his initial appearance "unnecessary" and unreasonable within the meaning of the Great State Rules of Criminal Procedure §118 thereby rendering appellant's confession and the evidence flowing from it inadmissible at trial?

2. When appellant has been interrogated by police without the presence of legal counsel and where appellant was in a state of apprehension after having been physically "roughed up" at the time of arrest and neither understood nor appreciated the legal implications of statements made to the police in such circumstances, does the appellant's confession lack the voluntariness required by <u>Miranda v. Arizona</u>, 384 U.S. 436 (1966), thus making it as well as any evidence flowing from it inadmissible against appellant?

3. When the trial court, in denying defense counsel's motions to suppress evidence, refers to defense counsel's statements as frivolous, does the interjection by the court of such remarks prejudice appellant's case and offend against the fundamental requirements of an unbiased and unprejudiced tribunal thereby denying defendant a fair and impartial trial and thus constituting reversible error?

History

This is a direct appeal from the imposition of sentence to imprisonment for a maximum of three years made by Order of the Criminal Court of Local County, Great State, at No. 1246 of 19XX.

A. Circumstances of the Criminal Conviction

Appellant was indicted in the Criminal Court of Local County at No. 1246 of 19XX on a bill containing counts of burglary and theft.

Motions to suppress evidence gathered following the arrest of appellant and search of his home were filed on July 10, 19XX. After a hearing before Judge Homer Grant, appellant's motions to suppress were denied on July 15,

19XX. While being represented by Henry Law, Esquire, appellant pleaded not guilty to all counts. On August 28, 19XX, a trial commenced before Judge Wolfe and a jury of twelve. Bob Barrister, Esquire, was the prosecuting attorney. On August 29, 19XX, the jury found the appellant guilty of burglary and theft.

On October 3, 19XX, appellant was sentenced to undergo imprisonment for a maximum of three years at the Little Town Correction Center.

The facts of the instant appeal can be briefly and accurately summarized as follows:

On May 20, 19XX, appellant was arrested by Big City police at 7:30 p.m., ...

B. Post-Trial Motions

On August 29, 19XX, the honorable trial court granted appellant leave to file a motion for new trial and in arrest of judgment which appellant filed on September 4, 19XX. After a hearing, en banc, before the Honorable Homer Grant, Richard Roe, and Shirley Wolfe, appellant's motion for new trial and in arrest of judgment was denied on September 16, 19XX. On October 3, 19XX, appellant was sentenced to imprisonment for a term of not more than three years. An appeal to your honorable court was filed on behalf of appellant on October 13, 19XX.

Argument

1. Under the circumstances of the case, delay between the arrest and initial appearance of appellant was unnecessary and unreasonable within the meaning of Great State Rules of Criminal Procedure § 118 thus rendering appellant's confession and the evidence flowing from it inadmissible at trial.

The mandate of Great State R. Crim. P. § 118 is clear: "When a defendant has been arrested without a warrant, he shall be taken without unnecessary delay before the proper judicial authority where a complaint shall be filed against him." In connection therewith, your honorable court has held: "All evidence obtained during unnecessary delay between arrest and initial appearance in inadmissible except that evidence which has no reasonable relationship to the delay whatsoever." Great State v. Futch , 447 G.S.

389, 394, 290 Z. 417 (19XR). See also Great State v. Wayman, 454 G.S. 79, 309 Z. 784 (19XS); Great State v. Dutton, 453 G.S. 547, 307 Z. 238 (19XS); Great State v. Tingle, 451 G.S. 241, 301 Z. 701 (19XS); Great State v. Dixon, 454 G.S. 444, 311 Z. 613 (19XS).

In the instant case, the initial appearance of the appellant before a magistrate was delayed after completion of the administrative processing associated with arrest and booking. This delay, of approximately one hour, was not caused by unavailability of a magistrate. Instead, the time was used for interrogation of appellant by the police without the presence of counsel and while appellant was in a state of apprehension after having been physically "roughed up" by police at arrest and concluded with appellant's inculpatory statement.

Delay for the purpose of obtaining incriminating statements from an arrestee is clearly impermissible under Rule 118 as construed in Great State v. Futch where at 447 G.S. 392 your honorable court quoted from Adams v. United States, 399 F.2d 574, 579 (D.C. Cir., 1968) (concurring opinion) as to what constitutes permissible delay between arrest and initial appearance:

> Necessary delay can reasonably relate to time to administratively process an accused with booking, fingerprinting and other steps and sometimes even to make same (sic) limited preliminary investigation into his connection with the crime for which he was arrested, especially WHEN IT IS DIRECTED TO POSSIBLE EXCULPATION OF THE ONE ARRESTED (Emphasis Added)

The one-hundred minute detention and delay before the initial appearance in the instant case was not consumed solely in "administratively processing the accused" nor was any of it "directed to possible exculpation of the one arrested." Instead, a delay of one hour was used to secure inculpatory statements. Such delay cannot be said to be either necessary or reasonable in terms of Rule 118. Thus it represents a clear violation of the requirements of that rule, and any evidence obtained as a result of the delay must be excluded.

2. . . . .

3. . . . .

Conclusion

For the reasons stated above, appellant submits that the verdict and judgment of the lower court must be reversed.

Respectfully submitted,

Henry Law

Attorney for Appellant

789 Main Street
Big City, Great State

---

transfer of the trial court records and docketing of the case with the supreme court. Henry knew he faced an uphill battle and anticipated the arguments that would appear in the brief, which the state, as the appellee, would file in response.

In the district attorney's office, Bob Barrister who engaged in trial, but not appellate, work discussed the case with the assistant district attorney, Mel Advocate, to whom the appeal had been assigned. Selected portions of the brief Mel prepared in reply appear in Form 11-5.[8] Notice the restatement of the questions presented to the court. Note, too, that he has included Judge Grant's findings of fact and conclusions of law in the history of the case. Those findings do not appear in the appellant's brief.

Oral Arguments

The case was marked for oral argument after the justices of the state supreme court reviewed the briefs. They decided they should hear more from both appellant and appellee with regard to the first question presented to them by the appellant. The set of facts contained in it was different from any which had been present in other cases they had decided involving Rule 118. It involved issues which were before the court for the first time: Did "without unnecessary delay" mean immediately? Did the Rule automatically make excludable all confessions obtained between

FORM 11-5. Appellee's Brief.

IN THE SUPREME COURT OF GREAT STATE

STATE OF GREAT STATE,	:	
Appellee	:	
v.	:	BRIEF FOR APPELLEE
HARVEY WORKER,	:	
Appellant	:	

. . . .

Counter Statement of Questions Presented for Review

1. Whether under the facts of this case the delay between the time of appellant's arrest and initial appearance was not unreasonable within the meaning of Great State v. Futch, 447 G.S. 389, 290 Z 417 (19XR) and therefore appellant's confession as well as the physical evidence seized subsequent thereto and flowing from such confession was properly admitted into evidence by the trial court.

2. Whether under the facts of this case appellant's confession did meet the standards required by Miranda v. Arizona, 384 U.S. 436 (1966), and therefore the confession and the evidence flowing from it were properly admitted into evidence by the trial court.

3. Whether the trial court's reprimand of defense counsel at a side bar conference was not prejudicial to appellant's case and thus did not give rise to an unfair trial.

Counter History

. . . .

In denying appellant's motions to suppress, Judge Homer Grant on July 15, 19XX, entered findings of fact and conclusions of law as follows:

. . . .

Argument

1. Under the facts of this case, the delay between the time of appellant's arrest and initial appearance was not unreasonable within the meaning of Great State v. Futch, supra, and therefore appellant's confession and evidence

flowing from it were properly admitted into evidence by the trial court.

Appellant contends that his confession and the evidence flowing from it were inadmissible against him at trial because the police failed to comply with Rule 118 of the Great State Rules of Criminal Procedure. It is the State's position that, under the facts of the instant appeal, the delay between arrest and initial appearance was reasonable and necessary and appellant's confession and the evidence flowing from it properly admitted into evidence by the trial court.

In the instant appeal, the time from arrest to initial appearance was less than two hours. In no case which has come before your honorable court has a time span of such short duration been deemed an unreasonable delay. See Great State v. Wayman, 454 G.S 79, 309 Z. 784 (19XS) (involving eighteen hours); Great State v. Dutton, 453 G.S. 547, 307 Z. 238 (19XS) (involving eight hours); Great State v Tingle, 451 G.S. 241, 301 Z. 701 (19XS) (involving twenty-one hours); Great State v Dixon, 454 G.S. 444, 311 Z. 613 (19XS) (involving fifteen hours). The first contention of the State, therefore, is that the time period involved in this case cannot be termed an unreasonable delay.

The State further contends that the delay between arrest and initial appearance was due to necessary police procedures. In Great State v. Futch, your honorable court at 447 G.S. at 392 commented that permissible activity between arrest and initial appearance included not merely booking and administrative procedures but also limited preliminary investigation into the accused's connection with the crime. Given the time constraints in the instant case, no more than such limited investigation could have taken place. Were all police questioning to be forbidden following arrest and prior to initial appearance, law enforcement agencies would be handcuffed in their fight against crime. It follows from the Futch decision that limited questioning by the authorities is permissible, for only after such questioning can it be determined if the material is inculpatory or exculpatory. Therefore, the State submits that all that occurred in the instant case between the time of arrest and the initial appearance falls within the ambit of permissible activity as determined by your honorable court in Futch.

The considerations which require prompt initial appearance after arrest were forcefully stated by Justice

Frankfurter in <u>McNabb v. United States</u>, 318 U.S. 332 (1943) wherein he stated:

> Experience has therefore counseled that safeguards must be provided against the dangers of the over-zealous as well as the despotic. The awful instruments of the criminal law cannot be entrusted to a single functionary. The complicated process of criminal justice is therefore divided into different parts, responsibility for which is separately vested in the various participants upon whom the criminal law relies for its vindication.

> The police in the case at bar did not resort to "awful instruments of the criminal law." They did not use coercive tactics such as administering a polygraph test and then confronting the defendant with the results, nor did they isolate the defendant for a lengthy period. Following his arrest defendant did not make repeated denials of guilt. In <u>Futch, supra</u>, the police used the 14-hour delay to put the defendant in a line-up without the benefit of counsel. Conversely, in the case at bar, appellant was at all times advised of his right to counsel.

> Therefore, the State submits that the appellant has failed to establish that the confession and evidence flowing from it resulted from unnecessary and unreasonable delay between arrest and initial appearance.

2. ....

3. ....

Conclusion

For the reasons stated above, the State submits that the verdicts of the lower court were proper and that they be, in all respects, affirmed.

Respectfully submitted,

James Bethann
District Attorney
BY *Mel. Advocate*
Assistant District Attorney

Room 705 Local County Courthouse
Big City, Great State

arrest and initial appearance? Was police interrogation permissible under Rule 118 before the initial appearance? Not only would their decision establish a precedent, but their interpretation of Rule 118 could have far-reaching effects upon police practice. The other two questions presented for review were more easily answered. The facts needed to determine voluntariness of the appellant's confession and prejudicial effect, if any, of the court's remarks were provided in the record of the suppression hearing and the trial. Had they been the only questions raised, no oral argument would have been scheduled.

That took place before the seven supreme court justices three weeks later. Henry was especially pleased with a portion of his argument to the court concerning Rule 118:

> The prohibition in Rule 118 against any unnecessary delay between arrest by an accusatorial authority and an initial appearance safeguards against unnecessary abridgement of a citizen's liberty. Such an abridgement would, of course, be unconstitutional. The danger of any such unnecessary and unconstitutional restriction of liberty diminishes significantly when a citizen is brought swiftly before a neutral judicial authority, there to be informed of the charges and provided with an immediate and reasonable opportunity to regain his liberty by the posting of a reasonable bail.

> The significance of Rule 118, requiring initial appearance without unnecessary delay, becomes fully apparent when that rule is read together with the requirements of Rule 119. Under Rule 119, at the initial appearance before a neutral authority, the citizen, who is presumed innocent, must be given a copy of the complaint, informed of his rights, and must be provided an immediate and reasonable opportunity to post bail. The fundamental purpose of the initial appearance is, therefore, to guarantee a citizen substantially the same rights to which he is entitled under both the United States and the Great State constitutions.[9]

Henry was aware that most of the justice's questions were directed to him. Some of the dialogue was as follows:

"Is it your contention that Rule 118 precludes any police questioning of an arrestee prior to the initial appearance?," Henry was asked.

"Yes," he replied, "except for securing that information which is necessary for booking purposes."

"Would not such severe limitation on the investigatory powers of the police adversely affect the apprehension of criminals and the solution of crime?"

"There is no limit on the information they can secure or the questioning that can be done of other persons. The arrested person's privilege against compulsory self-incrimination must be protected. It is not protected when the first-time offender, such as the appellant, succumbs to the subtle pressures arising from police questioning following arrest because of the fear engendered by the situation in which he finds himself and the lack of knowledge of police procedures."

At this point, the chief justice asked Mel Advocate:

"And what is your response to that?"

"It would be a strange rule of criminal procedure, indeed, that would not permit the police to accept the confession of a person who has just committed a crime when that confession is voluntarily offered. The purpose of Rule 118, as announced when it was first promulgated, is regulation of police practices. The rule is based on the presumption that reprehensible practices—the third degree, for want of better terminology—are not possible within the time of a reasonable delay. In this way it acts to preclude forced confessions, and it is these involuntary confessions that are the evil sought to be avoided by the Miranda requirements."

Henry thought that one question directed to him regarding the third issue was somewhat revealing:

"How can remarks of the court made at side bar—out of the hearing of the jury—be prejudicial to the defendant's case?"

"In this case it was a rebuke connected with the entrance of objections. In that way it can act to restrict or limit pursuit of the suppression of evidence, to lessen the aggression with which the attorney proceeds, and thus deny the client the full effect of a zealous advocacy."

"A zealous and aggressive advocacy is to be recommended, but should it not also be limited to reasonable bounds?"

"I agree. Any excess was not present in this case, however." That response brought smiles from everyone.

Postargument conference

At the conferences of justices following the oral argument, it was soon apparent that Henry's arguments were insufficient, in their opinion, to warrant a reversal. There was agreement that short shrift should be made of the second and third issues—those concerned with the involuntary confession and prejudicial effect of the judge's remarks at side bar. The court found sufficient evidence, "in appellant's own words" as one justice remarked, that Harvey had voluntarily waived his rights and that his confession had been voluntary. Henry's argument that Harvey did not understand all of the legal implications was unpersuasive. As the chief justice remarked:

"Followed to its logical conclusion, that argument would require that only lawyers would be able to waive their rights. And that is clearly inconsistent with the decision in *Miranda v. Arizona.*"

They also agreed that the trial judge's statement that defense counsel's motion for a mistrial was frivolous did not prejudice the defendant when

FORM 11-6. Opinion.

IN THE SUPREME COURT OF GREAT STATE

STATE OF GREAT STATE,   :
          Appellee   :
        v.   : Appeal from No. 1246 of 19XX
HARVEY WORKER,   :   Local County
         Appellant   :

CARY, J.   December 12, 19XX

OPINION

The appellant, Harvey Worker, was convicted of burglary and theft on August 29, 19XX following a jury trial. Post-trial motions were denied and the appellant was sentenced to a term of imprisonment not to exceed three years. This appeal followed.

Appellant was arrested without a warrant at approximately 7:30 p.m.,

. . . .

Appellant contends that his confession was the product of unnecessary delay between his arrest and initial appearance and therefore should have then excluded along with the evidence flowing from it. Prior to trial appellant requested suppression of both his inculpatory statement and the physical evidence. These requests were denied by the trial court.

In Great State v. Futch, 447 G.S. 389, 290 Z.417 (19XR) this court adopted the "federal approach" to evidence obtained during unnecessary delay prior to the initial appearance and announced a procedural rule excluding all evidence so obtained from admission at trial. (Congress repudiated this approach by enacting the Omnibus Crime Control and Safe Streets Act of 1968, Act of June 19, 1968, Pub. L. 90-351, 82 Stat. 210, 19 USC §3501.) Like its federal prototypes, McNabb v. United States, 318 U.S. 332, 63 S. Ct. 608 (1943) and Mallory v. United States, 354 U.S. 449, 77 S. Ct. 1356 (1957) our decision in Futch was not based on constitutional considerations. The exclusionary rule we promulgated was grounded on the Court's supervisory powers over the administration of justice in the courts of this state. The rule is directed entirely to police conduct prior to trial. The threat of exclusion operates to deter dilatory or illegal police conduct.

In Futch, 447 G.S. at 392 we adopted the reasoning of the D.C. Court of Appeals wherein Judge Burger, now Chief Justice Burger, stated in his concurring opinion in Adams v. United States, 399 F.2d 547, 579 (D.C. Cir., 1969) (concurring opinion):

> Necessary delay can reasonably relate to time to administratively process an accused with booking, fingerprinting and other steps and sometimes even to make same (sic) limited preliminary investigation into his connection with the crime for which he was arrested, especially when it is directed to possible exculpation of the one arrested.

The instant case does not involve the prolonged questioning and lengthy time lapse which occurred in those prior cases in which this Court has found unreasonable delay between arrest and initial appearance. Great State v. Wayman, 454 G.S. 79, 309 Z. 784 (19XS); Great State v. Dutton, 453 G.S. 547, 307 Z. 238 (19XS); Great State v. Tingle, 451 G.S. 241, 301 Z. 701 (19XS); Great State v. Dixon, 454 G.S. 444, 311 Z. 613 (19XS).

Nor is there any record of suspect or reprehensible practices commonly known as the "third degree." The time constraints permitted only limited preliminary questioning in addition to booking and other administrative processing. This is permissible under Futch. That such questioning result in exculpation is not a requirement. Reasonable, limited inquiry by the police is consistent with Rule 118.

We are satisfied that the delay in the instant case was occasioned by proper and necessary steps in the police process and cannot be said to be either unnecessary or unreasonable in light of the requirements of Rule 118. The trial court properly refused suppression of appellant's confession and the physical evidence seized as a result thereto.

Appellant next contends.........................

JUDGMENT OF SENTENCE AFFIRMED.

Kathleen Cary / J.

the response was given at a side bar conference out of the hearing of the jury. In addition, they were unanimous in their opinion that had it been the intention of the drafters of Rule 118 to require an "immediate" initial appearance, the word "immediate" would have been used rather than "without unnecessary delay." They also believed that the absolute restriction upon police interrogation following arrest which Henry advocated would unreasonably hamper police investigation of crime. Nor was such restriction constitutionally required.

However, the justices did decide there was a need to put in writing further explanation of Rule 118 in order to make clear that limited police questioning following arrest did not constitute "unnecessary delay." They also agreed that they should not set a specified time limit which would automatically become an "unnecessary delay," their thought being that this would vary with the circumstances of each situation. The newest member of the court, Judge Kathleen Cary, was assigned the task of writing the opinion, portions of which appear in Form 11-6.[10]

Filing of Opinion

The appellate procedure culminating in that opinion has been flow charted in Figure 11-4. A copy of the opinion was filed with the clerk of the supreme court who thereupon sent copies to Mel Advocate, to Henry, and to the Local County Criminal Court where it was forwarded to Judge Wolfe.

TO CORRECTIONS

Notice was sent to Harvey, the sheriff, and the Little Town Correction Center of orders directing the sheriff to take Harvey into custody and transport him to Little Town to begin his term of imprisonment.

Harvey was at first stunned, then bitter.

"It's all Henry's fault," he told his mother. "He should have made me plead guilty. Then I'd be on probation, not on my way to prison."

Bitterness turned to outrage when a bill for legal services came from Henry's office.

"Why should I pay him?" Harvey asked. "What did he do for me? Just sent me to prison, that's all."

It was Mary who eventually settled matters with Henry. They discussed the fact that Great State, unlike some other states, did not have a procedure for expunging criminal records following imprisonment and successful readjustment to society. The records of ex-offenders in Great State remained on file along with all the information gathered in the criminal process. That meant Harvey would later be looked upon by many as an "ex-con." This could limit his opportunities for employment and even to be licensed and enter certain professions.

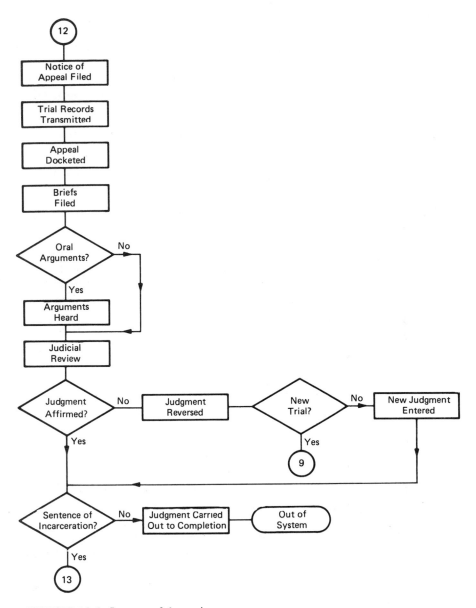

FIGURE 11-4. Process of Appeal.

Although Harvey said he was "through with lawyers," Mary attempted to persuade Harvey to talk with Henry about some other forms of postconviction relief. That eventually occurred, but not until Harvey had entered upon an entirely new phase of his life, one that will be discussed in the next chapter.

QUESTIONS

Since Harvey's new life is a direct result of the outcome of the trial, it seems appropriate to ask if Harvey's election to go to trial—and to a jury trial—was unrealistic judgment on his part? Should Henry have further encouraged or even insisted that Harvey plead guilty? Do you believe the judge would have placed Harvey on probation if he had pleaded guilty? If so, is he really being punished for having exercised a constitutional right to trial by jury?

Would the jury's verdict have been any different had Harvey taken the stand and testified in his own behalf? What would have been the effect of cross-examination? Why did Henry make the motions to demur to the evidence and for a directed verdict for acquittal? Wasn't it just as obvious to him as it was to the judge that they would not be granted? Is this not also true regarding his request for a new trial?

What value exists in the presentence report prepared for the judge by the probation officer? Did the judge really make use of it? If so, does this really mean that the person preparing the report, rather than the judge, becomes the real influence in determining sentence? Should this be so?

Do you agree with the judge's analysis of the sentencing alternatives and their appropriateness in Harvey's case? What sentence do you believe should have been imposed in Harvey's situation? Why? Nothing is said about the district attorney's reaction to Harvey's sentence. What do you think it was? Why?

At each stage of the criminal system through which Harvey has progressed, a different group of persons has played significant roles. In the beginning stages, it was the police. Then there were magistrates, next lawyers and judges, and a probation officer. Have you seen any interaction between these different groups of persons? Is there some means of coordination and integration, so that the effect is that of a whole system? Or, do you see these groups as working mostly by themselves, so that the final effect is one of separate and distinct systems loosely tied to each other? What suggestions have you for improvement?

What differences did you note between the criminal trial and the civil trial? Are these merely matters of form or are they of real substance?

Can you think of issues which Henry could have raised on appeal but which he did not? Why do you suppose he did not? Should cases like this one be appealed? Why? Do you agree with the appellate court's decision? Why?

If you were arrested and interrogated by the police in Great State for three hours before being taken to a magistrate for an initial appearance, would the *Worker* decision be precedent for inclusion or exclusion of any statement you might have made to the police during that time? Based on the *Worker* decision, would you need to know more than just the amount of time that elapsed? Why? Did the court in that decision define "without unnecessary delay?" If not, why not? If yes, what is that definition? When the court determined that Harvey had not been held "without unnecessary delay," was it making new law? In what way? When an appellate court interprets statutory law, does it really make new law? If so, why did this appellate court look to the specific wording of Rule 118? Why did the Great State Supreme Court in *Futch* rely upon a federal court's decision if Great State, rather than federal, law was involved? What effect did the Omnibus Crime Control and Safe Streets Act have on the Worker decision? Why would Congress pass such legislation after the United States Supreme Court had already made a contrary decision in both the *McNabb* and *Mallory* cases?

Should Harvey Worker seek additional attempts at relief? If so, which of the postconviction forms of relief would be appropriate? What hope of success has he? Should postconviction relief be more limited? in cases like Harvey's? Why?

CASES

Duncan v. Louisiana
391 U.S. 145, 88 S.Ct. 1444, 20 L.Ed. 2d 491 (1968)

Appellant was convicted of a misdemeanor, punishable by two years imprisonment and a $300 fine. Trial by jury was sought but the request denied because the Louisiana Constitution provided for jury trials only in cases in which capital punishment or imprisonment at hard labor might be imposed. Appellant was convicted and sentenced to serve 60 days in the parish prison and pay a fine of $150.

MR. JUSTICE WHITE . . . Because we believe that trial by jury in criminal cases is fundamental to the American scheme of justice, we hold that the Fourteenth Amendment guarantees a right of jury trial in all criminal cases which—were they to be tried in a federal court—would come within the Sixth Amendment's guarantee. . . .

The guarantee of jury trial in the Federal and State Constitutions reflect a profound judgment about the way in which law should be enforced and justice administered. A right to jury trial is granted to criminal defendants in order to prevent oppression by the Government.

Those who wrote our constitutions knew from history and experience that it was necessary to protect against unfounded criminal charges brought to eliminate enemies and against judges too responsive to the voice of higher authority. The framers of the constitutions strove to create an independent judiciary but insisted upon further protection against arbitrary action. Providing an accused with the right to be tried by a jury of his peers gave him an inestimable safeguard against the corrupt or overzealous prosecutor and against the compliant, biased, or eccentric judge. If the defendant preferred the common-sense judgment of a jury to the more tutored but perhaps less sympathetic reaction of the single judge, he was to have it. Beyond this, the jury trial provisions in the Federal and State Constitutions reflect a fundamental decision about the exercise of official power—a reluctance to entrust plenary powers over the life and liberty of the citizen to one judge or to a group of judges. Fear of unchecked power, so typical of our State and Federal Governments in other respects, found expression in the criminal law in this insistence upon community participation in the determination of guilt or innocence. The deep commitment of the Nation to the right of jury trial in serious criminal cases as a defense against arbitrary law enforcement qualifies for protection under the Due Process Clause of the Fourteenth Amendment, and must therefore be respected by the States.

Of course jury trial has "its weaknesses and the potential for misuse." We are aware of the long debate, especially in this century, among those who write about the administration of justice, as to the wisdom of permitting untrained laymen to determine the facts in civil and criminal proceedings. . . . At the heart of the dispute have been express or implicit assertions that juries are incapable of adequately understanding evidence or determining issues of fact, and that they are unpredictable, quixotic, and little better than a role of dice. Yet, the most recent and exhaustive study of the jury in criminal cases concluded that juries do understand the evidence and come to sound conclusions in most of the cases presented to them and that when juries differ with the result at which the judge would have arrived, it is usually because they are serving some of the very purposes for which they were created and for which they are now employed.

. . . in the late 18th century in America crimes triable without a jury were for the most part punishable by no more than a six-month prison term, although there appear to have been exceptions to this rule. We need not, however, settle in this case the exact location of the line between petty offenses and serious crimes. It is sufficient for our purposes to hold that a crime punishable by two years in prison is, based on past and contemporary standards in this country, a serious crime and not a petty offense. Consequently, appellant was entitled to a jury trial and it was error to deny it . . .

Commonwealth v. Martin
(Pa.) 351 A.2d 650 (1976)

Appellants (six) attack their sentences on the ground they were imposed in accordance with a presentence agreement among three judges of the trial court to impose sentence of three to ten years imprisonment plus fine for the sale of heroin, without giving consideration to defendants' individual characteristics. There was no evidence of a conspiracy among appellants, and no claim that identical sentences were imposed because of any conspiracy.

MR. JUSTICE ROBERTS . . . The record amply demonstrates that the three judges had agreed in advance that the sentence to be imposed for a sale of heroin was to be three to ten years imprisonment plus a fine, and all of the sentences were to run consecutively. In no case was a presentence report ordered. No meaningful inquiry was made into the appellants' backgrounds, individual characteristics, relative culpability or prospects for rehabilitation, despite clear evidence that the appellants' offenses were committed in varying circumstances. In short, all appellants' sentences were based on an abstract predetermination of the sentence to be imposed for the particular offense, without regard to the individual circumstances of particular cases. . . .

. . . At one time, sentencing by a court after a finding of guilt was purely ceremonial, since there was but one penalty at law for any given crime. However, during the nineteenth century, when incarceration became the primary mode of punishment, the practice of discretionary sentencing began. At first this took the form of executive pardons, and the judge's duty remained only to apply the sentence mandated by law. However, discretionary sentencing soon became an integral part of judicial procedure; the sentencing court had increasing discretion in its choice of sentence. This development reflected the move toward individualized sentencing, which attempted to rehabilitate, as well as punish, the offender.

The indeterminate sentence won early recognition in Pennsylvania. . . . The Legislature reinforced these provisions by allowing suspension of sentence and probation, at the sentencing court's discretion, in all but the most serious crimes. . . .

. . . Pennsylvania's procedure of indeterminate sentencing carries with it an implicit adoption of the philosophy of individual sentencing. This necessitates the granting of broad discretion to the trial judge, who must determine, among the sentencing alternatives and the range of permissible penalties, the proper sentence to be imposed. The importance of this discretion cannot be overemphasized; many commentators argue that it is one of the most important, and most easily abused, powers vested in the trial court today . . . .

The procedures employed by the sentencing court in the appeals before us today ignore the basic premises of Pennsylvania sentencing. Here . . . the nature of the criminal act was used as the sole basis for the determination of the length of sentence, and all sentences of imprisonment were to run consecutively. Thus the court failed to exercise its broad discretion in accordance with the applicable statutory requirements.

The sentence must be imposed for the minimum amount of confinement that is consistent with the protection of the public, the gravity of the offense, and the rehabilitative needs of the defendant. . . . At least two facts are crucial to such determination—the particular circumstances of the offense and the character of the defendant. . . . We hold that regardless of whether a presentence report is ordered, the sentencing court must at least consider these two factors in its sentencing determination. Failure to give such individualized consideration requires that these sentences be vacated . . . .

In these cases the court did not order any pre-sentence reports although it was authorized to do so . . . . Normally such reports should be used, although they are sometimes unnecessary because other sources of information are available. However, presentence reports are of obvious importance to the sentencing court. . . .

The ABA Project on Minimum Standards of Justice, Standards Relating to Probation §2.1 (Approved Draft, 1970), recommends that a pre-sentence report is peculiarly necessary in any of the following circumstances: 1) where incarceration for one year or more is a possible disposition; 2) where the defendant is less than twenty-one years old; and 3) where the defendant is a first offender. These situations require the utmost care in sentence determination . . . . Judgments of sentence vacated and cases remanded for sentencing.

Illinois v. Allen
397 U.S. 337, 90 S.Ct. 1057, 25 L.Ed. 2d 353 (1970)

Allen was convicted of armed robbery. Following unsuccessful appeal of his conviction to the Illinois Supreme Court, he petitioned for a writ of habeas corpus in federal court alleging that he had been wrongfully deprived of his constitutional right to remain present throughout his trial. During that trial, he had repeatedly interrupted the proceedings with loud talking, argued with the judge in abusive language, and at one point threatened the judge's life. Allen was removed from the courtroom twice and was permitted to return upon his promise to conduct himself properly. He was absent during part of the selection of the jury and during presentation of the prosecution's case, except for several instances of identification. The District Court found no constitutional violation and declined to issue the writ. The Court of Appeals reversed, ruled that a criminal defendant has an absolute right to be present at all stages of the proceedings even if it means that the trial judge must resort to shackling and gagging to restrain the defendant. The Supreme Court granted certiorari.

MR. JUSTICE BLACK . . . The Confrontation Clause of the Sixth Amendment to the United States Constitution provides that "In all criminal prosecutions, the accused shall enjoy the right . . . . to be confronted with the witnesses against him . . . ." We have held that the Fourteenth Amendment makes the guarantees of this clause obligatory upon the States . . . One of the most basic of the rights guaranteed by the Confrontation Clause is the accused's right to be present in the courtroom at every stage of his trial . . . .

. . . Although mindful that courts must indulge every reasonable presumption against the loss of constitutional rights, . . . we explicitly hold today that a defendant can lose his right to be present at trial if, after he has been warned by the judge that he will be removed if he continues his disruptive behavior, he nevertheless insists on conducting himself in a manner so disorderly, disruptive, and disrespectful of the court that his trial cannot be carried on with him in the courtroom. Once lost, the right to be present can, of course, be reclaimed as soon as the defendant is willing to conduct himself consistently with the decorum and respect inherent in the concept of courts and judicial proceedings.

It is essential to the proper administration of criminal justice that dignity, order, and decorum be the hallmarks of all court proceedings in our country. The flagrant disregard in the courtroom of elementary standards of proper conduct should not and cannot be tolerated. We believe trial judges confronted with disruptive, contumacious, stubbornly defiant defendants must be given sufficient discretion to meet the circumstances of each case. No one formula for maintaining the appropriate courtroom atmosphere will be best in all situations. We think there are at least three constitutionally permissible ways for a trial judge to handle an obstreperous defendant like Allen: (1) bind and gag him, thereby keeping him present; (2) cite him for contempt; (3) take him out of the courtroom until he promises to conduct himself properly . . . .

It is not pleasant to hold that the respondent Allen was properly banished from the court for a part of his own trial. But our courts, palladiums of liberty as they are, cannot be treated disrespectfully with impunity. Nor can the accused be permitted by his disruptive conduct indefinitely to avoid being tried on the charges brought against him. It would degrade our country and our judicial system to permit our courts to be bullied, insulted, and humiliated and their orderly progress thwarted and obstructed by defendants brought before them charged with crimes. As guardians of the public welfare, our state and federal judicial systems strive to administer equal justice to the rich and the poor, the good and the bad, the native and foreign born of every race, nationality, and religion. Being manned by humans, the courts are not perfect and are bound to make some errors. But, if our courts are to remain what the Founders intended, the citadels of justice, their proceedings cannot and must not be infected with the sort of scurrilous, abusive language and conduct paraded before the Illinois trial judge in this case. The record shows that the Illinois judge at all times conducted himself with that dignity, decorum, and patience that befits a judge. Even in the holding that the trial judge had erred, the Court of Appeals praised his "commendable patience under severe provocation."...

Reversed.

FOOTNOTES

[1] In federal cases, Article III, § 2, cl. 3 also applies.

[2] *Duncan v. Louisiana,* 391 U.S. 145 (1968).

[3] *Baldwin v. New York,* 399 U.S. 66 (1970).

[4] *Johnson v. Louisiana,* 406 U.S. 356 (1972), *Apodaca v. Oregon,* 406 U.S. 404 (1972).

[5] *Commonwealth v. Martin,* (Pa.) 351 A.2d 650 (1976).

[6] *Pointer v. Texas,* 380 U.S. 400 (1965).

[7] *Illinois v. Allen,* 397 U.S. 337 (1970).

[8] Parts adapted from Brief for Appellee filed in the Supreme Court of Pennsylvania in the case of *Commonwealth v. Whitson,* No. 177, March Term, 1974.

[9] Adapted from Opinion of the Court, *Commonwealth v. Dixon,* 454 Pa. 444, 311 A.2d 613 (1973).

[10] Parts adapted from *Commonwealth v. Whitson,* (Pa.) 334 A.2d 653 (1975).

CHAPTER 12

INCARCERATION AND RELEASE: CORRECTIONS SUBSYSTEM AND EXIT

Dread. Dejection. Despair. Degradation. All of these terms characterized Harvey's feelings at the moment. Handcuffed and accompanied by two constables, he sat in the back of their car on the way to the Great State Correction Center in Little Town, 140 miles away from Big City. Although he knew not what awaited him there, he was relieved to be out of the Local County jail. A traffic accident involving the sheriff's car had caused an unexpected delay in his transportation to Little Town. He had been taken to the jail to await completion of the arrangements for the trip. The short time he had been there had, without question, been the worst experience of his life. He did not believe he would survive if life at Little Town turned out to be anything like it was in that jail.

JAIL

He had been depressed as he entered the jail, following a tearful goodbye to his family. As electrically-controlled steel doors clanged open and then closed behind him, he was horrified at the unbelievable ugliness of the scene before him. The filth, the stench, and the reverberating animal-like sounds assaulted his entire being. A guard pushed him into a cell with these words:

"Get in there, you . . . punk . . . you."

"This one's for the country club," that guard had said to another.

"Judge Wolfe's in a hurry again; doesn't want any of her people here too long. Her orders say he has to be in Little Town by four-thirty today."

Harvey looked around. He did not even wish to sit down. There was no chair, just a cot covered with a torn and dirty mattress. Lice crawled over it. The lighting was extremely poor, but Harvey could distinguish plainly the peeling paint on the walls and the decaying particles of food on the steel bars of the cell door. A toilet and sink were at the other end of the cell. The concrete floor still contained evidence of the vomit of the last occupant. The rancid putridness coming from it together with the all pervasive smell of urine combined to assail Harvey's olfactory sense to the point at which he thought he could no longer breathe. Nor was there any escape from the sounds of cell doors loudly clanging, the screams of a drug user in the process of withdrawal, the senseless mutterings of the individual arrested for intoxication who was in the cell next to him, the incredible sounds coming from the cell across the way where a prisoner battered his head against the wall. As he stood there near the cell door, not knowing where to turn or what to do next, a passing prisoner spat at him.

Harvey found it hard to believe this was real. Was this not cruel and unusual punishment, as prohibited by the Eighth Amendment of the United States Constitution?[1]   (This provision has been held applicable to the states by the United States Supreme Court.[2]) How could human beings be expected to live in a place like this? He rejected an offer of lunch. He was filled with revulsion at just the thought of eating in this place. When at last a guard came to take him to the car for the ride to Little Town, he could hardly wait to get to the jail yard so that he could breathe the outdoor air again. He realized that he had been in jail for less than two hours. To him it seemed more like 200 years.

When Harvey talked with the two constables about his experience in the jail, they were not at all surprised. Harvey learned that more than 420 persons were currently housed in the jail, although it had been built over 50 years ago to accommodate no more than 300. One wing was set aside as a women's section, but persons under 16 years of age were taken to a separate juvenile detention facility in Big City. The constables told Harvey of problems at the jail, such as the incidence of homosexual assault and the increasing number of suicides.

They also assured him that Little Town was strikingly different. It was so recently constructed that the buildings still had the smell of new plastering. Although the constables had merely transported prisoners there and had never spent much time inside, they did know it had acquired a reputation for the "country club atmosphere" which was said to exist there. That brought Harvey some sense of relief, enough that he was able to engage in conversation with the constables about their work.

SHERIFF AND CONSTABLES

He learned that the constables in Local County worked under the direction of the sheriff. An elected official, the latter was the principal law enforcement officer of the county. His principal duties included

1. Maintaining the county jail and its prisoners;
2. Assisting the county court through the service of process, summoning jurors, conducting judicial sales, executing judgment, providing bailiffs and tipstaffs;
3. Keeping the peace in the unincorporated areas of the county.

The two constables with Harvey told him they were assigned to the county jail and worked principally with prisoners although, on occasion, they had assisted sheriff's deputies in effecting arrests and executing search warrants. They discussed a new county regulation which required all sheriff's deputies and constables to be graduates of the Big City police academy. It was not yet clear whether this new ruling would apply only to personnel to be hired in the future or whether it also pertained to those already employed. If the latter, both constables said they would have to find some way to take the course in order to keep their jobs.

MAXIMUM SECURITY FACILITY

A highway sign indicated the exit to Cul deSac just ahead. Harvey learned that the two constables sometimes transported prisoners to the state maximum security prison located there. Their description coincided with the image of prison Harvey had formed from his reading, the movies, and television. They told him how it was surrounded by a 25-foot high, thick stone wall with 35-foot guard towers manned around the clock by armed sentries. It has a population of about 1500 men. Neither women nor juveniles were sent there, and only infrequently men under the age of 25. The one electric chair still in existence in the state was located there, but it had not been used in the past ten years.

Life in the "pen," as the constables referred to the Cul deSac facility, had been described to them by a prison social worker. Men were confined to steel-barred cells, twenty of which were in a row, with rows six tiers high in each cell block. Prisoners moved from one place to another only in a company and under guard. They were required to march in twos, arms folded, with eyes straight ahead, and in silence. Meals were eaten in the mess hall, where the men filed through a cafeteria-type line, walked to the first unoccupied seat at a long table, and sat eating silently while facing the back of the man in front.

Inmates spent most of the time between the hours of 6:00 PM and

6:00 AM confined in their cells. Entering another man's cell was not permitted, nor was the passing of articles from one cell to another. Smoking was permitted in cells between the hours of 6:00 AM and 10:00 PM, which were the times for rising and retiring. Men were required to sleep with their feet toward the door and with their head uncovered, their shoes placed at the door and the rest of their clothing on the chair next to the door. Should a man fail to do this, he would be awakened by a guard.

Visiting by family and friends was permitted during scheduled hours on Sundays once a month. A small gymnasium and an outside prison yard provided limited recreational facilities. Fourteen teachers were employed full time at the institution to provide instruction in subjects varying from basic grammar to social studies. The staff also included four psychologists and five social workers. Inmates worked during the day in the prison laundry, bakery, and kitchen. Some were employed in making license plates and brooms.

Discipline was strict. Frequent or serious violation of the rules could result in solitary confinement. This meant the prisoner was kept locked either in his cell or in the "hole" 24 hours a day, placed on a restricted diet, and denied such privileges as visitation and receiving mail.

Harvey learned from the constables that the persons most likely to be sent there were those who represented a grave risk to the safety of the community because they were violently assaultive, had committed atrocious crimes, or were hardened criminals. He also learned that correctional institutions are classified as maximum-, medium-, and minimum-security facilities. The one to which he was being sent was a minimum-security institution. A medium-security facility differed from one of minimum security, he learned, in that the former had guards, was enclosed behind a high fence, generally had cells instead of dormitories, and limited residents to work and study programs within the institution.

STATE CORRECTION CENTER

"Do you have his papers back there?" the driver asked as they approached the highway exit to Little Town. He was referring to records related to Harvey's case, including the judge's order of commitment and the presentence report, which were being sent to the personnel at the Little Town facility.

Harvey's first surprise came as they arrived at the entrance to the Great State Correction Center. To him it looked just like a college campus. There were no guards; there was no entrance check point, no fence. He noted spacious and well-kept grounds, people moving freely about from one building to another, an absence of bars on windows. At the end of a serpentine driveway the car came to a stop outside a building marked "Reception Center."

Intake

The sense of prison returned as Harvey noticed the entrance to the building was electronically controlled. In the office, Paul Grace, intake officer, was expecting them. Harvey's file was turned over to Paul, and he signed the constable's form certifying delivery of the prisoner to the facility, noting time and date. He also made a mental note of what occurred as the constable removed the handcuffs from Harvey. Shaking hands with Harvey, the constable departed with these words:

"Gook luck, son."

In his fifteen years of working in corrections, Paul Grace had not found that to be the usual occurrence.

It was already past mid-afternoon. Paul said they would get Harvey settled and would wait until the next morning for further discussion. Once again Harvey experienced a sense of prison as he was searched and given a change of clothing. He welcomed a shower, feeling clean for the first time since leaving the jail. He was given a booklet containing regulations and information about the Center, and was assigned to a private room. It was small and sparsely furnished, but it was clean. Most importantly to Harvey, it was not a cell with steel bars. Hungry, he hoped that eating arrangements would be comfortable and the food palatable. He found that the dining room was not unlike that in his former college dormitory. There was a cafeteria line, with seating arrangements at round tables for eight. Another young resident recognized that he was new and asked him to join a group of four. Harvey did. He enjoyed the food but was uncomfortable with the conversation and with the other residents. He did, however, go with them after dinner to the lounge to watch TV and play ping pong. In a short while, he left for his room. He was physically tired and filled with a great sense of loneliness, of being cut off from the rest of the world. The feeling of being imprisoned remained until he fell asleep.

The following morning Paul Grace met with him and explained that Harvey would remain in the reception center for the next few weeks for an orientation program. Harvey was kept busy. He was given a medical and dental check-up. He seemed to be forever meeting with either counselors, case workers, or psychologists. To him they appeared to be most interested in his year of college, his knowledge of computers, his cypres hobby. He participated in a variety of recreational activities with some of the other residents. However, he did not develop even a feeling of ease with them.

Paul Grace presided at a staff meeting held for the purpose of discussing Harvey's assignment and program at the Center. Few of the other residents had either a background or interests similar to Harvey's. Therefore, in assigning him to a cottage, the staff decided solely upon the basis of placing him with other men of his age group. They also agreed that Harvey would probably be neither challenged nor happy with the programs currently available at the Center. They therefore looked to community resources. A work program in the cypres industry was not available in the locality. However, there did exist opportunity for employment in several firms with computer facilities. Furthermore, the nearby community college offered some cypres engineering and computer science courses in the evenings which should be of interest to Harvey. The staff also agreed that Paul Grace had developed the greatest rapport with Harvey and therefore appeared to be the best person to serve as his counselor.

As the meeting ended, Paul smiled to himself. Great State was currently in the process of converting from the practice of having the sentencing judge specify the prison to which a convicted individual should be sent to the kind of program which exists in most states where the judge merely sentences to the state correction system. The convicted individual is then sent to a reception and classification center, such as the one they were presently developing in Little Town. There, following screening and diagnosis by the professional staff, the sentenced individual is assigned to the most appropriate institution or program for corrective treatment. Paul Grace mused that, after weeks of study by a group of professionals, the staff had come up with the same recommendation as Judge Wolfe had. He found a certain irony in that, although it was obvious that Harvey's was an unusual case.

Rehabilitative Program

Harvey was happy with the news from Paul Grace. Moving to a cottage meant that he would be unrestricted in his movements about the grounds, and that the only locked doors would be those of the cottage at night. That freedom was one he had taken for granted until recently. He was very interested in the possibility of going out to work. Paul explained that there had been much controversy and resistance, as well as complaint in the small community, over the idea of having "prisoners" employed in local industry. However, he planned to seek out an appropriate job opportunity for Harvey. He also gave Harvey a bulletin listing courses offered at the community college, suggesting that Harvey take a few days to determine courses he might like to take.

Harvey asked if he might have some of his own clothes sent to him from home. Paul recommended that he invite his family to bring them, there being liberal visiting privileges. It was the happiest day Harvey had experienced since he arrived at the Center. He wrote to his mother. He declined a ride to the cottage to which he had been assigned. Although it was on the other end of the grounds, he walked the entire way in the rain.

It was now Paul Grace's turn to experience disappointment and frustration. Several firms whom he contacted about employing Harvey were cordial but insisted they could not afford the employee morale problems and poor public relations that would follow. Others simply refused outright. Gail Earl, who taught computer science at the community college and with whom Paul discussed Harvey's enrollment, provided helpful information. She said that the Planning and Research Division of the Great State Department of Corrections had undertaken a study of juvenile recidivism. The data were being processed at the computer center at the Juvenile Ranch, located twenty miles from Little Town. Since she was one of the consultants for the project, Gail knew that trained personnel were sorely needed.

Paul arranged for Harvey to be interviewed by Michael Patrick, director of the computer center at the Ranch. The Ranch was a medium-security facility for boys aged 13—15 who assisted in the operation of a large dairy farm while institutionalized. The offices of the Juvenile Division of the Great State Department of Corrections occupied one of the buildings on the grounds. There Harvey viewed the computer facilities and talked with Michael Patrick about his background. Michael asked a great many questions about the changes Harvey had made in The Firm's records in his attempt to cover up the theft of the cypres parts.

"I'll try him," Michael told Paul Grace over the telephone. "He knows more about computers than anyone else I have working here. Furthermore, he won't have the temptation he had with the cypres parts. About the only thing he could steal here would be office supplies."

When Paul told Harvey he had been hired, he emphasized that it would be on the condition that he prove himself. He also talked with him about arrangements for transportation to his job and to the classes at the community college two evenings a week in the Correction Center's minibus.

Family Visitation

When Mary Worker came to visit Harvey, she was not only pleased with the news about his job but also pleasantly surprised at the "unprison-like" characteristics of the Center. Henry Law accompanied her. In the course of their conversation, Harvey asked him about a "postconviction hearing." Residents of his cottage talked about it a great deal. Forms requesting such a hearing were available at the Center. Henry and Harvey quickly went through the contents of the form, a copy of which is shown as Form 12-1.

POSTCONVICTION HEARING

Henry explained that a post conviction hearing is a procedure established to provide relief to persons who have been convicted and

FORM 12-1. Petition Under PCHS.

PETITION UNDER POST CONVICTION HEARING STATUTE

_____

Court and Docket Numbers

(To Be Filled In By Clerk of Court)

STATE OF GREAT STATE

vs.

_____

(Name of Petitioner)

_____

Note: List below those informations or indictments and offenses for which you have not completed your sentence.

Information or indictment numbers: _____

I was charged with the following crimes: _____

_____

1. My name is: _____

2. I am now:

   (A) ____ On Parole   (B) ____ On Probation

   (C) ____ Confined in _____

3. I was sentenced on _____, 19____, to a total term of _____, commencing on _____, 19_____, following a

   _____ Trial by Jury

   _____ Trial by a Judge without a Jury

   _____ Plea of guilty

   _____ Plea of nolo contendere

4. I am eligible for relief because of:

   ____ The introduction of evidence obtained pursuant to an unlawful arrest.

_____ The introduction of evidence obtained by unconstitutional search and seizure.

_____ The introduction of a coerced confession into
evidence.

_____ The introduction into evidence of a statement
obtained in the absence of a lawyer at a time
when representation is constitutionally required.

_____ The infringement of my privilege against self-
incrimination under either federal or state law.

_____ The denial of my constitutional right to representation by a competent lawyer.

_____ A plea of guilty unlawfully induced.

_____ The unconstitutional suppression of evidence by
the state.

_____ The unconstitutional use by the state of perjured
testimony.

_____ The obstruction by state officials of petitioner's
right of appeal.

_____ Being twice placed in jeopardy.

_____ The abridgement of a right guaranteed by the
constitution or laws of this state or the constitution or laws of the United States, including
a right that was not recognized as existing at
the time of the trial if the constitution requires
retrospective application of that right.

_____ The unavailability at the time of trial of exculpatory evidence that has subsequently become
available and that would have affected the outcome of the trial if it had been introduced.

_____ The denial of my right to appeal through failure
to inform me of this right.

5. The facts in support of the alleged error(s) upon
which this petition is based are as follows: (State
facts clearly and fully; argument, citations or discussions of authorities shall not be included.)

A) I know the following facts to be true of my own personal knowledge:

_____

_____.

B) The following facts were made known to me by means other than my own personal knowledge. (Explain how and by whom you were informed.):

_____

_____.

C) In the event my appeal is allowed as requested under #4, the following are the matters which I intend to assert on that appeal. (Specify the matters to be asserted if appeal is allowed.)

_____.

6. Supporting Exhibits:

A) In support of this petition I have attached as exhibits:

____ Affidavits   [Exhibit(s) #_____]

____ Records   [Exhibit(s) #_____]

____ Other supporting   [Exhibit(s) #_____]
     evidence

B) I have not attached any affidavits, records or other

supporting evidence because _____

_____

7. I have taken the following action(s) to secure relief

from my conviction(s) or sentence(s):

____ Yes   ____ No

A) Direct Appeal: (If yes, name the court(s) to which appeal(s) was/were taken, date, term and number, and result.)

_____

_____

B) Previous Proceedings in the Courts of the State of Great State:

_____ Yes   _____ No

(If yes, name the type of proceedings--such as habeas corpus, etc., including former proceedings under the Post Conviction Hearing Statute, the Court(s) in which petition(s) was/were filed, date, term and number, and result, including all appeals.)

_____

_____

C) Habeas Corpus or other Petitions in Federal Courts:

_____ Yes   _____ No

(If yes, name the district in which petition(s) was/were filed, date(s), court number--civil action or miscellaneous, and result, including all appeals.)

_____

_____.

D) Other Legal Proceedings:

_____ Yes   _____ No

(If yes, give complete details--type of action, court in which filed, date, term and number, result, including all appeals.)

_____

_____.

8. Following my arrest, I was represented by the following lawyer(s): (Give the lawyer's name and the proceeding at which he represented you.)

_____

_____

_____.

9. The issues which I have raised in this petition have not been finally litigated or waived because: (State facts.)

_____

_____ .

10. Because of the foregoing reasons, the relief which I desire is:

   A) _____ Release from custody and discharge.

   B) _____ A new trial.

   C) _____ Correction of sentence.

   D) _____ Other relief (specify):

   _____

   _____ .

11. A) I Am ____ able/____ not able to pay the costs

   of this proceeding. I have $_____ in my prison account.

   B) My other financial resources are: _____

   _____ .

12. A) _____ I do not have a lawyer and I am without financial resources or otherwise unable to obtain a lawyer.

   (1) _____ I request the court to appoint a lawyer to represent me.

   (2) _____ I do not want a lawyer to represent me.

   B) _____ I am represented by a lawyer. (Give the name and address of your lawyer.)

   _____

   _____

                              _____
                              (Signature of Petitioner)

AFFIDAVIT

State of Great State

County of _____ ss

    Personally appeared before me, a notary public in and

for said county and state, _____,

                                      (Name of Petitioner)

who, being duly sworn [or affirmed] according to law, de-

poses and says:

That he is the petitioner herein and the facts as set forth in
this petition are true and correct to the best of his knowledge, information and belief.

                             _____

                             (Signature of Petitioner)

Sworn to and subscribed

before me this _____

day of _____,

19 _____.

    _____
            Notary Public

        _____

sentenced without due process of law. A prisoner in Great State could
apply for such relief by sending copies of the completed form, referred to
as a petition, to the clerk of the criminal court in which he had been tried.
His petition would have to show three things:

    1. That he was convicted of a crime;

    2. That he was currently imprisoned or on parole or probation in
Great State;

    3. That his conviction and sentence resulted from one or more of
the 13 unconstitutional legal grounds listed under question four on
the form.

Henry also explained that the petition must conform with the requirements of the Great State Postconviction Hearing Statute. He added that meeting this requirement had become easier since the printed petition form came into use. The form had been designed so that it was easily completed. Forms were made available to inmates of all penal institutions in the state. Henry added that many prisoners prepared the forms themselves, without the assistance of legal counsel. These often failed to meet requirements.

"What happens when a petition is completed and sent to the clerk of courts? " Harvey wanted to know.

Henry said that a copy was received by the judge who had presided at the trial, after the clerk of courts filled in identification numbers of the original proceedings. The judge then reviewed the petition to determine if it had merit. Should he decide that it did not, he would issue an order dismissing the petition. Otherwise the judge would direct that the second copy of the petition be sent to the district attorney with a request that the prosecutor show cause why relief should not be granted.

An answer to the petition would then be prepared by the district attorney who would either admit, deny, or explain the allegations made in the petition. The prisoner who originated the petition received a copy of this answer, as did the judge and any lawyer designated on the petition. The answer was used by the judge to arrive at a second decision. He could either dismiss the petition, based on information contained in the answer, or he could schedule a hearing at which evidence could be introduced regarding the matters stated in the petition. Following such a hearing, he would enter an order either granting appropriate relief or dismissing the petition. The relief granted might consist of discharge of the prisoner, retrial, or resentencing. The judge's order is a final judgment for the purposes of review by an appellate court.

The postconviction relief process has been flow charted in Figure 12-1. Henry explained to Harvey that the statute had been enacted to simplify procedure. As a result, the one process replaced several forms for postconviction relief previously used in the state, including *habeas corpus.*

HABEAS CORPUS

"Habeas corpus? Tell me about that. There's a lot of talk around here about it, too."

Henry said the literal translation of habeas corpus is "you have the body." A writ is written court order. Therefore petitioning the court for a writ of habeas corpus is an application for the release of a person held in custody. It is available at any stage of the criminal process, not just after a person has been imprisoned following sentencing. The issue involved in habeas corpus is not an individual's guilt or innocence, but whether his liberty has been restrained without due process.

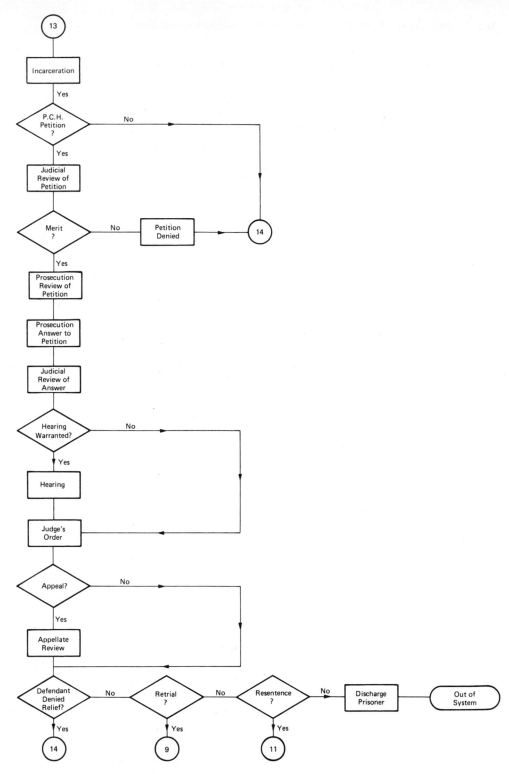

FIGURE 12-1. The Postconviction Hearing Process.

Henry went on to say that under the old common law habeas corpus was known as the Great Writ. The United States Constitution[3] provides that the privilege of the writ of habeas corpus shall not be suspended except when the public safety so requires in cases of rebellion or invasion. Under federal statute[4] recourse to the federal system for the writ is possible when, under a judgment of a state court, a person is held "in custody in violation of the Constitution, or laws, or treaties of the United States." However, the federal courts will not intervene where a state has provided an opportunity for full and fair litigation of a defendant's claim.[5] Of course, in the case of federal prisoners, application for habeas corpus is properly made in the federal courts.

If the petition for habeas corpus alleges facts that show deprivation of constitutional rights, a hearing follows. If the allegations are shown to be true, a writ is issued for the release of the individual. Otherwise, the petition is dismissed. As seen in Figure 12-2, which flow charts the process, appeal of the court's decision is possible.

Henry cautioned, however, that discharge of a prisoner under either of these two forms of relief does not automatically guarantee against the possibility of recommitment following retrial, a matter often overlooked by hopeful prisoner applicants based on misconceptions about the constitutional provision against double jeopardy.

"But why do you ask?" Henry directed the question to Harvey. "Are you interested in further pursuit of your case?"

Harvey was rather emphatic in stating that he did not wish to do so until he saw what happened to his fellow residents as they sought these various forms of relief.

"I have no desire to be a three-time loser," he said.

WORK RELEASE

In the weeks that followed Harvey began both his job and his classes. He not only enjoyed them, he did well at both. Eventually he was given responsibility for supervision of two teenagers who were residents at the Ranch and who were assigned to work in the computer center several hours each day. He found this to be especially rewarding and developed a fine working relationship with the two young persons.

For his work at the computer center, Harvey was paid a salary by the State Department of Corrections. His check was made payable to the warden at the center in trust for Harvey. Because he was employed, Harvey was required to make monthly payments to the institution for his maintenance. This amount was deducted from his salary and the remainder deposited in an account held in his name by the warden. Harvey authorized payment of most of that sum for restitution purposes. The small amount remaining was sufficient to cover his personal needs.

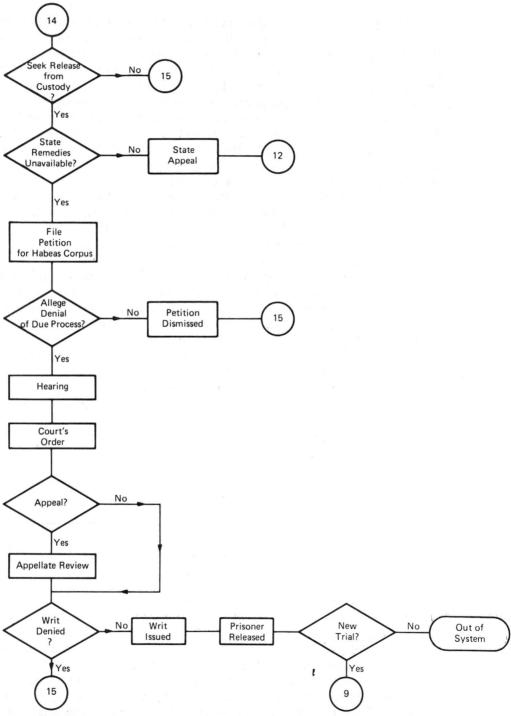

FIGURE 12-2. Procedure for Federal Writ of Habeas Corpus as Postconviction Relief.

JUVENILE PROGRAMS

Through his job related activities, Harvey gained some insight into the matter of juvenile offenders in Great State. Until now, he had given little thought to the delinquent juvenile. He was greatly impressed with the tremendous emphasis given to programs designed to help young people with their problems, to deter them from criminal activity, and to discourage youthful offenders from becoming recidivists.

Even more, he was surprised to learn that special programs dealing with treatment of juveniles were held for police officers in the state. Those particularly encouraged to attend were members of the smaller police departments that did not have the specially trained youth squads for working with juveniles that were to be found in the larger cities. Some of the topics discussed at these juvenile programs included

1. Police reaction at the time of first contact with juveniles and the impact upon youngsters of the manner in which police respond to the situation;

2. Dealing with youthful behavior that might be mischievous, insolent, arrogant, or annoying to others but did not constitute a violation of the law;

3. Handling "status offenders;" that is, youth charged with acts that would not be considered violations of the law were the actor an adult;

4. Police discretion, especially when the offense is of a minor nature and the youngster has no prior record of trouble with the law;

5. Community programs and treatment centers to which police might make referral of juveniles.

In addition, statewide standards had been promulgated that required each police agency to have written policies and guides regarding police discretionary authority at the first contact with a juvenile offender as well as at the police station. Written procedures related to the taking of a juvenile into custody included the following:

1. Who to notify and when,

2. Where the child could be detained,

3. Rules covering police interviews and interrogation,

4. Ground rules for police disposition without referral to the juvenile court,

5. When police should refer the child to the juvenile court,

6. Nature of police records and confidentiality of them, including fingerprinting and photographing.

The standards also required each juvenile court jurisdiction to work out procedures with local police governing discretionary diversion authority of police officers.   Diversion to community based programs and agencies outside the juvenile justice system was recommended when the welfare of the child and the safety of the community would not be jeopardized.

From Sam, a 14-year-old resident of the Ranch whom he supervised, Harvey learned a great deal about the juvenile court. Sam was at the Ranch after having been found guilty for the third time of stealing cars.

"But you're not even old enough to get a Great State driver's license," Harvey had said when Sam told him how he came to be at the Ranch.

"Yeah. The judge said something about that, too." Sam replied.

In the course of one of his conversations with Paul Grace, Harvey repeated this short conversation and added that he found it difficult to believe that Sam could be a car thief.

"He's such a decent kid. He's been honest about everything with me. I can depend on him. He's very intelligent—learns quickly. He's just not the kind of person you'd expect to be stealing cars."

Harvey was surprised at Paul's answer:

"That's very interesting. Sounds something like what the counselors around here say about you."

That comment made a deep impression upon Harvey. He thought about it over and over again. And each time he did, he asked himself a question that had been on his mind ever since the day he spent in the Local County jail.

"How did I ever get myself into this?" He still could not explain why he had ever started to steal; he only knew he would never do such a thing again.

One day Harvey had occasion to work with the report of the President's Commission on Law Enforcement and Administration of Justice[6] regarding a suggested juvenile justice system. It intrigued him, especially the flow chart of the system recommended by that Commission, which is shown in Figure 12-3. Harvey decided to compare it with the Great State system.

JUVENILE COURT

It was not too long until Harvey could say that he was acquainted with the procedure in juvenile courts in Great State from intake to final disposition. With the exception of homicide cases, all persons under the age of 16 accused of criminal activity in Great State were required to be processed through the juvenile system. Harvey learned that youngsters were referred to the juvenile court by the police when diversion to some community agency was not appropriate. In addition to the police, parents and schools frequently made referrals to the court. Neighbors, victims, and social agencies did so on occasion.

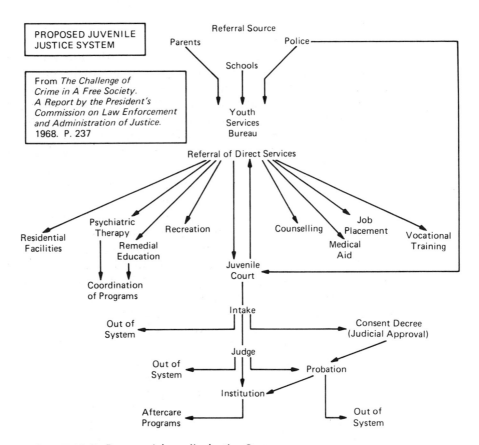

FIGURE 12-3. Proposed Juvenile Justice System

Referrals to the court might originate by an information filed with a district magistrate, by a police arrest report being sent in, by the police bringing the juvenile to the court following an arrest, or there might be a referral in person or by correspondence from a school, parent, or others.

Referrals came to the Intake Department of the court, which was staffed by officers experienced in working with juveniles. Intake officials reviewed each case, evaluating the situation and circumstances that led to the referral. Their first decision was whether an adjudicatory hearing was warranted. Such a hearing is held before a judge of the juvenile court. Evidence is heard to determine if the facts sustain a finding beyond a reasonable doubt that the youngster is guilty of criminal activity.

In Great State, over 40 percent of all referrals to the juvenile courts were disposed of other than by way of an adjudicatory hearing. In those cases, the usual recourse was diversion to an appropriate community agency. Sometimes this involved finding short-term residences or foster homes for youngsters in order to remove them from an environment which tended to encourage delinquency.

In Great State, each juvenile court jurisdiction was required to have written guidelines and procedures which set forth criteria for screening youngsters out of the juvenile justice system. When a diversion decision was made by the intake officer, with or without consultation with the prosecutor's office, the staff member who made it was required to state in writing the basis for the decision. These written reports were then reviewed periodically by one of the judges of the juvenile court, by the chief administrator of the juvenile probation services, and by the prosecutor's office, in order to insure that diversion programs were being operated as intended. The objective was to provide intake services for screening and referral to divert as many youngsters as possible from the juvenile justice system and to reduce detention of youngsters to an absolute minimum.

In cases in which the intake officer decided that an adjudicatory hearing should be held, a petition to the court would be prepared setting forth the charges against the juvenile. This petition was filed with the clerk of the court. A copy was sent to the juvenile and his parents or guardian together with notice of the date and time set for the hearing. (Notification of a juvenile's parent or guardian was automatic with regard to all action taken by the court.) For those cases referred to the juvenile court by an information from a magistrate, no such petition was necessary since the information served in its place.

At the time the petition was prepared, the case was assigned to one of the juvenile probation officers for investigation. He proceeded in much the same way as would an adult probation officer who was preparing a presentence investigatory report for one of the criminal court judges.

When an intake officer decided an adjudicatory hearing should be held, he also decided whether or not a detention hearing was necessary. The purpose of the second hearing was to obtain a judicial determination as to whether the youngster should be detained in a juvenile facility or returned home while awaiting the adjudicatory hearing. In some states, this determination is made by an intake or probation officer rather than by a judge as it was in Great State. The usual practice in Great State was to recommend detention only when some alternative disposition was not advisable, cases, for example, in which the youngster was a threat to himself or others, or he was a runaway risk, or home and family difficulties were the source of his problems.

An adjudicatory hearing can be held only in the juvenile court which has jurisdiction in the case. In Great State, that was the juvenile court in the youngster's home county or in the county where the offense allegedly occurred. In some unusual cases, such as an individual over the age of 14 who was charged with murder, the matter was transferred to the criminal court.

In Great State, the rules of evidence applied at adjudicatory hearings although the atmosphere was more informal than in the criminal court. A juvenile is entitled to due process.[7] He has the right to the assistance of counsel and the right to confront his accusers and to cross-examine them. Because he is also entitled to the privilege against self-incrimination, he must be advised of his constitutional rights as required in *Miranda v. Arizona.* Since there were questions as to a juvenile's ability to knowingly and intelligently waive his rights, Great State required that the Miranda warnings be given in the presence of either counsel or a parent or guardian. A further requirement was that the consent of such individuals be secured to waive any rights.

If the evidence did not reveal facts that would sustain a finding beyond a reasonable doubt that the youngster was guilty of unlawful activity, there could be no adjudication of delinquency and the judge would dismiss the case. This would be tantamount to a finding of not guilty in a criminal case. On the other hand, if the evidence led to an adjudication of delinquency, the judge would ask the juvenile probation officer for his report of the social history of the youngster and a recommendation regarding disposition. After receiving that report, the judge made a determination of disposition. His decision was announced either at a separate hearing or immediately following the adjudicatory hearing. The judge might decide upon commitment to a state or private institution or upon probation.

A prevalent belief among Great State juvenile authorities was that probation usually offered the best remedy at the least risk of damage to the child and at the least expense to the community. Many of the juvenile judges considered a good probation staff as the juvenile court's most effective tool. On the other hand, they also recognized that commitment might be necessary when a juvenile's aggressive actions presented danger to the community; when his family was a threat to the youngster's rehabilitation; or when the juvenile had special needs that could be met only under a closely controlled situation.

Great State provided by statute that a juvenile acquired no civil disabilities nor was he deemed to have committed a crime as a result of his appearance in juvenile court. A separate docket was kept for the court and withheld from indiscriminate public inspection. The legal records were in the custody of the clerk of courts. The social records were kept by the probation staff. All were required to be held strictly confidential.

Following the judge's disposition of the case and entry of his final order, a juvenile or his parents could request a rehearing. There was a 21-day limit in which this request must be made. If they were still not satisfied after the rehearing, they could appeal to the intermediate appellate court.

This entire process was flow charted by Harvey. His chart appears as

Figure 12-4. In preparing that flow chart, Harvey found many of the steps were analogous to those through which he had been processed. His interest, however, was not limited to procedure. The information generated by the computerized data system on which he was working also held his attention.

For instance, he noted the data showed a male, age 12, who had been before the juvenile court nine times; twice for possession and sale of drugs; twice for auto theft; once each for burglary, robbery, assault, disorderly conduct and intoxication, and finally for parole violation. Another, age 13, was there for the eighth time; once for assault, once because he had run away from home; once for disorderly conduct and intoxication; three times for retail theft; and twice for other theft. Harvey found this hard to believe. It was even more difficult to reconcile with the existence of extensive and many-faceted programs for youth in the state, coordinated in each county by a youth service bureau. When he talked with Gail Earl about it, she explained that one of the main purposes of the project was to identify factors common to juvenile recidivists and determine causal relationships. Harvey learned that during the past several years about one-third of the youngsters appearing before the juvenile courts in Great State were there for other than the first time.

PAROLE

As Paul Grace continued to receive good reports about Harvey's progress—reports that coincided with his own observations—he decided that Harvey should be recommended for parole at the first date on which he would be eligible.

Parole meant that Harvey would be released from prison, subject to supervision by a parole officer, and must, during the term of his parole, meet certain conditions. The conditions imposed in Great State were similar to those found in many of the other states. The parolee must

1. Remain employed;
2. Obey the law; conviction of another crime would result in automatic revocation of parole;
3. Refrain from "undesirable associations;" i.e., persons with whom he would be likely to lean toward criminal activity;
4. Refrain from the use of narcotics and use alcohol only in moderation;
5. Secure permission from the parole officer to travel out of state, to own and operate a car, to change employment or residence, to marry;
6. Neither possess nor make use of any weapon.

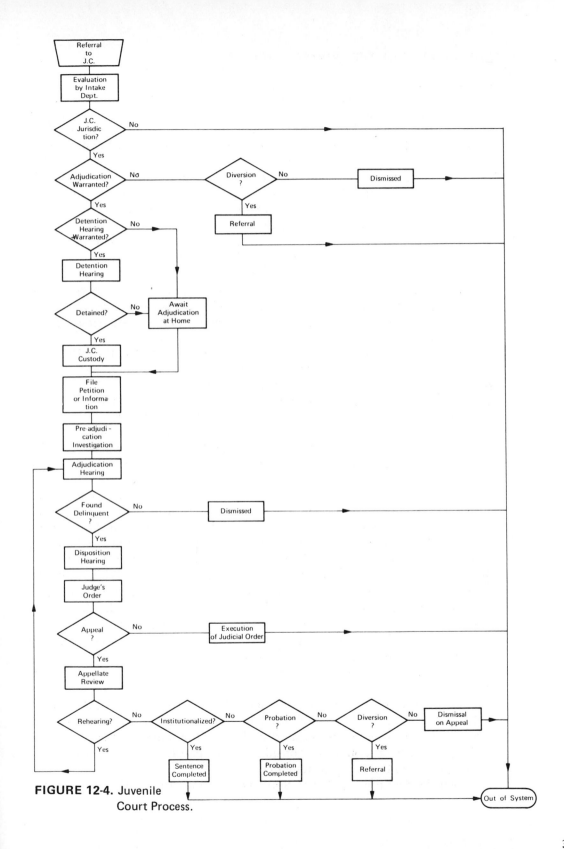

FIGURE 12-4. Juvenile Court Process.

Parole consists of serving the remainder of one's sentence in the community. As such, it is a controlled transition from prison life to life in society. Since the period immediately following release from prison is crucial for acceptable social adjustment and integration in the community, supervision is an important element.

That supervision is the function of a parole officer. While his concern is reintegration of the parolee into the community, there are some who view his function as more similar to law enforcement than to social work. In some localities, probation officers also serve as parole officers. Authorities do not all agree that this is in the best interests of either the parolee or the case worker. Parolees are considered to be more difficult to supervise than probationers. The ideal case load for a parole officer, according to many authorities, ranges from 35 to 50 persons. In Great State, parole and probation supervision was separated in the larger communities, such as Big City. In smaller communities, one person often did both.

Over two-thirds of the persons imprisoned in Great State were eventually released on parole. Few prisoners served their entire term except for those with minimal sentences such as one year. Persons who had not been returned to prison because of repeated offenses or parole violations generally secured favorable consideration upon application for parole provided they could present a definite plan of constructive life in the community following release. The Great State statistics compare with those of the nation as a whole, although there is great variation among the different jurisdictions.

Parole is an executive function and is generally granted by an administrative board or agency, as contrasted with probation, which is a function of the courts. As is true in most states, parole in Great State was the responsibility of a parole board. That board consisted of five persons, all of whom devoted full time to the task. They were appointed by the governor with the approval of the state legislature. While they had exclusive power over parole and recommitment for parole violations, their jurisdiction did not extend to persons sentenced to death or life imprisonment, to juveniles, or to persons whose sentence was for two years or less. In the latter case, Great State statutory law required that the judge retain complete control. In the case of persons serving indeterminate sentences, the board's jurisdiction did not begin until the minimum term had been served.

In Great State, the date of eligibility for parole might be fixed by the sentencing judge as Judge Wolfe had done with Harvey. In other cases, statutory provisions required that one-third of the sentence must be served before a prisoner could be considered for parole. This is a frequent, although not universal, requirement.

Parole decisions in Great State were completely within the board's discretion and not reviewable in any court. Factors considered by the board when it received an application for parole included

1. Prior history of the offender,
2. Sentence served,
3. Readiness and suitability for release,
4. Need for supervision and assistance in the community,
5. Reaction of the community to the offender's release.

The board held periodic interviews with all prisoners under their jurisdiction. The first time they met with a prisoner was two months prior to expiration of the minimum sentence or date of eligibility for parole. These were informal sessions held at the prison. Prisoners were given an opportunity to express themselves and to state reasons why they should be released on parole. The third week of each month the board also interviewed family, friends, or attorneys who wished to provide information regarding any of the parole applicants. Prison counselors assisted by advising the prisoner and his family with regard to procuring a job on release, and finding a home and community environment conducive to rehabilitation.

Therefore, in anticipation of helping Harvey with the preparation of his parole application, Paul Grace consulted Gail Earl and Michael Patrick concerning Harvey's prospects for employment in the computer field in Big City should he be released on parole. Following some checking with colleagues in Big City, Gail reported that Harvey would not have an easy time finding a job there. Economic conditions caused job opportunities to be scarce. In addition, many firms refused outright to employ a person with a criminal record, especially for work in computer centers where there could be access to sensitive information. Mike said he didn't know about Big City, but he would be more than happy to continue Harvey's employment at the Ranch.

In conversation with Paul, Harvey said he would not be reluctant to start a new life in another town, especially if it were Little Town. Paul therefore investigated living arrangements. One of the employees at the Ranch offered to rent a small apartment over his garage. Harvey liked the idea. As a result, in his application for parole he indicated that his future plans included continued employment at the Ranch, continued part-time attendance at the community college, and renting the apartment in Little Town.

When the time came for his parole hearing, Harvey met with the entire board. They had available the complete institutional file compiled regarding Harvey, the presentence investigative report prepared for Judge Wolfe, and records of his employment and course work while at the Center. They asked a great many questions about his desire to remain in Little Town. While several were hesitant about continued removal of Harvey from his family, the majority found Paul's recommendations to be most persuasive. Great State did not follow the practice of having legal counsel present to represent prisoners at parole hearings. While there has been much discussion of the advantages and disadvantages of this, there is no constitutional right to counsel at the hearing since it is not a hearing of an adversarial nature and parole is not a right.

In informing Harvey that his request would be granted, the board members stressed that parole is not a pardon. The latter is an act of forgiveness and remission of punishment which frees the individual from responsibility to the state with respect to the remainder of his sentence. They told him that, instead, his maximum term would remain unaffected during the time he was on parole. He would not lose credit for the time spent on parole. However, should he commit a new crime and be convicted of that, he faced the loss of all time spent at liberty. It would be added to the maximum term plus the new sentence. Should he violate parole conditions, he would be entitled to a full due process hearing prior to parole revocation, as required by the United States Supreme Court. Harvey mentally determined there would be no violation. Because there were few parolees in the Little Town area, Paul Grace was assigned to serve as his parole officer. That was good news.

Harvey later learned that the Great State parole board was somewhat unusual, in that the board personally informed parole applicants of the parole decision and the reasons for it. In many jurisdictions, a prisoner merely receives written notification of either approval or rejection of his parole application.

RELEASE

Harvey's parole was a success. When at the end of two years he was released from supervision and his sentence officially came to an end, he continued to live in Little Town and to work at the Ranch. His parole process has been flow charted in Figure 12-5. Although he was happy, his criminal record denied him several opportunities in the years that followed. One such instance was especially frustrating to him. When Michael Patrick was transferred to another location, he recommended Harvey as the person best qualified to succeed him. Harvey was informed he would not be given the job because of his criminal background. Hearing of this, Paul Grace intervened. He argued strongly that the Department of Corrections should be the leader in employing rehabilitated former prisoners. It was to no avail. Although ten years later Harvey did get that very job, he could not help but wonder how much his career had been held back as a result of his conviction.

When he spoke of this to Henry Law, whom he consulted in connection with the purchase of a small piece of land, Henry replied:

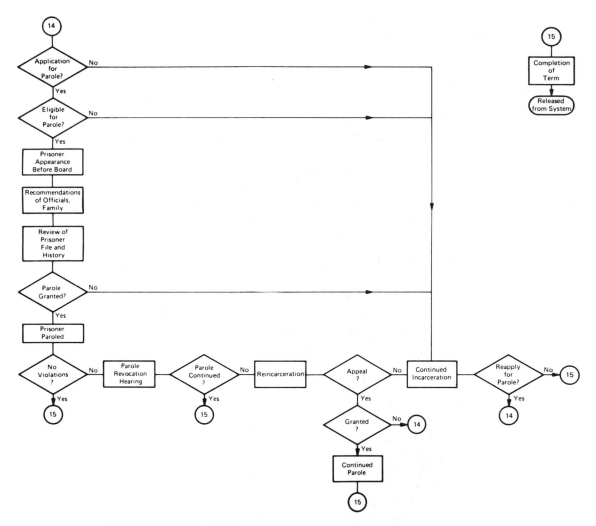

FIGURE 12.5. Parole Process.

"Have you ever wondered where you would be if you had never been sent to Little Town?"

Harvey thought that comment had the force of the one made by Paul Grace when Harvey had talked with him about Sam.

Many years later when Judge Wolfe came to Little Town to speak at a meeting of the civic clubs, Harvey sought her out. She did not remember him. After he had identified himself and told her of his experiences, she said:

"We don't have as many success stories as we should, but yours is certainly one of them. I am happy to see that the system can work. We desperately need to know the reasons why it doesn't do so more often."

And with these words of Judge Wolfe, the saga of Harvey Worker comes to an end.

QUESTIONS

Were Judge Wolfe to consult you regarding suggestions for meeting what she terms a "desperate need," what recommendations would you make?

When told of her statement, Henry Law said that, with all due respect, he would have to disagree. It was his thought that the real "desperate need" was to keep people out of the criminal system. Do you agree? What recommendations do you have for accomplishing that?

Harvey had been confined in two different correctional institutions, albeit only briefly in one. He also had described for him a third. Which do you think had the greatest effect upon Harvey's rehabilitation? Why? What type of facility produces real correction, that is, rehabilitation? Considering your answer, how do you explain the high recidivism rate in this country? Viewed from the perspective of the juvenile population, what accounts for the reappearance rate in the juvenile court of Great State? What relation, if any, do you see between that and the entire juvenile program in that state as described by Harvey? Should juvenile repeaters continue to be kept out of the criminal system in which adult offenders are processed when their records are similar to the two Harvey reported? Why?

What accounts for the fact that Harvey did not become a repeat offender? Had he been rehabilitated prior to release on parole? If so, what contributed the most to that? Should parole be restricted to persons similarly situated? What benefits accrue from parole? to the prisoner? to the community? Why is parole an executive function?

Where else in the criminal system did you see the executive branch of the government play a role? In the description of the Great State juvenile justice system, what coordination, if any, did you find between the branches of government? What coordination, if any, did you see between the corrections subsystem and the court subsystem? Do the three—control, courts, and corrections—actually operate as subsystems within the entire criminal system? Is it truly a system?

Did you find any examples of the effect of the demands of the public, of society as a whole, upon the criminal system? Where? Any examples of change within the system as society changes?

Can you answer Henry Law's question about what would have happened to Harvey had he not been sent to Little Town? To Harvey's question about how he ever got into this? Of all the persons who had some role in affecting Harvey's future, which one do you believe exerted the most influence? Why? How?

Compare the criminal and civil processes as "systems." What similarities, what differences do you see? what relationships to each other? to some larger system?

CASES

In Re Gault
387 U.S. 1, 87 S.Ct. 1428, 18 L.Ed. 2d 527 (1967)

MR. JUSTICE FORTAS . . . neither the Fourteenth Amendment nor the Bill of Rights is for adults alone . . . . Due process of law is the primary and indispensable foundation of individual freedom. It is the basic and essential term in the social compact which defines the rights of the individual and delimits the powers which the State may exercise. As Mr. Justice Frankfurter has said: "The history of American freedom, is in no small measure, the history of procedure."

. . . "Procedure is to law what 'scientific method' is to science."

. . . In *Kent v. United States* [383 U.S. 541 (1966)] we stated that the Juvenile Court Judge's exercise of power of the State as *parens patriae* was not unlimited . . . . We announced with respect to such waiver proceedings that while "We do not mean . . . to indicate that the hearing to be held must conform with all of the requirements of a criminal trial or even of the usual administrative hearing, but we do hold that the hearing must measure up to the essentials of due process and fair treatment." We reiterate this view, here in connection with a juvenile court adjudication of "delinquency," as a requirement which is part of the Due Process Clause of the Fourteenth Amendment of our Constitution . . . .

. . . Notice, to comply with due process requirements, must be given sufficiently in advance of scheduled court proceedings so that reasonable opportunity to prepare will be afforded, and it must "set forth the alleged misconduct with particularity." . . . Due process of law requires notice of the sort we have described—that is, notice which would be deemed constitutionally adequate in a civil or criminal proceeding. It does not allow a hearing to be held in which a youth's freedom and his parents' right to his custody are at stake without giving them timely notice, in advance of the hearing, of the specific issues that they must meet . . . .

. . . The probation officer cannot act as counsel for the child . . . . Nor can the judge represent the child . . . . A proceeding where the issue is whether the child will be found to be "delinquent" and subjected to the loss of his liberty for years is comparable in seriousness to a felony prosecution. The juvenile needs the assistance of counsel to cope with problems of law, to make skilled inquiry into the facts, to insist upon regularity of the proceedings, and to ascertain whether he has a defense and to prepare and submit it. The child "requires the guiding hand of counsel at every step in the proceedings against him." Just as in *Kent* . . . we indicated our agreement . . . that the assistance of counsel is essential for purposes of waiver proceedings, so we hold now that it is equally essential for the determination of delinquency, carrying with it the awesome prospect of incarceration in a state institution until the juvenile reaches the age of 21 . . . .

. . . We conclude that the Due Process Clause of the Fourteenth Amendment requires that in respect of proceedings to determine delinquency which may result in commitment to an institution in which the juvenile's freedom is curtailed, the child and his parent must be notified of the child's right to be represented by counsel retained by them, or if they are unable to afford counsel, that counsel will be appointed to represent the child . . . .

The privilege against self-incrimination is, of course, related to the question of the safeguards necessary to assure that admissions or confessions are reasonably trustworthy, that they are not the mere fruits of fear or coercion, but are reliable expressions of the truth . . . . One of its purposes is to prevent the State, whether by force or by psychological domination, from overcoming the mind and will of the person under investigation and depriving him of the freedom to decide whether to assist the State in securing his conviction . . . .

. . . It is true that the statement of the privilege in the Fifth Amendment, which is applicable to the States by reason of the Fourteenth Amendment, is that no person "shall be compelled in any *criminal case* to be a witness against himself." However, it is also clear that the availability of the privilege does not turn upon the type of proceeding in which its protection is invoked, but upon the nature of the statement or admissions and the exposure which it invites. The privilege may, for example, be claimed in a civil or administrative proceeding, if the statement is or may be inculpatory.

We conclude that the constitutional privilege against self-incrimination is applicable in the case of juveniles as it is with respect to adults. We appreciate that special problems may arise with respect to waiver of the privilege by or on behalf of children, and that there may well be some differences in technique—but not in principle—depending upon the age of the child and the presence and competence of parents. The participation of counsel will, of course, assist the police, juvenile courts and appellate tribunals in administering the privilege. If counsel is not present for some permissible reason when an admission is obtained, the greatest care must be taken to assure that the admission was voluntary, in the sense not only that it has not been coerced or suggested, but also that it is not the product of ignorance of rights or of adolescent fantasy, fright or despair . . . .

Morrissey v. Brewer
408 U.S. 471, 92 S.Ct. 2593, 33 L.Ed. 2d 484 (1972)

MR. CHIEF JUSTICE BURGER. Petitioner asserts he received no hearing prior to revocation of his parole . . .

In practice not every violation of parole conditions automatically leads to revocation . . . . Yet revocation of parole is not an unusual phenomenon, affecting only a few parolees. It has been estimated that 35–45 percent of all parolees are subjected to revocation and return to prison. Sometimes revocation occurs when the parolee is accused of another crime; it is often preferred to a new prosecution because of the procedural ease of recommitting the individual on the basis of a lesser showing by the State.

Release of the parolee before the end of his prison sentence is made with the recognition that with many prisoners there is a risk that they will not be able to live in society without committing additional antisocial acts. Given the previous conviction and the proper imposition of conditions, the State has an overwhelming interest in being able to return the individual to imprisonment without the burden of a new adversary criminal trial if in fact he has failed to abide by the conditions of his parole. Yet the State has no interest in revoking parole without some informal procedural guarantee.

In analyzing what is due, we see two important stages in the typical process of parole revocation.

a. *Arrest of Parolee and Preliminary Hearing.* The first stage occurs when the parolee is arrested and detained, usually at the direction of his parole officer. The second occurs when parole is formally revoked.

In our view due process requires that after the arrest, the determination that reasonable grounds exist for revocation of parole should be made by someone not directly involved in the case. The officer directly involved in making recommendations cannot always have complete objectivity in evaluating them. This independent officer need not be a judicial officer.

It will be sufficient, therefore, in the parole revocation context, if an evaluation of whether reasonable cause exists to believe that conditions of parole have been violated is made by someone such as a parole officer other than the one who has made the report of parole violations or has recommended revocation.

With respect to the preliminary hearing before this officer, the parolee should be given notice that the hearing will take place and that its purpose is to determine whether there is probable cause to believe he has committed a parole violation. The notice should state what parole violations have been alleged. At the hearing the parolee may appear and speak in his own behalf; he may bring letters, documents, or individuals who can give relevant information to the hearing officer. On request of the parolee, persons who have given adverse information on which parole revocation is to be based are to be made available for questioning in his presence. However, if the hearing officer determines that the informer would be subjected to risk of harm if his identity were disclosed, he need not be subjected to confrontation and cross-examination.

The hearing officer shall have the duty of making a summary, or digest, of what transpires at the hearing in terms of the responses of the parolee and the substance of the documents or evidence given in support of parole revocation and of the parolee's position. Based on the information before him, the officer should determine whether there is probable cause to hold the parolee for the final decision of the parole board on revocation. Such a determination would be sufficient to warrant the parolee's continued detention and return to the state correctional institution pending the final decision. No interest would be served by formalism in this process; informality will not lessen the utility of this inquiry in reducing the risk of error.

b. *The Revocation Hearing.* There must also be an opportunity for a hearing if it is desired by the parolee, prior to the final decision on revocation by the parole authority. This hearing must be the basis for more than determining probable cause; it must lead to a final evaluation of any contested relevant facts and consideration of whether the facts as determined warrant revocation. The parolee must have an opportunity to be heard and to show, if he can, that he did not violate the conditions, or, if he did, that circumstances in mitigation suggest the violation does not warrant revocation. The revocation hearing must be tendered within a reasonable time after the parolee is taken into custody. A lapse of two months, as the State suggests occurs in some cases, would not appear to be unreasonable.

We cannot write a code of procedure; that is the responsibility of each state. Most states have done so by legislation, others by judicial decision usually on due process grounds. Our task is limited to deciding the minimum requirements of due process. They include a) written notice of the claimed violations of parole; b) disclosure to the parolee of evidence against him; c) opportunity to be heard in person and to present witnesses and documentary evidence; d) the right to confront and cross-examine adverse witnesses (unless the hearing officer specifically finds good cause for not allowing confrontation); e) a "neutral and detached" hearing body such as a traditional parole board, members of which need not be judicial officers or lawyers, and f) a written statement by the fact finders as to the evidence relied on and reasons for revoking parole. We emphasize there is no thought to equate this second stage of parole revocation to a criminal prosecution in any sense; it is a narrow inquiry; the process should be flexible enough to consider evidence including letters, affidavits, and other material that would not be admissible in an adversary criminal trial.

We do not reach or decide the question of whether the parolee is entitled to the assistance of retained counsel or to appointed counsel if he is indigent. . . .

James v. Wallace
406 F.Supp. 318 (M.D., Ala.) 1976

Consolidated actions were filed by inmates of Alabama penal institutions for declaratory and injunctive relief in respect to alleged deprivation of their Eighth and Fourteenth Amendment rights. The District Court held that action was maintainable as a class action on behalf of all persons presently confined by Alabama Board of Corrections or who might be so confined in the future, . . .

Judgment for plaintiff.

JOHNSON, CHIEF JUDGE . . . this Court has a clear duty to require the defendants in these cases to remedy the massive constitutional infirmities which plague Alabama's prisons. It is with great reluctance that federal courts intervene in the day-to-day operation of state penal systems, . . . a function they are increasingly required to perform. While this Court continues to recognize the broad discretion required for prison officials to maintain orderly and secure institutions, . . . constitutional deprivations of the magnitude presented here simply cannot be countenanced, and this Court is under a duty to, and will, intervene to protect incarcerated citizens from such wholesale infringements of their constitutional rights. . . .

... There has been growing recognition by the courts that prisoners retain all rights enjoyed by free citizens except those necessarily lost as an incident of confinement. ... The Supreme Court recently identified three legitimate functions of a correctional system: deterrence, both specific and general; rehabilitation; and institutional security. ... *Pell v. Procunier,* 417 U.S. 817 (1974). ...

Prisoners are entitled to be free of conditions which constitute cruel and unusual punishment in violation of the Eighth and Fourteenth Amendments. The content of the Eighth Amendment is not static but "must draw its meaning from the evolving standards of decency that mark the progress of a maturing society.". ... There can be no question that present conditions of confinement in the Alabama penal system violate any current judicial definition of cruel and unusual punishment, a situation evidenced by the defendant's admission that serious Eighth Amendment violations exist. ...

The conditions in which Alabama prisoners must live, as established by the evidence in these cases, bear no reasonable relationship to legitimate institutional goals. As a whole they create an atmosphere in which inmates are compelled to live in constant fear of violence, in imminent danger to their physical well-being, and without opportunity to seek a more promising future.

The living conditions in Alabama prisons constitute cruel and unusual punishment. Specifically, lack of sanitation throughout the institutions in living areas, infirmaries, and food service—presents an imminent danger to the health of each and every inmate. Prisoners suffer from further physical deterioration because there are no opportunities for exercise and recreation. Treatment for prisoners with physical or emotional problems is totally inadequate. This Court has previously ordered that the penal system provide reasonable medical care for inmates in these institutions. ...

Prison officials are under a duty to provide inmates reasonable protection from constant threat of violence. ...

Not only is it cruel and unusual punishment to confine a person in an institution under circumstances which increase the likelihood of future confinement, but these same conditions defeat the goal of rehabilitation which prison officials have set for their institutions. ...

Prisoners are protected by the Due Process and Equal Protection Clauses of the Fourteenth Amendment; therefore, they must be free from arbitrary and capricious treatment by prison officials. ...

... However, a state is not at liberty to afford its citizens only those constitutional rights which fit comfortably within its budget. ... It is well established beyond doubt that inadequate funding is no answer to the existence of unconstitutional conditions in state penal institutions. ...

... a public official may be held liable where he, in subjective good faith, acts in disregard of a person's clearly established constitutional rights. The court now acts in these cases with a recognition that prisoners are not to be coddled, and prisons are not to be operated as hotels or country clubs. However, this does not mean that responsible state officials can be allowed to operate prison facilities that are barbaric and inhumane. Let the defendant state officials now be placed on notice that failure to comply with the minimum standards set forth in the order of this Court filed with this opinion will necessitate the closing of those several prison facilities herein found to be unfit for human confinement. ...

[The Court appended "Minimum Constitutional Standards for Inmates of the Alabama Penal System" containing specific standards detailing among other matters

Number of inmates to be confined to any one institution;

Number of prisoners to be confined to a single cell and size of cell;

Conditions and length of confinement in isolation;

Plan for classification of inmates;

Standards for food service;

Requirements for protection from violence;

Criteria for mental health care;

Staff requirements;

Standards for educational, vocation, work and recreational programs;

Correspondence and visitation privilege requirements;

Standards re living conditions.]

FOOTNOTES

[1] *James v. Wallace,* 406 F. Supp. 318 (M.D., Ala.) 1976. At 328, n. 12 states: "Federal courts in a number of states including Massachusetts ... Maryland ... Arkansas ... and Mississippi ... recently have had occasion to hold conditions in penal institutions in those states unconstitutional."

[2] *Robinson v. California,* 370 U.S. 660 (1962).

[3] Article I, § 9, cl. 2

[4] 28 U.S.C. § 2254

[5] *Stone v. Powell,* 428 U.S. 465 (1976).

[6] The President's Commission on Law Enforcement and Administration of Justice, *The Challenge of Crime in a Free Society* (Washington, D.C.: Government Printing Office, 1968).

[7] *In Re Gault,* 387 U.S. 1 (1967).

[8] *Morrissey v. Brewer,* 408 U.S. 471 (1972). In *Gagon v. Scarpelli,* 411 U.S. 778 (1973), the Court held that "a probationer, like a parolee, is entitled to a preliminary and a final revocation hearing, under the conditions specified in *Morrissey v. Brewer.*"

PART IV

DECISION ANALYSIS OF THE ADMINISTRATIVE LEGAL PROCESS

Administrative agencies have been established to regulate economic or social activities that are affected with a public interest. Even then the agencies must do so in a reasonable and nonarbitrary manner. Such activity of commercial firms, economic enterprises, social organizations, or individual action is subject to control in the public welfare. A state is free to adopt such policy as will enhance public welfare.

In two hundred years of growth of the United States and in the mechanisms developed to govern the nation and its people, the complexity of the problems increasingly faced has given rise to a tool little known until less than one hundred years ago—the administrative agency. This rather new mechanism is the seat of much power and, as such, has the potential for abuse. Yet it also represents great opportunities for the enhancement of public welfare, as was intended in its birth and development.

Part IV will present only a small sample of the activity of administrative law organizations in order to provide some awareness of the nature of their functioning and to provide a basis for comparison with older and more traditional means of regulation in society that have been illustrated by prior examples of judicial and executive action in this book.

CHAPTER 13
ADMINISTRATIVE LAW PROCESS: FAIR EMPLOYMENT

A few days after the funeral of John Q. Worker, Mary Worker was called on the telephone by Tom Newboy, the personnel director of The Firm. After again conveying his condolences to Mary he made it known that one of the workers in the cypres department recommended that her son Harvey might be interested in employment in The Firm in some capacity. "As you know," he said, "we have always tried to take care of our workers and their families. The Firm is a place where several members of the family often work together." It was emphasized, further, that Fred Famous always believed that hiring members of the same family was good business. In this case Tom Newboy had checked with Famous and the latter was enthusiastic about the idea. "It's one of the things we can do to help the Worker family," said the president.

JOB APPLICATION

Harvey was quite anxious to get a job because he realized that a lot of the burden for keeping the family together would fall on his shoulders. Besides, he would need money to finish college even though there was some financial aid for the family from sources such as Social Security. The next day he walked into the personnel office of The Firm and was greeted warmly by the receptionist who asked him to fill out the application form the company always required of their job applicants. Harvey went over to a large table in an adjoining room where several other persons, male and female, were filling out identical job application forms. Harvey then recognized a classmate of his at Local University, Benjamin C. Dreen, who was also filling out a form for employment. "Hey, man, what are you doing here," said Ben as he spotted Harvey entering the room. Harvey explained the tragic circumstances of his father's death and added the news of the company offers to help the family, including the opportunity extended to Harvey for a job with the company. "That's nice, man—a corporation with a heart—one to work for, for sure," replied Ben.

When they were finished with the preliminary paper work, both Harvey and Ben were asked to wait for an interviewer from the personnel department to go over the application form responses with them in an individual interview. Ben was asked how he heard about The Firm and whether he had applied in response to information about any specific job opening. Ben replied that many of his friends at the University worked here, especially in the summer, and all said it was a good place to work. He had no direct knowledge of any specific opening, he said. After a few more queries on other matters, the interviewer thanked Ben and the interview was over. As he walked out Ben noticed Harvey waiting for him. "Want a ride to school, Bennie, I'm going that way," said Harvey. The two left the plant grounds together.

Several days later Ben received a polite letter in the mail from Tom Newboy which said that The Firm's personnel were impressed with Ben's qualifications but that there were no openings at present. The Firm would keep his application on file, however, should something come up in the future. That afternoon in an accounting class they had together Ben told Harvey about the result of the application to The Firm. "Yeah," said Harvey, "they don't have many openings. I was lucky to get one as a stock clerk in the cypres department." Ben agreed that it was a lucky break for Harvey to get a clean job in a quiet corner of the plant.

The more Ben thought about it afterward, however, the more he got aroused by the fact that he had (he thought) been obviously passed up in favor of Harvey when he, Ben, had had superior qualifications. After all, he received higher grades in school than Harvey and had some experience as a stockroom clerk in Hoffmans Department Store for two summers. Harvey, he knew, had no such experience. Finally his indignation knew no bounds and he hastened to talk to a friend of his, Willie Sutton, the president of Emerging Black Economy (EBE—called by some "Earn, Baby, Earn"), a civil rights organization highly active in Big City. After hearing the whole story, Sutton suggested that Ben file a complaint alleging discrimination in employment with either the Equal Employment Opportunity Commission, a federal agency established under the Civil Rights Act of 1964[1] or with the Human Relations Commission, a Great State agency with an office in Big City. He also promised to meet with other officers of EBE and determine if something should be done by that organization in this situation.

DISCRIMINATION COMPLAINT

Ben decided that, since he was more familiar with state agencies he would pick the Human Relations Commission. There he was instructed by the secretary in the office in the mechanics of structuring his complaint. He found that the HRC was established under state legislation to accept complaints of discrimination and determine if a cause existed. If the investigation indicated that discrimination on the basis of race, sex, age, religion, or national origin did occur, within the previous 90 days[2] the commission was empowered to proceed to invoke those sanctions granted in the statute.

Ben was referred to a staff member, Larry Mensch, who interviewed him to determine if the complaint fell within the jurisdiction of the Commission. Mensch explained that the Human Relations Commission was established twenty years ago by the Great State Human Relations Act of 1956 prohibiting "certain practices of discrimination because of race, color, religious creed, ancestry, age, or national origin by employers, employment agencies, labor organizations and others." From the information given by Ben, Mensch determined that jurisdiction undoubtedly lay in the HRC and the specific incident may have been a violation of Section 5 (a), and possibly 5 (b) (4) of the Act (Table 13-1). Mensch then asked Ben to answer all of the questions regularly asked to get the facts of the case that would serve as the basis for a later investigation (Form 13-1). The basic information would then be put in a more legal form by the Commission's attorneys for a review by Ben (who would be known as the Complainant). Ben would then sign it and have it notarized (Form 13-2). The Commission would assign a docket number and send a copy of the complaint to The Firm (known as the Respondent).

Ben, curious about the steps in the entire procedure, asked Mensch to outline the process that would occur from that point on. "There will be a field representative assigned to your case. He will interview people at The Firm and will review pertinent documents and records." Mensch added that the field representative might call upon Ben again if there were any questions. If any new information came up, Ben was to call the representative. As a result of the investigation the Commission could find

1. Cause for the complaint and take further steps to end the discrimination.
2. No cause, in which case the Commission itself would move to dismiss the complaint.

If there is a no cause finding, Ben would be notified by letter from the HRC main office in the state capitol. "Suppose the Commission finds no cause and I disagree," said Ben. "What then?" He was assured that a hearing by the Commission would be held if he appealed within ten days.

TABLE 13-1. Great State Human Relations Act (excerpt)

SECTION 5. UNLAWFUL DISCRIMINATORY PRACTICES.

It shall be an unlawful discriminatory practice, unless based upon a bona fide occupational qualification, or in the case of a fraternal corporation or association, unless based upon membership in such association or corporation or except where based upon applicable security regulations established by the United States or the State of Great State:

(1) For any employer because of the race, color, religious creed, ancestry, age, sex, or national origin of any individual to refuse to hire or employ, or to bar or to discharge from employment such individual, or to otherwise discriminate against such individual with respect to compensation, hire, tenure, terms, conditions, or privileges of employment, if the individual is the best able and most competent to perform the services required. The provision of this paragraph shall not apply, to (a) termination of employment because of the terms or conditions of any bona fide retirement or pension plan, (b) operation of the terms or conditions of any bona fide retirement or pension plan, which have the effect of a minimum service requirement, (c) operation of the terms or conditions of any bona fide group or employee insurance plan.

(2) For any employer, employment agency or labor organization, prior to the employment or admission to membership, to (a) elicit any information or make or keep a record of or use any form of application or application blank containing questions or entries concerning the race, color, religious creed, ancestry, sex, or national origin of any applicant for employment or membership. (b) print or publish or cause to be printed or published any notice or advertisement relating to employment or membership indicating any preference, limitation, specification, or discrimination based upon race, color, religious creed, ancestry, age, sex, or national origin. (c) deny or limit, through a quota system, employment or membership because of race, color, religious creed, ancestry, age, sex, national origin, or place of birth. (d) substantially confine or limit recruitment of hiring of individuals, with intent to circumvent the spirit and purpose of this act, to any employment agency, employment service, labor organization, training school or training center, or any other employee-referring source which services individuals who are predominantly of the same race, color, religious creed, ancestry, age, sex, or national origin.

(3) For any labor organization because of the race, color, religious creed, ancestry, age, sex or national origin of any individual to deny full and equal membership rights to any individual or otherwise to discriminate against such individuals with respect to hire, tenure, terms, conditions, or privileges of employment, or any other matter, directly or indirectly, related to employment.

(4) For any employer, employment agency or labor organization to discriminate in any manner against any individual because such individual has opposed any practice forbidden by this act, or because such individual has made a charge, testified, or assisted, in any manner, in any investigation, proceeding, or hearing under this act.

(5) For any person, whether or not an employer, employment agency, labor organization, or employee, to aid, abet, incite, compel, or coerce the doing of any act declared by this section to be an unlawful discriminatory practice, or to obstruct or prevent any person from complying with the provisions of this act or any order issued thereunder, or to attempt, directly or indirectly, to commit any act declared by this section to be unlawful discriminatory practice.

(6) For any employment agency to fail or refuse to classify properly, refer for employment or otherwise to discriminate against any individual because of his race, color, religious creed, ancestry, age, sex, or national origin.

(7) For any individual seeking employment to publish or cause to be published any advertisement which specifies or in any manner expresses his race, color, religious creed, ancestry, age, sex, or national origin, or in any manner expresses a limitation or preference as to the race, color, religious creed, ancestry, age, sex, or national origin of any prospective employer.

FORM 13-1. Complaint Data Sheet

Complaint Data Sheet--Human Relations Commission

DETAILS OF ALLEGATION   DOCKET NO. _____

All of the following questions must be answered <u>prior</u> to docketing the complaint:

1. Give a detailed, chronological description of events leading up to /precipitating the alleged act(s) of discrimination. Thoroughly describe the specific act(s) of discrimination and explain why the complainant believes he/she has been discriminated against.

2. (a) What reason(s) for these acts did respondent give to complainant? When did this take place? Where?

    (b) Did complainant have an opportunity to respond to those reason(s) to respondent representatives? If so, what did complainant say, to whom, and when?

3. (a) List names, addresses and telephone numbers of all of the complainant's witnesses. Summarize what each person saw, overheard, or otherwise has first-hand knowledge of. If information is not first-hand, identify the original source of same. Describe the physical surroundings the witnesses were in, if necessary.

    (b) List names, addresses and telephone numbers of all persons the complainant knows are witnesses or are likely to be witnesses for the respondent's position. Summarize what each person saw, overheard, or may otherwise have first-hand knowledge of. Describe the physical surroundings these persons were in, if necessary.

4. What does the complainant understand the respondent's requirements for education, previous experience and other qualifications to be?

5. (a) What does the complainant cite as his/her related education, previous experience or other qualifications?

    (b) Did the respondent know about all of the complainant's education and other qualifications? How?

6. (a) What tests are given by respondent? Be specific and distinguish between paper and pencil tests and other criteria used in screening, selection or evaluation.

   (b) Who administered the test or applied the criteria? Describe the circumstances.

7. (a) What does the complainant understand the respondent's procedures, policies, rules/regulations or other requirements to be with respect to the specifics of the alleged act(s) of discrimination?

   (b) How, when and by whom was the complainant made aware of them?

8. How have these procedures, rules/regulations affected the complainant's employment situation?

9. (a) If respondent representatives have cited the complainant for any violations of any rules, what penalty(ies) was/were assessed? When, and for what periods of time?

   (b) Describe the complainant's account of each situation, specifying any mitigation reasons for any of the complainant's actions.

10. (a) What are the specific duties of the job sought?

    (b) Has the complainant ever been employed in a position requiring substantially the same duties/responsibilities as the position in question? If so, detail the duties, periods of time held, and with what employer(s).

11. What other persons have received the same treatment as the complainant? Identify as to race, etc., as applicable, and describe the circumstances. Have any of these persons filed any discrimination complaints?

12. What persons have NOT received the same treatment as the complainant? Identify as to sex, etc., as applicable, and describe the circumstances.

13. Identify the name, title, race, sex, etc., and physical description (if needed) all respondent personnel involved in the alleged act(s) of discrimination. Describe each person's exact involvement.

14. (a) Has the complainant filed the identical allegations

with any other Federal, State or local agency?
Which and date of filing? List EEOC's Case
Number.

(b) If filed, but allegations are not identical, specify
the differences.

15. Has complainant filed a Union Grievance? If so, name
the Union, its Officers, the basis of the grievance,
which step of the procedure it is in, and date filed.
Secure copy of same, or explain why complainant did
not provide it.

16. (a) Explore with the complainant and describe in detail
patterns of discrimination which the complainant has
either specified and provided information about, or
which appears to be inherent in the situation.

(b) Does complainant wish to file both individually and
as a member of the class? If not, why?

(c) Do others wish to join in this complaint with the
complainant or file on their own on the same or
similar issues? If yes, specify which option and
list name, address and telephone number of each
person.

17. Has the complainant lost:

(a) Earnings--specify as to amount and time period.

(b) Out-of-Pocket Expenses--specify as to amount(s),
items paid for, and date(s) spent.

18. (a) Has the complainant experienced emotional and/or
mental upset? Describe in detail.

(b) List names, addresses and telephone numbers of
anyone who has observed any of the complainant's
emotional and/or mental upset.

19. What remedy does the complainant wish to secure?

20. Itemize the documents the complainant has provided
relative to this complaint; explain the significance
and/or relationship of each to specific parts of the
complainant's allegation, where necessary.

21. (a) How many persons does the respondent employ?

(b) Is the complainant aware of any State or Federal

funding received by the respondent? If so, specify the sources.

22. Other relevant data:

Note: WHEN TAKING A HANDICAP/DISABILITY COMPLAINT, ATTACH THE SUPPLEMENTAL DETAILS OF ALLEGATIONS FOR HANDICAP/DISABILITY CASES

_____

HUMAN RELATIONS REPRESENTATIVE

_____

DATE OF INTERVIEW

SPECIFIC INFORMATION--EMPLOYMENT (Complainant)

Docket No. _____

Name _____ Birthdate _____

U.S. Military Service _____yes____no

Honorable Discharge _____yes____no

U.S. Citizenship ____yes____no

Union Membership ____yes ____no

Highest Educational Level Attained _____

Additional Training or Education _____

EMPLOYMENT EXPERIENCE
(Begin with Present Employment)

Employer _____ From _____ To _____

Address _____ Starting Salary _____

_____ Ending Salary _____

Position _____ Supervisor _____

Duties _____

Reason for Leaving _____

FORM 13-2. HRC Complaint

Human Relations Commission Complaint

COMPLAINT

Benjamin C. Dreen
(Complainant)

VS.

The Firm
(Respondent)

: GREAT STATE
GOVERNOR'S OFFICE
HUMAN RELATIONS
COMMISSION

: COMPLAINT
DOCKET NO. __76-1379__

1. The Complainant herein is:

    (Name) Benjamin C. Dreen

    (Address) Big City, Local County
        (City-Borough-Township-County-Zip Code)

2. The Respondent herein is:

    (Name) The Firm

    (Address) Big City, Local County
        (City-Borough-Township-County-Zip Code)

3. The Complainant(s) allege(s) that beginning on and/or occurring on and/or beginning prior and continuing on or about to wit ____October 1, 19XX____

    the Respondent(s) __The Firm, violated Section 5 of the__ Great State Human Relations Act, Act of September 1, 19XN, PL 744, as amended, by discriminating against complainant in the following manner, to wit:

    1. refused to hire complainant who was best able and qualified to perform the work required.

    2. elicited information and kept a record of race, color, and sex of applicant.

    3. Substantially confined recruitment with intent to circumvent the Act.

4. Denied or limited employment through a quota
   system based on race.

4. The allegations in paragraph 3 hereof constitute(s) an
   unlawful discriminatory practice or unlawful practice
   and is in violation of:
   Great State Human Relations Act (Act of September 1,
   19XN, P.L. 744, as amended). Section 5 of Sub-
   section(s) a and b

5. The Complainant allege(s) that the alleged unlawful
   discriminatory practice or unlawful discriminatory
   practices:
   ☒ is/are of a continuing nature which has/have per-
   sisted up to and including the present time.

6. No other action based on the aforesaid allegations has
   been instituted by the Complainant in any Court or before any other Commission within the Commonwealth
   of Great State except as follows:
   ☒ None
   ☐

7. The Complainant(s) pray that the Respondent(s) be
   required
   (a) To make the complainant(s) whole, including but not
       limited to compensatory and/or punitive awards
       such as back pay and "out of pocket expenses."

   (b) to eliminate all unlawful discriminatory practice(s)
       and procedure(s).

   (c) to remedy the discriminatory effect of past prac-
       tice(s) and procedure(s).

(d) to take further affirmative action necessary and appropriate to remedy the violations complained of herein.

(e) such further relief as the Commission deems necessary and appropriate.

STATE OF GREAT
STATE   :
                                           SS
COUNTY OF LOCAL   :

Benjamin C. Dreen, of full age, being duly sworn according to law deposes and says: that he is the Complainant herein; that he has read the foregoing complaint and knows the content thereof; that to the best of his knowledge, information and belief the facts alleged therein are true.

Benjamin C. Dreen
Signature of Complainant

Sworn and subscribed   :
before me this 5th day   :
of October, 19XX   :

Mark Diup
Notary Public
My Commission Expires
1/1/XZ

If the Commission field investigation finds cause, the respondent will be required to cease and desist in the alleged discrimination and implement action suggested by the Commission that is necessary for ending the practice. This phase is known as the Conciliation since the respondent is asked by the Commission to comply voluntarily.

If there is no settlement through the conciliation procedure the Commission may convene a public hearing. Three commissioners usually sit, but the respondent can agree to a hearing where just one commissioner will hear the case. At the hearing, testimony is taken under oath, the Commission makes a decision, and a legally enforceable order is issued.

If either Ben or The Firm would wish to appeal the decision, that appeal would be taken to the Commonwealth Court, the statewide appellate court with jurisdiction to hear appeals from decisions of all administrative agencies in the state.

"One last question," said Ben. "How long is this going to take?" Mensch responded, "Unfortunately, we are badly understaffed, so it may take about six months or a year to get to a finding." Mensch did mention, however, that if a complainant's case was not processed within a year, the complainant could file a proceeding in Common Pleas Court, the court of initial jurisdiction in the county. "We'll have the complaint ready for your signature in two weeks, though," added Mensch.

Ben thanked Larry and returned home. At that point he mentally reconstructed the entire process and drew a flow chart (Figure 13-1) using all the concepts he had picked up at Local University.

GROUP DEMONSTRATIONS

In the meantime, Willie Sutton met with the officers and board of EBE to decide what, if anything, they should do about the situation in which Ben Dreen found himself or, more importantly, what steps to take if they felt the situation called for a general attack on discrimination in The Firm. Several of the officers declared that The Firm was well known in Black circles as a company where few Blacks were hired and those few were always placed in menial positions. Because of this few Blacks applied for work there. Employment agencies almost never sent any Black candidates to The Firm because the agencies, too, were aware of the situation. Also widely known in the community was the company policy of hiring relatives of present employees if ability factors were equal. The consensus for further action became so strong that the officers of EBE decided to launch a campaign against The Firm and planned a news conference to get it moving.

Newspapers, as well as television and radio stations in Big City, provided extensive coverage of the news conference. EBE pledged to fight

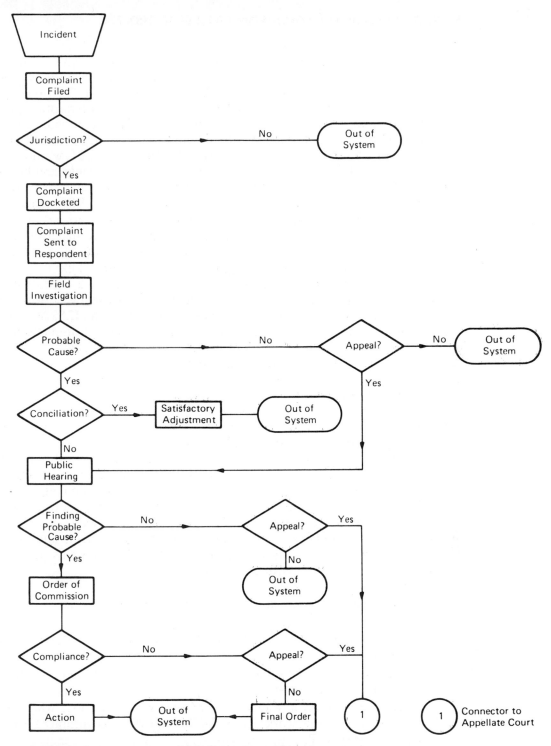

FIGURE 13-1. Process under Great State Human Relations Act.

discrimination at The Firm "and everywhere else, no matter what it takes." Much was made of the small number of Blacks in The Firm—less than three percent of the work force. EBE demanded that The Firm sign an agreement with them (EBE) that would set forth hiring quotas and a reporting system whereby EBE would monitor The Firm's compliance with the agreement. EBE president Sutton indicated that they would first engage in negotiations with The Firm but if those failed EBE would take the same steps they had employed in the past with some banks and hotels in Big City. Similar demands were pressed at that time and, after long and unruly demonstrations the target companies yielded to EBE·demands.

The following morning Fred Famous met with all the major officers of The Firm, as well as Leo Lex. Famous was furious as he discussed the situation. "This is so ridiculous I don't see why we should even reply." He was adamantly opposed to signing any agreement; Lex found it particularly obnoxious to be asked to provide reports of a confidential nature about employees to a private, nongovernment agency. "Who do those guys think they are, anyway; a private army above the U.S. or Great State Government?" added Fred Famous. After extensive discussion, it was finally agreed that The Firm should avoid being placed on the defensive or in a corner. A consensus emerged that, far from ignoring the attack as first proposed, The Firm would have to go to great lengths to put its case before the public. Fred Famous directed the director of public relations to meet with Cranston, Canter, Borden, and Gregory, the advertising agency employed by The Firm in order to plan and implement the campaign. "Do it now—soonest," roared Fred Famous.

In what is perhaps a record time for the development of a media campaign, the advertising agency and The Firm got the program started in two days. It consisted of a press conference to launch the campaign along with full-page ads in the two major dailies in the Big City metropolitan area. Editors of the two papers and of all suburban weeklies were sent press kits with complete materials and asked to view them, and write editorials on the topic if they wished. All material focused upon the following points The Firm wished to make

1. The Firm was dedicated to the policy of nondiscrimination in hiring and promotion.

2. There would be no agreement with a nongovernment agency to establish quotas.

3. No employee information would be submitted to a non-governmental organization.

4. The Firm would hire regardless of race but only those who were qualified to do the work, much of it important government work requiring great skill.

5. The Firm would accept its social responsibility to improve

economic conditions for all and, to do so, would enlist the aid of and take advice from all.

6. The Firm would communicate directly with the Great State Human Relations Commission and voluntarily provide quarterly information on the numbers and percentages of minority workers.

7. The number of minority persons in The Firm is much higher than the three percent figure used by EBE. That percentage refers only to Blacks.

8. Finally, The Firm, while recognizing the right to peacefully assemble and speak out in demonstrations, would not tolerate any violations of law in the process of demonstration.

These statements received much favorable comment through press editorials and in television or radio coverage.

The open letter sent by The Firm to the Chairman of the Great State Human Relations Commission contained the above points as well as an offer to meet with any responsible minority groups to discuss alleged discriminatory practices.

As a result of the willingness of The Firm to sit down with minority group representatives, a meeting was set up between a small group of The Firm's officers and the officials of EBE. The latter came to the meeting (they called it "coming to the negotiating table") with a long list of prepared demands to present to the officers of The Firm. Briefly, the list included demands that The Firm

1. Post equal employment notices widely and have all employment personnel reaffirm their adherence to that policy as well as communicate it to all outside agencies.

2. Create a human relations coordinator position.

3. Make special efforts to recruit Blacks and cooperate with Black groups to train candidates who cannot meet formal job requirements but who can receive on-the-job training by the company.

4. Submit to EBE the figures for hiring and turnover for the past year, broken down by race and job category.

5. Continue to provide a statistical breakdown of employees in the manner requested by EBE.

6. Provide names and addresses of those tested, interviewed, hired, and not hired as well as those who leave the company.

7. Hold regular meetings with EBE at which the desired statistics will be required.

8. Not issue press releases without prior EBE approval, after which they will be considered joint releases.

The rest of the meeting was, not unexpectedly, cool and stilted. The Firm, said Fred Famous, was unalterably opposed to the issuance of confidential information about employees to a nongovernmental group. "That breaches a trust in the company-worker relationship," mentioned the personnel director. The gathering of the statistics requested, moreover, would be fantastically expensive if not impossible to gather. The company would make attempts, all officers agreed, to provide on-the-job training to those who showed potential for skilled work but there could not possibly be an agreement on hiring a specific number of candidates to be sent from the Black community. That first meeting ended with those issues unresolved.

Subsequent meetings over a period of three months did not provide resolution of the basic problem issues presented. After the fifth meeting, which lasted a mere twenty five minutes, Willie Sutton abruptly announced that EBE was tired of talking and would contact the Human Relations Commission with their demands. "There will be no more meetings until we hear from the HRC," said Sutton. The letter to the HRC contained several questions that asked whether the HRC could act in discrimination cases, would make employment figures available to the public, and whether the HRC had the ability to check on the figures presented to it by The Firm.

Two weeks later Glenda Madison, the chairperson of the Human Relations Commission, replied in a lengthy letter to EBE. Because of its small size and limited funding, Ms. Madison stated, the HRC could not conduct extensive inquiries. It could and would, however, sample extensively through spot checks of employment patterns when the commission was empowered to do so. Technically the Commission swung into action only upon an individual complaint, or by the Attorney General or through a commission-initiated investigation of apparent discrimination. In those instances there was no doubt of the power to compel submission of pertinent data. If a company volunteers to submit information, there is obviously no need to resort to legal procedures. The commission chairperson stated further that, although policy on the point had not yet been formulated, it was likely that some information on employment within The Firm would be released to parties with a valid interest in the outcome.

The next few weeks were occupied with the issuance of press releases from the organizations involved. EBE released one that insisted that since the HRC could not check on the validity of employment data from The Firm, it was incumbent upon The Firm to provide that data to EBE, and The Firm was unreasonable when it refused to do so. The HRC announced that, yes, it could check on alleged discrimination and that spot checks on a limited basis were sufficient to determine whether discrimination existed in a specific organization. The Firm reiterated its previous position that it could not provide confidential information to a nongovernment agency. It also emphasized that the sessions with EBE were only meetings in which there was an exchange of ideas; they were not negotiations leading toward an agreement. The Firm's statement re-emphasized the company's desire to enhance economic opportunity for minorities, a willingness to listen to all constructive suggestions for the elimination of discrimination everywhere and the intent of The Firm to report pertinent data for evaluation by the HRC and other government bodies.

EBE promptly fired off a letter to The Firm containing the points presented earlier along with a new set that included demands such as inclusion of minority organizations in the conducting of recruiting programs; featuring Blacks in advertising, and recognition that The Firm's distinction between government and nongovernment agencies was arbitrary. When The Firm presented its first report to the HRC one week later it mentioned that the percentage of minority workers in The Firm was fourteen percent. EBE then issued a press release calling The Firm's method of reporting statistics inaccurate and misleading. Saying that the situation had reached the breaking point, Willie Sutton announced that EBE was going to take measures that would be more direct in nature.

What Sutton meant became readily apparent within a few days. EBE asked other organizations to join with them in a campaign to force The Firm to adopt its demands but continued at the forefront of extensive efforts to publicize the campaign. Demonstrations and marches took place at least once a week in various parts of Big City. Pickets were placed at the plant gates of The Firm to hand out leaflets and to solidify EBE pressure on the scene. "We'll have a victory," said Sutton; "they'll have to give in or we close up shop. What a beautiful use of economic power."

Marches and picketing continued for four months, although the pace slackened considerably as time went on. The Firm announced that it would not tolerate lawlessness and destruction of property. When such incidents occurred, a petition for an injunction from the Court of Common Pleas was sought and granted. The arrival of Sheriff's Deputies armed with the Court Writ, was ordinarily enough to calm a potentially explosive situation. Media coverage of the situation also declined with time and editorial comment became less favorable to the demonstrations with the passage of events.

COMPLAINT AND DEMONSTRATIONS

In the following spring another civil rights organization, the Right-On Federation (ROF) picked up where EBE left off and tried another approach using the same basic information. They enlisted the aid of still other organizations that were getting involved in the equal rights movement in Big City and together they lodged a complaint with the Office of Federal Contract Compliance (OFCC) alleging that The Firm failed to meet the requirements imposed by Title VII of the Civil Rights Act of 1964 and Executive Order 11246 in that the company failed to adopt personnel policies to ensure nondiscrimination in employment and promotion.

Using the material turned up earlier by EBE, the groups again alleged substantial discrimination by The Firm against minority group members. One continuing practice they concentrated upon was the avoidance of advertising of openings in the plants or main office; most referrals came from employees and preference was given to relatives of present workers or those who were recommended by the employees. Since there were still few Black workers in The Firm, there were limited applications from Blacks who might have known of the openings. Applicants from the Black community were even more limited by the general impression in that group that The Firm did not hire Blacks and it was useless to try to get a job there.

"In addition," said James Johnson, the president of ROF, "The Firm asks whether the applicant has had a criminal record. That clearly discriminates against ghetto dwellers who are predominantly Black." It was pointed out that the use of intelligence tests based on white cultural conditions was a further factor that discriminated. Most important, The Firm did not communicate a policy of nondiscrimination to the personnel department.

At the same time the Right-On Federation held a news conference at which they announced plans for a concerted effort to publicize the small number of blacks in The Firm. "The officials of The Firm are guilty of violating the law of the land," said James Johnson, "and we intend to use all means to eliminate this cancer and promote economic justice." It was emphasized further that this case would serve as an example for other employers in the area who were not exerting all effort to seek out and recruit workers from the Black community.

After the press conference, members of the ROF sat down with representatives of Local 135 of the United Cypres Operators Union in order to obtain support for the attempts to gain equal employment opportunity for minority groups. The Union officials agreed to support the efforts and pointed out that they had attempted to include a fair employment clause in the contract but had failed to achieve that end result. Local 135 representatives agreed with comments made by the ROF delegation to the effect that substantial unemployment could result from government contract cancellations, and there was imminent danger of this if the situation at The Firm continued.

The Union officers told ROF, however, that the Union could not take any step toward reopening the contract for negotiation of a nondiscriminatory clause, unless and until the membership of Local 135 decided to do so. ROF then extended its campaign to passing out leaflets to Firm workers at the plant gates and holding demonstrations and marches throughout the area. A week later the Local 135 membership met to consider authorizing the executive committee of the Local to negotiate a nondiscriminatory clause and propose a solution whereby Blacks could be hired on a preferential basis until the percentage of Blacks in The Firm reached the percentage they constituted in the local community. Since this preferential hiring would extend only to "new hires" there would be no effect on seniority rights of present employees, the officers told the membership. Thus reassured, a majority of the members voted to extend authorization as requested by the officers.

Fred Famous was quite agitated as a result of the complaint and the specific bases for the action. "This is plain foolishness," he roared. "One of the main reasons why we are so successful is because we are one big happy family. Close personal and blood ties make for a good and productive work force. We look out for each other." Tom Newboy, the personnel director, felt strongly, too, especially about the demands that The Firm mount a crash campaign to recruit Black workers through direct contacts with Black organizations and the extensive advertising in the Black newspaper or the radio station. He felt that this was "reverse discrimination" and was contrary to the good personnel policy and procedures he had learned in graduate school.

The personnel director also pointed out the collective bargaining agreement with Local 135 of the United Cypres Operators Union whereby any information with respect to vacancies must first be disseminated in the departments where they occur and then the information communicated throughout the plant.

Fred Famous asked Leo Lex what the difference was, if any, between alleging a violation of Title VII of the Civil Rights Act of 1964 and the invoking of Executive Order 11246. Lex pointed out that Title VII was a statute prohibiting discrimination on the basis of race, religion, age, sex, or national origin and it applied generally to activity in most organizations. Executive Order 11246 mandated affirmative action and sharpened enforcement of nondiscrimination by setting up the Office of Federal Contract Compliance to monitor companies with federal contracts.

The Secretary of Labor has the power to withdraw those contracts from and/or to prohibit the granting of new contracts to those companies found to be discriminating in violation of the policies enunciated in Title VII. It became clear to the participants in the meeting that serious efforts had to be made to challenge the allegations put forth.

Two weeks later The Firm received a notice from John D. Rector, director of the Office of Federal Contract Compliance, that the Office was instituting proceedings against the company. The Director indicated that he would proceed to terminate all government contracts The Firm currently held and to bar it from any contracts in the future. Rector stated further that the basis for his action was the failure of The Firm to comply with the requirements under Executive Order 11246, Sections 202 and 209, to maintain equal employment opportunity in the company.

After a lengthy session with his top officers and lawyer, Fred Famous determined that The Firm, as in the past with EBE, had to contest the charge because he still felt that there was little basis for the action. Perhaps more controlling in the decision was the recognition that the loss of the government contracts would do more than cause inconvenience; it would mean the difference between fiscal health of the company and severe financial difficulty, perhaps even bankruptcy. Fred Famous directed Lex to request a hearing; Lex immediately did so in writing.

Three months later the Secretary of Labor named a three man panel to hear arguments on both sides (the OFCC was placed under the Secretary of Labor by Executive Order 11246). One week later hearings were conducted in Great City and lasted three days.

In its arguments before the panel the OFCC concentrated on two points

1. The reliance by The Firm upon employing family members discriminated against Blacks.

2. The Firm did not take positive steps to remedy the effects of its practice.

Both conditions were a violation of the equal opportunity statutes and the duty to take affirmative action under them. The situation constituted a basis for the withdrawal of government contracts and subcontracts, as well as barring the granting of future government contracts.

The OFCC amplified each of the above points in its argument. It noted that The Firm had contended, in earlier investigations by the Department of Defense, that it had ended its policy of relying on employee referrals and nepotism but this policy was not communicated to others. It cited earlier testimony from civil rights groups that The Firm was well known for not encouraging Black applicants. Even other employee referral organizations were aware of the practice.

The Firm had stated continually that there was no intent to discriminate and no intent could be shown. In its argument the OFCC contended that this was not relevant since the actual outcome of a practice was the controlling factor and cited several court cases to support the position.[3]

The OFCC ended its argument with the conclusions that, while The Firm was not found to discriminate against any specific Black applicant, the system used is inherently discriminatory. Further, equal opportunity requires more than a passive policy statement or minimal action; it requires positive action to eliminate the discriminatory effects of a practice.

The Firm, in its appearance before the panel had its argument presented by Leo Lex. That argument contended, in short, that

1. Equal employment opportunity requires that nondiscrimination be practiced. Following the interpretation of the OFCC would mean discrimination that would contravene the intent of civil rights legislation.

2. The Firm practiced nondiscrimination and there is no evidence to the contrary.

The brief by Leo Lex supported the oral argument before the panel by citing long historical data that the original intent of early legislation in this area was to eliminate, in employment, distinctions based on race or color.[4] Under those legal concepts The Firm was to keep to procedures that were "color blind," a situation that did not result if it were forced to comply with the demands of the various Black organizations and the OFCC. Moreover, attention should be paid to those activities in which The Firm participated when allegations of discrimination were made. The Firm never actively recruited anyone but interviewed all who appeared. Allegations that The Firm discriminated in hiring were casual references made by individual members of the Black organizations involved in demonstrations against the company and are not supported by evidence. On the other hand, The Firm had established the reputation of being a good place in which to work and of employing highly skilled craftsmen as the result of good personnel policies.

After hearing further testimony the three-man panel adjourned. Four months later they issued a decision which they forwarded directly to the Secretary of Labor of the U.S. Department of Labor with a copy to The Firm. The panel found a violation of the equal opportunity clause of the Civil Rights Act of 1964 through the failure to open its recruitment activity to a point at which there would be an increase in the number of minority applicants. This was based upon the following supportive findings

1. There existed a recruiting program by The Firm and it tended to perpetuate the racial composition of the work force.

2. If there is doubt that this is discrimination, it hardly matters because the OFCC case is based upon the lack of an affirmative action program. This requires some company action to broaden the base of recruitment.

3. Adding minority applicants to the existing pool of white applicants does not contravene the provisions of Title VII of the Civil Rights Act of 1964; indeed, it promotes the equal employment opportunity sought under the act.

The panel then recommended that the Secretary of Labor direct The OFCC and The Firm to agree on a program of affirmative action, if no agreement could be reached, to convene another panel to hold a hearing to come up with specific recommendations, as well as sanctions for noncompliance.

Tom Newboy and his staff then began to work feverishly for three weeks on a program they felt could meet the recommendations of the panel and they continually consulted with Lex on the proposals. The program that emerged consisted of notices to every conceivable source of candidates that The Firm was an equal opportunity employer and made no distinctions based on race, sex, creed, or national origin. Job openings would be advertised and no preference would be made with respect to relatives or friends of employees. Recruiting statistics would also be available to OFCC upon request.

The OFCC was much more specific and aggresive in its proposals. In addition to requiring The Firm to go out into the Black community, it would be required to maintain a holding file with names of potential minority candidates not rejected. This file would serve to provide candidates when job opportunities arose in the future.

Tom Newboy and Leo Lex objected to the proposal of the holding file and Fred Famous backed them up. As a result, the OFCC and The Firm failed to come to an agreement. When the Secretary of Labor reconvened the panel six months later, another round of deliberations continued for two weeks. At that point, the panel reported to the Secretary of Labor that an agreement in principal was reached.

The Secretary, after being briefed on the details of the plan, indicated that he had reservations about the proposal. It would be preferable that further procedures to end discrimination be specified by The Firm and that it take steps to improve its image in the community, but its proposals to advise all constituencies that it is an equal opportunity employer and its maintenance of a file of all job applicants as well as minimum entry level qualifications were good evidence of substantial progress. In addition, all information would be reported bimonthly to the OFCC.

When they heard of the details of the plan and the acceptance of it by the Secretary of Labor, ROF leaders staged further demonstrations at the gates of the main plant of The Firm. They were unhappy with the actual percentage of new hires from the minority populations. "At this rate we'll never catch up to our rightful share of the jobs," yelled James Johnson, again leading the group of demonstrators.

Within a few weeks, however, it was evident that the campaign against The Firm lost strength. It was no longer big news in Big City, and union support faded when it became evident that cancellation of government contracts was no longer a threat.

INDIVIDUAL COMPLAINT CONTINUED

In the midst of the activity of the civil rights organizations, the complaint of Benjamin Dreen was served. Arrival of the complaint at The

Firm caused less concern than earlier legal actions, probably because by this time all participants had become enured to the long series of adversary proceedings. As in all important matters, Famous asked Tom Newboy to sit down with Leo Lex and discuss the response The Firm would make to the complaint. Lex pointed out that the complaint was filed by the aggrieved person; it could have been filed by the Human Relations Commission itself or the Attorney General of Great State. "Interestingly enough, even we, as an employer, could file a complaint," added Lex. Newboy had never had a discrimination case under Great State statutes filed by an individual against The Firm during his tenure so that he was interested in knowing what was coming.

Lex pointed out that a field investigator would visit The Firm and interview the personnel involved in the alleged discrimination as well as any other witnesses who could add to the case. Records and documents, if pertinent, would have to be made available and the investigator could also make an on-site inspection of The Firm and its operations. As a result of the investigation the Commission staff would make a finding of either probable cause or no probable cause. In the latter instance, the complaint would be dismissed (complainant can appeal). "If there is a finding of probable cause there is an opportunity for us to sit down with the HRC officer who acts as a conciliator," added Lex who then outlined the actions that would be required by The Firm

1. Make available to the complainant the job he didn't get.
2. Compensate him for losses incurred as the result of the discrimination.
3. Remedy injustices caused through violation of the act.
4. Correct practices leading to discrimination having an adverse effect on persons protected.
5. Take other affirmative action to eliminate discrimination.

These provisions would be incorporated into a conciliation agreement or consent order having the same effect as the formal order issued by the Commission after a public hearing.

"What happens if we don't agree?" asked Newboy. "Then we go before the Commission in a hearing open to the public," replied Lex. "That happens so seldom, about one percent of the time, that firms and individuals involved must really feel strongly about the particular matter if it does go to a hearing." Lex pointed out further that three commissioners, sitting at the hearing, heard testimony under oath, made a decision, and could issue an order that was legally inforceable, much as a court of original jurisdiction might. Appeals, if either the complainant or The Firm wished, would be taken to the statewide intermediate appellate court, which was established by statute to hear appeals from the decisions of administrative agencies.

Lex felt he had to add the information that a willful violation of the Commission's orders or interference with the performance of duty of a Commission representative was a misdemeanor, punishable by fines of up to $500 and/or imprisonment not to exceed thirty days.

At this point, both Newboy and Lex agreed that the situation called for an approach consistent with the responses The Firm was making to the demands and demonstrations of the various civil rights organizations. Both were well aware, too, of the strong feelings held by Fred Famous that the personnel policy of hiring relatives of workers was one of the finest examples of good employee relations. For this and other reasons, Newboy and Lex felt that a defense denying either an intent to discriminate or discrimination *per se* would have to be put forth by The Firm.

By some coincidence, the field investigator of the HRC who arrived at The Firm seven months later was Larry Mensch. Just as Lex had predicted, the field investigator interviewed everyone in the personnel department, starting with Newboy. Mensch was not able to interview Harvey Worker, who was no longer with The Firm, but he did take extensive notes from his talks with employees in the cypres department.

One month after he visited The Firm, Mensch discussed his findings with the HRC attorney and got agreement on the finding of probable cause of violation of the nondiscrimination statute. Mensch then drafted a letter with this information and requested that representatives of The Firm meet with him for the Conciliation.

The meeting was arranged for a midweek day two weeks later. Mensch simply repeated the finding and asked the representatives of The Firm to point out any errors they felt had been made or to make any additions that were necessary. After Newboy and Lex agreed as to the facts, Mensch discussed with them the possibility of a formal agreement by The Firm that would embody the recommendations of the Commission to remedy the situation as the field representative found it to be. Mensch had already drafted a conciliation agreement (Form 13-3).

Newboy and Lex thanked Mensch for his efforts and asked for some time to go over the proposed solution. "We will get back to you within a week," said Lex. "Is that all right?" Mensch indicated approval of that time projection and returned to his office.

Discussion on the subject among those at The Firm who were involved continued during the next day. Attention was focused upon the alternatives available in the situation. "I already know what the hearing is like in case we go that route," said Newboy, "but what happens if we disagree with the decision that emerges." Lex pointed out that the process of appeal was virtually identical with that in the civil suit involving Zagger Supply Co., Inc. (see Chapter 8) a case with which the officers of The Firm were familiar even though they were not directly involved.

There was general agreement that the appellate process, or even going to a hearing itself, was a costly and time-consuming ordeal. More to the point, however, was the recognition that signing the conciliation agreement would be in conformity with the results in the matters raised by the OFCC and the civil rights organizations, those events having just been concluded. In addition, there was an opening in the cypres department; as a matter of fact that slot was the very one that Harvey Worker had occupied before his unfortunate fate overtook him (Chapter 9). Under these circumstances it was decided that it would be best to have the matter end here. Fred Famous agreed and the conciliation form was signed by him.

FORM 13-3. HRC Conciliation Agreement

STATE OF GREAT STATE

GOVERNOR'S OFFICE

GREAT STATE HUMAN RELATIONS COMMISSION

Benjamin C. Dreen
:
:
:
:
:
:
:
:
:   Docket No. 76-1379
vs.
:
:
:
:
The Firm
:
:
:

CONCILIATION AGREEMENT

WHEREAS, on the ___5th___ day of ___October___ , 19 _XX_, a verified Complaint was filed with the Great State Human Relations Commission ("Commission") against: ___The Firm___

("Respondent(s)") by: ___Benjamin C. Dreen_____

("Complainant(s)"). This Complaint alleged that Respondent(s) had violated Section(s) __5a, 5b__ of the Great State Human Relations Act, 43 P.S. § § 951 et seq, as amended ("Act"), in that Respondent(s) committed or caused to be committed certain acts set out in said Complaint and now contained in Appendix "A", hereof; and

WHEREAS, Respondent(s) do(es) not admit any violation of the Act but wish(es) to avoid litigation; and

WHEREAS, Commission finds that the settlement terms, as set forth in Appendix "B" hereof, are reasonable under the circumstances and finds further that the public interest will be served by settlement of the case; and

WHEREAS, Respondent(s) for the reasons set forth above do(es) hereby waive all rights to a public hearing under Section 9 of the Act and the Regulations promulgated by the Commission, and do(es) hereby consent to the entry of this Conciliation Agreement as a Consent Order and Decree of the Commission, which shall have the same force and effect as a Commission Order and Decree following a Public Hearing by the Commission and shall be enforceable as such under Section 10 of the Act:

NOW, THEREFORE, Respondent(s) and Commission hereby agree to be legally bound as follows:

1. The foregoing preambles shall be included herein as if fully set forth.

2. The Respondent(s) admit(s) the jurisdiction of the Commission in this matter and hereby waive(s) all objections thereto.

3. All appendices annexed hereto are incorporated into this Agreement as integral parts hereof, as if fully set forth.

4. The term "Respondent(s)" as used herein shall include all agents, servants and employees of the Respondent(s) named above, in addition to the principal(s).

5. The execution and implementation of this Agreement shall not constitute any waiver of powers and duties conferred upon the Commission, nor shall this Agreement be deemed a declaration of policy or precedent by the Commission. This Agreement shall in no way affect the intake, processing, adjudication or disposition of future Complaints involving the Respondent(s), except that the Respondent(s) may in the course of any proceedings refer to this Agreement and to its (their) performance thereunder to the extent relevant to such proceedings.

6. Respondent(s) shall hereafter fully comply with all of the provisions of the Act and the Regulations promulgated by the Commission and shall fully comply with each of the terms of settlement set forth in Appendix "B" hereof.

7. It is expressly understood by the Respondent(s) that any violation of infraction of the terms and conditions set forth herein by Respondent(s) shall constitute a violation of an Order of the Commission pursuant to Section 11 of the Act.

8. The relationship between Complainant(s) and Respondent(s) shall be subject to and defined by Appendix "C" if attached hereto.

9. If any portion of this Agreement, or the application thereof to any person or circumstance, should for any reason be adjudged by any court of competent jurisdiction to be invalid or unenforceable, in whole or in part, such judgment shall not affect, impair or invalidate any other portion of this Agreement.

10. Commission and Respondent(s) enter into the Agreement with the intent to be legally bound thereby, This Agreement shall become final when approved and ratified by the Commission; and thereafter shall be binding upon and inure to the benefit of each of the parties hereto, and each of their respective heirs, successors and assigns, effective immediately from the date of such approval. If not so approved and ratified, it shall be null and void from its inception.

By the Respondent(s):

_Thomas Newbory_____   ___June 19, 19XX___
Title: Personnel Director   Date

_____   _____
Title: Date

ATTEST:

_Frederick Famous_____
Title: President

STATE OF GREAT STATE   :
                                              SS
COUNTY OF LOCAL   :

On the ___19th___ day of ___June___ , 19XX , each of the persons who have signed their names above personally appeared before me and, if not already known to me, satisfactorily proved identity as the persons whose names are signed above. Each of them signed this agreement freely and with full intent to be legally bound thereby, and clearly understanding that they are waiving their rights to a hearing by signing this agreement.

In testimony whereof, I have hereunto set my hand and seal on the day last above written.

_____
                              Notary Public

My Commission Expires:

_____

Recommended for approval by the Commission:

_____
                              Executive Director
Great State Human Relations Commission

Approved and ratified at a meeting of the Great State Human Relations Commission on the ___10th___ day of ___July___ , 19XX

_____
                              Chairperson
Great State Human Relations Commission

ATTEST: _____
                              Secretary
Great State Human Relations Commission

Appendix "A"

STATE OF GREAT STATE

GOVERNOR'S OFFICE

GREAT STATE HUMAN RELATIONS COMMISSION

Benjamin C. Dreen   :

                     :   Docket No. 76-1379

vs.   :

The Firm   :

COMPLAINANT(S) ALLEGATIONS

Discriminatory practices prohibited by Statute 5 a, b of the Great State Human Relations Act and utilized by The Firm prevented complainant from being employed when in fact he was the best qualified at that time for the work required. Complainant was discriminated against because of race and the recruitment practices which circumvented the purposes of the Act.

Appendix "B"

STATE OF GREAT STATE
GOVERNOR'S OFFICE
GREAT STATE HUMAN RELATIONS COMMISSION

Benjamin C. Dreen

              vs.

The Firm

           Docket No. 76-1379

TERMS OF SETTLEMENT

Pursuant to the agreement reached between the parties and consonant with the Human Relations Act of September 1, 19XN, The Firm agrees to the following:

1. Complainant will be employed at The Firm in the capacity of stockroom clerk in the cypres department.

2. Complainant will receive the wages established at the entry level for that position.

3. Respondent firm will pay complainant back wages beginning with a date three weeks after the initial job application.

4. Respondent firm will not keep records of race, color, or sex except those required by federal and state statutes.

5. Respondent firm will publicize widely in the community any job openings and will not rely solely on em-

ployee recommendations. Respondent firm, in support of its agreement with the above terms, will provide reports every six months to the Human Relations Commission.

Appendix "C"

STATE OF GREAT STATE

GOVERNOR'S OFFICE

GREAT STATE HUMAN RELATIONS COMMISSION

Benjamin C. Dreen	:
vs.	: Docket No. 76-1379
The Firm	:

CERTIFICATE OF SATISFACTORY ADJUSTMENT

I, Benjamin C. Dreen, Complainant in the above-docketed case, do hereby certify that my Complaint has been adjusted to my satisfaction in that:

An offer of employment in the position applied for, with back wages, has been made by The Firm.

I hereby request the Great State Human Relations Commission to close the above-docketed case.

Benjamin C. Dreen
_____
Complainant

STATE OF GREAT STATE

GOVERNOR'S OFFICE

GREAT STATE HUMAN RELATIONS COMMISSION

Benjamin C. Dreen	:	
vs.	:	Docket No. 76-1379
The Firm	:	

RELEASE

Know all persons by these presents that upon the condition that Respondent(s) shall fully comply with all the Terms of Settlement set forth in Appendix "B" of this Agreement, I do hereby release and forever discharge Respondent(s) from all manner of actions and causes of action and all suits, debts, claims and demands whatsoever based upon the allegations set forth in Appendix "A" of this

Agreement, including the present action, except as described below. This release shall in no way discharge, release or absolve Respondent(s) from liability for any violation of Section 5(d) of the Act (relating to retaliation) which may occur after execution of this Agreement, nor in any way limit my rights to bring suits or actions or file Complaints based in whole or in part on any violation of the Act or other applicable law which may occur in the future; (nor shall this release in any way limit my rights to seek additional relief for the acts complained of herein in a forum having jurisdiction and power to grant additional or greater relief.)

STATE OF GREAT STATE

GOVERNOR'S OFFICE

GREAT STATE HUMAN RELATIONS COMMISSION

Benjamin C. Dreen	:	
	:	Docket No. 76-1379
vs.	;	
The Firm	:	

FINAL ORDER AND DECREE

AND NOW, this____20th____ day of ____June____ , 19XK, upon consideration of the Conciliation Agreement submitted in the above captioned case it is hereby ORDERED AND DECREED that said Conciliation Agreement be entered into the official record of the Great State Human Relations Commission as a Final Order, to be given the same force and effect as if entered after a Public Hearing.

BY:

Glenda Madison.
_____
Chairperson
Great State Human Relations Commission

ATTEST:

Gail Monroe
_____
Secretary
Great State Human Relations Commission

Dated:____June 20, 19XX____   _Benjamin C. Dreen_
                               Complainant

STATE OF GREAT STATE   :
                       : SS
COUNTY OF ___LOCAL___ :

On the____20th____day of____June____ , 19XK, the Complainant named above, ___Benjamin C. Dreen___ personally appeared before me. He/she is known to me or proved his/her identity as the person who signed this release. He/she acknowledged that the release was freely signed, with full understanding of its contents and legal effect, and solely for the consideration and upon the conditions expressed therein.

Witness my hand and seal the day and year written above.

_____*Mark Six*_____
Notary Public

My Commission Expires _____ *1/1/19X2*_____

QUESTIONS

What differences in procedure have you noted in a comparison of administrative agency activities with those of court systems?

What are the probable end results of the two separate systems?

Are there any advantages in administrative agency law and procedures? To whom? Are there any disadvantages?

If you were a manager, would you prefer to operate under purely administrative agency procedures or would you opt for civil and criminal court processes? Why?

Who has more control over events—judges or administrative agency personnel?

CASES

Griggs v. Duke Power Company
401 U.S. 424, 91 S.Ct. 849, 28 L.Ed. 2d 158 (1971).

Black employees brought a class action against their company alleging a violation of the Civil Rights Act of 1964 in a company requirement of a high school diploma and a satisfactory intelligence test score for placement in jobs previously limited to white employees. The requirement was alleged to preserve the effects of the company's past racial discrimination. The Court of Appeals affirmed a District Court holding that the requirements were proper, absent a discriminatory purpose but reversed the holding that present effects of part discrimination were insulated from remedial action.

MR. CHIEF JUSTICE BURGER delivered the opinion of the Court.

We granted the writ in this case to resolve the question whether an employer is prohibited by the Civil Rights Act of 1964, Title VII, from requiring a high school education or passing of a standardized general intelligence test as a condition of employment in or transfer to jobs when (a) neither standard is shown to be significantly related to successful job performance, (b) both requirements operate to disqualify Negroes at a substantially higher rate than white applicants, and (c) the jobs in question formerly had been filled only by white employees as part of a longstanding practice of giving preference to whites. . . .

The objective of Congress in the enactment of Title VII is plain from the language of the statute. It was to achieve equality of employment opportunities and remove barriers that have operated in the past to favor an identifiable group of white employees over other employees. Under the Act, practices, procedures, or tests neutral on their face, and even neutral in terms of intent, cannot be maintained if they operate to "freeze" the status quo of prior discriminatory employment practices. . . .

In short, the Act does not command that any person be hired simply because he was formerly the subject of discrimination, or because he is a member of a minority group. Discriminatory preference for any group, minority or majority, is precisely and only what Congress has proscribed. What is required by Congress is the removal of artificial, arbitrary, and unnecessary barriers to employment when the barriers operate invidiously to discriminate on the basis of racial or other impermissible classification. . . .

The Act proscribes not only overt discrimination but also practices that are fair in form, but discriminatory in operation. The touchstone is business necessity. If an employment practice which operates to exclude Negroes cannot be shown to be related to job performance, the practice is prohibited.

On the record before us, neither the high school completion requirement nor the general intelligence test is shown to bear a demonstrable relationship to successful performance of the jobs for which it was used. Both were adopted, as the Court of Appeals noted, without meaningful study of their relationship to job-performance ability. Rather, a vice president of the Company testified, the requirements were instituted on the Company's judgment that they generally would improve the overall quality of the work force. . . .

The Company's lack of discriminatory intent is suggested by special efforts to help the undereducated employees through Company financing of two-thirds the cost of tuition for high school training. But Congress directed the thrust of the Act to the *consequences* of employment practices, not simply the motivation. More than that, Congress has placed on the employer the burden of showing that any given requirement must have a manifest relationship to the employment in question. . . .

Nothing in the Act precludes the use of testing or measuring procedures; obviously they are useful. What Congress has forbidden is giving these devices and mechanisms controlling force unless they are demonstrably a reasonable measure of job performance. Congress has not commanded that the less qualified be preferred over the better qualified simply because of minority origins. Far from disparaging job qualifications as such, Congress has made such qualifications the controlling factor, so that race, religion, nationality, and sex become irrelevant. What Congress has commanded is that any tests used must measure the person for the job and not the person in the abstract.

The judgment of the Court of Appeals is, as to that portion of the judgment appealed from, reversed. . . .

Washington v. Davis
426 U.S. 229, 96 S.Ct. 2040, 48 L.Ed. 2d 597 (1976).

A class action suit was brought by unsuccessful Black applicants for employment as police officers in the District of Columbia. The suit alleged racial discrimination and a violation of the due process clause of the Fifth Amendment through the use of written personnel tests of verbal skill. The District Court granted the defendant's motion for summary judgment. The Court of Appeals reversed and directed summary judgment for plaintiffs.

Mr. Justice WHITE delivered the option of the Court.

This case involves the validity of a qualifying test administered to applicants for positions as police officers in the District of Columbia Metropolitan Police Department. The test was sustained by the District Court but invalidated by the Court of Appeals. We are in agreement with the District Court and hence reverse the judgment of the Court of Appeals. . .

According to the findings and conclusions of the District Court, to be accepted by the Department and to enter an intensive 17-week training program, the police recruit was required to satisfy certain physical and character standards, to be a high school graduate or its equivalent and to receive a grade of at least 40 on "Test 21," which is, "an examination that is used generally throughout the federal service," which "was developed by the Civil Service Commission not the Police Department" and which was "designed to test verbal ability, vocabulary, reading and comprehension." 348 F.Supp., at 16.

The validity of Test 21 was the sole issue before the court on the motions for summary judgment. The District Court noted that there was no claim of "an intentional discrimination or purposeful discriminatory actions" but only a claim that Test 21 bore no relationship to job performance and "has a highly discriminatory impact in screening out black candidates." 348 F.Supp., at 16. Petitioners' evidence, the District Court said, warranted three conclusions: "(a) The number of black police officers, while substantial, is not proportionate to the population mix of the city. (b) A higher percentage of blacks fail the Test than whites. (c) The Test has not been validated to establish its reliability for measuring subsequent job performance." *Ibid.* This showing was deemed sufficient to shift the burden of proof to the defendants in the action, petitioners here; but the court nevertheless concluded that on the undisputed facts respondents were not entitled to relief. . .

It was thus not necessary to show that Test 21 was not only a useful indicator of training school performance but had also been validated in terms of job performance—"the lack of job performance validation does not defeat the Test, given its direct relationship to recruiting and the valid part it plays in this process." The District Court ultimately concluded that "the proof is wholly lacking that a police officer qualifies on the color of his skin rather than ability" and that the Department "should not be required on this showing to lower standards or to abandon efforts to achieve excellence". . . 348 F.Supp., at 18.

As the Court of Appeals understood Title VII, employees or applicants proceeding under it need not concern themselves with the employer's possibly discriminatory purpose but instead may focus solely on the racially differential impact of the challenged hiring or promotion practices. This is not the constitutional rule. We have never held that the constitutional standard for adjudicating claims of invidious racial discrimination is identical to the standards applicable under Title VII, and we decline to do so today.

The central purpose of the Equal Protection Clause of the Fourteenth Amendment is the prevention of official conduct discriminating on the basis of race. It is also true that the Due Process Clause of the Fifth Amendment contains an equal protection component prohibiting the United States from invidiously discriminating between individuals or groups. *Bolling v. Sharpe,* 347 U.S. 497, 74 S.Ct. 693, 98 L.Ed. 884 (1954). But our cases have not embraced the proposition that a law or other official act, without regard to whether it reflects a racially discriminatory purpose, is unconstitutional *solely* because it has a racially disproportionate impact. . .

Under Title VII, Congress provided that when hiring and promotion practices disqualifying substantially disproportionate numbers of blacks are challenged, discriminatory purpose need not be proved, and that it is an insufficient response to demonstrate some rational basis for the challenged practices. It is necessary, in addition, that they be "validated" in terms of job performance in any one of several ways, perhaps by ascertaining the minimum skill, ability or potential necessary for the position at issue and determining whether the qualifying tests are appropriate for the selection of qualified applicants for the job in question. However this process proceeds, it involves a more probing judicial review of, and less deference to, the seemingly reasonable acts of administrators and executives than is appropriate under the Constitution where special racial impact, without discriminatory purpose, is claimed. We are not disposed to adopt this more rigorous standard for the purposes of applying the Fifth and the Fourteenth Amendments in cases such as this.

A rule that a statute designed to serve neutral ends is nevertheless invalid, absent compelling justification, if in practice it benefits or burdens one race more than another would be far reaching and would raise serious questions about, and perhaps invalidate, a whole range of tax, welfare, public service, regulatory, and licensing statutes that may be more burdensome to the poor and to the average black than to the more affluent white. . .

The submission of the defendants in the District Court was that Test 21 complied with all applicable statutory as well as constitutional requirements; and they appear not to have disputed that under the statutes and regulations governing their conduct standards similar to those obtaining under Title VII had to be satisfied. The District Court also assumed that Title VII standards were to control the case identified the determinative issue as whether Test 21 was sufficiently job related and proceeded to uphold use of the test because it was "directly related to a determination of whether the applicant possesses sufficient skills requisite to the demands of the curriculum a recruit must master at the police academy." 348 F.Supp., at 17. The Court of Appeals reversed because the relationship between Test 21 and training school success, if demonstrated at all, did not satisfy what it deemed to be the crucial requirement of a direct relationship between performance on Test 21 and performance on the policeman's job.

We agreed with petitioners and the federal respondents that this was error. . .

FOOTNOTES

[1] Pub. L. 88–352, 78 stat. 241.

[2] The Statute of Limitations under EEOC legislation is 180 days.

[3] *Radio Officers v. Labor Board*, 347 U.S. 17 (1945); *Griggs v. Duke Power Company*, 401 U.S. 424 (1971).

[4] *Oyawa v. California*, 332 U.S. 633 (1948); *Hernandez v. Texas*, 347 U.S. 475 (1954).

CHAPTER 14
ADMINISTRATIVE PROCESS: OCCUPATIONAL SAFETY AND HEALTH

On the fateful August day that tragedy struck in the Cypres Department it was quiet for the remainder of the day as the employees, stunned by the death of one of the most popular persons in the department, John Q. Worker, took the rest of the day off. The atmosphere was even grimmer that evening as most of them congregated in the United Cypres Operators of America building. Initial shock soon gave way to slowly mounting anger among members of the group as they discussed the situation. Timothy O'Goode became one of the most vocal participants in the discussion. "Working on those zaggers is absolutely unsafe, and there is no reason why we should go back and use them as long as the present conditions exist. We must have some rights under that new occupational safety and health act that everybody is talking about." Robert Leader, the President of Local #135, and himself a machine operator who worked right next to John Q. Worker, took the floor. "Yes, I learned something at that supervisory development session at Local University about OSHA and we can file a complaint. This act, the Occupational Safety and Health Act of 1970, was set up to cover all businesses engaged in or affecting interstate commerce. It was passed to assure safe and healthful working conditions for all workers; each employer has to provide a safe and healthful set of working conditions either by following the specific standards set up by the government for particular work activities or through a general duty to provide a work place free from recognized hazards that cause or are likely to cause death or serious physical harm." Leader then mentioned further that a state agency would take charge if it were in existence and met the federal requirements for action but that Great State did not have an agency so qualified and he would have to go directly to the federal office. He knew there was an area office right here in Big City and that he could easily find it in the telephone directory under the listing of the U.S. Department of Labor, in which the Occupational Safety and Health Administration is located. Having gained the satisfaction that something was going to be done on their behalf, the members left for their homes.

IMMINENT DANGER

When he returned home Leader consulted the notes he had made when he attended the supervisory development session dealing with occupational safety and health. One of the first entries in the notes consisted of a discussion on imminent danger situations. The OSHA regulations provide for moves for a voluntary abatement of conditions that constitute an immediate danger to workers;[1] any condition or practice in which reasonable certainty exists that death or serious physical harm could be expected before regular enforcement procedures would take place. Upon notification the local OSHA office would send out an inspector and, if an imminent danger situation were found, the employer would be asked to abate the situation voluntarily.

After thinking about this, Leader felt sure that this was an imminent danger situation and that it was his duty to call the local OSHA office first thing in the morning.

Leader's call to OSHA early the next day was transferred by the receptionist to the area director, George Gem, who personally took all the information over the telephone. Gem soon came to the conclusion that this probably was an imminent danger situation and promised to send one of his compliance officers over for an immediate inspection of the cypres department.

"Can I call my men off the job until this is taken care of?" asked Leader. Gem informed him that there is no right to walk off the job because of potentially unsafe work conditions. If anyone did so the employer could take disciplinary action. There was a right, however, to refuse, in good faith, to expose oneself to a situation in which a "reasonable person" would conclude there is a real danger of death or serious injury in the situation and the employer refused to take steps to eliminate that danger when asked to do so. In addition, the employees would have to be aware of the fact that there was no time for normal enforcement procedures. Since Gem promised to have an inspection made that very morning, Leader did not consider the further possibility of telling the cypres operators to walk off the job.

Tom Newboy was a bit taken aback when, in the midmorning, the

OSHA compliance officer, Conrad O'Neil, appeared; Newboy had had no advance warning of the visit but knew enough about OSHA provisions that kept him from questioning the legality of the inspection. As he rushed out to join O'Neil, Newboy asked his secretary to put in a hurried call to The Firm's legal counsel, Leo Lex, and to alert Fred Famous, the president.

Newboy accompanied O'Neil on his inspection of the cypres department and made notes (just as O'Neil did) on the questioning of workers and other aspects of the inspection. After about an hour of this, O'Neil decided that there was some question about the ability of zaggers to remain intact under present work conditions. O'Neil acknowledged that there was no firm conclusion he could come to at this time, since the question was a very complex scientific one that required further analysis. At this point, however, O'Neil said he felt that suspension of the use of the zaggers in the production process would abate the imminent danger. He asked Newboy to have The Firm do this voluntarily without delay. O'Neil then advised all affected workers of the circumstances of the hazardous situation.

Newboy returned to the president's office with the news. Fred Famous was upset to hear of the abatement request. "If we don't use those zaggers, our whole production schedule gets thrown off. We could really take a bath, financially, on this," roared Famous. He turned to Lex and questioned him about the outcomes if The Firm considered the abatement request frivolous and refused to comply. Lex pointed out that OSHA, through its regional solicitor, would apply for an injunction or other appropriate remedy to the local Federal District Court and the Court was likely to act in favor of the petitioner. Under those circumstances, all felt there was little alternative but to comply with the request of the compliance officer for abatement.

"I wonder how they heard about this," asked Fred Famous. Lex reminded Famous that The Firm was obliged to report the fatality to OSHA within 48 hours, in any case. Lex was further concerned that Famous' comments could be interpreted by others as being an attempt to find out who "blew the whistle" and punish that person subtly in the process. Lex pointed out that anyone who felt discriminated against for reporting to OSHA could file a complaint. Action on that person's behalf by the Secretary of Labor, if favorable to the complainant, would result in penalties for the company in addition to the burden of litigation in the interim.

Leader was pleased with the outcome of the inspection and felt he had acted properly to cut down the time lag in the process by making the telephone call to OSHA. He felt he should proceed further, however, in personally following through in this area of occupational safety. He knew that another inspection by the OSHA office was forthcoming but he sensed an opportunity to play a more active role. At any rate, he felt that he should have more definitive information about OSHA in order that he could do his job as president of the union local.

FILING OF COMPLAINT

Two days later Leader drove to the area office of the Occupational Safety and Health Administration, located in the Federal Building in Big City, and asked to see George Gem, the Director, with whom he had spoken on the telephone. Leader asked Gem to provide him with some information as to OSHA procedures. Gem was happy to discuss the basis for OSHA, the reasons for jurisdiction and the various types of violations.

A *nonserious* violation, indicated Gem, has a direct relationship to occupational safety and health but is not one that can be considered a serious violation. A *serious* violation is present if there is a substantial probability that death or serious physical harm could result from a condition which exists, or from one or more practice, means, method, operation, or process which have been adopted or are in use, in such a place of employment unless the employer did not, and could not, with the exercise of reasonable diligence, know of the presence of the violation. A *willful* violation would occur where the employer intentionally and knowingly violated the act and was aware of such violation or was aware that a hazardous condition existed and made no reasonable effort to eliminate that condition even though he was not conscious of violating the act. A *repeated* violation occurs where the same violation is committed by the employer who was cited earlier for a violation. Gem then gave Leader a copy of the form, OSHA-7, (Form 14-1) in which the details of a complaint would have to be listed. Gem was careful to mention to Leader in this connection that his, Leader's, name would not be revealed to the employer should he wish to keep this confidential. Gem further indicated that upon receipt of the complaint, the area director would send out a compliance officer who would do a tour of inspection of the facilities in what was commonly called a "walk-around." If the inspection showed that conditions of the plant existed that did not comply with the provisions of the act, a citation would be issued for the alleged occupational safety and health violations. "Will you let us know ahead of time when you're inspecting?" said Leader. "Yes, because that would be helpful," was the response. "Representatives of the employees, usually the union officer, can accompany the compliance officer in his walkaround, as well." It was further pointed out by Gem that the employer would get advance warning if such warning would provide a quicker abatement of a hazard, or if it would facilitate entry into the plant. No more than 24 hours notice ahead of the visit could be given, however.

FORM 14-1.

U.S. DEPARTMENT OF LABOR
OCCUPATIONAL SAFETY AND HEALTH ADMINISTRATION

For Official Use Only		
Area	Date Received	Time
Region	Received By	Formal

COMPLAINT

Non Formal

This form is provided for the assistance of any complainant and is not intended to constitute the exclusive means by which a complaint may be registered with the U.S. Department of Labor.

Sec. 8(f)(1) of the Williams-Steiger Occupational Safety and Health Act, 29 U.S.C. 651, provides as follows: Any employees or representative of employees who believe that a violation of a safety or health standard exists that threatens physical harm, or that an imminent danger exists, may request an inspection by giving notice to the Secretary or his authorized representative of such violation or danger. Any such notice shall be reduced to writing, shall set forth with reasonable particularity the grounds for the notice, and shall be signed by the employees or representative of employees, and a copy shall be provided the employer or his agent no later than at the time of inspection, except that, upon request of the person giving such notice, his name and the names of individual employees referred to therein shall not appear in such copy or on any record published, released, or made available pursuant to subsection (g) of this section. If upon receipt of such notification the Secretary determines there are reasonable grounds to believe that such violation or danger exists, he shall make a special inspection in accordance with the provisions of this section as soon as practicable, to determine if such violation or danger exists. If the Secretary determines there are no reasonable grounds to believe that a violation or danger exists he shall notify the employees or representative of the employees in writing of such determination.

NOTE: Section 11(c) of the Act provides explicit protection for employees exercising their rights, including making safety and health complaints.

The undersigned *(check one)*

☐ Employee   ☐ Representative of employees   ☐ Other *(specify)* _____

believes that a violation at the following place of employment of an occupational safety or health standard exists which is a job safety or health hazard.

Employer's Name _____

Address   (Street _____ Telephone _____
  (
  (City _____ State _____ Zip Code _____

1. Kind of business _____

2. Specify the particular building or worksite where the alleged violation is located, including address. _____

3. Specify the name and phone number of employer's agent(s) in charge. _____

4. Describe briefly the hazard which exists there including the approximate number of employees exposed to or threatened by such hazard.

(Continue on reverse side if necessary)

(Continued on reverse side)

Form OSHA-7
Rev. Aug. 1976

5. List by number and/or name the particular standard (or standards) issued by the Department of Labor which you claim has been violated, if known.

_____

_____

_____

6. (a) To your knowledge has this violation been considered previously by any Government agency? _____

(b) If so, please state the name of the agency _____

(c) and, the appropriate date it was so considered. _____

7. (a) Is this complaint, or a complaint alleging a similar violation, being filed with any other Government agency?
_____

(b) If so, give the name and address of each. _____

8. (a) To your knowledge, has this violation been the subject of any union/management grievance or have you (or anyone you know) otherwise called it to the attention of, or discussed it with, the employer or any representative thereof? _____

(b) If so, please give the results thereof, including any efforts by management to correct the violation. _____
_____

9. Please indicate your desire:

☐ I do not want my name revealed to the employer.

☐ My name may be revealed to the employer.

COMPLAINANT'S NAME

NOTE: IT IS UNLAWFUL TO MAKE ANY FALSE STATEMENT, REPRESENTATION OR CERTIFICATION IN ANY DOCUMENT FILED PURSUANT TO THE OCCUPATIONAL SAFETY AND HEALTH ACT OF 1970. VIOLATIONS CAN BE PUNISHED BY A FINE OF NOT MORE THAN $10,000, OR BY IMPRISONMENT OF NOT MORE THAN SIX MONTHS, OR BY BOTH. (Section 17(g))

Signature _____   Date _____

Typed or Printed Name _____

Address
(Street _____   Telephone _____
(
(City _____   State _____   Zip Code _____

If you are an authorized representative of
employees affected by this complaint, please
state the name of your organization and your title. _____

Leader returned to the plant where he found some production problems because zaggers were not in use. Leader informed the men with whom he came into contact about his information gathering session at the OSHA office and got their suggestions in filling out the complaint (Form 14-1). "I'm going to be the employee representative accompanying the OSHA compliance officer when he conducts his inspection but I want a good idea ahead of time of all aspects of the unsafe conditions we think exist. There may be still other hazards, however, that we will want to point out to the compliance officer. I want to know where these are in the plant, how long they have existed, and the names and job titles of everyone who is exposed to the hazard, and if the firm has tried to remedy the hazards." Leader then indicated that he probably should have these notes arranged in the order in which the compliance officer would be likely to move through the plant. The most logical and usual route the officer would take would be to follow the order of manufacture, that is, he would start where the raw materials enter the plant and move through the usual manufacturing sequence to the point where the finished products were being shipped to customers. Leader also indicated that the compliance officer noted or commented upon findings in the order in which he proceeded. Having done all of this and filled in the complaint, Leader rushed back to the OSHA office to deliver it in person and to make sure that as little time was lost as possible.

Early the next morning the telephone rang in the office of Jim Boss, the plant manager for The Firm. At the other end of the line was George Gem who informed Boss that another complaint was filed by one of the employees of The Firm alleging further unsafe conditions that violated the Occupational Safety and Health Act of 1970. Boss was further informed that a compliance officer would inspect the premises of The Firm within six hours. This advance notice, while not generally done, was being given because it was likely to assure the presence of appropriate representatives of the company and employees. Gem further stated that such notice is often given if it will facilitate the inspection in any way or when special preparations are called for, as in an inspection conducted after regular business hours. Gem then telephoned Robert Leader with the same information.

As soon as he put down the telephone, Jim Boss rushed to the office of the President of The Firm, Fred Famous, with the information he had received. Famous immediately instructed his secretary to call Tom Newboy, Sam Scott, the plant engineer, and Leo Lex. Each participant recognized the additional burdens upon The Firm as they assembled and each was attentive to the information presented by Jim Boss. When Boss had finished, Famous turned to Newboy and asked, "The safety program is part of your responsibility, Tom. What's our situation with respect to this whole mess we've gotten into?" "Well, F.F.," responded Newboy, "you know that I've been handling all the safety matters on top of everything else in the personnel area and it's been quite a struggle. You know my request for a full slot for a safety director has been in channels here for a long time. We really needed one." Newboy further indicated that a better place to start would be for Leo Lex to give a short background on the statute and what was to be expected from this second visit of the compliance officer.

Leo Lex took over and gave the background of the purposes of the law. "The Occupational Safety and Health Act of 1970," he said, "is also known as the Williams-Steiger Act for its two sponsors in the Congress." It was passed "to assure safe and healthful working conditions for working men and women; by authorizing enforcement of the standards developed under the Act; by assisting and encouraging the states in their efforts to assure safe and healthful working conditions; by providing for research, information, education, and training in the field of occupational safety and health; and for other purposes."[2] The two main aspects affecting The Firm as well as other companies are a concern for a fulfillment of the general duty to provide a safer working environment and, second, the adherence to standards that were developed under the Act.

"Standards? What standards?" asked Fred Famous. Leo Lex responded by pointing out that these, like all other information about federal government action, were published in the *Federal Register*. The Occupational Safety and Health Standards were published in Volume 39 No. 125 of the *Federal Register* on Thursday, June 27, 1974. And they're very precise and specific in most cases," said Lex. "Well I think our association representatives in Washington should have kept us informed of all of this," replied Famous. Tom Newboy mentioned that he had been collecting some information in his office but was a little bit hazy on all the specifics of the standards as they applied to all of the manufacturing operations in The Firm. "We'll have to go over those parts of the standards that refer to zaggers in greater detail." Lex further indicated that the Secretary of Labor, through regional offices of the Department of Labor, was charged with the responsibility for ensuring that the specific standards were met and that the employers discharged their general duty of providing safe working conditions. "The compliance officer will probably tour the plant, this time paying close attention to the specific conditions alleged to be a violation. As you know, we have 48 hours to report a fatality or the hospitalization of five employees and the compliance officer would have been here anyway. Lex noted further the basic duty of the company to report and record specific types of injuries (Figure 14-1). Lex also noted that the compliance officer could take cognizance of any other unsafe conditions or practices, not just those mentioned in the complaint. "I already know about imminent danger but what about other complaints?" asked Fred Famous. "Well, if he finds that we have violated one or more standards, the officer will point that out and determine the seriousness of the violation." There are four types of violations for which a citation will issue along with a possible penalty. One situation, called a *de minimis* violation, will call for a notice but no citation (see Table 14-1).

TABLE 14-1. Determinations in occupational injury or illness (by compliance officer and area director).

Violation Type	Description	Action	Penalty (Possible)
Initial Violations			
Imminent Danger	hazard that can cause death or serious physical harm immediately or before the imminence of the danger can be eliminated through the procedure of the Act.	Citation	request for voluntary abatement or federal court order to abate
Serious	this violation refers to a substantial probability that death or serious physical harm will result.	Citation	$500 to $1000 for each violation
Nonserious	violation of a standard would probably not result in death or serious physical harm.	Citation	up to $1000 for each violation
De minimis	this violation has no direct or immediate relationship to the safety or health of an employee.	Notice	no penalty
Willful or Repeated Violations			
Willful or repeated violation	employer intentionally or knowingly violates the act and was aware of such violation or was aware that a hazardous condition existed and made no reasonable effort to eliminate the condition even though not conscious of violating the act.	Citation	up to $10,000 fine
Willful or repeated violation resulting in death		Citation	up to $10,000 fine and/or 6 months imprisonment

A serious violation of OSHA standards is one where the condition involves a "substantial probability of death or serious physical harm involving permanent or prolonged impairment of the body." In addition however, a violation of this category is not determined unless the employer also "knew or could have known of the violation." Lex noticed that the minimum penalty for this type of violation is $500. A nonserious violation is one that has a direct bearing on the safety or health of workers but which would probably not cause death or serious physical harm. The penalty may or may not be assessed in this type of violation.

A willful violation is where the employer commits a knowing violation of the act or where there was awareness of the condition with no reasonable

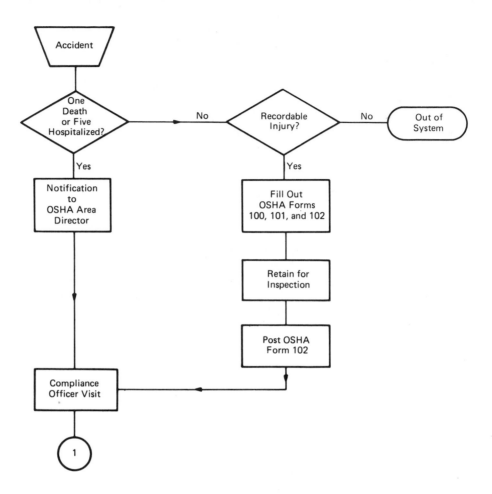

FIGURE 14-1. Employer Responsibilities in Occupational Injury or Illness.

effort to eliminate that hazard. For this violation to be charged it must be definitely shown that the employer knowingly permitted the dangerous condition to exist. Penalties of up to $10,000 are provided for this type of violation.

A *repeated* violation exists when the employer was already cited by OSHA for the same violation.

All these situations are in addition to the determination of imminent danger by the OSHA office, the determination already made earlier in the immediate aftermath of the death of John Q. Worker.

"Well," said Tom Newboy, "we'll just have to wait and see what the compliance officer will say when he gets here this time."

COMPLIANCE OFFICER VISIT

At 3:00 PM, promptly, Conrad O'Neil, already familiar with The Firm, appeared at the front gate and was promptly directed to the office of Tom Newboy in the Personnel Department since the guard was alerted by Newboy. Since both men had met, O'Neil did not have to present his credentials again, just the copy of the complaint. Newboy read over the complaint with the specific allegations of a violation of safety standards under OSHA. The allegation stated, in effect, that, "The Firm permitted unsafe operations of zaggers on the cypres machine in violation of Section 1910.215 of the Occupational Safety and Health Standards.[3] O'Neil also told Newboy that he wished to review the records kept on accidents and the summary record of accidents within the past year. O'Neil reminded Newboy that the company must keep three types of records. OSHA Form No. 100 (Form 14-2) is the "Log of Occupational Injuries and Illnesses." This form records details on each injury that occurs on the job. OSHA Form No. 101 (Form 14-3) is a "Supplementary Record of Occupational Injuries and Illnesses" that requires details of specific job mishaps. OSHA Form No. 102 (Form 14-4) is a Summary form for listing occupational injuries and illnesses along with totals for pertinent factors. O'Neil reminded Newboy that this last form must be posted for employees from February 1 to March 1 if the summary was for the previous calendar year. O'Neil then stated that he would take this opportunity to inspect the entire plant not just the cypres machine operation. He asked Newboy to call in Robert Leader as the representative of the Union in order that Leader accompany them through the plant on the walkaround.

When Leader reached the personnel department office the trio left on the inspection of the plant. As Leader had predicted, the compliance officer chose to begin the inspection at the logical beginning point of manufacturing operations, the receiving room for raw materials. Soon after they entered Leader pointed out some grease spots on an inclined roadway that apparently caused some slippage problems for the fork lift trucks shifting the pallets in the receiving room. Conrad O'Neil hurriedly made some notes covering this possibility. "Wait," said Newboy, "the union representative isn't supposed to butt in on the inspection, he is just supposed to watch." "No, according to the Compliance Operations Manual he can point out alleged violations or hazards," said O'Neil. Newboy responded—"are you going to issue a citation?" "The Manual states that I am not required to respond as to whether a citation will be issued but I can respond generally to give some indication as to whether a hazard exists or not. This looks like an easily abatable hazard and I think the foreman here can correct it immediately.'" O'Neil jotted down some further thoughts on his inspection sheet.

FORM 14-2.

OSHA NO. 100

RECORDABLE CASES: You are required to record information about: every occupational *death*, every nonfatal occupational *illness*; and those nonfatal occupational *injuries* which involve one or more of the following: loss of consciousness, restriction of work or motion, transfer to another job, or medical treatment (other than first aid). More complete definitions appear on the other side of this form.

Form Approved
OMB No. 44R 1453

LOG OF OCCUPATIONAL INJURIES AND ILLNESSES

CASE OR FILE NUMBER	DATE OF INJURY OR ONSET OF ILLNESS	EMPLOYEE'S NAME (First name or initial, middle initial last name)	OCCUPATION (Enter regular job title, not activity employee was performing when injured or at onset of illness.)	DEPARTMENT (Enter department in which the employee is regularly employed.)	DESCRIPTION OF INJURY OR ILLNESS — Nature of Injury or Illness and Part(s) of Body Affected (Typical entries for this column might be Amputation of 1st joint right forefinger Strain of lower back Contact dermatitis on both hands Electrocution—body)	Injury or Illness Code See codes at bottom of page.	EXTENT OF AND OUTCOME OF CASES — DEATHS (Enter date of death.)	LOST WORKDAY CASES — Enter a check if case involved lost workdays.	LOST WORKDAYS — Enter number of days of WORK AWAY FROM WORK due to injury or illness.	LOST WORKDAYS — Enter number of days of RESTRICTED WORK ACTIVITY due to injury or illness	NONFATAL CASES WITHOUT LOST WORKDAYS (Enter a check if no entry was made in columns 8 or 9 but the case is recordable, as defined above.)	TERMINATIONS OR PERMANENT TRANSFERS (Enter a check if the entry in columns 9 or 10 represented a termination or permanent transfer.)
	Mo./day/yr.						Mo./day/yr.					
(1)	(2)	(3)	(4)	(5)	(6)	(7)	(8)	(9)	(9A)	(9B)	(10)	(11)

Company Name _____
Establishment Name _____
Establishment Address _____

NOTE: This is NOT a report form. Keep in the establishment for 5 years.

Injury Code
10 All occupational injurie[s]

Illness Codes
21 Occupational skin diseases or disorders
22 Dust diseases of the lungs (pneumoconioses)
23 Respiratory conditions due to toxic agents
24 Poisoning (systemic effects of toxic materials)
25 Disorders due to physical agents other than toxic materials)
26 Disorders associated with repeated trauma
29 All other occupational illnesses

LOG OF OCCUPATIONAL INJURIES AND ILLNESSES

Each employer who is subject to the recordkeeping requirements of the Occupational Safety and Health Act of 1970 must maintain for each establishment a log of all recordable occupational injuries and illnesses. This form (OSHA No. 100) may be used for that purpose. A substitute for the OSHA No. 100 is acceptable if it is as detailed, easily readable and understandable as the OSHA No. 100.

Each recordable occupational injury and occupational illness must be timely entered on the log. Logs must be kept current and retained for five (5) years following the end of the calendar year to which they relate. Logs must be available (normally at the establishment) for inspection and copying by representatives of the Department of Labor, or the Department of Health, Education and Welfare, or States accorded jurisdiction under the Act.

INSTRUCTIONS FOR COMPLETING LOG OF OCCUPATIONAL INJURIES AND ILLNESSES

Column 1 - CASE OR FILE NUMBER

Enter a number which will facilitate comparison with supplementary records. Any series of nonduplicating numbers may be used.

Column 2 - DATE OF INJURY OR ONSET OF ILLNESS

For occupational injuries enter the date of the work accident which resulted in injury. For occupational illnesses enter the date of initial diagnosis of illness, or, if absence from work occurred before diagnosis, enter the first day of the absence attributable to the illness which was later diagnosed or recognized.

Column 3 - EMPLOYEE'S NAME

Column 4 - OCCUPATION

Enter regular job title, not the specific activity being performed at time of injury or illness. In the absence of a formal occupational title, enter a brief description of the duties of the employee.

Column 5 - DEPARTMENT

Enter the name of the department or division in which the injured person is regularly employed, even though temporarily working in another department at the time of injury or illness. In the absence of formal department titles, enter a brief description of normal workplace to which employee is assigned.

Column 6 - NATURE OF INJURY OR ILLNESS AND PART(S) OF BODY AFFECTED

Enter a brief description of the injury or illness and indicate the part or parts of body affected. Where entire body is affected, the entry "body" can be used.

Column 7 - INJURY OR ILLNESS CODE

Enter the one code which most accurately describes the case. A list of the codes appears at the bottom of the log. A more complete description of recordable occupational injuries and illnesses appears in "DEFINITIONS."

Column 8 - DEATHS

If the occupational injury or illness resulted in death, enter date of death.

Column 9 - LOST WORKDAY CASES

Enter a check for each case which involves days away from work, or days of restricted work activity, or both. Each lost workday case also requires an entry in column 9A or column 9B, or both.

Column 9A - LOST WORKDAYS–DAYS AWAY FROM WORK

Enter the number of workdays (consecutive or not) on which the employee would have worked but could not because of occupational injury or illness. The number of lost workdays should not include the day of injury or onset of illness or any days on which the employee would not have worked even though able to work.

NOTE: For employees not having a regularly scheduled shift., i.e., certain truck drivers, construction workers, farm labor, casual labor, part-time employees, etc., it may be necessary to estimate the number of lost workdays. Estimates of lost workdays shall be based on prior work history of the employee AND days worked by employees, not ill or injured, working in the department and/or occupation of the ill or injured employee.

Column 9B - LOST WORKDAYS–DAYS OF RESTRICTED WORK ACTIVITY

Enter the number of workdays (consecutive or not) on which because of injury or illness:

1) the employee was assigned to another job on a temporary basis, or

2) the employee worked at a permanent job less than full time, or

3) the employee worked at a permanently assigned job but could not perform all duties normally connected with it.

The number of lost workdays should not include the day of injury or onset of illness or any days on which the employee would not have worked even though able to work.

Column 10 - NONFATAL CASES WITHOUT LOST WORKDAYS

Enter a check for any recordable case which does not involve a fatality or lost workdays.

Column 11 - TERMINATIONS OR PERMANENT TRANSFERS

Enter a check if the entry in columns 9 or 10 represented a termination of employment or permanent transfer.

☆ U.S. G.P.O. 1976-621 736/5941

FORM 14-3.

OSHA No. 101   Form approved
Case or File No. _____   OMB No. 44R 1453

Supplementary Record of Occupational Injuries and Illnesses

EMPLOYER

1. Name _____

2. Mail address _____
                 (No. and street)   (City or town)   (State)

3. Location, if different from mail address _____

INJURED OR ILL EMPLOYEE

4. Name _____ Social Security No. _____
       (First name)   (Middle name)   (Last name)

5. Home address _____
            (No. and street)   (City or town)   (State)

6. Age _____   7. Sex: Male_____ Female_____ (Check one)

8. Occupation _____
         (Enter regular job title, *not* the specific activity he was performing at time of injury.)

9. Department _____
         (Enter name of department or division in which the injured person is regularly employed, even
         though he may have been temporarily working in another department at the time of injury.)

THE ACCIDENT OR EXPOSURE TO OCCUPATIONAL ILLNESS

10. Place of accident or exposure _____
                    (No. and street)   (City or town)   (State)
    If accident or exposure occurred on employer's premises, give address of plant or establishment in which
    it occurred. Do not indicate department or division within the plant or establishment. If accident oc-
    curred outside employer's premises at an identifiable address, give that address. If it occurred on a pub-
    lic highway or at any other place which cannot be identified by number and street, please provide place
    references locating the place of injury as accurately as possible.

11. Was place of accident or exposure on employer's premises? _____ (Yes or No)

12. What was the employee doing when injured? _____
                        (Be specific. If he was using tools or equipment or handling material,
_____
               name them and tell what he was doing with them.)

13. How did the accident occur? _____
                  (Describe fully the events which resulted in the injury or occupational illness. Tell what
_____
happened and how it happened. Name any objects or substances involved and tell how they were involved. Give
_____
full details on all factors which led or contributed to the accident. Use separate sheet for additional space.)

OCCUPATIONAL INJURY OR OCCUPATIONAL ILLNESS

14. Describe the injury or illness in detail and indicate the part of body affected. _____
                                         (e.g.: amputation of right index finger
_____
           at second joint; fracture of ribs; lead poisoning; dermatitis of left hand, etc.)

15. Name the object or substance which directly injured the employee. (For example, the machine or thing
         he struck against or which struck him; the vapor or poison he inhaled or swallowed; the chemical or ra-
         diation which irritated his skin; or in cases of strains, hernias, etc., the thing he was lifting, pulling, etc.)
_____
_____

16. Date of injury or initial diagnosis of occupational illness _____
                                             (Date)

17. Did employee die? _____ (Yes or No)

OTHER

18. Name and address of physician _____

19. If hospitalized, name and address of hospital _____
_____
    Date of report _____ Prepared by _____
    Official position _____

SUPPLEMENTARY RECORD OF
OCCUPATIONAL INJURIES
AND ILLNESSES

To supplement the Log of Occupational Injuries and Illnesses (OSHA No. 100), each establishment must maintain a record of each recordable occupational injury or illness. Workmen's compensation, insurance, or other reports are acceptable as records if they contain all facts listed below or are supplemented to do so. If no suitable report is made for other purposes, this form (OSHA No. 101) may be used or the necessary facts can be listed on a separate plain sheet of paper. These records must also be available in the establishment without delay and at reasonable times for examination by representatives of the Department of Labor and the Department of Health, Education and Welfare, and States accorded jurisdiction under the Act. The records must be maintained for a period of not less than five years following the end of the calendar year to which they relate.

Such records must contain at least the following facts:

1) *About the employer*—name, mail address, and location if different from mail address.

2) *About the injured or ill employee*—name, social security number, home address, age, sex, occupation, and department.

3) *About the accident or exposure to occupational illness*—place of accident or exposure, whether it was on employer's premises, what the employee was doing when injured, and how the accident occurred.

4) *About the occupational injury or illness*—description of the injury or illness, including part of body affected; name of the object or substance which directly injured the employee; and date of injury or diagnosis of illness.

5) *Other*—name and address of physician; if hospitalized, name and address of hospital; date of report; and name and position of person preparing the report.

SEE *DEFINITIONS* ON THE BACK OF OSHA FORM 100.

FORM 14-4.

| OSHA No. 102 | Complete no later than one month after close of calendar year. See back of this form for posting requirements and instructions. | Form Approved OMB No. 44R 1453 |

SUMMARY
OF
OCCUPATIONAL INJURIES AND ILLNESSES
FOR CALENDAR YEAR 19 ___

> Use previous edition of this form for summarizing your 1974 cases. This edition is for summarizing your cases for 1975 and subsequent years.

Establishment:
NAME _____
ADDRESS _____

INJURY AND ILLNESS CATEGORY		TOTAL CASES	DEATHS	LOST WORKDAY CASES				NONFATAL CASES WITHOUT LOST WORKDAYS	TERMINATIONS OR PERMANENT TRANSFERS
				Total Lost Workday Cases	Cases Involving Days Away From Work	Days Away From Work	Days of Restricted Work Activity		
CATEGORY	CODE	Number of entries in Col. 7 of the log. (1)	Number of entries in Col. 8 of the log. (2)	Number of checks in Col. 9 of the log. (3)	Number of entries in Col. 9A of the log. (4)	Sum of entries in Col. 9A of the log. (5)	Sum of entries in Col. 9B of the log. (6)	Number of checks in Col. 10 of the log. (7)	Number of checks in Col. 11 of the log. (8)
OCCUPATIONAL INJURIES	10								
Occupational Skin Diseases or Disorders	21								
Dust Diseases of the Lungs	22								
Respiratory Conditions Due to Toxic Agents	23								
Poisoning (Systemic Effects of Toxic Materials)	24								
Disorders Due to Physical Agents	25								
Disorders Associated With Repeated Trauma	26								
All Other Occupational Illnesses	29								
TOTAL—OCCUPATIONAL ILLNESSES (Sum of codes 21 through code 29)	30								
TOTAL—OCCUPATIONAL INJURIES AND ILLNESSES (Sum of code 10 and code 30)	31								

(Left margin vertical label: OCCUPATIONAL ILLNESSES)

| This is NOT a report form. Keep it in the establishment for 5 years. |

I certify that this Summary of Occupational Injuries and Illnesses is true and complete, to the best of my knowledge.

Signature _____
Title _____
Date _____

SUMMARY OF OCCUPATIONAL INJURIES AND ILLNESSES

Every employer who is subject to the recordkeeping requirements of the Occupational Safety and Health Act of 1970 must use this form to prepare an annual summary of the occupational injury and illness experience of the employees in each of his establishments within one month following the end of each year.

POSTING REQUIREMENTS: A copy or copies of the summary must be posted at each establishment in the place or places where notices to employees are customarily posted. This summary must be posted no later than February 1 and must remain in place until March 1.

INSTRUCTIONS for completing this form: All entries must be summarized from the log (OSHA No. 100) or its equivalent. Before preparing this summary, review the log to be sure that entries are correct and each case is included in only one of the following classes: deaths (date in column 8), lost workday cases (check in column 9), or nonfatal cases without lost workdays (check in column 10). If an employee's loss of workdays is continuing at the time the summary is being made, estimate the number of future workdays he will lose and add that estimate to the workdays he has already lost and include this total in the summary. No further entries are to be made with respect to such cases in the next year's summary.

Occupational injuries and the seven categories of occupational illnesses are to be summarized separately. Identify each case by the code in column 7 of the log of occupational injuries and illnesses.

The summary from the log is made as follows:

A.   For occupational injuries (identified by a code 10 in column 7 of the log form) make entries on the line for code 10 of this form.

Column 1—Total Cases. Count the number of entries which have a code 10 in column 7 of the log. Enter this total in column 1 of this
        form. This is the total of occupational injuries for the year.
Column 2 Deaths. Count the number of entries (date of death) for occupational injuries in column 8 of the log.
Column 3—Total Lost Workday Cases. Count the number of checks for occupational injuries in column 9 of the log.
Column 4—Cases Involving Days Away From Work. Count the number of entries for occupational injuries in column 9A of the log.
Column 5—Days Away From Work. Add the entries (total days away) for occupational injuries in column 9A of the log.
Column 6—Days of Restricted Work Activity. Add the entries (total of such days) for occupational injuries in column 9B of the log.
Column 7—Nonfatal Cases Without Lost Workdays. Count the number of checks for occupational injuries in column 10 of the log.
Column 8—Terminations or Permanent Transfers. Count the number of checks for occupational injuries in column 11 of the log.
CHECK: If the totals for code 10 have been entered correctly, the sum of columns 2, 3, and 7 will equal the number entered in column 1.

B.   Follow the same procedure for each illness code, entering the totals on the appropriate line of this form.

C.   Add the entries for codes 21 through 29 in each column for occupational illnesses and enter totals on the line for code 30.

D.   Add the entries for codes 10 and 30 in each column and enter totals on the line for code 31.

CHECK: If the summary has been made correctly, the entry in column 1 of the total line (code 31) of this form will equal the total number of cases on the log.

The person responsible for the preparation of the summary shall certify that it is true and complete by signing the statement on the form.

Use previous edition of this form for summarizing your 1974 cases. This edition is for summarizing your cases for 1975 and subsequent years. Forms for the 1974 summary can be obtained from the appropriate State statistical grant agency (if there is one in your State) or from the appropriate Regional Office of the Bureau of Labor Statistics. Addresses are in the booklet entitled Recordkeeping Requirements under the Occupational Safety and Health Act of 1970.

The inspection proceeded further without incident until the party arrived at the cypres department. Here Leader introduced the compliance officer to several of the employees who were most familiar with the important features of the job situation. Timothy O'Goode was interviewed first and pointed out the safety guard on each one of the machines, particularly the one that John Q. Worker was attending at the time of the fatal accident. "I believe that this is a violation of section 1910.215 of the *Rules and Regulations of the Occupational Safety and Health Standards*[4] covering machine guarding of abrasive wheel machinery," said O'Neil, as he sketched a diagram of the safety guard on the machine used by workers and made more notes.

O'Goode then pointed out the exact procedures for unpacking the new zaggers. He demonstrated the technique followed by the workers in removing the zaggers and mounting them on the machine. In addition to making notes, O'Neil took out a small camera and began taking photographs from several different angles. "Does the foreman here require the workers to do a ring test on each one of the zaggers before mounting?" asked O'Neil. "No, what's a ring test?" asked O'Goode. The compliance officer then explained that when the zagger is removed from the packing all the sawdust or packing material should be removed and then the zagger tapped with a nonmetalic instrument to determine whether it gave a clear sound. "Remember that organic bonded zaggers sound a little different from the Vitrified or silicate types," he said. The compliance officer then indicated that apparently this was not followed. "I could have you sign a statement to that effect but since I am interviewing you publicly and others have heard I don't think that it's necessary," he said as he scribbled more notes.

The rest of the tour proceeded without incident and eventually the inspection was completed. As they returned to the Personnel Department offices, O'Neil mentioned to Newboy that the *Compliance Operations Manual*[5] calls for a closing conference after the completion of the inspection. He turned to Leader and said "we sit down separately with the employer to advise him of all the conditions we feel may be violations of the act." "Do you have a closing conference with the employee representatives?" asked Leader. "Generally not, since you have participated in the inspection and given us your comments during that period. However, if you request a closing conference we can sit down and describe the results of the inspection in general and any alleged violations that could result in a citation." Leader thought for a minute and decided that he had pretty much pointed out, along with other employees, all of the possible violations that they thought existed and he left the room.

O'Neil and Newboy then sat down to go over the listing of violations. "This is to give the employer an opportunity to correct the violations as soon as he possibly can," said O'Neil. "What do you think, Mr. Newboy, is the length of time that it will take to correct these alleged violations?

Also, how much do you think it would cost to do so in each case?" O'Neil paid close attention to Newboy's responses because these would be considered when determining how long a period would be available for abatement and what penalty would be assessed, if any. O'Neil avoided any specific statement about a citation (except, of course, the reference to the easily correctable hazard he noted) nor would he discuss a length of time for abatement or a specific possible penalty. "Wait until I call in Sam Scott, the plant engineer. He should be able to give a better reading on what it will take to get this done." When Scott arrived he listened intently to the recitation of the alleged hazards as viewed by the compliance officer during the inspection. "We should be able to fix things up to your satisfaction within a week," said Scott. "Also, the cost for implementing these changes I estimate to be just under $1000."

At that particular point Conrad O'Neil thanked both men and returned to his office in the Federal Building.

DETERMINATION OF VIOLATION

The next morning Conrad O'Neil sat down with George Gem to discuss his findings. O'Neil knew that he could not issue a citation for a violation and assess a penalty without the direction of the area director to that effect except in the case of an easily abatable hazard when spotted or in what is known as a "instant citation" procedure. Both these are for more minor problems. The director's approval for a citation is still needed for serious violations. The two men also knew that they were required to issue a citation promptly following an inspection. This action must follow with "reasonable promptness," a time period that has been interpreted as no more than three days.

O'Neil's notes indicated two violations that he discovered

1. Violation of §1910.215 (d) (1) in that no "ring" test was made on the zagger prior to mounting on the wheel.
2. Violation of §1910.215 (b) whereby the safety guard mounted above the wheel left more than the maximum exposure permitted by the standards.[6]

O'Neil felt the standards were quite clear on these points and that the events constituted a violation of those standards.

Gem asked O'Neil his opinion of the level of violation. "This is clearly not a de minimis matter, I cleared up one of those on the spot," said O'Neil. He indicated that it was neither willful nor repeated violation, since there was no evidence that the employer committed an "intentional and knowing violation of the act or was conscious of that fact, or if not conscious of the act that he was aware that the condition existed and made no reasonable effort to eliminate it." There was no earlier violation so this could not be a repeated one, O'Neil told Gem. He felt this was more than a nonserious violation, since that category indicated no probability of serious injury or death.

O'Neil and Gem then sat down with the OSHA Compliance Manual and found the detailed formulas and factors used in calculating penalties for the violation. They started calculating at a maximum $1000 penalty for each violation (a penalty adjustment up to a maximum of 50 percent is allowed based upon the history of violations in the past, size of the company, and employer good faith). The men calculated that The Firm would receive the maximum 50 percent adjustment so that the penalty for each of the two violations was $500, for a total of $1000.

Had the violation been determined by the two men to be nonserious, the penalty would have been calculated according to a more complicated formula that could provide more reductions than the serious penalty. In addition to the same penalty adjustment as serious violations called for, there would be an adjustment with respect to gravity of violation as well as an abatement credit which would reduce the adjusted penalty up to 50 percent if the violation were corrected by the employer within the stated time period.

The men remembered that a de minimus violation called for no penalty. The willful violation calls for a maximum fine of up to $10,000 for each violation. O'Neil and Gem had never assessed this type of violation and knew that it was very rarely found. This type of violation occurs only where it was clear that an employer permitted the violation intentionally and knowingly or was aware that a hazardous condition existed and made no reasonable attempt to correct it.

The two OSHA officials then had to decide on the abatement period. It was clear that a long complicated program to eliminate the true hazards was not necessary and the two men felt that a period of fifteen (15) days was appropriate.

Gem then had his secretary fill out the citation form, OSHA-2 (Form 14-5). It described the alleged violations and specified conditions of posting. Two copies were sent to the employer along with a booklet of information which included details about the conditions under which the employer can contest the citation, either in an informal discussion with the area director of the U.S. Department of Labor or in a formal appeal to the OSHA Review Commission in Washington, D.C. If neither of these steps is taken the citation is considered a final order of the Review Commission and is not subject to review by any court or agency. An appeal to the OSHA Review Commission must be made within 15 working days and can contest the citation of the violation itself, the penalty assessed, or the abatement period. A contest of the citation by the employer stops the abatement period, which would not begin to run until a final order of the Commission.

FORM 14-5.

U.S. DEPARTMENT OF LABOR
OCCUPATIONAL SAFETY AND HEALTH ADMINISTRATION

CITATION and NOTIFICATION OF PENALTY

¹ ISSUANCE DATE	² OSHA NUMBER
³ REGION	⁴ AREA	⁵ PAGE OF

INSPECTION DATE:

INSPECTION SITE:

TYPE OF VIOLATION·S	CITATION NO

TO:

PENALTIES ARE DUE WITHIN 15 DAYS OF RECEIPT OF THIS NOTIFICATION UNLESS CONTESTED (See enclosed Booklet)

This Section May Be Detached Before Posting

OSHA AREA OFFICE MUST DETACH THIS SECTION BEFORE MAILING OR FILING IN CASE FILE

THE LAW REQUIRES that a copy of this Citation be posted immediately in a prominent place at or near the location of the violation(s) cited below. The Citation must remain posted until the violations cited below have been corrected, or for 3 working days (excluding weekends and Federal holidays) whichever is longer.

This citation describes violations of the Occupational Safety and Health Act of 1970. The penalty(ies) listed below are based on these violations. You must correct the violations referred to in this citation by the dates listed below and pay the penalties proposed, unless within 15 working days (excluding weekends and Federal holidays) from your receipt of this citation and penalty you mail a notice of contest to the U.S. Department of Labor Area Office at the address shown above. (See the enclosed booklet which outlines your responsibilities and courses of action and should be read in conjunction with this form.)

⁶ ITEM NUMBER STANDARD, REGULATION OR SECTION OF THE ACT VIOLATED: DESCRIPTION	⁷ DATE BY WHICH VIOLATION MUST BE CORRECTED	⁸ PENALTY	⁹ NBR INST.	¹⁰ REC	¹¹ MOD

¹² AREA DIRECTOR

NOTICE TO EMPLOYEES — The law gives an employee or his representative the opportunity to object to any abatement date set for a violation if he believes the date to be unreasonable. The contest must be mailed to the U.S. Department of Labor Area Office at the address shown above within 15 working days (excluding weekends and Federal holidays) of the receipt by the employer of this citation and penalty.

EMPLOYER RESPONSIBILITIES AND COURSES OF ACTION — The enclosed booklet outlines employer responsibilities and courses of action and should be read in conjunction with this notification.

EMPLOYER DISCRIMINATION UNLAWFUL — The law prohibits discrimination by an employer against an employee for filing a complaint or for exercising any rights under this Act. An employee who believes that he has been discriminated against may file a complaint no later than 30 days after the discrimination with the U.S. Department of Labor Area Office at the address shown above.

TOTAL PENALTY FOR THIS CITATION
Make check or Money Order Payable To "DOL OSHA" Indicate OSHA No on Remittance

TOTAL PENALTY FOR THIS PAGE

CITATION AND NOTIFICATION OF PENALTY

OSHA 2 REV. 5/76

▲ DETACH HERE

The secretary finished typing up the forms, had them signed by Gem, and sent them off immediately by certified mail to The Firm.

The arrival of the citation at the office of The Firm caused a certain amount of consternation in the offices. Tom Newboy immediately took a copy of OSHA-2 and posted it in a conspicuous place near the site of the fatal accident. Any failure to do so would have incurred the penalties stipulated under the act.

APPEAL

When Newboy returned to his office there was a message asking him to join the meeting the president was having with Leo Lex. Fred Famous was quite upset by the whole thing as he had always felt himself to be very solicitous of the welfare of his men and now looked upon this citation as impugning his good motives in personnel matters. "I don't think we're getting a fair shake on this," said Famous, "what can we do about it?" Leo Lex outlined the entire procedure from beginning to end (Figure 14-2) and pointed out the immediate steps such as discussion with the area director, or the formal appeal to the Occupational Safety and Health Review Commission. Fred Famous was of the opinion that the area director had already made up his mind and that it would be fruitless to have a discussion with him. He asked what the Review Commission was like and what it did.

Lex described the procedure for appeal and identified the composition of the Commission. The OSHA Review Commission is a three-person independent board appointed by the President of the United States to make final determinations on OSHA citations. The Review Commission has the power to "affirm, modify or vacate" the cited violations, penalties, or abatement period orders. Upon appeal, the case is heard by an OSHA Administrative Law Judge in one of nine offices strategically placed throughout the United States. After a hearing on the matter, one of the judges issues a decision. After the decision either the employer or a representative of the employees may request a review by the commission but a review does not take place unless a commissioner requests a full commission review of the judge's decision within thirty days after that decision has taken place. When the commission hears a case, it must issue a majority decision. If no review is requested the decision becomes a final order of the commission after the end of the thirty day period. At this point an appeal is possible to the United States Court of Appeals in the circuit in which the case arises.

"It is my opinion that we should simply accept the abatement period and pay the fine," said Lex.

"This is a strong matter of principle for me and I want you to contest

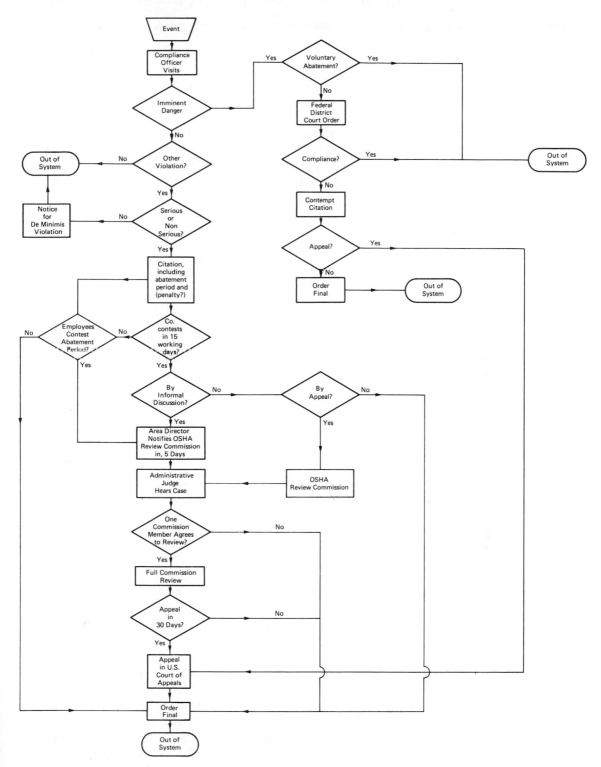

FIGURE 14-2. General Sequence of Events in OSHA Case.

the citation," stormed Fred Famous. Lex then informed him that a copy of the appeal and any supporting documents must be given to the authorized employee representative.

Back in the cypres room the employees gathered around the posted notice and commented in various ways. One of them stated his opinion that the fines for the incident were much too low and insulted the memory of a fine man. There was a suggestion of an appeal by the Union representatives on this matter but Leader informed them that the employees could contest only the matter of the abatement period and not the amount of the fine levied. He further pointed out the fact that the abatement period did not begin to run until the date of the Commission's final order, and he happened to know that there was quite a backlog in these cases. That could mean that the company could have something like six months or more before they were required to institute the changes that would bring the working conditions up to the standards required by the act.

At the direction of Fred Famous, Lex proceeded with the appeal and filed it within the 15-day period required by the statute. Lex also provided a copy of the appeal and all support documents to Leader, the authorized employee representative. This, too, was as mandated by the law. Had he not appealed within the time set, the citation would have become a final order of the Commission and would not have been subject to review.

Two weeks after the appeal was filed a Notice of Hearing was mailed to The Firm. It contained information as to

1. Time, place, and nature of the hearing.
2. The legal authority under which the hearing would be held.
3. Specification of the issues of fact and law.
4. The designation of a hearing examiner appointed under 5 U.S.C. 3105 to preside.

Immediately upon receipt of the notice, Lex began preparing for the hearing.

The case was duly assigned to Mark Sensor, one of the Administrative Law Judges appointed for the specific purpose of hearing appeals from citations under OSHA. The hearing procedure allows for the filing of briefs for the record and presenting evidence, even from the employees' representative. After the hearing Sensor set to work on his decision and issued it within two weeks, a fairly short period in these matters.

No OSHA Commissioner requested a Commission review of the decision within 30 days; the decision, therefore, became a final order of the Commission. Lex told Famous that this was the usual situation as only about 20 percent of the decisions were ever reviewed by the commission. When asked by Famous whether there was any further recourse, Lex noted that the final order of the commission was subject to review by the U.S. Court of Appeals. This review was even rarer as only about 1 percent of the decisions ever went as far as the Court of Appeals. Lex added that when these appeals are carried that far the U.S. Department of Justice argues the government's case.

At this point Fred Famous was willing to accept the advice given him earlier by Lex to accept the stipulations of the citation and pay the fine. He directed Lex and Newboy to proceed with action in conformity with the OSHA final order.

QUESTIONS

Legislation such as OSHA has what may be inevitable consequences in our society. What impact is likely upon the various constituencies involved?

The standards promulgated under OSHA are extensive and specific. What are the advantages of this approach? Disadvantages?

Local OSHA citations become final if no appeal is made within the strict time limit of 15 days. Are there any problems with this? Can you think of ways in which problems, if any, can be overcome?

CASES

(To give the reader more familiarity with the outcomes of the process, the following court decision is being reprinted in its entirety.)

United States Court of Appeals
For the Third Circuit
No. 75-2334
In the Matter of Establishment of:

RESTLAND MEMORIAL PARK
990 Patton Street
Monroeville, Pa. 15146
Restland Memorial Park, Appellant

(D.C. Civil No. 75-1189)

On Appeal From the United States District Court
for the Western District of Pennsylvania
Submitted June 22, 1976
Before: Adams, Hunter and Weis, *Circuit Judges*

Robert E. McKee, Jr., Esq.
Feldstein Bloom Grinberg
Stein & McKee
Pittsburgh, Penna. 15219

Attorneys for Appellant

William J. Kilberg
Solicitor of Labor
Benjamin W. Mintz
Assoc. Solicitor for
Occupational Safety
and Health
Michael H. Levin
Counsel for Appellate
Litigation
Allen H. Feldman
Asst. Counsel for Appellate
Litigation
Sidney M. Nowell
Attorney
U.S. Department of Labor
Washington, D.C.

Counsel for Appellee

OPINION OF THE COURT
(Filed July 30, 1976)

ADAMS, CIRCUIT JUDGE. During the consideration of the bills which ultimately became the Occupational Safety and Health Act of 1970 (OSHA), the intention to make the maximum use of the commerce power was repeatedly expressed by various Congressmen.[1] The Act is by its terms applicable to every "person engaged in business affecting commerce who has employees."[2] In this proceeding, a cemetery company seeks some definition of the scope of the phrase "affecting commerce." The issue is raised by way of an appeal from the district court's denial of a motion to quash a civil search warrant authorizing an inspection of the cemetery's business premises.

I.

Restland Memorial Park, a cemetery, is operated by a corporation whose shares are owned by a husband and wife. These two shareholders and their son comprise three of the four employees of the company. The cemetery is located in Pennsylvania; a very high portion of those buried in it were Pennsylvania residents; its supplies and equipment are purchased from Pennsylvania dealers. The Secretary asserts that the caskets used for the burials in Restland have often been imported into Pennsylvania, that each year several persons who died outside of Pennsylvania are buried there, and that Restland's equipment is operated on public highways.

---

[1] *See* Brennan v. OSHRC, 492 F.2d 1027, 1030 (2d Cir. 1974).
[2] 29 U.S.C. § 652(5) (1970).

The operations of the cemetery require the use of a backhoe, mowing machinery, and two trucks. In view of the safety hazards created by such equipment, principally amputations that result from improperly guarded mowers, the agency has assumed the responsibility of inspecting cemeteries, golf courses, and similar establishments. At Restland, however, OSHA's representative was ordered off the premises. The Secretary then sought, and obtained, an inspection warrant. Despite this, his representative was again refused entry.

Before the Secretary could obtain enforcement of his warrant from the district court, Restland petitioned that court to quash the warrant, contending that the operations of the cemetery do not bring it within the jurisdiction of the agency under the interstate commerce clause and the provisions of the Act. The district court denied the petition to quash the warrant and ordered the officials and employees of the corporation to permit an authorized safety officer to enter the premises and conduct a resonable inspection.

Restland has appealed the decision of the district court. We have jurisdiction under 28 U.S.C. §1291.[3]

II.

Pursuant to his duties under the Act, the Secretary is authorized to enter any place of employment "affecting commerce," and to inspect that place, its structures, and equipment for violations of OSHA standards.[4] *Whether the agency is authorized to enter Restland Memorial Park depends on whether the cemetery is an employer "affecting commerce."* Restland seeks a determination of that issue prior to permitting entry by the Secretary or his representative. This Court, however, is precluded from considering that question at this stage of the proceedings.

The Occupational Safety and Health Act has created a central forum for adjudications in the Occupational Safety and Health Review Commission,[5] which is authorized to pass on all factual and statutory defenses available against the enforcement actions of the Secretary.[6]

---

[3]The present action is independent of, although ancillary to, any enforcement proceeding that may subsequently be pursued under OSHA. The order of the district court refusing to quash the warrant provides "a final and indisputable basis of action as between the [agency] and the [cemetery] . . . ." ICC v. Brimson, 154 U.S. 447, 487 (1894). The matter reverts to the processes of the Department of Labor, and there is nothing further for the district court to do. *See* Cobbledick v. United States, 309 U.S. 323, 329–30 (1940).

[4]29 U.S.C. §657 (a) (1970).

[5]*Id.* §661. See Atlantic & Gulf Stevedores v. OSHRC, No. 75-1584 (3d Cir. March 26, 1976); Frank Irey, Jr., Inc. v. OSHRC, 519 F.2d 1200 (3d Cir. 1974, *aff'd en banc* 1975), *cert. granted*, 44 U.S.L.W. 3531 (U.S. March 22, 1976) (No. 75-749); Budd Co. v. OSHRC, 513 F.2d 201 (3d Cir. 1975) (per curiam); Brennan v. OSHRC (Hanovia Lamp Div.), 502 F.2d 946 (3d Cir. 1974).

[6]29 U.S.C. §§651 (b) (3); 659 (a), (c) (1970).

The Review Commission would appear competent to consider the scope of the Act's coverage. If a citation is issued, and if the employer chooses to contest the citation, the Secretary is obliged to serve a formal complaint setting forth, *inter alia*, the basis for jurisdiction.[7] The Review Commission must then decide whether the agency has exceeded its jurisdiction by attempting to enforce the Act against an employer who does not affect commerce—an employer such as Restland claims to be. The decision of the Commission would then be subject to review by a Court of Appeals.[8]

Where Congress has designated a specific forum for the review of administrative action, that forum is exclusive, and a concerned party must exhaust his administrative remedies prior to seeking relief from the courts.[9] As the Supreme Court explained in Myers v. Bethlehem Shipbuilding Corp., "[N]o one is entitled to judicial relief for a supposed or threatened injury until the prescribed administrative remedy has been exhausted."[10] Give these principles and the structure of the administrative process created by OSHA, this Court has held that the doctrine of exhaustion of administrative remedies applies under that Act.[11]

The doctrine of exhaustion of administrative remedies is well established, and is "required as a matter of preventing premature interference with the agency processes, so that the agency may function efficiently and so that it may have an opportunity to correct its own errors, to afford the parties and the courts the benefit of its experience and expertise, and to compile a record for judicial review."[12] In addition, the doctrine exemplifies judicial recognition of the autonomy of the executive branch, whose dominion the courts will not invade unless the agency has clearly exceeded its jurisdiction.[13]

In the Occupational Safety and Health Act, Congress has delegated to the Secretary of Labor broad jurisdiction under the interstate commerce clause. Because of the policy considerations underlying the doctrine of exhaustion, we conclude that *until Restland has exhausted its administrative remedies, the courts should not consider the question of the Secretary's jurisdiction.* If a citation is issued, appealed from, and then upheld by the Review Commission, Restland may, in its petition for review,

[7]29 C.F.R. § 2200.33 (a) (2) (1) (1975).

[8]29 U.S.C. § 660 (1970).

[9]Whitney Nat'l Bank v. Bank of New Orleans, 379 U.S. 411, 422 (1965). *See* McKart v. United States, 395 U.S. 185, 193-95 (1969); Myers v. Bethlehem Shipbuilding Corp., 303 U.S. 41, 48 (1938).

This is not to say, however, that exhaustion of remedies is required under all circumstances; when not compelled by statute, exhaustion may not be required in every instance. *See* United States ex rel. Sanders v. Arnold, No. 75-1080 (3d Cir. 1976) (Adams, J. dissenting).

[10]303 U.S. at 50-51.

[11]*See* Keystone Roofing & Harold E. Sweeney Corp. v. OSHRC, No. 75-2101 (3d Cir. 1976). *See generally* cases cited in note 5 *supra*.

[12]Weinberger v. Salfi, 422 U.S. 749, 765 (1975).

[13]*McKart*, 395 U.S. at 193-94.

present to this Court the matter of the Secretary's jurisdiction under the interstate commerce clause and the Act.[14]

Accordingly, the judgment of the district court will be vacated, and the proceeding remanded with instructions to dismiss for failure to exhaust administrative remedies.

A True Copy:
Testee:

> *Clerk of the United States Court of Appeals*
> *for the Third Circuit.*

Lake Butler Apparel Co. v. Secretary of Labor
In the United States Court of Appeals for the Fifth Circuit. No. 73-3518(1975)

A compliance officer on a routine inspection found several minor violations for which the employer was not assessed any nonabatement penalties. The employer, a clothing manufacturer employing over 100 sewing machine operators contested the citations on the ground that the provisions were unconstitutional in that they had a "chilling" effect on the right to seek review. The employer further contended that OSHA inspections and constitute illegal searches, violated the Fourth Amendment. Finally, the requirement to post a notice of the citation was alleged to be a violation of the employer's rights to freedom of speech under the First Amendment.

Before Brown, Chief Judge, and Thornberry and Ainsworth, Circuit Judges.

In [Atlas Roofing Co. v. Brennan (5 Cir. 75)] we analyzed and rejected two of the Lake Butler arguments: (i) the due process issue-penalties that become final absent employer initiated review are in violation of due process, citing *Snidach v. Family Finance Corp.,* 1969, 395 U.S. 337, 89 S. Ct. 1820, 23 L.Ed. 2d 349; and (ii) the Sixth Amendment argument-civil penalties under OSHA are essentially criminal in nature invoking the protections of the Sixth Amendment. There remains to be considered Lake Butler's arguments that (iii) the OSHA provisions for nonabatement penalties have the effect of "chilling" the employer's right to seek review; (iv) the Fourth Amendment is violated by the OSHA provisions allowing warrantless administrative searches without probable cause; (v) the authority vested in the Secretary of Labor to assess penalties usurps the powers of the judiciary under Article III. . .

Although we noted the importance of this argument in *Atlas,* we concluded there that the petitioner lacked standing to raise the point because the abatement date was stayed by the Commission and no nonabatement penalties were therefore possible. Unlike Atlas Roofing Company, Lake Butler has not received such a plenary stay. Instead, OSHRECOM ordered only the penalties assessed be stayed. According to Lake Butler, such a selective stay leaves the company vulnerable to a later determination

---

[14]Prior judicial intervention would tend to disrupt a statutory scheme which is designed to provide swift issuance of abatement orders to protect employees endangered by the conditions of their work. *See* 29 U.S.C. § 659 (1970).

by OSHRECOM that the review proceeding was not initiated in "good faith" after which the abatement period could be considered to have retroactively commenced on the date originally specified in the citation. Thus, if such a determination were made, Lake Butler might be assessed a nonabatement per day penalty running retroactively from the original abatement deadline. Although no Court has yet so held, Lake Butler argues that such a possible penalty operates to "chill" the exercise of the employer's right to seek review proceedings. *Lance Roofing Company v. Hodgson,* N.D. Ga., 1972, 343 F. Supp. 685, 689–90, aff'd, 409 U.S. 1070, 93 S. Ct. 679, 34 L.Ed. 2d 659.

However, in order to challenge these specific provisions, Lake Butler must present this Court with a realistic case or controversy. *U.S. Const. Art. III* § 2. We do not judge the hypothetical. To put those statutory provisions at issue Petitioner must show a demonstrable threat of future citations by the Secretary and that an employer would reasonably be dissuaded from invoking the elaborate review procedures of the Act by the possibility of cumulative fines. By our consideration at length of this case the Secretary could not possibly conclude this to be a bad faith appeal. The record contains no indication that the Secretary would intend to exercise these nonabatement sanctions. In any event, the possibility does not exist until after our affirmation of this case. If then the Secretary sought to invoke these retroactive penalties, they would—as we read the statute—be subject to the same administrative proceedings as might any original violation. 29 U.S.C.A. § 666(d). However, if there is any question that these employers would have a right of review in the Court of Appeals over such nonabatement penalties, it certainly is a sanction as to which the APA 5 U.S.C.A. § 704 affords judicial review. We would not hold the provisions unconstitutional "in advance of its immediate adverse effect in the context of a concrete case.". . .

Lake Butler contends that OSHA authorizes warrantless inspections by its compliance officers in violation of the Fourth Amendment. Lake Butler would have this Court void the administrative hearing because the violations were discovered pursuant to an illegal search. In response, the government argues that business enterprises subject to OSHA inspections should fall under the "implied consent" exception to the Fourth Amendment. *United States v. Biswell,* 1972, 406 U.S. 311, 92 S. Ct. 1593, 32 L.Ed. 2d 87. In the past this exception has been limited to businesses the government has had "historically broad authority" to regulate, e.g., the liquor industry, and any attempt to expand the concept must be cautiously analyzed.

But here we need not reach the issue because, looking at the total circumstances of the search, we find that it was purely consensual. In fact, Lake Butler has never contended that the compliance officer did not have the fullest permission of the President of Lake Butler. The OSHA officer, on a routine inspection of plants in the Lake Butler area, presented himself to Stephenson who then accompanied him through the plant. The violations that were discovered during that walking tour-ungrounded machines, lack of color [coding] coating on the fire extinguishers, etc.—where in plain, obvious view. There was no search here of drawers or other sequestered areas. For that reason Lake Butler may not rely on the *Camara/See* precedent. In each of those instances appellants sought to avoid criminal punishment for the assertion of their Fourth Amendment rights. Lake Butler cannot obtain a ruling on constitutionality when it did not assert its rights at the time of the inspection. . .

Lake Butler argues that the provision of OSHA that permits the Commission to assess civil penalties for violation of the Act, 29 U.S.C.A. § 666, usurps the powers of the judiciary under Article III by making the compliance officer "investigator, legislator, factfinder, prosecutor and judge." 29 CFR § § 1903.7 and 1903.14. This argument is closely akin to an argument raised by the appellant in *Atlas*—that the absence of a jury in OSHA proceedings makes it violative of the Seventh Amendment. We reject the argument now for similar reasons.

It has long been recognized that it is well within the powers of Congress to entrust the enforcement of statutory rights to an administrative process and limit the participation of the Courts by the substantial evidence standard. *NLRB v. Jones & Laughlin Steel Corp.;* 1937, 301 U.S. 1, 57 S. Ct. 615, 81 L.Ed. 893. Most recently, the Supreme Court reiterated this in *Curtis v. Loether,* 1974, 415 U.S. 189, 94 S.Ct. 1005, 39 L.Ed. 2d 260. The administrative proceedings under OSHA present no unusual features that would cause us to deviate from this rule. . .

Lastly, Lake Butler argues that the OSHA requirement that the information sign be posted at its clothing factory violates its First Amendment rights to freedom of speech. 29 CFR § 1903.2(a). However, Lake Butler does not cite us to any cases on the issue and we are hard put to find any. The argument is seemingly nonsensical for if the government has a right to promulgate these regulations it seems obvious that they have a right to statutorily require that they be posted in a place that would be obvious to the intended beneficiaries of the statute—Lake Butler's employees. The posting of the notice does not by any stretch of the imagination reflect one way or the other on the views of the employer. It merely states what the law requires. The employer may differ with the wisdom of the law and this requirement even to the point as done here, of challenging its validity. He may as we once said "take his views to a McGahey marked grave." *NLRB v. McGahey,* 5 Cir., 1956, 233 F. 2d 406, 409. But the First Amendment which gives him the full right to contest validity to the bitter end cannot justify his refusal to post a notice Congress thought to be essential.

Affirmed.

FOOTNOTES

[1] 29 CFR 1903.13.

[2] Public Law 91-596 (29 USC 651 et seq., 84 STAT. 1590 et seq.)

[3] 29 CFR 1910.215.

[4] 29 CFR 1910.215.

[5] *Compliance Operations Manual* (Washington, D.C.: U.S. Government Printing Office, (1975).

[6] 29 CFR 1910.215 (b) and (d) (1).

PART V
SUBSTANTIVE LAW

Part V provides a short overview covering major areas of substantive law: contracts, business organizations, commercial transactions, torts, criminal law, and socioeconomic regulation.

CHAPTER 15
CONTRACTS

A contract, in the minds of many people, is identified with a formal written document embodying the legal rights and duties of the parties in an exceedingly complicated transaction. So it may be with many contracts. Yet it is also true that a great many other contracts arise out of such ordinary occurrences as buying a loaf of bread or a pair of shoes, subscribing to a magazine, having a car repaired, renting a garage for that car, or obtaining employment. There may be no writing at all involved in a contract. Some contracts are completed without even spoken words, the parties understanding one another's intentions from their actions.

While the word *contract* refers to a specific legal relationship arising between individuals, it is also used at times to refer to the writing that recites the arrangements or agreement of the parties who have entered into a contractual relationship. It is the legal concept of contract with which this chapter is concerned.

CONTRACT DEFINED

What, then, is a contract? A short, popular definition is that it is an agreement or promise enforceable at law. Perhaps the most frequently used and widely recognized definition is this: "A contract is a promise or a set of promises for the breach of which the law gives a remedy, or the performance of which the law in some way recognizes as a duty." (*Restatement of Contracts §1*)

In other words, the concept of contract is of a legal obligation arising from voluntary agreement or promises made by persons to each other. The agreement of the parties may be privately made, but their promises are recognized and enforceable by the courts. Since it involves promises, a contract relates to what shall or shall not be done in the future. Thus, it may be said that a contract deals with the future, emerges from the promises and agreement of the parties involved, and carries the sanction of law.

THE LAW OF CONTRACTS

The law of contracts is to be found mainly in the common law. An exception exists with regard to contracts for the sale of goods when provisions of the Uniform Commercial Code are paramount. Throughout this chapter, reference will be made to Code provisions in the discussion of those areas in which the Code and the common law differ. A comprehensive act dealing with the law of commercial transactions, the Code, as explained in previous chapters, is a prime example of uniform state legislation. (Louisiana, however, has not adopted Article 2 of the Code—the part that deals with sales.)

ELEMENTS OF A CONTRACT

In order for a valid contract to exist, certain requirements must be met. There must be

1. An offer and an acceptance,
2. Competent parties,
3. True assent,
4. Consideration (as required),
5. Legality of subject matter,

If the contract is to be enforceable, there must also be compliance with the form required by law.

Validity

The absence of one or more of these essential elements may result in an agreement that is null insofar as any contractual relationship is concerned. Such an agreement is termed *void*. On the other hand, a *valid* contract is one that meets all of the requirements of the law and is legally binding upon both parties. In some situations, lack of an essential element may result in a contract that is *voidable*. This means that the contract is valid and enforceable against one of the parties but, because of circumstances, the other party has the right to set aside or withdraw from the contract if he so desires.

The effect of each of these essential elements upon the validity of a contract is considered in the following sections.

AGREEMENT

A contract requires an *agreement*. This is the mutual expression by the parties of their intentions, assent, and willingness to be legally bound. It consists of an *offer* made by one party, referred to as the *offeror*, and an *acceptance* made by the other party, known as the *offeree*. Different means of expression may be used. When the expression of the parties is by word and language, either oral or written, the contract is referred to as *express*. When the parties express their intentions through action or conduct, it is customary to refer to the contract that follows as one *implied in fact*.

Distinction must be made between the terms "contract implied in fact" and "contract implied in law." Contract *implied in law* is the expression used by some persons to refer to a legal obligation created by the law to prevent unjust enrichment of a person who, generally with knowledge, receives and continues to accept benefits conferred upon him by another party, often through mistake. Because it is not based on any voluntary agreement of the parties, it is not a true contract. For that reason, it is also known as a *quasi-contract*.

Offer Defined

An *offer* is a manifestation by the offeror of his desire to enter into a contract with the offeree. It is the promise of the offeror to do or to refrain from doing something in return for some promise, act, or forbearance upon which it is conditioned. In other words, the offeror communicates to the offeree his assent to a certain undertaking or course of action provided the offeree will assent to the same. An offer must be made with the intention of creating a legally binding obligation, or be made in such a manner that a reasonable person would so construe it.

Acceptance Defined

An offer creates in the offeree the power to create a contract by acceptance of the offer. *Acceptance* is the offeree's exercise of that power. It is his manifestation of intent to be bound by the terms of the offer. Acceptance is the offeree's act, forbearance, or promise as requested in the offer and his assent to the offer. This must be made in the manner and method indicated in the offer and by the party to whom the offer was made.

Many offers require acceptance by a promise. When both offer and acceptance are promises—one promise being made in exchange for another promise—the contract is referred to as *bilateral*. A *unilateral* contract exists when only one party makes a promise. In that case, acceptance of the offer is usually by some action.

OFFER

One requirement of an offer is that it be made with the intention of creating a legal obligation. Therefore, statements made in jest, in the heat of excitement, or for the purpose of creating social rather than legal obligations do not constitute offers. Distinction must also be made between an offer and statements made prior to and leading up to an offer, often referred to as *preliminary negotiations*. The latter term refers to those communications made prior to the expression that creates a power of acceptance. In common parlance, preliminary negotiations are known as "bargaining," "dickering," or "haggling."

Invitation to do Business

A mere statement of plans or intention about the future, such as "I am going to sell this book for $15," does not constitute an offer. Advertisements—whether they be carried by newspaper, magazine, radio, or television—are generally not considered to be offers. Instead, they are invitations to do business with the advertiser. This is also true of catalogues, brochures, billboards, price lists, circulars, price quotations, invitations to submit a bid, and displays of merchandise containing a price tag. However, any of these can be turned into an offer by a positive statement consisting of a promise and indicating the action the other party must take to accept. It is also possible, in these situations, for an offer to arise because customs of the trade or prior course of dealings are such that both parties know the intent to create the power to accept exists.

Definiteness

An offer must be definite. Vagueness or uncertainty with regard to essential matters will prevent a contract from arising. The reason is that the courts would be unable to determine exactly what it is that should be enforced. Omission of minor details or immaterial matters will not affect the validity of an offer. The definiteness required is such specificity that, when the offer is combined with the acceptance, it will be possible to determine with reasonable certainty the nature and extent of the obligations of the parties. The Uniform Commercial Code provides that a contract for the sale of goods will not fail for indefiniteness even though one or more terms are left open if the parties intended to make a contract and there is a reasonably certain basis for giving an appropriate remedy (UCC 2-204).

Communication

An offer must be communicated to the offeree. In fact, it is not effective until that communication takes place. An offeree cannot accept an offer about which he does not know. Because of this, problems sometimes arise in connection with offers of a reward for the return of lost property or the arrest of a criminal. These are offers for a unilateral contract. Acceptance of these offers is by performance of an act. Most states provide that a person who learns of a reward only after he has effected the return of the property or the arrest of the criminal cannot collect the reward.

Termination

The power of acceptance created by an offer remains in effect either until acceptance takes place or until the offer is terminated. An offer may be terminated by

1. Lapse of time,
2. Revocation by the offeror,
3. Rejection by the offeree,
4. Counteroffer,
5. Death or disability of either party,
6. Destruction of subject matter,
7. Operation of law.

Barring prior acceptance, an offer remains open for the time period stated in the offer. When the offer does not indicate how long it will remain open, the offer terminates after lapse of a reasonable length of time. What constitutes a reasonable time depends upon the surrounding facts and circumstances. The nature of the subject matter involved, the prevailing market conditions, and the means of communication used by the offeror are examples of factors that are relevant in determining what is a reasonable time. For instance, a reasonable time for the existence of an offer for the sale of land is generally deemed to be greater than that for the sale of a crop of newly harvested vegetables subject to quick spoilage. So, too, when the parties are negotiating in the presence of each other, a response to an offer is ordinarily expected at once.

Option

A promise by an offeror to keep an offer open for a specified time is ordinarily not binding upon the offeror unless he has been furnished consideration for so doing. When there is consideration, there is a contract to keep the offer open for a definite period of time. This is referred to as an *option*. While it thus binds the offeror, an option imposes no duty upon an offeree to accept the offer. The Uniform Commercial Code creates an exception to the option rule in connection with the sale of goods. There, a merchant's signed and written offer to hold an offer open is binding upon him, even in the absence of consideration, for the time stated or for a reasonable time, but not in excess of three months (UCC 2-205).

Withdrawal Estopped

There is a trend by courts to recognize exceptions to the general rule that an offeror may withdraw his offer at any time prior to acceptance. One occurs when an offeree justifiably relies upon an offer to the extent that he changes his position because of it and the offeror either knows or should have known this. This situation is referred to as *detrimental reliance*. It results in the offeror's being estopped from revoking his offer. To be *estopped* means that, because of his prior action or failure to act, one is prevented by law from stating or denying a fact. Another exception applies to offers for a unilateral contract in which the offeree has performed some substantial act toward acceptance. An increasing number of courts hold that the offeror is thereby estopped from revocation until a reasonable period of time has been provided the offeree in which to complete performance.

Revocation

Revocation of an offer is effective when it is communicated to the offeree. This communication may be made directly by the offeror or it may be in the form of an indirect notice from a third person. It may consist of reliable information supplied to the offeree to the effect that the offeror has changed his position in such a manner that he can no longer perform according to the promise contained in his offer. This could occur when a third person informs an offeree that property which had been offered for sale to him has been purchased from the offeror by another person. An offer made to the general public is effectively revoked when the revocation is made in substantially the same manner as the offer was made. The effectiveness of such a revocation is not lost because a person who knows of the offer does not hear of the revocation.

Rejection

An offer is terminated when it is rejected by the offeree. Termination occurs when the offeror receives notice of rejection. No specific method of communication is required for this. Rejection should be distinguished from an offeree's solicitation of additional information from the offeror regarding the terms of the offer. Such inquiries by the offeree do not terminate the offer.

Counteroffer

An offeree who responds to an offer by changing the terms of the offer or by conditioning acceptance upon a change in the terms of the offer has made a *counteroffer*. This causes the original offer to terminate. A counteroffer is a substitute offer as well as a rejection of the original offer. The original offeree now becomes the offeror. A counteroffer can result in a binding contract if it is accepted by the original offeror, who has now become the offeree.

UCC Provisions

With regard to contracts for the sale of goods, the Uniform Commercial Code is more flexible regarding a change of terms in an acceptance. The code provides in Section 2-207 as follows:

(1) A definite and seasonable expression of acceptance or a written confirmation which is sent within a reasonable time operates as an acceptance even though it states terms additional to or different from those offered or agreed upon, unless acceptance is expressly made conditional on assent to the additional or different terms.

(2) The additional terms are to be construed as proposals for addition to the contract. Between merchants such terms become part of the contract unless:

(a) the offer expressly limits acceptance to the terms of the offer;

(b) they materially alter it; or

(c) notification of objection to them has already been given or is given within a reasonable time after notice of them is received.

Termination for Other Reasons

Death or insanity of either the offeror or offeree automatically terminates an offer. Termination also occurs when the subject matter of an offer is destroyed prior to acceptance, provided this was not caused by either party. For instance, an offer to sell a specific car is terminated when that car is destroyed by an earthquake prior to acceptance.

An offer can also be terminated by operation of law, as when the promise contained in an offer becomes illegal after the offer has been made. This would be true in the case of an offer to sell a particular substance when a law prohibiting the sale of that substance was enacted after the offer had been made but had not yet been accepted.

ACCEPTANCE

Ordinarily, an offeree is under no legal obligation to accept an offer. As a general rule, acceptance requires a manifestation of assent. It cannot be forced upon the offeree because of his silence or inaction. Exceptions may exist as a result of prior course of dealings or usage of the trade.

Method of Acceptance

Generally, an offer may be accepted at any time prior to its revocation or rejection. Acceptance is possible only by the offeree. Offers made to the public may be accepted by any member of that public. Acceptance must take place in the manner and within the time constraints required by the offer. Ordinarily, no acceptance takes place when it is attempted in a manner at variance with the requirements of the offer. In that case there is, instead, a counteroffer. Some offers contain a suggested rather than a required mode of acceptance. Failure to follow a mere suggestion does not preclude acceptance. It results only in delaying the time of acceptance until its receipt by the offeror. When the offer does not mention any specific manner of acceptance, any means reasonable under the circumstances may be used. In the absence of extenuating circumstances, use of the same method as was followed in making the offer is considered to be reasonable.

Time of Acceptance

When the means of transmitting an acceptance is either

1. that which is required by the terms of the offer, or

2. in the absence of any suggestion in the offer regarding method of accepting, the same as was followed in making the offer,

then acceptance takes place at the time the acceptance message is given to the transmitting agency for delivery to the offeror. For instance, when the offer was either made by mail or requires acceptance by mail, the acceptance takes place at the time a correctly addressed and stamped letter of acceptance is placed in the mail. (This is commonly known as the *Mail Box rule*.) A contract exists from that moment, even if the letter of acceptance is never received by the offeror. The latter can always protect himself from such a contingency by stating in the offer that acceptance will not take place until received. When the offer was either made by telegram or requires acceptance in that manner, the acceptance takes place at the time the message is delivered to the telegraph company for transmission. Acceptance by telephone takes place when the offeree speaks the words constituting an acceptance. In the case of an offer for a unilateral contract in which performance of a certain action is required for acceptance, a contract ordinarily does not come into existence until completion of the necessary act.

The time and place of a contract are those of the acceptance, unless the parties specify otherwise. In the absence of agreement by the parties to the contrary, a contract is binding from the time it comes into being, even though the parties intend to put their agreement into writing later. In situations in which a contract is in existence but the legal obligations of the parties have not yet been fulfilled, the contract is referred to as *executory*. Once those obligations have been fulfilled, it is an *executed* contract.

COMPETENT PARTIES

A valid contract requires two legally competent parties. A person cannot contract with himself. The parties to a contract need not be natural persons. A corporation or a partnership may be one of the parties to a contract. A party may also consist of a number of persons. The parties to a contract are presumed to be legally competent to enter into a contract in the absence of proof to the contrary.

Protected Classes

For purposes of their own protection, certain kinds of persons who are recognized as having the legal capacity to enter into a contract have the right to avoid a contract if they so wish. In other words, their contracts are voidable by them. Unless the right to avoid the contract is exercised by those persons, the contract is considered to be valid. In all cases, the legally competent party to the contract is bound and cannot escape his legal obligations because he has contracted with a person who is within one of the protected classes. Those classes include minors or infants, persons of unsound mind, and intoxicated persons.

Minors or Infants

A *minor* or an *infant* is a person who has not yet reached the age of legal majority. In most of the states, that age is 18. A few states, still following the common law tradition, consider an individual to be a minor until he has reached age 21.

With certain exceptions, the contracts of a minor are voidable by him. In the absence of state statute to the contrary, this is true even if the infant has intentionally misrepresented his age. In that case, however, the other party may avail himself of the remedies for fraud or misrepresentation.

Disaffirmance by Minor

An infant avoids a contract by expressly indicating his desire to *disaffirm*; that is, to withdraw from the contract. He will also be considered to have disaffirmed when his actions are inconsistent with continued recognition of the contract as valid. For instance, an infant who, having an executory contract to sell his bicycle to B, delivers the same bicycle to P and accepts payment for it, has by his actions indicated disaffirmance of the contract with B. Disaffirmance by a minor must occur either during his infancy or within a reasonable time after he has reached his majority. What constitutes a reasonable time depends upon the circumstances. There is one type of contract, that affecting the title to real property, which an infant cannot avoid until he reaches his majority.

When a minor avoids a contract, he must return to the other party all property, monies, or other consideration that he received under the contract. However, his right to disaffirm is not lost if he no longer has all of what he received or if it is in damaged condition. In such situations, he need return only what he does have and return it in its present condition. Generally, this is all that is required of him. However, in some states (and there appears to be a trend in this direction) he must return the other party to the condition of *status quo ante*; that is, the position of that party prior to the making of the contract.

A minor who avoids a contract can generally recover all of that with which he has parted or its value in money. Recovery of property is possible, even if it has been transferred to a third party. An exception to this occurs, however, when the contract disaffirmed was for the sale of goods. The Uniform Commercial Code provides that a good faith purchaser for value (the third party) acquires a good title from a seller with a voidable title (party with whom the infant contracted) (UCC 2-403).

Necessaries

Contracts entered into by an infant for necessaries are treated differently. A minor is legally obligated for the reasonable value of necessaries supplied to him. Note that he is not liable for the contract price but, instead, for the reasonable value of necessaries and then only for those which have actually been furnished to him. The reason is that this obligation does not arise out of contract but is of a quasi-contractual nature. It has been imposed by the law so that persons who supply necessaries to minors will be paid for them. Were it not for this requirement, the great reluctance of many persons to contract with infants would make it extremely difficult for minors to secure the necessaries of life.

What constitutes a necessary depends upon the infant's status in life. Food, clothing, and shelter, which are not otherwise provided for him, are normally deemed to be necessaries. In some cases, a college education or a car that provides transportation to and from his place of employment have been considered to be necessaries. Determination of what are necessaries is based upon the minor's socioeconomic condition and what is reasonably needed for his maintenance.

Parents are ordinarily not responsible for contracts entered into by their minor children. An exception occurs when the infant is acting as the agent of the parent. In that case the contract is that of the parent and not the infant. A parent who has neglected to provide for his children as required by law is liable for necessaries furnished to his children.

Protection of Adult Party

In some cases, the party with whom a minor is dealing refuses to enter into a contract unless the infant secures a person of legal age to act as a cosigner. When that occurs, the cosigner becomes legally obligated and bound by the contract as his own even if the minor avoids the contract.

By statute in some states, an infant cannot avoid certain contracts. Examples are contracts approved by a court, or those made by a minor while operating his own business.

Ratification at Majority

Once he reaches the age of legal majority, an individual may expressly ratify the contracts he made during his infancy. Such ratification—frequently in written form—is required in some states. Actions consistent with ratification, such as performance of his part of the contract or acceptance of performance by the other party, are viewed as evidence of an intention to ratify.

Insane Persons

As a general rule, contracts made by a person while he is insane are voidable by him. In cases in which a person has been adjudged insane, a guardian is appointed by the court to handle the individual's business affairs. In that situation, the insane person's contracts are void.

In order for his contracts to be voidable, a person must be so impaired mentally that he neither understands that he is entering into a contract nor the consequences of what he is doing. For that reason, contracts made by an insane person during lucid intervals are valid.

Sane persons, who neither know nor can reasonably be expected to know the mental condition of an insane person with whom they contract, have a right to be returned to the status quo ante if the contract is avoided. On the other hand, when a sane person enters into a contract with an individual whom he either knows or should know to be insane, return to the status quo ante is not required.

Persons who regain their full sanity have the option of either ratifying or disaffirming the contracts they made while insane.

Other Incompetent Parties

Contracts entered into by persons who are so intoxicated that they do not know they are entering into a contract are treated the same as those of insane persons. Upon reaching sobriety, the individual may disaffirm or ratify contracts made while intoxicated.

In some states, the capacity of persons in a drugged condition to enter into valid contracts is limited. At times, there may exist restrictions on the rights of aliens and prisoners to contract. Today there has been a change from the old common law under which a married woman could not contract.

TRUE ASSENT

A contract arises from an agreement to which there has been mutual assent by two competent parties. Sometimes, however, the assent of the parties is not real or genuine. This may occur because there has been mistake, fraud, misrepresentation, duress, or undue influence. Each of these will have an effect upon the enforceability of the agreement.

Mistake

A mistake exists when one or both of the parties believe that a material matter relating to the past or present is true when it actually is not. A mistake is *unilateral* when only one of the parties is in error; it is *mutual* or *bilateral* when both parties are. A matter is *material* when it is of such importance or significance to the transaction that a party would not have entered into the contract had he known the truth.

Different kinds of mistakes may occur in connection with a contract. There may be

1. A unilateral or bilateral mistake;
2. A mistake of fact or a mistake of law;
3. A mistake in preparation of the written document evidencing the contract; a mistake as to expectations; or a mistake of judgment.

The kind of mistake will determine the effect it has upon the agreement.

Effect of Unilateral or Bilateral Mistake of Fact

As a general rule, a unilateral mistake as to a material fact does not affect the validity of the contract. However, if one party either knows or should have known of the other party's erroneous belief, the mistaken party may rescind the contract. To *rescind* is to cancel or avoid, placing the parties in a position of status quo ante. *Rescission*, which is the act of rescinding, must take place within a reasonable time, otherwise the right is forfeited. It is in this way that the law prevents one party from taking advantage of the other's mistaken belief to the detriment of the latter. However, relief is generally not available when the mistake results from an individual's own negligence, as when a party either fails to read or carelessly reads a document and later alleges he did not realize or understand what it was that he signed.

On the other hand, bilateral mistake as to a material fact generally results in a void agreement. Examples of the kinds of mutual mistakes of fact which make an agreement void are: error as to the existence of the subject matter of the contract, as to the identity of the subject matter, or as to the possibility of performance.

Effect of Mistakes of Law

Mistakes of law generally will not affect enforceability of an agreement. This is in keeping with the old adage that ignorance of the law is no excuse. However, some states treat mutual mistakes of law as they do those of fact.

Effect of Other Kinds of Mistakes

Sometimes mistakes in drafting occur when the parties prepare a written document with the intention that it shall recite their agreement. The result is a writing which does not conform with the actual agreement. In that case, a court will reform the document so that it does express the intention of the parties. However, if the language in the document is ambiguous and the parties reasonably and honestly place different interpretations upon the language, the agreement is void. No reformation is available in such situations, since the courts will not make a contract for the parties.

Errors in judgment or as to expectations normally have no effect upon the validity of a contract and do not, therefore, form a basis for relief. The courts will not relieve a party of his contractual obligations merely because he has made a "bad deal" or a "bad bargain," or because he exercised poor business judgment.

Fraud and Misrepresentation

Mistake is sometimes induced by the representations of one of the parties to the contract. A false representation as to a present or past material fact upon which the other party to the contract justifiably relies is known as a *misrepresentation* when it is made innocently, without intention to deceive. If the falsehood is made deliberately or with reckless disregard for the truth and with the intention of having the other party rely upon it, there is *fraud*. The difference between fraud and misrepresentation, therefore, lies in whether the false statement was unintentional or deliberate.

Both fraud and misrepresentation require that the falsehood be about a present or past material fact. Predictions about the future are not considered to be statements of fact. Mere expressions of opinion do not form the basis for either fraud or misrepresentation.

Relief Available for Fraud or Misrepresentation

Relief is available to a party who is injured when he justifiably relies upon misrepresentation or fraudulent statement. There is no justifiable reliance if the injured party has either knowledge or opportunity equal to that of the misrepresenting party to learn the truth. In the case of either fraud or misrepresentation, the injured party may rescind the contract. He must, however, do so within a reasonable time. If there is fraud, the injured party may keep the contract and seek damages in a tort action for fraud or deceit. Compensatory damages are available and, in some instances, punitive damages may also be awarded. *Compensatory damages* are those that make reparation to an individual for injury he has suffered; *punitive damages* are in addition to what is necessary for compensation and are imposed as a form of punishment because of the intentional nature of the wrongdoing. The Uniform Commercial Code provides that both rescission and an action for damages are available to the party injured by fraud in connection with contracts for the sale of goods (UCC 2-721). In the case of other contracts, the individual ordinarily must make a choice of which remedy he wishes to pursue.

Concealment of Information

Does the concealment of information constitute fraud? In the absence of specific questions, a party is generally not required to volunteer information he possesses even though it be material. However, there is a discernible trend toward requiring a seller to volunteer to a buyer material facts regarding which a buyer would not be likely to inquire. In such cases, concealment constitutes fraud. When parties are in a fiduciary relationship, there is a duty to reveal matters that are to the other party's material interest. Failure to do so is fraud. Fraudulent concealment may also occur when important matter is placed in extremely fine print or under misleading headings on written documents with the expectation and intention that the other party will not read it.

Duress and Undue Influence

When a contract is the result of coercion, whether it be physical or mental, there is no real assent of the parties to the agreement. Therefore, contracts made under duress or undue influence are voidable by the innocent party.

When there is threat or serious injury, either to the person himself or to close relatives, when a threat is sufficient to overcome the free will of a reasonable person, and when the threat is made by an individual whom a reasonable person would believe has the ability to carry out the threat, there is *duress*. In other words, duress is the wrongful use of force or threat of force with the intention of causing a person to do what he otherwise would not do. Duress obviously destroys the voluntariness of contract.

Threat or physical force is not the only form of duress. Threat of criminal prosecution, withholding of goods to compel payment of exorbitant sums, and treat of a civil suit which would bring financial ruin may, in some cases, constitute duress. Ordinarily, threat of economic loss is not considered to be duress.

Undue influence arises out of a confidential relationship in which a person in a dominant position takes advantage of the relationship by exerting wrongful pressure upon the other party to enter into a contract for the unjust benefit of the dominating party. Parent and child or attorney and client are illustrative of the forms of confidential relationship in which undue influence may develop. Frequently the situation is one in which a relative or friend of long standing takes advantage of another in a weaker position. In order for undue influence to exist, there must be more than mere persuasion. The person in the weaker position must be deprived of his free will and coerced into a contract which provides unusual or unjust benefit to the dominant party.

Relief for Duress or Undue Influence

Relief is available when by wrongful means a person has been coerced into an unjust or unconscionable contract. In the case of duress, the injured party may either rescind the contract or may seek damages for any amount over a reasonable sum which he has been forced to pay. Where undue influence can be shown, the contract is voidable by the injured party.

CONSIDERATION

Unenforceable Promises

One example of a promise which is rarely enforceable at law is a promise to make a gift. A gift is something rendered voluntarily, with no expectation of return or compensation. Lack of consideration is its very essence, and consideration is necessary if the promise is to rise to the status of a contract. While an executory promise which is not supported by consideration will not be enforced, lack of consideration will not cause an executed gift to be rescinded.

Consideration Defined

Consideration has been defined as the "bargained for exchange." It has also been described as a legal benefit which the promisor exacts and receives for his promise, and a legal detriment to the promisee. By *legal benefit* is meant something to which the party is not already entitled under the law. A *legal detriment* may consist either of giving up a legal right or of assuming a legal obligation, one that the individual is not already bound to perform. In most contract situations, each of the parties receives a legal benefit and suffers a legal detriment. One example is the exchange that takes place in a sale.

Forbearance

Consideration is usually in the form of money or some type of property. It may also take the form of services, conduct, or forbearance. *Forbearance* consists of abstaining from action, such as when one promises not to bring a law suit. When a person has cause to bring legal action to enforce a valid claim, forbearance to sue constitutes consideration when it is given in return for a promise. On the other hand, forbearance to sue on a fictitious claim cannot be consideration since there is no legal right which is being given up. Nor can forbearance—or anything else, for that matter—be consideration when it is not given in exchange for a promise.

Moral Consideration

Moral consideration is that which is given because of a moral obligation or out of love, affection, or friendship. An example is the promise of a child to care for his aged parents. Moral consideration is ordinarily unacceptable as consideration to support a contract.

Past Consideration

The same is true of *past consideration*, which consists of that which has already been performed. Thus, valuable services rendered by an employee to an employer over the past forty years cannot serve as consideration to support a promise to pay $100 when that promise is made by the employer at the time of the employee's retirement. The forty years of service is past; it was not bargained to be performed in exchange for the $100. If the payment of $100 at retirement had been part of the agreement entered into at the time the employee was hired, the forty years of service would have been bargained for in exchange for it plus any other agreed-upon consideration. Or, had the employee promised to retire early in exchange for the $100, then there would be valid consideration and an enforceable contract would exist.

Pre-Existing Obligations

So, too, a promise to pay a pre-existing debt to the person to whom it is owed at the time, place, and in the amount owed is not valid consideration. Since that promise represents something which the party is already legally bound to do, he will suffer no legal detriment. Nor will the creditor receive anything to which he does not already have a legal right; therefore, there is no legal benefit to him. Other examples of obligations which are pre-existing and therefore cannot be consideration are: to obey the law, to fulfill the duties of one's office or job, to carry out the promises of an existing contract. For example, it sometimes happens in connection with construction contracts that unexpected difficulty is encountered. A contractor may find rock when excavating where rock was not anticipated or may learn that there has been an increase in the price of building materials. A promise by the other party to pay the contractor an additional sum of money to complete the contract as originally agreed would not be supported by consideration and would, therefore, be unenforceable.

Modification of Existing Contracts

Modification of an already existing contract results in the creation of a new legal duty, a duty that did not previously exist. If not supported by consideration, a promise to fulfill that new duty is a promise of a gift and, consequently, unenforceable. However, a promise to pay a contractor an additional sum if he will do something he is not already required to do under an existing contract is enforceable. So, too, is the promise of a creditor to accept a sum smaller than the amount owed to him in return for the promise of the debtor to pay prior to the due date or in a place different than originally promised. It should be noted that the general rule requiring that modification of a contract be supported by consideration is not applicable in the case of contracts for the sale of goods. The Uniform Commercial Code provides that modification of those contracts needs no consideration to be binding (UCC 2-209).

Illusory, Requirements, and Output Agreements

Promises that lack valid consideration include those that are *illusory*. An example would be my promise to buy your car for $4000 if I should ever decide to buy a car. That promise creates no obligation and therefore cannot be consideration. However, requirements contracts and output contracts are enforceable. An agreement to purchase from a particular supplier all of the oil one needs to run his factory for a year is an example of a *requirements contract*, while an agreement to purchase all of the wool produced by a certain manufacturer during one month is an example of an *output contract*. These contracts are not considered to be illusory in spite of the fact that the quantity or amount involved may be uncertain at the time promises are exchanged.

Charitable Contributions

For reasons of public policy, promises or pledges to contribute to recognized charities are generally enforceable. In some states, however, the promise does not become enforceable until the charity has incurred obligations in reliance upon the subscription. This is an example of *detrimental reliance*. It can result in enforcement of an agreement even though reliance of the party was not the bargained-for-exchange. When the promisee acts to his detriment in reliance upon the promise of the other party, when such reliance is reasonable and foreseeable under the circumstances, the promisor may be prevented from asserting lack of consideration as a defense to avoid carrying out his promise. Known as *promissory estoppel*, this doctrine is applied by the courts to avoid the injustice that would result were the promisor not required to fulfill his promise.

Adequacy of Consideration

Adequacy of consideration is not a requirement. The bargained for exchange need not be equal. However, when a great discrepancy in values occurs and is combined with other circumstances that might give rise to an unconscionable transaction or is combined with evidence of fraud or duress, the courts may make inquiry into the matter of adequacy. When identical matter—such as money—is exchanged, equality is required. If consideration of a nominal sum (such as $1) is recited in a written document merely for the sake of giving the appearance of consideration, that will not be considered as valid consideration to support the contract.

Consideration may be furnished by a third party, such as when a wife promises to pay a merchant for a coat purchased by her husband.

Composition of Creditors

The settlement of debts sometimes poses problems of consideration. *Liquidated debts* are those that are fixed or settled. In connection with them, it may happen that a debtor who owes several creditors is hard pressed financially. When two or more (although not necessarily all) of those creditors agree to accept a pro-rata portion of what is owed in full satisfaction of their accounts, there is a *composition of creditors.* Such arrangements are legally enforceable, the consideration for such agreements being the mutual promises of the creditors.

Accord and Satisfaction

When an honest dispute exists as to whether there is a debt at all or as to the amount of the debt, the debt is referred to as *unliquidated.* Often the parties in such situations are able to work out a settlement to their mutual satisfaction. That kind of compromise is referred to as an *accord and satisfaction.* Consideration is recognized as existing in such an arrangement, since each of the parties has foregone his right to bring legal action concerning the alleged debt.

UCC Provisions

In some states, a seal may act as a substitute for consideration, a practice originating in the common law. In the majority of states, however, the seal no longer has that effect. Provisions of the Uniform Commercial Code make the seal inoperative in contracts for the sale or offers to buy or sell goods (UCC 2-203). The Code also provides that consideration is not required in contracts for the sale of goods for the following:

1. An agreement to modify an existing contract (UCC 2-209);
2. A written discharge of a claim for alleged breach of contract (UCC 1-107);
3. A merchant's firm offer in writing (UCC 2-205).

Whether the Code's flexibility and latitude with respect to consideration will be applied in the case of other contracts remains to be seen.

ILLEGALITY

The law condemns the making and performing of agreements that are illegal. Examples are agreements to commit a crime or a tort, agreements which are prohibited by statute, agreements which are opposed to public policy.

Effect of Illegality

Ordinarily, illegal agreements are void and will not be enforced by the courts. In fact, the courts will usually do nothing to assist either party to an illegal agreement. Instead, a court will leave the parties where it finds them. Neither party will be aided, either to enforce the illegal promise or to get back that which he gave as part of the agreement. The underlying theory is that such inaction will serve as a deterrent to illegal agreements. An exception occurs when the effect of refusing assistance would be to defeat the very purpose for making the transaction illegal. In such cases, relief may be granted.

Wagering or Gambling Agreements

In most states, gambling, wagering, betting, raffles, and lotteries are prohibited by statute. If a prize is awarded by lot or chance and either a purchase or the payment of money is required to participate, there is a *lottery*. Sales promotions which meet these criteria are lotteries. Some states by statute make legal state-run lotteries and certain kinds of race track betting.

Insurance

Contracts for insurance are not wagers when the insured has an insurable interest in the life or property covered by the policy. An *insurable interest* means that it is to the insured's benefit that the particular risk which is insured against not occur, since having it take place would cause him financial or other personal loss. A wager or bet involves creation of a risk which did not exist previously for the purpose of bearing that risk, but insurance involves shifting of the burden of a risk which did have prior existence. It is that which differentiates the two.

Transactions in the Stock Market and Future Goods

Regular stock market transactions or dealings in the commodities exchange are not illegal. However, wagers based on changes in price on either the stock or commodity markets are illegal. A contract for the sale of goods which presently do not exist but which will exist and be delivered in the future is not illegal.

Usury

Statutes in most states stipulate a maximum rate of interest which may be charged by a money lender for the use of money. Charging a higher rate than that permitted by law is *usury*. In most states, a higher maximum rate is applicable in the case of small consumer loans. Provisions differ regarding service charges and fees for late payment. Usury laws are not violated when the *interest is discounted*; that is, deducted in advance so that the amount received by the borrower is the face amount of the loan minus the interest. State provisions also differ regarding the effect of usury upon an agreement. In some, the agreement is void. In others, only the lawful rate of interest is payable and recoverable. In still others, the lender can recover no interest at all.

State statutes generally provide that installment sales are not loans. Therefore, the usury laws are not applicable to finance charges on an installment purchase. (See Chapter 20.)

Illegal Discrimination

The Fourteenth Amendment to the United States Constitution provides that no state can deny to any person within its jurisdiction the equal protection of the laws. This provision is contained in what is known as the *equal protection clause*. Agreements that deprive persons of their rights under that clause or that are in contravention of equal opportunity or civil rights acts will not be enforced by the courts. (See Chapter 20.)

Licensing of Trades and Professions

Many businesses, professions, and trades are regulated by statute. A frequent provision requires that an individual obtain a license before engaging in such professional activity. When the purpose of the licensing requirement is to protect the public by requiring proof of skill and character of persons before a license is obtained, the statute is considered to be *regulatory*. Where such statutes exist, the agreements of unlicensed persons to perform services are illegal and void. However, a distinction must be made between regulatory statutes and those which require a license for the purpose of revenue raising. Generally, if the statute provides that a license may be issued to anyone upon payment of the fee, without regard to evidence of skill and character, it will be considered to be for the purpose of *revenue raising*. In that case, the agreement of an unlicensed person to perform services is generally valid.

Sunday Contracts

Many state statutes prohibit the transaction of certain types of business on Sundays. Provisions of the statutes are far from being uniform. Some make an agreement void if it is made or performed on a Sunday, while others make void only agreements that are completed on a Sunday. In some states, the sale of merchandise other than necessaries is prohibited on Sundays. There is a growing tendency to dispense with restrictions on Sunday sales.

Restraint of Trade

Agreements that are in unreasonable restraint of trade are illegal. Examples include agreements made for the purpose of creating a monopoly and those made among competitors to fix prices, to divide territories, or to restrain production. (See Chapter 20.)

Reasonable restrictions for the protection of valid interests are, in some cases, permitted. An example is the contract for the sale of a business where the seller agrees not to compete with the buyer of the business. Another common situation is that of an employment contract in which an employee agrees not to compete with his employer. In both cases, these "no compete" provisions are just part of a larger agreement and are ancillary to it. Provided the time and geographic restrictions are reasonable and the restraint is no greater than necessary for the reasonable protection of the other party, the courts will generally enforce such provisions. When the restraint is not considered to be reasonable or necessary by the court, that much of the restraint which is reasonable will usually be enforced. An agreement not to compete, in and of itself and not as part of another agreement, is illegal.

Agreements Against Public Policy

Some contracts are illegal because they are against public policy. Actions that endanger the welfare of society or that offend the standards of conduct generally accepted by the community as a whole are considered to be contrary to public policy. As social conditions and values change, so too do concepts of what is good for the public welfare. That is not to say, however, that there currently exists no generally accepted view as to the kinds of agreements that are contrary to public policy. Agreements in that group include the following:

1. Agreements that obstruct justice,
2. Agreements that cause neglect of duty,
3. Agreements that, although legal in themselves, lead to accomplishment of an illegal purpose by one or both of the parties.
4. Agreements that are unconscionable.

Obstruction of Justice

Agreements made for the purpose of adversely affecting or interfering with the proper administration of justice are illegal. Examples include agreements to commit perjury or to secure another person to do so, to conceal evidence of a crime, to give consideration or to use influence in order to prevent prosecution of a person accused of crime, to use one's influence to secure appointment of a judge to a higher court in return for his rendering a decision in favor of a particular party in a legal dispute.

Corruption of Public Officials

Agreements that tend to corrupt a public official, to use personal influence or other improper means to induce a public official to act in one's favor, or to offer a bribe to a public official are illegal. A distinction must be made between making known one's thoughts about desirable legislation to a legislator—a right guaranteed in a democracy—and offering a legislator favors, either personal or pecuniary, in order to influence his action. The latter is illegal, whether done by an individual, a corporation or other form of organization, or a person hired for the express purpose of doing so.

Neglect of Duty

It is equally illegal to cause a person who has a private duty to neglect that duty. Persons in this group include those who are under an obligation to act on another's behalf, such as agents, trustees, or corporate officers or directors. Examples of illegal agreements would be agreement to pay a corporate director to vote for the employment of another person as an officer of the corporation at a specified salary, or payment to a newspaper editor for running editorials in support of a particular candidate for office.

The legality of agreements in which one party promises to exempt the other from liability for negligence depends upon the surrounding circumstances. If the parties are of relatively equal bargaining power, if the transaction is free from duress and undue influence, if the parties fully understand the agreement, and if the interests involved are purely the private ones of the parties involved, the agreement to relieve one party of nonwillful negligence can be legal. However, the transaction will be against public policy and therefore illegal if the duty is one owed to the public, such as in the case of a common carrier's responsibility for the safety of passengers, or when there is great disparity of bargaining power, as in the case of an employer and employee.

Agreement to Accomplish Illegal Purpose

A contract that, in and of itself, would be perfectly legal may become illegal if it is made to accomplish an illegal purpose. Under normal circumstances, the leasing of a dock would be legal. When its use is sought for the purpose of smuggling, however, the lease can become illegal. So, too, the sale of a gun may be legal. It obviously becomes illegal when the sale is knowingly made for the express purpose of committing a crime, such as providing a gun for use in killing another person.

It frequently happens that one of the parties to a contract is ignorant of any unlawful purpose. If he has no such knowledge and does not participate in accomplishment of the illegal act, the courts usually hold that he may bring suit against the other party to enforce the contract provisions. However, if he knows of the unlawful purpose at the time the agreement is made, the entire agreement is illegal (and therefore unenforceable) when the wrongful act involves commission of a serious crime.

When an illegal agreement has been rescinded prior to execution, the courts permit recovery of any consideration that has been paid. When an agreement is *divisible* (that is, its provisions include a number of promises for which there is corresponding consideration) and when one part is legal and the other illegal, the courts will generally enforce the legal aspect while holding the other part to be void. When there is a matter of serious moral turpitude, however, the entire agreement will be considered void. When the agreement is indivisible and partly illegal, the entire agreement is void.

Unconscionable Agreements

Agreements that are so grossly unfair to one of the parties as to be oppressive may be said to be unconscionable and this may be the basis for relief by the courts. When a contract has been reduced to a writing which consists of a standard form prepared by a party with greater bargaining and economic power and when the other party has little or no opportunity to go elsewhere or to deal with others in order to satisfy his needs, the contract may be classified as one of *adhesion* and may be set aside because of unconscionability if greatly oppressive provisions are imposed upon the weaker party. In the case of contracts for the sale of goods, the Uniform Commercial Code specifically provides that the courts may refuse to enforce unconscionable contracts (UCC 2-302).

FORM REQUIRED BY LAW

In order to be enforceable, certain kinds of contracts must ordinarily be evidenced by a writing. This requirement arises from the Statutes of Frauds, which have been adopted by the various states. The purpose of these statutes is to prevent fraud and perjury in the proof of contracts. Although statutory provisions vary from state to state, those types of contracts usually required to be in writing are discussed here.

Contracts that, by their nature, cannot be performed within one year of the date the contract came into being. The decisive question is whether performance is possible within one year. Thus, when the contract is to extend for some indefinite time, such as for a person's lifetime or "for as long as necessary" the statute is not applicable. In the majority of states, when one party to a bilateral contract has completed performance within a year, the contract is taken out of the statute even though the other party cannot complete his performance within a year.

A collateral or secondary promise made to a creditor to pay or guarantee payment of the debt or obligation of another person should the latter default. Distinction must be made between contracts that are primarily for the benefit of the promisor (these are not required to be in writing) and those in which the promise to pay the debt is ancillary to that of the primary or original contract (these must be written under the statute). Furthermore, the promise must be made to the creditor rather than to the debtor. For example: rich Uncle Joe promises Tom Haberdasher that if Tom will extend credit to Nephew George, Uncle Joe will pay for the clothes George buys if George cannot pay for them. Note that Uncle Joe's promise is ancillary to George's contract to buy clothes. Furthermore, Uncle Joe's promise is not for his own benefit, but for that of George. In addition, Uncle Joe made his promise directly to Tom, not to George. That being the case, Uncle Joe's promise will not be enforceable against him unless it is in writing.

So, too, the promise of the executor or administrator of a decedent's estate to pay the debts of the deceased from the personal funds of the executor or administrator, as distinguished from funds of the estate, must be in writing to be enforceable.

Contracts for the transfer of an interest in real property. This includes contracts to sell or to mortgage real estate and those granting easements or leases. In most states, special statutory provisions deal with the writing requirements for the leasing or rental of real property.

Miscellaneous requirements. In some states, promises made in consideration of marriage must be in writing. There may be other writing requirements provided by specific statute. A common example is the need for a written policy in connection with insurance contracts.

UCC Provisions

The Uniform Commercial Code provides that contracts for the sale of goods must be evidenced by a writing when the price is $500 or more, except for the following times:

1. When there has been payment for the goods;
2. When there has been receipt and acceptance of the goods by the buyer;
3. When the goods are to be specially manufactured and are not fit for sale to others, and the seller has made a substantial beginning toward their manufacture or a substantial commitment to the procurement of the necessary raw materials for their manufacture,
4. When existence of a contract is admitted in judicial proceedings (UCC 2-201).

Kind of Writing Required

Requirements concerning the kind of writing necessary under the various statutes vary. Most states provide that a note or memorandum is sufficient. This may consist of several writings. It may be in the form of letters, receipts, telegrams, or a formal contract. Except for contracts for the sale of goods, the writing must contain all of the material terms of the contract: normally, the names of the parties, a description of the subject matter, the price or other consideration, and the terms of payment.

The writing must be signed by the party sought to be charged (or an agent of that party). Absent statutory provision to the contrary, the signature may be at any place on the writing. It need not consist of a fully signed name but may take the form of initials. It may be typewritten or stamped. The signature requirement may be satisfied by a mark or symbol.

In the case of contracts for the sale of goods, the Uniform Commercial Code provides that the writing requirement is satisfied if the writing indicates that a contract of sale has been entered into between the parties. However, enforceability is limited to the quantity of goods stated in the writing (UCC 2-201).

Failure to Execute a Writing

Failure to execute the necessary writing is a defense to an action brought either to enforce the contract or to seek damages for failure to perform. Part performance may take the contract out of the statute.

Furthermore, reliance on an oral promise may give rise to promissory estoppel and may prevent assertion of failure to meet statutory requirements as a defense. When recovery on the contract is not permitted, a party who has performed in reliance on an oral promise may recover the value conferred on the basis of quasi-contract.

INTERPRETATION OF A WRITING

To ask a court to enforce a contract is to request that it effectuate the intentions of the parties. However, the language, words, and other manifestations of the intent of the parties to a contract are not always clear and unambiguous. Therefore, before a court can enforce a contract, it must first determine what the intentions of the parties are. This process is referred to as *interpretation* of contracts. Over the centuries, the courts have evolved some principles or standards for such interpretation and these are discussed below.

The transaction is viewed as a whole. This is especially important when the contract consists of several writings, or some writing supplemented by oral statements. If the entire agreement has been reduced to one writing, that document is viewed from all four corners. Only in this way can the main purpose of the contract be determined.

Conduct of the parties after execution of the written document is considered. Action of the parties is often revealing of the meaning they place upon the manifestation of their intentions. Repeated conduct over a period of time by the parties may estop either or both of them from alleging a meaning inconsistent with such conduct.

The contract is construed strictly against the party preparing the written document, especially when the drafter of the contract is one skilled in preparation of such agreements. This is often the case with insurance policies.

In the absence of circumstances indicating a contrary intention, the following apply:

(a) the ordinary or plain meaning of a word or words is preferred;

(b) technical terms are given their technical meaning;

(c) usage of a trade, profession, locality or community will be followed in the contracts of members of such groups. When one of the parties is a member of such a group but the other party is not, special usage or meaning of terms will not be followed unless the nonmember either does or can reasonably be expected to know and intend the special meaning.

When a term is missing in a contract, the court will first determine if the silence was intentional. If it was not, custom and prior practice will be referred to in order to determine the missing term. Oral evidence may be admitted to supply missing terms in accordance with provisions of the parol evidence rule.

When several interpretations are possible, a contract will be construed to be legal as opposed to illegal; and as avoiding injustice, undue hardship, or unfairness to one or both of the parties.

In case of inconsistencies, typewritten words will be considered to prevail over printed words; written, over typewritten; words, over figures.

The law of the forum will determine the conflicts of law rules that are applicable. In some contracts, the parties indicate within the written document which state's law will be controlling. Such a provision is enforceable under the Uniform Commercial Code provided the state named "bears a reasonable relation" to the transaction (UCC 1-105).

Generally, interpretation is by the judge when a writing is certain and unambiguous. However, when parol evidence must be introduced to explain or clarify what is ambiguous or indefinite, then it is for the jury to determine the intentions of the parties.

Parol Evidence Rule

When the parties have incorporated their intentions in a writing or writings and have come to regard such writing as the final expression of their intentions, then it may not be contradicted by evidence of any prior or contemporaneous oral agreement; in other words, by other expressions that have taken place in connection with that transaction. The intentions of the parties are deemed to be incorporated entirely within the four corners of the writing. Oral evidence may be introduced, however, to explain or clarify the writing. This is known as the *Parol Evidence Rule.*

RIGHTS OF THIRD PARTIES

Third-Party Beneficiaries

In some situations, persons other than the parties to the contract may derive some benefit from it. These are known as *third-party beneficiary* contracts. In fact, the parties may expressly provide by terms of the contract for benefits to others.

When the benefit is a gift to the third person, he is known as the *donee beneficiary*. A common example is life insurance, whereby the insurer agrees in consideration for premiums paid by the insured to pay the face amount of the policy to a named beneficiary upon the death of the insured. A donee beneficiary has the right to bring suit on the contract. In fact, the promisee also has a right of action and can recover nominal damages.

In other instances, the benefit to the third party is for the purpose of satisfying a legal obligation owed to that person. In that situation, the third party is known as a *creditor beneficiary*. For instance: A sells to B in return for which B promises to pay A's debt to C. A's purpose in securing B's promise is to confer a benefit upon his creditor, C. C is the creditor beneficiary. As such, he can proceed against either A or B if B does not perform.

A third type of beneficiary is created when a third party obtains a benefit from a contract which was entered into for the benefit of the two contracting parties and without intention to benefit a third person. Such a person is known as an *incidental beneficiary*. Incidental beneficiaries are often created as a result of contracts entered into by government bodies. An example would be in the case of a municipality's contract with a paver for improvement of a street. Persons owning property along that street receive the benefit of the improvements resulting from the contract. An incidental beneficiary has no rights under the contract.

A third party beneficiary acquires only those rights that are granted by the terms of the contract, and he is limited to its terms.

Assignment

In the case of some contracts, it may be necessary or desirable to transfer either the rights or duties arising out of the contract. The law permits such transfers when the contract is not personal in nature. Such a transfer is known as an *assignment*.

A contract may, by its terms, contain prohibitions against assignment. Some prohibitions are expressed as conditions which make a contract void. Others are only promises not to assign. In some states, the courts consider a nonassignment clause to be contrary to public policy. As a general rule, the courts tend to construe in favor of assignability when several interpretations of the clause are possible.

The person making a transfer under a contract is known as the *assignor*. The person to whom the transfer is made is known as the *assignee*. Except when there is agreement to the contrary, an assignor remains bound by the legal obligations imposed upon him by the original contract. He must perform if the obligor does not. So, too, the rights acquired by an assignee are no greater than those the assignor had under the original contract. An assignee may bring legal action in his own name, as a general rule.

Ordinarily, a person can transfer his rights to receive the payment of money or goods under a contract. The securing of another person to perform one's duties under a contract is referred to as a *delegation of duties*. Delegation is permitted if the work to be performed is such that it does not require special skill, training, ability, or personal characteristics.

For that reason contracts for personal services, such as those for employment, are not assignable. Duties that are routine or standardized may be delegated.

An assignment generally requires no special form. It may be oral or written, except for those cases in which, by statutory provision, a specific written form must be executed. One situation in which this frequently occurs is the assignment of wages.

Although notice may not be required for an assignment to be effective or valid, notice does provide protection to the assignee. An obligor who does not know of the assignment will have discharged his contractual obligation by performing for the assignor according to the original terms of the contract. Once notified of an assignment, however, the obligor is legally bound to perform for the assignee.

An assignor who receives payment after an assignment has been made holds the payment as trustee for the assignee and is legally obligated to him for that amount.

When successive assignments of the same rights are made to two different and good faith assignees, the first assignee will prevail over any others according to the American rule. Courts that follow the English rule permit the assignee who first gives notice of the assignment to prevail. An assignor who makes successive assignments of the same right is liable to those assignees who acquire no rights as a result.

An assignor makes an implied warranty to the assignee that he has made a valid assignment, that the contractual obligation has neither been discharged nor rendered unenforceable prior to assignment, that he has transferred good title, and that he will do nothing to defeat the value of the assignment. If a written instrument is involved, he warrants that it is genuine and is in all respects what it purports to be. The parties may by agreement either limit or enlarge these warranties.

UCC Provisions

In the case of contracts for the sale of goods, the Uniform Commercial Code provides that such contracts may be assigned unless the parties otherwise agree and except when the assignment would materially change the performance of the other party. Furthermore, an assignment of "the contract" is an assignment of rights. Unless the language or circumstances indicate the contrary, it is a delegation of performance of the duties of the assignor and its acceptance by the assignee constitutes a promise by him to perform those duties. The Code also provides that unless the circumstances indicate the contrary, a prohibition of assignment of "the contract" is to be construed as barring only the delegation to the assignee of the assignor's performance (UCC 2-210).

CONTRACT TERMINATION

The bringing to an end or termination of the legal duties which represent the contractual obligations of the parties is referred to as a *discharge*. Discharge may occur as a result of

1. *Performance*; that is, carrying out the promises made. This is the usual method of discharge and, when done satisfactorily, gives rise to no cause of action.

2. Failure of a condition to occur. Ordinarily, this discharges the parties of their obligation but does not give rise to a cause of action.

3. *Breach*; that is, failure of one or both of the parties to fulfill their contractual obligations. This gives rise to a cause of action.

4. *Rescission* or mutual agreement by the parties to cancel or revoke their contract. When rescission is by mutual agreement, there is no cause of action.

Performance: Effect of Conditions

Discharge by *performance* occurs when both parties have satisfied their contractual obligations in accordance with the terms of the agreement. Although the duty to perform is created by and exists from the creation of the contract, the time when performance is required may be conditioned upon the occurrence of a future event. Such a provision in the contract is known as a *condition precedent*. An example is a fire insurance policy, in which the condition precedent to performance is the occurrence of a fire. Note that failure of the condition to occur results in no obligation to perform. When the parties agree that they may be relieved of the duty to perform by some future occurrence, there is a *condition subsequent*. Again, fire insurance provides a good illustration. A frequent policy provision is that no action may be brought against the company unless notice of the fire is given within one year after the loss occurs. Failure to do so within that time would, therefore, be a condition subsequent and would relieve the company of the duty to perform.

It can be seen that the term *condition* in a contract refers to some event or fact, other than just the lapse of time, upon which the obligation to perform depends. In some contracts, conditions may be *concurrent*. For instance, the promise to pay may be conditioned on the tender of goods by the seller, and the buyer's promise to deliver may be conditioned upon the tender to pay. *Tender* is a word meaning an offer to perform. Performance by both parties must occur at the same time when conditions are concurrent.

Conditions may be implied, either in fact or by law. More frequently, they are expressed. Often the clue to their existence is provided by wording such as the following: "condition," "provided that," "as soon as," "after," and "when." The existence of a condition is a matter of contract interpretation. In many contracts, the promises made by the parties are independent. Thus, the duty to perform exists without any conditions being attached to it.

The parties can agree that an event will be both a promise and a condition. A promise creates a legal duty. It is both an intention and an assurance regarding performance in the future. A condition is a fact or event. It is neither an expression of intention nor an assurance, but rather a factor modifying performance. A promise is made for the purpose of creating a duty. The purpose of a condition is to postpone a duty. Failure to perform a promise gives rise to cause of action for breach of contract. Nonoccurrence of a condition discharges the contractual obligation and gives rise neither to breach of contract nor to a cause of action.

Discharge by Performance

Performance may be either satisfactory or substantial. When the parties fulfill the obligations they have promised to undertake, performance is complete. It is *satisfactory* when performance is made as promised. This would be true in the case of payment in full for goods purchased or delivery of goods which meet the specifications required by the order.

Some contracts require that the legal duty be performed to the satisfaction of particular individuals. For instance, construction contracts frequently condition payment upon production of an architect's or an engineer's certificate. Production of the certificate is the criterion by which satisfactory quality of performance is determined. The courts will uphold it as a condition precedent to payment, unless the contractor can show that the certificate is being withheld dishonestly or for reasons that indicate lack of good faith.

In some contracts, the agreement is that performance must be to *personal satisfaction*. An example is a contract for the painting of a portrait, in which personal taste is the measure for determining whether the purchaser will find performance to be satisfactory. In such cases, the courts will require that the individual named be satisfied with the performance, except when dishonesty or lack of good faith on that person's part can be shown. However, if the contract involves performance of a job, the quality of which can be measured in a more objective way, for example, in the paving of a road, the courts will consider performance to be satisfactory if a reasonable person would be satisfied with what has been done. A justifiable expectation in such contracts is that performance be in a "good and workmanlike manner."

When performance unintentionally results in slight deviations from the agreement, when the finished job is of a quality only slightly below that of satisfactory performance, there is said to be *substantial performance*. If improvement is neither possible nor made to bring the performance up to a state where it can be considered to be satisfactory, the courts will ordinarily require payment of the contract price less a sum for damages in an amount to compensate for the defective condition.

Breach of Contract

When a promisor either fails to perform or performs with major deviations from his promise, there is *breach of contract* and a cause of action is created. A material breach gives the injured party the right either to reject the tendered performance or to accept it and recover damages. There will be no breach, however, if a party acts in such a manner as to prevent performance. A party has an obligation to cooperate with the other party, so that the latter can carry out his promise under the contract. For instance, a property owner who has entered into an agreement for improvements to his property is expected to cooperate with the contractor by permitting the entry of workers upon the premises as is necessary to make the improvements. If the party's actions cause delay or make performance more expensive, as distinguished from preventing performance, there is no discharge but the injured party is entitled to damages.

Impossibility of Performance

A party may be excused from performance of his promise because of impossibility. If the subject matter is destroyed through no fault of either party, the party's obligations cease. For instance, in a contract for the sale of the original copy of the Declaration of Independence, performance would be excused if the original were destroyed by an accidental fire. So, too, the contract of employment of a major league baseball pitcher terminates if he is killed in an automobile accident.

A contract may end with a change in the law subsequent to creation of the contract and prior to its execution. For instance, a contract for the employment of a 16-year-old student to serve as a part-time driver would be terminated should a law be passed raising the minimum age for driving to 18.

UCC Provisions

Provisions of the Uniform Commercial Code make possible release of contractual obligations because of "impracticability," a more liberal provision than the impossibility required for release under common law.

Hence, in contracts for the sale of goods, the duty to perform may be ended because of the occurrence of a contingency, the nonoccurrence of which was assumed when the contract was made (UCC 2-615). This might be in the nature of a raw material shortage due to war, embargo, unforeseen shutdown of major sources of supply, or major crop failure, which result in marked increases in cost or prevent the securing of supplies.

No such relief is possible when the contract does not come under the Code. The fact that performance will cost more money, can be made only with great inconvenience, or will result in a loss does not excuse performance under the common law. For instance, a contractor who finds that his construction in process has been destroyed overnight because of a hurricane must start all over again from the beginning at his own expense, absent a saving clause in the contract. Many modern courts recognize "commercial frustration" as a valid basis for termination of contractual duties, such frustration occurring when unforeseen developments result in greatly increased costs or extreme difficulty of performance.

Mutual Rescission and Waiver

Mutual agreement of parties to rescind or revoke a contract is valid, since the consideration of each party to such an agreement is the giving up of a legal right under the contract. Not only may the parties mutually agree to cancel or rescind, but one party may voluntarily forego certain of his rights under the contract. Thus, acceptance of incomplete or defective performance without objection is a waiver of the right to strict and satisfactory performance. However, a party cannot first waive his rights and then later bring an action because of failure to receive those same rights. When defective performance occurs, a party's failure to give notice of the defect can sustain a reasonable belief that there has been a waiver and he may be estopped later from asserting any rights. A party may accept a defective performance but reserve his right to seek damages. Such would be the case when a party is in urgent and immediate need of a good. He may accept delivery of material of lower quality than ordered because of that need yet still wish to reserve the right to seek damages. A reservation of right may be oral, but it is preferably written.

When the parties agree to rescind an existing contract and enter into a new one which modifies or changes terms of the original contract, the first contract is said to be discharged by *substitution*. The substituted contract must, of course, meet all the requirements for a valid contract including the presence of consideration. When the new contract results from release of a party to the original contract from his obligation to perform and substitutes another person to take his place, the second contract is referred to as a *novation*.

UCC Provisions

In the case of contracts for the sale of goods, the Uniform Commercial Code provides in Section 1-107 that "any claim or right arising out of an alleged breach can be discharged in whole or in part without consideration by a written waiver or renunciation signed and delivered by the aggrieved party." The Code also provides that when contracts for the sale of goods call for successive performances but are of indefinite duration, reasonable notification must be given for termination except on the happening of an agreed-upon event (UCC 2-309).

REMEDIES FOR BREACH OF CONTRACT

An injured party who seeks a remedy because of breach of contract must take action within the applicable Statute of Limitations. The time period for this under the Uniform Commercial Code is normally four years after the cause of action accrues (UCC 2-725). In the case of other contracts, the allowable time varies from state to state. A common provision is six years for simple contracts, and 21 years for contracts under seal.

In some instances, a party may declare prior to the time for performance that he does not intend to perform when the time for him to do so comes. When he does so declare, the injured party may take one of three courses of action.

1. He may ignore the declaration and insist on performance according to the contract;

2. He may accept the delcaration as an anticipatory breach and sue for damages; or

3. He may accept the declaration as a breach of contract and rescind. Furthermore, he may take either of these actions as soon as he learns of the other party's intention not to perform. For instance, this may occur when he learns that the specific goods or property to be sold to him under the contract has been sold to a third person.

In the case of breach of contract, the remedy at law is for damages. The injured party has a duty to *mitigate damages*. That means he must prevent an increase in damages and cannot act in a manner that would result in their becoming any greater. Nor can he make a profit from the breach. The purpose of damages is to place him in the same position he would have occupied had the contract been satisfactorily performed. Damages are of several kinds: compensatory, consequential, punitive, nominal, liquidated, and unliquidated.

As noted previously, *compensatory damages* refer to the sum necessary to make up for the actual loss incurred as a result of the breach. It is the amount the injured party is out as a result of nonperformance. In the case of the sale of property, it is frequently computed as the difference between contract price and market price, calculated so as to enable the injured party to replace the goods through another source of supply.

Consequential damages are those that do not arise directly from the breach but from unusual circumstances attendant the contract. For instance, in a contract to provide air conditioning service for a retailer for whom a faulty mechanism caused an interruption of service, consequential damages resulted when a customer of the store fell and was injured because the defective mechanism leaked, resulting in a slippery surface when water spilled onto the floor.

Punitive damages, also known as *exemplary damages*, are generally not recoverable in a contract situation. An exception occurs when there has been wanton, reckless, and irresponsible action. *Nominal damages* are those for a token amount, such as one dollar, and are awarded if there is no reasonable certainty as to the occurrence of a loss. Such an award would be based upon mere speculation. A person, however, may recover for losses that would be sustained in the future if he can prove such losses will occur.

Liquidated damages refer to those which are stated in the contract as due to be paid in case of breach or default. Courts are reluctant to enforce such provisions unless it can be shown that the amount specified is not excessive, that it is reasonable and proportional to the presumed loss, that the contract is such that it would be difficult either to prove damages or that damages anticipated are uncertain, and that the parties intended to liquidate damages in advance. Liquidated damage provisions that require payment of an unreasonable sum or a sum not related to the possible damages to be incurred are looked upon as a penalty and are considered by most courts to be void. When the liquidated damage provisions of a contract are not enforced, compensatory damages will be awarded upon sufficient proof.

When damages are inadequate as a remedy, equitable relief is possible in the form of specific performance. Generally, this is sought when the injured party seeks to have a contract for the sale of realty enforced or seeks enforcement of a contract for the sale of goods that are unique or unusual. Another equitable remedy is an injuction. Frequently this is sought when artists or athletes of great prominence threaten to breach a contract of employment by performing for a third party. An injunction enjoins employment of their talents for any but the party to the original contract.

UCC Provisions

In the case of contracts for the sale of goods, the Uniform Commercial Code provides that the remedies available under the Code are to be liberally administered so that the injured party is put in "as good a position as if the other party had fully performed." Neither consequential nor punitive damages are available unless specifically provided for in the Code (UCC 1-106).

Other specific remedies are detailed in the Code. Since discussion of these is more appropriate in connection with treatment of the law of sales, it has been included in Chapter 17 rather than in this chapter.

CHAPTER 16
BUSINESS ORGANIZATIONS

The entities that operate in a business setting can be structured in several different ways, but only three basic types need to be considered in any detail.

1. Sole proprietorship,
2. Partnership,
3. Corporation.

Most common is the sole proprietorship, a business unit organized, owned, and conducted by one person. Partnerships involve two or more persons working in a close relationship. Corporations are relatively recent creations composed of many persons in a legal entity that has certain rights and corresponding duties. In terms of size of operations and impact, the corporation is by far the most significant of the three types.

Each form of ownership of a business has its advantages and disadvantages. A sole proprietorship is easy to organize and manage since it is a one-person operation. That gives the proprietor greater freedom to operate and the fact that profits are not shared with anyone else provides motivation. Because one person is the decision maker, however, a great deal of burden falls upon the sole proprietor in that one individual cannot provide more than a limited amount of managerial skill to the ongoing business. Taxes are apt to be lower than in a corporation, but the proprietor is responsible personally for all activities and debts.

A partnership is a business entered into by two or more persons. The partners agree as to the sharing of responsibilities and benefits as well as more specific details of location, length, division of profits, managerial duties of each, and the dissolution procedures to be followed. Partnerships are like sole proprietorships in the ease of establishment, operation and dissolution. They are free of much governmental regulation and are not subject to federal income tax as a unit since only the partners are liable to taxation as individuals. Partnerships are superior to sole proprietorships in that more capital is usually available, managerial talent is apt to be broader in scope, and motivation may be higher in employees, since they may have a chance to participate in the future as partners in the firm.

The form of organization under which most business activity takes place today is the corporation. The corporation is an entity that is considered by the law as a "person" with many of the rights of a natural being. A corporation is formed by individuals (or other corporations) who apply for a charter from a state in order to begin business. Individuals invest money in the enterprise and receive shares of stock as evidence of their ownership. These shareholders, the owners of the company, meet and transact business in a yearly meeting and elect directors to develop policies for action and select executive officers to manage the enterprise. All this is under the charter of incorporation and according to the bylaws developed for the corporation under the laws of the state granting the charter.

There are many different ways corporations may be classified. A basic functional breakdown is

1. Corporations for profit,
2. Corporations not for profit,
3. Public or quasi-public corporations.

Profit corporations distribute earnings as dividends to their stockholders; *not for profit* corporations are charitable or service organizations. Both of the above are usually (but not always) *private* corporations, that is, they are owned by the individual stockholders. Public corporations are operated by a government body. Other designations are further descriptive of some corporations. *Open* corporations have stock that anyone may purchase, and *closed* corporations have stock held by a limited number of individuals. *Domestic* corporations are called that by the state in which they were incorporated; *foreign* corporations are those of another state while *alien* corporations are those chartered in a foreign country. These classifications depend upon either the purpose for which they are to exist or the circumstances under which they were formed.

A corporation provides many advantages over the sole proprietorship or partnership form of organization. Because it is a legal entity or a "person" under the law it has many of the rights that real persons do, including the right to sue. Usually because more people are involved, the corporation has an easier task of raising capital, either from lending institutions or because it can issue stock to other individuals who then become owners, with limited liability, of a share of the corporation. The increased size and financial ability also makes the corporation better able to employ managers and specialists for the many jobs required in the company. The extension of the corporation beyond the abilities and the lifetimes of a few individuals is perhaps the greatest of the advantages of the corporation over the other forms.

There are some disadvantages, however. Because the corporation is a legal person it must first be recognized as such by the state in which it will exist, that is, it must be chartered. The cost in getting organized in this way can be high. Control by government agencies means a further expense as reports and fees continue. Taxes, overall, are apt to be greater as the corporation pays taxes and the shareholders pay taxes on the earnings that are declared as dividends to them.

Other forms of organization are not widely used or, at times, are treated as one of the three major types. An *unincorporated association* is a loose organization for the furtherance of a common nonprofit purpose. It has no legal existence apart from its members and therefore has none of the advantages of a corporation. A *cooperative* is an unincorporated association unless special state statutes give it a status resembling that of a corporation. A *business trust* (or *Massachusetts trust*) exists when owners of property transfer ownership of it to trustees to be managed for the benefit of the original owners. Most courts follow the basic law of trusts in determining rights and duties of the parties. A *syndicate* is an association formed to conduct business. It can become incorporated, but, if not, the association will be regarded as a partnership with most of the elements of partnership law controlling.

PROPRIETORSHIP AND AGENCY

The legal constraints of a sole proprietorship are very much like those facing an individual in everyday activity as well as business. About the only additional feature that must be faced is the necessity, in most jurisdictions, to register the name of the business with the state and local authorities. Anything other than just the name of the proprietor is considered to be a fictitious name. "The John Smith Company" would be required to register. In addition, the proprietorship would be responsible to apply for any health or other permits required by the local municipality or county.

In the course of business, the proprietor usually hires someone to work for him within the company or an outside party may also act for the benefit of the proprietor from time to time. Both the employer-employee and the proprietor-outside party (principal and agent) relationships are covered by the area of law called *agency*. In this relationship one person agrees to act for the benefit of another (or in some circumstances, seems to act for another) and the law regards the relationship to be governed by the law of agency.

The principles of agency are important in a discussion of the functioning of a proprietorship but it must be emphasized that the principles of agency apply as well to partnerships, corporations, and other forms of organizations. What is stated here will generally apply to the further discussions of partnerships and corporations below.

Types of Agency

Agency relationships are basically of two types

1. Employer-employee,
2. Principal-agent.

The employer-employee relationship is sometimes called a master-servant one. The employer ordinarily has physical control over the employee during hours of employment. The principal-agent relationship also involves control of conduct of the agent by the principal but the activity of each with third parties is that determined by law rather than an employment relationship. An employee can be an agent for his employer, the principal. There are also agents, sometimes professional ones like brokers or lawyers, that operate independently but under some control of the principal for whom a task is performed. There may also be work done by an independent contractor with no specific control by the principal. An agent can also be a *general* agent who can act for the principal in many ways or a *special* agent whose authority is limited to the performance of a specific action. Acts of agents are those of the principal when the principal consents to setting up the relationship. There may be an agency relationship under certain circumstances, however, even when neither the principal nor agent intended it. Why this last statement is so can be explained under the concepts of authority and ratification.

Authority and Ratification

The agent is given authority to act for the principal, either through conduct of the principal or words to that effect. The authority of the agent is either

1. Express,
2. Implied, or
3. Apparent.

Express authority is explicitly stated in spoken or written words. *Implied* authority is the extension of express authority to cover those acts reasonably called for to carry out the assignment made under the express authority. *Apparent* authority arises when a third party might reasonably conclude that an agent has authority because a principal has acted in such a way as to give indication of authority vested in the agent.

Ratification is an act of a person accepting the actions of another who purportedly functioned as an agent though in fact was not authorized. The entire process is retroactive to the time when the "agent" acted but the person who ratifies must have been in a position whereby he could have authorized the original move when it was performed. The "principal" must ratify all of the transaction, not just part, and rights of third parties cannot be adversely affected.

Principal-Agent Relationship

The activity that binds the agent and the principal usually calls for a close relationship requiring responsibilities and providing rights on both sides.

Duties of principal

The principal is required to compensate the agent for the performance of his duties. Usually such compensation is specified in an agreement between them, but, if not, a reasonable payment is deemed to be forthcoming.

Liability of the principal

Torts of an agent in employment make a principal liable for them if the torts are committed in the course of performance of duties and within the scope of employment. Liability of the principal/employer is absolute and does not depend upon authority of the agent/employee or fault of the employer. If there is a departure from duty or abandonment of employment then any tort committed by the departing employee is not attributable to the employer.

In a few other instances liability for torts will not normally be imputed to the employer. The acts of a professional agent are not ordinarily attributable to the employer since the professional agent is, in his acts, considered to be an independent contractor. In the tort of deceit, the principal may escape liability if the agent made fraudulent misrepresentations despite clear instructions by the principal to the contrary. If the principal ratifies those acts, then he will of course be held liable. An injured party can sue both principal and agent, jointly and severally.

Extent of authority

An agent has no authority to either pledge his principal's credit or to sign or endorse the principal's name to a negotiable instrument. Such action can only occur through express authority or because the nature of the activity is such that it is absolutely necessary for the agent to do so.

If the agent is authorized to appoint subagents, the principal is liable for the acts of those subagents that are within the scope of authority of the original agent. The agent can delegate to the subagent only those duties that do not involve discretionary decision making; the agent may not delegate authority to a subagent if the agent's selection was based upon his skill and discretion, that is, abilities that are important in the agent's activities.

Agent and Third Persons

An agent acting within the scope of his authority from a disclosed principal is not liable in a contract to third parties unless he elects to make himself a party to the contract by an express agreement. If the principal is undisclosed or partially disclosed, the agent becomes a party to the contract, except that in the case of a partially disclosed principal, the third party can agree that the agent escapes liability and the principal can be identified. The agent will be liable on a negotiable instrument if the name of the principal does not appear on the instrument. If a person purports to act as an agent for another, that person is liable unless the third party agrees to the contrary. When the agent is liable, however, he does have all the defenses that would ordinarily have been available under the contract. There will be no liability of the agent of a principal who does not have the capacity to contract unless he hides or misrepresents the status of the principal.

If an agent has no authority but acts as if he had, then the purported agent will be held liable to the third party with whom he deals. If the third party is justified in relying on the misrepresentation and suffers damages while thus relying on the misrepresentations, the purported agent escapes liability only if the third party knew or had reason to know of the misrepresentation or if the purported principal would not have been bound had he been in existence.

Principals and Third Parties

Many of the agency conclusions relating to legal relationships between principals and other parties arise from questions as to the awareness of the third persons of the existence of a principal rather than assuming that they are dealing only with the agent. When a principal is disclosed there is seldom a problem; when a principal is not disclosed or partially disclosed, there are varying possibilities in the legal outcomes.

The following conditions are the descriptions of the relationships:

1. *Disclosed principal*—the third person knows of the existence of the agency and the identity of the principal.

2. *Partially disclosed principal*—the third person knows of the agency but does not know the identity of the principal.

3. *Undisclosed principal*—neither the existence of the agency or identity of the principal are known to the third person.

Ordinarily the agent of a disclosed principal does not intend to be a party to the transaction but is a party to that activity when the principal is partially disclosed (unless there is an express agreement to the contrary in both cases). When the principal is undisclosed, the third party has the option, upon discovering the agency, of holding either the principal or the agent liable in the transaction.

To indicate either a disclosed or partially disclosed principal, the agent should indicate the name of a principal, or that one exists, in the writing covering the transaction and should sign specifically as "agent." If the writing is a contract under seal or a negotiable instrument, however, the principal must be named. Since in the case of an undisclosed principal the third party can elect to hold either principal or agent liable, the undisclosed principal can be held liable for all actions of his agent, even those acts that were unauthorized. The undisclosed principal may take over in the transaction but takes it subject to claims, defenses, and rights of third parties; in this case the principal is in the same position as the assignee of a contract (Chapter 15).

In the development of a transaction the principal is held liable for the representations of his agent; principals may try to protect themselves by having agents use printed forms stating that representations are limited to those in the form. Despite this provision, a third party may rescind a contract entered into under misrepresentations by an agent if that third party justifiably relied on the misrepresentations. This might come about if the agent's statements were those of a nature generally made in the trade. Notice the agent receives in return is binding on the principal even if not communicated unless it is information that is

1. Not related to the business,

2. Not within the scope of the agency,

3. Not from a reliable source,

4. The result of collusion between agent and third party,

5. Where interests of agent conflict with those of principal,

6. Based on criminal activity (that requires intent on the part of the principal for culpability).

In other ways the actions of an agent are binding on the principal because agency law imputes knowledge of the agent to the principal.

PARTNERSHIP

A partnership is an association of two or more persons organized to engage in business for their financial benefit. Partners may consider the partnership an entity separate from themselves but the law looks directly to the partners as individuals. There are few legal requirements for organization and the conduct of business under a partnership is free of most governmental regulation. In about four-fifths of the states *The Uniform Partnership Act* has been adopted as the governing set of statutes for partnerships.

Organization

A partnership comes into existence when two or more persons agree, or act as if they had agreed, to operate a business as a partnership. In most states no more is needed than evidence of participation in management and a sharing of profits and losses. The persons may be natural or artificial persons, but they must have the capacity to give consent. An infant or an insane person not declared insane may become a partner but the infant may disaffirm at any time and the declaration of insanity provides the same end result for an insane person. A corporation, in most states, may be a person in a partnership. In this connection it is important to note that corporations sometimes enter into a *joint venture*, a relationship that is limited to a specific transaction or venture and is to be dissolved at the conclusion of the activity of the venture. Though they act together, members of a joint venture are limited in the ability to bind other members.

The description of partners so far has referred to *general* partners, the ordinary type. A partner may also be a *limited* partner, one who is limited in his liability as well as lacking participating control of partnership business. If a limited partner does take part in the control of the business he becomes as liable as a general partner. A partnership that has general and limited partners is called a limited partnership. There can be no limited partnership, however, unless the statutes of the state permit one to be maintained.

Relationship Among Partners

Duties and rights among the partners are similar to those under the concepts of agency that relate to principal and agent. Each partner owes the other a fiduciary duty; loyalty to the other partners and the partnership and full disclosure of all material facts of any transaction within the partnership or in dealings with third parties is called for under partnership law. These basic rules govern even though the partnership draws up partnership articles which otherwise define the course of conduct under the relationship.

The partner owes a duty to exercise reasonable care when conducting partnership business. There is no liability for losses resulting from honest errors of judgment but negligence or failure to exercise reasonable care does make the acting partner liable to the others. There is a duty to devote full attention and energy to the conduct of the business but not a right to wages unless the partnership agreement provides to the contrary.

A partner can engage only in those transactions that are authorized by the partnership. If a partner engages in unauthorized transactions resulting in a loss, he is liable to the other partners for such losses. If he profits from unauthorized activity or because of misrepresentation there must be an accounting to the other partners for any gains from those transactions.

Management of the partnership is entrusted equally to all partners, unless there is an agreement to the contrary. Each partner has one vote in the conduct of business even though there may be a difference in the extent of the contribution each has made to the capital of the partnership. No partner can be excluded, and if any disagreement continues without settlement there can be no course other than dissolution of the partnership.

Ownership

Property of the partnership is determined by the agreement. What belongs to the partnership and what remains the property of the individuals must be determined, otherwise all property brought into the partnership or acquired later with its funds is deemed to be that of the partnership. Title to property is acquired and held under the partnership name, although each partner has a right to use the partnership property for partnership purposes.

Whether the individual or the partnership owns the property is important if they encounter financial difficulties. Creditors of the individual partners have first claim on the individual property, whereas creditors of the partnership have first claim on the partnership property. Creditors of an individual partner may have a claim on the partner's share of the partnership, but no more than that. A creditor may obtain a "charging order" against any individual partner and thus have a court-appointed receiver obtain sufficient funds from the partnership to satisfy the creditor or, in some cases, even sell the partnership interest.

Real property, if held in the partnership name, may be conveyed by a partner. Even if real property is not held in the name of all the partners, a conveyance will pass good title to an innocent purchaser for value if conveyed by those partners who are named.

Good will and the name of the partnership are property and are considered to be partnership property.

The power to borrow money depends upon the type of venture and the circumstances under which the partnership was formed. If the usual practice is to borrow money in an enterprise such as manufacturing or retailing, for instance, it would be the usual practice to establish credit and borrow money in order to conduct business. In this case a partner would have the power to borrow money in the name of and for the partnership. In a professional partnership such as a law or accounting firm a partner would not ordinarily possess the authority to borrow. The partnership is responsible for repayment of funds borrowed even though a partner may have converted it to his own use. Financial powers extend to such matters as the ability to endorse negotiable instruments for deposit, power to pledge assets as security for repayment of money borrowed, and ability to sign checks if it is normally, like borrowing, a part of business procedures in that type of venture.

Termination of the Partnership

Dissolution is the change in partner relationships caused by a partner ceasing to be associated in the business and may occur in various ways. It may be voluntary, through the deliberate choice of one or more partners, or by the accomplishment of the objectives set, or the expiration of a term agreed upon. Dissolution may also occur in an involuntary way either through the death or bankruptcy of a partner or at the dissolution by decree of a court. In the case of a creditor with a charging order, the court can rule the partnership dissolved. A court can act in the same way in the case of insanity or incapacity of a partner or when one partner continues to act in a manner detrimental to the partnership.

Notice must be given to persons who have dealt with the partnership. Without this notice the partners run the risk of being liable to third parties who may be justified in believing that the partnership continues. Creditors must have actual notice, while those who have dealt with the partnership in other ways may be given *constructive notice*—a notice in a newspaper of general circulation in the area is sufficient.

Upon dissolution, the partnership must wind up its business in an orderly and proper manner. The partnership continues and each partner retains a fiduciary duty until partnership assets are liquidated, creditors paid, and remaining assets distributed among the partners. In the termination process the authority of partners is limited to those activities necessary for the winding up of partnership affairs and does not extend to the conduct of any new business.

If a partnership ceases because of the death of a partner the deceased partner's estate may require a speedy winding up of the partnership and the payment of the proper share of the liquidated assets. In many cases the partnership agreement includes provisions for handling the contingency of a partner's death, a situation that may specify methods of payment to the deceased's estate by the remaining partners or be handled through insurance that will pay the estate upon the death of a partner. It is also possible to have the remaining partners organize a new partnership in which the deceased partner's estate is a new partner.

A similar result occurs if a partnership is terminated by the bankruptcy of a partner. Either payment of that partner's share or a speedy winding up of the partnership is a right in this instance.

Any change in the membership of a partnership means that the partnership is dissolved, even though the activity of that partnership may continue by having the remaining partners conduct the business. Rights and liabilities under the conditions of change vary. A partner who has withdrawn is still liable unless persons extending credit have notice or knowledge of withdrawal. If remaining partners acquire the interest of a withdrawing partner the new partnership is still liable for the obligations of the old partnership. If a partner sells his interest to a third person, the new partner is liable only for those obligations arising after he enters the partnership, unless that new partner promises to substitute for the old, take on the debt burden, and there is a release from the creditors to that effect (a novation). In bankruptcy or death of a partner, the bankrupt or the deceased's estate is not liable for the debts of the remaining partners.

Distribution of the assets in a solvent partnership is seldom a problem; under the Uniform Partnership Act, (Section 40) distribution from an insolvent partnership puts creditors before partners. Creditors of the partnership have a priority claim to partnership assets, whereas creditors of partners have priority as to assets of partners. The specific distribution is in the order: creditors, then to partners for amounts owed other than capital or profits, partner's capital, and, finally, partner's profits.

CORPORATIONS

A corporation is an organization recognized by the law as an entity apart from its owners and managers. It is considered a "person" with most of the legal rights possessed by natural persons. It is ordinarily the most advantageous form of conducting business because of the characteristics already mentioned above—a legal entity, liabilities accruing only to the unit and not to its shareholders, ability to raise capital, greater opportunity to secure professional management, and continuing existence beyond the lifetimes and skills of its participants. Most of what can be written about corporations applies to three basic functional types

1. Corporations for profit,
2. Corporations not for profit,
3. Public (government) corporations.

There are a few differences and it should be kept in mind that the variations may be of some importance in a specific instance. The following discussion, however, will focus on the corporation for profit as it is the pivotal part of our economic system.

Although activities under the laws of different jurisdictions do vary from state to state, more than half of the states have adopted the Model Business Corporation Act. Even those states that have developed their separate statutes for corporations have been influenced by the Model Act, so that it would not be too misleading to focus on this act as the source for subsequent discussions of corporations.

Formation of the Corporation

Beginning a corporation is known as incorporation. There are certain specific steps that must be taken before a corporation can legally exist and do business. Incorporation generally takes place under the laws of specific states (there are a few federally chartered corporations). A state grants life to the corporation, regulates its activities, and determines whether it can continue and how it can go out of business. Federal regulation occurs, too, if the corporation is to conduct interstate business or sell securities beyond state lines.

The choice of the state in which to incorporate is dictated by the scope of operations. A corporation planning to be active within a state would obviously wish to incorporate in that state. A corporation planning multistate operations would wish to choose a state where the laws and taxes are most beneficial. For this reason many corporations choose to incorporate in the state of Delaware with its statutes that allow great freedom for developers and managers. The corporation would be, in that case, a *domestic* corporation in Delaware.

A *foreign* corporation is one that has been chartered in another state. In order to do business in still another state, a foreign corporation must be authorized by that other state after an application requiring data similar to that supplied by the domestic corporation. It must maintain a registered office and agent within the state, as well as file reports, and pay the required fees and taxes.

A foreign corporation does not need to become authorized to do business within the state if it engages only in interstate activity. Some of this may be regarded as intrastate, however, and the corporation would be required to qualify in the state. Courts differentiate type of activity that constitutes doing business within the state as well as that requiring the filing of reports and paying the required fees and taxes. More activity in the state would be needed for the corporation to be required to qualify than if the corporation were to be taxed or subject to suits in the state court by its citizens. Even minor activity within the state such as entering into a contract with one of its citizens will be recognized as sufficient to enter suit in the state courts. The power of the state to tax requires more than remote contacts across state lines. Inventory stored in a state may be subject to taxation but not goods ordered and shipped in.

Incorporation under state statutes makes the corporation a legal person with a domicile in that state. In this position the corporation assures many advantages for shareholders, including limited liability, since corporations and shareholders are separate entities. If the incorporation is for the purpose of fraudulent activity or the accomplishment of an illegal purpose, the law will "pierce the corporate veil" and hold either stockholders of a closely held corporation or the parent corporation liable for the acts of the corporation.

The process of incorporation must proceed according to the statutes of the state chosen. Generally the following steps must be taken

1. Drafting of the articles of incorporation,

2. Signing by one or more incorporators (persons or corporation),

3. Filing with the appropriate state official, usually the Secretary of State,

4. Paying the required fees,

5. Contribution by stockholders of a minimum amount of capital,

6. Issuance of the certificate of incorporation by the state,

7. An organizational meeting of the board of directors to adopt bylaws and elect officers.

The corporation is then ready to do business.

The articles of incorporation are usually specific in identifying the proposed character and functioning of the corporation: Name, registered office and agent, purposes, amount of consideration and classes of shares, as well as names and addresses of incorporators and directors. The number of incorporators will vary from state to state, ranging from a minimum of one to at least three. Most states, however, permit as few as one shareholder of either publicly held or closely held corporations. The bylaws of the corporation specify the further powers, functions, and duties of officers and members of the board of directors of the corporation. Shareholders are bound by all bylaws not contrary to the state statutes, but outside parties are ordinarily bound only by those provisions of the bylaws of which they have notice.

In most states the name of the corporation in full must include a word or its abbreviation such as *Incorporated*, *Limited*, or *Corporation*. Furthermore, the name must not resemble the name of another corporation so as to be deceptive, nor can it mislead as to the type of business to be carried on. There can be a variation from state to state with respect to the existence of the corporation, whether for a set time limit or perpetual existence. Rights inherent in different classes of stock ownership and the requirements for capital structure will also vary according to the laws of the state of incorporation.

Incorporators of a corporation also may be promoters. Before the corporation exists a person who sets about trying to organize it cannot be considered an agent of the future corporation nor can he be an agent of those who are prepared to invest their time and money in the corporation-to-be. The promoter does have a responsibility, however, to those who are active in the organization of the corporation. He owes a fiduciary duty to disclose all facts concerning purchases and sales for the prospective corporation. Any profits made by the promoter due to misrepresentation or nondisclosure can be recovered by the interested parties although they can consent to the exchange of those assets for stock in the corporation at an agreed upon figure. Contracts made by the promoter before the corporation comes into existence cannot be said to have been made by the corporation and it is not, therefore, responsible for those contracts after it comes into existence unless the new corporation accepts the benefits under the contract. Even so, that contract must have been one in which the corporation could legally act and the corporation must accept it in its entirety. Adoption of the contract by the corporation does not relieve the promoter of liability unless there has been a *novation* (see Chapter 15, Contracts) where the third party agrees to substitute the corporation for the promoter.

If there is some failure to meet all the requirements for incorporation under state statute, the business may act as if it were a corporation when in fact or law it is not. Corporations under question may be classified as

1. *De jure* corporations,
2. *De facto* corporations,
3. Not a corporation at all.

A *de jure* corporation is one that has met all of the requirements of the statute and its existence under the law cannot be questioned. A *de facto* corporation is one in which there has been a failure in a material respect to meet the requirements of statute, despite an honest attempt to do so. In the case of a *de facto* corporation only the state may bring proceedings against the *de facto* corporation attacking the validity of its existence under that organizational form. Neither the corporation nor third parties attacking it may use as a defense the failure to comply completely with statute and therefore allege that no corporation exists. A failure of promoters and other persons interested in the corporation to meet even the minimal requirements of a *de facto* corporation result in their being considered partners and their liability is determined on that basis.

Management of the Corporation

The first step in structuring the corporation and determining its function takes place after the charter has been granted from the state of incorporation. At an organizational meeting, the board of directors is elected, drafts and adopts the bylaws and elects officers. The Model Act (Section 35) calls for the board of directors to manage the business and affairs of the corporation, although these powers and duties may be conferred on such persons as shall be provided by the articles of incorporation.

The authority of the corporation to act stems from the granting of powers from the state through the incorporation. The state continues to exercise control over the activities of the corporation, but the corporation generally may exercise all the corporate powers reasonably necessary to achieve the purposes stated. The corporation does not, however, have powers that can exceed those conferred upon them by the state. In the case of certain types of corporations there may be further special statutes that limit the scope of operations of those corporations. Banks, for instance, often operate under special state restrictions as do utilities and insurance companies.

If a corporation acts beyond its legal authority, it is said that the corporation acts *ultra vires*, that is, beyond its powers. While this doctrine is not often successfully applied as a defense by the corporation to third-party actions under an existing agreement, shareholders often have the power to enjoin corporations from engaging in activities that are beyond powers granted to that corporation.

Directors

It has been noted that under the corporate form the corporation has an existence separate from its stockholders. The corporation makes its bylaws and can acquire and sell property in its own name. The stockholders have control of the corporation, however, because they own it. This ownership calls for a placement of the management of the corporation in the board of directors who determine the policy of the corporation and elect officers to carry on the normal daily activities of the corporation. With the exception of those decisions reserved to the stockholders by state statute or the articles of incorporation, the board of directors have the responsibility of conducting the affairs of the corporation. The board of directors is responsible for:

1. Determining the major objectives and policies,
2. Establishing consideration to be paid for shares of stock,
3. Writing, amending, or repealing bylaws,
4. Selling, mortgaging, or leasing corporate assets,

5. Selecting officers and determining their duties,

6. Approving major financial transactions,

7. Declaring dividends.

Less important and mundane matters are delegated to officers and employees of the corporation.

After the initial organizational meeting of the board of directors, the directors are elected at future annual meetings of the shareholders. There may be only one member of the board of directors under the Model Act, (Section 35) but the bylaws or the articles of incorporation may specify more than that number. Members of the board need not be shareholders of the corporation, unless there is a provision in the bylaws or statutes to the contrary. Directors may be elected to serve until the next annual meeting or for some other specified term; in any case they serve until their successors are duly elected and qualified.

Business of the board of directors is usually conducted at meetings at which a quorum is present, but many state statutes permit action to be taken without a formal meeting provided that all directors give written consent. A majority of directors constitutes a quorum for doing business unless a larger number is specified.

Some directors have, in the past, served without compensation, but most corporations now provide some compensation for their directors. Some directors are more active than others; corporate bylaws frequently provide for an executive committee composed of certain members, usually those who are more readily available for meetings beyond the regular meetings of the board of directors. The executive committee is empowered to act in certain matters between meetings of the full board.

Officers

Corporate officers are usually designated as the president, one or more vice presidents, a secretary, and a treasurer, and the Model Act provides specifically for those officers. In the Model Act (Section 50) any two offices may be held by the same individual except for the office of president and secretary. In addition to these offices many corporations have a chairman of the board who conducts the business of the board of directors.

The duty of the officers is to carry out a normal business of the corporation, and, in doing so, they are acting under powers granted to them by the bylaws or the board of directors. The president of the corporation has broad powers to conduct the ordinary business of the corporation while the powers of other officers are more strictly confined. Vice presidents are charged with duties that are more narrowly determined. The treasurer of a corporation is ordinarily responsible for custody of corporate funds and for receiving and dispersing those under specific authority granted him by the board of directors. He does not ordinarily have the power to borrow money. The secretary prepares the minutes of all shareholders and board meetings, keeps those records, and maintains all other appropriate records, as well. A secretary also has control of the corporate seal and there is a presumption that documents with the corporate seal affixed are duly authorized documents. Officers may delegate their authority or part of it to other employees of the corporation, in which case the principles of agency law, as discussed above, apply.

Fiduciary Duties

Directors and officers have certain fiduciary duties to the corporation and its shareholders. In general they are required to act

1. With care and diligence in conducting the affairs of the corporation,

2. In good faith for the benefit of the corporation,

3. Within the powers granted to the corporation and their own scope of authority.

Officers and directors must perform with the degree of skill and care that is expected of reasonably prudent men in the circumstances under which they act. Good faith and diligence are expected of them, and, even though they may rely on professional staff or consultants such as accountants or lawyers, they are not absolved from liability for lack of knowledge when such knowledge could have been gained by the director or officer through reasonable diligence. The activity of directors and officers is limited by the authority granted by the state in the articles of incorporation or statutes regulating the conduct of corporations; a director or officer may be liable personally for any damage sustained through exceeding the scope of authority unless there are grounds to believe that he acted within the authority or his actions are later ratified by shareholders. Directors and officers are barred from profiting from any actions that are self-serving to the detriment of the corporation and the shareholders. A corporate fiduciary may not avail himself of a business opportunity if the corporation is able to undertake it. If such transactions do take place the corporation or its shareholders may void the transaction. If, however, the corporation enters into a transaction with another company in which the director has an interest, the transaction may be permitted to stand provided the director made full disclosure and his vote was not necessary for carrying the motion.

Officers and directors may not use inside information in any transaction involving stocks to the detriment of shareholders or to other potential buyers and sellers of the corporations stock. Such trading of stock is called insider training, and subsequent profits under such activity will result in liability for the insiders and a recovery of the profits for the benefit of the corporation shareholders.

The rights of minority shareholders are protected under the fundamental concept that officers and directors must act in the best interests of the entire corporation and all its shareholders. Injured minority shareholders may sue for damages or obtain an injunction to restrain the abuse of normal business activity that results in the detriment of the minority shareholders.

Various statutes regulate activity of officers and directors, particularly at the federal level under the Securities Act of 1933 and the Securities Exchange Act of 1934. Individuals are punishable under criminal statutes, or civil penalties may be levied for violations, but, in addition, under the laws of agency, corporations are liable for the torts committed by their employees in the scope of their employment. A corporation can also be liable for a criminal act since the act can be determined to have taken place in the course of activity for the corporation and the requisite intent may be determined from the acts of the officials or employees of the corporation.

Directors may be removed by the shareholders for cause involving misconduct or acts detrimental to the corporation; bylaws or articles grant this power to the directors themselves, as well. Directors may not be removed without cause, unless there is specific authority for that action.

SHAREHOLDERS

Ownership of a corporation is in the hands of shareholders—not any specific property is owned by shareholders as the corporation is the owner of its property. A shareholder owns a share of the corporation, a fractional interest in the total property of the corporation and a right to a fractional distribution of earnings (dividends) or of assets upon dissolution.

Stock

Evidence of ownership lies in *stock certificates* issued by the corporation. Stock certificates are not absolutely necessary to indicate shareholding but the practice is convenient and widely followed. The Model Act (Section 23) requires the following in a certificate:

1. statement that it is organized under the laws of this State
2. name of person to whom issued
3. number and class of shares, as well as series
4. par value of each share, or statement that shares are without par value.

Interest cannot be transferred without delivery of the certificate (UCC Article 8-301).

515 Business Organizations

Shares of stock may be acquired by *subscription* or *transfer*. Subscription is a contract to purchase stock when issued. Transfer takes place between a shareholder and the corporation.

If a subscription is made before incorporation, the Model Act (Section 17) provides that the subscription is irrevocable for six months unless indicated otherwise or all subscribers consent to a revocation (in this as in other matters state statutes can vary). Subscriptions made after incorporation are governed by the ordinary rules of contracts—there must be an offer and an acceptance, as well as other elements of a valid contract.

Transfer of shares may be made to anyone unless a reasonable prohibition is provided by statute. Giving the corporation the right to repurchase is a valid restriction but other such provisions are not valid against a purchaser of the certificate unless noted on the certificate or the purchaser has knowledge. Any interpretation is apt to be made in favor of transferability.

Shares of stock are known as *equity* securities because they represent ownership of a part of the corporation. *Debt* securities make the holder a creditor of the corporation rather than an owner.

There may be different classes among shareholders in terms of rights to which they are entitled. Classes of stock may be designated as:

1. *Common,* or
2. *Preferred*.

The preferred shareholders participate first, before common shareholders, in distribution of earnings or of assets in dissolution. Preferred stock may be further designated as:

(a) cumulative, or
(b) noncumulative.

Dividends on cumulative preferred stock add up each year if not paid. If noncumulative preferred stock does not pay dividends in one year those are not payable in subsequent years.

Preferred stock may also be:

(a) participating, or
(b) nonparticipating.

Participating shareholders not only are preferred in distribution of dividends as to certain percentage but also participate later along with the common shareholders.

Preferred stock may also be made *redeemable* in that the corporation may retain the right to buy it back.

While preferred shareholders participate first in distributions, the common shareholders ordinarily have more control of corporate affairs.

If there is only one class of stock it is designated as common stock.

A corporation is limited, under the Uniform Commercial Code (Article 8-104), to the issuance of no greater number of shares than it is authorized to issue. The corporation is liable for the issuance of any unauthorized stock by an employee or agent to a bona fide purchaser for value. A corporation may buy back issued stock; this is known as *treasury* stock.

Regulation of securities

Both federal and state legislation controls the issuance of and trading in securities. At the federal level the Securities Act of 1933 and the Securities Exchange Act of 1934 control while most states have laws, often popularly known as "blue sky" laws, to supplement the federal acts and protect investors from fraudulent activity in connection with stock issues and trading.

The Securities Act of 1933 primarily regulates the issuance of securities. Under the Act, a corporation planning to offer securities across state lines must register with the Securities Exchange Commission (SEC) and provide the Commission and the public with specific information. Interested persons must be provided with a prospectus containing important details of the issue. The corporation must provide the Commission with information concerning organization, capitalization, expenses, prospective use of capital and other factors in management and control of the corporation. Civil and criminal penalties are provided, as well, for deceptive and misleading statements.

The Securities Exchange Act of 1934 focuses upon trading of securities. Periodic reports must be made to the SEC on financial information, as well as on the trading in corporate securities by officers, directors, and large shareholders. Manipulation of securities or deceptive practices are prohibited and profits made by "insiders" may be recovered by the corporation.

Shareholder meetings

The articles of incorporation, bylaws, or state corporation statutes define the activity of shareholders, most of it taking place at an annual meeting. Shareholders act on the specific matters listed for the meeting including the following:

1. Election of directors,
2. Removal of members of the board,
3. Merger, consolidation, sale, or mortgage of assets,
4. Changes in the articles of incorporation,
5. Other extraordinary matters not in the regular course of business.

Notice of the meeting is required to be given to shareholders "of record," those shareholders listed on the books of the corporation at a specific time. Only shareholders of record are entitled to vote but they may sign a *proxy*, a statement designating some other person to cast a vote in their name. The Model Act (Section 33) requires that a proxy be in writing although some state statutes do not require it. If nonvoting stock exists, the holders are not able to vote except in limited extraordinary situations such as merger proposals.

Each share of stock is entitled to one vote on matters before the shareholders at the meeting. In the election of directors, however, some states or corporations allow or mandate *cumulative* voting, that is, a shareholder may lump his votes for one candidate who would then receive the number of votes represented by the number of shares held multiplied by the number of directors to be elected. Cumulative voting gives a better opportunity for minority shareholders to elect directors to the board.

Rights

Shareholders have a right to inspect the minutes, record of account, and record of shareholders of a corporation if they have a proper purpose for doing so. The Model Act gives shareholders the right, if the request is in writing, to receive the latest financial statements in reasonable detail (Section 52).

Fundamental changes in the structure of the corporation are to be voted upon by the shareholders and normally more than a majority vote is required for action such as amendment of the articles of incorporation. Shareholders have the right to vote on other extraordinary matters such as mergers, consolidation, or dissolution of the corporation. Dissenting shareholders in such actions have the right under the Model Act (Section 81) to receive fair value for their shares rather than continue as shareholders under the new circumstances as long as they give notice within the required time.

Shareholders have a right to bring a suit against the corporation in their own name when there has been an action that violates their rights under the relationship with the corporation such as recovery of a dividend or inspection of the books when proper. While shareholders do not ordinarily have the right to bring a suit in their own name on behalf of the corporation, a "derivative" suit may be brought by shareholders for the benefit of the corporation when action by officers or directors has been detrimental to the interests of the corporation or its shareholders.

Dividends

A shareholder has no absolute right to receive dividends but when declared at the discretion of the directors, there is a right to a proportionate share of those declared dividends according to the preferential order established.

Corporation statutes limit the distribution of dividends. Directors may declare a dividend out of earned surplus or, under some conditions, out of net profits. No dividends can be declared unless assets are greater than the liabilities plus outstanding shares. Creating a surplus on paper in the corporation's books by increasing the value of assets or decreasing the capital stock does not permit the declaring of cash dividends although some states permit the declaration of *stock dividends* under these conditions. When dividends are made in stock the surplus is, in effect, made part of the capital of the corporation. Shareholders retain their proportionate interest as before. Stock dividends must be distinguished from a *stock split*. In the case of a stock split the number of shares held is multiplied. A shareholder with 100 shares, for instance, would receive 200 shares if the stock split two for one. The additional shares are not dividends but only a new unit representing the same proportionate share of the corporation.

The recipient of the dividend is the shareholder of record on the books of the corporation. If the stock has been sold, the agreement between the parties determines the recipient of the dividend but the corporation is not liable if the corporation acts according to its records in sending the dividend to that shareholder on the record. If there is no agreement with respect to the dividend, the purchaser receives the dividend if

1. The sale was before the record date, or
2. On the stock exchange, the sale came "ex dividend" or five days before the record date.

When a dividend has been declared it is a debt owing to the shareholder and the shareholder may enter suit to obtain dividends improperly withheld. Cash dividends may not be rescinded although stock dividends may be withdrawn.

Preemptive rights of shareholders are those developed to protect the shareholder in maintaining existing proportionate interest in the corporation. If a corporation would attempt to issue more stock to some shareholders than others, the proportionate control of the corporation would be altered. Preemptive rights of stockholders means a right to subscribe to new issues of stock in the same proportion as currently held by the shareholder. Preemptive rights do not extend to shares issued for a merger, consideration other than cash, or for shares reacquired by the corporation (treasury shares).

Shareholder liability

A shareholder who receives dividends, knowing them to have been declared on an illegal basis, is bound to return them to the corporation. Actual knowledge is not even a requisite when payment was made under insolvency of the corporation. If stock has been "watered," that is, stock issued for less than proper consideration, the shareholder may be liable for the difference between the actual sum and the one paid in. There is also liability for any unpaid balance on an original subscription contract for the shares even though the corporation becomes insolvent in the meantime.

DISSOLUTION

As in all other spheres of activity of corporations, state statutes regulate the termination of corporate life. There are many ways in which a corporation may go out of existence. The charter may have been filed with a specific termination date. After a breach of its charter or by suit of minority shareholders courts may declare a dissolution. The corporation itself may end its existence through voluntary dissolution or by entering into a merger by consolidation and thus becoming a new entity.

No dissolution takes place until there has been compliance with the statute, whether voluntarily through shareholder approval or involuntarily by court proceedings. The ordinary business may come to a standstill while assets are sold, creditors paid, and remaining assets distributed among the shareholders; the corporation continues until all the procedures called for in the statute are followed.

CHAPTER 17
COMMERCIAL TRANSACTIONS

In the course of their everyday lives, most persons become involved in such transactions as the purchase, rental, and sale of goods and perhaps even of real estate; the financing of purchases, often by securing credit; making and receiving payment with bank checks or other kinds of commercial paper. These are often referred to as commercial transactions. Obviously, an understanding of the law which is applicable in such situations is of importance not just to the merchant or business person but also to the consumer.

This chapter focuses on legal areas which are of particular relevance to commercial transactions. It deals with the law of

1. Property,
2. Sales,
3. Commercial paper,
4. Secured transactions.

It should be noted that contracts are the basic framework for commercial transactions. Therefore, an understanding of contract law is essential to an understanding of these other areas.

PROPERTY

Definition and Classification

The word "property" is frequently used to refer to those things that a person can acquire, possess, own, enjoy, use, and of which he can dispose.   In the law, *property* refers to all those legal rights and interests which an individual has in any one thing, tangible or intangible.

A distinction is made between real property or realty and personal property or personalty.   *Real property* refers to land and that which is firmly affixed to the land, whether it be growing or erected upon the land. Buildings and such perennials as trees are examples of realty. Everything that can be owned and that is not realty is considered to be *personal property*.   Personalty is sometimes thought of as having a movable and temporary nature as contrasted with the permanent and immovable characteristics associated with realty.

The concept of property is closely aligned with possession, ownership, and title.   *Possession* refers to an individual's custody or assertion of control over property. *Ownership*, on the other hand, is the ultimate in legal rights and interests with respect to an item of property. It is the complete power, as allowed by law, to use and dispose of a thing. Obviously, possession and ownership are not synonymous. One may be obtained without the other.   *Title* is often used interchangeably with ownership. It is the union of all the elements that constitute ownership. Title is also used to refer to evidence of one's legal rights in property.

Multiple Ownership

Property can be owned by more than one person. Multiple ownership of property takes several forms: tenancy by the entireties, joint tenancy, tenancy in common, and community property.

Tenancy by the entireties is a form of ownership which is possible only by husband and wife. In some states and in the absence of provision to the contrary, real estate acquired by husband and wife automatically results in ownership by the entireties. This type of ownership cannot be destroyed by the independent act of either spouse. Nor can creditors of only one spouse reach property held by the entireties. However, a creditor holding the joint obligation of husband and wife can do so. Upon the death of one spouse, the survivor continues in ownership of the property.   Therefore, the deceased by will cannot dispose of the property.   A tenancy by the entireties comes to an automatic end with divorce. Some states have abolished this type of tenancy.

Two or more persons, whether they be related to each other or not, can own property as *joint tenants* or as *tenants in common*. Joint tenants must own equal shares of the property. Tenants in common need not. Joint tenancies must be created at the same time. This is not necessary with a tenancy in common.

A right of survivorship is a distinguishing feature of joint tenancy. Upon the death of any one of the joint tenants, his interest automatically passes to the surviving tenants. For this reason, he cannot dispose of it by means of his will. The right of survivorship associated with joint tenancy is not favored by the law and some states have abolished joint tenancy.

A tenancy held either jointly or in common may be sold or encumbered by act of one tenant. A tenant also may petition the court to divide or partition the property. In addition, each tenant has the right of use and possession of the property. Each must respect the interests of the other tenants and permit them to exercise their property rights. Joint and common tenants share income as well as expenses. Where two or more persons own the same property and the type of ownership has not been indicated, the law ordinarily presumes it to be a tenancy in common. Joint tenancy frequently occurs with bank accounts, safe deposit boxes, stocks, and bonds.

In some states, by statutory provision, property acquired after marriage is the *community property* of husband and wife. Most community property statutes place limitations upon disposition of the property and contain provisions regarding transfer of the property interest at the death of either spouse.

Real Property

Interests in Realty

Interests in real estate include a fee simple, a life estate, a leasehold, and an easement. The greatest interest one can have in property is a *fee simple*. It gives the owner an unconditional right to the entire property, unqualified and unlimited as to duration, disposition, and descendability. Therefore, the owner can dispose of the property as he wishes during his lifetime. At his death, the fee simple passes to his heirs. This differs from a *life estate*, which is an interest that is limited to the lifetime of an individual or individuals. A person with a life estate is known as a *life tenant*. He must act in connection with the property in such a way so as not to destroy the interests of those who will succeed to it at his death.

A *landlord-tenant* relationship arises when a person acquires from an owner the right of possession of realty for a time. The agreement entered into by the parties is referred to as a *lease*, and the interest acquired by the tenant is referred to as a *leasehold*. An *easement*, on the other hand, is a nonpossessory interest in realty which gives a person the right to use the property of another. A common example of an easement is that of a right of way across the land of another. An easement is distinguished from a *license*, which is not considered to be an interest in realty. Rather it is a privilege to use and enjoy another's property in some specific way. Often it is permission to enter upon another's land for a particular purpose.

Fixtures

A *fixture* is an item of personal property which is so firmly attached to realty that it comes to be regarded as part and parcel of it. Controversy sometimes arises between landlord and tenant as to whether additions made to the property leased by the tenant are fixtures. The reason is that a tenant who brings personal property onto leased premises may remove them when his lease expires. Fixtures, however, remain with the realty. In the case of personalty that is used in carrying on a business for which real estate is leased, the courts have usually held that it is a *trade fixture* and may be removed by the tenant at the expiration of his lease. Exceptions occur where the attachment is such that removal will destroy or weaken the structure.

Conveyance of Real Estate

The transfer of title to realty is known as a *conveyance*. Generally this is done by execution and delivery of a deed. A *deed* is the written instrument in which the owner of the realty (known as the *grantor*) conveys his interest in the property to another (the *grantee*). It should be distinguished from a contract for the sale of real estate, which is the agreement between buyer and seller. The latter document sets forth such terms as price, the kind of deed the buyer will get, etc. State regulations frequently specify the form a deed shall take and requirements regarding recording of deeds.

A *quitclaim deed* is one in which the grantor conveys whatever title he has—good, poor, or none at all! Obviously, this gives the grantee no legal claim should there be a defect in the title. A *warranty deed*, on the other hand, makes guarantees against defects in title. Generally, a deed must be signed, sealed, and witnessed. Usually title does not pass until there has been delivery of the deed. This is ordinarily done in person; however, it may be by mail or otherwise. Acceptance by the grantee is required, although this is usually presumed to exist in the absence of an expression to the contrary.

A conveyance of real estate is distinguished from a transfer of title to personal property. Realty and personalty can be acquired, among other ways, by purchase, inheritance, and gift.

Personal Property

An individual may have personal property rights in articles that are tangible, such as clothing and cars, or those that are intangible, such as copyrights, accounts receivable, insurance, and contract rights. The term *chattel* is frequently used to refer to items of personal property. Another term, *goods*, is often used to refer to personal property.

Acquisition by Gift

One method for the transfer of ownership of personal property is by gift. The person making the gift is known as the *donor*, and the recipient as the *donee*. A gift between living persons is known as an *inter vivos* gift. If, however, the gift is made in contemplation of death, there is a gift *causa mortis*.

As explained in the chapter dealing with contracts, an executory promise to make a gift is ordinarily not enforceable by the courts. Three elements are necessary to effectuate a gift:

1. An intention on the part of the donor to transfer ownership;
2. Relinquishment by the donor of control over the property through delivery of either the property, the means of control of the property, or documents of title;
3. Acceptance of the gift by the donee (usually not a problem).

An inter vivos gift is effective from the time these three elements have been performed. A gift causa mortis, on the other hand, is conditioned on the donor's death. If a donor has made delivery of the property, he may recover it if he does not die, if he revokes his gift before his death, or if the donee should die before the donor.

Acquisition by Possession

Persons who find personal property that has been lost or abandoned may not only come into possession but also into ownership of the property. Property is *lost* when the owner has no idea where he left it. The original owner retains title to lost property. A finder acquires only possession and must give up the property to the true owner once that person is located. By statutory provision in some states, a finder of lost property acquires title to it after he complies with certain prescribed requirements, such as advertising.

Property is *mislaid* when an owner, having placed it in a particular location, forgets about it. Because of a presumption that the owner will eventually remember where the article is and return for it, the owner of the premises where mislaid goods are found is entitled to possession.

Property is *abandoned* when the owner has the intention of giving up title to the property and also gives up possession of it. Ownership of abandoned property is acquired by the first person who takes it into his possession.

Bailment

You can create a legal relationship known as a *bailment* when you leave your car at a service station to be repaired, when you borrow a book from the library, when you ship your possessions to a new home. Note that each of these examples involves

1. Personal rather than real property,
2. Transfer of possession of that property to a person other than the owner for a particular purpose and limited time,
3. Delivery of the property to the other person,
4. No transfer of title and no intention of such a transfer,
5. An agreement,

6. Intention of return or other disposition of the property in accordance with the owner's instructions.

Those are the essential elements of a bailment. The person turning the property over to another is known as the *bailor*. This is usually the owner or someone acting for him, one with the goods in his possession. The individual to whom the bailor delivers possession of the property is known as the *bailee*. In a bailment situation, title or ownership of the chattel bailed remains with the owner. The bailee acquires the right of use and possession and does so under the terms and conditions of the agreement between the parties.

Bailment is a contractual relationship. The contract may be express or it may be implied either in fact or at law. The latter occurs when one discovers that he is in possession of property that the owner has mislaid.

A bailment does not arise if the bailor has not either actually or constructively delivered possession of the chattel to the bailee. Thus, some courts find a difference between the legal relationship which arises when one parks his car in a parking lot, locks it, and keeps the keys, and when that same person drives into a parking lot, gives the car or keys to an attendant who parks, and later returns the car to the owner. In the former case, it can be said there has been no delivery. Thus, there is no bailment. There is, instead, a lease of the parking space. In the second situation, a bailment can be created because there has been a delivery.

Note should be made of the situation that exists when an employer permits an employee to have use or custody of the employer's property so that the employee may be able to carry out the duties of his job, the employer neither intending to not actually surrendering legal possession of the property to the employee. In that case, custody alone exists and must be distinguished from a bailment.

No bailment exists if the bailee does not realize he is in possession of the goods. Such would be the case if you checked your coat but did not inform the attendant that valuable stock certificates were in the pocket of the coat. While there would be a bailment of the coat, there would not be one of the stock certificates. The general rule followed is that goods normally found in a container are deemed to be bailed when the container is bailed. When it is unusual that the item be found in the container and the bailee would not ordinarily realize its presence, the item is not considered to be bailed unless the parties have expressly agreed otherwise.

Rights and Duties under a Bailment Contract

Consistent with the terms of the bailment agreement, a bailee has the right to possession and use of the bailed chattel. At the same time, he has a duty to exercise reasonable care under the circumstances with respect to the goods. What is reasonable depends upon such factors as the nature of the chattel, its normal uses, its value, and the bailment facilities and location. A bailee is liable for damage caused by neglect of his duty of care, including that resulting from unauthorized use of the chattel either by himself or a third person. The latter may lead to an action for conversion. *Conversion* is a tort and consists of the wrongful appropriation of the personalty of another.

A bailee, however, is not an insurer of the bailed property. Damage to the chattel that is caused by an act of God or for which no one is at fault rests with the bailor. By agreement, the parties may, within the bounds of reasonableness, expand or limit the bailee's liability. However, deliberate or willful damage is ordinarily not subject to limitation because of public policy considerations. An example of limitation of a bailee's liability can be found where signs are posted conspicuously in parking lots announcing the bailee's limitation of liability to specified amounts. Courts generally uphold such limitations if they are clearly called to the bailor's attention or if the circumstances are such that the bailor is chargeable with notice of the terms.

The bailee has a duty upon termination of the bailment to return the bailed property in undamaged condition. He will be excused from such redelivery if the property has been disposed of or damaged without his fault. Ordinarily he is expected to return the same goods that were bailed. In the case of fungible goods, (those such as wheat and oil, where one unit is the equivalent of any other unit), his duty is to return only an equal quantity of goods of the same description and quality as those bailed.

An unpaid bailee has a lien on the bailed property and may therefore keep possession of it until he has been paid. A *lien* is a claim on property for payment of a debt. By statutory provision, he may be authorized to sell the property if he remains unpaid. To meet constitutional requirements, there must ordinarily be both prior notice and a hearing as to the existence of the claim if a sale is to take place.

A bailor has a duty to inform a bailee of latent, that is, hidden defects in the bailed property. If the bailment is for the mutual benefit of the parties, the bailor must make reasonable investigation to determine that the chattel is safe for the use intended under the bailment. A bailor who fails to exercise these duties will be liable if either the bailee or his employee is injured as a result of a defective condition of the chattel.

Special bailment situations exist in connection with common carriers and public warehousing.

Common Carriers

A *common carrier* is one who engages in the transportation of goods for the general public. As such, he is the bailee of goods for hire. He is distinguished from a *private carrier*, who is also a bailee, but who carries property only of one person or selected persons. Since the days of the early common law, a common carrier has had a greater duty of care than does a private carrier. A common carrier has absolute liability for damage or loss of property unless it results from an act of God, the public enemy, the state, or the shipper, or it results from the nature of the goods.

When shipment of goods is to be made by carrier, a *bill of lading* is generally issued. The term is a corruption of the original term, bill of loading. In the case of air transportation, the document is known as an *air bill*. The bill of lading or air bill has several functions. It is a contract for the transportation of the goods. It is also a receipt for the goods. In addition, it is a *document of title*. Title to the goods being carried may be transferred by a transfer of the document.

A *negotiable* bill of lading is one which provides for the delivery of the goods to either the order of a named person or to the bearer of the document, and the carrier will give up the goods only upon surrender of a bill of lading that is made out to or indorsed over to the bearer. A *nonnegotiable* or *straight* bill of lading provides for delivery of goods to a specified person only. When a bill of lading is transferred from one person to another, several implied warranties exist in the absence of provision to the contrary. Those implied warranties are that the document is genuine, that its transfer is rightful, and that the person doing the transferring has no knowledge of anything that would affect the validity or worthiness of the document.

Common carriers are subject to considerable statutory regulation. Article 7 of the Uniform Commercial Code deals with bills of lading. Provisions of the Federal Bills of Lading Act are applicable in the case of interstate shipment. Transportation rates are subject to regulation by the Interstate Commerce Commission as well as state commissions.

When a common carrier has not been paid for services rendered, he has a lien on the goods transported. He also has a right to *demurrage*. This is a charge for equipment or cars that are unreasonably detained by the shipper or receiver of the goods.

Warehousing

One who is in the business of storing goods for a fee is known as a *warehouseman*. He is also a bailee of the goods stored. He is a public warehouseman if his services and facilities are available to the general public. In most states, the warehouseman is subject to regulation by statute. Common provisions deal with charges and rates, condition and suitability of storage facilities, and protection of clients through bonding requirements. An unpaid public warehouseman has a lien on the property stored. This may result in a sale, provided constitutional requirements of notice and a hearing are met.

A *warehouse receipt* is a document of title. It may be negotiable or nonnegotiable. It serves also as a receipt for the goods and as the contract between the parties. In general, the same requirements for surrender of the document apply as in the case of a bill of lading and the same warranties are applicable.

SALES

A *sale* is the transfer of ownership or title of movable personal property for a consideration. It is based upon a contract. The contracting parties are the sellor or *vendor* and the buyer or *vendee*. The consideration—whether it be in money, services, or other property—is known as the *price*.

Article 2 of the Uniform Commercial Code deals with sales. It restricts sales to transactions in goods. *Goods* are defined as personal property of a movable nature. Investment securities, stocks and bonds, secured transactions, negotiable instruments, and money in which the price is paid are not considered to be goods. However, *future goods*—that is, those not currently existing and identified—may be the subject of a contract of sale (UCC 2-105).

The UCC reflects business practice and custom. It gives contracting parties much flexibility with regard to the terms of their agreement. At the same time, the Code imposes upon the parties an obligation to deal with each other in good faith (UCC 1-203). Another important Code provision is that contract terms may be explained or supplemented by reference to prior course of dealings or usage of the trade (UCC 1-205). Furthermore, the Code specifies methods for determination of terms which the contracting parties do not specify.

Price and Delivery

Price, for instance, is a term which may be left open. If the parties have not set forth the means for fixing the price, it will be a reasonable price at the time of delivery (UCC 2-305). This is usually market price. With regard to quantity, the parties may agree that it shall be the entire output of the seller (output contract) or all that is required by the buyer (requirements contract) (UCC 2-306).

Transfer of possession of goods from seller to buyer is known as *delivery*. When the place of delivery is not stated, it is the seller's place of business. If he has none, it is his residence. If the goods are in possession of a bailee, the seller must *tender* (that is, proffer) a negotiable document of title (UCC 2-308). Tender of delivery requires that the seller put and hold conforming goods at the buyer's disposition and give the buyer any notification reasonably necessary to enable him to take delivery (UCC 2-503). The parties must act reasonably: tender must be at a reasonable hour; the seller must keep the goods available for a reasonable time to enable the buyer to take possession; and the buyer must, in the absence of agreement to the contrary, furnish facilities reasonably suited to the receipt of the goods (UCC 2-503). Unless otherwise agreed, all of the goods called for by a contract of sale must be tendered in a single delivery (UCC 2-307). When the time of delivery is not specified, it is a reasonable one (UCC 2-309). What constitutes a reasonable time may be determined from usage of the trade, prior course of dealings, or reasonable commercial conduct under the circumstances.

The taking of physical possession of the goods is referred to as *receipt*. Payment is due at the time and place at which the buyer is to receive the goods (UCC 2-310). Except for COD shipments, the buyer has the right of inspection of the goods before paying for them (UCC 2-513).

Shipping Terms

The code deals with the legal effect of use of such standard shipping terms as FOB, FAS, and CIF. *FOB* (free on board) *shipping point* obligates the seller to deliver conforming goods to the carrier, properly prepared for shipment. The seller bears the expense and risk of putting them into the possession of the carrier. The goods are at the risk of the buyer during transit. *FOB destination* requires the seller at his own expense and risk to deliver goods to that place. *FOB vessel or car* requires that the seller at his own risk and expense load the goods on board. If the terms are *FAS* (free alongside) *vessel*, the seller at his own expense and risk must deliver the goods alongside the vessel in the manner usual in that port. *CIF* means that the total price includes cost of the goods, insurance, and freight. The seller must at his own risk and expense load the goods, obtain insurance for the buyer, and pay for the freight.

Title

In the absence of provision to the contrary, title to the goods passes to the buyer at the time and place at which the seller completes his performance of delivery of the goods. Passage of title is not affected by any reservation of a security interest. It cannot, however, take place prior to identification of the goods to the contract (UCC 2-401).

If the contract requires the seller to ship the goods to the buyer but does not require delivery at destination, title passes to the buyer at the time and place of shipment. If delivery at destination is required, title passes when delivery is tendered to the buyer there. Sometimes delivery is to be made without moving the goods, such as when they are in possession of a warehouseman or other bailee. If the seller in such a situation is to deliver a document of title, then title passes at the time and place where the necessary documents are delivered. However, if the goods are already identified at the time of contracting and no documents are to be delivered, title passes at the time and place of contracting. If a buyer, whether justifiably or not, refuses to receive or retain the goods or justifiably revokes acceptance of the goods, title revests in the seller by operation of law (UCC 2-401).

A general rule of property law is that a buyer ordinarily acquires a title no better than that of the seller. However, the Code provides that a person with voidable title has the power to transfer a good title to a good faith purchaser for value (BFP) (UCC 2-403).

A seller who is permitted to retain possession of the goods after the sale has been completed may transfer good title to a *buyer in the ordinary course of business*. The Code (UCC 1-201) defines the latter as a person who, in good faith and without knowledge. that the sale to him is in violation of the ownership rights or security interest of a third party, buys in the ordinary course from a person in the business of selling goods of that kind. Permitting the seller to retain possession is an *entrusting* of goods. When the seller is a merchant who deals in goods of that kind, the entrustee can pass good title. This is because of the justifiable reliance by the second buyer upon the seller's apparent ownership of the goods.

Sale on Approval

Goods are sometimes delivered under terms that permit the buyer to use them for a period of time in order to permit him to determine if he actually wishes to purchase them for use. This is referred to as a *sale on approval*. In such cases, title and risk remain with the seller until the buyer accepts the goods. Return is at the seller's risk and expense.

Sale or Return

When goods are delivered to a buyer for the purpose of resale, with the understanding that they may be returned to the seller should resale not occur, the transaction is known as a *sale or return*. In that case, risk and title are in the buyer. Return of the goods is at his expense and risk.

It is important to distinguish these transactions. Goods held on approval are not subject to the claims of the buyer's creditors until acceptance. However, goods held on sale or return are subject to such claims while in the buyer's possession (UCC 2-326).

Consignment

Goods may be delivered to a person for the purpose of sale by him to others. No title passes to him, however. Instead, a consignment is created. The consignee remits to the consignor the proceeds of any sale minus a commission for his selling efforts. The consignee has the power to transfer good title to a purchaser. If the consignee maintains a place of business in which he deals in goods of the kind but under a name other than that of the consignor, the goods will be considered to be on sale or return insofar as claims of creditors of the consignee are concerned (UCC 2-326).

Bulk Sales

When a merchant sells the major part of his stock in trade or inventory not in the ordinary course of business, it is referred to as a *bulk sale* or transfer. The Code requires that in order to protect his creditors, the merchant must give advance notice to them. If he does not, unpaid creditors may reach the goods after the sale, even though those goods be in the possession of a purchaser (UCC 6-107).

Seller's Responsibility for Goods Sold

A seller has a responsibility with respect to the goods he sells. If a product sold is defective and causes harm, it is possible that action may be brought against the seller in tort on the basis of negligence or strict liability. A seller may also be required to meet product standards imposed by statute or agency regulation. The Consumer Product Safety Act and similar acts are of importance in this connection, as discussed in Chapter 20.

Warranty

Responsibilities of a seller in connection with the goods sold also include those arising from Code provisions regarding warranties, both express and implied. A *warranty* is a representation by the seller of goods which is made with respect to the title, quality, or character of the goods. It is made as a part of the contract or sale and contains the seller's promise that certain facts are as he has represented them to be. A breach of warranty may give rise to an action by the buyer against the seller for breach of contract. If there was an intentional misrepresentation by the seller, the buyer may elect to bring an action in tort for fraud and deceit.

Express Warranties

An express warranty is created when the seller makes to the buyer as a part of the basis of the bargain any affirmation of fact, promise, or description that relates to the goods or when he provides a sample or model of the goods (UCC 2-313). The seller need not use the words "warranty" or "guarantee" or even state that he has a specific intention to create a warranty. A statement that is merely a seller's opinion or commendation of the goods, however, does not create a warranty. Statements that are only "sales talk" or "puffing" are not ordinarily considered to be warranties.

Implied Warranties

The Code provides that every seller impliedly warrants that the title he is conveying is good; that he has the right to transfer that title; and that the goods are free of any security interest, lien, or encumbrance (UCC 2-312). This warranty may be excluded by an express statement. It is also excluded if the circumstances are such that the buyer has reason to know that the seller is not guaranteeing the title, such as in the case of a sheriff's sale.

An implied *warranty of fitness for a particular purpose* exists if the seller had reason to know of any special purpose for which the buyer required the goods, the buyer relied upon the seller's skill or judgment to furnish suitable goods, and the seller knew or had reason to know of the buyer's reliance (UCC 2-315). If the seller is a merchant with respect to goods of the kind, there is an additional implied warranty—that of *merchantability*. To be merchantable, goods must at least be fit for the ordinary purposes for which such goods are used; pass without objection in the trade under the contract description; if fungible, be of fair average quality within the description; run, within the variations permitted by the agreement, of even kind, quality, and quantity within each unit and among all units; be adequately contained, packaged, and labeled; and conform to the promises or affirmations of fact on the container or label (UCC 2-314).

When there are both express and implied warranties in connection with a sale, they are construed, to the extent that is reasonable, as being consistent with each other (UCC 2-316).

Disclaimer of Warranties

The Code provides for disclaimer of implied warranties. A *disclaimer* is a denial of responsibility. Exclusion or modification of an implied warranty or fitness must be made by a writing and must be conspicuous. In the case of an implied warranty of merchantability, the language must mention "merchantability" and the writing must be conspicuous. Furthermore, implied warranties are excluded when goods are sold, "as is," "with all faults," or with similar wording; when the buyer has either examined or refused to examine goods, sample, or model; or by prior course of dealing or usage of the trade (UCC 2-316).

In some states, consumer legislation curtails warranty disclaimers. At the federal level, the Magnuson-Moss Warranty Act of 1975 establishes standards for written warranties on consumer products. This is discussed in more detail in Chapter 20.

Third-Party Beneficiaries of Warranties

Third party beneficiaries of both express and implied warranties include any natural person who is a member of the buyer's family or household or who is a guest in his home, if it is reasonable to expect that such persons may use the goods (UCC 2-318). The Code also provides that a seller may not exclude or limit his liability to such persons.

Traditionally a contractual relationship, or privity of contract, was a requirement in a suit for breach of warranty. That meant that only the buyer could recover from the seller. Today, this requirement has been abolished in almost every state, especially in cases involving personal injury.

Duties of Buyer and Seller

A seller has the duty to deliver or tender delivery of conforming goods at the proper time and place. Tender of delivery is a condition to the buyer's duty to accept and pay for the goods (UCC 2-507).

Buyer's Rights and Remedies

If the goods or tender of delivery fail to conform to the contract, a buyer may accept or reject the whole or he may accept any commercial units and reject the rest (UCC 2-601). A *commercial unit* is that which by commercial usage is considered as a single whole for purposes of sale and would be materially impaired in value by division (UCC 2-105). The buyer who accepts nonconforming goods may seek damages for breach of contract from the seller provided he sends notification of such breach to the seller within a reasonable time (UCC 2-607).

Rightful rejection of nonconforming goods must be within a reasonable time after delivery or tender of delivery. It is not effective unless the buyer reasonably notifies the seller (UCC 2-602). The reason for rejection must be provided to the seller, since it enables him to determine if the nonconformity is correctable. A seller has the right of *cure*, that is, the right within a reasonable time to effect correction of a defect in performance.

If the buyer has taken physical possession of the goods prior to rejection, he must hold them with reasonable care at the seller's disposition for a sufficient time to permit the seller to remove them

(UCC 2-602). A buyer who has made payment on the price of the goods prior to rejection has a security interest in them to the extent of the payment. He may resell them in satisfaction of it and may also recover any expenses incurred because of the rejection (UCC 2-711).

If the buyer is a merchant and the seller has no agent or place of business where the rejection occurs, the buyer must follow reasonable instructions from the seller as to what is to be done with the rejected goods (UCC 2-603). In the absence of such instructions, the merchant buyer must make reasonable effort to sell the rejected goods for the seller's account if the goods are perishable or subject to rapid decline in value. When such resale is made, the merchant buyer is entitled to reasonable reimbursement for his expenses as well as to a selling commission (UCC 2-603). When he receives no instructions regarding rejected goods, a merchant buyer either may store the goods for the seller, he may ship them back to the seller, or he may resell them (UCC 2-604).

A buyer accepts goods if, after a reasonable opportunity to inspect them, he informs the seller either that the goods are conforming or that he will take them in spite of their nonconformity; if he fails to make an effective rejection; if he does any act inconsistent with the seller's ownership (UCC 2-606). The buyer must pay the contract rate for the goods accepted (UCC 2-607).

A buyer may revoke his acceptance when he accepted nonconforming goods in the reasonable belief that cure would be effected and it has not been, or when he did not discover the nonconformity prior to acceptance because of difficulty of such discovery of the seller's assurances (UCC 2-608). The seller must be notified of revocation of acceptance within a reasonable time after the buyer discovers or should have discovered the reason for revocation (UCC 2-608). After revocation of acceptance, the buyer has the same rights and duties as if he had rejected the goods.

A buyer who accepts nonconforming goods has the burden of establishing breach. Furthermore, his failure to give the seller notice of nonconformity within a reasonable time will bar him from any remedy (UCC 2-607).

A buyer who has paid all or part of the price of goods may recover goods still in the seller's possession if they have been identified to the contract and the seller becomes insolvent within ten days after payment of the first installment (UCC 2-502). A buyer has the right of replevin for goods identified to the contract if, after reasonable effort, he is unable to effect a cover. *Replevin* is a legal action brought to recover possession of the goods. *Cover* refers to a purchase of goods in substitution for those due from the seller (UCC 2-712). In the case of goods which are unique, a buyer's remedies include specific performance (UCC 2-716).

Seller's Rights and Remedies

If the buyer wrongfully refuses to accept the goods or repudiates the contract, the seller may seek as damages the difference between market price at the time and place for tender and the unpaid contract price. He may also recover incidental damages (UCC 2-708). If this would not put the seller in as good a position as performance would, then the measure of damages is the profit, including reasonable overhead which the seller would have had from full performance plus incidental damages (UCC 2-708).

An unpaid seller has the right to sue for the contract price of the goods if the buyer has accepted the goods, if the goods were lost or destroyed after risk passed to the buyer, or if resale of the goods was impracticable (UCC 2-709). A seller who has possession of goods that were intended for a buyer who has either breached or repudiated the contract may resell the goods. The resale may be private or public. Notice to the buyer is required except in cases where the goods are perishable or subject to quick decline in value. The seller may purchase at the resale (UCC 2-706). The difference between the resale price and contract price is recoverable from the buyer. The seller need not account to the buyer for any profit made on a resale (UCC 2-706 and 2-710).

If a seller learns of a buyer's breach when the goods are unfinished, he may complete the manufacture and identify the goods to the contract, cease manufacture and resell unfinished parts for salvage, or take any other reasonable action. He must exercise reasonable commercial judgment in making this election (UCC 2-704).

If a seller discovers that the buyer is insolvent, he may refuse to make delivery except for cash, he may recover goods in transit from the carrier, or he may reclaim goods which are in the buyer's possession upon demand within ten days after their receipt by the buyer (UCC 2-702). In addition to stopping delivery of goods in transit to an insolvent buyer, a seller may stop delivery of a carload, truckload, planeload, or other large shipment when the buyer repudiates or fails to make a payment due on or before delivery (UCC 2-705).

Remedies under the Code

In considering remedies available to buyer and seller, two provisions of the Code should be borne in mind:

1. That, unless displaced by code provisions, the principles of law and equity supplement its provisions (UCC 1-103).

2. That remedies provided by the code are to be liberally administered with the objective of putting the injured party in as good a position as if the other party had fully performed (UCC 1-106).

When payment for goods is made by check, the law with regard to commercial paper can be of significance to a sales transaction. Payment in that case is conditional and is defeated between the parties by dishonor of the check on proper presentment (UCC 2-511). Presentment and dishonor are discussed in more detail in the next section.

COMMERCIAL PAPER

Article 3 of the Uniform Commercial Code deals with the law of commercial paper; Article 4, with checks and bank collections.

Commercial paper refers to a written promise or order to pay money. It is a special type of contract and functions as a substitute for money or as an instrument of credit. One of its distinctive features is the ease and readiness with which it can be transferred from person to person. Commercial paper may take several forms: checks, notes, drafts, and certificates of deposit.

Forms of Commercial Paper

Certificates of deposit and promissory notes are examples of commercial paper which contains a promise to pay. A *certificate of deposit* is "an acknowledgement by a bank of the receipt of money with an engagement to repay it" (UCC 3-104). Given by a bank as evidence of a time deposit, it contains the promise of the bank that issues it to make repayment to the person to whom it has been issued. In some cases, certificates of deposit contain a notation that they are "not subject to check," meaning that the depositor cannot write checks against the deposit represented by the certificate. A promise to pay money, other than a certificate of deposit, is a *promissory note* (UCC 3-104). It is signed by the person making the promise to pay, who is known as the *maker*. The party to whom it is payable is the *payee*.

Checks and drafts or bills of exchange are examples of commercial paper which contains an order to pay. A *draft*, also known as a *bill of exchange*, is a three-party paper as contrasted with notes and certificates of deposit which are two-party paper. The person who signs the draft is known as the *drawer*. The drawer orders or directs another person, referred to as the *drawee*, to make payment to a third person, the *payee*. A draft drawn by a seller of goods upon the buyer for the price of goods is known as a *trade acceptance*. A drawee obligates himself to make payment when the draft is due by *accepting* it. He does this by writing his name on its face.

A *check* is a draft drawn on a bank (the drawee) and payable on demand (UCC 3-104). It is the most frequently used form of commercial paper. A check is a special kind of draft. The drawer is a customer of the drawee bank and has funds on deposit in a checking or, as it is also known, a commercial account in that bank.

Checks and Bank Collections

When a person opens a checking account at a bank, he enters into a contractual relationship with the bank. The bank agrees to serve as the customer's agent. Its duties include honoring, that is, paying, checks drawn on it by the customer provided there are sufficient funds in his account. In fact, a bank is liable to its customer for damages proximately caused by wrongful dishonor of a check (UCC 4-402). *Dishonor* occurs when payment of the check is refused by the bank.

A bank must follow reasonable orders directed to it regarding payments to be made from a customer's account. Orders to make payment are contained in the checks written by the bank's customers. A bank is charged with knowledge of the signatures of its customers. Those signatures are on file at the bank. A drawee bank which honors a check on which the signature of the drawer has been forged ordinarily cannot charge the customer's account. In the case of a check which has been altered, a bank which makes payment in good faith may charge a customer on the check as it was originally drawn (UCC 4-401). There are exceptions to this general rule, such as where the forgery or alteration occurs because of the drawer's negligence.

When a customer issues a stop payment order, the bank has a duty not to honor the check provided the stop payment order has been received at a time and in a manner which gives the bank reasonable opportunity to act on it before the bank has paid or otherwise committed itself on the check. An oral stop payment order is binding upon the bank for 14 days unless confirmed in writing within that time. A written order is effective for six months (UCC 4-403).

Ordinarily checks are not "accepted" by the drawee. A check, however, can be accepted by having it *certified* by the drawee bank. When this occurs, the bank deducts the amount of the check immediately from the depositor's account and sets the sum aside. This makes it possible for the bank upon certification to undertake payment on the check regardless of the status of the depositor's account at the time the check is presented for payment. Unless there has been agreement to the contrary, a bank has no duty to certify a check. Its refusal to do so is not considered to be dishonor.

Nor has a bank an obligation to its customer to pay a check (with the exception of 'a certified check) that is presented for payment more than six months after its date. Such checks are sometimes referred to as "stale checks." However, the bank may charge the customer's account for payment made after six months if such payment is made in good faith (UCC 4-404). A bank may pay or certify checks drawn by a customer for ten days after the date of the customer's death unless it receives a stop payment order by a person claiming an interest in the account (UCC 4-405).

A customer has a duty to examine cancelled checks returned to him by the bank with the statement of his account and to report forgeries and alterations. If the customer does not report checks which have been altered or on which the customer's signature has been forged to the bank within one year from the time the bank statement and cancelled checks were returned to him or does not report forged indorsements appearing on his cancelled checks within three years, he is barred from asserting such matters against the bank if it made payment on the check in good faith (UCC 4-406).

When a customer deposits a check in his account, the bank provisionally credits the customer's account. The bank then becomes the customer's agent for the collection of the check. Until final settlement for the check is made, the depositor (as owner of the check) bears the risk of loss in case of its nonpayment. The *depositary bank* (the first bank to which a check is transferred for collection) then sends the check on its way to the bank by which the item is payable, known as the *payor bank*. When the payor bank honors the check, *settlement is final*. All prior provisional transactions become final also. The depositary bank then becomes the debtor of its customer: the situation is as though the customer had deposited cash in his account. On the other hand, if the payor bank dishonors the check, the provisional settlements are revoked and the dishonored check is returned to the drawer. When this occurs, the depositary bank charges the amount of the check against the customer's account. In other words, the effect is to cancel the deposit.

Negotiable Instruments

Commercial paper may be transferred by assignment. In that case, the rules of contract law with respect to assignment are applicable. If the paper meets the legal requirements for a negotiable instrument, it can be transferred by negotiation. The advantage of negotiation is that the transferee may acquire greater rights in the instrument than the transferor had and that an assignee would ordinarily acquire. To qualify as a *negotiable instrument*, the paper

1. Must be in writing and signed by the maker or drawer,
2. Must contain an unconditional promise or order to pay a sum certain in money,
3. Must be payable on demand or at a definite time, and
4. Must be payable to order or bearer (UCC 3-104).

Writing and Signature

No particular form of writing is required. Handwriting, printing, and typewriting are among the acceptable forms (UCC 1-201). Requirements concerning the signature are liberal: a typewritten or rubber stamp signature is acceptable, as is one consisting of the person's name, his initials, or an identifying mark. It is customary for commercial paper to be signed on the face in the lower right-hand corner; however, this is not required.

A signature may be made for a person by his agent or other authorized representative. The agent will be personally liable on the instrument if, in signing, he neither names the person he represents nor shows that he is signing in a representative capacity (Item A, Table 17-1). If the signature partially discloses the agency and representative capacity of the person signing, the agent may be personally liable on the instrument to third persons. However, if the agent is sued by the person with whom he dealt, parol evidence is admissible to prove that party knew the agent was acting only for his principal and that the parties intended that the principal would be bound. Partial disclosure exists if the instrument does not name the person represented but does show that the agent signed in a representative capacity (Item B, Table 17-1), or if the instrument names the person represented but does not show that the agent signed in a representative capacity (Item C, Table 17-1). The agent can escape personal liability when the signature contains the name of an organization (or principal) preceded or followed by the name and office of the agent (Item D, Table 17-1) (UCC 3-403). A signature that is unauthorized is wholly inoperative as that of the person whose name is signed. That person, however, may ratify the signature (UCC 3-404).

TABLE 17-1. Agent's signature and liability

	Signature	Liability
A	Fred Famous	Fred Famous is personally liable.
B	Fred Famous, President	Fred Famous may be personally liable to third parties, but may prove his agency status if sued by the party with whom he dealt.
C	The Firm, Inc. Fred Famous	'' ''
D	The Firm, Inc. by Fred Famous, President	The Firm is liable; Fred Famous escapes personal liability.

Promise or Order to Pay

To be negotiable, the instrument must contain a promise or order to pay that is unconditional. It cannot be qualified in any way. However, a mere acknowledgement of a debt—such as "I owe you" or "Due Fred Famous"—will not satisfy the requirements of a promise or order to pay. Addition of information to the instrument, such as a statement of the reason for which the instrument was given or of the collateral which constitutes the security for the instrument, does not destroy negotiability (UCC 3-105).

The instrument must be payable in money. A promise or order to pay in goods is not negotiable. The sum payable must be definite. There must be some way of determining how much the instrument is worth. A statement that the sum due is payable with interest at a specific rate, such as "with interest at 6% per year," would make that determination possible. However, interest "payable at the rate in effect at the date of maturity" lacks the necessary certainty. Provision for payment in installments does not destroy negotiability (UCC 3-106).

Time of Payment

To be negotiable, the instrument must be payable at a definite time or on demand. Most checks and drafts are payable on demand. Most notes are time instruments. They may be payable at such times as "one year after date" or "on January 1, 19XX." These are definite times, as contrasted with a statement that the instrument will become payable "30 days after my favorite ball team wins the pennant"—an occurrence that is uncertain and indefinite. The fact that the instrument is undated, antedated, or postdated does not affect negotiability if this is done in good faith and there is no intention to defraud (UCC 3-114). When the date has been omitted, the date of the instrument is considered to be that on which it was executed and delivered to the payee. Any holder of the instrument may insert the true date. *Postdating*, that is, dating the instrument as of a time later than that when it was made, does not destroy negotiability.

Words of Negotiability

The instrument to be negotiable must be payable to bearer or to the order of a named payee. "Bearer" and "order" are words of negotiability. When the payee is identified as "Cash" or "Bearer," the instrument is payable to the person who has possession of it and it is known as *bearer paper*. *Order paper* exists when there is a named payee to whose order the instrument has been made payable. Ordinarily, it will contain expressions such as these: "Pay to the order of John Q. Worker," "Pay to John Q. Worker or bearer," or "Pay to John Q. Worker or order." An instrument payable "to John Q. Worker" is not negotiable because it lacks words of negotiability.

Negotiation

Bearer paper may be negotiated by delivery alone. Negotiation of order paper requires indorsement in addition to delivery (UCC 3-202).

Although indorsement may not be required for negotiation under the provisions of the Code, some transferees insist upon it in order that the liabilities of an indorser will be borne by the transferor.

Indorsement

An instrument is *indorsed* when the holder of the instrument signs his name on the back of it or on a paper attached to it in such a way that it becomes a part of the instrument itself. Such an attachment is called an *allonge*. Indorsements may be of several kinds:

blank,
special or full,
qualified,
restrictive.

When an indorser signs only his name, the indorsement is referred to as a *blank indorsement*. This makes the instrument bearer paper. Because the paper can now be negotiated by delivery alone, many persons hesitate to use this type of indorsement if there is any possibility that the instrument may be lost, mislaid, or fall into the hands of unauthorized persons.

A *special indorsement* specifies the person to whom or to whose order it makes the instrument payable. An instrument specially indorsed becomes payable to the order of the special indorsee and requires his indorsement for further negotiation (UCC 3-204). "Pay to the order of Mary Worker, John Q. Worker" is an example of a special indorsement. The indorsement has the effect of making the instrument order paper. However, the indorsement need not contain the words "order" or "bearer."

A holder can convert a blank indorsement into a special indorsement by writing above the indorser's signature a statement that the instrument is payable to him (UCC 3-204). A *holder* is a person who is in possession of an instrument which has been drawn, issued, or indorsed to him or to his order, to bearer, or in blank (UCC 1-201).

A *restrictive indorsement* indicates the use to which the paper is to be put. Examples are: "For deposit. John Q. Worker" or "For collection. John Q. Worker." A restrictive indorsement does not destroy negotiability. However, the first taker of the instrument under such an indorsement must pay or apply any value given consistently with the indorsement (UCC 3-206). Many business firms make a practice of depositing the checks they receive and indorse them "for deposit only" in order to prevent their use or negotiation for any other purpose. The restrictive indorsement, however, will not prevent the bank that receives the instrument from transferring it to such other banks as may be involved in the process of deposit and collection of the check.

"Without recourse.   John Q. Worker" is an example of a *qualified indorsement* (UCC 3-414).   This is a disclaimer of contractual liability by the indorser in case of default by the maker or drawee.   This indorsement does not destroy negotiability.

When an instrument is payable to a person whose name has been misspelled or in a name other than his own, indorsement may be in that name, in his own name, or in both.   A person paying or giving value for the instrument may require both (UCC 3-203).

An instrument may be payable to the order of two or more payees, such as "to John Q. Worker and Mary Worker," or it may be payable to them in the alternative such as "to John Q. Worker or Mary Worker" (UCC 3-110).   The former requires indorsement by both payees.   The latter may be negotiated by either payee (UCC 3-116).

Indorser Warranties

A person who transfers an instrument by unqualified indorsement and who receives consideration warrants to his transferee and to any subsequent holder who takes the instrument in good faith that

1. He has good title to the instrument or is authorized to obtain payment for another, and the transfer is otherwise rightful;
2. All signatures are genuine or authorized;
3. The instrument has not been materially altered;
4. No defense of any party is good against him; and
5. He has no knowledge of any insolvency proceedings against a maker, or drawer, or acceptor (UCC 3-417).

Each indorser makes these warranties to the following indorser. Indorsers are liable to one another in the order in which they indorse, which is presumed to be the order in which their signatures appear on the instrument (UCC 3-414).

Forged Indorsements

As a general rule, a forged indorsement cannot operate as that of the person whose name has been signed.   If that person's indorsement was required for proper negotiation of the paper, anyone who has possession of the instrument cannot be a .holder.   When payment is made on an instrument to one claiming through a forged indorsement, the payor is ordinarily liable to the rightful owner of the instrument.

However, an indorsement by any person in the name of a named payee is effective:

1. If an imposter has induced the maker or drawer to issue the instrument to him in the name of the payee (this is known as the imposter rule); or

2. If the person signing the instrument intends the payee to have no interest in the instrument; or

3. If an agent or employee of the maker or drawer has supplied him with the name of the payee intending the latter to have no interest in the instrument. (An example is a payroll clerk who prepares checks payable to fictitious employees and then indorses them himself.) (UCC 3-405)

Ordinarily, a customer who deposits an instrument for collection should indorse it. If he does not, however, a depositary bank may supply the missing indorsement. This rule is a matter of practical convenience, to save the time that would be needed to send the item back for indorsement.

Holder in Due Course

The status of holder in due course places a person in a favorable position with regard to commercial paper. This is because a holder in due course can enforce payment even though there be personal defenses to the instrument. Only real defenses are effective against him. Examples of *real defenses* are: infancy or other incapacity of parties, fraud in the inception, illegality, discharge in bankruptcy, forgery, or material alteration. Examples of *personal defenses* are: lack of consideration, slight duress, unauthorized completion, failure of a condition precedent.

The effect of a Federal Trade Commission rule which became effective in 1976 is to eliminate the doctrine of holder in due course in connection with consumer purchases. The rule for the "Preservation of Consumers' Claims and Defenses" makes it an unfair or deceptive act or practice for a seller directly or indirectly to take or accept a consumer credit contract which fails to contain a notice in bold type that "Any holder of this consumer credit contract is subject to all claims and defenses which the debtor could assert against the seller of goods or services obtained pursuant hereto or with the proceeds hereof." A common form of financing consumer purchases is to have the buyer sign an installment note for the price of the goods. Sellers in need of cash frequently sell such notes to a finance company. Under the holder in due course doctrine, the finance company (provided it could meet the qualifications for a holder in due course) would take the note free of personal defenses of the consumer against the seller. Should the goods prove to be defective, the consumer could not make use of his most effective weapon—that is, to discontinue payments to the finance company. His only recourse would be against the seller. The FTC ruling enables him to exert personal defenses against the finance company; thus, he may discontinue payments to them.

The holder in due course doctrine, however, still exists in the case of commercial transactions between business persons. It should be noted that there can be no holder in due course on an instrument which is not payable to order or to bearer (UCC 3-805).

In order to be a holder in due course, one must first be a holder. It should be noted that a thief or finder may be the holder of a bearer instrument. However, a thief or finder has no rights in order paper.

To be a holder in due course, a holder must take the instrument

1. For value,
2. In good faith,
3. Without notice that is overdue or has been dishonored, and
4. Without notice of any defenses or adverse claims (UCC 3-302).

A payee or a bank may be a holder in due course.

A person takes an instrument for *value* when he performs the agreed upon consideration, when he takes the instrument as security for a debt, or when he acquires a security interest in the paper. *Good faith* means "honesty in fact in the conduct or transaction concerned" (UCC 1-201).

Notice of Defenses

A person who takes paper which is incomplete or irregular on its face may be charged with notice of defenses. An instrument is considered to be *incomplete* when a term which is material has been omitted. A *material term* is one that affects the legal obligations of the parties. Examples include the payee's name or the amount. Because he is charged with notice, a person cannot be a holder in due course if he takes an instrument which contains omissions of material terms at the time he takes it. However, if blanks on an incomplete instrument are filled in by any person according to instructions of the maker or drawer, the instrument becomes effective as completed. A person who takes such an instrument can be a holder in due course and can enforce the instrument as completed (UCC 3-407). On the other hand, when the instrument is not completed in accordance with instructions, it is considered to be altered (UCC 3-115). If such paper is received by a holder in due course, it can be enforced by him as completed. Loss falls upon the person who made the alteration possible by signing an incomplete paper (UCC 3-406). A person who is not a holder in due course, however, would be subject to the defense of improper completion.

A paper is *irregular* when its face contains noticeable alterations, when it has been marked paid, or when there is anything else on the instrument which would put a reasonable person on notice that something is wrong, causing him to investigate further. A person taking such an instrument cannot be a holder in due course, nor can a person who takes an instrument which is overdue.

A holder who acquires an instrument from a holder in due course usually acquires the rights of the holder in due course.

Presentment and Payment

Presentment is a demand for either acceptance or payment, which is made upon the maker, drawee, or other payor of an instrument by or on behalf of a holder (UCC 3-504).

Presentment for acceptance does not apply to promissory notes. It is, however, required to charge, i.e., to hold liable, the drawer and indorsers of a draft in the following instances:

1. When the instrument provides that such presentment must be made,

2. When it is payable at a place other than the business or residence of the drawee, or

3. When it is payable at a fixed time after presentment or on sight (UCC 3-501).

Presentment for acceptance is made to the drawee of a draft. Until and unless he accepts, he is not liable on the instrument. Furthermore, he is under no duty to the holder to accept. Once he does accept, he becomes primarily liable for payment on the instrument. His acceptance is his assent to be bound by the instrument.

In the case of certification of checks, a bank may certify a check at the request of either the drawer or a holder. Certification at the request of a holder discharges the drawer and all prior indorsers from liability on the check.

Presentment for payment is necessary to charge any indorser of a negotiable instrument (UCC 3-501).

Time and Manner of Presentment

The time and manner of presentment is prescribed in the Code. Presentment must be made within a reasonable time. What is reasonable is determined from the nature of the instrument, custom and usage of banking and the trade, and by the facts and circumstances of the case (UCC 3-503). In the case of checks, a reasonable time to charge a drawer is 30 days after date, and a reasonable time to charge an indorser is seven days after his indorsement (UCC 3-503). If presentment is due on a day which is not a business day, presentment becomes due on the next day which is a full business day for both parties. Presentment must be made at a reasonable hour. If it is made at a bank, it must be during its banking hours (UCC 3-503).

Presentment may be made in person, by mail, or through a clearing house (UCC 3-504). The party to whom presentment is made may, without dishonoring the instrument, require the exhibition of the instrument and reasonable identification of the person making the presentment as well as evidence of his authority to make it if he is making it for another (UCC 3-505). A signed receipt for full or partial payment or surrender of the instrument upon payment in full may be demanded. Failure to comply with these requirements invalidates the presentment, but the person presenting is given a reasonable time in which to comply (UCC 3-505).

Failure to present an instrument when due, without excuse, completely discharges indorsers. Discharge to the extent that proper presentment caused them a loss is accorded to drawers, to the acceptor of a draft or the maker of a note payable at a bank (UCC 3-502).

Dishonor

An instrument is *dishonored* when presentment has been duly made and acceptance or payment is refused or cannot be obtained within the prescribed time; or, in the case of bank collections, the instrument is returned by the midnight deadline. The *midnight deadline* is midnight of the next banking day following the one on which the bank received the item. Dishonor also occurs when presentment is excused and the instrument is not duly accepted or paid. Upon dishonor, the holder has an immediate right of recourse against the drawer and indorsers (UCC 3-507).

Notice of Dishonor

Unless excused, notice of dishonor is necessary to charge any indorser. Failure to give notice discharges indorsers completely. Notice of dishonor is also necessary to charge any drawer or the acceptor of a draft or maker of a note payable at a bank. Failure to give notice discharges such persons only to the extent that they have suffered a loss because of failure to receive notice.

Notice may be given in any reasonable manner. It may be oral or written. It must identify the instrument and state that it has been dishonored. Sending the instrument bearing a stamp, ticket, or writing stating that acceptance or payment has been refused is considered to be sufficient notice (UCC 3-508).

Notice may be given to any person who may be liable on the instrument. It may be given by or on behalf of the holder or any party who has himself received notice or any other party who can be compelled to pay the instrument (UCC 3-508).

Protest is a certificate of dishonor made under seal of an authorized person. It is a formal method of giving notice of dishonor and is required only for drafts drawn or payable outside the United States (UCC 3-509).

Excused Presentment, Notice of Dishonor, Protest

Delay in presentment, protest, or notice of dishonor is excused when the party is without notice that it is due. It is also excused when the delay is caused by circumstances beyond his control and he exercises reasonable diligence.

Presentment, notice of dishonor, and protest may be excused when the party to be charged has waived it or has himself dishonored the instrument or when, in the exercise of reasonable diligence, it cannot be made.

Waiver of protest is also waiver of presentment and notice of dishonor even though protest is not required (UCC 3-511).

Discharge

The legal obligation of a party in connection with a negotiable instrument is discharged when he pays the amount due on the paper to a holder or his agent (UCC 3-601). Discharge is to the extent of payment or satisfaction of the holder. This is true even though it is made with knowledge of a claim of another person to the instrument. However, the party making such a claim can enjoin payment or satisfaction by court order. He can also defeat discharge by posting adequate indemnity prior to payment (UCC 3-603).

There is no discharge of a party who in bad faith pays or satisfies a holder who acquired the instrument by theft. Nor is there discharge of a party who pays or satisfies an instrument which has been restrictively indorsed and does so in a manner inconsistent with the terms of the restrictive indorsement. The Code makes exceptions for certain banks in the collection process in this connection (UCC 3-603).

The holder of commercial paper may, without consideration, discharge any party by intentionally cancelling either the instrument or the party's signature by destruction or mutilation. He may also renounce his rights in a signed writing or by surrender of the instrument to the party to be discharged. Neither cancellation nor renunciation without surrender of the instrument affects the title to the paper (UCC 3-605).

A holder who discharges any party to the instrument without reserving the rights of others against that party also discharges such other persons from liability on the instrument. If a holder unjustifiably impairs any collateral which has been given, the parties on whose behalf it has been given are discharged (UCC 3-606).

Discharge of commercial paper brings to an end the legal obligations of the parties with regard to that paper.

SECURED TRANSACTIONS

Article 9 of the Uniform Commercial Code deals with yet another topic that can be of great importance in connection with a sale, and that is the secured transaction. This section discusses provisions of the 1972 revised version of Article 9. At the time of this writing, however, that version had not yet been adopted by many states who not only retain the earlier version but have also enacted numerous amendments to it. As a result, the law with regard to secured transactions is in a transition stage and far from uniform. Persons interested in any one state's specific provisions, therefore, are urged to check that state's law.

The seller of goods on credit often desires some assurance of payment when physical possession of the goods is given to the buyer. In that case, the seller may protect his rights by means of a security interest consisting of the right to repossess the goods should the buyer fail to make the required payments or otherwise breach the contract. This is an example of a secured transaction.

Definitions

A *secured transaction* is one that, regardless of form, is intended to create a security interest in personal property or fixtures (UCC 9-102). A secured transaction takes place when a debtor or buyer gives an interest in personal property to a creditor or seller (known as the *secured party*) to secure payment of a debt or performance of an obligation. The interest need not be possessory and is referred to as a *security interest*. The obligation involved is not restricted to the payment of money, although that is perhaps the most common.

Secured transactions of various forms are covered by Article 9 of the Code. For instance, they may be in the nature of lien or title retention contracts. The latter is exemplified in a *conditional sale*; that is, one in which the seller retains title to the goods until final payment for them has been made. Another example of a secured transaction is a *pledge*. This is a transaction in which a creditor or lender is given, as security for a debt, physical possession of personal property until such time as the obligation is paid in full. Some security interests, including landlord liens and certain statutory liens, are not covered by the Code (UCC 9-102 and 9-104).

Except for fixtures, the property that serves as the security must be personal rather than real property. It is referred to as the *collateral*. Various kinds of personalty may serve as the collateral, including goods;

documents, such as bills of lading and warehouse receipts; instruments, such as stocks, bonds, and commercial paper; intangibles, such as accounts, contract rights, good will, patents, and copyrights; and chattel paper, such as a conditional sales contract executed in connection with a note (UCC 9-102). Whether title to the collateral is in the secured party or in the debtor is immaterial (UCC 9-202). The security interest exists in the collateral itself, and, unless there is agreement to the contrary, also in its proceeds (UCC 9-306). *Proceeds* consist of whatever is received when the collateral is sold or otherwise disposed of (UCC 9-306). Proceeds may be cash or other property.

Creation of the Security Interest

The security interest is created by agreement between the secured party and the debtor. This is known as the *security agreement*. It must be in writing, signed by the debtor, and contain a description of the collateral (UCC 9-203). An exception to the writing requirement exists when the security arrangement is possessory so long as the secured party has possession of the goods (UCC 9-113).

The description of the security is sufficient if it reasonably identifies the collateral (UCC 9-110). No security interest arises in property which is not included in the description. Except in the case where the collateral consists of consumer goods, the agreement may provide that the obligations covered by it are to be secured by afteracquired collateral (UCC 9-204). This is the case with a "floating lien," that is, a security interest which exists in a rapidly changing stock of goods, such as a retailer's inventory.

Article 9 of the Code provides for four classifications of goods:

1. *Consumer goods*—those that are used or bought for use primarily for personal, family, or household purposes.
2. *Equipment*—property that is used or bought for use primarily in business, farming, or a profession.
3. *Inventory*—goods that are held by a person for sale, lease, or to be furnished under a contract of service. Inventory includes raw materials, work in process, or materials used or consumed in a business.
4. *Farm products*—crops, livestock, or supplies used or produced in farming operations (UCC 9-109).

The classification of the collateral is often determinative of requirements and rights of the parties.

Attachment

The security interest attaches to the collateral as soon as the agreement has been executed, value has been given, and the debtor has rights in the collateral. *Attachment* means that the security interest is enforceable against the debtor with respect to the collateral (UCC 9-203).

Perfection of Security Interest

It sometimes happens that creditors to the debtor, other than the secured party, attempt to attach or effect a lien on the property which is serving as collateral for a secured transaction. When the secured party's interest is effective against third parties, the interest is said to be *perfected*. Perfection gives the secured party priority over others who may claim an interest in the collateral. Perfection of a security interest generally requires notice to third parties of the secured party's interest in the collateral.

The most frequently used method of perfecting is by filing a *financing statement* in the proper public office. This document is separate and distinct from the security agreement. It must be signed by both the debtor and the secured party, give their names and addresses, contain a description of the collateral, and state that the parties have entered into a security agreement. The Code contains a suggested form for the statement (UCC 9-402).

Filing is not required for perfection in all cases. Perfection occurs automatically when the secured party takes and retains possession of the collateral. Perfection also occurs without filing when the security interest attaches in the case of a purchase money security interest in consumer goods that are not fixtures. A *purchase money security interest* is a security interest by the seller of the collateral to secure all or part of its purchase price. It may also exist when money is lent for a debtor's purchase of the collateral (UCC 9-107).

Requirements for filing differ among the states. In some, the filing must be done at the county level; in others, at the state capitol; and in still others, in both places. Filing is effective for five years, after which time the security interest will end unless a continuation statement is filed. This extends the time for another five years. When the debt has been paid, a termination statement should be addressed to the filing officer who can then remove the financing statement from the files. Filing of a termination statement is required in the case of consumer goods (UCC 9-404).

As a general rule a perfected security interest is retained intact for four months if collateral is taken into another state. After that time, filing is necessary for continuation of the perfected security interest (UCC 9-103).

The Code makes special provision for articles that have a certificate of title, such as motor vehicles (UCC 9-302). These generally require licensing and notation of a security interest on the title in accordance with state law. Filing may be necessary for perfection in some states (UCC 9-103).

Priority of Claims

Provisions of Article 9 set forth the priorities which exist when there are conflicting interests in the same collateral. As a general rule, a secured party's rights in collateral are superior to those of an unsecured creditor or one who has no lien. The claims of the holder of an unperfected security interest are ordinarily subordinate to those of a lien creditor who is without knowledge of the unperfected interest (UCC 9-301). A secured party with a perfected interest takes priority over a creditor with an unperfected security interest, an unsecured creditor, and even a debtor's trustee in bankruptcy. Should there be more than one secured party with a perfected interest in the same collateral, priority is in the order of filing (UCC 9-312). When a person in the ordinary course of business furnishes services (such as repairs) for goods subject to a security interest, a lien upon goods in the possession of that person for his services takes priority over a perfected security interest in the absence of statutory provision to the contrary (UCC 9-310).

Purchase money security interests have priority over certain secured interests which may be prior in time. A purchase money security interest in collateral other than inventory is superior to conflicting security interests in the same collateral provided the purchase money security interest is perfected at the time the debtor receives the collateral or within ten days thereafter. One who furnishes inventory on a purchase money basis can prevail over a prior secured party if the supplier notifies the prior secured party in writing that he expects to get a purchase money security interest in the goods (UCC 9-312). When the debtor has given a security interest in after-acquired inventory to a creditor other than the supplier of inventory, this provision is of importance. Conflicts with regard to other interests, such as those with regard to crops and fixtures, are also covered by the Code.

Sale or Transfer of Collateral

A debtor may transfer his rights in the property which is the collateral for a secured transaction. The debtor's right to transfer the goods cannot be defeated by a provision in the security agreement either prohibiting such transfer or making it a default (UCC 9-311). Ordinarily the transferee cannot acquire any rights greater than those of the debtor and therefore he generally holds the goods subject to the security interest.

Certain transferees, however, are protected. In the case of consumer goods, a buyer takes free of a security interest even if it is perfected if he buys without knowledge of the security interest, for value, and for his own personal, family, or household purposes. However, this is not true if a financing statement has been filed prior to the purchase (UCC 9-307).

A buyer in the ordinary course of business is also protected. Except for persons buying farm products from an individual engaged in farming operations, a buyer in the ordinary course of business takes free of a security interest created by his seller even though the security is perfected and even though the buyer knows of its existence (UCC 9-307). This enables merchants to give valid title to customers even though the merchant's inventory has been financed through a security interest.

Duties of Secured Party

A secured party must use reasonable care in the custody and preservation of any collateral in his possession (UCC 9-207). In the absence of agreement to the contrary, all reasonable expenses (such as insurance or taxes) incurred in the custody or use of the collateral are chargeable to the debtor and are secured by the collateral. Risk of accidental loss or damage is on the debtor to the extent it is not covered by insurance (UCC 9-207).

Default

Default occurs when the debtor fails to make payment when due. Unless otherwise agreed, a secured party has the right to take possession of the collateral upon the debtor's default. He may do so without recourse to legal process if repossession can be accomplished without breach of the peace (UCC 9-503).

After default and before the secured party disposes of the collateral, the debtor may redeem the property by tendering the payment due plus any expenses (UCC 9-506).

The secured party may sell, lease, or otherwise dispose of the repossessed property. Resale may be public or private, at any time or place and on any terms, provided all of these are commercially reasonable. Unless the collateral is perishable or will decline rapidly in value, the secured party must give the debtor reasonable advance notice of resale. The secured party may purchase at a public resale and, if widely distributed standard price quotations for the goods exist, at a private sale (UCC 9-504).

If, in the case of a purchase money security interest in consumer goods, the debtor has paid 60 percent of the cash price, a secured party who has repossessed the collateral must dispose of it by resale within 90 days after taking possession unless the debtor has signed a waiver. If the secured party does not comply with these requirements, the debtor may recover for conversion or may proceed otherwise against the secured party for failure to comply with Code requirements (UCC 9-505).

The proceeds of resale are applied first to recover reasonable expenses of repossession and resale, and after that to satisfaction of the indebtedness plus interest and any legal fees. The secured party must account to the debtor for any surplus and, unless otherwise agreed, the debtor is liable for any deficiency (UCC 9-504). A resale discharges the security interest and transfers to a purchaser for value all of the debtor's rights in the goods.

Sale of Accounts

Article 9 of the Code also applies to the sale of accounts or chattel paper. Certain such transfers are excluded, however. These include a sale of accounts or chattel paper as part of a sale of the business out of which they arose, an assignment of accounts or chattel paper which is for the purpose of collection only, a transfer of a right to payment under a contract to an assignee who is also to do the performance under the contract, or a transfer of a single account to an assignee in whole or partial satisfaction of a pre-existing indebtedness (UCC 9-104). An *account* is any right to payment for goods sold or leased or for services rendered which is not evidenced by an instrument or chattel paper, whether or not it has been earned by performance (UCC 9-106). No financing statement is required to be filed to perfect an assignment of accounts or contract rights which does not transfer a significant part of the outstanding accounts or contract rights of the assignor (UCC 9-302).

The provisions of Article 9 are far reaching in their effect upon credit transactions. Other statutory requirements affecting credit are discussed in Chapter 20 dealing with socio-economic regulation.

CHAPTER 18
TORTS

A tort in the legal sense is a civil wrong usually arising from an act that harms. The term comes from the Latin *tortus*, or twisted, implying conduct that is not straight or right. A tort has always been difficult to define. Most of the definitions have focused upon what it is not; it has been described as an act, neither a crime nor a breach of a contract, that provides a basis for legal action.

In this situation the best definition may be an operational one, that is, a definition that points to actual instances of behavior and lets those examples combine to provide the definition. This entire chapter, then, defines a tort.

There are various ways of classifying torts, including the following one based upon the originating act:

1. Intentional;
2. Nonintentional:
   (a) Negligence,
   (b) Strict liability;
3. Combinations of the above.

All torts involve some act (possibly words as well as physical movement) or an omission when there is a duty to act. The act must be shown to cause an injury to a party who can recover monetary damages in a civil legal action as a result.

What makes a great deal of difference in the legal action, however, is the variation between the categories of torts in terms of what is required in developing the cause of action in court. Different standards of care, scope of duty, and burden of proof are present.

CONSTRAINTS UPON ACTIONS

In each of the classifications several other factors must be taken into consideration when evaluating the activity and judging whether it is indeed an actionable wrong.

Sovereign Immunity

The general rule is that a state cannot be sued for tort unless there is a statute that permits an action to be taken. State officers engaged in official acts are not liable for the negligence incurred in pursuing a governmental function. There is no immunity, however, in proprietary functions, that is, activities that can be pursued by private enterprise. Negligence in the operation of a police or fire department or a school district cannot be the basis for a suit; maintaining highways, parks, airports, or playgrounds has been labeled a proprietary function and in many states recovery has been allowed for negligence in connection with such activities.

Charitable Immunity

Nonprofit organizations that presumably work for the public welfare (hospitals, schools, etc.) have been held to be immune to tort liability. Increasingly courts have either eliminated this immunity completely or severely restricted its application.

Wrongful Death and Survival Actions

At common law tort actions did not survive the death of the injured party nor was there a tort action possible for a wrongful death. At present all jurisdictions have statutes permitting some suits in both these areas. There is, however, a wide variation among states as to the extent of the right to sue.

Relationships

Persons in the same family generally cannot sue each other in a tort action; this immunity extends to husband, wife, parents, and children.

In some cases persons may be liable for the torts of others; parents, in many jurisdictions, are liable for the torts of their children. Under the doctrine of imputed liability a master may be liable for the tort of a servant.

INTENTIONAL TORTS

Intentional torts may be subdivided into two categories—torts to the person, and torts to property. Each of the two categories has a variety of examples with some unique elements and each has the same range of variation in terms of the defenses that are possible to raise or any specific privileges that arise in the situation.

Torts to the Person

Torts to the person involve the actual invasion of the life space of an individual or the threat of doing so.

Battery

Battery is an intentional touching without consent. There must be some volitional movement by a person; it must be shown that the actor intended the harmful touching of another or must have known that the harmful effect would follow. If, however, the actor actually intended to touch A but touches B instead, no matter, for courts will apply the "transfer of intent doctrine" to fix liability on the toucher for the battery. Reasonable damages as the result of the injury will be awarded by the court.

Assault

The tort of assault arises from a menacing movement that makes one apprehensive of one's personal safety; assault does not involve a touching although mere words alone will not be enough to constitute an assault. For an assault to take place there must be an intentional act that results in placing a person in apprehension of an immediate offensive or harmful touching. Apprehension is sufficient to show the tort even if the person threatened knows there may be a way out.

False Imprisonment

A confinement of a person within fixed boundaries for some period of time as a result of an intentional act is the tort of false imprisonment. Confinement by actual or threatened physical force to a person or a member of his family or the exclusion of a person from his home all represent confinement. There may also be confinement through the use of mere words, when there is an assertion of legal authority, as in an arrest. There is no confinement, and therefore no tort, if the person either does not know he is confined or is aware that there is a reasonable means for him to escape.

Defenses or Privileged Invasions

Situations can exist in which invasion of personal interests, even though intentional, are not actionable torts.

Consent

One of the most common of these is when a person consents to an invasion; there may be actual consent or consent may be implied from conduct (apparent consent). A third type of consent may be implied by law as when an operation is necessary for the saving of a person's life if the person is unable to give consent. There is no consent, however, in a situation where the actor goes beyond the act the person understood would take place. Under the doctrine of informed consent, for instance, a physician has a duty to inform the patient completely of the dangers inherent in the treatment. There is no consent, furthermore, if such consent were obtained under duress or fraud.

Self-defense

Reasonable reactions to threats of bodily harm when the force is not likely to cause death or serious bodily injury are available to one acting in self-defense. There is a duty to retreat or try to explain if the threat arises through negligence or mistaken identity.

The use of force likely to cause death or serious bodily harm in self-defense is available to a person who can reasonably believe that he is under immediate threat of death or serious bodily harm. There is, however, a duty to retreat although in some states there is no duty to retreat in one's home or when it would be dangerous to the person. A defense of third persons would generally fall under the same guidelines with the additional factor that there be a socially recognized duty to protect a third person and a belief that the third person is not able to defend himself.

Defense of real or personal property

Unprivileged intrusions upon property may be resisted by force not likely to cause serious bodily harm or death if such force is believed necessary. There must first be a demand, however, that the intruder cease and desist. Deadly force can be used only in defense of a dwelling place and only when there is a threat of serious bodily harm or death to the resident. Mechanical devices such as traps or electric fences may be used in defense of property only when such means are reasonable and customary, adequate warning is given, and an intrusion does in fact threaten serious bodily harm or death to the owner.

Reasonable and nondeadly force can be used to regain personal property unlawfully taken (a pickpocket case) or when someone has been wrongfully dispossessed of his land. When there has been no initial wrongful dispossession redress must be through the courts.

Arrest

The extent of privileged actions in arrest situations depends upon whether a warrant has or has not been issued, whether the actor is an officer of the law or a private citizen, and whether the original act is a felony or a misdemeanor.

There is no tort liability for an arrest under a warrant free of defects that a reasonable man might discover and the person named in the warrant is the person arrested (again within a reasonable range of mistakes). Liability for arrests without a warrant varies. If an officer of the law has a reasonable belief that a felony has been committed he may arrest a person he suspects of committing the felony. A private citizen may make an arrest without a warrant only if a felony has in fact been committed and he has a reasonable belief that the person arrested did commit the felony. Both officers and private citizens are under the same constraints with respect to a misdemeanor. There must have been a misdemeanor committed in their presence and the person arrested must in fact be guilty. Some jurisdictions allow reasonable belief of guilt as grounds for an officer to arrest without liability.

Torts To Property

Invasion of interests in real and personal property are known as trespass or conversion. As with other kinds of torts there are privileged invasions and defenses.

Trespass to Realty

Intentional invasion of a right to possession of land by actual entry or failure to leave when required is actionable. Only the lessee may bring an action during the term of the lease.

Of increasing importance is the consideration of rights to air space above the land. Courts vary in the designation of the extent of rights—potential or actual use by the landowner may be the determining factors but legitimate invasions can be privileged (aircraft are increasingly put in this category).

Trespass or Conversion

Personal property interests may be invaded by dispossession, theft, or destruction of a chattel. Dealing with stolen property or misdelivering it is also basis for a tort action. Recovery in trespass is for damages while conversion actions bring recovery for the value of the chattel plus damages.

Defenses or Privileged Invasions

One can enter land to recover dispossessed chattels with reasonable nondeadly force (except when it is his own fault). Such action is also privileged if entry is necessary to avert a danger to the public (but not a public nuisance). There is a privilege to enter land to abate a private nuisance if there is first a demand that the nuisance be abated.

NEGLIGENCE

This area of torts provides more legal action than any other; court calendars are often jammed with personal injury suits.

A negligence action looks to four elements that must be present to provide a basis for recovery:

1. Duty to conform to a certain standard of care,
2. Failure to conform to that standard,
3. Causal connection between conduct and injury,
4. Actual damage or loss.

Of all four elements the most complex is the question of the duty owed.

Duty

The duty generally owed by one person to another is the "duty of due care" or what a "reasonable man" may be expected to do. This may, at times, be supplemented by standards imposed by statutes or court decision.

The duty of due care means that which the reasonable man might objectively follow in the circumstances under study. Conditions do make a difference; the greater the risk involved or skill needed, the higher the standard. Physicians or lawyers, for instance, are expected to follow a higher standard than a layperson in certain circumstances.

There may be duties imposed by statutory or case law that are in addition to the basic duty of due care. Violation of the statute would be negligence *per se*, if the legislature intended the statute to stop those acts committed. Traffic violations may be the basis for negligence per se or the selling of liquor to an intoxicated person may make the seller liable for third party injuries. An employer may be liable for a tortious act committed by an employee in the course of employment (*respondeat superior*). In many states parents are now liable for the torts of their children (where they were not so liable under common law). Bailees for hire are at least liable for exercising due care but may even be strictly liable.

Under certain circumstances there may be a duty of care standard different from or less than the level required of a reasonable man. Occupiers of land, for instance, may have limited liability. Generally there is no liability to those outside the land except for due care to inspect things like fences or protruding trees. With respect to trespassers, the occupier is under no duty to unknown trespassers; the occupier must exercise due care with respect to all risks for known trespassers and risks of serious bodily harm for constant trespassers—those who are in the habit of doing so. The standard is higher in most jurisdictions with respect to young children who trespass upon land containing an "attractive nuisance." Here the occupier must exercise due care to protect immature infants from artificial conditions with a risk of serious bodily harm.

Businesses must be alert also to the standard of care to be exercised with respect to persons who come onto the business premises for a specific purpose. Such persons are known as "invitees." The duty of the occupier of the premises is to inspect and discover any invitees, any natural or artificial conditions that may cause harm, and warn invitees of these or make the conditions safe.

The *scope* of the duty owed is another difficult problem for the legal system to resolve. Much of the activity in negligence cases may revolve around the question—to whom is the duty of care owed. A classic case (*Palsgraf v. Long Island R. Company*, 248 N.Y. 339) held that the duty of care extended to only a "foreseeable plaintiff" or one who was in a foreseeable "zone of danger." A much broader view is that the duty of care extends to anyone injured as the proximate result of a breach of duty. This latter view has become the accepted approach in most jurisdictions at the present time.

Failure to Conform

A breach of duty occurs when the conduct of a defendant in a negligence action can be shown to fall short of the standard of care required. In some instances the mere fact that an act takes place is evidence enough of the breach of duty. The doctrine of *res ipsa loquitur* (Latin for "the thing speaks for itself") may be invoked for showing breach of duty. This concept of liability, however, requires four specific factors:

1. A device in the prior exclusive control of the defendant,
2. An event that would not have happened in the exercise of due care,
3. No voluntary act by the plaintiff contributing to the event,
4. The event is more readily explained by the defendant than the plaintiff.

Some courts look upon *res ipsa loquitur* as permitting an inference of negligence while other courts view it as a presumption that is rebuttable. In the latter case the burden of proof shifts to the defendant to get a satisfactory explanation.

Cause

A further necessary element for the establishment of negligence is to show that the action of the defendant was the actual and proximate cause of the injury. Actual cause will be shown if the plaintiff would not have been injured but for the act of the defendant. If acts of a third party combine with those of the defendant and the plaintiff would not have been injured except for the two acts occurring together, both acting parties may still be liable. If either defendant alone is a material factor in causing the injury, both are still liable.

Proximate Cause

Demonstrating an act as causing an injury is not enough to establish liability—there must also be a determination that the act was the *proximate* cause of the injury. If there is direct causation (no intervening forces) there is little doubt of the proximity even though there is actually a long chain of events. That long sequence may have been entirely unforeseen but that makes no difference (courts may draw the line at some reasonable point, however).

Intervening Acts

Most of the difficulty in determining liability comes when there are intervening forces between the original act of the defendant and the injury sustained by the plaintiff. Generally if the intervening act is a normal one or to be expected, any aggravation of injury does not relieve the defendant of liability. Injury as part of a rescue or poor medical attention might be foreseeable or one of the common risks (determined by the jury). Unforeseeable results or "Acts of God" are the kinds of intervening forces that relieve the defendant of liability.

Actual Damage or Loss

The last element is, perhaps, the easiest of the four to determine insofar as occurrence is concerned; what is more difficult, however, is the conversion of damage or injury to a monetary figure. How much is a life, limb, or reputation worth? The necessity for providing specific answers taxes the abilities of all involved in the calculation of legal damages.

Defenses in Negligence Actions

If a party is injured under a set of circumstances where he understood the dangers to be met and voluntarily undertook them, it may be said that he expressly or impliedly consented to take the chances involved. This is *assumption of the risk*. Most courts hold, for instance, that spectators at a hockey game assume the risk of flying pucks.

Agreements holding one party free from liability (such as releases or waivers) may be upheld if the bargainers had equal power but it is deemed to be against public policy for disadvantaged parties in bargaining to be bound by such agreements. Even if such agreements are valid they are not so in "willful" or "gross" negligence.

Contributory negligence is conduct of a party that helps to cause his injuries and, as a result, serves as a bar to recovery. The standard of self-care to be met by a plaintiff is that of the reasonable man or that behavior required by statute (as use of seat belts in an automobile). Contributory negligence alone serves as a defense; unless other factors are present that contributory negligence would bar recovery. If the defendant had the *last clear chance* of knowingly avoiding the accident and did not, the plaintiff would not be barred, despite his negligence.

There is a trend toward the determination by the court of relative contribution to an accident by the parties. Under the doctrine of *comparative negligence* recovery would be allowed according to the proportion of the contribution to the accident.

STRICT LIABILITY

Legal policy holds that there are some situations in which an injured party must recover even though there was no intent or negligence on the part of a defendant. Absolute liability exists for the act or omission even if it is otherwise legally and morally correct. Strict liability, in general, requires the same elements as does an action under negligence with the important addition of the existence of an absolute duty to make a situation safe.

Needless to say, there is a good reason for restricting the scope of this category of torts and courts are reluctant to expand coverage.

Scope of Liability

There is an absolute duty to make an "extra-hazardous" activity safe for "foreseeable" plaintiffs. The danger that comes from the extra-hazardous activity must be foreseen to be the kind of danger that normally arises from it and must be a proximate cause of the accident. While courts will differ on this and other points, there is a tendency to eliminate strict liability for certain activities as they become more common and under control (i.e., blasting) and to expand into newer areas where increased protection is deemed necessary (manufacture of defective equipment).

Types of Situations

Extra-hazardous activities and dangerous animals can be the occasion for determining strict liability. The activities must be such that they are not in common usage in the community and involve a risk of serious harm to persons or property that cannot be eliminated by the use of due care. Different courts have included virtually everything from manufacturing of explosives to fumigating (at one time automobiles and airplanes were included by some). There is a further trend in holding manufacturers or suppliers of defective products liable in the concomitant move away from the necessity of showing privity between user and manufacturer in order to establish a cause of action. In these new cases, however, a defect must be shown.

Animals with a dangerous propensity (threat to life and limb) and understood as such "by a reasonable man" make the possessor strictly liable. Watchdogs with dangerous propensities come under the same rule as mechanical devices protecting property (above).

Defenses

Assumption of the risk is a good defense. Teasing an animal or accepting the benefits of a dangerous situation can be said to be good evidence that the party assumed the risk. Contributory negligence is not a defense unless it is the actual cause of the accident.

TORTS WITH MIXED BASIS

An extended list of torts exists that may be actionable on more than one basis. The same tort may be shown to have intentional elements or be based on negligence and/or strict liability.

Defamation

A publication that tends to lower the person in the estimation of a portion of the community or cause others not to associate with him is actionable. The elements of defamation are

1. Publication (in various forms),
2. Defamatory meaning,

3. Understood to refer to plaintiff in defamatory manner,
4. Damage caused by the act.

This tort is a good example of a mixed basis. Intent or negligence must be shown in publication but strict liability is the basis for the other elements. That the matter is defamatory is enough even though there was no intent that it be defamatory.

Libel is defamation in written or printed form. *Slander* is usually oral in nature although gestures may also be slanderous. Intent to publish defamatory material that is understood to refer to the plaintiff are elements of both libel and slander. The major difference between the two comes in the matter of damages and defenses.

In libel most courts presume general damages from the mere fact of publication but actual (special) damages may also be shown. In slander actual damages must be shown except that certain defamations are actionable *per se*: charges that the person has committed a serious crime, has a loathsome disease, is unchaste (if a woman), conduct incompatible with an office or profession (don't refer to a lawyer as a "shyster").

Truth is a defense to defamation regardless of the motivation of the publisher, but a minority opinion holds that justifiable motives in publishing the truth must be shown. The defense of absolute privilege is available to legislators, top government executives, and participants in judicial processes if statements are relevant to their activity. Utterances within the family are also privileged.

Emotional Distress

Causation of distress may be intentional or through negligence. Intent to cause severe emotional distress that could be foreseen to lead to physical injuries makes a defendant liable. Words or gestures are sufficient. The same result through lack of due care establishes liability.

Invasion of Privacy

While not recognized by all states, a majority of states recognize the right to be left alone or not have one's life exposed to undue public scrutiny. Offensive unauthorized use of a name or picture, divulgence of confidences, and intrusion into personal affairs with reckless disregard can be the basis of this tort. If there is a legitimate public interest in the information the invasion may be privileged; invasion of the private life of a celebrity is not privileged even though his public life may be.

Business Torts

Interference with economic relationships or advantages gives rise to tort actions. *Disparagement*, or making false statements as to quality of product or title to goods, is a basis for special damages. *Interference* with contracts or prospective advantage also impose tort liability (see Chapter 20).

Improper Use of Legal Process

Wrongful institution of criminal process is the tort of *malicious prosecution*. The comparable tort in civil matters is *malicious prosecution of civil proceedings*. Both require a malicious intent and lack of probable cause, i.e., no reasonable belief in the truth of the charge. *Abuse of process* is the use of process for a purpose other than the one intended when the legal remedy was established. Use of the process of attachment in order to coerce payment is one example.

Nuisance

An unreasonable interference in use of land or other interests of an individual is a private nuisance; obstruction of common rights is a public nuisance for which a person may not maintain an action unless an injury peculiar to him is sustained. Substantial and unreasonable harm to use and enjoyment of land may be the result of intentional or nonintentional acts or on the basis of strict liability.

Misrepresentation and Deceit

A material false representation of fact which causes justifiable reliance to the detriment of another is actionable. The representation may be intentional, nonintentional, or under strict liability; the three conditions differ in certain aspects. Intentional misrepresentations of fact made by ordinary persons are required to support an action in deceit. Misrepresentation by individuals in the business of providing expert guidance is the basis for negligence actions. The scope of liability to others is more limited in negligent misrepresentations. Actions in strict liability are those resulting from situations such as the failure of products to perform as advertised generally. Defenses to negligence actions are assumption of the risk and contributory negligence. Assumption of the risk is the only defense in strict liability cases.

Products Liability

Physical harm to persons or property caused by a defective product is the basis for this tort. Past actions under common law have been based on either tort or contract (breach of warranty) but in either case privity had to be shown. Courts have moved away from this requirement and have sometimes gone beyond negligence to strict liability as a basis.

There is little question of the liability of a manufacturer who knows a product to be defective. Much of the difficulty comes in the majority of cases where no intent is present. There is a duty owed to all parties foreseeable in use of the product but damages are generally still limited. The manufacturer remains liable even if liability also attaches to a middleman who passes on inherently dangerous products. A further discussion of liability under recent statutes appears in Chapter 20.

CHAPTER 19
CRIMINAL LAW

This chapter deals with the substantive criminal law. It is that area of law which defines conduct that is criminal and provides for the punishment to be imposed for such conduct. Most criminal law is developed under state statute rather than federal law. The origin of many of the provisions is the law of crimes as developed in the early English common law. Frequently it is in code form, the states having supplemented or modified, and some having replaced, the common law by statute. One crime, treason, is mentioned in the United States Constitution. Similar provisions appear in most state constitutions.

Crimes are public wrongs. A crime is an act or omission which is prohibited by law and for which an offender is prosecuted by the state. Punishment upon conviction may be by fine, imprisonment, or both. It may also be by death, although that is infrequent today.

CLASSIFICATION OF CRIMES

The early common law divided crimes into three major groups according to the gravity of the offense: treason, felonies, and misdemeanors. The classification of a crime is important and can have far-reaching consequences. For instance, today it can be determinative of whether arrest for commission of the act is permissible without a warrant, whether a specific court has jurisdiction over the matter, whether probation or parole will be granted to a person convicted of the act, and whether a convicted person will have the right to serve on a jury or to practice a particular profession.

For procedural purposes, crimes are often divided into major crimes (treason, felonies, and misdemeanors) and petty offenses. The latter are also known as summary offenses since they commonly come within the jurisdiction of a magistrate who has the authority to dispose of the matter summarily, as explained in Chapter 9.

In the United States today, the most important classification of crime is that of felony and misdemeanor. Felonies are the very serious crimes; misdemeanors, less serious. Under federal law, a felony is any crime for which the penalty is death or imprisonment for more than one year. Federal misdemeanors are those offenses for which the penalty is imprisonment for less than a year.

State criminal codes frequently set up categories related to the sentences for crimes. The classification made by one state in its code is illustrative and is shown in Table 19.1. Note that murder in the first degree has been distinguished from other crimes and placed in a category by itself.

TABLE 19.1. Categories of crimes by sentence

Crime	Sentence	
	Maximum Fine	**Term of Imprisonment**
Murder in the first degree	—	Life (death penalty alternative)
Felony of the first degree	$25,000	More than 10 years
Felony of the second degree	$25,000	Maximum of 10 years
Felony of the third degree	$15,000	Maximum of 7 years
Misdemeanor of the first degree	$10,000	Maximum of 5 years
Misdemeanor of the second degree	$ 5,000	Maximum of 2 years
Misdemeanor of the third degree	$ 2,500	Maximum of 1 year
Summary Offense	$ 300	Maximum of 90 days

Mala in Se and Mala Prohibita

Crimes are sometimes described as crimes *mala in se*, those consisting of actions that are wrong in themselves or inherently evil, and crimes *mala prohibita*, those consisting of actions that are not inherently evil but are wrong only because they are prohibited by statute. This distinction is of limited usefulness. One use is in determining whether certain homicides constitute involuntary manslaughter.

Ordinance Violations

There is some difference of opinion as to whether violations of ordinances enacted by counties, cities, townships, and other municipalities are crimes even though the penalties include fine and imprisonment.

Generally these violations are disposed of by a municipal, city, or police court. The matters involved usually deal with regulation of traffic, garbage, pets, and the like.

Corpus Delicti

An individual's guilt or innocence in connection with a crime becomes relevant only after it has first been established that a crime has been committed. To do this, a prima facie case must be established. Those elements which the prosecution must plead and prove to show that a particular crime has been committed are referred to as the *corpus delicti* of the crime. Each crime has its own distinctive elements. If one or more is missing, the particular crime could not have been committed.

The corpus delicti of each crime consists of a *mens rea*, or criminal state of mind, and an *actus reus*, the commission of some prohibited act.

Mens Rea

The mens rea is the mental element necessary to a crime. For most crimes, proof of a general mens rea is sufficient. The requirement is that the accused meant to do what he did. (An exception exists in those cases in which negligence is the basis of criminal liability.) Some crimes require, in addition, proof of a specific mens rea, such as a particular intent.

Some statutory violations are labelled criminal although there is no requirement of a mens rea. In the case of these offenses, a person is held strictly liable upon commission of a prohibited act. This occurs most frequently in connection with acts that are against the public welfare, such as the sale of adulterated food. There is a question of whether there can be a "true crime" without a mens rea.

Actus Reus

A crime requires an act; the law does not punish a person for mere thought. The criminal act may be one of commission or omission. If the criminal act is one of omission, it must be of a possible and legally required performance. Failure to meet moral or ethical standards, when there is no legal requirement involved, is not a crime.

Causation

An accused's criminal act must be the legal cause of the injuries for which the state is prosecuting. Essentially, the standards for the requisite, legally recognized causation are the same as those for proximate cause in the law of torts.

Anticipatory Acts as Crimes

Acts which are anticipatory to the commission of a particular crime may be crimes in themselves. These include solicitation, conspiracy, and attempt.

Solicitation occurs when, having the intention that another person commit a crime, an individual entices, encourages, incites, or otherwise induces that person to commit a felony or misdemeanor. It is not necessary that the crime being solicited actually be committed.

Conspiracy is a combination between two or more persons to accomplish a criminal or unlawful act, or to do a lawful act by criminal or unlawful means. The common law crime of conspiracy requires merely the forbidden combination; no additional act is necessary. By statutory provision in some jurisdictions, some overt act in furtherance of the unlawful plan is required.

An attempt to commit a crime can be a crime in itself. The crime of *attempt* requires that there be both an intent to commit a particular crime and an act in pursuance of that intent which goes beyond mere preparation but which falls short of actual commission of the crime. Determination of whether an act has gone sufficiently beyond preparation is often difficult. The intended crime must be legally possible of commission, and there must be apparent ability to commit that crime. Attempt cannot be a crime unless the attempt, if completed, would have constituted a crime.

Parties to a Crime

Criminal culpability, that is, blame or fault, can rest not only with the person who actually commits the criminal act but also with other persons who aid and abet in any significant way in the commission of the crime. Under the common law, the perpetrator of a felony is a *principal in the first degree.* Persons other than perpetrators who are present at the time of the commission of a felony and who aid and abet in its commission are *principals in the second degree.* Nonperpetrators who aid and abet and who are not present when the felony is committed are *accessories.* They may be designated as accessories before or after the fact. In the case of misdemeanors, all culpable persons are considered to be principals except for accessories after the fact who are not considered to be parties to the crime at all. Modern criminal statutes tend to treat all parties as principals, whether they be perpetrators or merely aid and abet. In some jurisdictions, the designation "accessory after the fact" has been retained in felony cases to distinguish them from principals.

CRIMINAL RESPONSIBILITY

Capacity of Parties

Responsibility for the consequences of one's actions is basic to the criminal law. Lack of capacity may diminish that responsibility and therefore be a defense to criminal charges.

Insanity

Legal insanity is a defense to criminal charges. A person cannot be convicted of a crime if at the time he committed the offense his mind was so defective he was incapable of forming the requisite criminal intent. The courts, however, are not agreed as to what constitutes insanity.

The M'Naghten Rule, so named because it was formulated in 1843 by an English court in the murder trial of Daniel M'Naghten, is frequently used as the test for insanity. The court in that case said:

> to establish a defense on the ground of insanity it must be clearly proved that, at the time of the committing of the act, the party accused was labouring under such a defect of reason, from disease of the mind, as not to know the nature and quality of the act he was doing; or, if he did know it, that he did not know he was doing what was wrong. (*Daniel M'Naghten Case*, 10 Cl. & F. 200, 8 Eng. Reprint 718 (1843)).

This test for legal insanity is popularly known as the "right or wrong" test.

Not all jurisdictions have found it to be totally acceptable. As a result, other tests for legal insanity have developed. Some states have added to it the "irresistible impulse rule" and find "insanity" if the criminal act was the result of an irresistible impulse even though the accused had the capacity to distinguish between right and wrong as to the particular act. A few states adopted the Durham rule, developed by the court in *Durham v. United States*, 94 U.S. App. D.C. 228, 214 F.2d 862 (1954). That court held that "an accused is not criminally responsible if his unlawful act was the product of mental disease or mental defect" and left it to the jury to decide if the offense was such a product.

A midway position is found in the test for insanity set forth in §4.01 of the American Law Institute's Model Penal Code. It provides:

> A person is not responsible for criminal conduct if at the time of such conduct, as a result of mental disease or defect he lacked substantial capacity either to appreciate the wrongfulness of his conduct or to conform his conduct to the requirements of the law.

Most courts take the position that below-average mental ability does not excuse a criminal act. Degrees of insanity are not recognized.

A person is presumed to be sane at the time he commits an offense. The prosecution must prove the accused's sanity only when insanity is raised as a defense. Substantive criminal law is concerned with sanity or lack thereof at the time of commission of the offense. Procedural questions, however, may arise concerning an accused's mental capacity to stand trial. This can lead to postponement of a trial until a person is determined to be competent.

Intoxication

Involuntary intoxication is generally a defense to criminal charges when the intoxication is to such a degree that the accused cannot be held responsible for his acts. Voluntary intoxication, on the other hand, is generally not a defense to criminal charges. If, however, the crime requires proof of a specific mens rea, evidence of intoxication may be admitted to determine if the accused was capable of the necessary intent. Whether the degree of intoxication was sufficient to prevent formation of the intent is a jury question.

Many jurisdictions apply the same rules regarding intoxication to mental states and conditions resulting from the use of narcotics and dangerous drugs.

Infancy

Under the common law, children are not always considered to be sufficiently mature to form a criminal intent. A child under the age of seven is conclusively presumed to be incapable of committing a crime. In the case of a child aged 7 to 14, presumption of incapability is rebuttable. This means that the prosecution can offer evidence to show the particular child was capable of forming the requisite intent. Without proof that this is so, the child cannot be convicted. Children over 14 are treated as adults. Some states have made statutory changes in these presumptions, generally in the direction of restricting infancy as a defense.

Corporations

In some cases, a corporation may be held criminally liable for crimes committed on its behalf by its employees and agents. There is some question as to whether a corporation can commit a crime requiring a mens rea. Some courts answer this question by imputing the mens rea of the firm's agents or employees to the corporation.

Mistake

Ignorance or mistake of fact may negate criminal intent. The mistake must be genuine and consist of a reasonable belief in facts which, if they did exist, would either make the act an innocent one, justify it, or excuse it. Ignorance or mistake of the law, on the other hand, is seldom an excuse.

Coercion

Coercion or compulsion, consisting of threat of death or serious bodily harm to the accused or a member of his family, may constitute a defense to a crime requiring criminal intent, except under the common law in the case of homicide. Duress does not excuse the killing of another human being.

Self-defense

An individual is justified in using nondeadly force in self-defense if a reasonable person would have been put in apprehension of immediate harm and if the force used was reasonable under the circumstances. *Deadly force* is that which is likely to or does cause death. It is justified in only a few situations. As a general rule, it can be said that deadly force is never justified if nondeadly force will accomplish one's purpose. Deadly force is not justified in the defense of property even if it is in one's home. Only when an atrocious felony which threatens life or serious bodily harm is being committed may deadly force be used and then only as a last resort.

In most jurisdictions a person has a duty to retreat as far as possible before one is justified in taking another's life in self-defense or in defense of another person. An exception ordinarily exists in defense of human life in one's home, office, or place of business, provided such force is necessary under the circumstances. One normally has the same rights to use force in defending others as he has in defending himself.

A law enforcement officer may be justified in the use of deadly force to prevent commission of an atrocious felony, but not to prevent commission of a misdemeanor. So, also, deadly force used in making an arrest or to prevent escape can be justified only in felony cases, and then only if there is no other means of apprehending the felon. Some jurisdictions further require that the felony committed be one of violence and surprise. An officer acts at his peril if he uses deadly force upon mere suspicion that a felony has been committed.

Consent

In the case of some crimes, such as rape, consent of the victim means that there may be no crime at all. Aside from such crimes, consent is not a defense for an act which results in a public injury, such as one which causes breach of the peace or constitutes an affront to public morals.

Entrapment

Entrapment is a valid defense to criminal charges. It consists of conduct by a law enforcement officer which instigates the commission of a crime by another. When the officer merely provides an opportunity for commission of a crime, there is no entrapment.

Statute of Limitations

Expiration of the time period provided by the applicable Statute of Limitations may be a defense in criminal cases, just as it is in civil cases.

CRIMES

In the following section, crimes will, for the most part, be defined first according to the common law. This will be followed by discussion of changes in the common law frequently found in statutory provisions. Crimes against the person will be considered first, then those against property.

CRIMES AGAINST THE PERSON

Homicide

Homicide is the killing of a human being by another human being. Not all homicides are criminal. Homicide that is either justifiable or excusable is noncriminal.

Homicide is *justifiable* when it is commanded or authorized by law, when it is done in the performance of a legal duty or exercise of a legal right where the slayer is not at fault. Examples include execution by court order of a convicted capital offender, necessary killings by police officers in preventing atrocious felonies or in capturing a felon, necessary killings in self defense and in the defense of others.

Homicide is *excusable* when the slayer may be at fault to some extent but not to a degree sufficient to impose criminal sanction. An example of excusable homicide is a killing by a person, such as an infant or insane person, incapable of committing a crime. Homicide may be excusable when a slaying results from an accident or misadventure, such as when a person runs in front of a moving vehicle, the driver of which is unable to avoid hitting and fatally injuring the person.

Killings which are neither justifiable nor excusable are criminal. Criminal homicide may be either murder or manslaughter.

Murder

Murder is the unlawful killing of a human being by another with malice aforethought. While the malice cannot be an afterthought, killing on the spur of the moment is not precluded by the requirement of "malice aforethought." *Malice* means a specific intention to act in such a way that death of a human being may result. The requisite intention, sometimes referred to as a "man endangering state of mind," exists when there is:

1. Intent to kill or to inflict great bodily injury, or
2. Intent to act with wanton and willful disregard of unreasonable risk to human life, or
3. Intent to resist lawful arrest with force, or
4. Intent to commit a dangerous felony.

Therefore, malice aforethought may be said to exist in the case of killing by firing a loaded gun into the eyes of another, intending to blind him; by deliberately setting fire to a home with knowledge that persons are asleep therein; by fatal blows to the head received by a law enforcement officer in a struggle with the accused who was resisting arrest being made with legal authority and in a reasonable manner; by actions committed in perpetration of such violent crimes as rape, arson, and robbery. The latter is the basis for the *felony murder rule*, which is that an unlawful killing caused by actions in the attempt or perpetration of another felony inherently dangerous to human life is murder whether it is intentional or not.

When the person killed is different from the intended victim, the slayer's malice aforethought as to the intended victim is considered to be transferred to the actual victim. This is known as the doctrine of transferred intent. (It is applicable in the case of other crimes, as well.) For instance, when a husband, with intent to kill his wife, fires a gun in her direction but fatally wounds, instead, a neighbor who is standing beside her, he will be deemed to have the requisite malice as to the neighbor.

Unlike the common law, modern statutes recognize degrees of murder. Ordinarily, murder is classified as of the first degree when it is committed by means of poison; by lying in wait; by any other kind of willful, deliberate, and premeditated killing; or in the commission of such felonies as robbery, rape, arson, burglary, or kidnapping. It is not uncommon to find all other kinds of murder classified as of the second degree.

Manslaughter

Manslaughter is the unlawful killing of one human being by another without malice aforethought. Manslaughter may be voluntary or involuntary.

Voluntary manslaughter is an intentional killing, committed without premeditation or malice aforethought in a sudden heat of passion caused by legally adequate provocation by the victim. The provocation must be sufficient to inflame a reasonable person to passion. Words alone are never sufficient, nor ordinarily are insulting gestures, simple assault, or technical battery. On the other hand, seduction of a man's wife or mutual quarrel and combat can constitute adequate provocation.

Heat of passion consists of more than mere anger and is less than insanity. The provocation must so arouse and inflame the slayer that he does not know what he is doing. At the time of the killing the slayer must still be acting in the heat of passion. If it has cooled to the point where he knows what he is doing, the homicide is murder. Lapse of time is an important, but not the sole, determining factor in deciding whether cooling has taken place.

Causal connection must be shown. The provocation must have caused the heat of passion which caused the homicide.

It is also voluntary manslaughter if a person intentionally kills another, believing unreasonably at the time of the killing that the circumstances are such as to justify the killing.

Involuntary manslaughter is an unintentional and unlawful killing, without malice aforethought. It covers unintentional killings that occur in connection with unlawful, inherently dangerous, mala in se acts as well as unintentional killings which are the result of criminal negligence. Examples include a killing caused by careless use of a loaded firearm and death of a pedestrian caused by a drunken driver. In the latter case, it should be noted that some jurisdictions have a separate crime, manslaughter committed in the operation of a motor vehicle.

Classification

Murder and manslaughter are felonies, with the exception of involuntary manslaughter which is classified as a misdemeanor in some jurisdictions.

In connection with homicide, much discussion and debate have been focused recently on the criminal status, if any, in the killing of a fetus that has not yet been "born alive" and the withdrawal of life support systems from persons with "brain death."

Assault and Battery

At common law, *battery* is the intentional, nonconsensual, unlawful touching of another. There is a battery no matter how slight the injury to the victim. Some jurisdictions require that the touching be a rude, angry, revengeful act, but the more common requirement is simply that the touching be willful.

Common law *assault* consists of an attempted battery or placing a person in apprehension of an immediate battery. Unlike battery, assault requires no physical contact. As a general rule, words alone are not sufficient to constitute an assault; the words must be accompanied by some threatening or menacing act.

Both assault and battery are misdemeanors at common law. Modern statutes tend to combine the two into one crime, usually assault. The Pennsylvania criminal code, for instance, provides that "a person is guilty of assault if he:

1. attempts to cause or intentionally, knowingly or recklessly causes bodily injury to another; or
2. negligently causes bodily injury to another with a deadly weapon; or
3. attempts by physical menace to put another in fear of imminent serious bodily injury."

The common law crime of *mayhem*, which consists of removing or permanently disabling some part of a person's body, may be included in statutory assault. Permanent disfigurement is usually also covered by the crime. Statutes usually provide for different types of assault, such as aggravated assault (involving serious bodily harm), assault with a deadly weapon, assault on a police officer, and simple assault. The first three are usually classified as felonies; the latter, a misdemeanor.

Rape

Rape is defined by the common law as unlawful sexual intercourse with a female without her consent. Because the intercourse must be unlawful to be rape, sexual relations between husband and wife are not criminal regardless of consent. However, a husband may be guilty of rape of his wife if he aids and abets another man in committing the crime.

The slightest sexual penetration is sufficient to complete the crime of rape. In its absence, the crime committed may be attempted rape or assault with intent to ravish. Emission is not required. Lack of consent is an important element of this crime. Consent is not real if it results from force, threat of force, or is given under duress. Nor is it real if the woman is incapable of giving consent, such as would be true if she were unconscious, intoxicated, drugged, asleep, or insane at the time. Rape is defined in some modern criminal codes as sexual intercourse with another person who is not one's spouse by forcible compulsion or threat of such or with a person incapable of consent. This crime is sometimes referred to as forcible rape to distinguish it from the crime of statutory rape.

Statutory rape consists of sexual intercourse with a person under a statutorily specified age (16, for example) whether the person consents or not. It is based on the presumption that a person under that age is incapable of understanding the full implications of giving consent. Mistake as to the age of the person is ordinarily not a defense to statutory rape.

Rape is a felony. Increased attention has been focused in recent years upon treatment of victims of rape.

Other Sex Offenses

State statutes make criminal other offenses related to sexual activity. The trend in recent years has been to remove criminality from sexual acts between consenting adults, except where such acts are performed for money or are incestuous. Criminal sex offenses include involuntary deviate sexual intercourse, indecent exposure, indecent assault, corruption of minors, and prostitution.

Involuntary deviate sexual intercourse is ordinarily a felony. It is involuntary when it is forced, when one of the parties is incapable of giving consent because of age or mental incapacity, or when one of the parties is under a statutorily specified age. Sodomy is referred to as deviate sexual intercourse in a number of criminal codes. The statutory offense is usually defined as sexual relations between persons who are not husband and wife consisting of contact between the sex organs of one and the mouth or anus of the other. Bestiality, or sexual intercourse by a human being with an animal, is also included in the offense in some jurisdictions.

Indecent exposure is generally defined as exhibition of one's genitals under circumstances where such conduct is likely to cause affront or alarm and for the purpose of arousing or gratifying the sexual desires of the exhibitionist or others. Usually it is a misdemeanor.

Indecent assault, also usually a misdemeanor, consists of sexual contact with another person not one's spouse when one knows that the contact is offensive to the other person, or the other person is incapable of appraising the nature of the conduct, or the other person is unaware such contact is being committed, or the other person is not able to resist because of a drugged, intoxicated, or like condition.

Corruption of a minor is generally defined as any act which corrupts the morals or contributes to the sexual delinquency of a minor. It is usually a misdemeanor.

Prostitution consists of engaging in sexual activity as a business. Statutory provisions ordinarily make it a crime not only to engage directly in prostitution but also to promote, compel, procure, encourage, or solicit prostitution. Persons of both sexes can commit prostitution. It is usually a misdemeanor. Prostitution is generally considered to be an offense against public decency rather than a crime against the person. Some, in fact, consider it to be a victimless crime.

Kidnapping

Kidnapping, as generally defined by federal and state statute, is the intentional and unlawful confinement or movement from one place to another of a person against his will. It is a felony and may even be a capital offense if there is a ransom demand. The federal crime of kidnapping requires that there be movement across state lines.

Other offenses, related to deprivation of a person's liberty include false imprisonment and interference with custody of children or committed persons. They are usually misdemeanors.

False imprisonment consists of knowingly and unlawfully restraining another so as to interfere substantially with his liberty. *Interference with custody* occurs when a person, not privileged to do so, knowingly or recklessly takes or entices a minor from the custody of the parent or guardian, or a committed person away from lawful custody.

CRIMES AGAINST PROPERTY

Burglary

At common law, *burglary* consists of breaking and entering the dwelling house of another in the night time with the intent to commit a felony. In most jurisdictions today, burglary has been expanded by statute so that it consists of either breaking or unlawful entry; it includes buildings other than dwelling houses; it can occur during the day as well as at night; and it includes the intent to commit any crime, not just a felony. An example of present-day statutory definition of burglary is as follows:

> A person is guilty of burglary if he enters a building or occupied structure, or separately secured or occupied portion thereof, with intent to commit a crime therein, unless the premises are at the time open to the public or the actor is licensed or privileged to enter.

Burglary is a felony. A closely related offense is *criminal trespass*. It consists of entering or remaining in a building without license or privilege to do so. In some jurisdictions, it is a felony; in others, a misdemeanor.

Larceny or Theft

Common law *larceny* consists of taking and carrying away the personal property of another with the intent to permanently deprive the owner of his property. Two other common law crimes, embezzlement and obtaining property by false pretenses, are closely related to larceny. Common law *embezzlement* consists of unlawful appropriation of another's goods by one who obtained lawful possession of them by virtue of his office or employment. *False pretenses* is the criminal act of obtaining both possession and title to the property of another through false representations.

By statutory change in many jurisdictions, these three common law crimes have been classified as types of theft. *Theft* is ordinarily defined as unlawfully taking or appropriating another's property for one's self or one's benefit. Separate offenses may be designated when the theft is accomplished by other than a taking. For instance, there is *theft by deception*. This occurs when one deprives another of his property by some falsity, including deceiving the other person by false impression or by other fraudulent means.

Theft by extortion is often referred to as blackmail. It consists of obtaining the property of another by threat, intimidation, or fear of accusation or exposure. The threat may be to inflict bodily injury, to publicly expose matters which hold another up to contempt or ridicule, to take or withhold some form of official action, to bring about or to continue a strike or boycott, to disrupt or injure another's business. *Theft by failure to make required disposition* is committed by a person who obtains property upon agreement or subject to legal obligation to make specified payment or other disposition of that property. The offense occurs when that person intentionally deals with the property as his own and fails to make the required payment or disposition. It is also not uncommon to find theft of services, retail theft (commonly known as shoplifting), unauthorized use of motor vehicles, and theft of trade secrets designated as separate crimes.

Theft may be a felony or misdemeanor. In some states, theft is a felony when the amount involved exceeds $2000 or if a firearm, airplane, or motor vehicle has been stolen. It is also not uncommon for theft to be a felony when property is taken by threat or in breach of a fiduciary obligation. Other thefts are ordinarily misdemeanors.

Receiving and Concealing Stolen Goods

Closely associated with theft is the offense of *receiving and concealing stolen property*. Either receipt or concealment is sufficient to constitute a crime. A person may be the receiver of stolen goods if he exercises dominion and control over the property. It is not necessary that he actually have the goods in his hands. Nor is it necessary that the accused receive the stolen goods directly from the thief. In fact, he need not know the true owner. Furthermore, it is not material that he received them from a person who knows that the property was stolen.

Concealing stolen property does not require that an accused physically hide the goods. All that is necessary is that he aid the thief in doing something with the property to prevent the true owner from using and enjoying his goods or that he assist in securing the goods to the benefit of the thief. This might consist of such actions as removing identification or serial numbers, painting or otherwise changing the color of the article.

In the absence of express statutory provision, it is unclear whether knowledge that goods were stolen is requisite to the crime or whether mere suspicion is sufficient. The intent required is the same as that for theft: to deprive the true owner of his property.

Many states classify receipt and concealment of stolen goods as a felony when the receiver is in the business of buying and selling stolen property. Whether it is a misdemeanor or felony is ordinarily otherwise determined by the value and kind of property involved.

Robbery

Common law *robbery* is the unlawful taking and carrying away of the personal property of another from his person or in his presence by violence or by threat of violence. Robbery is larceny from the person by force or intimidation. Robbery differs from larceny in two ways.

1. Robbery requires force or threat of force. The slightest force—even a shove or a tug—is sufficient.

2. Robbery requires a taking from a person of in his presence. Any place within his hearing or sight is ordinarily deemed to be sufficient.

Some jurisdictions, by statute, have expanded the concept of robbery so that a person is guilty of the crime if, in the course of committing a theft, he inflicts or threatens another with serious bodily injury or he commits or threatens to commit a serious felony.

Robbery is itself a felony. Different degrees of felony may be designated, based upon whether the theft involved was accompanied by mere threat or by actual physical injury. Armed robbery is ordinarily a very serious felony.

Arson

Common law *arson* consists of the willful and malicious burning of the dwelling house of another, by day or by night. The crime has been expanded by statute to include buildings other than a dwelling house and to include one's own property. In some jurisdictions, the burning of another's personal property, when it is valued at more than a statutorily specified minimum, constitutes arson. In some, arson includes causing an explosion even though there be no burning. It is not uncommon to find a specific statutory crime for the burning of property with the intent to defraud an insurer, regardless of whether that property is owned by the accused or by another.

Arson is a felony. Closely related to arson are crimes, ordinarily classified as felonies, which consist of causing or risking catastrophe by reckless employment of fire, explosives, or other such dangerous means.

OTHER CRIMES

Many other crimes exist under the common law and by statutory provision. Common law *perjury* is the willful taking of a false oath in a judicial proceeding with regard to a material matter. Modern statutes have expanded the crime to include false affidavits under oath, and to almost every kind of governmental proceeding. Generally, falsity of an accused's sworn statements must be established by the evidence of two witnesses. Perjury is normally a felony. *Subornation of perjury* is a separate offense. It consists of procuring another to commit forgery.

Counterfeiting is the unlawful making of false money and has been extended by statute to include any obligation or security of the government.

Bribery is an offer or tender of anything of value to a person who holds public office, or the receipt of anything of value by a public office holder. The intention is that such official be influenced in the performance of his duties. Note that both giving and accepting a bribe is a crime. It is a felony under most statutes.

Forgery is the false making or material alteration of a written instrument, with the intent to defraud. The writing must be one that, if genuine, could be the foundation of a legal liability. Such writings include deeds, wills, checks, and securities. Forgery is ordinarily a statutory felony.

Treason is defined in Article III, §3 of the United States Constitution as levying war against the United States, adhering to this nation's enemies or giving them aid and comfort.

Other crimes include rioting, disorderly conduct, public intoxication, loitering, harassment, carrying concealed weapons, dealing in the use of dangerous drugs and other controlled substances, furnishing obscene material to minors, cruelty to animals, obstruction of justice, falsifying business records, issuing and negotiating a bad check, fraudulent use of a credit card, and issuing false financial statements. Still other crimes may be found by reference to the criminal codes of the various jurisdictions, and other specific criminal penalties exist in some socio-economic areas discussed in the next chapter.

CHAPTER 20
SOCIOECONOMIC REGULATION

Maintenance of the public welfare through administration of social and economic activity is a basic power of governmental entities under constitutions, statutes, and court decisions. A "free enterprise" system is not entirely without controls, although there is a continuing controversy as to the extent to which agents of government ought to be involved in group and individual economic or social activity. Basic policy questions are at the bottom of all discussions of government regulation.

The power to regulate business is a police power to promote the public welfare (Article II, United States Constitution). The power is restricted by safeguards in the same document in that laws must be uniformly applied to members within the same class and that there be no deprivation, without due process, of life or property (under the Fifth and Fourteenth Amendments of the Constitution). This "Due Process Clause" is seldom a basis these days, however, for striking down state or federal legislation that regulates conditions of work or broader social behavior.

Individual civil as well as economic rights are receiving more attention from governmental agents. The right to privacy, equal opportunity in employment, physical protection in the environment, fair dealing in financial matters or in the market place are all examples of the emphasis put upon individual rights. These rights are being enforced in all spheres of society—in organizations other than business as well as in industrial and commercial entities. Often the regulation of business represents the implementation of individual rights of those persons in contact with the corporation.

ECONOMIC REGULATION

The regulation of broad and fundamental activity in economic matters represents, at present, the development of some of the longest and most active approaches to control of enterprises. Concern that too few control too many has been present in the thoughts and acts of many public servants and private citizens alike. Maintenance of efficient service to society has been the aim of such governmental regulation.

Antitrust

One of the earliest governmental actions toward regulation of business was the enactment of the Sherman Act of 1890. The Sherman Act is known as the Antitrust Act because it was intended to prevent monopolies or combinations in restraint of trade. Section 1 of the Act provides that "every contract, combination in the form of trust or otherwise, or conspiracy, in restraint of trade or commerce among the several States, or with foreign nations, is hereby declared to be illegal." Section 2 makes it a misdemeanor for any person to "monopolize or attempt to monopolize, or combine or conspire. . .to monopolize" in the same area of trade or commerce as in Section 1 of the Act.

The Sherman Act provides a maximum penalty of $100,000 fine for a person, a million dollars if a corporation and three years imprisonment, or both in a 1974 amendment and other legislation has supplemented it in providing protection from monopolies.

Early judgments by the courts in interpreting the Sherman Act caused later legislation to emerge. The Clayton Act of 1914 and its later amendments tightened some of the provisions of antitrust statutes. Whereas the Sherman Act was interpreted to prohibit actual unreasonable restraint of trade, Section 7 of the Clayton Act now says that a merger of corporations shall be illegal when the effect "may be substantially to lessen competition, or to tend to create a monopoly" (15 USC Section 18). The Clayton Act also prohibits the purchase of stock in one corporation by another when that same result (monopoly and restraint of trade) would be effected.

The Clayton Act prohibits, if in restraint of trade, the imposition of an *exclusive dealer agreement* whereby a dealer must agree not to handle goods of a competitor of the manufacturer. The Act also prohibits the use of a *tie-in* sale or lease where the buyer of goods promises to purchase or lease only from the seller. Such provisions are permissible only if their use does not lessen competition or create a monopoly. If, for example, a product can only be served by specific supplies from the seller or a machine could not be run without the materials furnished by the manufacturer, the tie-in restrictions would not be struck down. If there are alternate sources of supply, however, tie-in provisions are in violation of the statute.

The Clayton Act drafters included pricing as one further aspect of maintenance of competition in the economy. The Act prohibited price discrimination when the intent was to lessen competition or tend to create a monopoly. Differences arising from product quality, quantity of goods, costs of transportation, or bonafide attempts to meet competition are allowable. These exceptions were later reinforced by the Robinson-Patman Act of 1936 which made illegal price discrimination a criminal offense. The Act prohibited the granting of promotional and advertising aid by sellers to buyers unless all buyers were included in receiving the same assistance. Sellers are permitted to choose their customers, however, unless the intent of the choice was to restrain trade.

The fixing of prices between parties on the same level in the production or distribution system, *horizontal price-fixing*, is a violation of federal law. *Vertical resale price agreements* had been deemed valid under federal and many state statutes but have been declared invalid. The so-called *Fair Trade* laws enacted by many States during the Big Depression of the 1930s provided for just this maintenance of retail prices because of a feeling that this would support the economic order.

Further curbs on unfair methods of competition and the establishment of an agency to police such activity came with the enactment of the Federal Trade Commission Act. The Federal Trade Commission (FTC) was to monitor adherence to existing laws but also has determined an extensive number of practices to be in violation of the law. Practices condemned include those such as coercion, disparagement of a competitor, discrimination or boycott, making gifts to obtain benefits, pretended free trial offers or premiums, offers with no intention to deliver, inducing breach of contracts, spying on a competitor, appropriating trademarks or simulating a competitor's goods, using deception in labels or brands, false or misleading advertising and any other "unfair methods of competition."

It must be added that most States have statutes that prohibit the same activities on the commercial scene. Under tort law, these activities also may be actionable as the tort of unfair competition (Chapter 18).

Regulation of Transportation and Communication

Control in these areas occurs primarily under federal legislation although state statutes control intrastate activity. The Interstate Commerce Commission Act of 1881 established the governmental commission of the same name and provided a set of regulations covering the transport of goods in commerce throughout the country on freight and passenger lines. Since at that time the primary carriers were the railroads, the impact on them had considerable effect on the economy generally. The growing importance of other carriers either extended

ICC regulation or led to the development of other federal and state regulatory agencies. The Federal Aviation Agency (FAA) and the Civil Aeronautics Board (CAB) share regulatory powers in air transportation. Agencies comparable to the ICC at the state level are given names such as "Public Utility Commission" as they may regulate all quasi-public services such as telephone communication in addition to transportation.

The Federal Communication Commission (FCC) licenses and monitors radio and television broadcasting.

LABOR-MANAGEMENT RELATIONS

The relationship of employer and employee is undoubtedly the most important in business and industry. In the past half-century this relationship has shown significant changes; representation by labor unions has grown in intensity and importance and the body of labor law has expanded commensurately.

The National Labor Relations Act (Wagner Act) in 1935 established the right of employees to form a union and have it represent them in collective bargaining with an employer. In 1947 Congress passed the Labor Management Relations Act (Taft-Hartley Act) amending many of the provisions of the earlier act. Another twelve years later the Labor-Management Reporting and Disclosure Act of 1959 (Landrum-Griffin Act) provided additional controls over labor and management activity.

While these three are the major pieces of federal labor legislation, other statutes have been enacted to supplement them. The Norris-LaGuardia Act (1932) is best known for limiting injunctions by employers in labor disputes. The Railway Labor Act (1926) is an example of legislation similar to all of the above but with specific reference to a particular industry. In addition, many states have adopted labor statutes to cover intrastate activity, particularly in establishing the basic right of employees to organize and utilize other benefits similar to the Wagner Act.

The National Labor Relations Act created the National Labor Relations Board (NLRB) in order to assure the right of self-organization and bargaining representation of employees through the establishment of rules and regulations pursuant to the Act and monitoring the labor activities under it.

Union Representation

The National Labor Relations Act and the Railway Labor Act were enacted to encourage democratic association among employees for the establishment of better working conditions and minimizing labor unrest. The acts ensure the right of representation in bargaining by a union chosen by the majority in an appropriate employee unit.

The first step in the representation process comes when a petitioning group presents satisfactory evidence to the NLRB that at least thirty percent of the target group have indicated support of the request for an election. Signed and dated "authorization cards" are required.

After the petition is filed with the NLRB the Board determines whether it has jurisdiction, the bargaining unit is appropriate, and the requisite thirty percent of that unit have signed cards. If so it will conduct the elections. If a majority of employees votes to be represented by a union the board certifies that union as the bargaining agent.

The union, as sole representative of the employees, engages in collective bargaining with the employer in order to establish the contract under which the workers will function on the job. Both sides are under an obligation to bargain in good faith (although there is no duty to reach an agreement). No other representation is permitted by law in bargaining for a contract with the employer. Not all employees are required to be union members but the union is the representative of all employees, union members or not, and must represent all fairly and without discrimination. All matters under the contract are handled by the union representative.

Union representation has various forms. A *closed shop* is one in which the employer agrees with a union that no one will be employed who is not a member of that particular union. The Taft-Hartley Act of 1947 prohibited a closed shop but permitted a *union shop*. In this situation an employer is free to hire but after a period of not more than thirty days the new employee must join a union in order to retain his job. A third variation is the *agency shop* in which nonunion persons may be employed but must pay the union a sum equaling the union dues. State laws may govern with respect to the legality of the agency shop.

The employer, for his part, is prohibited from contracting with an employee that he not join any union under penalty of discharge. This was known as the *yellow-dog* contract.

It is an unfair labor practice for the employer to interfere with unionization or to discriminate against any employee because of union activity. The right to comment on the issues, however, is ensured by the Taft-Hartley Act. Views, arguments, or opinions are not an unfair labor practice as long as these expressions do not represent force, threats of reprisals, or promises of benefits.

It is an unfair labor practice for the union, as well, to interfere with the organization by employees of a union. To stop work or try to persuade others to do so, to cause an employer to discriminate against employees for their attempts on behalf of other unions or work for no union, is prohibited.

A later challenge to representation may be made by filing a *decertification* petition with the NLRB, again with signatures of thirty percent of the unit required. A decertification election follows.

Labor and Management Practices

Union tactics in obtaining a favorable end result include strikes, picketing, and boycotts. A strike is a group effort in stopping work while picketing is the stationing of persons outside the workplace in order to inform all others of the nature of the dispute. A boycott is an effort to persuade others not to labor for or use the services and products of the employer.

When employees picket or boycott at the workplace of the employer their activity is called a *primary* boycott or picketing; when employees extend the scope of their operations to other employers involved in business with their employer the action is known as a *secondary* boycott or picketing. Secondary boycotts are generally considered to be unfair labor practices.

The NLRB classifies strikes into three broad categories.

1. Economic strike;
2. Employer unfair labor practice strike;
3. Union unfair labor practice strike.

The economic strike takes place through demands for improvement in wages, hours, and working conditions. An employer unfair labor practice strike is one protesting against employer tactics such as refusal to bargain collectively or discrimination against union members. Union unfair labor practice strikes are those that are either unprotected or proscribed by law. Violation of no-strike agreement, forcing an employer to stop dealing with another person, forcing an employer to join an employer organization, or requiring recognition after another union has obtained bargaining rights are all examples of strike activity that is prohibited.

A *jurisdictional* strike occurs in a dispute between two or more unions, each of which claims exclusive or unique rights from the employer as when each of two trades feels its workers are the ones to do a certain job. A *wildcat* strike is one where the union disclaims responsibility as this kind of strike purportedly arises on a spontaneous basis.

Other work stoppages can occur within the workplace. Employees may conduct a *sitdown* strike where they remain on the job site but no work is done. A *slowdown* strike is similar except that work continues but the pace is reduced so that little output is generated.

Various other practices to ensure security of union members or extraordinarily favorable conditions are encountered. Make-work practices, or *featherbedding*, may restrict the level of output on the job or require the hiring of additional workers to do a job. Make-work practices are generally valid except that where pay is exacted for services not performed there is a violation of the act. Wasteful and duplicative idiosyncrasies of a trade are not considered violations.

Further efforts to assure union security such as excessive initiation fees and dues (so that the number of available workers will be reduced) are violations of the statute.

Employers, on the other hand, have used *lockouts*, a closing of the workplace, as a weapon in a labor dispute. Court injunctions have been useful in limiting the scope of the union activity to legally recognized methods in a strike and picketing. The Norris-La Guardia Act prohibited the granting of injunctions where no damage to property was involved although the NLRB may obtain an injunction to stop unfair labor practices.

The NLRB also serves as a quasi-judicial agency of the federal government in determinations of the validity of labor practices under the National Labor Relations Act and its amendments.

Whenever an unfair labor practice is alleged, the NLRB will issue a complaint, notifying the party of the allegations and giving notice of a hearing. The board, after the hearing, makes findings of fact and conclusions of law. It either dismisses the complaint or takes such actions as would effectuate the policies of the Act. The action may range from stopping an unfair labor practice to the more positive reinstatement or reimbursement of an aggrieved employee.

Appeals from NLRB decisions may be made to the U.S. Court of Appeals. It is important to note that in this area of activity, as in most others, there are often state statutes that provide for civil, criminal, or administrative agency remedies. If the state and federal laws are in conflict, however, the federal law pre-empts the state statutes.

Duties of Unions

Concern with union conduct of members' interests led to specific action in the Taft-Hartley Act (1947) but more so in the Landrum-Griffin Act, the Labor-Management Reporting and Disclosure Act of 1959. The 1947 amendments prohibited the imposition of excessive and discriminatory dues or fees or to have dues deducted by the employer unless authorized by each member. Campaign contributions from dues are also prohibited. Detailed reports, with copies to members, are to be sent to the Secretary of Labor.

The Act of 1959 imposed still other duties upon unions and their officers. Unions are required to adopt constitutions and bylaws and file them with the secretary along with detailed financial statements. The right of union members is guaranteed with respect to information on financial matters, voting, the contract, and other specific matters. Persons convicted of major crimes are barred as officers or employees for a specific time, and communists are barred from office. Controls are imposed upon union officials and assets to prevent theft or embezzlement. Loans to officers and employees are limited and all officers with interests that may conflict with union activities are required to file a report.

CONDITIONS OF EMPLOYMENT

Concern for conditions of work, from the right to consideration for employment, later organizational activity on the job, and safety at work has an extensive history. Equal opportunity for employment, standards for hours and wages, compensation under unemployment or as the result of injury are some of the major areas covered by federal or state legislation.

Wages and Hours

The Fair Labor Standards Act of 1938 sets minimum wages for workers in interstate commerce and industry. The act, known by many as the Wage and Hours Act, also regulates the hours worked and stipulates that work over 40 hours in a week must be paid at time-and-a-half for overtime. Similar special provisions cover employees of railroads which limit the number of hours worked while moving trains or engaged in duties relating to that activity, such as handling communication.

Contractors for materials and services to the United States government are further regulated by several acts. The Public Contracts Act (Walsh-Healey) provides that contracts with the federal government for more than $10,000 meet all wage and hour standards of the Act or those set by the Secretary of Labor. The Public Works Contracts Act (Davis-Bacon) requires contractors in building for the United States to pay the prevailing wages determined by the Secretary of Labor. In addition employers are prohibited from requiring employees to return or "kickback" any part of their wages.

Equal Opportunity

The *Equal Pay Act of 1963* began a long series of related acts by mandating equal pay for equal work by men and women. The most extensive legislation, however, came the next year in Title VII of the *Civil Rights Act of 1964* which (as amended) requires that the employer not discriminate in privileges, terms, and conditions of employment on the basis of race, religion, sex, or national origin. The *Age Discrimination in Employment Act of 1967* added the prohibition with respect to age forbidding discrimination against job applicants between ages 40 and 65. Further legislation came in the *Equal Employment Opportunity Act of 1972* amending the 1964 Act and in *Executive Order 11246,* which regulates contractors doing business with the federal government.

The Civil Rights Act of 1964, Title VII, as amended by the Equal Employment Opportunity Act of 1972 prohibits discrimination because of race, color, religion, sex, or national origin. The act makes it unlawful for an employer to discriminate on the above basis in:

1. Failing or refusing to hire or discharge any individual or discriminate with respect to compensation or conditions of employment.
2. Limiting an employee or classifying him in any way adversely affecting his status.

Employment agencies may not refer or refuse to refer on the basis of the demographic variables mentioned above.

It is also an unlawful employment practice for a labor organization to discriminate, as above, by:

1. Expelling or excluding from membership;
2. Limiting, segregating, or classifying its members in any way that deprives or limits employment opportunities;
3. Causing an employer to discriminate.

Any further activity in apprentice or training programs that discriminates is also unlawful. Advertising or printing of notices contrary to the provisions of Title VII is prohibited as is any discrimination arising because a person has filed a complaint or assisted in an investigation of a matter arising under this title.

Certain activities are not considered to be violations of the Act. Different standards of compensation are permitted when they relate to performance measures of quality and quantity pursuant to a bona fide seniority system, or work at different locations, provided that there is no intent to discriminate.

Administering and acting on the results of professionally developed tests are not unlawful if acted upon or developed with no attempt to discriminate. The tests must be "job related" and the resulting use must not be discriminatory. The lack of intent to discriminate is not enough, there must also be an actual nondiscriminatory effect (*Griggs v. Duke Power Co.* 401 U.S. 424 (1971)).

A further exception is where religion, sex, or national origin is a bona fide occupational qualification reasonably necessary in the operation of the business. The exception is being narrowly construed and, as the Act indicates, there is no exception on the basis of race or color.

Title VII of the Civil Rights Act of 1964 also established the Equal Employment Opportunity Commission (EEOC) in order to investigate and eliminate discrimination. Where a state agency with comparable powers exists, a complainant must first file a complaint with the state agency. After sixty days or completion of the state proceedings, a complaint may be filed with the EEOC. The commission investigates and, if there is cause to believe discrimination exists, conciliation will be attempted. Should conciliation fail, the commission is empowered to initiate court actions for the complainant under the Equal Opportunities Act of 1972 which amended Title VII. The EEOC also has the authorization, since 1972, to initiate class action suits and those demonstrating "pattern and practice" in discrimination.

Courts have the power to grant injunctions against discriminatory practices and to issue affirmative orders to reinstate workers, with or without back pay.

Executive Order 11246 goes further in requiring *affirmative action* plans on the part of bidders on federal government contracts. These plans must be specific prosposals to achieve equal employment opportunity with analyses of present conditions, goals and commitments, timetables, and data supporting the effort, particularly in those areas targeted by the government for special attention. The Executive Order gives the Secretary of Labor the duty of coordinating the efforts; the Secretary of Labor has established the Office of Federal Contract Compliance (OFCC) to administer all activity under Executive Order 11246. Supervision under the Order is not limited to those of governmental agencies. In the construction industry voluntary local efforts are encouraged and some are already in effect in major cities. If no such local plan exists the OFCC has indicated that it will impose the so-called "Philadelphia Plan," which, among other conditions, requires bidders to agree to meet specific established goals and timetables.

Work Safety

"Preservation of human resources" and assurance of safe and healthful working conditions is the intent of Congress in enacting the Occupational Safety and Health Act of 1970 (The Williams-Steiger Act). The OSHA law applies to all employers engaged in business affecting commerce. Federal and state employees are not included (but may be covered by other equally effective requirements). Employees in certain occupations are excluded because they have already been covered by earlier specific statutes. Employers have the duty of providing a safe place of work by following the standards promulgated under the Act while employees have the duty to comply with the regulations.

The Act established the Occupational Safety and Health Administration in the Department of Labor and a new agency, the Occupational Safety and Health Review Commission, a quasi-judicial board of review.

Any employees who believe immediate danger exists or that physical harm is threatened because of a violation of standards may request an inspection by the Department of Labor. If such inspection reveals a violation, the Department will issue a citation, fix a reasonable time for abatement, and notify the employer of the penalty.

Citations for *serious* violations incur mandatory monetary penalties of up to $1000. Serious violations are those where a substantial probability exists that death or serious physical harm could result. A *willful* violation resulting in an employee death is punishable by fine up to $10,000 or imprisonment for up to six months. A *de minimis* violation having no direct relationship to safety or health receives a notice only.

If the employer wishes to contest the citation or penalty he may request a hearing before the Occupational Safety and Health Commission.

Employers have the further duty of maintaining specific records and making periodic reports of work-related deaths, injuries, and illnesses.

Discharge of or discrimination against any employee who exercises a right under the Act is prohibited.

FINANCIAL PROTECTION

Development of programs looking to the financial welfare of workers, or the regulation of existing ones, is a major concern of government. Few problems cause as much unease as those faced by the old and out-of-work with limited financial resources.

Unemployment Compensation

Some semblance of financial security for workers when they are without work through no fault of their own is provided by unemployment compensation programs in all states. The Social Security Act of 1935 encouraged states to set up programs and today the federal base is built upon to different levels in each state; requirements with respect to time needed to qualify and the amount of benefits vary.

An unemployed worker who meets the tests of the acts draws payments regardless of need. Workers qualify if they

1. Worked in an industry covered by the acts (certain industries are exempt).

2. Worked a minimum number of weeks or earned a minimum salary.

3. Lost work through no fault of their own and do not quit voluntarily.

4. Are not discharged for proper cause.

5. Do not refuse other suitable work offered them.

The programs are financed from the federal unemployment tax (now 3.2 percent of payroll, at a maximum) but credit up to 2.7 percent is made for employer payments into a state fund. Actually, all money is deposited into the Federal Unemployment Trust Fund to be drawn upon by states in paying unemployment benefits (and only those benefits). An employer with good experience rating (the company that has less unemployment and fewer claims) may have his payments reduced.

Social Security

Federal legislation establishing a system of aid and assistance to the needy and elderly came with enactment of the Federal Social Security programs; the most direct federal support comes in the area of Old Age and Survivor's Disability Insurance, most frequently known simply as Social Security. Unemployment compensation, maternal and child care services, and general welfare activity are programs operated by states with the extensive support of the federal government if the state plan is approved.

The Social Security Act of 1935 provided the first income security for a limited number of persons but the coverage has expanded to the point at which 90 percent of the workers in the country are included. Social Security payments by employees are deducted from their wages, matched by employer contributions and generally deposited in an authorized bank with quarterly reports made to the Internal Revenue Service. Earnings affected by retirement, death, or disability make the worker or his family eligible for monthly payments. A recently enacted *Medicare* program provides hospital and health insurance for those over age 65.

Retirement Plans

Private pension plans are strengthened by provisions of the Internal Revenue Code. Employee contributions to a qualified plan are excluded from taxable income and payments from the annuity fund are taxed to the recipient only when received after retirement. Employer contributions to a retirement fund under a qualified plan may be claimed as tax deductions. A qualified plan is one that meets IRS requirements to assure broad coverage of employees, not just a favored few at a particular managerial level.

Concern aroused by a large number of deficient retirement plans led to the enactment of the Employee Retirement Income Security Act of 1974 (ERISA). The Act imposes strict funding requirements to assure a strong financial base as well as providing a means whereby some equity in annuities earned is available to the employee ("vesting" of benefits). In the past many employees had worked for years and departed with no benefits because they did not reach retirement under the plan. Strong actuarial programs and insurance coverage under the Pension Benefit Guaranty Corporation are requirements of a qualified plan. Vesting is immediate as to the employee's contributions and those from the employer must be fully vested in ten years or a stated gradual vesting over fifteen years.

Civil suits may result in damages for aggrieved parties or an injunction may be sought by private parties or the Secretary of Labor. There are some violations of the act that are criminal in nature.

CONSUMER PROTECTION

Protection of persons in consumer activity, as well as in the general environment, is a valid exercise of police powers under the Constitution of the United States and subsequent federal and state statutes. Health and purity standards received their first important impetus under the Food and Drug Act of 1906 but except for intermittent flurries of regulation in food and drug commerce, little happened in the intervening period. Not until the decade from 1965 to 1975 did the most extensive activity in legislation looking to the preservation of the health of the nation's citizens take place.

Health and Safety

A review of some of the federal statutes may give an idea of the extent of the societal interest. Controls over depressant and stimulant drugs were strengthened in the Drug Abuse Control Amendments of 1965 to the Food, Drug and Cosmetic Act. The Fair Packaging and Labeling Act of 1966 provided further consumer protection in terms of the accuracy and validity of designations external to the product. The Public Health Cigarette Smoking Act of 1969 required the now well-known warning on cigarette packages of the hazard to health as determined by the Surgeon General.

The Consumer Product Safety Act of 1972 established the Consumer Product Safety Commission and charged it with the responsibility of determining safety standards for all consumer products and regulating most aspects of their manufacture and distribution. Manufacturers are required to maintain extensive inspection procedures and notify the Commission and general public if a product is found to be defective. Products may be removed from the market and each violation may carry with it a penalty of $2000 up to a maximum of half a million dollars.

Business Practices

Consumer protection in the course of business focuses upon the prohibition of deceptive trade practices or the mandating of sufficient information for the making of an informed decision.

The Federal Trade Commission Act prohibits deceptive or unfair practices with respect to consumers. False or misleading advertising is a frequent target of Federal Trade Commission activity. Other tactics such as "bait and switch," misbranding, using names deceptively similar to other products, and disparagement of the products of others (see below) are also subject to legal action by the commission.

The Consumer Product Warranty Act of 1975 (Magnuson-Moss Warranty—FTC Improvement Act) establishes that written warranties be given in simple and understandable terms and conditions. Informal settlement procedures prior to litigation are also issued by the Federal Trade Commission. Manufacturers need not issue a warranty but if they do the language must be such as to be understood by the buyer.

If a product costing more than $15 has a warranty, the warranty must be labeled "full" or "limited." A defective product with a full warranty must be repaired or replaced without charge within a reasonable period of time. Limited warranties must be clear in their limitations.

The Consumer Goods Pricing Act of 1975 eliminates the practice of "fair trade" laws in all states still having such laws in effect. The so-called fair trade laws date from the great depression of the 1930s and permitted the manufacturer to fix the price of merchandise at the retail level. Public policy in maintaining a healthy economy was given as the reason for such price-fixing legislation but it did stifle price competition.

The Real Estate Settlement Procedures Act of 1974 requires disclosure of all costs in a real estate transaction. Purchasers or borrowers must be made aware of all closing costs, appraisal fees, title changes, and loan discount "points." A point is a charge by the lender and each point equals one percent of the total sum considered. The complete statement must be given to the buyer/borrower at least the day before the closing.

Other practices prohibited by the act are kickbacks, charging for a service not performed, requiring title insurance from a particular company, and a placing of more than one month's advance deposit in escrow for taxes and insurance.

Credit Protection

Various facets of consumer protection in financial matters are embodied in the Consumer Credit Protection Act. The primary feature of the act has become known as the Truth in Lending law (Title I—Consumer Credit Protection Act). The Act is intended to provide consumers with extensive knowledge of the costs and conditions of credit in order that they may be able to make better financial plans and decisions. The Act mandates that those who extend credit or arrange for it to be extended are required to communicate specific details to the borrower. The finance charge must be stated by the creditor as a dollar amount and in the annual percentage rate. The finance charge, as disclosed, is the sum of all charges—interest, carrying charges, required insurance, or any other charges. The seller must also state the cash price, down payment, difference between the two, amount to be financed, payments, repayment dates, late payment charges, and the finance charge in dollars, as well as percentage rate.

The Consumer Credit Protection Act includes provisions covering the issuance and use of credit cards. The act prohibits issuance of a credit card without an application for it. The cardholder must be notified of the rights and obligations surrounding the use of the card and be provided with a simple method of notification of loss or theft of the card. In the case of unauthorized use of the card, the act limits the liability of the cardholder to fifty dollars.

Other provisions of the act relate to real property transactions. The giver of a mortgage or lien on a home has a three day period during which the deal can be rescinded; the creditor is required to give written notice of the availability of the right to cancel.

The Consumer Credit Protection Act also places a limit on the percentage of wages that may be garnished as the result of debt delinquency. The act also prohibits an employer from discharging the wage earner as the result of the garnishment.

The Fair Credit Billing Act of 1974 is an amendment to the Truth in Lending Law, which gives consumers additional rights in credit card usage. The right to assert claims against the issuer in the case of a dispute concerning the product is a substantial gain for the consumer. Other rights in a dispute with respect to billing are additional features.

The Equal Credit Opportunity Act of 1975 attempts to put women seeking credit on an equal basis with men. Discrimination on the basis of sex or marital status in the giving of credit is prohibited.

Credit Reporting

The amount of information being collected on private individuals without their knowledge or control has aroused widespread concern. A major legislative response in the credit area was the enactment of the Fair Credit Reporting Act (Title VI of the Consumer Credit Reporting Act).

The Act provides an opportunity for a party to become aware of most of the information collected in a report. Ordinarily the report is assembled as the result of investigations connected with applications for credit or employment. Inquiries as to personal character or general reputation often descended into collecting gossip or inaccurate information.   The subject of the report has the right under certain conditions to inspect his/her file and have the credit agency check the accuracy of the material.   Disputed points may be responded to with a short statement to be placed in the file by the person and included in all future reports.   Obsolete information must be removed on request— usually that over seven years is considered to be in that category.

Generally, the individual is entitled to be informed of the conduct of an investigative report and may request to be informed, in addition to the content of the report, of the names of persons or organizations to whom the report is being sent.

Access to the reports is limited by the act. There may be consent by the subject of the file, of course. Businesses with a bona fide need for the information may obtain it or access may be gained by court order.

Securities

The Securities Act of 1933 and the Securities Exchange Act of 1934 regulated the issuance and transfer of securities by a corporation. Many of the requirements placed upon corporations in security dealings (Chapter 16) were introduced as protection for the purchasers and traders of securities. Violations make the corporation liable in both criminal and civil (tort) actions.

BUSINESS PROTECTION

Business activity enjoys some benefits of regulation or access to courts when rights are threatened. The due process clause of the Constitution provides fundamental protection of persons and property. This may be said to be extended by specific statutes establishing rights in material or intellectual products and in the right to be free of economic interference.

Rights to Intellectual Products

In order to promote economic activity for the general welfare of the nation, the federal government established, at a very early stage of the development of the United States, a system of protection of rights to inventions and literary or artistic works.

A *patent* represents an exclusive right to make and sell an invention for a set period of time.   Patents are issued only on new and useful inventions, improvements, or designs not known in the trade or in use for more than a year prior to application. Infringement is the making of a device that produces the same result as the patented one. A patent holder can sue the infringer for damages and loss of profits.

A *copyright* enables the holder to maintain an exclusive right to publish and sell a literary, musical, and artistic work, or photographs and drawings for a time limit represented by the life of the author plus fifty years. The Copyright Act, under the amendments of 1976, provides for a limited amount of copying for spontaneous educational purposes, but not for the monetary profit of the copier. Infringement calls for actual or statutory damages.

A *trademark* is a distinctive mark, design, or picture by which consumers can identify a product of service. The Lanham Act of 1946 established a Principal Register for the registration of trademarks. Rights to trademarks rest with the developer.

Rights Under Tort Law

Interference with the business activities of another may provide a basis for legal action under the law of torts. This general offense may come about in many different ways—one may disparage the goods of another, interfere in contractual relationships, infringe upon patents, copyrights, and trademarks, or engage in unfair competition. Some of these torts may be actionable under federal and state statutes as well. Review of the more general invasions of property rights such as *deceit*, *conversion*, and *trespass* is also appropriate in so far as they relate to business activity (Chapter 18).

Disparagement

A wrongful publication of false statements that interferes with the prospects of the business gives rise to this action, sometimes known as *trade libel* or *slander of title*. Derogatory statements as to quality of product, service, or general reputation of the business (good will) are actionable if factually untrue. Statements of opinion such as "my zaggers are better than yours" are not a basis for action.

Interference

Tort liability may exist for activities that interfere with present or prospective business interests. There are two types of torts—*interference with contract* and *interference with prospective advantage*. Interference with a valid contract that produces damage is actionable if the interferor did so with intent to disrupt the relationship. The same elements must be present to make out the tort of interference with prospective relations (except, of course, no contract need be in existence). Valid competitive methods are permissible as is peaceful picketing and boycotting by labor organizations.

Infringement of Economic Privilege

Rights established through the granting of patents, copyrights and the registry of trademarks are protected by the law establishing the systems (above). Infringement of these rights gives rise to a tort action.

Other Statutory Bases

Violations of antitrust laws expose the violator to a civil suit in tort by parties suffering damages as a result of the illegal activity. This is in addition to any criminal action that may be brought by state or federal authorities. The injured party may bring an action for treble damages and a prior successful suit by the government can be proof of the violation.

The National Labor Relations Act prohibits unfair labor practices. Violation of the act give rise to civil actions in tort by the aggrieved parties.

The causes of action arising from these statutory violations can usually be fitted under the forms of tort action already mentioned above.

ENVIRONMENTAL PROTECTION

Concern over the quality of life space has been mounting with the passage of time, reaching high and active levels in the past decade. The response has come in the form of community action on a wide front and extensive legislation at all governmental levels, particularly the federal. The National Environmental Policy Act expresses well the purposes to be met in the legislation:

> To declare a national policy which will encourage productive and enjoyable harmony between man and his environment; to promote efforts which will prevent or eliminate damage to the environment and biosphere and stimulate the health and welfare of man; to enrich the understanding of the ecological systems and natural resources important to the Nation; and to establish a Council on Environmental Quality.

The act builds upon this statement of purpose by setting broad policy goals, determining duties for federal agencies with respect to the environment. The purpose of the Council on Environmental Quality (CEQ) is to gather information, analyze it, issue guidelines, and make recommendations to the President on environmental matters.

Much of the activity as the result of the act comes in the requirement that all federal agencies provide a detailed statement of the environmental impact of all major federal actions or proposals for legislation. The Environmental Impact Study (EIS) has been the source of considerable litigation as agencies and courts have attempted to meet the requirements of an act when the provisions have not always been clear.

In 1970 further administrative and regulatory coordination came with the establishment of the *Environmental Protection Agency* (EPA) under the President's Reorganization Plan No. 3. Regulation of air quality, water pollution, solid waste, radiation, and pesticides was transferred from a wide variety of agencies to the new agency in order to provide more effective administration of laws designed to improve the quality of life.

Water Quality

Regulation of water pollution has a longer history than most other areas. The Water Pollution Control Act of 1948 attempted to bring strong federal controls to what was already being perceived as a major problem (there was very early legislation, the River and Harbor Act of 1899, but it was seldom enforced). Significant amendments that represented a "sweeping" campaign to "prevent, reduce and eliminate water pollution" were passed in 1972. Two major goals of the legislation were the achievement of water clean enough for swimming by 1983 and no discharges of pollutants into the Nation's waters by 1985. All waters are covered, not just interstate ones, and the EPA is empowered to step in speedily if states do not act. An immediate court injunction may be obtained if there is an imminent and substantial danger to public health. The EPA has the power to inspect, and information, except for trade secrets, will be made public. Penalties range from $2500 to $25,000 per day and up to a year in prison for the first offense.

Guidelines for control of water pollution are set out in a form outlined as "best practicable" and "best available" but if these do not meet the standards the state may impose stricter controls.

Federal aid to local governments for sewage facilities is available and small business may obtain loans from the Small Business Administration in order to meet the standards.

Air Quality

Air pollution controls developed slowly from the mid 1950s reaching a high level in the Clean Air Act amendments of 1970. The amendments require the EPA administrator to formulate air quality standards, set a timetable for development and monitor their implementation. The administrator also approves state plans and, while state officials enforce air quality standards within the state, the EPA can play an active role in inspection and in litigation if standards are not met. If an inspection determines that there is noncompliance with an air quality standard, the administrator will issue a notice and, after thirty days, seek relief in a civil action or a restraining order if there is an imminent and substantial danger. Failure to comply with an order or the implementation plan can bring a penalty of up to $25,000 per day or one year in prison, or both.

Solid Waste

An increase in population and affluence carries with it a commensurate growth of waste products of that society. Agricultural and mineral wastes make up over half the total produced. While wastes from homes and businesses make up a small part of the whole, their impact on individuals is likely to be greater because those wastes build up where people live.

The major legislation in the regulation of solid waste is the *Solid Waste Disposal Act* of 1965 and its major amendments of 1970. It is recognized under the act that this is primarily a state or local problem but the EPA is authorized to provide technical and financial assistance to state and local governments as well as interstate agencies. Research support and training grants are also made available to foster development of new methods of processing, recycling, or disposing of solid wastes.

Noise Control

The adverse effects of "noise pollution" have long been noted. In response to continuing concern over the contribution of excess noise to physical and emotional problems, Congress passed the *Noise Control Act of 1972.* The main thrust of the act is toward the control of noise emission in manufactured items rather than control of noise in the general environment. Manufacturers must meet EPA standards if products are identified as a major source of noise. Distribution of a product that does not meet the standards or removal of a noise control device is prohibited by law. Violation brings a fine of $25,000 per day or one year in prison, or both. Private citizens, as well as the EPA, may bring a civil action to force compliance with the Act.

Chemical and Radiological Control

The primary chemical danger to the quality, or even existence, of life occurs in connection with the widespread use of insecticides. Admittedly the problem of control is accentuated by the obvious fact that our society has been able to flourish, based to a great extent upon the ability to feed the population at low cost. That outcome has been reached largely through the use of fertilizers to increase yields and pesticides to prevent the ravages of insects.

The Insecticide, Fungicide and Rodenticide Act of 1947 (amended 1973) provided some regulation over the uses of potentially hazardous use of chemicals in pest control. Later the *Environmental Pesticide Control Act* of 1972 added more provisions covering the use of pesticides. The Act requires pesticides to be registered with the EPA and adhere to extensive and specific standards with respect to labeling, effectiveness, and application. The EPA is required to determine whether the pesticide may have "unreasonable adverse effects on the environment" before it may be distributed for general or restricted use. The EPA also has wide authority to inspect, halt sales, order seizure, or suspend registration of a pesticide to prevent an imminent hazard.

Radiation pollution control is exercised under several of the above acts. The Water Pollution Control Act and The Clean Air Act are two of the major pieces of legislation that contain provisions relating to radiation pollution. Coverage extends from problems connected with nuclear facilities to such simple household products as microwave ovens or color television sets.

GLOSSARY

A

A PRIORI: in logic, what goes before must necessarily be followed by an effect.

AB INITIO: from the beginning.

ABANDONMENT: relinquishing or giving up property or rights.

ABATEMENT: a reduction or diminution of payment, action, or the removal of a nuisance.

ABROGATE: to annul or repeal a former law.

ACCEPTANCE: act of complying with offer or receiving goods with intention to retain.

ACCESSORY: one who contributes to or helps the principal actor in a criminal act, before or after the fact.

ACCOMMODATION PAPER: a bill or note to which an accommodation party puts his name, without consideration, in order to benefit another party raising money.

ACCOMPLICE: one who knowingly combines with the primary offender in the commission of a crime.

ACCORD AND SATISFACTION: an agreement whereby one who has a right against another agrees to accept something different.

ACQUITTAL: a release by jury verdict.

ADJUDICATION: the act of judging claims of parties before the courts.

ADMINISTRATIVE LAW: that branch of the legal system dealing with executive or quasijudicial duties delegated to it by the legislative or executive branch.

ADMINISTRATOR: in a general sense, one who manages. In decedent's estates, one who is appointed by the court to administer the estate of the deceased.

ADULTERY: sexual intercourse between a married person and one who is not married to him/her.

ADVERSE POSSESSION: to claim title by adverse possession one must be in continuous possession of the land or property for the duration of the period prescribed by law.

AFFIDAVIT: a written statement of facts confirmed by oath of the party making it.

AGENCY: the acting for or representing of another under authority.

AMICUS CURIAE: "friend of the court;" a third party who provides the court with information.

ANALYSIS OF DECISIONS SYSTEMS: the approach developed in this text that focuses upon the decision making in steps of an ongoing process.

APPARENT AUTHORITY: authority conferred by law upon an agent in that the actions of a principal led others to suppose it to exist.

APPELLANT: the initiator of an appeal from a court decision.

APPELLATE COURT: a court to which appeals and reviews may be taken.

APPELLEE: one against whom an appeal has been taken.

ARBITRATION: submission of a controversy to a private, selected person for determination.

ARREST: the deprivation of a person's liberty under legal authority.

ARSON: malicious burning of a building (in common law, the dwelling of another).

ASSAULT: a threat of bodily injury.

ASSIGNMENT: a transfer of a right in action relating to property or the property itself.

ASSUMPSIT: a form of action alleging a breach of contract.

ASSUMPTION OF THE RISK: may be used as a defense in a negligence action. One who voluntarily assumes the risk cannot claim damages.

ATTACHMENT: a writ or process seizing a person's property in order to bring that person before the court or to save the property for debtors.

AUTHORITY: legitimate power; power delegated to an agent by a principal in agency.

B

BAIL: procuring the release of a person from custody by pledging a later appearance in court.

BAILMENT: delivery of goods under a contract, to be returned to the bailor after a particular purpose is fulfilled.

BANKRUPTCY: an election under law by a financially burdened person or his creditors to have a court determine a distribution of assets among creditors and allow the person a new start.

BATTERY: an unlawful touching of another without his consent.

BEARER: one holding a check, draft, or security payable to bearer or endorsed in blank.

BIGAMY: marrying while a previous marriage still exists.

BILATERAL CONTRACT: a contract by which one promise is given in exchange for another.

BILL OF EXCHANGE: an unconditional written order by a person to another to pay a sum to order or bearer on demand or at a set time. Also known as a draft.

BILL OF LADING: a document from a carrier noting presence of goods and the terms for transportation.

BILL OF SALE: a writing by a seller describing a sale of personal property to a buyer.

BINDER: a contract of insurance by a memorandum before execution of the written policy.

BLANK INDORSEMENT: an indorsement that does not name the person to whom the paper is negotiated.

BLUE-SKY LAWS: state statutes to protect the public from sellers of worthless securities.

BONA FIDE: actual, real, valid, not fraudulent.

BOND: a promise or obligation, generally in writing under seal, by representatives or trustees.

C

CANCELLATION: changing the legal effect of an instrument or eliminating part of it through an agreement or court decree.

CAPITAL: net assets of a corporation.

CAPITAL STOCK: money value of corporate stock outstanding.

CAUSE OF ACTION: a plaintiff's right to relief and/or damages when an unlawful act of defendant occurs.

CAVEAT EMPTOR: Latin for "let the buyer beware."

CAVEAT VENDITOR: Latin for "let the seller beware."

CERTIORARI: an order grainting standing in an upper court for review.

CHARTER: authority from the state to a corporation to initiate its existence, shown by a certificate of incorporation.

CHATTEL: property, *personal* chattels (objects) or *real* chattels (leases).

CHATTEL MORTGAGE: transfer of title to personal property by a debtor to a lender as security for a debt (now a "secured transaction" under the Uniform Commercial Code).

CHECK: a depositor's order to a bank to pay a sum of money to a party (payee).

CHOSE IN ACTION: a claim in the form of intangible property such as wages.

CIRCUMSTANTIAL EVIDENCE: facts surrounding an incident from which deduction may be made by a trier of fact in a legal action.

CIVIL LAW: the system of law in European countries based upon Roman law; in the Common Law system, that branch of law dealing with controversies concerned with private rights and duties.

CLEAN HANDS: in equity, relief can be denied to one who is himself guilty of inequitable conduct.

CLOSED SHOP: a place of work where only union members may be offered employment; prohibited by the Taft-Hartley Act.

CODE: collection of laws, systematically arranged, enacted by a legislative body.

CODICIL: a writing adding to or modifying a will.

COINSURANCE: a requirement that the insured maintain a certain amount of insurance or otherwise be liable for losses up to that amount.

COLLECTIVE BARGAINING: the process of determining the conditions of employment through negotiations between representatives of employer and employees.

COLLECTIVE BARGAINING UNIT: the unit participating in an election of an individual union to represent them in collective bargaining.

COLLUSION: an agreement between two or more persons to defraud others or the courts.

COLOR OF TITLE: appearance of ownership when in fact no valid title is present.

COMMERCIAL PAPER: short-term negotiable instruments resulting from commercial transactions, i.e., checks and promissory notes.

COMMON CARRIER: a carrier serving the public generally for compensation.

COMMON LAW: a body of law based upon the following of unwritten customs and usages of the community; used as a designation for the Anglo-American legal system.

COMMON STOCK: stock without priorities in dividends or distribution.

COMMUNITY PROPERTY: cotenancy of husband and wife in property acquired during marriage; applicable in certain states.

COMPLAINT: means of initiating an action in the legal process by a plaintiff.

COMPOSITION OF CREDITORS: an agreement among creditors to accept part rather than full payment.

CONFIDENTIAL RELATIONSHIP: a relationship which, because of law or actual conditions, imposes a trust upon one for the guidance of another.

CONFLICT OF LAWS: substantive law that determines which state law applies when more than one state is involved in a case.

CONSTITUTION: the fundamental law of a state, nation, or association establishing its basic framework and organization.

CONSTRUCTIVE: adjective that qualifies a situation implied to exist in law if not in fact, as in a *constructive* trust.

CONTINGENT BENEFICIARY: the person receiving the benefit of a life insurance policy when the primary beneficiary predeceases the insured.

CONTRACT: a lawful agreement between competent parties which, if breached, will be the basis for a legal remedy.

CONTRIBUTORY NEGLIGENCE: negligence of the plaintiff contributing to his injury and barring him from recovering.

CONVEYANCE: transfer of an interest in land.

COOLING-OFF PERIOD: a delay of a strike as required by statute.

COPYRIGHT: a right granted to an author for exclusivity in publication.

CORPORATION: an organization, considered a fictitious person, created under authority granted by the state.

COUNTERCLAIM: a claim by the defendant in an action brought by the plaintiff.

COVENANTS OF TITLE: a legal declaration that the seller has valid title or that no other factors will prevent the buyer from full enjoyment of rights to the property.

CREDITOR BENEFICIARY: a third-person creditor of a promisee benefited by the performance of a contract by the promisor.

CRIME: a violation of law to which the government applies sanction.

CRITICAL PATH METHOD: a form of network analysis that illustrates a flow of activity through a system.

CROSS COMPLAINT: a complaint made by the defendant against the plaintiff in response to the original complaint.

CROSS-EXAMINATION: examination of a witness by the attorney for the adverse party.

CUMULATIVE VOTING: voting by shareholders for directors of a corporation in which the number of votes an elector may cast equals the number of shares owned times the number of directors to be elected, which votes may be allocated as desired.

CY-PRES DOCTRINE: a carrying out of the wishes of the settlor of a trust as close as possible to the intent when the original use is not possible.

D

DAMAGES: a sum of money awarded in redress of a legal wrong.

DECEIT: fraudulent misrepresentation.

DECISION: judicially, a judgment of a court settling a controversy; in management of systems, a conscious selection among alternatives.

DECLARATORY JUDGMENT: determination by a court of the rights of the parties without ordering anything to be done.

DECREE: judgment of a court of equity.

DEED: an instrument indicating the transfer of title to land from the owner (grantor) to the purchaser (grantee).

DE FACTO: existing in fact.

DEFAMATION: a publication exposing one to ridicule, contempt, or otherwise injuring a reputation; a term encompassing both libel and slander.

DEFENDANT: the party against whom the law suit is brought.

DEFICIENCY JUDGMENT: judgment for a sum still due the mortgagee after foreclosure of a mortgage.

DE JURE: existing in law or as of right.

DELEGATION: transfer of power from one person to another.

DE MINIMIS: Latin for "a trifle" or "of minor interest." Short form of "de minimis non curat lex" or "the law is not concerned with trifles."

DEMONSTRATIVE EVIDENCE: physical objects or other concrete forms of evidence.

DEMURRER: a pleading attacking an adverse pleading as not stating a cause of action; a defense.

DEPOSITION: testimony under oath taken outside of court.

DEPOSITARY BANK: first bank to which an item is transferred for collection even though it is also the payor bank (UCC 4-105).

DESCRIPTIVE MODEL: a representation that is intended to portray the real situation as it exists.

DETERMINISTIC MODEL: a model in which the outputs from the inputs are determined to be certain in outcome.

DEVISE: realty passing under a will or the process of passing under a will.

DIRECTED VERDICT: a verdict complying with a direction by the court to a jury to return a verdict in favor of one party in the action.

DIRECTOR: an individual elected by shareholders of a corporation to direct the activity of the corporation.

DISCHARGE IN BANKRUPTCY: discharge of a debtor from most creditors' claims under an order of the bankruptcy court.

DISCHARGE OF CONTRACT: a contract terminated through performance or other action or by operation of law.

DISCOVERY: the use of procedures for determining pertinent facts before trial in order to eliminate surprise.

DISHONOR: refusal to accept or pay commercial paper (draft, bill of exchange).

DISMISS: (a pleading) to terminate an action on the basis that plaintiff has not pleaded a cause of action.

DISPARAGEMENT: false and malicious statements of the quality of goods of another.

DIVIDEND: a payment of cash or stocks to shareholders out of surplus of the cor-corporation.

DOMESTIC BILL OF EXCHANGE: a draft drawn in one state and payable in that or another state.

DOMESTIC CORPORATION: a corporation so designated by the state in which it is incorporated.

DOMICILE: location considered as the home of a person rather than impermanent abode or, in the case of a corporation, the state of incorporation.

DONEE BENEFICIARY: a third person benefiting from the contract as a gift from the promisor.

DOUBLE INDEMNITY: a life insurance provision for payment of double the set amount if death occurs under accidental circumstances.

DOUBLE JEOPARDY: the protection against double jeopardy refers to the principle that no one can be tried twice for the same offense.

DRAFT: an unconditional written order by a person to another to pay a sum to bearer or order on demand or at a set time. Also known as a *bill of exchange*.

DUE CARE: the standard of care to which reasonable man would adhere in order to avoid harm.

DUE PROCESS OF LAW: the constitutional guarantee that no person would be deprived of life, liberty or property through arbitrary or unfair procedures.

DURESS: action that deprives another of the exercise of free will; it may be the basis for setting aside transactions under it.

DYNAMIC MODEL: a model showing activity in an ongoing process.

E

EASEMENT: a right in another's land, such as a right to pass through.

ELEEMOSYNARY: charitable or benevolent, usually applied to an organization formed for such purposes.

EMBEZZLEMENT: unlawful conversion of property intrusted to the violator in a fiduciary manner.

EMINENT DOMAIN: the power to take private property, with compensation to the owner, for public purposes.

EMPIRICAL: based upon data gathered in an organized manner.

ENCUMBRANCE: a charge against property, such as a mortgage or judgment lien, held by another.

EQUITY: the value of an interest in property; also, the body of law developed in Anglo-American courts as the result of the inadequate rules under common law forms.

ESCROW: delivery of property or an instrument to a custodian who is to make final delivery to another upon the fulfillment of a condition.

ESTATE: a decedent's property at time of death; also, the extent of interest in land, as in *estate in fee simple,* the absolute ownership of land.

ESTOPPEL: a principle barring a person from pursuit of an action or asserting a point of law because it would be unfair to permit it.

EVIDENCE: information presented for determination of fact by a tribunal or trier of fact.

EXCEPTION: an objection to an act in the legal process, as in the introduction of improper evidence in court.

EXECUTION: the carrying out of a court judgment.

EXECUTOR: one named to administer the will, upon the testator's death.

EXEMPLARY DAMAGES: punitive damages in excess of exact compensation in order to serve as an example.

EXONERATION: an agreement that a party will not be liable for a loss, as a surety getting agreement that another party be liable first on a claim.

EXPERT WITNESS: one who has superior knowledge through education or experience with regard to a particular subject.

EX POST FACTO: Latin for "after the fact," usually applied to a law that makes illegal an act that was legal when done. Such statutes are prohibited.

EXTRAORDINARY BAILMENT: a bailment imposing special duties upon the bailee, such as a common carrier.

F

FACTOR: a bailee to whom goods are delivered for sale.

FAIR EMPLOYMENT PRACTICE ACTS: laws enacted to eliminate discrimination in employment on the basis of certain personal characteristics.

FAIR LABOR STANDARDS ACTS: statutes enacted to eliminate unfair employment conditions relating to hours, pay, and child labor.

FAIR TRADE ACTS: statutes authorizing agreements to maintain retail prices; now generally eliminated.

FALSE ARREST: the unlawful detention of a person under color of law by an agent of the government.

FALSE IMPRISONMENT: the tort of confining a person without proper authority.

FEATHERBEDDING: an unfair labor practice wherein payment is demanded for services not performed.

FEE SIMPLE: a full and complete interest in realty.

FELLOW SERVANT RULE: a common law rule barring a suit by an employee against the employer for an injury by a fellow employee.

FELONY: a criminal offense so designated and punishable by imprisonment or death.

FIDUCIARY: a person occupying a position of trust or confidence.

FINANCIAL RESPONSIBILITY LAWS: statutes requiring proof of financial responsibility by those involved in automobile accidents.

FIRM OFFER: an offer to be held open for a specified time.

FIXTURE: personal property that becomes part of the realty by its attachment to the real estate.

FORBEARANCE: refraining from doing an act.

FORECLOSURE: enforcing rights under a mortgage by public sale of the mortgaged property.

FOREIGN CORPORATION: a corporation incorporated under the laws of another state (other than the one making that designation).

FORGERY: a fraudulent making or changing of an instrument that apparently alters the rights of another.

FORUM: a court.

FRAUD: the making of statements that are or should be known to be false with the intent to cause injury and the achievement of that end.

FULL FAITH AND CREDIT: the required recognition by one state of the laws and proceedings of other states.

FUNGIBLE: the designation of the homogeneous nature of materials, as when one unit of goods is recognized as the equivalent of each other unit.

G

GAME MODEL: models operating under conditions of uncertainty in which outcomes are faced without specific knowledge of conditions.

GARNISHMENT: designation in some states for an attachment; a process whereby a person's property is applied to payment of that person's debt to a third person.

GENERAL APPEARANCE: act of defendant agreeing to jurisdiction of a court for all purposes.

GENERAL CREDITOR: a creditor with a claim against a debtor that is not secured by a lien on the property or through a judgment.

GENERAL DAMAGES: damages that ordinarily follow naturally and reasonably from the injury caused by an act of the defendant.

GENERAL LEGACY: a legacy to be paid out of assets of a testator without specifying the source of funds.

GENERAL PARTNERSHIP: a partnership managed by all partners as co-owners with unlimited liability.

GOODS: movable personal property.

GRAND JURY: a jury that considers evidence of a crime and either prepares indictments to bring violators to trial or dismisses cases, now generally being replaced by the process of information.

GRANT: a conveyance of real property.

GRATUITOUS BAILMENT: a bailment without compensation to the bailee.

GRIEVANCE: a dispute in a work situation under a labor contract.

GUARANTY: an undertaking to pay the debt of another should the creditor not be able to recover against the debtor after a suit.

H

HABEAS CORPUS: (Latin), a court order releasing a person held unlawfully.

HEARING: a court proceeding to hear arguments and determine facts.

HEARSAY: out of court evidence offered as proof of statements made, generally not admissible.

HEIR: person designated by statute to inherit estate not passing under a will.

HOLDER: person in possession of commercial paper payable to him as payee or indorsee or made payable or indorsed to bearer.

HOLDER IN DUE COURSE: a holder who, under certain circumstances, is given favorable treatment, including rights in the instrument despite certain defenses.

HUNG JURY: a petit jury that had been unable to reach a verdict.

I

ICONIC MODEL: a model that possesses some characteristics of the thing it represents, as, for instance, a model airplane or train.

IMPLIED CONTRACT: a contract deduced from facts or conduct.

IMPUTED: action by one attributed to another, such as acts of an agent charged to the principal.

INCIDENTAL AUTHORITY: authority necessarily related to that granted and needed for an agent to act under express authority.

INDEMNITY: a right to be reimbursed for loss under certain conditions.

INDEPENDENT CONTRACTOR: one who undertakes a task under contract free from control of another party and responsible only for a specified result.

INDICTMENT: an accusation of crime made by a grand jury.

INHERITANCE: the passing of an interest from a decedent to an heir.

INJUNCTION: a court order in equity that orders persons to refrain from an act.

INSOLVENCY: a condition where assets are exceeded by debts or liabilities.

INTANGIBLE PERSONAL PROPERTY: a nonphysical interest in personal property such as a claim under a contract or stock in a corporation.

INTERLOCUTORY: referring to a step in the legal process that is not final.

INTERPLEADER: an action by a person faced with conflicting claimants in order that the court decide which claim is to prevail.

INTER SE: Latin for "between parties themselves."

INTER VIVOS: a transaction among living persons on matters before their deaths.

INTESTATE: describing the situation of dying without a will.

IPSO FACTO: Latin for "the act in itself."

IRREBUTTABLE PRESUMPTION: a position in the law in which contrary facts cannot be put forth.

IRREPARABLE INJURY: an injury of such unique nature that it cannot be compensated through money damages or material replacement.

J

JOINT AND SEVERAL: descriptive of a condition under which two or more persons have rights or liabilities alone and together.

JOINT STOCK COMPANY: an association wherein members' shares are transferable and control is delegated to a board.

JOINT TENANCY: an estate held by two or more persons with right of survivorship.

JOINT VENTURE: a combination of two or more persons sharing profits and losses from a single undertaking.

JUDGMENT: a final decision or order of the court at the end of a legal action.

JUDGMENT NOTE: a promissory note with a clause authorizing the holder to enter judgment against the maker if payment is overdue.

JUDGMENT N.O.V.: (judgment *non obstante veredicto*, or, notwithstanding the verdict)—judgment in favor of one party although the verdict was for the other party.

JUDGMENT ON THE PLEADINGS: a judgment that may be entered based on the pleadings because it is clear from them that the petitioner is entitled to the judgment.

JUDICIAL SALE: a sale under order of the court.

JURISDICTION: the power of a court to act in the case of a defendant or to hear particular cases.

JURISDICTIONAL DISPUTE: a labor dispute between two unions, each of which claims the right to work on the tasks under contention.

JURY: a body of persons charged with determining the factual basis of a legal action and arriving at a verdict.

JUSTIFIABLE DISCHARGE: the right of an employer to fire an employee for just cause.

L

LACHES: a rule in equity that denies equitable relief to one who has waited too long to file an action.

LAND: earth and all things attached thereto.

LAST CLEAR CHANCE: the rule in tort law that considers the defendant liable for the injury of a contributorily negligent plaintiff if the defendant could clearly have avoided the accident at the last moment.

LAW OF THE CASE: a rule that matters decided in litigation are binding in later phases of the case.

LEADING QUESTION: a question that suggests an answer to a witness or assumes a fact in dispute.

LEASE: an agreement wherein an owner of property gives possession of it to another for consideration (rent).

LEGACY: personal property given by a decedent's will.

LEGAL TENDER: money regarded as lawful payment.

LETTERS OF ADMINISTRATION: a formal writing authorizing a person to act as an administrator of an estate.

LETTERS TESTAMENTARY: a formal writing authorizing the person named as executor/executrix in the will to act accordingly.

LEVY: physical or constructive seizure of property pursuant to a judgment of a court.

LEX LOCI: Latin for "law of the place." Refers to place where facts for legal action occurred.

LIBEL: defamation in written or visual form made without legal justification.

LICENSE: a privileged entry upon land of another, less than an easement or right to possession. Example: setting up a sign.

LIEN: a right or claim against property; for example, one that can arise through the entry of a judgment and levy by a court against the owner.

LIFE ESTATE: an estate in property for a lifetime of a person.

LIMITED JURISDICTION: legal restrictions upon the power of a court to hear and adjudicate cases.

LIMITED LIABILITY: maximum liability, as in the case of a stockholder whose loss is limited to contributed capital.

LIMITED PARTNERSHIP: one in which a partner is limited in loss to his contribution provided he takes no part in management of the partnership.

LIQUIDATED DAMAGES: stipulated sum in an agreement identifying amount of damages in the case of a breach of contract or default.

LIQUIDATION: the conversion of property into money; the process of winding up and settling affairs of a firm.

LIS PENDENS: Latin for "pending the suit nothing should be changed," a legal doctrine maintaining that certain pending actions are notice to others that rights are preserved pending the outcome of a legal action.

M

MAGISTRATE: commonly used to refer to a member of the minor judiciary, such as a justice of the peace or the judge in a city or traffic court; a public judicial official who has the power to issue search and arrest warrants, to preside at preliminary arraignments and preliminary hearings and to make final disposition of petty offenses and small civil claims; in a wider sense, the term refers to any public civil official with executive, legislative, or judicial powers.

MAJORITY: the chronological age specified by law at which an individual is no longer presumed to be an infant but is deemed to be capable of managing his own affairs.

MAKER: with regard to promissory notes, that party who promised to pay; the signer of a note; one who executes and signs certain negotiable instruments.

MALA IN SE: an act which is wrong in itself.

MALA PROHIBITA: an act not wrong in itself but prohibited by law.

MALICE: a state of mind in which there is intention to act wrongfully without excuse or justification; more generally, a state of mind indicative of a "hard heart."

MALICIOUS PROSECUTION: institution of charges against another without probable cause but with malice.

MANDAMUS: a writ issued by a court ordering a party to do a specific thing.

MANSLAUGHTER: the unlawful killing of a human being without malice; the absence of malice distinguishes it from murder.

MARSHAL: a federal official whose duties in executing the law are similar to those of a sheriff.

MAXIM: statements concerning generally accepted rules of law, usually used in connection with "equitable maxims."

MECHANICS LIEN: a claim against real property created by law to secure payment for material and labor provided in either repair or construction of that property.

MENS REA: the state of mind required if an act is to be criminal, often described as "criminal intent."

MERCHANT: a person who by occupation buys and sells goods; a person who deals in goods of the kind or by occupation holds himself out as having knowledge or skill peculiar to the practice or goods involved in the transaction (UCC 2-104).

MERCHANTABLE: a quality referring to goods sold, indicating they are fit for the ordinary purpose for which such goods are sold and used (UCC 2-314).

MERGER: with reference to corporations, an entity resulting from a transfer of the assets of one or more corporations to another, the latter to be the sole organization remaining in existence after the transfer.

MIDNIGHT DEADLINE: midnight of the next banking day following that on which a bank received an item or notice from which the time for taking action begins to run, whichever is later (UCC 4-104).

MINOR: person under the age of majority or legal competence; an infant.

MISDEMEANOR: a crime less serious than a felony.

MISREPRESENTATION: a false or incorrect statement of fact made without intent to deceive.

MISTRIAL: a trial that is invalid because of some irregularity.

MITIGATION OF DAMAGES: action by the party injured through breach of contract to prevent increase of the damages due him by the offending party.

MODEL: a representation of reality; a replica.

MONOPOLY: such control and power as to have the exclusive ability to carry on a particular kind of business; ability to restrain trade, to stifle competition.

MOOT: a matter already resolved or for other reason not capable of being settled by action of the court; one for which judicial decision would be merely theoretical, not practical in result.

MUTUALITY: in connection with contract, the binding of both parties. Mutuality of obligation refers to the duty of each party to a contract to perform in accordance with his promises. Mutuality of assent refers to agreement of both parties to the same thing.

N

NECESSARY: in connection with minors, such things as are needed, within reason, to provide for a person's maintenance according to his station in life.

NEGLIGENCE: failure to exercise that degree of care which a reasonable person would use under the circumstances.

NEGOTIATION: in connection with commercial paper, transfer in such a manner that the transferee becomes a holder (UCC 3-202).

NEGOTIABLE INSTRUMENT: commercial paper signed by the maker or drawer, containing an unconditional promise or order to pay a sum certain in money, made payable to order or to bearer, and payable on demand or at a definite time (UCC 3-104).

NOLLE PROSEQUI: decision by the government or state's attorney not to proceed with the prosecution.

NOLO CONTENDERE: plea of an accused in which he indicates he will not contest a criminal action and on which he may be sentenced.

NOMINAL DAMAGES: the sum recoverable when no actual damages have been sustained, consisting of a paltry sum indicating a technical invasion of legal rights.

NON OBSTANTE VERDICTO: n.o.v.; judgment notwithstanding the verdict.

NONSUIT: judgment against a plaintiff who is unable to prove a prima façie case or who does not proceed with the trial, leaving the issues unresolved.

NORMATIVE MODEL: a model that prescribes the functioning in a situation, as, for instance, how a system should operate.

NOTARY PUBLIC: a public official who has the authority to administer oaths and attest to certain documents.

NOTICE: providing information or knowledge of certain facts. It may be either actual or constructive, the latter being knowledge implied by law from the circumstances.

NOVATION: substitution of one contract or obligation for another; it may be between the same or different parties.

NUISANCE: that which is annoying or disturbing and which prevents the reasonable use and enjoyment of one's property or causes discomfort to the person.

O

OBITER DICTUM: (frequently referred to simply as dictum)—statement or expression by the court in an opinion which is neither necessary nor bears upon resolution of the issues involved in the case.

OBJECTION: in the course of a trial, expression by counsel of disapproval for some matter or method of proceeding, usually accompanied with reasons therefore.

OBLIGATION: this may have many meanings; the term is used to refer to a duty, whether it be moral or ethical or is imposed by law, by promise, or by contract; it also refers to a debt.

OBLIGEE: a person to whom a promise is made; a creditor.

OBLIGOR: a person who makes a promise; a debtor.

OFFER: in connection with contracts, a proposal made with the intention that it may be accepted by the person to whom it is made and will lead to a legally binding obligation.

OFFEREE: a person to whom an offer is made.

OFFEROR: a person who makes an offer.

OPENING STATEMENT: in a trial, statement of counsel to the jury, prior to testimony by witnesses, advising the jurors of the general nature of the trial, the issues, and forthcoming proceedings.

OPINION OF A COURT OR JUDGE: a statement explaining and giving the legal reasons for a court's decision and upon which its judgment is based. An opinion differs from a decision. The *decision* is the court's judgment; the *opinion* gives reasons for that judgment.

A *concurring* opinion is a separate opinion by a judge in which he agrees in result with the majority but expresses his own reasons for arriving at the result; these may either reinforce or be in disagreement with the reasons expressed by the majority. A *dissenting* opinion is also the separate opinion of a judge; it is one in which that judge states his disagreement with the result reached by the majority and gives his reasons therefore. A *per curiam* opinion is one in which all members of the court agree, but no judge is indicated as the author of the statement.

P

PANEL: list of names of persons summoned to serve as jurors, either for a particular court or trial.

PARDON: a release, granted to an offender by the governor or president, from all punishment and disabilities connected with a crime.

PARI DELICTO: equally guilty.

PAROL EVIDENCE: oral evidence. The parol evidence rule provides that oral evidence may not be introduced to contradict or modify a written contract that contains the final and complete expression of the agreement of the parties but may be introduced for such limited purposes as explaining the writing.

PAROLE: release of a prisoner upon condition that he comply with certain requirements; failure to meet such condition results in return to incarceration.

PARTY: person or persons who take part in or engage in a particular transaction, such as a party to a law suit (plaintiff, defendant) or to a negotiable instrument (payee, maker, drawer, drawee).

PARTITION: a division of property held by joint tenants or tenants in common into portions to be held severally.

PARTNERSHIP: association of two or more persons to carry on as co-owners a business for profit. (Uniform Partnership Act, §6 (1)).

PAT DOWN: search of a suspect's outer clothing, primarily for weapons.

PAYEE: one to whom commercial paper is made payable.

PAYOR BANK: a bank by which an item is payable as drawn or accepted (UCC 4-105).

PER CURIAM: by the court; with regard to an opinion, one written by the court with a specific author not designated.

PEREMPTORY: absolute. A peremptory challenge is an objection made to having a person serve as a juror, with no reasons having to be given for objecting.

PERJURY: a false statement made under oath.

PERSONALTY: personal property; things which are movable, such as chattels and goods.

PERSONAL REPRESENTATIVE: the administrator or executor of the estate of a deceased person.

PERSONAL SERVICE: service of process which is actually (as opposed to constructively) delivered to the defendant.

PLAINTIFF: the party who initiates a law suit.

PLEA: the formal reply of a defendant to a charge; an answer in a court proceeding.

PLEA BARGAINING: negotiations between prosecutor and defendant, often resulting in the accused's entering a plea of guilty in exchange for reduction of charges or recommendation of leniency by the state.

PLEADINGS: written statements of the parties to a law suit consisting of a claim for relief and such denials and defenses as are submitted in response; the process by which the parties to a law suit arrive at the issues.

PLEDGE: delivery of goods to a creditor as security for a debt or obligation.

POLICE COURT: a court with jurisdiction over minor offenses.

POLLING JURY: calling the name of each juror for the purpose of determining that juror's verdict.

POSSESSION: exercise of power over property for one's own use and enjoyment; physical custody and control of property.

PRAYER: a request that a court grant the relief desired.

PRECEDENT: an already decided case used as authority for deciding a present controversy.

PREDICTIVE MODEL: a model developed for the primary purpose of predicting future outcomes of activity of a system.

PRELIMINARY HEARING: a hearing, generally presided over by a magistrate, for the purpose of determining if there is probable cause to believe the accused committed a crime and should be held over for trial.

PREPONDERANCE: the greater weight; preponderance of the evidence is that which has greater credibility, that which creates the stronger impression and is more convincing.

PRESENTENCE REPORT: a report prepared, generally by a probation officer, at the request of a sentencing judge to provide the latter with information to be considered in determining the sentence to be imposed.

PRESENTMENT: in criminal procedure, a written statement by a grand jury charging there is reasonable ground for believing a particular person has committed a crime, having the same effect as a bill of indictment.

PRETRIAL CONFERENCE: a meeting, prior to trial, of counsel for both parties with the judge for the purpose of discussing matters related to the trial.

PRIMA FACIE CASE: one which has been established by sufficient evidence but which may be discredited by rebuttal of the opposing party.

PRINCIPAL: in criminal law, the actor or perpetrator of a crime, also one who aids and abets in perpetration of the crime; in agency, the person for whom another acts.

PRIVACY: the right to be let alone, to be free from unwarranted intrusion into one's personal affairs.

PRIVITY: in connection with contracts, that relationship which exists between the contracting parties.

PROBABILISTIC MODEL: models based upon expectations of outcomes, i.e., using probabilities of occurrence.

PROBABLE CAUSE: reasonable grounds, such as would warrant a prudent person in believing certain facts are true; it is more than mere suspicion but less than beyond a reasonable doubt.

PROBATE COURT: a court with jurisdiction over the administration of the estates and affairs of deceased persons. To probate a will is to prove a will.

PROBATION: a sentence served in the community rather than by incarceration.

PROCEDURE: the various steps involved in the conduct of a law suit and in enforcing a legal right. The law of procedure is sometimes referred to as adjective law as distinguished from substantive law.

PROCESS: the method by which a court achieves a result; commonly used to refer to the means of compelling a defendant to appear; an order issued by a court to acquire jurisdiction over a person or his property.

PRODUCT LIABILITY: liability of a seller or manufacturer for injury caused by a defect in the goods.

PROOF: a conclusion derived from the evidence; establishing the truth of a matter or a fact by means of the evidence.

PROMISSORY NOTE: a form of commercial paper consisting of the written promise of one person to pay money to another.

PROPERTY: all of those interests, rights, and privileges which a person has with regard to a particular thing.

PROSECUTE: to proceed with criminal charges against a person.

PROSECUTOR: the person who brings criminal action in the name of the government against another.

PROXIMATE CAUSE: the natural and foreseeable cause of an injury.

PUNITIVE DAMAGES: damages over and above those necessary to compensate for injury which are imposed as a penalty.

PURCHASE MONEY SECURITY INTEREST: a security interest by the seller to secure the price in whole or in part.

Q

QUANTUM MERUIT: obligation imposed by law to prevent injustice.

QUASH: to annul, to declare to be void.

QUASI CONTRACT: a legal duty imposed by law, in the absence of a valid contract, in order to prevent injustice.

QUIET TITLE: a proceeding to establish a person's title in realty wherein a person with an adverse claim is brought into court and required either to prove his claim or to refrain from asserting it.

QUIT CLAIM: a deed containing no warranty by which the grantor transfers to the grantee only that interest which the grantor has in the property.

R

RAPE: unlawful sexual intercourse, by force and without consent.

RATIFICATION: approval of a prior act.

REALTY: real property; real estate. Land and all that which is permanently affixed to the land, such as buildings.

REASONABLE CARE: that degree of care exercised by the ordinarily prudent person under similar circumstances.

REBUTTAL: evidence offered to overcome, disprove, or contradict the evidence presented by the adverse party.

RECOGNIZANCE: an obligation owed to a court to do some particular act, such as to appear before the court as required.

RECORD: in practice, the written notation of a court's action, step by step. As a verb, the term refers to the act of placing a document on file in a public office.

RECORDER OF DEEDS: official charged with the duty of receiving, filing, and preserving deeds, mortgages, and other documents related to realty.

RECROSS EXAMINATION: at trial, that examination of a witness following redirect examination which is made by the attorney representing the opposing party.

REDIRECT EXAMINATION: at trial, that examination which is made of a witness following cross-examination and which is made by the attorney representing the party for whom the witness has been called to testify.

REFORMATORY: place of incarceration for youthful offenders.

REGISTER OF WILLS: in some states, the clerk of the probate or orphans court; official charged with receiving, filing, and preserving wills as well as other documents related to the administration of the affairs and estates of deceased persons.

REJOINDER: in a trial, that stage following the plaintiff's rebuttal in which the defendant may present additional evidence.

RELEASE ON OWN RECOGNIZANCE (ROR): pretrial release of an accused on his promise to appear for court as required: used as an alternative to bail of a pecuniary nature.

RELIEF: redress for a wrong; that remedy granted by the court in satisfaction for a harm.

REMAND: to send back. With reference to a case, sending it back to the court from which it came for such action as indicated. In a criminal context, to send a prisoner back to jail or prison following a hearing or other action.

REMEDY: the action or object sought through legal process as a means of redressing an injury.

REMOVAL: in relation to causes of action, the transfer of a case from one court to another.

REPLEVIN: legal action to recover possession of personal property unlawfully taken.

REPLY: in connection with the pleadings, the written response of the plaintiff to the defendant's answer.

RES: Latin for a thing.

RESCISSION: setting aside; in connection with contracts, the setting aside of a contract so that the effect is as if it had never been made.

RES GESTAE: Latin; an exception to the hearsay rule, words or acts which are a part of and uttered or done during the course of a particular event.

RES IPSA LOQUITUR: Latin for "the thing speaks for itself."

RES JUDICATA: Latin for "the thing has been decided." It refers to the fact that a final judgment by a court of proper jurisdiction is conclusive of the matter.

RESPONDEAT SUPERIOR: the master is liable for the acts of his servant; the doctrine that an employer is liable for the torts of his agent or servant committed within the scope of employment and during the course of such employment.

RESPONDENT: in equity, a person who replies to another's pleadings; similar to a defendant in a suit at common law.

RESTITUTION: restoring or making good by giving the equivalent for damage or harm done.

RESTRAINING ORDER: a temporary injunction.

RESTRICTIVE INDORSEMENT: an indorsement limiting further transfer of the instrument.

RETAINER: payment of a fee to an attorney for the purpose of employing him to the extent that the client has the right to expect legal services when such are requested.

RETURN: act of a sheriff, marshal, or constable in bringing back to court such forms or copies of documents as he was obliged to execute or serve, together with his statement of action taken, such as time and method of serving or inability to do so.

ROBBERY: a crime which consists of taking personal property from another's person and against his will by force or threat of force.

S

SATISFACTION: discharge of a legal obligation by performing according to requirements. Satisfaction of a judgment occurs when there is payment made of the sum awarded to a party by the court.

SATISFICE: a term coined by Herbert Simon to designate the making of decisions with a requisite amount of data rather than the theoretical maximum.

SCIENTER: with knowledge; commonly used to indicate the defendant's knowledge of the wrongfulness of his actions.

SEAL: a stamp, mark, or impression affixed to an instrument for the purpose of indicating the formal execution of the document.

SECURITY: that which is given to a creditor by a debtor to make sure payment of a debt or obligation, forfeiture of the object to occur upon nonpayment.

SECURITY INTEREST: an interest in personalty (or fixtures) given to a creditor to insure payment of a debt or obligation.

SENTENCE: judgment of a court declaring the form of a punishment imposed upon a defendant who has been convicted of a crime.

An *indeterminate* sentence is one in which the period of incarceration includes a spread of time between a minimum and maximum date when the prisoner will be eligible for parole.

A *suspended* sentence is one where incarceration is postponed, often permanently, and release into the community occurs instead.

SERVANT: an employee; a person hired to work for another and subject to direction and control of that person as distinguished from one who pursues an independent calling.

SERVICE: delivery by a person authorized by the court of a notice or writ for the purpose of providing official notification regarding legal action. Service of process consists of delivery of such notice for the purpose of securing jurisdiction over a defendant.

Personal service occurs when the writ or notice is delivered to the individual named in person. *Constructive* service occurs when there is other than personal service, such as notice by mail or through publication in a newspaper. *Substitute* service also occurs when there is other than personal service, such as when notice is served upon an agent or other person who has authority to accept service.

SETTLEMENT: agreement of the parties to a dispute to a particular method or means of disposing of the matter; commonly used to refer to acceptance by an aggrieved party of a sum of money in payment for injuries without going to trial.

SEVERALTY: distinct, separate. Ownership in severalty refers to sole ownership.

SHERIFF: a public, elected, county official whose duties include keeping the peace and rendering assistance to the courts in such matters as service of process, conduct of judicial sales, summoning persons for jury duty.

SIMULATION: a model of a situation too complex for the use of other models to picture reality.

SLANDER: spoken defamation. Oral false and malicious statements about another which injure his reputation.

SOLICITATION: in criminal law, enticing another person to commit a crime.

SOLICITOR: an attorney; used frequently in this country to refer to the attorney who represents some governmental unit.

SOLICITOR GENERAL: an assistant to the United States attorney general who represents the government in cases before the United States Supreme Court and the Court of Claims.

SOVEREIGN IMMUNITY: exemption of a state or nation (and political subdivisions) from legal liability when engaged in governmental functions.

SPECIAL APPEARANCE: appearance for a limited purpose only of a person in court by his attorney. This does not result in the court's securing jurisdiction over the person as is true with a general appearance.

SPECIAL INDORSEMENT: an indorsement which names the person to whom the instrument is indorsed.

SPECIAL VERDICT: jury verdict consisting of answers to specific questions put to it, as distinguished from a general finding for one party as is true with a general verdict.

SPECIFIC PERFORMANCE: an equitable remedy in which a court orders that a contract be carried out in accordance with the agreement of the parties.

STARE DECISIS: Latin for "to stand by the decision," to follow precedent; use of a prior court decision as a guide in reaching a decision in a similar case.

STATIC MODEL: a model that does not reflect changes over time.

STATUS QUO: the state of things at a particular time; with regard to contracts, the status quo ante refers to the state of things prior to the time of contacting.

STATUTE: a law enacted by a legislative body, often referred to as "written" law to distinguish it from the common or "unwritten" law.

STATUTE OF FRAUDS: a statute which requires that certain transactions be written if they are to be enforced, the purpose being to prevent fraud in the form of perjury.

STATUTE OF LIMITATIONS: a statute that sets specific time requirements for the bringing of legal action.

STAY: to stop, to hold in abeyance. A stay of execution refers to stopping execution on a judgment. A stay of proceedings refers to a temporary halt in an action, ordinarily to permit time for accomplishment of some act relevant and essential to the suit.

STIPULATION: an agreement between counsel for opposing parties regarding some matter related to a legal action.

STOCK: with regard to corporations, stock refers to the firm's capital derived from contributions of subscribers upon the sale of shares. It represents the right of ownership in the corporation.

Preferred stock is a class of stock to which some priority is attached such as with respect to dividends. Common stock is that class without any preference.

STRICT LIABILITY: tort liability which is imposed for harm or injury caused without regard to negligence; commonly in connection with defective products or with the use of dangerous or hazardous activities.

STRIKING A JURY: selection of jury members from a panel through the process of striking off certain persons until the desired number is reached.

SUA SPONTE: on one's own, without request.

SUBORNATION OF PERJURY: a crime committed by securing another to commit perjury.

SUBPOENA: a court order directing the appearance of a witness in court.

A subpoena duces tecum commands a person to bring with him to court records or instruments which are in his possession.

SUBROGATION: substitution of one person for another in connection with some legal claim, such as an insurer, having made payment for injury to an insured, who substitutes himself for the insured as the party in a legal action brought against the person or persons who caused the injury.

SUBSTANTIAL PERFORMANCE: performance of all the major aspects of a contract.

SUBSTANTIVE LAW: that part of the positive law which relates to the rights and duties of persons, as distinguished from adjective or procedural law.

SUIT: a legal proceeding in which the plaintiff seeks enforcement of a right of redress for an injury. Ordinarily it refers to a civil action as distinguished from a criminal action. It is frequently used in connection with equity, in distinction to an "action at law."

SUMMARY JUDGMENT: judgment of a court upon motion of one of the parties when there is no issue as to any material fact but only as to law and based upon information contained in pleadings, affidavits, depositions, admissions, and answers to interrogatories.

SUMMING UP: at trial, summary of the evidence presented to the jury by counsel for each party in their closing statements. The judge sometimes "sums up" evidence in the charge to the jury.

SUMMONS: a writ or court order notifying a party that legal action has been instituted against him and requiring that he answer the charges and allegations made against him.

SUPERSEDEAS: a writ or court order to stay the proceedings.

SUPERVENING CAUSE: a cause, second in time, which acts independently to proximately cause injury or harm.

SUPPRESSION MOTION: a motion to hold back or prevent revelation of certain matters.

SURETY: one who undertakes responsibility for performance of another's obligation in case the obligor does not perform. According to UCC 1-201, a surety includes a guarantor.

SURVIVAL ACTION: a legal action which survives the death of the injured party.

SYMBOLIC MODEL: a representation of a situation using a designation that stands for the real thing, as a mathematical or other symbol does.

SYSTEM: an orderly and methodic arrangement of parts into a whole in such a combination as to achieve particular objectives or goals.

SURVEILLANCE: police investigation by means of observation, sometimes including listening, for the purpose of gathering information about suspected criminal activity.

SYNERGY: the working together of products or medicines to provide a result greater than would be achieved by simple addition.

T

TENANCY: an interest in realty.

TENANT: one who has an interest in property; commonly used to refer to a lessee. Tenancy by the entirety refers to an interest held by husband and wife whereby each is seized of the entire estate and the survivor takes all upon the death of the other. A joint tenancy refers to the interest held in the same property at the same time by two or more persons, ordinarily accompanied by a right of survivorship. A tenancy in common is an undivided interest held by two or more persons in the same property, with no right of survivorship.

TENDER: to offer to perform an obligation.

TERM OF COURT: that period of time during which a particular court transacts business or holds sessions.

TESTAMENT: a will; a declaration of the disposition one wishes to be made of his property and effects upon his death.

TESTAMENTARY: relating to a will.

TESTATOR: one who makes a will. (Testatrix is sometimes used to indicate female gender.)

TESTES: witnesses.

TESTIMONY: answers to questions provided by witnesses under oath. It is distinguished from evidence in that the latter may consist of more than testimony, documents and exhibits being evidence.

THEFT: the crime of larceny; the taking of the personal property of another without his consent with the intention of depriving the owner of its use and of appropriating it to one's own benefit.

TITLE: in connection with property, the combination of legal rights which represent ownership.

TORT: a breach of a duty imposed by law; a private wrong as distinguished from a crime which is looked upon as a public wrong.

TORT FEASOR: one who commits a tort.

TRADE ACCEPTANCE: a bill of exchange drawn by the seller on the buyer of goods.

TREASON: a crime involving betrayal of one's country or state.

TRESPASS: inflicting harm or injury to person or property by the doing of a lawful act in an unlawful manner or the doing of an unlawful act. Frequently used in the sense of the common law trespass *quare clausum fregit*, that is, unlawful entry upon the property of another.

TRIAL: a legal proceeding in a court with proper jurisdiction in which there is inquiry into and determination of issues of law and fact. A bench trial is one without a jury.

TRIER OF FACT: generally refers to the jury, although in a bench trial or in equity it refers to the judge.

TRUST: the transfer of property by one person to another to be held for the benefit of a third person or the transferor.

TRUSTEE: the person charged with management of another's property.

TRUSTY: a convict deemed to be reliable.

U

ULTRA VIRES: an act which is beyond the power or authority of a corporation.

UNCONSCIONABLE: that which shocks the conscience.

UNDUE INFLUENCE: persuasion which overpowers the will of a person, inducing him to act as he would not do on his own.

UNIFORM LAWS: laws drafted by the National Conference of Commissioners on Uniform State laws, many of which have been adopted in the various states. One example is the Uniform Commercial Code.

UNION SHOP: a place of employment where employees must join a union or be discharged after a trial period of a maximum of 30 days.

UNWRITTEN LAW: a term usually used to refer to the common law.

USAGE OF THE TRADE: a mode of dealing so commonly observed as to result in the justifiable expectation it will be followed in the transaction at hand.

USURY: interest in excess of that permitted by law.

V

VACATING: setting aside; to vacate a judgment is to set aside a judgment.

VALID: legal; not void.

VENIRE: the writ summoning a jury.

VENIREMAN: a person who is a member of a jury panel.

VENUE: the location or place where a case is to be tried.

VERDICT: decision of a petit jury.

VOID: having no legal effect.

VOIDABLE: capable of being made void.

VOIR DIRE: preliminary examination of jurors.

W

WAIVE: to voluntarily dispense with a right or an opportunity.

WANTON: reckless disregard for the rights of others.

WARDEN: a chief officer, frequently used in connection with a prison or jail.

WAREHOUSEMAN: one engaged in the business of storing goods for others.

WARRANT: as a noun, the term refers to the written order issued by an authorized judicial officer directing certain action to be taken, such as an arrest or a search. As a verb, the term refers to the making of a promise that certain facts are true.

WARRANTY: a guarantee.

WATERED STOCK: stock issued as fully paid up but for which the consideration is less than par value.

WITNESS: as a noun, the term refers to a person who testifies regarding that about which he has knowledge. As a verb, the term refers to the act of observing the execution of an instrument and subscription of one's name thereon attesting to such.

WORKMEN'S COMPENSATION: payment to employees who suffer injury in the course of their employment, without regard to negligence by either employer or employee.

WRIT: a written instrument, generally used in connection with an order of a court compelling certain action, such as a writ of habeas corpus.

Z

ZONING ORDINANCE: a regulation imposing restrictions upon the use of property.

INDEX

NOTE: This revised Index replaces the one directly following the Glossary. Please refer here for the correct page references.

Date Due